The Origins of the Hundred Years War

Hertfordshire
COUNTY COUNCIL
Community Information

Please renew/return this item by the last date shown.

So that your telephone call is charged at local rate, please call the numbers as set out below:

	From Area codes 01923 or 0208:	From the rest of Herts:
Renewals:	01923 471373	01438 737373
Enquiries:	01923 471333	01438 737333
Minicom:	01923 471599	01438 737599

L32b

The Origins of the Hundred Years War

The Angevin Legacy 1250–1340

MALCOLM VALE

CLARENDON PRESS · OXFORD
1996

Oxford University Press, Walton Street, Oxford OX2 6DP

Oxford New York
Athens Auckland Bangkok Bogota Bombay
Buenos Aires Calcutta Cape Town Dar es Salaam
Delhi Florence Hong Kong Istanbul Karachi
Kuala Lumpur Madras Madrid Melbourne
Mexico City Nairobi Paris Singapore
Taipei Tokyo Toronto

and associated companies in
Berlin Ibadan

Oxford is a trade mark of Oxford University Press

Published in the United States
by Oxford University Press Inc., New York

British Library Cataloguing in Publication Data
Data available

Library of Congress Cataloging in Publication Data
Data applied for
ISBN 0-19-820620-8

1 3 5 7 9 10 8 6 4 2

Printed in Great Britain
on acid-free paper by
Bookcraft Ltd,
Midsomer Norton, Bath, Avon

For Timothy and Patrick

Foreword to the Clarendon Paperback Edition

SINCE the publication of this book in its original edition (1990) a relatively small number of contributions to the study of Anglo-French relations between 1250 and 1340 have appeared. They have been added to the Bibliography. None has, however, seriously contested a fundamental argument of this book: namely, that the retention by the Plantagenets of the residue of their Angevin inheritance in France gave rise to tensions and conflicts which were, ultimately, to lead to the Hundred Years War. Some degree of consensus appears to have been reached and, it is argued, 'historians now generally accept that Edward [III's] war-aims in 1337 were first and foremost to secure sovereignty over his continental possessions'.[1] What is less generally agreed is the relative significance of the Gascon problem in relation to other sources of Anglo-French friction. Varying degrees of emphasis have always been put upon the component elements in the explosive mixture that was detonated under Edward III. To what extent was the Plantagenet presence within France – whether as sovereign or merely immediate lord over Aquitaine and Ponthieu – responsible for drawing the English and French monarchies into the long-lasting conflict that broke out in 1337?

At least one reviewer of this book has considered the role of Gascon affairs to be somewhat exaggerated, and that 'other, more significant matters' brought England and France to war.[2] But it is certainly not my intention to isolate Aquitaine, especially during the 1330s, from the complex imbroglio into which both monarchies had been · drawn, and in which Scottish, Flemish, and German (or imperial) issues played very important parts. The fundamental, intractable problem of Aquitaine, however, served to inject a degree of thematic continuity into the ebb and flow of war and diplomacy. It remained unresolved until the mid-fifteenth century. The Hundred Years War began – and ended – with Gascon issues well to the fore, and I make no apology for restating this view. But the current climate of historical research is no more favourable to the close and detailed study of Anglo-French relations – especially through a consideration of what may on the surface appear to be merely regional or local issues – than it was when the first edition of this book appeared.

---

[1] C. J. Rogers, 'Edward III and the dialectics of strategy', *TRHS*, 6th ser., iv (1994), p. 85.

[2] See the review in *History*, lxxvii (1992), p. 286. The 'other, more significant matters' are not specified.

Studies of the English monarchy itself, however, have recently proliferated. Two substantial books have appeared on the reign of Edward III, two books on Edward II's Gascon favourite Piers Gaveston, a study of Simon de Montfort, and an interesting new volume on the representation of kingly power under the Plantagenets.[3] Royal ceremonial, matrimonial policy, social and sexual behaviour, and the architectural and iconological expression of royal authority continue to exercise historical minds.[4] In France, the study of power – its nature, exercise, and representation – has notably advanced, although the concentration there has tended to be upon monarchical rather than princely or seigneurial authority.[5] But little further sustained work has as yet been done to set Capetian or Valois kingship into a more general context of relationship and comparison with other powers. A surge of interest in the military history, broadly defined, of the fourteenth century has, however, been a marked feature of recent research. A number of studies have argued for a 'military revolution' in fourteenth-century England which transformed the armies which had suffered humiliation by the French in the war of 1294–8 and disastrous defeat by the Scots at Bannockburn in 1314 into the highly successful fighting machine of Edward III's reign.[6] Although some stress is laid upon continuities between the military organizations of Edward I and Edward III, the dominant note which has recently been sounded is one of far-reaching change. The emergence of England as a front-rank military power in fourteenth-century Europe is attributed more to English strategic superiority, skilful tactical deployment of dismounted men-at-arms and archers, and effective use of the *chevauchée* as a battle-seeking device than to French internal divisions, tactical misjudgements, and poor command structures.[7] There is much truth in this, but talk of 'military

[3] W. M. Ormrod, *The Reign of Edward III. Crown and Political Society in England, 1327–1377* (New Haven and London, 1990); S. L. Waugh, *England in the Reign of Edward III* (Cambridge, 1991); J. S. Hamilton, *Piers Gaveston, Earl of Cornwall, 1307–1312. Politics and Patronage in the Reign of Edward II* (Detroit, 1988); P. Chaplais, *Piers Gaveston. Edward II's Adoptive Brother* (Oxford, 1994); J. R. Maddicott, *Simon de Montfort* (Oxford, 1994); P. Binski, *Westminster Abbey and the Plantagenets. Kingship and the Representation of Power, 1200–1400* (New Haven and London, 1995).

[4] See, for some examples, E. A. R. Brown, 'Diplomacy, adultery and domestic politics at the court of Philip the Fair: Queen Isabelle's mission to France in 1314', in *Documenting the Past. Essays in Medieval History Presented to George Peddy Cuttino*, ed. J. S. Hamilton and P. J. Bradley (Woodbridge and Wolfeboro, 1989), pp. 53–83; E. A. R. Brown and N. F. Regalado, '*La grant feste*: Philip the Fair's celebration of the knighting of his sons in Paris at Pentecost of 1313', in *City and Spectacle in Medieval Europe*, ed. B. A. Hanawalt and K. L. Reyerson (Minneapolis, 1994), pp. 56–86. See also Binski, *Westminster Abbey and the Plantagenets*.

[5] See *Représentation, pouvoir et royauté à la fin du Moyen Age*, ed. J. Blanchard (Paris, 1995); and *Renaissance du pouvoir législatif et genèse de l'Etat*, ed. A. Gouron and A. Rigaudière (Montpellier, 1988).

[6] For examples, see C. J. Rogers, 'The military revolutions of the Hundred Years War', *Journal of Military History*, lvii (1993), pp. 249–57 and 'Edward III and the dialectics of strategy', pp. 83–102. Also A. Ayton, *Knights and Warhorses. Military Service and the English Aristocracy under Edward III* (Woodbridge, 1994) and 'English armies in the fourteenth century', in *Arms, Armies and Fortifications in the Hundred Years War*, ed. A. Curry and M. Hughes (Woodbridge, 1994).

[7] See Rogers, 'Edward III and the dialectics of strategy', pp. 88–90, 99–102; Ayton, *Knights and Warhorses*, pp. 9–25.

revolutions' may exaggerate the extent and character of change at the expense of continuity. Mounted raiding expeditions, for example, had been the very stuff of warfare in Aquitaine, Scotland, and elsewhere for a long time, and the origins of the *chevauchée* could be sought in such practices, adapted to the needs of Edward III's aggressive war effort.[8]

It is perhaps the transition from essentially defensive wars against France in 1294–8 and 1324–7 to the aggressive tactics of the 1340s and 1350s that stands out most clearly in this context. Furthermore, Edward III's shift from the recruitment of large, mixed armies composed of foreign allies and mercenaries, as well as his own subjects, to the smaller, more disciplined and united Anglo-Gascon forces which won him his victories after 1340 also deserves more consideration in an analysis of the reasons for the rise of English military power to the front rank.[9] This emphasis upon aggressive warfare did not, however, mean that the defence of English continental possessions was neglected: the sustained war effort in Aquitaine, and the continued survival of Plantagenet rule there, gave the Black Prince the necessary base from which to launch his *chevauchées* and the Poitiers campaign in the 1350s. Recovery of lost Plantagenet territory, as well as the pursuit of his claim to the throne of France, remained a significant element in Edward III's war-aims. It was, after all, at Crécy in the *comté* of Ponthieu – held by the Plantagenets from 1279 until the French confiscations of 1337 – that he achieved his first great victory in land warfare against the French.

A renewed tendency to seek for signs of emergent national identity – if not of nationalism – during the later Middle Ages has also been discernible in some recent works.[10] This approach underscores the view that the Hundred Years War was a 'national' – rather than a dynastic or feudal – conflict from its outset. This book, on the contrary, attempts to stress the cosmopolitanism and internationalism of court society, dynastic politics, and the world of the higher aristocracy. If it came from anywhere, 'national sentiment' at this time may have come from below, often barely distinguishable from xenophobia and, at times of crisis, exploited by governments for their own ends.[11] Popular consciousness of English national identity, in so far as it transcended regional and local boundaries, could thus be utilized and orchestrated to galvanize tax-paying subjects into action. But it could also cut across and sometimes hamper attempts to conclude agreements and compromises with the French. A divergence between the so-called 'community of the realm' and its rulers may be apparent here.

Furthermore, a tendency to emphasize differences rather than similarities between England and France has been increasingly apparent, especially in

---

[8] See below, pp. 210–11.   [9] See below, pp. 264–5, 269.

[10] For an early example, from which subsequent work has derived, see C. Beaune, *Naissance de la nation France* (Paris, 1985). An able exposition of the view that 'national honour', as well as dynastic pride, informed the attitudes of Henry III and his subjects towards Crusading schemes is to be found in S. Lloyd, 'King Henry III, the Crusade and the Mediterranean', in *England and her Neighbours, 1066–1453. Essays in Honour of Pierre Chaplais* (London and Ronceverte, 1989), esp. pp. 104–6.

[11] See below, pp. 4–6.

recent art-historical literature.[12] Much of this revisionism is to be welcomed, because it combats a prevailing orthodoxy which has tended to proclaim French cultural supremacy and to assume that England was peripheral to European developments. But the issues tend to become somewhat clouded by nebulous arguments about stylistic influences and the existence (or, nowadays, non-existence) of 'court styles' which are in some manner thought to reflect deeper truths about the individuals and societies which they purport to represent. The latter-day Hegelians are out in force. In more general cultural terms, however, I see no good reason to abandon the view that the royal courts and households of England and France at this period were broadly francophone and shared many common social and cultural features. This is not to imply that there was any implicit or recognized French superiority in this sphere. English responses to, and adaptations of, French cultural models could be original, creative, and inspired.

One could speculate about the underlying causes of current trends towards a more nationalistic outlook in some recent historical writing. In some cases they may stem from the recent recrudescence of political nationalism in Europe, and from greater emphasis in some quarters on a 'Europe of national sovereignties'. Such tendencies often see the nation state as an organic growth rather than as an artificial construct. But searches for historic identity can often lead to distortion and anachronism. For example, the extent to which ruling dynasties consciously attempted to harness specifically 'national' – rather than dynastic or simply exemplary – saints' cults to their political aims and ambitions remains debatable. Devotional and chivalric attitudes and aspirations – as well as allegedly propagandist aims – have to be taken into account in this process. The English monarchy at this period began to foster the cult of the legendary, chivalric, and certainly non-English soldier-saint George, while continuing to promote the existing veneration of the indigenous St Edward the Confessor and St Edmund the Martyr.[13] Their French neighbours were soon to take up that of the distinctly non-French St Michel (the Archangel). Arguments on both sides can all too easily be overstated, especially in view of the rise, on the one hand, of ideas about 'national curricula' for the teaching of history – in which, for some apologists, the nation state should ideally loom large – and, on the other, of ambitious and far-reaching plans for further European integration. These tensions can, in time, hardly fail to influence historical writing.

Reviewers and critics of the original edition have kindly pointed out slips and other failings, which I have striven to correct in this edition. I have benefited from the helpful comments of many scholars, including Professor J. B. Henneman, Professor Werner Paravicini, Dr J. H. Dunbabin, and Dr S. Lloyd. I have not, however, substantially rewritten any part of the book. All remaining

---

[12] See, for instance, Binski, *Westminster Abbey and the Plantagenets*, esp. pp. 7–9.

[13] See J.-P. Genet, 'La monarchie anglaise: une image brouillée', in *Représentation, pouvoir et royauté*, pp. 98–100. A similar point could be made with reference to the cult of St Stephen and the building of St Stephen's chapel at Westminster after 1292 (ibid., pp. 99–100).

omissions and errors remain my sole responsibility. I am, finally, grateful to the Delegates of Oxford University Press and to Tony Morris, its History Editor, for giving me the opportunity to reissue the book in its present form.

M. V.

St John's College, Oxford
September 1995

Contents

Abbreviations   xv

List of Plates   xvii

Preface   xix

Acknowledgements   xxi

A Note on Currency   xxii

1   Introduction   1

2   Anglo-French Civilization   9
    2.1   The Legacy of the Angevin Empire
    2.2   The World of the Courts
    2.3   A Common Culture

3   Anglo-French Tensions   48
    3.1   Homage for Aquitaine
    3.2   The Plantagenet Presence in France, 1259–1294

4   Politics and Society in Aquitaine – I: The Nobility   80
    4.1   The Structure and Political Behaviour of the Gascon Nobility
    4.2   Private War

5   Politics and Society in Aquitaine – II: Town and Countryside   140
    5.1   Economic Activity and Social Texture
    5.2   New Settlements
    5.3   Faction and Conflict

6   Anglo-French Conflict   175
    6.1   The Causes of War in 1294
    6.2   War, Finance and Military Organization
    6.3   The Aftermath of War

7   The Coming of the Hundred Years War   227
    7.1   The War of St Sardos and its Consequences
    7.2   The Defence of Aquitaine, 1326–1340

8   Epilogue   266

Appendix I   Family Trees   270

Appendix II   The Costs of the Gascon War   281

Appendix III   Maps   283

Bibliography   288

Index   303

Abbreviations

ADG	Archives Départementales du Gers
ADPC	Archives Départementales de Pas-de-Calais
AHG	*Archives Historiques du département de la Gironde*
AHR	*American Historical Review*
ALG	Archives Départementales de Lot-et-Garonne
AM	*Annales du Midi*
AM Agen	*Archives Municipales d'Agen*
AMB	Archives Municipales de Bordeaux
AN	Archives Nationales
APA	Archives Départementales des Pyrénées-Atlantiques
ATG	Archives Départementales de Tarn-et-Garonne
BEC	*Bibliothèque de L'Ecole des Chartes*
BIHR	*Bulletin of the Institute of Historical Research*
BL	British Library
BN	Bibliothèque Nationale
Bod. Lib.	Bodleian Library
BACTH	*Bulletin Archéologique du Comité des travaux historiques et scientifiques*
BPH	*Bulletin Philologique et Historique du Comité des travaux*
CCR	*Calendar of Close Rolls*
CPR	*Calendar of Patent Rolls*
CR	*Comptes Royaux*
EHR	*English Historical Review*
EcHR	*Economic History Review*
HT	*History Today*
JMH	*Journal of Medieval History*
JWCI	*Journal of the Warburg and Courtauld Institutes*
MA	*Le Moyen Age*
Olim	*Les Olim*
Ordonnances	*Ordonnances des rois de France de la troisième race*
PBA	*Proceedings of the British Academy*
PP	*Past and Present*
PRO	Public Record Office
RG	*Rôles Gascons*
RHB	*Revue Historique de Bordeaux*
RH	*Revue Historique*

RHDFE	*Revue Historique de droit français et étranger*
Rot. Parl.	*Rotuli Parliamentorum*
RS	Rolls Series
RQH	*Revue des Questions Historiques*
SHF	*Société de l'Histoire de France*
TRHS	*Transactions of the Royal Historical Society*

List of Plates

2.1 Tomb effigies of Henry II and Eleanor of Aquitaine at the abbey of Fontevrault 10

2.2 The Triumphant Virtues of *Largesce* and *Débonereté* (Westminster, Painted Chamber) 24

2.3 Seal and counterseal of Aymer de Valence 28

2.4 The Valence Casket 29

2.5 Effigy of William de Valence (d.1296) 31

2.6 Peter de Dene's window, York Minster 36

3.1 Tomb slab of Aliénor de Vipont (d.1270) 76

4.1 Villandraut castle 107

4.2 Effigy of a Gascon noble 109

4.3 Keep of Lesparre castle 117

6.1 Views of Libourne and Fronsac (1612) 185

6.2 Seal and counterseal of Sir John St John 191

6.3 View of Bayonne (1612) 195

6.4 Monument to Edmund of Lancaster (d.1296) 213

6.5 Effigy of Edmund of Lancaster 214

6.6 Seal of John de Hastings, lord Abergavenny 222

7.1 Tomb effigy of Sir Oliver Ingham (c.1340) 243

Preface

The legacy of continental rulership bequeathed by the Angevin kings of England (1154–1216) to their Plantagenet successors forms the subject of this book. Although the French possessions of the English monarchy shrank in territorial size during the first half of the thirteenth century, Plantagenet concern to retain their residual Angevin inheritance in France was to determine the course of much English activity abroad. Intermittent conflict with the crown of France was, I shall argue, largely determined by this legacy of continental lordship. A dynasty which had once held vast dominions in France did not adapt easily to their loss. The later French wars of Edward III and Henry V were to some extent attempts to recover and re-create a continental presence which had been substantially eroded. My purpose is thus essentially twofold: to examine the aftermath of the Angevin Empire's disintegration, and to trace the subsequent growth in hostility between England and France. This was to lead to sustained warfare between the two kingdoms under Edward III and his successors.

The book is the product of some seven years' work on the sources for Anglo-French relations during the century before the Hundred Years War. I have inevitably incurred many debts during the course of my researches: above all, to the British Academy, the Oxford Faculty of Modern History and St John's College, Oxford, for grants of funds and of sabbatical leave which have enabled me to work in French archives and libraries. I am very grateful indeed to these bodies for their support. The staff of the Public Record Office (Chancery Lane), the British Library, the Bodleian Library, the Archives Nationales, the Archives Municipales de Bordeaux, and the Archives Départementales of Pyrénées-Atlantiques (Pau), Gers (Auch), Lot-et-Garonne (Agen), Tarn-et-Garonne (Montauban) and Pas-de-Calais (Arras) have been unfailingly helpful. Without their assistance this book would never have been written. I am especially indebted to Professor Jean Favier, Directeur des Archives de France, for permission to consult documents in the Archives Nationales in the original, rather than on microfilm; to M. Jacques Staes and Mme Annie Lafforgue and their staff at Pau and Montauban for much valuable help and advice; and to the SNCF for the ease with which my rail journeys to French archives have been accomplished. Although recent tendencies in historical research have led to some neglect of political, administrative and diplomatic history in the later Middle Ages, my debt to the work of other scholars will be obvious to the reader. I particularly acknowledge the influence, encouragement and advice of Dr Pierre Chaplais, the late Professors John Le Patourel and Pierre Capra, M. Jean-Philippe Genet, Dr M. C. E. Jones, Dr J. E. Vale, Dr J. H. Dunbabin, Mr. P. S. Lewis and Dr M. H. Keen.

Malcolm Vale
St John's College, Oxford

Acknowledgements

The author and publisher are grateful to the following for their kind permission to reproduce plates: Bibliothèque Nationale, Paris, 6.1, 6.3; By courtesy of the Board of Trustees of the Victoria and Albert Museum, London, 2.4; Bodleian Library, Oxford, 7.1; Caisse Nationale des Monuments Historiques et des Sites © Arch. Phot. Paris/SPADEM/DACS 1989, 2.1, 4.1, 4.3; Cliché Musée d'Aquitaine, Bordeaux, France, All Rights Reserved 3.1, 4.2; Crown Copyright. Public Record Office, London, 2.3 (E 329/87), 6.6 (E 26/2 No. 74), 6.2 (E 26/2 No. 5); Royal Commission on the Historical Monuments of England, 2.5, 2.6, 6.4, 6.5; Society of Antiquaries of London, 2.2. Cover illustration: Crown Copyright, by permission of the Controller of Her Majesty's Stationery Office.

A Note on Currency

There were a number of monetary systems within later medieval France. Rates of Exchange tended to fluctuate and it is impossible to establish equivalent values over long periods, especially during the reign of Philip the Fair (1285–1314). The major systems to which references are made in this book were:

Pounds sterling of England (*l.st.*): 1 *l.* = 20 *s.*   1 *s.* = 12 *d.*

Livres tournois (*l.t.*): The money of Tours came to dominate coinage minted by the French crown during the fourteenth century, replacing the earlier *livres parisis* (*l.p.*) of the Capetian royal domain. A fixed rate of 1 *l.t.* = 16 *sous parisis* was established by the 1220s.

Livres bordelais (*l.b.*): Money of Bordeaux. A rate of between 100 and 160 *sous bordelais* to the pound sterling operated during the period 1290–1340. 1 *l.t.* was worth about 25 *sous bordelais*.

Livres arnaldenses (*l.arn.*): Money of Agen. 1 *l.t.* = 25 *s. arn.*

Livres chapotenses (*l.ch.*): Money of Bigorre. 1 *l. t.* = 25 *s.ch.*

Livres morlanenses (*l.morl.*): Money of Morlàas, minted by the *vicomtes* of Béarn. A rough equivalence of 1 *l.b.* to 2 *l.morl.* can be established.

For further details of exchange rates see P. Spufford, *Handbook of Medieval Exchange*, Royal Historical Society Guides and Handbooks, vol. XIII (London, 1986).

1

Introduction

We British are as much heirs to the legacy of European culture as any other nation. Our links to the rest of Europe, the continent of Europe, have been the dominant factor in our history. . . . Visit the great churches and cathedrals of Britain, read our literature and listen to our language: all bear witness to the cultural riches we have drawn from Europe – and Europeans from us.

Margaret Thatcher, addressing the College of Europe, Bruges, 20 September 1988

The importance of England's links with the continent of Europe during the Middle Ages is undeniable. Henry III's Westminster Abbey, Edward I's Eleanor crosses, the tombs at Westminster of Edmund of Lancaster (d. 1296) and Aymer de Valence (d. 1324), or the Tickhill, Peterborough and Arundel Psalters – to name just a few examples – bear witness to the strength of English cultural and artistic connections with the continent.[1] Dating from the century (1250–1340) before the Hundred Years War with France, these surviving artefacts demonstrate that England undoubtedly shared in, and contributed to, 'the legacy of European culture'. So much is common knowledge. But tensions were already developing between England and its closest continental neighbour which were in the long term to lead towards sharper cultural divergence and greater political insularity. The Hundred Years War (1337–1453) was to further the growth of separate nation states on each side of the English Channel. The modern French nation state, for example, has inherited concepts of sovereignty first formulated under the later Capetian and Valois kings which, when allied to a pronounced sense of national identity, were to create a proud and autonomous continental nation.

But the exercise of hindsight introduces a tendency to see such developments as predetermined and inexorable. When the Hundred Years War began in 1337, the continued tenure by the Plantagenets of inherited continental possessions on the mainland of France contradicted Valois claims to exercise full and effective sovereignty over their kingdom. When it ended in 1453 the issue had largely been resolved in favour of the Valois monarchy. But there was nothing inevitable about the process. The long road leading towards absolute monarchy and the French nation state was not free from

---

[1] See below, pp. 35–9.

obstacles. The medieval English kingdom, on the other hand, formed the precociously centralized precursor of a nation state which was, later in its history, to look beyond Europe to a wider world and a distant empire. Differences between Englishmen and Frenchmen were to become more marked during the course of the Hundred Years War and its aftermath. They were expressed through cultural, linguistic and ultimately religious dissimilarities. Mutual incomprehension and misunderstanding often accompanied this development. The subject of this book therefore concerns the medieval origins of an Anglo-French estrangement which, until the comparatively recent past, has been an undeniably dominant feature of British history.

The book also stems from a certain dissatisfaction with existing explanations of Anglo-French conflict in the later Middle Ages. My debt to previous studies of the origins of the Hundred Years War will be obvious, nevertheless, and areas of agreement with them are not hard to find. No historian, for example, would confidently reject the argument that Plantagenet tenure of continental lands generated Anglo-French tension between 1250 and 1340. But the Plantagenets' homage to the French crown for those dominions, and its implications for the status and autonomy of the English monarchy, was only part of the story. Much medieval history inevitably tends to focus on the ruler, but this perspective sometimes ignores the attitudes and behaviour of those whom he ruled. In this period the interests and concerns of those inhabitants of non-royal France whose immediate lord was the Plantagenet king-duke of Aquitaine stood between the two monarchies as they attempted to exercise authority there. Meanwhile the ruling houses of England and France intermarried and made alliances together, and a common Anglo-French culture was shared by the clerical and secular elites of both kingdoms. The tension between this relative harmony and the hostility generated by the Plantagenets' tenure of their French inheritance is therefore a major theme of this book. Diplomacy, however, is not its primary concern. Diplomatic history can explain how a conflict developed and deepened, but does not always account for its causes. I have not therefore attempted a detailed narrative of diplomatic relations between England and France; indeed, this has already been provided by other historians. The emphasis lies rather upon political, social and economic conditions in the Plantagenet dominions, set against a background of Anglo-French dynastic and cultural connections. Harmony between Capetians and Plantagenets depended not merely upon mutual acknowledgement of their 'feudal' relationship, but upon their subjects' behaviour in regions of France noted for their turbulence and unruliness.

The origins of the Hundred Years War have normally been sought in the specific political and tenurial relationship established between the ruling houses of England and France in 1259. Any search for the 'origins' of a historical phenomenon presents problems of definition.[2] Are we looking for

---

[2] See M. Bloch, *The Historian's Craft*, tr. P. Putnam (Manchester, 1954), pp. 29–35.

beginnings, or causes, or both? Marc Bloch wrote that 'in popular usage, an origin is a beginning which explains. Worse still, a beginning which is a complete explanation'.[3] But the immediate occasion of a conflict can be distinguished from its underlying causes so that origin is not confused with explanation. We must examine Anglo-French relations over a longer period in order to establish some of the underlying considerations which predisposed the men of the 1330s towards war rather than peace. War was not inevitable, but the breakdown of old restraints and peace-keeping procedures unleashed a conflict which was to dominate the political life of western Europe for over a century.

Some historians would indeed argue that the term 'Hundred Years War' is itself a misnomer which artificially isolates a period of Anglo-French relations. In England, K. B. McFarlane saw a certain degree of unity in the period from 1290 to 1536, partly because it was 'filled . . . by what we have agreed to miscall the *Hundred* Years War, fought from the time of Edward I to that of Henry VIII and Wolsey'.[4] Others have seen Edward III's and Henry V's wars with France merely as phases in a 500-year conflict between England and France which began soon after the Norman Conquest. Any attempt at periodization is artificial and potentially misleading, but McFarlane's concept of 'the French wars of Edward I (1272–1307) and his successors' is adopted here.[5] Many of the 'origins' of later tensions and conflicts lay in the 1290s, and the experience of Anglo-French war during that decade left lasting impressions on both kingdoms. The political, financial and tenurial problems which were both causes and consequences of the war served to heighten Anglo-French tensions and made them more difficult to resolve. Considerable space has therefore been devoted to a study of Edward I's French war.[6]

It would, however, be extremely misleading to present Anglo-French relations during the century or so before 1337 in terms of consistent and continuous hostility. There were still too many ambiguities and contradictions in the relationship between the two powers and their ruling classes to admit of a simplistic interpretation. In 1922, T. F. Tout characterized the period as one of close and fertile interaction between the two kingdoms.[7] Armed clashes between England and France accounted for a mere handful of

---

[3] Bloch, *Historian's Craft*, p. 30.

[4] K. B. McFarlane, *The Nobility of Later Medieval England* (Oxford, 1978), p. 5. See also S. J. Gunn, 'The French wars of Henry VIII', in *The Origins of War in Early Modern Europe*, ed. J. Black (Edinburgh, 1987), pp. 28–51.

[5] McFarlane, *Nobility of Later Medieval England*, p. 19; for the notion of an intermittent conflict lasting for 500 years, see P. S. Lewis, 'France and England: the growth of the nation state', in *Essays in Later Medieval French History* (London, 1985), p. 235.

[6] See below, chapter 6.

[7] T. F. Tout, *France and England: Their Relations in the Middle Ages and Now* (Manchester, 1922), pp. 77–8. See also his *Chapters in the Administrative History of Medieval England*, i (2nd edn, Manchester, 1937), pp. 7–8.

years during this period: intermittent conflict was judicial, jurisdictional and diplomatic, rather than military. The prevailing atmosphere was cosmopolitan, enhanced by personal connections between the ruling families and members of their courts. The breakdown in political and diplomatic relations which led to war thus demands explanation.

Tout accounted for the rupture between England and France by adducing two major reasons: first, the increasingly difficult position into which the king of England was forced as a result of the homage which he owed as duke of Aquitaine and count of Ponthieu to the king of France.[8] Secondly, the similarity between the aims of both French kings and Plantagenet king-dukes produced greater friction: both strove to achieve sovereignty over all their possessions and to exercise an authority superior to that of any of their subjects. Edward I was attempting to construct a 'centralized state' even in his continental dominions and to act there as sovereign *de facto*. Two 'state-building enterprises' were set on a collision course – a view taken up more recently by John Le Patourel.[9] The clash of Capetian and Plantagenet claims to exercise authority over Aquitaine became a constant refrain of Anglo-French relations, and when a new dynasty assumed the crown of France in 1328 the position deteriorated even further. National sentiment fuelled the conflict on both sides and more recent studies have argued a case for viewing the so-called Hundred Years War as a war between nations from its outset. Professor George Cuttino has concluded that 'feudal and national claims were incompatible' in the 1330s and that 'the cosmopolitanism and suzerainty of 1259 had become the nationalism and sovereignty of 1339'.[10] The causes of Anglo-French war have therefore been sought in what has been described as a breakdown in feudal relationships. Professor Philippe Wolff supported this interpretation, believing that feudal structures had become unable to contain new, non-feudal sovereignties.[11] How, in the political and tenurial conditions of the 1330s and 1340s, asked Wolff, could two rulers who regarded themselves as sovereigns with equal authority play the old game of lord and vassal?

Interpretations such as these which see a transition from 'feudalism' to 'nationalism', from feudal monarchy to nation state, taking place in the space of about fifty years, impose certain strains on one's credulity. Recent work has suggested that the concept of 'feudalism' should in any case be aban-

[8] Tout, *France and England*, p. 114. A similar view was advanced by E. Perroy, *The Hundred Years War*, tr. W. B. Wells (London, 1945), p. 69, and G. Templeman, 'Edward III and the beginnings of the Hundred Years War', *TRHS*, 5th ser., ii (1952), p. 71.

[9] J. Le Patourel, 'The king and the princes in fourteenth-century France', 'The origins of the Hundred Years War' and 'France and England in the Middle Ages', in *Feudal Empires. Norman and Plantagenet*, ed. M. Jones (London, 1984), pts XV, pp. 155–83; XI, pp. 28–50, XVIII, pp. 1–14.

[10] G. Cuttino, *English Diplomatic Administration, 1259–1339* (2nd edn, Oxford, 1971), pp. 28, 111.

[11] P. Wolff, 'Un problème d'origines: la Guerre de Cent Ans', *Eventail de l'histoire vivante: Hommage à Lucien Fèbvre*, ii (Paris, 1953), pp. 147–8.

doned by historians.[12] The propaganda of rulers and their agents during this period can also mislead, and historians may easily find themselves overinfluenced by rhetoric about the 'French people' or the 'English nation', emanating from propagandist tracts and other contemporary sources. Of course we must be wary of transporting modern political doctrines and concepts of the state into thirteenth- and fourteenth-century conditions.[13] The inhabitants of the kingdom of France, for example, shared neither a common nationality nor a common language. In England, the ruling and propertied classes spoke and read French (or its Anglo-Norman form) and their way of life was in many ways closer to that of their French contemporaries than their English subjects and tenants. 'National' sentiment was fed by xenophobia and was played upon, especially in England, at periods of crisis in Anglo-French relations in a bid to justify war taxes, aids and exactions.[14] The Capetian and Valois monarchy found it difficult to kindle any sense or sentiment of common French nationality among their subjects, especially in the south. Nevertheless, historians have tended to see nationalism as a force in Anglo-French political relations at a relatively early date.[15]

An increase in national consciousness might explain why the Hundred Years War lasted so long but not how or why it started. The emergence of national sentiment as a political force was more probably a result than a cause of the war.[16] The Anglo-French war began in the same way as previous clashes and its early stages were little different from them. It was precipitated by Gascon problems and by the implications of Edward III's status as a vassal of the French crown. It was the severing of this feudal relationship in

[12] E. A. R. Brown, 'The tyranny of a construct: feudalism and historians of medieval Europe', *AHR*, lxxix (1974), pp. 1063–88; S. Reynolds, *Kingdoms and Communities in Western Europe, 900–1300* (Oxford, 1984), pp. 1, 9, 254.

[13] Tout, *France and England*, p. 8; Reynolds, *Kingdoms and Communities*, pp. 251–4.

[14] For the prevalence of French among the English knightly class, see AN J.633, nos 36–7 where a Gascon notary recorded that Philip V's letters summoning Edward II to perform homage for Aquitaine in October 1317 were translated aloud from Latin to French for the benefit of Gilbert Pecche, knight, the English seneschal of the duchy. The letters were read to him in French, his 'mother tongue' (*lingua materna*) as he did not understand Latin and Philip V's commissioners reported that 'nous feismes lire les lettres dessus dites, lesquelles nous li exposames apres *en langue française*'. For the use of propaganda designed to appeal to anti-French feeling among the English from 1295 onwards see the writ of summons to the clergy in W. Stubbs, *Select Charters* (9th edn, Oxford, 1960), p. 480 where Edward I claimed that the French intended to 'destroy the English language' (*linguam Anglicam*). The claim was repeated in 1344 and 1346 in similar circumstances (*Rot. Parl*, ii, pp. 147, 158).

[15] See, for example, C. Allmand, *The Hundred Years War. England and France at War, c.1300–c.1450* (Cambridge, 1988), p. 7.

[16] The terms *natio gallicana* and *natio anglicana* are found in documents dating from the second decade of the fourteenth century. They are best translated as 'people' rather than 'nation' and this appears to be the sense in which the phrase 'la nacion Dengleterre' was used under Edward III in diplomatic memoranda of the 1330s. See PRO, C 47/28/5, nos 17, 18, 34; cf. Cuttino, *English Diplomatic Administration*, p. 27.

1340 – when Edward III assumed the title 'king of France' – which turned
a dispute between lord and vassal into a dynastic war for the French
succession. But this owed little or nothing to national ideas or sentiments at
this period. The clash of rival sovereignties now became overt, but the old
issue of authority over the duchy of Aquitaine lay at the heart of the dispute.

That is why this book accords so prominent a place to Aquitaine in its
treatment of Anglo-French tensions. The duchy was all that remained of the
Plantagenets' Angevin inheritance. It was therefore a vital component of any
future strategy to recover their extensive continental dominions. The term
'Aquitaine' is here used in preference to 'Gascony' when referring to the
south-western French possessions of the Plantagenets. Gascony was a linguistic entity; Aquitaine (or Guyenne) described a political and administrative
area.[17] Similarly, 'English' is not used to describe the tenure and administration of Aquitaine and other continental possessions by the English crown.
('Plantagenet rule in Aquitaine' thus replaces such potentially misleading
terms as 'English rule in Gascony', 'English Bordeaux' or 'English officials in
south-west France'.) Aquitaine was not a colony, its rulers and their officers
were not 'English' in the modern sense, and the Plantagenet dominions were
not governed according to 'English' laws and customs. The king-dukes spoke
French throughout our period and considered themselves to be continental
princes as well as monarchs of an island kingdom. In this analysis considerable emphasis has therefore been laid upon the common culture which
bound the courts of England and France together. Similarly, the particular
internal problems and tensions within Aquitaine provide the framework for
an examination of the Plantagenets' role as dukes, as reflected in their
dealings with the region's nobility, clergy and towns. All these issues exercised a direct influence upon the course of Anglo-French relations.

Although much has been made by historians of the fundamental significance of Aquitaine in the growth of Anglo-French hostility, they have focused
primarily upon rulers rather than their subjects. Royalists to a man, both
English and French historians have – with few exceptions – treated Aquitaine and its inhabitants as an anomalous impediment to the inexorable
progress of the nation state.[18] But of course there were many other interests
at stake besides the aims and ambitions of rulers. In particular, the turbulent
and independently minded inhabitants of south-west France interposed their
own preoccupations and concerns between Capetian and Plantagenet claims
to exercise sovereignty over Aquitaine. This demands a change in focus away

[17] See C. Bémont, *La Guyenne pendant la domination anglaise, 1152–1453* (London and New York,
1920), p. 7.

[18] See, for example, Perroy, *Hundred Years War*, p. 320: 'everything encouraged the Gascons to
resist the French monarchy's attacks: their self-interested loyalty towards the ducal dynasty,
their long-standing habit of political autonomy, the trade links with England which ensured
their prosperity', and p. 330: 'the provincial nationalisms dangerously supported the activity of
the princes, a danger against which the State was not yet able to safeguard itself'.

from the conference table and the royal audience chamber towards the castles and communes of the south-west. I have therefore attempted to give some idea of the political, social and economic condition of the duchy of Aquitaine and its neighbouring territories during this period. Gascon society itself had certain characteristics (such as a tradition of private war, considerable urban faction and the sudden growth of new settlements) which arguably contributed to Anglo-French tensions.[19] Apparently regional or local issues therefore assume a much wider significance when they are viewed as determinants of conflict between two of the major powers in western Europe.

The sources for this study are scattered and diverse. A dearth of chronicles in south-west France where, unlike northern France and the Low Countries, there was no vigorous tradition of historical writing, makes the historian reliant upon archival records of war, diplomacy, finance and administration. These survive in great bulk in the Public Record Office: the practice of Chancery enrolment of all formal letters sent by the Plantagenets to Aquitaine produced the long series of Gascon Rolls, and the Exchequer accounts for their French possessions are also invaluable sources. These include the Foreign Accounts Various, Wardrobe and Household and Enrolled Accounts. Diplomatic material is found in the published papal registers and letter collections; in unpublished Chancery Miscellanea and Diplomatic Documents (Exchequer); and the remarkably copious class of Ancient Correspondence contains reports, newsletters and other missives sent from Aquitaine to England and vice versa from a relatively early date (c.1240). This unrivalled collection of letters can be supplemented by the files of Ancient Petitions, comprising supplications and requests from the king-dukes' Gascon subjects. Some of this documentary material was printed by Thomas Rymer in his *Foedera* and by other scholars, but a great deal remains unpublished. There no real equivalent in France, nor indeed in western Europe (with the possible exception of the archives of the *Corona de Aragon*) to this great archive of medieval secular government. The Archives Nationales (Paris) possess valuable but incomplete series of treaties, homages and financial accounts but there is an almost complete dearth of diplomatic and other correspondence. Very few petitions or letters relating to Aquitaine survive, while the unpublished records of the Paris Parlement are fragmentary and of procedural rather than political interest. Much of the French material in this book is therefore derived from the provincial Archives Départmentales which, as a result of the confiscation by the state of ecclesiastical and seigneurial archives in 1790, hold extensive medieval records. Among them, the collections of seigneurial and notarial documents in the Archives Départmentales of Pyrénées-Atlantiques, Gers, Tarn-et-Garonne and Pas-de-Calais have been exploited, as well as a smaller body of material in the Archives Municipales at Bordeaux. Town archives in this region have been generally well edited and extensively published: this is the case at

---

[19] See below, chapters 4 and 5.

Bordeaux, Bayonne and Agen. The reader will readily appreciate that the great collections of seigneurial archives (such as the records of the families of Albret, Armagnac, Foix-Béarn and L'Isle-Jourdain) are indispensable sources for the political behaviour and family structure of the Gascon nobility during this period.

Although the records of Anglo-French relations during the Middle Ages are now divided among the archives of two autonomous and self-contained nation states, both kingdoms shared a common civilization and culture in the thirteenth and early fourteenth centuries. As we shall see, political and institutional divergence was not yet accompanied by cultural distinctiveness among their articulate elites and ruling classes. The specifically 'English' and 'French' forms and genres which were to produce the vernacular cultures of a later date had not yet emerged and Middle English had not yet become a literary or administrative language. The English court was still cosmopolitan and eclectic in its tastes and personnel. Moreover, the tenure of extensive continental possessions by the Plantagenets was still fresh in contemporary memories during the 1250s. The future of these lands was uncertain then, and their disintegration demanded a readjustment and realignment of Plantagenet attitudes and ambitions. The following chapter will discuss the implications of the loss of the Angevin Empire for Anglo-French political, dynastic and cultural connections.

2

Anglo-French Civilization

2.1 The Legacy of the Angevin Empire

A few days before Christmas 1286, Edward I of England was in his duchy of Aquitaine. On 20 December he sent six pieces of cloth of gold to the abbess and convent at Fontevrault, which he had recently visited. These were to be placed upon the tombs of his ancestors who lay buried there – Henry II, Richard I, Eleanor of Aquitaine and Isabella of Angoulême (see plate 2.1).[1] In 1330 his grandson Edward III continued the practice of his forbears and was still giving alms to Fontevrault, the mausoleum of the Angevin dynasty.[2] Well before 1330 the Angevin Empire had ceased to be the dynamic and significant political force that it had been in the mid and late twelfth century. Yet dynastic memory kept it alive as a concept which still exercised a certain influence over the behaviour of the Plantagenets. In December 1291, Edward I confirmed and renewed all the grants of privilege bestowed by his Angevin ancestors on Fontevrault, and Henry III's heart was dispatched (albeit tardily) for burial there.[3] An undated letter from the abbess to Edward, probably written at this juncture, wished him prosperity in his affairs and reminded him of the convent's special relationship with the English crown.[4] By Edward I's reign (1272–1307) the continental possessions of his house had shrunk to a fraction of their former vast extent – by 1290 they consisted solely of the duchy of Aquitaine and *comté* of Ponthieu – but the notion that

---

[1] PRO, E 36/201, p. 93. For earlier Plantagenet relations with the abbey in general see T. S. R. Boase, 'Fontevrault and the Plantagenets', *Journal of the British Archaeological Association*, 3rd ser., xxxiv (1971), pp. 1–10. Edward was at Fontevrault on 1 September 1286.

[2] E 101/166/1, fo. 36[r]. Edward gave 40 *l.t.* from the revenues of the constable of Bordeaux 'quas . . . Henricus rex quondam Anglie eisdem abbatisse et conventu in helemosina dedit et concessit pro anniversario suo et parentum suorum' (1329–30).

[3] *Foedera*, I, ii, 758.

[4] SC 1/17, no. 120; also nos 115–18. See also E 101/160/1, m. 2[r] (oblations to the convent, 1303–5), and SC 1/13, no. 61: letter of Edward I ordering Jean de Grilly, seneschal of Gascony, to pay arrears of revenues granted to the convent from the tolls and customs of Marmande, as these had been given 'a clare memorie predecessoribus nostris ipsis in puram et perpetuam elemosinam' (3 March 1283).

2.1 Tomb effigies of Henry II (d. 1189) and Eleanor of Aquitaine (d. 1204) at the abbey of Fontevrault. This Angevin foundation was patronized by the Plantagenets until the reign of Edward III.

the Plantagenets had a continental role to play remained firmly embedded in their minds and in those of their subjects on both sides of the Channel.[5]

Continental involvement of this kind immediately brought the Plantagenet king-dukes of Aquitaine into contact with the Capetian monarchy of France. Dynastic sentiment, however strong, could not overcome the realities of thirteenth-century power-politics. The chronicle of Plantagenet losses in the reigns of Philip Augustus (1180–1223), Louis VIII (1223–6) and Louis IX (1226–70) could not be unwritten. Henry III's heart might, literally, be in Anjou, but 'by the end of his reign [he] was indisputably an English king and men were beginning to think of the Plantagenets as an English dynasty'.[6] Such may have been the common view, but it was not shared by the Plantagenets themselves. A dynasty which had ruled a great network of continental territories, larger in geographical extent than those of the Capetian kings of France, could not easily forget that legacy, nor readily adjust to the changed political conditions of the later thirteenth century. Their am-

---

[5] See Appendix III, maps 1 and 2; J.-P. Trabut-Cussac, *L'Administration anglaise en Gascogne sous Henry III et Edouard I de 1254 à 1307* (Geneva, 1972), xi–xvii for a description of the duchy of Aquitaine in the mid thirteenth century.

[6] J. Gillingham, *The Angevin Empire* (London, 1984), p. 84.

bitions and aspirations abroad – to adopt an Anglocentric point of view – are a major theme of this book, and the spectre of Henry II and his sons cannot be easily exorcized. The implications of this legacy were manifold, leading not only to strains and tensions in the Plantagenets' relations with their English subjects but also to positive benefits for the kingdom of England.

At its fullest extent, the Angevin Empire had comprised most of western France and its Atlantic seaboard. Normandy, Maine, Touraine, a sympathetic Brittany, Anjou, Poitou, Limousin, Saintonge, Périgord, Quercy, Gascony and the Agenais formed, Renouard argued, 'un empire en latitude, en aucun point il ne mord profondément sur le continent'.[7] This view tends to underrate the eastward extension of Plantagenet territories, which penetrated quite deeply into Auvergne and the Central Massif at certain points. But its centres of gravity lay firmly in western France – at Rouen, Tours, Poitiers, Saintes, Limoges, Bordeaux and Bayonne. None of these cities stood in a direct relationship to the Capetians, and the people of the southern lands were sharply differentiated from those of northern France by language, law and custom. Yet these divergences did not necessarily mean that the Plantagenet dominions were an incoherent and 'overextended' political, economic, geographical and cultural agglomeration.[8] A measure of unity was provided by routes of communication, on land and sea. The sea-ports of western France – Rouen, Nantes, La Rochelle, Bordeaux, Bayonne – were linked in common dependence upon England and the Iberian peninsula.[9] Natural antagonisms and rivalries between their maritime communities were accentuated after the Plantagenet loss of Normandy (1204), the reduction of the Seine valley to Capetian obedience (thereby providing Paris with a direct outlet to the sea) and the dispossession of Henry III at La Rochelle (1224). But in the preceding half-century it would be possible to speak in terms of an Angevin seaborne as well as land-based empire.

Land routes also defined the geographical shape of the Angevin dominions. If it had a centre, that lay in the triangle formed by the cities of Angers, Tours and Poitiers. 'The strip of road which passes . . . from Tours through Poiters', wrote Powicke, 'commanded, throughout the Middle Ages, the whole of north-western France, and was the key to the north and south.'[10] Further integration of western France under one dynasty was brought to a halt, and the loss of Touraine and the Loire valley was as crucial to the

---

[7] Y. Renouard, 'Essai sur le rôle de l'empire angevin dans la formation de la France et de la civilisation française aux xiie et xiiie siècles', in *Etudes d'histoire médiévale*, ii (Paris, 1968), p. 849.

[8] See J. C. Holt, 'The end of the Anglo-Norman realm', *Proceedings of the British Academy*, lxi (1975), pp. 226–7, 252–3; C. W. Hollister, 'Normandy, France and the Anglo-Norman *regnum*', *Speculum*, li (1976), pp. 202–42, esp. pp. 235, 241–2.

[9] Gillingham, *Angevin Empire*, pp. 42–6.

[10] F. M. Powicke, *The Loss of Normandy, 1189–1204. Studies in the History of the Angevin Empire* (2nd edn, Manchester, 1961), p. 9.

collapse of the Angevin Empire as that of Normandy. But imperial ambitions die hard; only in 1259 did Henry III 'in whose veins the blood of southern nobles mingled with the blood of Rollo [of Normandy] and Fulk Nerra [of Anjou] surrender . . . his claim to unite Aquitaine, Normandy and Anjou'.[11] Under Edward I, as we shall see, the surrender of the greater part of the Plantagenet's continental inheritance was a fact of very recent history. In northern France a similar process was at work. The acquisition of Artois and the Amiennois through inheritance by Philip Augustus in 1191 brought very substantial gains to the Capetians *before* the recovery of Normandy.[12] A 72 per cent increase in the yield of the Capetian royal domain took place between 1180 and 1203, before the annexation of the Plantagenet territories.[13] Revenues from the forests of northern France and from the extremely valuable tolls on merchandise at Bapaume (Artois) contributed substantially to the war treasury with which Philip Augustus fought Richard I and John.[14] Just as Paris was to be linked to the sea via the Seine estuary after Philip's conquest of Normandy, so the emergent capital of Capetian France was brought into a closer relationship to the wealth of the Low Countries through the absorption of Artois. It was on the northern borders of France and the Empire, moreover, that the last act in the drama of John's defeat was to be played out – at Bouvines on 27 July 1214, when the coalition between the Plantagenets, Flanders and the German Empire was routed by Philip Augustus's army. Plantagenet intervention against France in the Low Countries and the Empire was not to be revived until the last decade of the century.

A shift in Plantagenet aims and ambitions on the European stage can be discerned after these setbacks. The collapse of the Hohenstaufen dynasty in Germany and Italy between 1254 and 1268 created a power vacuum in imperial politics. Opportunities for intervention arose which Henry III was quick to grasp. The election of Richard, earl of Cornwall (d. 1272), Henry's brother, as king of the Romans (or German monarch) in May 1257 set the seal on this new direction of Plantagenet policy.[15] His marriage to Beatrix (d. 1277), daughter of Dirk II, lord of Valkenburg (Fauquemont) in Limburg, was an attempt to integrate the Plantagenets into the politics of the Franco-imperial borderland.[16] As 'queen of Almain' (*regina Allemanie*) Beatrix

---

[11] Powicke, *Loss of Normandy*, p. 8; he made a similar point about Edward I's 'southern-ness' in *Henry III and the Lord Edward* (Oxford, 1947), p. 688.

[12] J. W. Baldwin, *The Government of Philip Augustus. Foundations of French Royal Power in the Middle Ages* (Berkeley, Los Angeles and London, 1986), pp. 155–61; Holt, 'End of the Anglo-Norman Realm', pp. 237–8.

[13] Baldwin, *Government of Philip Augustus*, pp. 155, 248, 257–8.

[14] Baldwin, *Government of Philip Augustus*, pp. 111–12, 249, 251–7.

[15] N. Denholm-Young, *Richard of Cornwall* (Oxford, 1947), pp. 57–60; Powicke, *Henry III and the Lord Edward*, i, pp. 242–4.

[16] Powicke, *Henry III and the Lord Edward*, i, p. 244; *Age of Chivalry. Art in Plantagenet England, 1200–1400*, ed. J. Alexander and P. Binski (London, 1987), p. 290; S. H. Steinberg 'A portrait of

was depicted as donor of a surviving stained-glass panel, probably to the Franciscan convent at Oxford where she was buried, wearing the crown of Germany.[17] Her husband had contributed his symbolic share to the insignia of German monarchy by giving a dove-topped sceptre (in the English style) to Aachen cathedral in 1262. This was, he decreed, to be used at subsequent coronations of the kings of the Romans, together with a crown, vestments and a gilt apple.[18] Henry III's schemes – in Germany, Italy and Sicily – ultimately collapsed, to his cost, but they represented a Plantagenet response to the events of 1204–59 which had resulted in the dynasty's displacement from their central and prestigious place in European politics. An essential precondition for this shift of emphasis lay in peace with France. Henry III's admiration for and emulation of Louis IX is well known. At Westminster a second Paris was created, with a great abbey church, a palace and a palace chapel on the French pattern, a cult of the relics of saintly ancestors and a permanent administrative centre.[19] A new phase in Anglo-French relations had begun.

The transition from a hostile to a pacific relationship between the houses of Plantagenet and Capet took place between 1224 and 1259. Philip Augustus had concentrated his efforts against Henry II and his sons in northern and central France. The loss of La Rochelle and much of Poitou in 1224–5, however, reflected a new threat to the survival of the Plantagenet inheritance.[20] A French attack was mounted on the duchy of Aquitaine, but the day was saved by the able lieutenancy exercised there by Richard of Cornwall, and by large loans to him from the cities of Bordeaux and Bayonne. 'The fall of La Rochelle', writes Dr Gillingham, 'marked the end of the Angevin Empire.'[21] But the issue still remained in the balance for a further twenty years. Capetian successes in Poitou and Aquitaine were heavily dependent upon the volatile loyalty of the great magnates and nobles of Poitou. Hugh X de Lusignan, count of La Marche, had led the French campaigns against Aquitaine in 1224–5 but in 1241–2, influenced by his wife, Isabella of Angoulême, played turncoat and defied Louis IX.[22] Louis's successful Taillebourg expedition of that year was perhaps the real turning-point in Capetian–Plantagenet rivalry. Poitou was now securely in Capetian

Beatrix of Falkenburg', *Antiquaries Journal*, xviii (1938), pp. 142–5; F. R. Lewis, 'Beatrice of Falkenburg, 3rd wife of Richard of Cornwall', *EHR*, lii (1937), pp. 279–82.

[17] *Age of Chivalry*, p. 290 (cat. no. 226) for a plate.

[18] E. Grimme, 'Der Aachene Domschatz', *Aachener Kunstblätter*, xlii (1972), no. 51; *Age of Chivalry*, p. 203 (cat. no. 14).

[19] See below, pp. 35–7; P. Binski, *The Painted Chamber at Westminster*, Society of Antiquaries Occasional Paper, n.s., ix (London, 1986), p. 112.

[20] The most recent account of the campaigns in Poitou is R. C. Stacey, *Politics, Policy and Finance under Henry III, 1216–45* (Oxford, 1987), pp. 160–8.

[21] Gillingham, *Angevin Empire*, p. 82.

[22] Stacey, *Politics, Policy and Finance*, pp. 184, 194–6; C. Bémont, 'La Campagne de Poitou (1242–1243), Taillebourg et Saintes', *AM*, v (1893), pp. 289–314.

hands, given as an apanage to Louis IX's brother, Alphonse of Poitiers, as part of his great southern endowment.[23] Aquitaine was then surrounded on all sides (except the sea coast) by fiefs which stood in a more immediate relationship to the Capetians than ever before.

Before 1242–3 Henry III had journeyed to France in order to recover his lands by military force. In 1253–4 he went peacefully to visit Louis IX at Paris and, as duke of Aquitaine, to arbitrate a feud which was dividing his city of Bordeaux into two powerful factions.[24] The negotiations between him and Louis in the late 1250s heightened the atmosphere of harmony and concord. When Henry became Louis's vassal for Aquitaine in 1259, there was every sign that what Louis clearly regarded as a family quarrel had been resolved – at least among its leading protagonists.[25] The alliance between the houses of Plantagenet and Capet, secured and cemented by the treaty of Paris, and by marriage proposals, was intended to bring peace to a strife-torn Europe and the furtherance of a Crusade to recover the holy places. Yet the subjects of both parties to that alliance were less eager to embrace its terms. Henry III's dependence upon Louis IX for support against his own vassals in England was much resented by them, and Louis was thought by some of his own counsellors to have 'given away too much' to his Plantagenet kinsman in 1259.[26] A community of interest was forming between the ruling houses; but the community of interest between ruler and ruled within England began to crumble. 'Henry', argues Dr Clanchy, 'found himself in difficulties because he was so persistent in giving preference to his overseas inheritance and ambitions than to England itself.'[27] The spectacle of mutual kingly self-congratulation was not pleasing to some of their subjects. The close affinities between Henry III's and Louis IX's view of kingship were exemplified in Louis's arbitration of Henry's dispute with his baronage in January 1264.[28]

The 'Mise' or *Reformatio pacis* given by Louis IX at Amiens on 23 January 1264 referred to Henry III as 'our dearest kinsman' (*carissimus consanguineus noster*) and declared that he should have 'full power and free authority in his kingdom' (*plenam potestatem et liberum regimen*) over his subjects.[29] Louis, after the fullest deliberation, concluded that the baronial provisions of 1258–9

---

[23] L. Delisle, 'Mémoire sur une lettre inédite addressée à la Reine Blanche par un habitant de La Rochelle', *BEC*, xvii (1856), pp. 513–33.

[24] *CPR, 1258–66*, p. 608; J.-P. Trabut-Cussac, 'L'essor politique et administrative', *Histoire de Bordeaux, III*, ed. Y. Renouard (Bordeaux, 1965), pp. 102–8.

[25] See Jean de Joinville, *Histoire de St Louis*, ed. J. Natalis de Wailly (Paris, 1868), p. 245.

[26] Joinville, *Histoire de St Louis*, p. 245; P. Chaplais, 'Le traité de Paris de 1259 et l'inféodation de la Gascogne allodiale', *MA*, (1955), p. 124; M. Gavrilovitch, *Etude sur le traité de Paris de 1259* (Paris, 1899), pp. 41–2. See below, pp. 48–56.

[27] M. T. Clanchy, *England and its Rulers, 1066–1272* (London, 1983), p. 260.

[28] See C. T. Wood, 'The Mise of Amiens and St Louis' theory of kingship', *French Historical Studies*, vi (1970), pp. 300–10.

[29] *Documents of the Baronial Movement of Reform and Rebellion, 1258–67*, ed. R. F. Treharne and I. J. Sanders (Oxford, 1973), pp. 280, 288.

had greatly harmed the 'rights and honour of the king' (*juri et honori regio*) and gravely disturbed the realm of England.[30] The Provisions of Oxford were thus quashed and declared null and void, while the King was to retain control over his choice of those counsellors, whether native or alien, whom he thought faithful and useful to him.[31] An identity of interest between rulers was set out here, even though those rulers were now bound together in a 'feudal' relationship whereby one was a liegeman of the other. A similar assumption, that lords possessed common interests against their own men, is found in Edward I's dealings with his troublesome Gascon vassal Gaston VII, *vicomte* of Béarn in 1277–8. Edward's envoys told Philip III of France that their lord had been insulted and dishonoured by Gaston, but Edward had placed his trust in Philip and his court to redress his grievances.[32] On Edward's behalf, Philip was therefore requested to 'remedy this matter so that it will redound to your honour . . . and to the honour of monarchy [*roiauté*] and of all lords against their men' (*a touz seigneurs contre leurs hommes*).[33] The appeal to kingly honour was to be repeated on several occasions until the Anglo-French breach of 1294 led to war.

The feudal relationship between the Plantagenets and Capetians will be considered at greater length at a later stage, but some discussion of its implications before 1290 is appropriate at this point. Historians have indicated a 'structural weakness' in the Angevin Empire which stemmed from the obligations of its rulers to perform homage to the French crown from 1151 onwards for most of their continental dominions.[34] They never paid homage specifically for the duchy of Aquitaine (in particular, for that part to the south of the Garonne), and this partly explains how their south-western French possessions were able to survive Capetian attacks. The ancient duchy of Gascony, united with Aquitaine in the later eleventh century, had never been subject to the French crown.[35] In the registers recording military and other services from their kingdom compiled under Philip Augustus, Louis VIII and Louis IX, the archdioceses of Bordeaux, Auch and their provinces were not included. In the south-west, the French kingdom extended no further than Poitiers.[36] The Capetian kings had little conception of what

[30] *Documents of the Baronial Movement*, p. 286.

[31] *Documents of the Baronial Movement*, p. 188. Louis's award also quashed the baronial provision that 'the realm of England should in future be governed by native-born men'.

[32] SC 1/55, no. 6 (probably November 1277).

[33] SC 1/55, no. 6; SC 1/13, no. 7, where Philip is requested by Edward to respect 'your and our honour' (7 February 1278).

[34] See J. Le Patourel, 'The Norman Conquest, 1066, 1106, 1154', in *Proceedings of the Battle Conference on Anglo-Norman Studies*, i, 1978 (Woodbridge, 1979), p. 118; Gillingham, *Angevin Empire*, pp. 87–8.

[35] Chaplais, 'Le traité de Paris de 1259', pp. 128–32, 136–7.

[36] See G. Sivery, 'La description du royaume de France par les conseillers de Philippe Auguste et par leurs successeurs', *MA*, xc (1984), pp. 72, 78; R. Fawtier, 'Comment le roi de France, au début du xive siècle, pouvait-il se representer son royaume?', *Mélanges . . . P.-E. Martin* (Geneva, 1961), pp. 65–77.

these remote lands were like, and little connection with the Gascon nobility or towns. Unlike the great families of the Norman and Poitevin marches, the nobles of Aquitaine were not in the habit of appealing to the king of France's court, as the Lusignans had done in 1202, against the actions and decisions of their Plantagenet overlord.[37] Perhaps taking Aquitaine as their model, some pro-Angevin writers of the later twelfth century asserted a parity of status between the Angevins and Capetians. The *Draco Normannicus* written in 1168 by Etienne de Rouen, a monk of Bec, saw Henry II as a great continental prince, negotiating on equal terms with Frederick Barbarossa and with Henry the Lion, his own son-in-law.[38] He wrote that the Lion of Saxony: 'Mandat ne regi Francorum subiciatur, / Cum sibi par virtus, par honor atque thronus, / Non par set major . . .'.[39] Honour, virtue and regal dignity made Henry II more than equal to Louis VII in the writer's mind. The demeaning aspects of the homage ceremony could, moreover, be overcome by such devices as its performance on the frontiers between lordships held by lord and vassal (*hommage en marche*).[40] An element of this notion survived into the fourteenth century, when the French kings were sometimes prepared to accept Plantagenet homage at Amiens or Boulogne rather than Paris. Richard I had been crowned duke of Aquitaine and count of Poitou in 1172 at Limoges and Poitiers, and the *ordo ad benedicendum* (coronation order) made no reference to the kings of France. He was invested with a coronet (*circulum aureum*) lance, banner, sword, spurs and ring, and the two ceremonies were 'a ritual expression of Aquitaine's *de facto* independence from the King of France'.[41] Echoes of these symbolic assertions of ducal autonomy were also to be heard at later periods.

Yet the marked expansion in the French kingdom's territorial size between 1204 and 1259 could not fail to have an impact upon such claims to autonomy and independence. The ability of Philip Augustus and his immediate successors to translate what had for long been no more than theoretical claims into judicial, and sometimes geographical, reality changed the balance of forces. By offering protection and recourse to royal justice to all, breaches were gradually made in the dykes of princely and seigneural resistance to Capetian authority over their subjects. The process was very gradual, but the evolution from an essentially contractual relationship between king and magnates to one which acknowledged some form of sovereignty (*superioritas*) had taken place by the end of the thirteenth century.

[37] Powicke, *Loss of Normandy*, pp. 145–9; Gillingham, *Angevin Empire*, pp. 67–9.

[38] *Draco Normannicus*, in *Chronicles of the Reigns of Stephen, Henry II and Richard I*, ed. R. Howlett, ii (*RS*, London, 1885), p. 720; Holt, 'End of the Anglo-Norman Realm', p. 244.

[39] *Draco Normannicus*, ll. 735–7.

[40] See J. F. Le Marignier, *Recherches sur l'hommage en marche et les frontières féodales* (Lille, 1945), pp. 3–8, 177–80.

[41] J. Gillingham, *Richard the Lionheart* (London, 1978), pp. 58–9; M. Bloch, *Les Rois Thaumaturges* (Paris, 1961), p. 194, n. 1.

The terminology of French royal ordinances began to change, from the contractual language of *c*.1200–30 to the maxims and formulae drawn from Roman law of the 1290s.[42] In 1279 Philip III ceded the Agenais to Edward I, as duke of Aquitaine, 'saving sovereignty and *ressort* . . . to the king of France' (*salvis superioritate et ressorto . . . regis France*), but the inhabitants of the region were to accept and obey Edward as immediate lord.[43] Although, as Beaumanoir stated at this time, the magnates were 'sovereigns within their baronies', they were supposed to execute the crown's ordinances – which often meant that they anticipated royal legislation by legislating in their own name for their own domains.[44] But the notion of intervention by the crown of France as a result of default or denial of justice by a magnate, even by a peer of France or his officers, had begun to develop. In 1277, Gaston VII of Béarn had claimed 'false judgement and . . . default of justice' against Edward I's courts in the Paris Parlement.[45] Philip III was therefore able to intervene as a result of this appeal. Such actions could only be activated at the request of the immediate lord's vassal and the notion of French royal sovereignty remained largely theoretical and judicial throughout this period. The French king could act, but only by default. Philip the Fair's interventions in the 1290s were still guided and determined by the appeals of the allegedly wronged and disaffected vassals of the magnates, the greatest of whom was the king-duke of Aquitaine.

The tenacity with which the king-duke, his officers and agents defended his rights and prerogatives in the duchy of Aquitaine testified to its value. Not only was it a matter of dignity and prestige that the remaining continental possessions of the Plantagenets should be preserved, but political and material forces were at work to maintain the Anglo-Gascon connection. England's 'union avec l'Aquitaine', wrote Renouard, 'l'a maintenue integrée dans l'Europe, la faisant participer aux vicissitudes politiques comme à toutes les formes de la civilisation du continent'.[46] The benefits of the relationship were essentially threefold: political, economic and cultural. When they were joined, as we shall see, to the constant diplomatic presence maintained by the Plantagenets at Paris after 1259, England's latent isolationism was effectively countered.[47] English historians have sometimes lamented the retention of continental possessions by the English crown in the later Middle Ages, maintaining that they distracted English kings from their

---

[42] Sivery, 'La description du royaume de France', p. 73, and the observations on the nature of the *regnum* in Baldwin, *Government of Philip Augustus*, pp. 359–62.

[43] *Archives Municipales d'Agen. Chartes (1189–1328)*, ed. A. Magen and G. Tholin (Villeneuve-sur-Lot, 1876), p.j. no. lx, p. 85 (9 August 1279).

[44] See P. Chaplais, 'La souveraineté du roi de France et le pouvoir législatif en Guyenne au début du xiv\u1d49 siècle', in *Essays in Medieval Diplomacy and Administration* (London, 1981), pt V, pp. 449–67.

[45] SC 1/55, no. 6 (?November 1277).

[46] Renouard, *Etudes d'histoire médiévale*, ii, p. 875.

[47] See below, pp. 39–40.

proper purpose: the reduction of the British Isles to obedience and the formation of an island nation state.[48] This is to misread the preoccupations of England's medieval rulers. The continental inheritance served too many useful purposes to the abandoned, and claims to territory abroad had important implications for the dynastic and matrimonial policies of the ruling house.

The demands made upon England, in money and manpower, for the defence of the Angevin inheritance are well known and have been intensively studied.[49] But the line could never have been held in south-west France without the active collaboration and support of its inhabitants. Firstly, the Angevin government in Aquitaine commanded the support of the most prosperous and populated towns.[50] Bordeaux was described as a 'commune' by John in 1206 and it clearly possessed many rights of self-government. By 1225 the loss of Poitiers and La Rochelle made it the effective capital of the remaining Plantagenet dominions.[51] But the towns of the south-west were not allowed to move very far towards the autonomous, quasi-republican institutions either of Languedoc or of Flanders. From about 1205 onwards, the Plantagenets began to exert tighter control over them by granting them the constitutions known as the *Etablissements de Rouen*.[52] These northern French prescriptions for town government granted to the isle of Oléron in 1205, Bayonne in 1215 and Bordeaux by 1253–4, awarded them many urban privileges and liberties. But an essential facet of the *Etablissements* was the stipulation that the king-duke should appoint a mayor and *jurats*, or municipal council, in each of the communes.[53] He was also to receive the military service of the communal militias when he summoned them to his aid. These were exceptionally valuable and important powers. The looser structure of many Languedocian and meridional towns, with their *consuls* and *syndics*, never developed in the south-west, and from 1261 onwards the

---

[48] For perceptive comment see Clanchy, *England and its Rulers*, pp. 30–5; and R. W. Southern, 'England's first entry into Europe', in *Medieval Humanism and Other Essays* (Oxford, 1970), pp. 135–57.

[49] See J. C. Holt, *The Northerners* (Oxford, 1961), pp. 143–74; Gillingham, *Richard the Lionheart*, pp. 303–4; G. L. Harriss, *King, Parliament and Public Finance in Medieval England to 1369* (Oxford, 1975), pp. 14–26, 28–39; and most recently, J. C. Holt, 'The loss of Normandy and royal finances', in *War and Government in the Middle Ages. Essays in Honour of J. O. Prestwich*, ed. J. Gillingham and J. C. Holt (Woodbridge, 1984), pp. 92–105; Stacey, *Politics, Policy and Finance*, pp. 160–200, 237–59.

[50] See F. B. Marsh, *English Rule in Gascony, 1199–1259* (Ann Arbor, 1912), esp. pp. 152–6.

[51] Renouard, in *Histoire de Bordeaux, III*, pp. 28–9.

[52] See A. Giry, *Les Etablissements de Rouen*, i (Paris, 1885), *passim*; Renouard, *Etudes d'histoire médiévale*, ii, pp. 858–60, 977–92.

[53] *Archives Municipales de Bordeaux. Livre des Coutumes*, ed. H. Barckhausen (Bordeaux, 1890), pp. 273–309; C. Bémont, 'Les institutions municipales de Bordeaux au Moyen Age: la mairie et la jurade', *RH*, cxxiii (1916), pp. 274–90; and 'La mairie et la jurade dans les villes de la Guyenne anglaise: La Réole', *AM*, xxi (1919), pp. 23–33.

tendencies which Bordeaux showed towards becoming a city-republic were tempered by ducal intervention to appoint its mayor and *jurats*.[54] Although somewhat modified by southern customs deriving from the written Roman law of the Midi, the constitutions of Bordeaux, Bayonne and smaller towns such as Libourne, La Réole or St Emilion were primarily northern French in derivation and inspiration. Such relative uniformity may also have given greater cohesion to the Angevin Empire, for its major towns from Rouen to La Rochelle and Bayonne shared the *Etablissements*.[55] The price to the ruler was, at Bordeaux as elsewhere, the grant of extensive commercial privileges. Exemption of the bourgeois from customs payment on their wine, and the concession of a virtual monopoly whereby the produce of vineyards in the *haut pays* of the Dordogne and Garonne was held back until Bordeaux wine was sold, were considerable stimulants to the loyalty of the commune.[56] In 1203–4, 1205 and 1242 these concessions were rewarded by the financial and military support given to the Plantagenets by Bordeaux and other towns against both Castilian and French attacks on the duchy.[57]

A further benefit which England gained from continued possession of the residual Plantagenet inheritance was maritime supremacy. Control of the sea and of sea-routes was crucial to the economic symbiosis established within the Angevin Empire. The importance of Bayonne, for example, especially after the loss of La Rochelle in 1224, remained fundamental to a network of communications established from the bay of Biscay to the Tweed. England's economic and commercial contacts with Spain and with North Africa depended in large measure on the shipping of Bayonne.[58] The Cinque Ports received an admiral on the pattern of Bayonne's admiral, created in 1295, and ships from Bayonne brought supplies of wine, corn, flour and other victuals to Edward I's army in Wales during March and April 1283.[59] English ports and the Bayonnais together provided ships in which Bordeaux's wine was carried, and England's reliance on Aquitaine for wine – for both liturgical and secular consumption – helped to give birth to an English mercantile marine. Gascon vintners and middlemen resided in the Vintry ward of London, and Henry le Waleys served as mayor of London in 1273–4 and of Bordeaux in 1275.[60] In the early thirteenth century in Bordeaux we can observe the rise of certain bourgeois dynasties whose economic interests lay predominantly in a continuing relationship with England. Among them

---

[54] Trabut-Cussac, in *Histoire de Bordeaux, III*, pp. 103–12.

[55] Renouard, *Etudes d'histoire médiévale*, ii, pp. 991–2; Gillingham, *Angevin Empire*, pp. 45–6.

[56] Trabut-Cussac in *Histoire de Bordeaux, III*, pp. 562–3.

[57] A. Richard, *Histoire des comtes de Poitou, 778–1204*, ii (Paris, 1903), pp. 445–6, 455; Trabut-Cussac in *Histoire de Bordeaux, III*, pp. 94–6; Bémont, 'La Campagne de Poitou', pp. 289–314.

[58] *Foedera*, I, ii, pp. 795, 828; C 47/27/3, no. 34; *RG*, iii, nos 3883, 4134, 4477 and p. clxxxix.

[59] *CPR, 1281–92*, pp. 58, 59, 64; C 47/29/4, no. 26(b).

[60] J. Stow, *A Survey of London*, ed. C. L. Kingsford (Oxford, 1908), pp. 238–40; G. A. Williams, *Medieval London: From Commune to Capital* (London, 1963), pp. 246–7, 333–5.

the Colom and the Caillau were the most conspicuous. These two families were bound to the export trade in wine, although some of their members (such as Gaillard Colom) were general merchants who supplied the king-duke with horses, cloth and spices during the crisis of 1242.[61] But a 'new commercial elite' had emerged with exceptionally strong English connections. These were to prove especially valuable to the Plantagenet regime in times of crisis.

The possession of Aquitaine and, after 1279, Ponthieu also gave opportunities for individual advancement in the king-duke's service. Clerks, nobles, knights and merchants rose in wealth, status and dignity through their service in Aquitaine.[62] Some of their careers will be considered in later chapters, but they were not essentially different from those Angevin officers, such as Robert of Thornham, who had served as seneschal of Poitou and Gascony during the crisis of 1202–4.[63] At a higher social level the lives and fortunes of individuals continued to be bound up with the continental possessions. The Plantagenet dominions played an essential part in the dynastic policies of the three Edwards towards their families. Henry III had set the pattern by endowing the future Edward I with Gascony in 1254.[64] Edward I himself employed his closest kinsmen – Edmund of Lancaster and Henry Lacy, earl of Lincoln – in his south-western French lands at critical periods.[65] Edward II gave Aquitaine to his son, the future Edward III, in 1325.[66] The provisions made by Edward III for his large family are celebrated, culminating in his creation of a principality of Aquitaine for the Black Prince in 1362.[67] A recent thesis argues that the similarities between Henry II and Edward III in this respect are striking. Both had succeeded to a battered inheritance and both had chosen an expansionist policy in order to quell unrest in England and provide lands for their numerous offspring.[68] Plantagenet claims to hold more extensive territories in France, which the period 1259–1340 was to do little to quell, are clearly worthy of serious consideration in any analysis of the origins of the Hundred Years War. As

---

[61] Trabut-Cussac in *Histoire de Bordeaux, III*, pp. 72–4, 91.

[62] Trabut-Cussac, *L'Administration anglaise*, pp. 141–59, 218–46, 289–97 and the lists of officials on pp. 371–9; F. M. Powicke, *The Thirteenth Century* (Oxford, 1954), pp. 274–6; M. Vale, 'Nobility, bureaucracy and the "state" in English Gascony, 1250–1340: a prosopographical approach', in *Génèse de l'etat moderne: prosopographie et histoire*, ed. F. Autrand (Paris, 1985), pp. 308–10.

[63] Holt, 'End of the Anglo-Norman realm', pp. 251–2; Richard, *Histoire des comtes de Poitou*, ii, pp. 443–5, 448.

[64] J. R. Studd, 'The Lord Edward and Henry III', *BIHR*, I (1977–8), pp. 4–19.

[65] See below, pp. 206–12. See also plates 6.4 and 6.5.

[66] For Edward's homage to Charles IV for the duchy of Aquitaine and *comté* of Ponthieu see AN,J 634, no. 14 (14 September 1325).

[67] R. Barber, *Edward, Prince of Wales and Aquitaine* (London, 1978), pp. 170–2, 177–80.

[68] W. M. Ormrod, 'Edward III and his family', *Journal of British Studies*, xxvi (1987), pp. 407–8.

claimants to French lands and titles, the Plantagenets and their kinsmen and kinswomen were representatives of an Anglo-French civilization, and it is this cosmopolitan political and cultural world common to the courts of England and France which will now be examined.

2.2 The World of the Courts

It is sometimes forgotten that Anglo-French relations in the thirteenth and early fourteenth centuries in many ways resembled a family history. Sir Maurice Powicke rightly emphasized the domestic character of high politics, when so much depended upon dynastic marriages, connections and alliances within an enlarged family circle.[69] Henry III, Louis IX, Richard of Cornwall and Charles of Anjou were all kinsmen, French-speaking and French-cultured. 'It was this cordiality', wrote Tout, 'that made easy the mutual renunciations of the treaty of Paris of 1259.'[70] The world of the European courts was linked by both marriage and kinship ties. Henry III married into the house of Provence; Edward I was allied by marriage to Castile and then (after 1299) France; Edward II to France; Edward III to Hainault. It is sometimes argued that 'however close their links with the Continent, under-lined especially by their marriage ties, the Plantagenet Kings were Englishmen'.[71] If that were indeed the case their Englishness was certainly no impediment to involvement in a cosmopolitan, international world in which French speech and culture was shared. The close ties of kinship between the ruling houses of England and France overrode symptoms of incipient national sentiment at this time. In April 1305, for example, Edward I requested the English clergy to offer masses and prayers for the soul of Jeanne of Navarre, late queen of Philip the Fair of France, half-sister-in-law of Queen Margaret of England, mother of the future Queen Isabella.[72] Edward II acted in a similar manner in December 1314 when he requested masses and prayers for Philip the Fair, and we know that all London churches celebrated masses to this end.[73] The French monarchy reciprocated at the deaths of their Plantagenet kinsmen and women.

Powicke believed that 'historians incur a grave danger of misconception if they divorce what are called political tendencies from the interplay of

---

[69] Powicke, *Henry III and the Lord Edward*, pp. 156–61; *Thirteenth Century*, pp. 234–5, 245, where Edward I is pictured 'moving about in a detached, even desultory sort of way, in a large family circle', and see the comments in R. W. Southern, 'Sir Maurice Powicke, 1879–1963', *PBA*, 1 (1964), p. 293.

[70] T. F. Tout, *France and England: Their Relations in the Middle Ages and Now* (Manchester, 1922), p. 90.

[71] *Age of Chivalry*, p. 194 and see above, n. 6; see also Appendix I, tables 1 and 2.

[72] J. R. Wright, *The Church and the English Crown, 1305–34* (Toronto, 1980), p. 348; *CCR, 1302–7*, pp. 326–7.

[73] Wright, *Church and English Crown*, p. 352; *CCR, 1313–18*, p. 204; *Annales Paulini* in *Chronicles of the Reigns of Edward I and Edward II*, ed. W. Stubbs (*RS*, London, 1882), i, p. 277.

personal relations'.[74] Anglo-French affairs were to a large degree regulated by personal connections, not only at the level of the ruling houses. As relations between Edward II and Charles IV of France deteriorated in April 1324, Queen Isabella was urged to use her influence with the French monarch by asking him to 'have regard for us and our children who are so close to you, and for the alliances between them, and especially for the alliance made in our own person, which all the world knows was concluded to nourish and sustain peace and love between the two kingdoms, and to prevent wars and disputes'.[75] Kinship between the Capetians and Plantagenets was a string played upon by many intermediaries and arbitrators, but there is also evidence for genuine expressions of affection. During the Anglo-French war of 1294–8, Edward I's letters to his kinswomen Marie of Brabant, former queen of France, Jeanne of Navarre, queen of France, and Margaret of Anjou assured them that, although the kingdoms were in 'discord', he had no quarrel whatever with them (12 August 1295).[76] After the Anglo-French reconciliation of 1303, Edward wrote to Marie of France thanking her for her letters in which she expressed her desire for a meeting and conversation between him and her stepson, Philip the Fair. Edward assured her that he also desired to speak with Philip personally and would arrange a meeting (7 April 1304).[77] Queen Isabella, wife of Edward II, intervened more directly in political matters in 1314 when she petitioned her father, Philip the Fair, to remedy outstanding grievances relating to Aquitaine. Cases pending in the Parlement of Paris concerning *bastides* in the Agenais should be resolved because, she said, 'there should be no pleas between father and son'.[78] Family relationships could, of course, turn very sour and friction inevitably developed. But concord and harmony were the professed and accepted norm for the conduct of relations. Writing to the bishop of Bruges in January 1325, Edward II told him that Charles IV had attacked Aquitaine, irrespective of the 'state or condition of kinship and affinity' (*statum aut condicionem consanguinitatis vel affinitatis*) between them.[79] It was a theme that was to be taken up by mediators between the two kingdoms until the outbreak of the Hundred Years War.

It is evident from surviving correspondence and from reports of diplomatic

---

[74] Powicke, *Thirteenth Century*, p. 236.

[75] *The War of St Sardos (1323–25). Gascon Correspondence and Diplomatic Documents*, ed. P. Chaplais, Camden Society, 3rd ser., lxxxvii (London, 1954), p. 42 (April 1324).

[76] SC 1/13, no. 28 (12 August 1295): 'hiis diebus alique discordie fuit suborte, non tamen intendimus erga personam vestram illustrem idcirco quicquam contencionis habere'; *Foedera*, I, ii, p. 824. See also Powicke, *Thirteenth Century*, p. 234.

[77] SC 1/13, no. 30 (7 April 1304). Edward ordered the Frescobaldi and Bellardi to pay Marie of France a gift of 1000 *l.t.* on 4 October 1304. (*Foedera*, I, ii, p. 967).

[78] E 30/1530 (?March 1314): 'ne doie estre aucun plect, ainsi que ne doit estre entre pere et filz'.

[79] C 61/36, m. 8ᵛ (18 January 1325) where Edward requested the bishop to support his cause before Charles IV and to inform other French magnates of the true state of affairs.

missions that contemporaries expected relationships between the courts of England and France to reflect the accepted tenets of courtly *politesse* and courtesy. Terminology can be misleading, and can mask political realities, but the emphasis on certain qualities and attributes of *courtoisie* in the surviving documentation is noteworthy. Among these *débonaireté*, with its connotations of patience and good nature, is particularly common. In a letter, probably written at Stirling in April 1304, Edward I referred to letters from Philip the Fair 'in which you [Philip] have asked us that we should be *débonaires* and merciful [*merciables*]' to the Scots who were about to meet him. He would do so, wrote Edward, 'out of love for you who are our lord and cousin and our very dear friend', but only when the Scots obeyed him as their liege lord.[80] An undated letter, probably sent in the summer of 1297 by Geoffroi de Joinville to Aymer de Valence, discussed the qualities possessed by Raoul de Clermont-Nesle, constable of France and Valence's father-in-law.[81] The constable had responded to Joinville's requests *débonairement et ... en bon manere*, and had given him a knight as an escort who 'by his ordinance and advice expedited affairs *débonairement*'. A literary usage was reflected here. The heraldic poem on the *Siege of Caerlaverock* (1300) spoke of Edward I's leopard-like ferocity to his enemies:

For none experience his bite
Who are not envenomed by it.
But he is soon revived
With sweet good-naturedness [*débonaireté*]
If they seek his friendship,
And wish to come to his peace.[82]

The Triumphant Virtue of *Débonereté* was one of those personified in the wall paintings (now lost) of the Painted Chamber at Westminster, commissioned by Henry III between 1263 and 1272.[83] With *Largesce*, *Verité* and *Fortitude*, this Virtue was depicted, birching *Ira* (Anger) with a switch, in a setting where audiences and councils often took place (see plate 2.2). These images were inherited by Edward I and his successors, and also reminded them and

---

[80] SC 1/13, no. 35 (22 April? 1304). For *débonnaire*, its etymology and appearance in the *Chanson de Roland*, see O. Bloch and W. von Wartburg, *Dictionnaire Etymologique de la langue française* (Paris, 1932), p. 18.

[81] SC 1/58, no. 17: a reference in the letter to the fact that a reply to the constable about infractions of a truce was urgently desired before mid-August must date it to the summer of 1297. See also J. R. S. Phillips, *Aymer de Valence, Earl of Pembroke, 1307–24. Baronial Politics in the Reign of Edward II* (Oxford, 1972), p. 23; *Foedera*, I, ii, pp. 881–2.

[82] *The Roll of Arms of the Princes, Barons and Knights who Attended King Edward I to the Siege of Caerlaverock*, ed. T. Wright (London, 1864), p. 9.

[83] The most recent and authoritative discussion of the paintings is P. Binski, *The Painted Chamber at Westminster*, Society of Antiquaries Occasional Paper, n.s., ix (London, 1986), pp. 33–69. See also plate 2.2.

2.2 The Triumphant Virtues of *Largesce* and *Débonereté* (c.1263–72) from the wall paintings (destroyed in 1834) in the Painted Chamber at Westminster. *Débonereté* is personified by a female figure who birches *Ira* (Anger) upon whom she stands, and was one of the virtues most commonly admired in Anglo-French aristocratic society. (Watercolour by C. A. Stothard, 1819. Society of Antiquaries of London.)

their counsellors of the ideal qualities attributed to one of their illustrious predecessors.[84] The presence in the Painted Chamber of scenes depicting Edward the Confessor's coronation, and his gift of a ring to a St John in disguise, suggests that 'at Westminster the Virtues represent the ideals of the court and household of Henry III envisaged in terms of the chaste presence of St Edward; Edward is . . . the debonair king *par excellence*'; his arms are also found painted in the block borders beside the figure of *Débonereté*.[85] To be *duz et débonaire*, as the Confessor allegedly was, represented not merely a literary convention but a normal part of diplomatic and courtly intercourse. The personal and familial connections between the ruling classes of Plantagenet England and Capetian France were conducted, ideally and in practice, in terms of common assumptions shared by a courtly milieu.

The importance of this common culture should not be underrated. It could not prevent conflict and the outbreak of armed clashes between England and France, but it meant that considerable efforts were made, on both sides, to avert disputes or to seek a speedy reconciliation. The creation of a fitting environment for the conduct of diplomacy and the negotiation of marriage alliances may indeed have prompted Edward I's campaign of works at Westminster in the 1290s.[86] The Maccabean histories which were painted there, perhaps between 1292 and 1297, may reflect his desire to provide an impressive setting in which to conduct negotiations for his remarriage.[87] In this context, the use of kinsmen and women as intermediaries, both formal and informal, was of vital importance. The closest kinsmen of Edward I, for instance, played important 'cross-channel' roles. Edward's brother Edmund of Lancaster (Crouchback) married Blanche of Artois in 1275 and became governor of the northern French *comté* of Champagne on her behalf.[88] The heiress to Champagne, Jeanne of Navarre, was a minor and, until she married Philip the Fair in 1284, the *comté* was effectively held by Edmund of Lancaster, bearing the courtesy title of count of Champagne. It was very advantageous for Edward to have his brother in so central a position, adjacent to the Capetian demesne. A letter survives from Edmund to his brother the king which must date from 1282. In it he told the king that he

[84] Binski, *Painted Chamber*, pp. 36–42.

[85] Binski, *Painted Chamber*, p. 43; see also *Lives of Edward the Confessor*, ed. H. R. Luard (*RS*, London, 1858), p. 50, vv. 872–3 for the mid-thirteenth-century *Estoire de Seint Aedward* and its references to the Confessor's *débonnaireté* (cited in Binski, *Painted Chamber*, p. 42, n. 69).

[86] Binski, *Painted Chamber*, p. 112; *The History of the King's Works*, ed. H. M. Colvin (London, 1963), i, pp. 504–5.

[87] Philip the Fair's activities on the Ile-de-la-Cité and at the Louvre during this decade may have stimulated Edward. See J. Guerout, 'Le Palais de la Cité à Paris des origines à 1417: essai topographique et archéologique', *Mémoires de la Fédération des Sociétés Historiques et Archéologiques de Paris et de l'Ile-de-France*, ii (1950), pp. 23–44.

[88] Powicke, *Thirteenth Century*, pp. 239–41; W. E. Rhodes 'Edmund, Earl of Lancaster', *EHR*, x (1985), pp. 213–16. See also plates 6.4 and 6.5.

had heard of the outbreak of war in Wales while 'ordering and attending to the state of my affairs in Champagne'.[89] He did not yet know whether Edward wished him to bring to Wales any of his nobles of Champagne to serve there. He had warned many Champenois that they were to be ready to follow when so commanded and, he wrote, 'they willingly agreed'. He would bring news of his dealings with Philip III when he arrived in England, and hoped that his English retinue would suffice for Edward's needs until he knew his brother's wishes about the nobles of Champagne. An 'English' magnate was in effect offering the services of men, technically subject to the crown of France, to the king of England in his capacity as king, rather than as duke of Aquitaine. Edmund of Lancaster, loyal to the end, was to play a major part in the Anglo-French diplomacy of the 1290s and died representing his brother as lieutenant in Aquitaine at Bayonne on 5 June 1296.[90] His entrée to the court of France was an essential facet of Anglo-French relations. To buy out Edmund's rights and interests in Champagne after Jeanne de Navarre's marriage in 1284 cost Philip the Fair at least 14,200 *livres tournois* (*l.t.*).[91] The personal interests of an Anglo-French magnate and his wife made the absorption of this great and valuable fief a far costlier operation for the French crown.

Another kinsman who acted as an intermediary between England and France was Jean of Brittany, earl of Richmond. In 1261, Henry III's daughter Beatrix had married another Jean, eldest son of the duke of Brittany.[92] A son, aptly named Arthur, was born to them in 1262, described in a familiar and affectionate letter from Blanche, duchess of Brittany to Henry III as 'mout bon enffant et mout beil, la Dieu merci'.[93] A second son, Jean, was born in 1266. Beatrix died in 1275 and Jean was brought up in England, apparently in Edward's household. His sister Eleanor became a nun at Amesbury and was later elected abbess of the mother house at Fontevrault.[94] The Angevin connection was thus represented by a close kinswoman of Edward I. Jean of Brittany's talents were more suited to diplomacy than to warfare (although he served against Philip the Fair in Aquitaine, between 1294 and 1297), while his close connections with both the French court and the nobility of western France clearly helped to ease tension at periods of crisis. He was a valuable go-between. In 1306, after a career of service to Edward I in Wales, Scotland, France, Ponthieu and

---

[89] SC 1/16, no. 138, dated at La Ferté-Milon, Wednesday before Pentecost ?1282.

[90] Rhodes, 'Edmund of Lancaster', pp. 233–4; see below, pp. 187–92, 212.

[91] AN, J 631, no. 3, dated at Paris, 9 January 1287.

[92] Powicke, *Henry III and the Lord Edward*, pp. 257, 412.

[93] *Diplomatic Documents, 1101–1272*, ed. P. Chaplais (London, 1964), i, no. 368, datable to late summer 1262. See also nos 360, 396.

[94] I. Lubimenko, *Jean de Bretagne, comte de Richmond (1266–1334)* (Lille, 1908), p. 1. Edward I's daughter Marie was also a nun of Fontevrault, often residing at Amesbury. For gifts of wine and firewood to her see *Foedera*, I, ii, p. 758 (2 January 1292).

Aquitaine, Jean was given the earldom of Richmond by a king notoriously mean in his endowment of earls. He survived, unmarried, into the reign of Edward III, returning to Brittany shortly before his death in 1334.[95] There were few diplomatic encounters between England and France during this period at which he was not present.

Similarities between Jean of Brittany's position and that of Aymer de Valence, earl of Pembroke (c.1270–1324), have been pointed out.[96] Aymer's father, William de Valence (d. 1296), was one of Henry III's Lusignan half-brothers, and his close ties with his nephew Edward I brought the family to the very centre of power. Aymer de Valence was therefore cousin to Edward II and played a prominent part in his reign as a defender of the monarchy (see plate 2.3). His most recent biographer has observed that 'because Aymer de Valence held the English earldom of Pembroke and spent his entire career in English service it is easy to forget that in origin he was almost entirely French and that he retained very close links with France throughout his life'.[97] Yet this did not necessarily make him 'an outsider in English society', readily employed by Edward II against the magnates.[98] Pembroke was one of the ordainers of 1310 and his part in the death of Piers Gaveston hardly demonstrated his sympathy for Edward's obsessive relationship with his favourite. Both his marriages were with French noblewomen – Beatrice (d. 1320), daughter of Raoul de Clermont-Nesle, constable of France, and Marie de St Pol (d. 1377) daughter of Guy de Châtillon, count of St Pol, butler of France. Aymer thus stood in the midst of a ramified genealogical network relating him to many families within the French nobility. The connections of the Valence with other continental dynasties are exemplified in heraldic form by the so-called 'Valence casket' (see plate 2.4). This enamelled box, made either for Aymer or his father, displays the arms of England, Valence, Brittany (Dreux), Angoulême, Brabant and Lacy.[99] Further ties bound Aymer de Valence to other 'Anglo-French' nobles who will be discussed below – Amaury de Craon and Geoffroi de Joinville.

---

[95] Lubimenko, *Jean de Bretagne*, pp. 2–3, 12–26, 135–6. See below, pp. 204–5. For his brother Henry of Brittany (d. 1284), also brought up in Edward's household, see A. J. Taylor, *Studies in Castles and Castle-building* (London, 1985), p. 286.

[96] Phillips, *Aymer de Valence*, p. 13. For his seal see plate 2.3.

[97] Phillips, *Aymer de Valence*, p. 1. See *Complete Peerage*, ed. G. E. Cokayne, x (London, 1945), pp. 382–8; and see also plate 2.3.

[98] Phillips, *Aymer de Valence*, p. 271. His marriages to the daughters of nobles with high offices at the French court may represent a desire to retain influence there on Edward I's and Edward II's behalf.

[99] For his marriages, see Phillips, *Aymer de Valence*, pp. 5–7, 202, 206, 209; H. Jenkinson, 'Mary de Sancto Paulo, Foundress of Pembroke College, Cambridge', *Archaeologia*, lxvi (1915), pp. 401–6; and for the 'Valence' casket, see M. M. Gauthier, *Emaux du Moyen Age Occidental* (Fribourg, 1972), no. 143; *Age of Chivalry*, pp. 357–8. See also plate 2.4.

2.3 Seal and counterseal of Aymer de Valence, earl of Pembroke (d. 1324). He was a major figure in Anglo-French diplomacy from the 1290s onwards. (London, Public Record Office.)

2.4 The Valence casket, probably French (Limoges), c.1290–1324. Its enamelled decoration displays the arms of England, Valence, Angoulême, Brittany (Dreux), Lacy and Brabant, emphasizing the relationships between these families. (London, Victoria and Albert Museum, 4 – 1865.)

The tenure of lands in France strengthened the Valence family's position as intermediaries between the two kingdoms. It also gave them an additional incentive in their efforts to keep the peace between Plantagenets and Capetians, for they stood to lose lands and revenues through confiscation in time of war. On his father's death Aymer de Valence inherited the French lordships of Bellac, Rançon and Champagnac, near Limoges, and of Montignac, near Angoulême. He appointed a seneschal, receiver and auditors to administer his French lands and employed a proctor-general for French affairs to represent his interests at law.[100] Although he never seems to have performed military service in person for Philip the Fair, he certainly did homage for his French lands in 1300.[101] A somewhat distant claimant to the Lusignan inheritance – the great *comtés* of La Marche and Angoulême – he was nevertheless bought out by Philip the Fair for 1000 *l.t.* in 1308–9. The Valence family were representatives of an earlier dynastic alliance between

[100] See the lists in Phillips, *Aymer de Valence*, p. 293.
[101] J. Burias, 'Géographie historique du comté d'Angoulême, 1308–1531', *Bulletin et Mémoires de la Société archéologique et historique de la Charente*, (1955) (Angoulême, 1957), pp. 229–33.

the Plantagenets and the Lusignans which had promoted coalitions against the Capetians in Poitou, Limousin and Angoumois. The dissolution of the Lusignan lands was not to be completed until 1328 when the last claimants were finally compensated by the French crown.[102] But Aymer, and after him his widow, remained in possession of their Limousin and Angoumois lordships until Charles V of France confiscated them only five years before her death in 1377.[103] By his second marriage, to Marie de St Pol, at Paris in July 1321, Aymer was related to a family which held lordships in Artois and the Pas-de-Calais very close to the Channel ports at Boulogne and Wissant.[104] On the other side of the English Channel, the concentration of eleven Valence manors in Kent (at Brabourne, Egerton, East Sutton, Sutton Valence and Wickham, for example) may have facilitated his constant journeying to and fro by providing staging posts on the road to and from the coast. His father died at Brabourne in May 1296 (see plate 2.5), returning from an embassy to Cambrai.[105] It is known that Aymer was in France in 1299, 1301, 1302, 1303, 1304, and made at least twelve visits between 1307 and 1324, three of them in 1313. He died suddenly in France on 23 June 1324, at or near one of his wife's lordships (Tours-en-Vimeu), while on his way to Paris to negotiate Anglo-French differences over Aquitaine.[106]

By 1307 the English baronage included three out of eleven earls who were of 'foreign' origin – Pembroke (Aymer de Valence), Richmond (Jean of Brittany) and Cornwall (Gaveston).[107] The continental links of other baronial families such as Lancaster, Lacy and Warenne meant that Pembroke was 'by no means untypical of the leading English magnates of his time'.[108] Most were members of a court society which was essentially cosmopolitan. They had 'as much in common with members of their own class in other European states in their interests and assumptions as they did with their feudal inferiors'.[109] The role of 'aliens' in England under John and Henry III as targets for baronial opposition to the crown has perhaps led historians to see too sharp a polarization of attitudes among the English ruling classes at this time.[110] In the relatively small and somewhat isolated world of the courts, men of 'foreign' origin acted as natural and essential intermediaries between England and Europe. Members of the families of Grandson (or

---

[102] See below, n. 127; *Registres du Trésor des Chartes*, ed. R. Fawtier, J. Glénisson and J. Guerout, i (Paris, 1958), nos 470 (February 1309), 1527 (May 1312). Also see Appendix I, table 2.

[103] Jenkinson, 'Mary de Sancto Paulo', pp. 410–12; Phillips, *Aymer de Valence*, pp. 3–4.

[104] *Annales Paulini*, p. 291; Jenkinson, 'Mary de Sancto Paulo', pp. 402–3.

[105] Phillips, *Aymer de Valence*, p. 9. See also plate 2.5 for William's tomb effigy.

[106] Jenkinson, 'Mary de Sancto Paulo', pp. 405–6; Phillips, *Aymer de Valence*, pp. 233–4, concludes that he died near St Riquier.

[107] See *Complete Peerage*, x, pp. 382–8 (Pembroke); 814–18 (Richmond); iii, pp. 433–4 (Cornwall).

[108] Phillips, *Aymer de Valence*, p. 13.

[109] J. Alexander, 'The making of the "Age of Chivalry"', *History Today*, xxxvii (1987), p. 7.

[110] See Clanchy, *England and its Rulers*, pp. 261–2.

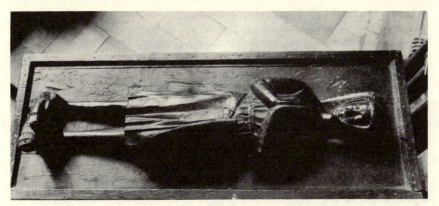

2.5 French chased and enamelled copper effigy of William de Valence (d. 1296), Henry III's Lusignan half-brother. It was probably made at Limoges. (London, Westminster Abbey, c.1290–1300.)

Grandisson), Joinville (or Geneville), Grilly (or Grailly), Geneva, Fiennes, Valence and Craon served the English crown in diplomacy, administration and warfare, while holding lands abroad. So did those Gascon nobles who were retained with fees or pensions in the king's household. In June 1286, there were forty Gascons in Edward I's household, including four knights banneret, three knights bachelor and twenty-one king's esquires.[111] Among those receiving liveries of robes from Edward III for the winter of 1330, at least seventeen Gascon knights and esquires are recorded as members of his household.[112] There was therefore a group of 'aliens' among the king's *familiares* which long outlived the political turmoil of Henry III's reign.

The knightly families of French, Burgundian and Savoyard origin who served Edward I and Edward II were especially important in dealings with France. The Savoyard knight Odo de Grandson (d. 1328) was among Edward I's most trusted lieutenants and missions of the highest significance were allotted to him.[113] He was, for instance, among those charged to receive Clement V in Aquitaine after his election to the papacy, in July 1305, and ordered the giving of gifts to the French envoys to the new pope when they were at Bordeaux. These included Louis of Evreux (Philip the Fair's brother), the duke of Burgundy and the count of Dreux.[114] Grandson was with Edward

---

[111] Trabut-Cussac, *L'Administration anglaise*, p. 79, n. 21; E 101/351/25 and 26 (2 June 1286).

[112] E 101/385/4: indenture between the keeper and clerk of the great wardrobe listing those members of the king's 'familie et retencionis' receiving robes (1330). They included '3 knights banneret of the *familia* of the lord pope' (John XXII).

[113] See C. L. Kingsford, 'Sir Otho de Grandison', *TRHS*, 3rd ser., iii (1909), pp. 125–95; Edward I's Savoyard connections are studied, with special reference to castle-building activities, in Taylor, *Castles and Castle-building*, pp. 1–51, 63–97, and F. Mugnier, 'Les Savoyards en Angleterre au xiiie siècle', *Mémoires et Documents de la Société Savoisienne*, xxix (1890).

[114] E 101/160/4, m. 2 (6 July–4 September 1304); *RG*, iii, pp. cxcix–cc.

I during his visit to France and Aquitaine in 1286–9, and was constantly employed by him in business at the courts of France and Aragon during those years.[115] His nephew, John de Grandisson (1292–1369), became bishop of Exeter in 1327 and before his election had continued the family's role in diplomacy, especially at the papal court. Odo de Grandson's fellow-Savoyard, Jean de Grilly (d. 1303), was Edward's lieutenant and seneschal in Aquitaine (1266–8, 1278–87) and built up considerable expertise in French and Gascon affairs.[116] His grandson, Pierre, inherited his Gascon lordships of Benauges and Castillon and married into the captaux de Buch.[117] The history of their service to the Plantagenets and Lancastrians is well known.

Less familiar is the evidence for service to the English crown, both diplomatic and military, by members of the Joinville (Champagne) and Craon (Anjou) families. Geoffroi de Joinville, lord of Vaucouleurs (c.1226–1314) was a younger brother of Jean de Joinville, the biographer of St Louis.[118] By 1252 he had come to England, married Maud de Lacy, and as co-heir to the Lacy inheritance received some of their Irish lands. He was in Aquitaine with the Lord Edward in 1255 and by 1280 is found as an envoy, with Jean de Grilly, to Paris, engaged in negotiating a Franco-Castilian peace. In April 1282 he fought in the Welsh war with one knight and one serjeant and in the following year made over his English and Welsh lands to his son, Pierre de Joinville. He was very active in the events of 1297–9, serving as marshal of Edward I's ill-fated army in Flanders (1297) and with Odo de Grandson and Aymer de Valence in the consequent peace negotiations with the French.[119] By November 1308 he had apparently renounced the world and entered the Irish Dominican house at Trim, where he died on 21 October 1314.[120] His son, Pierre, held his father's lands in Shropshire and Herefordshire but died in 1292, leaving three small daughters. His widow, Jeanne, held the Joinvilles' English lands but, like Aymer de Valence, agreed to renounce her claim to a part of the Lusignan inheritance (1308–10), although she held four Poitevin and Limousin lordships in reversion until her death in April 1323.[121] The Irish lands of the Joinville descended to Geof-

[115] Kingsford, 'Otho de Grandison', pp. 132–6.

[116] Trabut-Cussac, *L'Administration anglaise*, pp. 371, 373, 374–5, for the dates of his service.

[117] His eldest son Pierre had pre-deceased him and he instituted his grandson as heir in a testament drawn up in June 1303 (ATG, A 297, fos 1060^v–1068^v).

[118] See *Complete Peerage*, v, pp. 628–31; G. W. Watson, 'The families of Lacy, Geneva, Joinville and La Marche', *The Genealogist*, xxi (1904), pp. 13–16.

[119] *Gascon Register A (Series of 1318–19)*, ed. G. P. Cuttino and J.-P. Trabut-Cussac (Oxford, 1975), nos 311, 314, 324 (June 1299). On 31 August 1283 he was described as a counsellor of Edward I (no. 103) with Jean de Grilly and Anthony Bek, bishop of Durham. For his career in general, see Watson, 'The Families of Lacy . . .', pp. 13–16.

[120] *Complete Peerage*, v, p. 631.

[121] Watson, 'The families of Lacy . . .', p. 78; *Complete Peerage*, vi, pp. 632–3. Jeanne was widow of Bernard-Ezi IV, lord of Albret (d. by 1281), daughter of Hugh XII de Lusignan, count of La Marche and Angoulême. Hence her claim to the Lusignan inheritance.

froi's fifth son, Simon, who served as a 'strenuous' knight for Edward II in Scotland (1315–22) and Aquitaine (1324–5) and was still being summoned to fight the Scots in May 1335.[122] Another son, Gauthier, in fact assumed the French lordships of the family in Champagne by September 1298, was serving Philip the Fair against the Flemings in July 1302, and died at their hands two years later in the battle at Pont-à-Vendin, near Lens in Artois.[123] The political crisis of 1294–1303 had undoubtedly enforced a tenurial separation within the family, and during this period Gauthier de Joinville, lord of Vancouleurs, could not serve both the English and French crowns.

The Angevin legacy inherited by the Plantagenets found a late embodiment in the career of Amaury III de Craon (lord of Craon and Sablé and the last hereditary seneschal of Anjou, Maine and Touraine) who was seneschal of Aquitaine for Edward II in 1313–16 and 1320–2.[124] His appointment was in part a result of the amicable Anglo-French gathering which took place at Paris and Poissy in June–July 1313 for the knighting of the sons of Philip the Fair.[125] Outstanding issues between Edward II and Philip were to be resolved and the appointment of a seneschal of Aquitaine from within the Capetian court circle was probably thought to assist the process. Amaury de Craon was an assiduous and competent officer, and his tenure of a second term of office suggests that he commanded a degree of confidence. The letters appointing him spoke of the 'dissensions recently arisen' in the duchy of Aquitaine where he was to act 'to pacify the said land' (*circa stabilimentum terre predicte*), thereby incurring additional expenses (which were to be recompensed) at the Paris parlement and in the duchy itself.[126] With Aymer de Valence, Jean de Joinville and Elie-Rudel, lord of Pons, he too had a claim on the Lusignan inheritance. In a series of acts dating from 1317, 1322 and 1328 he was compensated for any losses sustained through the renunciation of that claim.[127] By the accession of Philip VI of Valois, therefore, the old Angevin and Lusignan fiefs had at last been absorbed by the French crown. This gradual process was in its way just as significant as the more dramatic

---

[122] Watson, 'The families of Lacy . . .', pp. 74–5. His sons married into Irish families.

[123] Watson, 'The families of Lacy . . .', pp. 15–16. His death is wrongly given there as 18 April 1303. See *Chronique Artésienne (1295–1304)*, ed. F. Funck-Brentano (Paris, 1899), p. 79; *Annales Gandenses*, ed. H. Johnstone (Oxford, 1985), p. 54, where he is described as a 'valentissimus miles', killed with seven or eight others on 'magnificent chargers' as they vainly tried to force a passage through a Flemish force guarding a narrow pathway through the marshes.

[124] *RG*, iv, pp. xxxi–xxxii; B. de Brousillon, *La Maison de Craon, 1050–1480* (Paris, 1893), ii, pp. 246–67; J. Petit, *Charles de Valois, 1270–1325* (Paris, 1900), pp. 275–6.

[125] J. R. Strayer, *The Reign of Philip the Fair* (Princeton, 1980), pp. 19–20, and for concessions to Edward II and Isabella made at Poissy and Paris in July 1313, see *Registres du Trésor des Chartes*, i, nos 1970–5, 2002–15, 2017–20, 2024, 2026–33. Amaury de Craon was appointed seneschal on 5 July 1313, at Poissy (*RG*, iv, no. 969).

[126] C 61/33, m. 7, dated at Dover, 22 July 1320.

[127] Watson, 'The families of Lacy . . .', *The Genealogist*, xxii (1905), pp. 240–1. For his ancestry, and the chivalric reputation of his family, see R. Harvey, *Moriz von Craûn and the Chivalric World* (Oxford, 1961), pp. 49–53. See also Appendix I, table 2.

annexations of former Angevin territories. But it did not eliminate the need for an Anglo-French nobility to mediate between the two powers.

Amaury de Craon wrote to Edward II from Sablé in November 1323 telling him that the 'great uneasiness of heart that I feel as a result of the dispute between you and your brother the king of France, our lord, and a desire to find ways, according to my humble ability, to prevent it, has emboldened me to write the following things'.[128] He spoke of the 'perilous conflict' between Edward and Charles IV and of his desire for peace between them which, if broken, would put 'the greater part of Christendom in peril'. To Hugh le Despenser on the same day, he expressed similar views and put himself at Despenser's disposal as an intermediary with Charles IV.[129] Amaury de Craon served both Plantagenets and Capetians in many capacities, fighting in Flanders for Louis X in September–October 1315 and January–February 1316 while holding office from Edward II as seneschal of Aquitaine.[130] He was among the last representatives of this kind of Anglo-French noble before the Hundred Years War, and the peace that subsisted between 1303 and 1324 enabled him to remain loyal to both his overlords.

Besides their encounters in war and diplomacy, English and French nobles and knights met on more specifically chivalric occasions. Participants from England were found at tournaments in northern France and the Low Countries – at Compiègne in 1278 and at Mons in 1310.[131] Pierre de Grilly and a 'Robert l'Englois' (perhaps Robert Clifford) attended the tournament at Chauvency in 1285.[132] French knights also tourneyed in England. In October 1279, Edward I wrote to Philip III informing him that Jean de Prie, the French king's knight, had come to England and, hearing of a tournament there, had hastened towards it 'as a knight should' although a tournament ban had been proclaimed by Philip.[133] Jean de Prie also participated in the events at Chauvency.[134] Similarly in 1290 Jean de Nesle, knight, took part in a tournament staged on the occasion of Jean, duke of Brabant's visit to England for the marriage of his son to Edward I's daughter, Margaret.[135] English rolls of arms at this time contain a considerable number of coats borne by 'foreign' knights especially from northern France, the Low Countries and the Franco-imperial borderlands.[136] A common chivalric culture – expressed in tournaments, *festes*, and the cult of Arthurian knighthood –

[128] *St Sardos*, p. 1 (4 November 1323).

[129] *St Sardos*, pp. 1–2.

[130] *RG*, iv, pp. xxi, 568–9; E 101/309/22; 376/7, fos 14ᵛ–5ʳ.

[131] See J. Vale, *Edward III and Chivalry. Chivalric Society and its Context, 1270–1350* (Woodbridge, 1982), pp. 22–3.

[132] Vale, *Edward III and Chivalry*, pp. 23, 98, n. 3, 162.

[133] SC 1/13, no. 12 (14 October 1279).

[134] Vale, *Edward III and Chivalry*, p. 59.

[135] SC 1/13, no. 38 (undated); J. de Sturler, *Les Relations politiques et les échanges commerciaux entre le duché de Brabant et l'Angleterre au Moyen Age* (Paris, 1936), p. 143–4.

[136] Vale, *Edward III and Chivalry*, pp. 22–3 and notes on pp. 109–10.

bound the courts of England and France together, adding a further dimension to the complex web of relationships between the two nobilities.

2.3 A Common Culture

The political and genealogical relationships which have already been examined were grounded in a shared culture, itself in part determined by the church. The pope was the greatest intermediary in western Christendom, and much diplomatic intercourse was in the hands of papal legates, bishops and clerks at this time. A reflection of clerical involvement in the world of the courts may be glimpsed in the large stained-glass window given to York Minster by Master Peter de Dene, king's clerk, probably between 1307 and 1310 (see plate 2.6).[137] Dene was employed as an envoy to the papal court in June 1294, charged with certain weighty matters, and was one of eleven masters ordered by Edward II to assist his envoys to Avignon in 1316.[138] His window at York celebrates his court connections and its profuse heraldic display refers to the alliances of the ruling houses of England and France. The arms of the Empire, England, France, Provence, the king of the Romans, Castile and Leon, Jerusalem and Navarre reflect the continental connections of Edward I and Edward II. Beside them the crossed keys of St Peter (for the see of York) express the Church's direct concern with the affairs of secular rulers. This theme was also found in the embroidered textiles listed in Clement V's inventory of the papal treasury in 1311.[139] Among the eighty-two items of *opus anglicanum* were an altar frontal, a bedcover and curtains worked with the keys of St Peter and the arms of England, France and Pope Boniface VIII.[140] These were assertions of papal and clerical association with, and intervention in, the world of the secular courts.

The courts of England and France shared common cultural influences and strove to imitate and emulate each other. The building programmes begun by Henry III, continued under Edward I, at Westminster and the contemporaneous development on the Ile-de-la-Cité and at the Louvre in Paris under Louis IX and Philip the Fair were similar in intention. As H. M. Colvin has observed 'what Reims and St Denis were to the house of Capet, Westminster should be to the house of Plantagenet'.[141] Influences were

---

[137] For the common intellectual background of many clerks see B. Smalley, *English Friars and Antiquity in the Early Fourteenth Century* (Oxford, 1960), p. 74; D. E. O'Connor and J. Haselock, in *A History of York Minster*, ed. G. E. Aylmer and R. Cant (Oxford, 1977), pp. 349–50; C. Winston and W. S. Walford, 'On an heraldic window in the north aisle of York cathedral', *Archaeological Journal*, xvii (1860), pp. 22–34; *Age of Chivalry*, pp. 198–9. See also plate 2.6.

[138] *Treaty Rolls, i, 1234–1325*, ed. P. Chaplais (London, 1955), nos 218, 220, 221 when Dene is described as 'our clerk' (20 June 1294); *Foedera*, II, i, p. 305 (25 December 1316).

[139] *Regestum Clementis papae V, Appendices*, i, ed. Monachorum OSB (Rome, 1892), pp. 429–60.

[140] *Regestum Clementis papae V*, i, pp. 429, 438–9.

[141] *King's Works*, i, p. 133.

2.6   Peter de Dene's window in the north nave aisle, York Minster, c.1310. Dene was a clerical
      diplomat with court connections and the canopy of his window depicts figures of the kings
      of France (*left*) and England (*right*).

mutual, and Philip the Fair's cult of the sainted kingship of Louis IX may
have been partly inspired by Henry III's and Edward I's promotion of
Edward the Confessor.[142] It is known that Edward III, another great royal
builder, compared Westminster favourably with the apocryphal resting-
place of the Three Kings at Cologne. John of Reading reported that in
September 1359, after hearing mass in St Stephen's Chapel, the king said
that he would much rather be buried where the Confessor, Henry III and
Edward I lay than at Cologne. A burial place at Westminster among the

---

[142] See Binski, *Painted Chamber*, p. 45.

aforesaid three illustrious kings was 'more fitting and more beautiful'.[143] A cult of Plantagenet kingship, closely comparable to that of the Capetians, with a distinctive ideology and historical focus, was a product of the reigns of Henry III and Edward I.

It would be irrelevant to the purpose of this chapter to conduct a detailed discussion of the purely stylistic aspects of artistic influence and cross-fertilization during this period. But a brief survey may establish points of comparison and contrast. The English response to the French Rayonnant style in architecture certainly produced characteristic and idiosyncratic results.[144] English manuscript illumination, as we shall see, also developed some qualities of its own which were not determined by French models.[145] But there can be little doubt that French styles and French cultural patterns were a major influence on the art forms and patronage of English Gothic. The incorporation of French-inspired architectural designs and motifs into English wall-paintings, stained glass and illuminated books was evident after about 1250.[146] There was a clear French model, for example, for Edward I's Eleanor crosses, erected at stopping-places along the route of Queen Eleanor's coffin as her body was brought to Westminster for burial in 1290. A 'recent French court prototype' was adapted to serve Edward's purpose of commemorating his first wife in a series of cenotaphs.[147] The crosses erected at stages on the route of St Louis's body as it came from Tunis to Paris for burial at St Denis were 'freely imitated in the Eleanor crosses of England'.[148] Although destroyed in 1789, the French crosses bore figures of kings, just as the Eleanor crosses contained a figure of the queen, and the *Montjoies* of St Louis must have been a formative influence on Edward's decision to act as he did.

In the related field of tomb sculpture, French motifs were increasingly absorbed in England. Henry III imitated French royal tombs in his own and his queen's effigies, and the introduction of 'weepers' on to the side of tomb-chests followed a pattern established thirty years earlier in France.[149] The English court was eclectic in its import of new techniques and artistic styles from Europe – in wall-painting, the French court's 'rich applied

---

[143] *Chronicon Johannis de Reading*, ed. J. Tait (Manchester, 1914), pp. 132–3.

[144] For a recent assessment see C. Wilson, 'The English response to French Gothic architecture', in *Age of Chivalry*, pp. 74–82.

[145] See below, pp. 38–9, 43.

[146] Binski, *Painted Chamber*, pp. 58–63 for a full discussion.

[147] Binski, *Painted Chamber*, p. 112; R. Branner, 'The Montjoies of St Louis', in *Essays in the History of Architecture presented to Rudolf Wittkower*, ed. D. Fraser, H. Hibbard and M. Lewine (London, 1967), pp. 13–16.

[148] Branner, 'The Montjoies of St Louis', pp. 13, 15.

[149] See *Art and the Courts. France and England from 1259 to 1328*, ed. P. Verdier, P. Brieger and M. F. Montpetit, i (exhibition catalogue, Ottawa, 1972), p. 30; L. Stone, *Sculpture in Britain: The Middle Ages* (Harmondsworth, 1955), pp. 146–7; H. A. Tummers, *Early Secular Effigies in England. The Thirteenth Century* (Leiden, 1980), pp. 29–30. See also plate 6.4.

polychromy'; in interior- and tomb-decoration, mosaic techniques from Rome and Avignon; and in tomb sculpture, the use of bronze and of Limoges enamel.[150] Edward I chose essentially French themes to complete the decorations of the Painted Chamber at Westminster and a 'particularly strong French influence' has been detected in a number of English works dating from the period *c*.1290–1320.[151] Imagery drawn from Maccabean sources associates the Westminster paintings of that time with a French, rather than English, stock of images and iconography.[152] Contemporary preoccupation with the personification of virtues and vices found expression in the illuminations by Master Honoré to the *Somme le Roi*, written by Laurent, Philip III's Dominican confessor.[153] Dating from the 1290s, these form part of an allegorical tradition similar to that which determined the representations of the Triumphant Virtues and Vices for Henry III in the Painted Chamber at Westminster, and in the sculptures of the chapter house at Salisbury.[154] Furthermore, it has been established that the Parisian miniaturist Honoré also illuminated a Book of Hours, now at Nuremberg, for an English patron.[155] Parallels between it and such English works as the Alphonso Psalter (*c*.1284–1300) reflect the very close connections between English and northern French manuscript painting and book production from which the so-called 'court style' of the decades around 1300 was derived.[156]

These works, including the Queen Mary and Isabella Psalters, have led Dr Binski to conclude that 'a big French illustrated Old Testament suddenly became known and influential from *c*.1290 in England, and that knowledge of it spread to various centres'.[157] The popularity of the *Bible Moralisé*, with profuse illustrations, was common to both English and French patrons. So was the taste among court circles for romances, devotional treatises and service books ornamented with stylistically related images. Since there was normally free passage between England and France at this time, 'there was

---

[150] Binski, *Painted Chamber*, p. 109.

[151] Binski, *Painted Chamber*, pp. 89–93; J. J. G. Alexander, 'Painting and manuscript illumination for royal patrons in the later Middle Ages', in *English Court Culture in the Later Middle Ages*, ed. V. J. Scattergood and J. W. Sherborne (London, 1983), pp. 141–3, 160–1.

[152] Binski, *Painted Chamber*, pp. 88–9: the 'material from Judges, Kings and Maccabees which characterise the Painted Chamber . . . implies at first sight access to French, rather than English iconography'.

[153] *La Somme le Roy, Attributed to the Parisian Miniaturist Honoré*, ed. E. G. Millar (Oxford, Roxburghe Club, 1953), plates I–XVII, XXIII–XXXIV; E. G. Millar, *The Parisian Miniaturist Honoré* (London, 1959), pp. 10, 20, 24, 26, 18, 30 and plates 5–8.

[154] Binski, *Painted Chambers*, pp. 38–9, 42; R. B. Green, 'Virtues and vices in the chapter-house vestibule in Salisbury', *JWCI*, xxxi (1968), pp. 148–58. See also plate 2.2.

[155] Nuremberg, Stadtbibliothek, MS Solger 4.4°; A. Martindale, *Gothic Art* (London, 1967), p. 127 and Figure 97.

[156] *Age of Chivalry*, p. 355; L. F. Sandler, *Gothic Manuscripts, 1285–1385. A Survey of Manuscripts Illuminated in the British Isles*, v (London, 1986), i, pp. 13–14.

[157] Binski, *Painted Chamber*, p. 90.

an intermingling of styles that often make it difficult to determine the place of origin of a manuscript and its artists'.[158] The Bible of William of Devon (*c.*1260–70), the Cuerden Psalter (*c.*1270) and the Douce Apocalypse (*c.*1270) showed marked affinities with Parisian workshop production, and the post-1290 influence of the *style Honoré* represented a continuation of this tendency.[159] Direct derivation can sometimes be established. The miniatures which decorate a volume of French poems and *lais* by Adenet le Roi, Marie de France and others, made in Paris for Marie de Brabant (1260–1321), second wife of Philip III, in about 1300, appear to have furnished models copied by the English illuminator of the Arundel Psalter, which date from before 1339.[160] A representation of the Three Living and the Three Dead in both volumes is strikingly similar, and it is known that Amadeus, count of Savoy, bought two panels depicting the same subject when he was in England in 1302–3.[161]

The precise means whereby these contacts and cross-currents were established in individual cases are often unclear. But the emergence in England of the French 'broad-fold' idiom – a 'style that was undoubtedly coming to transform the appearance of the figurative arts'[162] – in the 1260s might be related to the close and active relationships created between the two kingdoms by the diplomatic and judicial consequences of the treaty of Paris in 1259. Henry III's *rapprochement* with Louis IX between 1254 and 1259 had brought the two courts into a closer relationship, while the diplomatic and juridical presence at Paris which it necessitated thereafter strengthened English connections with northern France.[163] As early as October 1262, Henry III was retaining Englishmen as proctors to represent his interests, as duke of Aquitaine, before the court of France.[164] A letter dated 11 October 1262 from Roger de Doncaster, king's clerk, to John de Kirkby, the chancellor, tells us something about the activities of these men in the French capital.[165] Doncaster had arrived in Paris on Michaelmas day, where he encountered Roger de Missenden and Thomas de la Ley, king's clerk, seated at dinner 'jocose, sanos et hillares'. He waited until the festive meal had ended before giving them Kirkby's letter. This rather cooled their high spirits, because

---

[158] *Art and the Courts*, i, p. 51.

[159] See *Age of Chivalry*, pp. 351–2, 354; Binski, *Painted Chamber*, pp. 61–5.

[160] *Art and the Courts*, i, pp. 79–80. The *Recueil de poésies françaises* is Paris, Bibliothèque de l'Arsenal, MS 3142.

[161] A. J. Taylor, 'Count Amadeus of Savoy's visit to England in 1292', *Archaeologia*, cvi (1979), p. 123: 'in duabus tabulis depictis trium mortuorum et vivorum . . . 40s. 6d'.

[162] Binski, *Painted Chamber*, pp. 52–3; G. Henderson, 'Studies in English manuscript illumination', *JWCI*, xxx (1967), pp. 91–120.

[163] See below, pp. 67–70.

[164] *Diplomatic Documents*, i, no. 370; F. Aubert, *Histoire du Parlement de Paris*, i (Paris, 1894), p. 207.

[165] *Diplomatic Documents*, i, no. 370. For instructions to Henry III's proctors in the Paris parlement in February (?) 1263, see no. 375.

Missenden's failure to do what was required of him about some case of ecclesiastical preferment was criticized. Doncaster, however, absorbed current rumours and news from the court from them: Henry III, then in Paris, was still convalescing from an illness and was unlikely to move before Christmas. Less formal matters were then attended to by Doncaster. He reported his search for a tapestry at Paris, to cover the walls of the chancellor's hall at Westminster, but had not yet found one suitable. All kinds of business – from the lobbying of cardinals at the court of France to the purchase of fine saddles for warhorses or palfreys – could be conducted as a by-product of the 'peace' of Paris.

The emergence of the French capital as the greatest centre of learning and the arts in northern Europe was to have an important impact upon Anglo-French relations. In terms of artistic production the city of Paris reached its apogee between 1250 and 1330.[166] Artists and craftsmen came to the city, not only from northern France and Flanders, but also from England. They 'shared a profoundly similar cultural background' and the names of some of them are known.[167] English scribes were to be found living in Paris in the first quarter of the fourteenth century. A copy of Gratian's *Decretum* was written there by the English copyist Thomas de Wymondeswold in 1314, who also signed a large two-volume Bible.[168] He was an accredited bookseller (*libraire juré*) for the University of Paris in 1323.[169] His compatriot Robert Billing wrote the text of another Bible in a beautifully formed hand in 1327 with illuminations by the finest Parisian artist of his day, Jean Pucelle.[170] Between 1297 and 1330, a number of masons and sculptors of English origin were also working in France. One of these was probably the carver known as 'Guillaume de Nourriche' (William of Norwich) in documentary sources.[171] He executed two statues of apostles for the chapel of St James of Compostella in Paris between 1319 and 1324 and was associated with other English craftsmen working in northern France and for the papal court at Avignon.[172] They

[166] See F. Avril, *Manuscript Painting at the Court of France. The Fourteenth Century* (London, 1978), pp. 9–12; R. Cazelles, *Paris de la fin du règne de Philippe-Auguste à la mort de Charles V, 1223–1380* (Paris, 1972), pp. 72–96.

[167] Avril, *Manuscript Painting*, p. 9; F. Baron, 'Enlumineurs, peintres et sculpteurs parisiens des xiiiᵉ et xivᵉ siècles, d'après les rôles de la taille', *Bulletin archéologique du Comité des travaux historiques et scientifiques*, n.s., iv (1969), pp. 37–121.

[168] *Art and the Courts*, i, p. 80; *Les Fastes du Gothique. Le siècle de Charles V* (exhibition catalogue, Paris, 1981), pp. 287–8. The Bible is now Bibliothèque de la Sorbonne MS 9.

[169] *Fastes du Gothique*, p. 188; R. Freyhan, 'Ein englischer Buchmalerei in Paris zu Beginn des 14 Jahrhunderts', *Marburger Jahrbuch für Kunstwissenschaft*, vi (1931), pp. 1–9.

[170] *Fastes du Gothique*, p. 291; K. Morand, *Jean Pucelle* (Oxford, 1962), pp. 45–7.

[171] *Age of Chivalry*, p. 418; F. Baron, 'Le décor sculpté et peint de l'Hôpital St-Jacques-aux-Pélerins', *Bulletin Monumental*, cxxxiii (1975), pp. 29–72.

[172] Baron, 'Le décor sculpté', pp. 42–5; *Age of Chivalry*, pp. 416–17 for the tomb of Pope John XXII at Avignon (1316–34), 'whose every detail can be paralleled at Canterbury or in St Stephen's Chapel, Westminster'.

were integrated into the large body of at least 229 painters and makers of images recorded in the taxation rolls for Paris between 1292 and 1313.[173] As the largest European city – with an estimated population of 200,000 in 1300 – Paris exerted a magnetic attraction for all those who served the ruling classes and ministered to their needs and pleasures.[174] The city was a centre of banking, money-lending, textile supplies, goldsmiths' work and many other crafts, including the increasingly popular art of enamelling using the *champlevé* technique. After 1313 all works produced by Parisian goldsmiths and enamellers bore a hallmark depicting a fleur-de-lis within a lozenge and these objects were disseminated all over Europe, not least to England.[175] In 1292, Amadeus V of Savoy bought thirty-six silver cups with silver feet, an almsboat, a set of knives and other plate from a Parisian goldsmith on his way to visit Edward I.[176] Seven years later, the list of plate and jewels bought in Paris for Margaret, Philip the Fair's sister, before her marriage in 1299 to Edward I reads like the contents of Aladdin's cave. Crowns, circlets, spoons, plates, bowls, hanapers, chalices and crosses of precious metal were supplied by Parisian goldsmiths. One crown cost 700 *l.t.* and a gold cross for her chapel 579 *l.* 9 *s.t.*[177] When Edward III wished to offer an especially lavish gift of twelve table vessels of pure gold, a great cup and ewer, twenty-four spoons, and forks 'on which to hold meat' to Pope Benedict XII on the eve of the Hundred Years War in 1337, his agent still bought them in Paris.[178]

Anglo-French diplomacy before the Hundred Years War provided opportunities for 'cultural' connections to be exploited and sustained. Richard de Bury, later bishop of Durham, profited from his diplomatic missions to the French court by buying and exchanging books in Paris. He was a member of the embassies to France in 1325–6, 1331 and 1336 and he used his position as envoy and representative of Edward III to further his book-collecting activities.[179] He was at this time an exponent of the benefits of Anglo-French

---

[173] *Art and the Courts*, i, pp. 21–3; Baron, 'Enlumineurs, peintres et sculpteurs parisiens', pp. 43, 58, 69–70, 91. The presence of English craftsmen in northern France is also suggested by names such as 'Raoul Lengles' and 'Jehan Lengles' in the accounts for works at the count of Artois's castle at Hesdin (ADPC, A 180, m. 4; 181, nos 1–2; 1297–1302).

[174] For population estimates see L. Genicot, 'Les grandes villes d'Occident en 1300', in *Economies et sociétés au Moyen Age. Mélanges offerts à Edouard Perroy* (Paris, 1973), pp. 199–205, 214–15; B. Geremek, 'Paris, la plus grande ville de l'Occident médiéval', *Acta Poloniae Historica*, xviii (1968), pp. 18–37.

[175] *Art and the Courts*, i, pp. 22–4.

[176] Taylor, 'Count Amadeus of Savoy's visit to England', p. 124. Examples of the purchase of luxury goods at Paris could be multiplied from household accounts. For saddles, embroidered horse trappers and decorated harness bought for Robert II, count of Artois, at Paris see ADPC, A 38, no. 78 (1293); A 132, no. 3 (1292).

[177] AN, J 631, no. 4. The document purports to record purchases for Isabella, Edward II's queen, but internal evidence suggests an earlier date.

[178] E 101/311/25. These items cost 2686 l. 8s. 4d.st. *in toto*.

[179] N. Denholm-Young, 'Richard de Bury (1287–1345)', *TRHS*, xx (1937), pp. 135–68; *CPR*,

peace and in the *Philobiblon*, attributed to him and written in 1344–5, one chapter was entitled 'the Complaint of Books against Wars'. Its *incipit* began with the prayer: 'Almighty Author and lover of peace, scatter the nations that delight in war, which is above all plagues injurious to books'.[180] The treatise includes a eulogy of Paris, which tells us that 'there . . . opening our treasuries and unfastening our purse-strings we scattered money with joyous heart and purchased inestimable books with worthless coin.'[181]

He was evidently a good customer for Parisian booksellers. The fact that Paris was so rich a source of books – from de luxe manuscripts to 'soiled tracts and battered codices'[182] – in part stemmed from its position and reputation as the greatest northern European centre of learning. Richard de Bury spoke of its 'academic meadows shaken by the tramp of scholars'.[183] Some of those scholars, moreover, were Englishmen and some of them certainly served as proctors and representatives of the Plantagenets at Paris.

The affinity between France and England at this time could be illustrated by the fact that the diplomatic representatives of both kingdoms studied at Paris.[184] The organization of medieval universities into separate 'nations' must be taken into account, but study by English clerks at Paris may well have influenced the manner in which legal and diplomatic business was transacted with the French. There are many examples of Englishmen at the University of Paris before 1340, and some of the king's clerks most active in Anglo-French diplomacy had studied there. John de Hildesley and Thomas Cobham (later bishop of Worcester) were among them. In 1309 and 1311, Hildesley was granted licences to study at Paris for two-year periods. He was an Oxford bachelor of canon law by 1317 and served Edward II and III in France, Gascony and Aragon.[185] His most important assignment was his appointment as proctor for Edward at the court of France in 1330 and 1331 to discuss Edward's homage for Aquitaine and Ponthieu. He was still employed on missions to negotiate truces with the French in 1343.[186] His extensive knowledge, and training at Paris, doubtless served him well.

1324–7, pp. 166–71; and the account for Edward's expenditure as duke of Aquitaine on preparations for his mission to France, of which Bury was a member, in August–September 1325 (Bodleian Library, Oxford, MS Bodley 751, fo. 4ᵛ).

[180] Richard de Bury, *Philobiblon*, ed. M. Maclagan (Oxford, 1960), pp. 70–71.

[181] *Philobiblon*, p. 87. Bury had also collected some of the letters which he copied into his formulary, the *Liber Epistolaris*, at Paris. See *The Liber Epistolaris*, ed. N. Denholm-Young (Roxburghe Club, Oxford, 1950), nos 410–11, pp. xx, xxiv–xxv.

[182] *Philobiblon*, p. 83. For a vivid summary of his book-collecting see B. Smalley, *English Friars and Antiquity in the Early Fourteenth Century* (Oxford, 1960), pp. 68–9.

[183] *Philobiblon*, p. 84.

[184] Tout, *France and England*, p. 28.

[185] A. B. Emden, *A Biographical Register of the University of Oxford to 1500*, ii (Oxford, 1958), pp. 933–4 (Hildesley); i (Oxford 1957), pp. 450–1 (Cobham).

[186] Emden, *Biographical Register*, ii, p. 934; G. P. Cuttino, *English Diplomatic Administration, 1259–1339* (Oxford, 2nd edn, 1971), pp. 143–4.

Master Henry of Canterbury, responsible for many of Edward II's diplomatic memoranda, had also studied law at Paris, and his professional judgement upon Anglo-French affairs was invaluable.[187] 'Foreign policy' was partly determined by the appreciation of possibilities, based upon precedents, formed by these experts. Their function was to advise the Plantagenets on the best means of sustaining their interests as dukes of Aquitaine and counts of Ponthieu before the Paris parlement. Some were still doing this on the eve of war in 1336.[188] If these men were often Paris graduates as well as graduates of Oxford or Cambridge, they at least knew the thought-processes and tactics of their French counterparts well.

More will be said in a later chapter about the implications of Plantagenet representation in France at this level.[189] We should never forget the salient cultural fact that the *lingua franca* of clerical diplomats was Latin. Something of this cultural cosmopolitanism may be gauged from the fortunes of the psalter given in 1318 to Cardinal Gaucelme Duèse, papal nuncio to England and nephew of John XXII, by Geoffrey of Croyland, abbot of Peterborough.[190] This sumptuous and densely illuminated book written entirely in Latin, was then bought by Philip VI of France in *c.*1328. It was begun by an illuminator working in the Anglo-French 'court' style of *c.*1300, and was completed by associates who display features of the so-called 'East Anglian' style of the early fourteenth century.[191] But a common taste for lavish illumination was evidently shared by an English abbot, a Gascon cardinal and the first Valois king of France. 'National' differences pale into insignificance when the predilections of patrons and purchasers of illuminated books are considered. Secular culture shared in this 'internationalism' among those born or trained to rule. The *lingua franca* of courtly discourse, imaginative literature, and record-keeping was French, and remained so for most of the fourteenth century.

Analysis of early fourteenth-century letter-collections would show that a form of French, perfectly comprehensible to both Frenchmen and Englishmen alike, was the normal language of secular correspondence. Of 719 letters issued under the privy seal of Edward, prince of Wales (later Edward II) between 1304 and 1305, 676 were in French and the remaining 43 in Latin.[192]

---

[187] G. P. Cuttino, 'Henry of Canterbury', *EHR*, lvii (1942), pp. 298–311.

[188] Cuttino, *English Diplomatic Administration*, pp. 39, 57–9.

[189] See below, pp. 67–70.

[190] See Wright, *Church and the English Crown*, pp. 293–6 for his career as nuncio, and tenure of English benefices; L. F. Sandler, *The Peterborough Psalter in Brussels and other Fenland Manuscripts* (London, 1974), pp. 109–10.

[191] *Age of Chivalry*, pp. 450–1; Sandler, *Gothic Manuscripts*, ii, no. 40, pp. 45–7; i, figures 88–90.

[192] H. Suggett, 'The use of French in England in the later Middle Ages', *TRHS*, 4th ser., xxviii (1946), pp. 60–83; for general discussion of the language question in England see M. T. Clanchy, *From Memory to Written Record. England, 1066–1307* (London, 1979), pp. 151–4, 197–201.

The latter were all addressed to the pope or to foreign prelates. French was therefore the language used by Edward's officials to address recipients as diverse as English local officers and Italian merchants. Of 331 letters sent by Philippa of Hainault between 1330 and 1336, 203 were in Latin and 128 in French.[193] The predominance of Latin in this sample reflects the fact that many letters were addressed to bishops, and that Latin was used for the more solemn and formal instruments emanating from her chancery. But the language of everyday correspondence was undoubtedly French, and the many news-letters and reports sent to English recipients during the Anglo-French war of St Sardos (1324–5) were overwhelmingly French.[194] The first surviving letters patent issued in French by the English royal chancery date from 1258.[195] It was perhaps no coincidence that French was adopted by English departments of state during the Anglo-French *rapprochement* of that time.

Although much of their business was conducted in Anglo-Norman (which developed a literature of its own) there is little to suggest that 'English' magnates were ignorant of the best written French. The books (especially the romances) in their libraries, and their letter collections, bear witness to that.[196] Yet a consciousness of Anglo-French differences was already apparent – it was based upon irrational prejudices and linguistic dissimilarities, and had existed since the mid to late twelfth century. In his verse romance *Jean de Dammartin et Blonde d'Oxford*, for example, written in the 1270s or 1280s, Philippe de Beaumanoir (knight and author of the *Coutumes de Beauvaisis*) reveals the attitude of a representative thirteenth-century French nobleman towards England and his English contemporaries.[197] There is no inherent ill will towards Englishmen. Indeed, the hero of the tale, Jean, son of the count of Dammartin, not only inherits his father's French lordships but the earldom of Oxford as well. The tale revolves around Jean's career as a young *gentilhomme* who seeks his fortune in England. Parallels with Simon de Montfort, the Valence and Joinville families are not entirely inappropriate.[198] Beaumanoir may indeed have visited England shortly before 1270, and the settings of his romances are in Scotland and England. Jean de Dammartin, in Beaumanoir's story, met the earl of Oxford's retinue on the road from Dover to London on their way to parliament. His appearance attracted the earl's attention, and Jean

---

[193] Suggett, 'Use of French', pp. 63–4, 80.

[194] *St Sardos, passim*, and pp. vii–viii.

[195] Clanchy, *From Memory to Written Record*, pp. 171–4; Suggett, 'Use of French', p. 61.

[196] Suggett, 'Use of French', pp. 64–70; M. B. Parkes, 'The literacy of the laity', in *The Medieval World*, ed. D. Daiches and A. Thorlby (London, 1973), pp. 555–62.

[197] *Oeuvres poétiques de Philippe de Rémi, sire de Beaumanoir*, ed. H. Suchier (Paris, 1884), i, x–xii; ii, *passim*; P. Rickard, *Britain in Medieval French Literature* (Cambridge, 1956), pp. 124–9.

[198] *Oeuvres poétiques*, i, x–xii; ii, *passim*; P. Rickard, *Britain in Medieval French Literature*, pp. 124–9.

greeted him in French
And the earl replied fluently
(Because he understood French very well,
And had learnt it in France . . .)[199]

Oxford's linguistic ability is sharply contrasted with that of Jean's rival for
the hand of Blonde, Oxford's daughter. This is the blustering earl of
Gloucester, whom Jean again meets on the road. Gloucester recognizes Jean
as a Frenchman because of his tunic, which he thinks means that he was born
near Pontoise. The poem goes on:

[Gloucester] tried to talk to him in French
But his tongue turned into English [i.e. Anglo-Norman]
(Gloucester): 'Amis, bien fustes vous vené!
    Coment fu vostre non pelé?' [i.e. for appellé][200]

Gloucester offers to buy Jean's riding horse (palfrey) but, with heavy irony,
Jean demands what he most desires from the earl in payment. Gloucester
expostulates

'Nai [for 'non'], par la goiffre biu, nai, nai!'
[i.e. 'la coiffe Dieu' or Crown of thorns]
Quo deble! [= Provençal] Ce sera trop chère . . .[201]

Much amusement was no doubt derived by Beaumanoir's audience from the
villain's massacre of the best Ile-de-France French through solecisms and
Anglo-Norman constructions. Yet this was not so very different from the
linguistic parodies found in other French narrative verse of the period. In the
Tournoi de Chauvency (1285) there are jokes about Picard French, and very
funny and elaborate parodies of Alsatian speech.[202] The practice of linguistic
comedy was not confined to stories which involved the English: all kinds of
foreigners were the butt of linguistic satire. In *Jean et Blonde*, the hero's
beloved, although English, is described in terms of perfection, and the fact
that 'There was just a suspicion in her speech / That she had not been born
at Pontoise'[203] is a very minor and venial offence against *courtoisie*. Jean then
set about teaching her the finest French 'Par quoi ele mout chier le tint' ('for

[199] *Oeuvres poétiques*, ii, ll. 129–32: 'En son Franchois l'a salué, / Et li quens n'i a delué / (Que
le Franchois seut bien entendre, / En France eust este pour apprendre).'
[200] *Oeuvres poétiques*, ii, ll. 2635–6, 2639–40: 'Si vaut a lui parler franchois, / Mais sa langue
torne en Englois . . . / "Amis, bien fustes vous vené! / Coment fu vostre non pelé?"'
[201] *Oeuvres poétiques*, ii, ll. 2658–9.
[202] See J. Vale, *Edward III and Chivalry. Chivalric Society and its Context, 1270–1350* (Woodbridge,
1982), p. 9, n. 62.
[203] *Oeuvres poétiques*, ii, ll. 358–9: 'Un peu paroit a son langage / Que ne fu pas nee a Pontoise.'

which she held him very dear'). There are also in the poem a number of jokes by English characters at Jean's expense. Gloucester and his retinue describe him as 'ce sot français', but his *sottises* are clearly misunderstood by them.[204] Their reaction is partly linguistically determined – they simply do not appreciate the word-play of courtly French and, as a result, Gloucester is worsted in his courtship of Blonde. All ends happily, with a splendid scene of Anglo-French *entente* where the aged earl of Oxford decides to pass his remaining time in the company of his English daughter and French son-in-law, spending two years at Dammartin and two years in England by turns.[205] On his death, Jean becomes both earl of Oxford and count of Dammartin.[206] Though fictitious, his 'cross-Channel' landholdings and family connections put him into the company of Geoffroi de Joinville or Aymer de Valence.

The purpose of this chapter has been to summarize the consequences for Anglo-French relations of the collapse of the Angevin Empire and to examine the common features which still bound the two kingdoms together. Anglo-French tension and conflict is the subject of later chapters.[207] The Valois accession of 1328 to the French throne, it will be argued, was productive of increased friction and heightened tension which was to lead to protracted warfare. So much may appear clear to us today, but to contemporaries the thought of a century-long struggle between England and France was probably inconceivable. Writing seven years after the outbreak of the Hundred Years War, Richard de Bury showed no overt prejudice against the French. He still wrote of Paris as a 'worldly paradise' (*paradisium mundi*).[208] But the relative harmony of the period 1259–1328 had broken down. By Edward III's death in 1377, Anglo-French peace was becoming a remote and nostalgic memory. When the aged Marie de St Pol, widow of Aymer de Valence, bequeathed in her will of that year 'a sword that I have which has no point' to Charles V of France she was no doubt emphasizing her hope for peace and her neutrality in the Anglo-French conflict.[209] But there was perhaps a sense of regret for times past when, in July 1321, she had been welcomed to England by all the earls and barons 'who had come to the king's Parliament' as the new countess of Pembroke.[210] Peace-making had failed. It remains to be seen why this was so. Just as Beryl Smalley's study of

---

[204] *Oeuvres poétiques*, ii, l. 404.

[205] *Oeuvres poétiques*, ii, ll. 2685–6.

[206] *Oeuvres poétiques*, ii, ll. 6135–9, 6144–7.

[207] See below, chapters 3, 5 and 6.

[208] *Philobiblon*, pp. 84, 105–7.

[209] Jenkinson, 'Mary de Sancto Paulo', pp. 411–12; 434: 'Item, je devise a mon tresredoubte seigneur le Roi de France une espee que jai qui est sanz pointe et que mon bien ame Willecok de ma chambre la lui porte ou autre qui lui sache dire de quele maniere elle est.' She had also drafted statutes for Pembroke College, Cambridge which included provision for French scholars.

[210] *Annales Paulini*, i, p. 292.

connections between English clerks and the continent concludes that 'clerical Europe in the late thirteenth and early fourteenth centuries was still a family with its centre at the Curia',[211] so this chapter suggests that in some respects the higher Anglo-French aristocracy formed a family with its centre in Paris. But families can be notoriously quarrelsome.

[211] Smalley, *English Friars and Antiquity*, p. 74.

3

Anglo-French Tensions

3.1 Homage for Aquitaine

It is generally agreed by historians that the treaty concluded between Henry III and Louis IX at Paris in 1259 lay behind many of the problems from which subsequent Anglo-French tensions stemmed.[1] To understand the nature of relations between the two kingdoms between 1250 and 1340 we must consider the manner in which the treaty was made, and the implications of its clauses. As the treaty was concerned with rights to lordship and territory, their nature is clearly of considerable importance. Sovereignty, homage and fealty, and the 'domainal liberties' of the Plantagenets, are sometimes considered in a theoretical light but they must also be put as firmly as possible into the more pragmatic context of Anglo-French relations. There is nearly unanimous agreement among historians about the significance of the 'impossible situation' in which the Plantagenet king-dukes of Aquitaine found themselves in the later thirteenth and early fourteenth centuries.[2] Rulers who were kings in their own right were placed in a subordinate 'feudal' relationship to the kings of France as a result of their continental inheritance. At the same time, a notion that the Capetian king was not only an overlord but 'sovereign' in his kingdom had also evolved.

[1] The literature on the subject is extensive. The following works are particularly important: M. Gavrilovitch, *Etude sur le traité de Paris de 1259* (Paris, 1899); P. Chaplais, 'The making of the treaty of Paris and the royal style', *EHR*, lxvii (1952), pp. 235–53; 'Le traité de Paris de 1259 et l'inféodation de la Gascogne allodiale', *MA* (1955), pp. 121–37; 'Le duché-pairie de Guyenne: l'hommage et les services féodaux de 1259 à 1303', *AM*, lxix (1957), pp. 5–38. These three articles are reprinted in Chaplais's *Essays in Medieval Diplomacy and Administration* (London, 1981), pts I, II, III. My debt to them will be obvious in the following chapter.

[2] Again there is a very extensive bibliography. Among the more significant contributions are G. P. Cuttino, 'Historical revision: the causes of the Hundred Years War', *Speculum* (1956), pp. 463–77; Cuttino, *English Medieval Diplomacy* (Bloomington, Ind., 1985); P. Wolff, 'Un problème d'origines: la Guerre de Cent Ans', *Eventail de l'histoire vivante: Hommage à Lucien Fèbvre*, ii (Paris, 1953), pp. 141–8; G. Templeman, 'Edward III and the beginnings of the Hundred Years War', *TRHS*, 5th ser., ii (1952) pp. 69–88; J. Le Patourel, 'The origins of the war', in *The Hundred Years War*, ed. K. Fowler (London, 1971), pp. 28–50, reprinted in Le Patourel, *Feudal Empires. Norman and Plantagenet*, pt XI, ed. M. Jones (London, 1984), pp. 28–50.

What was 'sovereignty'? What could a sovereign do that others could not? Firstly, he could exercise his so-called *regalia* (regalian rights) and judge *cas royaux* (regalian law-suits). The first gave him a degree of control over appointment to benefices in the Church; the second referred certain cases to his court and gave him certain prerogative powers. These were reserved to the crown in, for example, grants of *apanages* such as that conferred by Louis IX on Charles of Anjou in 1246.[3] Although formally set out only at a later date (c.1372), they came to include the rights to create notaries, to legitimize bastards, to grant letters conferring the status of bourgeoisie and nobility, to issue pardons and remissions, to license fairs and markets, to permit suitors to be represented at law by proctors, and to legislate for the common weal of the kingdom. But, above all else, there was the supreme attribute of judicial sovereignty – the right to exercise 'superior justice' as 'emperor in his kingdom', or as 'prince and superior lord in the kingdom of France'.[4] No appeal was therefore permitted from the Capetian's supreme court, the incipient parlement of Paris. It was in a literal sense the 'last resort' (*dernier ressort*). Such authority could not be shared with, nor alienated to anyone; the notion was already fully developed under Philip the Fair by 1294: 'the king of France is subject to no one', wrote Guillaume de Nogaret, expressing the doctrine which could make vassals subjects and was absolute.[5] It did not, as has been claimed, need a Louis XI to act as its midwife in the fifteenth century.[6] That was the theory – did it work in practice?

To answer this question, we must first assess the significance of homage and fealty in the later thirteenth century: how important were they as expressions of subordination of one ruler to another? Did the obligations implied by them have any marked practical effects? Louis IX apparently thought the issue of homage highly significant. Joinville reported the king's reply to his counsellors who opposed the treaty with England of 1259: 'it seems to me that what I give him [Henry III] I am employing well, because he was not my man, and now he enters into my homage'.[7] Louis was to some degree right; since 1202 no homage had been performed to a king of France by any Plantagenet king for his residual continental possessions. Homage could be a demeaning ceremony for a ruler who was sovereign in his own

---

[3] See P. Chaplais, 'La souveraineté du roi de France et le pouvoir legislatif en Guyenne au début du xive siècle', *Essays in Medieval Diplomacy*, pt V, pp. 449–67; C. T. Wood, 'Regnum Francie: a problem in Capetian administrative usage', *Traditio*, xxii (1967), pp. 117–47.

[4] Chaplais, 'La souveraineté du roi de France', pp. 450–1, 466–7; A. Bossuat, 'La formule "Le roi est empereur en son royaume"', *Revue historique de droit français et étranger*, (1961), pp. 371–82.

[5] See J. R. Strayer, *The Reign of Philip the Fair* (Princeton, 1980), pp. 381–2, 389–90.

[6] Cf. B.-A. Pocquet de Haut-Jussé, 'Une idée politique de Louis XI: la sujétion éclipse la vassalité', *RH*, ccxxvi (1961), pp. 383–98.

[7] Jean, sire de Joinville, *Histoire de St Louis*, ed. Natalis de Wailly (Paris, 1868), p. 245: 'me semble que ce que je li doing emploi je bien, pour ce que il n'estoit pas mes hom, si en entre en mon houmaige'; Gavrilovitch, *Etude sur le traité de Paris*, pp. 41–3.

right to perform. The kings of France paid homage to no one. The king of England was indeed emperor in his own kingdom, but he was expected to swear an oath of homage and fealty to another sovereign or *princeps et dominus superior*. Under the Angevins, it has been argued, 'the legal relationship between a king of France and a king of England who held territories on the continent meant that it was relatively easy for the king of France to legitimize his own actions as part of a legal process'.[8] This still held good under Henry III and Edward I. But there were at least two means whereby the unwelcome connotations of homage for the king-duke of Aquitaine could be made more acceptable. Firstly, by appointing a proxy to perform the oath, and secondly, transferring the fief and his rights over it to another person. By Gascon custom, observed in 1254 by Henry III and in 1306 by Edward I, this could only be the king-duke's eldest son.[9] He would hold the fief and render the homage. Edward, earl of Chester, the future Edward III, did precisely this for Edward II on 10 September 1325.[10] But the matter was not such a simple one. What happened if the king-duke had no son? One privilege of his Gascon subjects was that the duchy could never be alienated to anyone except an eldest son – hence the outbreak of conflict under Richard II when John of Gaunt (the king's uncle) was made duke of Aquitaine (1390–4).[11]

Furthermore, when the king-duke died, his eldest son would succeed to the English throne, thus necessitating a new transfer of Aquitaine. What happened if (as was the case in 1327) the new king had no son, or he was a minor? He would simply have to perform homage in person. Edward III was in that position until the birth of Edward of Woodstock in June 1330. He was therefore obliged to perform homage to Philip VI in 1329.[12] If the king-duke decided to alienate the fief, the king of France's permission (as sovereign) was technically required, because he was entitled to exact the feudal payment of relief when a fief changed hands. In 1325 a relief of 60,000 *livres parisis* was demanded from Edward II when he gave Aquitaine to his son. It was never paid. But evasion of personal homage could be potentially expensive.[13]

What then was the form of homage exacted for the continental lands of the

[8] J. Gillingham, *The Angevin Empire* (London, 1984) p. 88.

[9] Chaplais, 'Le duché-pairie de Guyenne', pp. 8–10.

[10] AN, J 634, no. 14, dated at the 'maison roial dou bois de Vincennes', 14 September 1325. The English envoys' supplication was made through Master Guillaume de Breuil, the celebrated advocate at the Paris Parlement.

[11] See J. J. N. Palmer, *England, France and Christendom, 1377–99* (London, 1972), pp. 144–5, 149–63; and my review of this book in *EHR*, lxxxviii (1973), pp. 848–51.

[12] AN, J 634, no. 21: a form of homage was then agreed upon 'selonc la forme de pais faictes entre ses devanciers' (6 June 1329). The final form of homage was only acknowledged by Edward in March 1331 in the words 'combien que nous le feismes par paroles generales fu, est, et doit estre entendez lige' (AN, J 635, no. 6; 30 March 1331). But the ceremony of liege homage never appears to have been performed by him.

[13] Chaplais, 'Le duché-pairie de Guyenne', p. 9; *Foedera*, II, i, pp. 606–8; AN, J 634, no. 22.

English crown? The distinction between liege and simple homage had begun
to be made in the course of the twelfth century. There is no doubt, from the
terms of the 1259 treaty, that Henry III's was intended to be liege homage:
on 4 December 1259 he performed liege homage to St Louis in the garden of
his palace on the Ile-de-la-Cité. Henry, as peer of France, was now holding a
new *duché-pairie* in the south-west.[14] The implications of liege homage were
twofold: it combined both homage and fealty – although the latter was not
sworn by the monarch in person, but by proxy. To swear the oath of
exclusive personal loyalty contained in fealty would certainly have derogated
from the majesty of the king of England. The point was vividly made at
Amiens on 29 June 1320, when Edward II performed homage to Philip V of
France before the high altar of the cathedral.[15] Three or four days later,
according to an eyewitness report, a meeting took place between the two
monarchs and their advisers in the French king's chamber there in order to
renew an alliance of perpetual friendship concluded in 1303 by Edward I and
Philip IV. During the discussion, one of the French counsellors proposed
that Edward was bound to swear fealty, as well as homage, to Philip V.[16]
Edward's own words in reply to what he clearly considered an outrageous
suggestion survive: they were spoken without the advice of his council,
apparently because they had difficulty in hearing the king's whispered words
and he lost patience. Edward turned away from the assembled prelates and
nobles of his council and addressed Philip V as follows:

> We well remember that the homage which we performed at Boulogne [1308] was
> done according to the form of the peace treaties made between our ancestors,
> after the manner in which they did it. Your father [i.e. Philip IV] agreed to it, for
> we have his letters confirming this, and we have performed it already in the same
> fashion; no one can reasonably ask us to do otherwise; and we certainly do not
> intend to do so. As to the fealty [oath] we are certain that we should not swear it;
> nor was it ever asked of us at that time.[17]

The French council was stunned into silence by this intransigent retort.
Eventually, one of them tactfully suggested to Philip V that the perpetual
alliance should simply be sworn, and also a mutual oath not to harbour
enemies or those banished from either kingdom.[18] This presupposed parity of
status was to have important implications. No further allusion was made
to the issue of fealty, and Edward II himself replied 'with an amiable

[14] Chaplais, 'The making of the treaty of Paris', p. 247.

[15] See E. Pole-Stuart, 'The interview between Philip V and Edward II at Amiens in 1320',
EHR, xli (1926), pp. 414–5, printed from C 47/29/9, no. 25, (30 June 1320).

[16] Pole-Stuart, 'Interview between Philip V and Edward II', p. 413; Chaplais, 'Le
duché-pairie de Guyenne', pp. 153–4.

[17] Pole-Stuart, 'Interview between Philip V and Edward II', p. 414; Chaplais, 'Le
duché-pairie de Guyenne', p. 154.

[18] C 47/29/9, no. 25.

countenance': 'We willingly wish this to be done [i.e. the alliance to be renewed], for it is right.'[19] But the eyewitness who reported the scene noted that all could see from his face that he was greatly irritated by the French counsellor who had attempted to alter the terms of his homage and exact a fealty oath. That the king should feel it necessary to speak for himself in these discussions is striking – the theoretical concepts of sovereignty, homage and fealty clearly had important implications.

The bond of liege homage posed a further difficulty for one who was sovereign in his own right: how could the king of England perform services to the king of France which ran counter to his own previous alliances? If, for instance, the king of France was at war with the king of Aragon or Castile and called upon the king of England, as duke of Aquitaine, to serve him according to his oath, how could former treaties of alliance between England and Aragon or Castile be broken? One way round such thorny issues was the insertion of a clause in all subsequent alliances excepting the vassals' fealty to his liege lord. Edward I did this in alliances with Castile, Navarre, Aragon and Flanders.[20]

All this may seem cut and dried, and potentially restrictive, if not damaging to the interests of the Plantagenet king-duke of Aquitaine. But by 1273, when both the original parties to the 1259 agreement were dead, the issues were by no means so clear-cut. On 6 August 1273 Edward I paid homage to Philip III. The form of words that he used were these: 'Lord king, I do you homage for all the lands which I *ought* to hold from you'.[21] By this conditional statement, Edward clearly referred to the non-performance of the territorial clauses of the 1259 treaty. Before he would perform liege homage, he must be invested with the lands and rights which were agreed between his father and Louis IX. Again, on 5 June 1286, Edward performed homage to Philip IV of France, using the words: 'I become your man for the lands which I hold from you on this side of the sea according to the form of peace made between our ancestors'.[22] By this, he and his diplomatic agents maintained, was meant the fully implemented terms of the 1259 agreement. If, as was palpably obvious, those terms had not been properly executed, liege homage was to be postponed until such time as satisfaction had been obtained. Hence, with the exception of Henry III's action of December 1259, liege homage (in its full and proper form) had not been performed for Aquitaine prior to the accession of Philip IV in 1285. Homage was deemed conditional upon the putting into effect of what came to be called 'St Louis's peace'. To understand the reasons behind that agreement we must look more closely at the context in which it was made.[23]

---

[19] Pole-Stuart, 'Interview between Philip V and Edward II', p. 414.

[20] Chaplais, 'Le duché-pairie de Guyenne', pp. 11–12.

[21] *Flores Historiarum*, ed. H. R. Luard (RS, London, 1890), iii, p. 31.

[22] *Foedera*, I, iii, p. 665; BL, Add. MS 32, 045, fo. 112ᵛ.

[23] For the circumstances surrounding the treaty see F. M. Powicke, *Henry III and the Lord*

The treaty can be divided into four main parts. Firstly, Henry III of England took the somewhat unwise step of renouncing his fiefs in Normandy, Anjou, Touraine, Maine and Poitou. His heirs and successors were not to lay claim to them. Secondly, this was conditional upon Louis IX of France ceding to Henry all rights 'that he has and holds in these three dioceses and three cities: that is to say, Limoges, Cahors and Périgueux, in fiefs and in domains'. Thirdly, the Agenais, claimed by the king of England, was to remain in French hands until the question of his legal right was determined. That was only done twenty years later, in 1279. Lastly, all that Louis IX abandoned in favour of Henry III – his fiefs and domains in Limousin, Quercy, and Périgord (the so-called 'three dioceses') and all that remained to the Plantagenets of the ancient duchy of Aquitaine – was to be held by the king of England as an hereditary fief. He must take an oath of fealty and liege homage to his suzerain, the king of France, for it. In return Henry III was granted a peerage of France. He became one of the twelve peers of the kingdom, taking his place beside the count of Flanders, the duke of Burgundy and the count of Anjou.[24]

The treaty created conditions which, for three reasons, would arguably result in conflict: it was soon apparent that Louis IX possessed very little in the three dioceses worth ceding to Henry III: they were what Le Patourel called 'a complex and varying bundle of rights and jurisdictions, often barely effective, a fruitful source of disputes and appeals'.[25] In addition, some lords, both ecclesiastical and secular, were privileged (*privilegiati*) in that they could not be forced to transfer their allegiance to another lord against their will.[26] This was a rich, fertile field for those judicial disputes upon which many throve – especially the lawyers and officers in the pay of either side. In this area, therefore, Anglo-French rivalry should be viewed in judicial, legal and proprietary terms, rather than in a purely military framework. If war was a continuation of legal proceedings over rights by other means, then those legal proceedings were a result of the treaty of 1259.

Secondly, Henry III's renunciation of all his rights to Normandy, Anjou, Touraine, Maine and Poitou was a more serious matter than some contemporaries thought. The fact that Henry was not in possession of those areas in 1259 did not mean that he or his successors might not actively revive their claims. His renunciation also rested upon a dubious legal sentence of 1202, a punitive measure against King John by Philip Augustus. Ought this to be

Edward (Oxford, 1947), i, pp. 248–58; Chaplais, 'The making of the treaty of Paris', pp. 238–47.

[24] Chaplais, 'Le duché-pairie de Guyenne', pp. 5–7; Le Patourel, 'The king and the princes in fourteenth-century France', *Feudal Empires*, pt XV, pp. 155–6, 179–83.

[25] Le Patourel, 'The origins of the Hundred Years War', in *Feudal Empires*, pt XI, p. 34.

[26] Gavrilovitch, *Etude sur le traité de Paris*, pp. 68–71; J. R. Studd, 'The "privilegiati" and the treaty of Paris, 1259', in *La "France Anglaise" au Moyen Age*, ed. R.-H. Bautier (Paris, 1988), pp. 175–89. See also E. Albe, 'Les suites du traité de Paris de 1259 pour le Quercy', *AM*, xxiii (1911), pp. 472–91.

enforced in different circumstances against John's innocent son and heir?[27] And how did the inhabitants of those areas feel? The barons of Normandy and Poitou were not innately unfavourable towards a Plantagenet lord and, as their successors were to discover after 1337, a choice of allegiance could be a very useful weapon in the course of disputes with the Capetian monarchy.

Thirdly, by agreeing to hold the duchy of Aquitaine as an hereditary fief from the crown of France, Henry III was putting both himself and his heirs into an untenable position since a king in his own right was to perform liege homage to another king. Two sovereigns of equal authority in their respective kingdoms were put on an unequal footing because one of those sovereigns held land from the other. To hypothesize, it was as if the king of France held the earldom of Cornwall or Lancaster from the king of England, who could therefore exert some degree of control over the foreign policy and behaviour of the king of France. Conversely, it was theoretically to the advantage of the French kings to have the Plantagenets as feudal inferiors, rather than to expel them from their remaining continental possessions.[28]

Professor Cuttino has concluded that the peace of Paris 'which re-created the feudal relationship which led eventually to war, was the result of English commitments towards Sicily and the desire to secure wealthy territory'.[29] As such, he argued, it was a mistake. Henry III was indeed morally and financially committed to support the policies of Pope Innocent IV and his own brother, Richard of Cornwall, towards Sicily. His problems with the English baronage in 1258–9 also necessitated a settlement with France of the status of his remaining continental possessions. As we have seen, Louis IX's support against the troublesome magnates was highly desirable.[30] Yet there were also incentives for Louis IX to come to terms: Joinville reports that Louis replied to his critics, who asked why he should give away 'so great a part of your land, that you and your ancestors have conquered, and which has been forfeited', that he had given Henry, Aquitaine, Gascony and the three dioceses 'to create affection between my children and his, who are cousins-germain'.[31] The domestic circle was thus to be brought closer together. After all, Henry III, Richard of Cornwall, Louis IX and Charles of Anjou were brothers-in-law – they had all married daughters of the count of Provence. Margaret, Louis IX's queen, was the sister of Eleanor, queen of England, and maintained the closest connection with both Henry III and Edward I.[32] In January 1262, for instance, one of Henry III's proctors at Paris, Pierre de Limoges, wrote to Walter de Merton, chancellor of England,

---

[27] See Chaplais, 'Le traité de Paris', pp. 124–5; Le Patourel, 'The Plantagenet dominions', *Feudal Empires*, pt VIII, pp. 301–2.

[28] Le Patourel, 'The origins of the Hundred Years War', pp. 43–6.

[29] Cuttino, 'Historical revision', p. 472.

[30] See above, pp. 14–15.

[31] Joinville, *Histoire de St Louis*, p. 245; Gavrilovitch, *Etude sur le traité de Paris*, pp. 41–2.

[32] See above, pp. 21–2.

to tell him that Queen Margaret was so occupied in the business of negotiations that she had no time to write to him.[33] He was accordingly writing to
give the views which the queen would otherwise have sent. Again, in October
1281, Edward I wrote to her, saying that she had always striven to keep the
peace between Henry III and Louis, and between Philip III and himself. She
had laboured hard 'on behalf of this harmony for which', Edward wrote, 'we
thank you with all our heart'.[34]

Dynastic concord and family harmony were, however, bought somewhat
at the expense of the two princes' subjects. Henry and Louis had in effect
entered upon a private treaty of peace, against the wishes of many of their
most powerful subjects. In France, it was thought by Louis's noble counsellors that Henry III's homage had been far too dearly bought. The inhabitants of some areas ceded by Louis to Henry were similarly unenthusiastic
about the treaty, and the people of some places in the three dioceses actually
refused to celebrate St Louis's feast-day after his canonization in 1297.[35] In
England the chronicler of Meaux accused Henry of making a 'shameful
concord', and Matthew Paris singled out Richard, earl of Gloucester, as the
scapegoat in this dishonourable peace.[36] Yet the strongest opposition to the
treaty came from the very highest ranks of English society: from the Lord
Edward, and from Simon de Montfort and his wife Eleanor. Gervase of
Canterbury tells us that Edward objected especially to Henry's renunciation
of his rights to Normandy and to the infeudation of Gascony: although
Edward had agreed to its terms by 25 July 1259, he was to change his mind
in 1260 and allege that Normandy had been sold to the French.[37] He refused
to accompany his father to pay homage to Louis IX in November 1259.[38]
More immediately serious were the objections of de Montfort. Eleanor,
countess of Leicester, Simon's wife, had substantial claims against Henry III
for her dowry as widow of William Marshal. Abetted by her husband, she
refused to countenance the renunciations which Henry was to make in the
peace treaty. Although a form of peace had been agreed upon on 28 May
1258, it was not until 4 December 1259 that Eleanor de Montfort actually
accepted the renunciations and agreed that she would not revive her claims
to her French lands. She was in effect bought out for 15,000 marks.[39] It was

---

[33] *Diplomatic Documents, 1101–1272*, ed. P. Chaplais, ii, no. 348 (29 January 1262).

[34] *Foedera*, I, i, p. 599 (10 October 1281).

[35] Gavrilovitch, *Etude sur le traité de Paris*, p. 193.

[36] *Chronica Monasterii de Melsa*, ed. E. A. Bond (RS, London 1867), ii, p. 129: 'facta pudenda
concordia'; Matthew Paris, *Chronica Majora*, ed. H. R. Luard, v (RS, London, 1880, pp. 744–5.

[37] Gervase of Canterbury, *Historical Works*, ed. W. Stubbs (RS, London, 1879–80), ii, p. 210;
C 76/2, m. 4.

[38] Chaplais, 'The making of the treaty of Paris', pp. 245–7; and for tensions between Henry
III and Edward see J. R. Studd, 'The Lord Edward and Henry III', *BIHR*, 1 (1977–8), pp.
4–19.

[39] See Chaplais, 'The making of the treaty of Paris', pp. 244–47 for a full account of Eleanor
de Montfort's role in the negotiations.

upon such essentially private issues that so-called 'international' agreements could founder in the thirteenth century. Here, modern concepts of diplomacy and international relations are often at variance with those of this period.

Yet the treaty of 1259 did introduce a momentous change into the relations between the two powers. Henry III, unlike his three Angevin ancestors, could now no longer style himself 'king of England, lord of Ireland, duke of Normandy and Aquitaine and count of Anjou'.[40] His great seal had formerly born those titles, with an image of the king seated on a throne (or Norman stool) grasping a sword. By 9 September 1259 a new seal had been made – it bore the legend 'Henry, by the grace of God, king of England, lord of Ireland and duke of Aquitaine', with a representation of the king seated upon a Gothic chair, bearing not a sword, but a sceptre.[41] Yet the new royal style was initially used only for diplomatic relations with France: the old style was employed by some departments of English government until June 1260.[42] In effect, Henry acted in breach of the treaty of Paris by using his style as duke of Normandy and count of Anjou for acts of English internal administration. These apparently included documents concerning Gascony: for example, a letter to Oléron on 3 September 1259,[43] but this did not provoke any kind of diplomatic incident or crisis in Anglo-French relations. Louis IX did not apparently take any steps to prevent Henry from using an obsolete and illegal instrument. But the reaction might have been different if Philip the Fair, rather than St Louis had been king of France at that time. French susceptibilities over sovereignty had not yet developed to the extent that they were to do by 1294.

On 18 October 1260, however, the 'last symbol of English resistance to the conquests of Philip Augustus' disappeared.[44] A short ceremony in the king's chamber at Westminster marked the end of the Angevin Empire, in the form which it had assumed under Henry II and his sons. The new great seal was handed to the king, and the old seal broken by the king's command. Henry III then gave the new matrix to Master Nicholas de Ely who took the oath to keep it faithfully. With his own hand, the king characteristically gave the fragments of the old seal's silver matrix to one of his clerks for donation to some poor religious house.[45] So ended the formal history of the Angevin dominions – Henry III and his successors were to retain only their south-western French lands de jure and de facto, held as fiefs of the French crown in liege homage, a form of tenure which normally implied feudal service.

Did the performance of an oath to the king of France in fact entail the subsequent performance of feudal services by the king-dukes? There is some

---

[40] See, for a late example, BL, Add. ch. 11,299 (9 February 1259).

[41] A. B. and A. W. Wyon, *Great Seals of England* (London, 1887), no. 43.

[42] Chaplais, 'The making of the treaty of Paris', pp. 250–51, and n. 3.

[43] Chaplais, 'The making of the treaty of Paris', p. 252 (Appendix I (b)).

[44] Chaplais, 'The making of the treaty of Paris', p. 251.

[45] *CCR, 1259–61*, p. 130.

evidence that this was the case, although it is sometimes negative in nature. In May 1275 Edward I wrote to Alphonso of Castile, excusing himself from an alliance with Castile against France because he was bound by his homage and fealty to Philip III.[46] But in 1282 he received a direct summons from Philip requesting him to serve in arms in the proposed French expedition to Aragon of that year.[47] Edward was addressed as duke of Aquitaine and count of Ponthieu, and the summons was received in the duchy by his seneschal, the Savoyard Jean de Grilly. Grilly's action was noteworthy. On receipt of the summons, he sent a copy to Edward (who was in Wales), and immediately wrote to the nobles and communes of the duchy, ordering them to prepare themselves to serve 'with arms and horses' (cum armis et equis), and to make ready so that they might obey Edward's command when it was known.[48] In his circular letter to the Gascons, Grilly had made no mention of the fact that Philip III of France had issued the summons. He waited for Edward's decision but, in a second letter, took the opportunity of reminding him that his son, Pierre de Grilly, was eligible for knighthood and that Edward had promised to knight him. Jean desired this and as 'the king of France has given permission to make war in this land', Pierre could serve in Aragon.[49] In the event, there was no expedition to Aragon in 1282.[50] But on 21 July, Edward I ordered Jean de Grilly to obey Philip III's summons and to make ready to perform military service; but in his reply to the king of France he was to stress that in the 1259 treaty 'the certainty of the said service has not yet been found'.[51] The Aragonese were politely told by Edward (in January 1283) that 'we are bound by kinship and by homage to the king of France, nor does it behove us to rebel against him in any way, nor to do anything to arouse his anger nor give him offence'.[52] Military service to France was actually performed by Edward in 1283, in so far as Edward's seneschal of Ponthieu arrived at Bordeaux with a contingent of men-at-arms, ready to serve in Aragon, but they soon returned home.[53]

There were, however, very strong Gascon objections to the performance of feudal services by their duke to the French crown. The clergy, nobility and communes of Gascony and the Agenais sent Edward a petition urging him to refuse feudal services in the Aragonese war.[54] But they requested that his refusal should not be transmitted by appeal to the court of France (that is, to the king and peers), for that would be to recognize the superiority of Philip III's court in a matter which was by no means certain. As Philip's summons

---

[46] Foedera, I, ii, p. 522.

[47] SC 1/18, no. 67.

[48] RG, ii, no. 607; SC 1/18, no. 67.

[49] SC 1/18, no. 68.

[50] Chaplais, 'Le duché-pairie de Guyenne', p. 21.

[51] RG ii. no. 607: 'nondum reperitur dicti servicii certitudo'.

[52] SC 1/12, nos 35, 36 (12 January 1283).

[53] RG, iii, no. 5061.

[54] C 47/30/1, no. 5. The document is a copy from the reign of Edward III.

had been issued only on the fragile authority of a single peace treaty, its validity had to be established by other means.[55] The Gascons demanded that such issues, which gravely threatened the liberty and hereditary rights of both Edward I and themselves, be settled by those they called 'common judges' or wardens (*esgardiatores*) who should judge the case according to marcher law. Gascony and the Agenais were frontier areas; they were marches in the sense that the borders towards Scotland and Wales were to become marches, subject to their own customs and the jurisdiction of their two wardens.[56] This doing of justice *en marche* could beelevated to encompass the creation of *ad hoc* Anglo-French commissions (with a strong Gascon element) empowered to adjudicate disputes over services and obligations outside the formal appellate jurisdiction of the French crown. Questions arising from the 1259 treaty were, after an ordinance of Edward's Westminster Parliament in 1285, to be resolved by such commissions, and the so-called 'processes' of Montreuil, Périgueux and Agen were pragmatic applications of this idea.[57] Yet they took place only after the Anglo-French war of 1294–8. The French under Philip the Fair had gone too far towards reducing the issues posed by the treaty of Paris to the level of lawsuits between lord and vassal in the Paris parlement.

After 1303, however, no feudal service was performed by Edward I to the crown of France. A request for military aid against Flanders from Philip the Fair in March 1304 certainly met with Edward's support: twenty ships were promised.[58] But they were only to be offered upon condition that this created no precedent. This aid was interpreted as a product of the treaty of alliance concluded between the two sovereigns in 1303. It was not obligatory feudal service for Aquitaine and Ponthieu, but the friendly assistance of one sovereign, acting of his own free will, to another. In the event the ships do not appear to have been sent, although payment for preparing them was certainly made by the Exchequer at York to Roger Savage and Peter of Dunwich.[59] A letter of excuse was apparently sent to Philip, to be taken by three messengers including Savage and Dunwich.[60] Edward II, however, gave a measure of active assistance to Louis X of France against Flanders in

---

[55] C 47/30/1, no. 5: they referred to the 'infinitibus oneribus et injuriis et dampnis inestimabilibus' which the king-duke and they themselves would sustain if the case went to the 'court of France' (*curiam Francie*).

[56] See Chaplais, 'Règlement des conflits internationaux franco-anglais au xive siècle (1293–1377)', in *Essays in Medieval Diplomacy*, pt IX, pp. 275–7.

[57] P. Chaplais, 'Règlement des conflits . . .', *Essays in Medieval Diplomacy*, pt IX, pp. 269–302; G. C. Cuttino, *English Diplomatic Administration 1259–1339* (2nd edn, Oxford, 1971), pp. 62–111; and his 'The Process of Agen', *Speculum*, xix (1944), pp. 161–78.

[58] *Foedera*, I, ii, pp. 961–2.

[59] E 101/12/33: account of Roger Savage and Peter of Dunwich for expenses 'circa providenciam viginti navium domino regi Francie concessarum in subsidium guerre sue Flandrie'.

[60] *Gascon Calendar*, no. 414 (p. 40): transcript of letters 'de excusacione navium non missarum'.

September 1315, when he ordered two English admirals to sail towards the Flemish coast with their six ships, and issued a letter permitting Amaury de Craon, seneschal of Aquitaine, to serve Louis personally in Flanders.[61] We have no other details of this aspect of Anglo-French relations before the outbreak of the Hundred Years War. In effect, it seems safe to conclude that the performance of feudal services by the King of England as duke of Aquitaine and count of Ponthieu was very largely a non-issue. The question of homage, on the contrary, was another matter: its significance lay not in the amount of service which it might subsequently furnish to the kings of France, but in the principle which it enshrined. Henry III's *damnosa hereditas* made two sovereigns unequal when they became involved in the affairs of the surviving remnants of the Angevin Empire in south-west France.

It is important to be clear about the extent and status of those south-western French possessions. If, as is usually argued, the course of Anglo-French relations before the Hundred Years War was largely dictated by disputes over them, their nature is highly significant. They have been mistakenly described, with the Channel Islands and the Isle of Oléron (off La Rochelle) as component parts of 'England's first Empire', the first 'overseas dominions' of the English crown.[62] Their administration has been intensively studied and seen as part of what John Le Patourel called the 'converging and ultimately clashing development of the government of [the Angevin Empire], or what was left of it . . . and the development of royal government in the kingdom of France. It was more than the feudal relationship between king and king-duke, it was the overlapping and ultimately the conflict of two growing structures of government.'[63] To lift the conflict of England and France above the protracted legal wrangles and diplomatic bickering produced by the feudal relationship on to another, loftier, plane is no easy task. Talk of 'structures of government' may distort rather than illuminate, and the centrality of the personal relationship between rulers can be too much played down. Institutions can directly reflect political circumstances, and there can be no divorce between the implications of that feudal relationship and its expression in 'constitutional' forms – in appellate jurisdiction, in the devices used to delay homage or evade services, or in the administrative expedients whereby rights and revenues were upheld and increased.

In 1259 the status of Henry III's Gascon possessions was uncertain. Were they all in fact part of the kingdom of France? Did Louis IX really have a sound title to act as sovereign over them at that time? It is a notable feature of English diplomatic activity in the late 1290s that Edward I's lawyers argued that Gascony was not in effect part of the kingdom of France at all: it

---

[61] Chaplais, 'Le duché-pairie de Guyenne', pp. 143–7; *Foedera*, II, i, pp. 277–8; E 101/376/7, fos 12[r], 14[r], 15[r]: see above, pp. 33–4.

[62] M. Burrows, *The Family of Brocas of Beaurepaire and Roche Court* (London, 1886), p. 18; M. W. Labarge, *Gascony: England's First Colony* (London, 1980), pp. xi–xii, 23.

[63] Le Patourel, 'The origins of the Hundred Years War', pp. 39–40.

was an allodial land, held only from God.[64] The 'duchy of Aquitaine' in the mid-thirteenth century can, however, only be described in relation to the kingdom of France. One striking characteristic of the French kingdom throughout this period (1259–1340) was its fluctuating size. It was a bundle of rights and privileges, both claimed and exercised.[65] Its extent expanded and contracted according to many external and internal pressures. Philip the Fair's adviser, Guillaume de Nogaret, saw the *regnum* as the total area of Capetian jurisdiction – and that might not correspond to its territorial extent at a given time.[66] The use of royal letters of protection could annex territories – often enclaves – to the crown (Lyon, Valenciennes or the *comté* of Bar) but these might subsequently revert to other hands.[67] Outside his own domain (the Ile-de-France) the king often had no more than powers of general protection. The precise extent of those powers was the subject of constant dispute, and at this stage in constitutional development the play of politics still had a direct influence upon the definition of the king's rights, especially his rights of justice. How he chose to exercise those rights differed from time to time and from province to province. It has been rightly said that in the thirteenth century the king of France (unlike the king of England) possessed no direct control over the whole kingdom: 'outside the domain, default alone allowed him to act'.[68] It was only when seigneurial justice or administration broke down, or otherwise went awry, that the king could act directly to intervene in his vassals' conduct of their affairs.

How then did the south-western French domains of the Plantagenets rank in the hierarchy of fiefs which made up the kingdom of France? Dr Pierre Chaplais has argued that Henry III's action, by which he acknowledged Louis IX's superiority over the whole duchy of Aquitaine, was more damaging to both Plantagenet and Gascon interests than may at first appear.[69] The treaty of 1259 transformed a Gascon allod into a fief, and extended the French kingdom, for the first time, as far as the Pyrenees.[70] For the first time, an English king held the duchy from the French crown in liege homage. In other words, before 1259 the duchy of Aquitaine – or a substantial portion of it – had been an independent and autonomous unit, held by a duke who performed neither homage nor feudal services to the Capetians. It might bear comparison with Normandy in some respects – there, a separate ducal

---

[64] See H. Rothwell, 'Edward I's case against Philip the Fair over Gascony in 1298', *EHR*, xlii (1927), pp. 572–82; P. Chaplais, 'English arguments concerning the feudal status of Aquitaine in the 14th century', *BIHR*, xxi (1946–8), pp. 203–13.

[65] See Wood, '*Regnum Francie*', pp. 137–41; G. Sivery, 'La description du royaume de France par les conseillers de Philippe Auguste et par leurs successeurs', *MA*, xc (1984), pp. 65–85.

[66] Wood, '*Regnum Francie*', p. 140; and *Mémoire relatif au paréage de 1307 conclu entre l'evêque Guillaume Durand II et le roi Philippe le Bel*, ed. A. Maisonobe (Mende, 1896), pp. 3–6, 521–32.

[67] Wood, '*Regnum Francie*', pp. 140–2; Strayer, *Reign of Philip the Fair*, pp. 340–64.

[68] Wood, '*Regnum Francie*', p. 143.

[69] Chaplais, 'Le traité de Paris', pp. 135–37.

[70] BL, MS Cotton, Julius D. V, fo. 33^r (4 December 1259).

administration continued to function even after its so-called integration into France in 1204. Louis IX legislated for Normandy and for the kingdom in separate ordinances and he heard appeals not at Paris, but at Rouen. Professor Wood has noted the paradox that in Normandy 'the rights and powers of its rulers [i.e. the dukes] so far exceeded those possessed by the king that it was desirable to maintain the duchy as a territory apart, and provide for its continued semi-autonomous existence'.[71] Much of this statement could be applied to Aquitaine.

In the south-west of France, however, complete autonomy had, it seems, prevailed before 1259. The duchy of Aquitaine was not of ancient or Carolingan origin. It represented the tenure after 1063 of the two ancient duchies of Gascony and Guyenne (the Gallicized form of 'Aquitaine') by one ruler.[72] The earlier duchy of Aquitaine had been part of the *comté* of Poitou, but the duchy of Gascony was an independent entity. Very roughly, the boundary between the two lordships was the river Garonne. The early charters of the dukes of Gascony dating from the tenth and eleventh centuries make no mention in their dating clauses of the reigning king of France, and the dukes certainly possessed such rights as the striking of coins. From 1063 to 1202, the duchy of Gascony was held with Aquitaine by the counts of Poitou, but it was, unlike Poitou, held as an autonomous domain.[73] In 1152, Henry Plantagenet (later Henry II) became duke of Aquitaine, then part of the *comté* of Poitou, and as such recognized his vassalic status towards Louis VII of France.[74] But the duchy of Gascony, lying between the Garonne and the Pyrenees, remained inviolable, and the lands 'in Wasconia ultra Guaronam', as Richard I described them in 1191, were in fact allodial territories, held without superior lord.[75] So were the *vicomtés* of Béarn (independent of the French crown until 1612) and Turenne (independent until 1736).[76] The very fact that Philip Augustus made no serious attempt to invade or attack Gascony in the campaigns of 1202–4 may be more than simply a comment upon the military limitations of the French crown. It could have meant that the Capetians acknowledged that they possessed no realizable claims to the allodial duchy of Gascony. As we shall see, this area of the south-west was the source of much of the opposition to the crown of France between 1294

---

[71] Wood, '*Regnum Francie*', pp. 134–5; see also J. R. Strayer, *The Administration of Normandy under St Louis* (Cambridge, Mass., 1932), pp. 12–31.

[72] See Le Patourel, 'Plantagenet dominions', pp. 301–2; F. Lot, *Fidèles ou vassaux?* (Paris, 1904), pp. 49–52.

[73] Chaplais, 'Le traité de Paris', pp. 129–30.

[74] L. Delisle, *Recueil des actes de Henri II, Introduction* (Paris, 1909), pp. 127–31.

[75] Richard constituted his wife Berengaria's dower from 'ea omnia quae habemus in Wasconia ultra Guaronam' in 1191: Martène and Durand, *Veterum scriptorum et monumentorum amplissima collectio*, i (Paris, 1724), col. 995, cited in Chaplais, 'Le traité de Paris', p. 133. The term 'ultra flumen Garone' was applied to land invaded by the French in 1294–7. See AN, JJ 38, fos 12ᵛ–13ʳ (4 August 1298).

[76] See P. Tucoo-Chala, *Gaston Fébus et la vicomté de Béarn, 1343–91* (Bordeaux, 1960), pp. 39–41.

and 1303, and where traditional loyalties to the Plantagenet regime were most deeply rooted.[77]

The Gascons themselves were well aware that the 1259 treaty had led to an immediate change in their status. The *Livre des Coutumes* of Bordeaux contains a note that '[In 1259] king Henry did homage for Bordeaux, Bayonne and all the land of Gascony [*Gasconha*] which was [then] free allod [*franc en alo*] to Louis, king of France . . . but let it be known that this Gascony was the most free allod that the king of England had, before . . . king Henry received it back from the French king in homage'.[78] By the peace of Paris, the inhabitants of 'Gascony beyond the Garonne' had become *arrière-vassaux* of Louis IX, although in 1224 they had refused to transfer their ultimate allegiance to the king of France.[79] They performed no feudal services, military or otherwise, to the French crown, and they owed no suit of court outside strict territorial limits. There was therefore every reason for them, and for those who served the interests of the Plantagenet king-dukes, to try to undo the treaty's effects. Henry III's political miscalculation had to be set right, and it was imperative that the status of the Gascon lands be redefined. The new *duché-pairie* in Gascony had to be dismantled and an independent duchy re-created. If the actual performance of liege homage could be staved off by Henry's successors until the territorial clauses of the 1259 treaty were properly implemented, then it could be claimed that the duke was acting as *de facto* sovereign in his duchy until such time as the agreement was fulfilled. Given the objections of interested parties, such as the lords known as the *privilegiati* in the three dioceses, this was unlikely to be a speedy process.[80] Edward I's behaviour may be seen partly in this light. A theory of ducal sovereignty was in effect to be formulated between 1294 and 1300, which was to set important precedents for other peers and magnates of France to follow.[81] Capetian claims to the exercise of sovereignty evoked a hostile response from the magnates, led by the duke of Aquitaine and count of Flanders, which was not to be stilled by the death of Philip the Fair in 1314.[82] But it was only after Philip's seizure of Aquitaine (in 1293–4) that this response was brought out into the open. Was a workable *modus vivendi* then possible between the rulers of England and France, even within the limits set

[77] See below, pp. 194, 202–4, 207.

[78] *Archives Municipales de Bordeaux, Livre des Coutumes*, ed. H. Barckhausen, (Bordeaux, 1890), pp. 612, 614.

[79] See *Gesta Ludovici Octavi*, in *Recueil des Historiens des Gaules et de la France*, xvii, pp. 305–6.

[80] See above, n. 26.

[81] Le Patourel, 'Plantagenet dominions', p. 305; Chaplais, 'English arguments concerning the feudal status of Aquitaine', pp. 203–13; Le Patourel, 'The king and the princes', pp. 162–3, 181–3.

[82] See P. Contamine, 'De la puissance aux privilèges: doléances de la noblesse française envers la monarchie aux xive et xve siècles', in *La Noblesse au Moyen Age*, ed. P. Contamine (Paris, 1976), pp. 237–47.

by the peace of Paris? The answer cannot be found without closer scrutiny of the Plantagenet presence in France.

3.2 The Plantagenet Presence in France, 1259–1294

Sir Maurice Powicke reminded his English readers that 'Edward [I] was a southerner by blood, and, through his dukedom of Aquitaine, by circumstance'.[83] It is not therefore altogether surprising that he should have spent the years 1254–5, 1261–3, 1273–4 and 1286–9 in south-west France; nor that his mind was often preoccupied with French and Gascon affairs both before and during his reign. He knew the duchy well and, Powicke concluded, 'he never wished, even if it were possible to do so, to relax his grasp upon the affairs of his distant province'.[84] He arrived in Gascony in September 1273, for example, before he had even returned to England as king, to deal with the actions of Gaston VII, *vicomte* of Béarn, against his authority as duke of Aquitaine.[85] Edward remained in Gascony until the end of April 1274, fully occupied with the settlement of the case of Gaston VII in which Edward was represented at the Parlement of Paris by one of the best civil lawyers in Europe, Francesco Accursius of Bologna. He was busy negotiating alliances with the Spanish kingdoms, receiving oaths of homage from all his Gascon vassals, conducting a great inquiry into feudal tenures in Gascony (the so-called *Recogniciones feodorum* of 1273–5), which had parallels with the Hundred Rolls and *Quo Warranto* proceedings in England, and summoning assemblies of the three estates of the duchy, and of the 'court of Gascony' to adjudicate (among other things) the case of Gaston de Béarn.[86]

All this took place in the space of ten months – Edward was nothing if not energetic at this period. But the duchy also required government and administration during the absences of its ruler. Obviously the king-duke could not be everywhere in his far-flung territories at once, so delegation was presupposed; Henry II had used his son Richard (later Richard I) or Queen Eleanor as viceroys. Day-to-day government was from an early date conducted by an officer called a seneschal, with vice-ducal powers, and a council. This was the origin of the office held by the king's ordinary representative in the duchy of Aquitaine until 1453.[87] By the mid-thirteenth century, another permanent officer appears: the constable of Bordeaux, responsible for the financial administration of duchy, who is first documented in 1253–4. After 1292, he accounted to the Westminster exchequer.

---

[83] F. M. Powicke, *The Thirteenth Century*, (Oxford, 1954), p. 234.

[84] Powicke, *Thirteenth Century*, p. 280.

[85] J.-P. Trabut-Cussac, *L'Administration anglaise en Gascogne sous Henry III et Edouard I de 1254 à 1307* (Geneva, 1972), pp. 42–4. The following pages owe much to this exhaustive study.

[86] *Recogniciones feodorum in Aquitania*, ed. C. Bémont (Paris, 1914), esp. nos 140–73.

[87] Trabut-Cussac, *L'Administration anglaise*, pp. 141–59 and Appendix II (ii) pp. 372–6 for a list of seneschals from 1253 to 1305.

The reign of Edward I was a period of development and definition. He was the last English king to spend time (as king) in Gascony: ten months in 1273–4; two years in 1286–9; so there was a need to establish an administration there which would function without the king-duke's presence at all. The way towards permanent absentee government was prepared at the beginning of Edward's reign when the king was actually in Gascony. What the Normans and Angevins had done in England was now done in Gascony.[88] The great inquiry into Gascon tenures initiated by Edward I in September 1273 was, however, based upon sound precedent. In 1259, Henry III's seneschal of Gascony – Dreu de Barentin – had been ordered to inquire into feudal tenures in exactly the same manner as Louis IX's brother, Alphonse de Poitiers, had begun to do in his *comté* of Toulouse.[89] As was often to be the case, action by the French in lands adjoining the duchy of Aquitaine provoked the Plantagenet regime to do likewise. The inquiry of 1259 was never put into effect, and it has been suggested that one reason for Edward's visit to Gascony in 1273 was the 'desire to proceed to this measure'.[90] Edward had seen the confusions into which the administration of his duchy might fall through ignorance of vassalic obligations and regional customs. If cases were to be properly judged in Aquitaine, kept out of the Paris Parlement or adjudicated successfully by *ad hoc* commissions in either Gascony or (if a petition to the king in parliament had been made) in England, then knowledge of tenurial conditions, rights, duties and privileges was essential. Ignorance could spell ruin, as Edward's administration was well aware. The state of confusion surrounding such issues was such that he was obliged to allow forty days' grace to many of his ninety or so loyal vassals assembled at St Sever in September 1273, so that they might consult their title-deeds, old charters, relatives and aged kinsmen.[91]

The results of Edward's Gascon inquiry of 1273–5 were not entirely dissimilar to those of his subsequent inquest in England which led to the Hundred Rolls and the statute of Gloucester (1280).[92] Although there is no extant record of special itinerant commissioners taking information upon oath, the product of Edward's summonses to his tenants in Gascony was analogous. A comprehensive survey of feudal and allodial tenures (in the Bordelais only) was made, and it is significant that Edward's demands for military service from Gascon vassals in 1294 closely followed the lists of vassals in the *Recogniciones feodorum* of 1273–5.[93] In the Gascon inquest there is little suspicion, however, of rigorous *quo warranto* proceedings. The nobility,

---

[88] See R. W. Southern, 'England's first entry into Europe', in *Medieval Humanism and Other Studies* (Oxford, 1970), pp. 139, 152.

[89] Trabut-Cussac, *L'Administration anglaise*, pp. 17, 45, 46.

[90] Trabuc-Cussac, *L'Administration anglaise*, p. 45.

[91] *Recog. feod.*, nos 140–73.

[92] Powicke, *Thirteenth Century*, pp. 295–6.

[93] See below, pp. 66, 202–7.

clergy and communes of the region were not expected to produce justifications for their tenures, and there was no waving of rusty swords by irate
tenants-in-chief (as in England). The nearest approach, however, to the
inquiry which produced the Hundred Rolls was a letter of Edward, as lord of
Aquitaine for his father, in November 1259, whereby his seneschal was
required to 'certify to us . . . all rights, liberties, and other matters belonging
to our lordship, in cities, towns and vills, as elsewhere in our province
[*districtu*] of Gascony'.[94] His vassals were asked to swear on the Gospels what
these rights and obligations (*deveriis*) were, and the thrust of the inquiry
appears to have been towards municipal and communal liberties. In 1273, on
the other hand, the clergy and nobility were prominent – indeed dominant
– among those paying homage and fealty and declaring their services.
Edward may well have been thinking of exploiting his Gascon possessions
militarily, as well as financially, and the frequent references to military
service in the *Recogniciones* were to be put to good use.

The kind of information derived from Edward's Gascon inquiry can best
be illustrated by citing the declarations of two vassals, both of whom paid
homage to him at Bordeaux on 19 March 1274. First, one of the barons of the
Médoc, Senebron, lord of Lesparre, declared under oath that he held:

> the castle of Lesparre, with the honour and appurtenances of the said castle,
> paying 12 *l.* relief at change of lord, from the lord king of England, lord of Ireland
> and duke of Aquitaine. . . . Item, he said and recognised that he should perform
> homage and an oath of fealty to the said lord at change of lord. Item, he said he
> recognised that he owed military service with two knights; and if the lord king
> was himself in the army, he should personally serve with one esquire. Item, he
> said that he had no allods, nor had he, nor his predecessors, alienated anything
> of the above. He was to be judged before the seneschal of Gascony.[95]

From this declaration Edward and his officers knew the amount of relief to
be levied from Lesparre, the amount of military service owed and the status
of the tenures. This was useful information for any lord and it is indicative of
the confused and turbulent state of south-west France that the Plantagenet
regime had not recorded its tenurial condition before 1273.[96] The second case
concerns a somewhat lesser man: Guillaume-Sanche de Pommiers, *damoiseau*,
who spoke on behalf of his two co-heirs and co-seigneurs, Pierre and
Pierre-Amanieu de Pommiers, when he acknowledged that they 'held in fee,
immediately from the . . . king of England, lord of Ireland and duke of
Aquitaine, the castle of Pommiers with the honour, and all that these co-heirs
hold in the parishes of Morizès and Escaude, and at Tremblet, and the toll
which they levy on land at Garges, near La Réole'. For these, they owed

[94] *RG*, i (supplément), p. lxxxvii, no. 4.
[95] *Recog. feod.*, pp. 57–8.
[96] Trabut-Cussac, *L'Administration anglaise*, pp. xxvi–xxxiv.

service in the host with one knight; they paid 300 *s.bordelaises* in relief at change of lord and they owed the king-duke a meal with ten attendant knights whenever he came to Gascony, at the castle of Redort. If the king-duke did not order a specific meal, they were to be ready with pork, beef, cabbages (*caulibus*), mustard, and hens; and if one of the co-seigneurs was knighted, he was to wait upon the king-duke wearing 'red hose of scarlet and gilded spurs or shoes' while he ate.[97]

Some details of this tenure are reminiscent of a former age, not least the obligation to provide hospitality (*gîte*) and domestic service to the king-duke when he visited Aquitaine. Yet it emphasizes the close personal bonds which had existed between the dukes of Aquitaine and their vassals: the Pommiers were an ancient family, members of the ducal household, and it was to this kind of traditional relationship that appeal could be made by a largely absentee king-duke at periods of crisis. The ancestral obligations of Gascon nobles, recorded in the *Recogniciones feodorum*, were not only strengthened by Edward I's Gascon visits of 1273–4 and 1286–9. In the French war of 1294–8, as we shall see, they could be exploited by the king-duke so that French occupation of the whole of the duchy was effectively prevented.[98] Regional, local, even parochial loyalties, and the strength of Gascon conservatism were forces with which every ruler – Plantagenet or Capetian – had to reckon. International relations were determined by local factors as well as the interplay of political intrigue and diplomatic negotiation at the highest level: what Powicke rather dismissively described as 'a chapter in French local history' cannot be ignored if one is to explain the ebb and flow of events and the rapid transition from peace to war in this region.[99]

Once his officers had been provided with a comprehensive register of the homages and other obligations of Gascon vassals, Edward could set about the task of governing his duchy with some confidence. Since his administration there had to function without his presence, it was crucial to its development that competent seneschals should be appointed to represent him. From 1274 to 1289 there was a tendency towards increasing definition of the functions of the seneschals and other officers in the duchy.[100] On the road towards autonomy there were a number of obstacles, some easily surmountable, others notoriously resistant. Most resistant of all perhaps was the appellate jurisdiction of the crown of France. This meant that two essentially judicial functions were exercised by the seneschal of Gascony under Edward I: first, an annual progress through the duchy to preside over *assises* at Bazas, Dax and St Sever, although the seneschal, who had much business elsewhere, often empowered a lieutenant to serve in his place. But seneschals still itinerated when they arrived in the duchy to take up office – receiving oaths

[97] *Recog. feod.*, pp. 73–4 (19 March 1274).
[98] See below, pp. 204–7.
[99] Powicke, *Thirteenth Century*, p. 275 and pp. 296–7.
[100] Trabut-Cussac, *L'Administration anglaise*, pp. 154–62.

from the king-duke's Gascon subjects and swearing a reciprocal oath to them.[101] Secondly, he was appointed to represent his lord, the king-duke, at Paris. Below the seneschal and constable of Bordeaux were a swarm of local officials – *prevôts* and *baillis*, a financial controller and keepers of seals for contracts. Before Edward's reforms of 1289–91, offices were normally farmed out to the highest bidder. They were often in the hands of the local nobility, who took the revenues of such offices as one price of their loyalty to the king-duke. So, as Le Patourel commented, 'with a seneschal, an official council, sub-seneschals, a constable, receivers, and judges, a clear chain of command and a workable distribution of duties, the ducal government seemd competent to deal with anything short of an overwhelming emergency'.[102] But emergencies could and did arise, as they were to arise in 1293–4 and 1323–4. By the later thirteenth century, Aquitaine, like Brittany and to some extent the *comté* of Flanders, showed every sign of becoming an autonomous principality. After their loss of Normandy in 1204 the king-dukes were all the more concerned to hold on to their southern lands.

The shadow of the 1259 treaty inevitably fell over the history of the Plantagenet administration of the duchy of Aquitaine in the later thirteenth century. The appellate jurisdiction of the Paris Parlement not only over the three dioceses of Limoges, Câhors and Périgueux, but the whole of the duchy, meant that a constant ducal presence at Paris was necessary. This was what sovereignty really meant – the king of France's right to hold a supreme court of appeal. The king-duke's rights had therefore to be defended by his proctors at Paris and, above all, by the seneschals of Aquitaine themselves. Hence the office became almost a non-resident one in the 1280s. The appointments of two celebrated lawyers, Jean de Vaux and the Englishman John of Havering, as seneschals in 1287 and 1288 was a direct product of the need to represent the king-duke at the Paris Parlement against usurpations of his authority and against false or frivolous appeals.[103] The seneschals' functions had therefore become largely judicial.

The very existence of French appellate jurisdiction over the duchy clearly made Plantagenet rule potentially more difficult than it would otherwise have been. But the status of the duchy was in essence no different from that of the other great principalities – Flanders, Artois, Burgundy or Anjou. A constant irritant was contained in the possibility of the king-duke's Gascon subjects appealing to the court of France, and thereby removing themselves,

---

[101] It was during such an oath-taking tour of the duchy by the seneschal that the incident which sparked off the war of St Sardos took place. See *The War of St Sardos (1323–25). Gascon Correspondence and Diplomatic Documents*, ed. P. Chaplais, Camden 3rd ser. lxxxvii (London, 1954), p. 8, n. 2. Ralph Basset, the seneschal 'necessario habebat ire apud Sanctum Severum, Baionam, Aquens . . . et recipiendo juramenta fieri consueta in novitate cuiuslibet senescalli' (October 1323). See also C 47/26/17 for the oaths.

[102] Le Patourel, 'The King and the princes', p. 161.

[103] PRO, E 36/201, pp. 79, 93; *RG*, ii, no. 1050; *CPR, 1281–92*, p. 279.

if only temporarily, from the Plantagenet jurisdiction.[104] Subterfuges were devised and pressures were applied to prevent appeals going up to Paris.

The later thirteenth century demonstrated the difficulties of the relationship created by the treaty of 1259. The practice of appeal from ducal courts of first instance in the duchy to the Paris Parlement led ultimately to the formulation of the theory of independent Plantagenet sovereignty over Gascony. However, we should note that this took place only after the confiscation of the duchy (1294–1303) by Philip the Fair, after which English attitudes perceptibly hardened. During peace negotiations of 1298, Edward I's representatives, led by Master Philip Martel, introduced the idea of Gascony as an allod. The duchy was said to be a 'free land where the king of England holds complete jurisdiction'.[105] It was held from God alone, and no earthly superior was acknowledged. It was not therefore a part of the kingdom of France. The king-duke was sovereign and was not bound to pay any homage, fealty or feudal service to the crown of France. In the event, things ended in a compromise: by the peace treaty of 1303 the status quo was restored. But the 1298 claim had set a precedent which was to be used again – especially by Edward III.[106] And the claim to autonomous ducal sovereignty over a duchy was soon to be taken up by other princes – the dukes of Brittany, Normandy and, ultimately, Burgundy. If the king-duke could not be a *de jure* sovereign in his duchy of Aquitaine then he had to be made one *de facto*. The claims of 1298 are thus an acknowledgement that the relationship created by the treaty of Paris of 1259 could break down, but only when an assertive and belligerent French monarchy acted to enforce its rights.[107]

In the very early fourteenth century, Edward's lawyers also argued that the treaty was in any case no longer valid. Two reasons were adduced: firstly, Louis IX had not surrendered the lands promised to Henry III in the treaty.[108] Edward had gained only the Agenais in 1279 and southern Saintonge in 1286, although these were valuable additions to his lands, partly because of the number of new settlements or *bastides* previously founded in the Agenais by Alphonse de Poitiers, count of Toulouse, between 1259 and his death without heirs in 1271.[109] Such were the complexities of the tenurial

---

[104] AN, J 654, no. 26: where the subject of frivolous appellants was cited in complaints by Edward II's representatives at Paris against French royal officials. They were allegedly receiving such appeals from certain malefactors in the duchy who 'sub velamine appellacionis . . . defendant se cum armis contra gentes ducis'.

[105] H. Rothwell, 'Edward I's case against Philip the Fair over Gascony in 1298', *EHR*, xiii (1927), pp. 574–6; citing C 47/19/4, no. 9.

[106] Chaplais, 'English arguments concerning the feudal status of Aquitaine', pp. 210–11; Rothwell, 'Edward I's case against Philip the Fair', p. 577; Le Patourel, 'The king and the princes', pp. 162–3.

[107] See below, pp. 176–83.

[108] Chaplais, 'Le duché-pairie de Guyenne', pp. 32–3.

[109] See J.-P. Trabut-Cussac, 'Bastides ou forteresses?', *MA* (1954), pp. 81–135; *Enquêtes administratives d'Alfonse de Poitiers (1249–71)*, ed. Fournier et Guerin (Paris, 1959), pp. 231–2;

rights in these areas that one *bastide* – Castillonès (created in 1260) – was shared between the Plantagenets and the Capetians. The frontier of the Agenais ran right through the middle of the town. It did not fall wholly into Edward I's hands until the peace of 1303.[110] Secondly, it was alleged by Edward's envoys that Louis IX had never formally invested Henry III with the duchy of Aquitaine.[111] On such grounds, the treaty of 1259 was deemed to be invalid. But the old problem of Gascon appeals remained. It proved impossible to translate the theory that the duchy was an allod into practice. There was resistance not only from the crown of France but from some local interests as well. It was greatly to the advantage of certain Gascon subjects of the king-duke to have a source of judicial appeal outside the duchy. The possibility of using it as a tactical weapon against the king-duke was too valuable an asset to be abandoned. In *c.*1308 it was even suggested that some Gascons, especially from the Agenais, might have rebelled openly against their duke had it not been for the existence of French sovereign jurisdiction as a kind of safety valve.[112] The officials of the king-duke could be corrupt, and some behaved in a partisan fashion. Under Edward II two of his seneschals (the Genoese Antonio di Pessagno and the Englishman Ralph Basset of Drayton) were removed from office within a year of their appointments, in 1318 and 1324 respectively.[113] Edward I and Edward II had two principal courses of action open to them in their rivalry with the king of France over judicial supremacy in Aquitaine. Their position in this respect was little different from that of other great magnates of France.

Firstly, they could send requests to Paris asking for the abolition or limitation of the judicial control of the Parlement in Paris over the duchy's courts.[114] Secondly, they had to find some means of reducing the volume of Gascon appeals to Paris to as low a level as possible. The slow erosion of ducal authority through the fluctuating number of Gascon appeals (some of them quite frivolous) had somehow to be countered. The king-duke had to try to suggest that such appeals as were made were not his personal responsibility. One device which was tried was to claim that the appeal was

---

M. W. Beresford, *New Towns of the Middle Ages. Town Plantation in England, Wales and Gascony* (London, 1967), pp. 352–59.

[110] G. P. Cuttino, *Le Livre d'Agenais* (Toulouse, 1956), pp. xiv–xvi; MS Bodley 917, fos 25ᵛ–26ʳ.

[111] Chaplais, 'Le duché-pairie de Guyenne', p. 33.

[112] The suggestion was, however, made by the French, very much in their own interests: AN, J 654, no. 8 (*c.*1308).

[113] C 47/25/2, no. 30; 24/3, no. 16; SC 1/29, no. 196 where the difficulties of governing Aquitaine were partly attributed to the 'deficiency, fault . . . and negligence of the ministers [*ministrorum*] and officials' of Edward II. This had in part been responsible for the number of frivolous appeals to Paris (23 May, *c.*1311).

[114] See, for example, AN, J 654, no. 24 for a petition from Edward II to Philip the Fair for an extension of the time in which cases sent back from Paris to the duchy's courts could be heard and for limitation of frivolous or illicit appeals.

only an appeal against one of the king-duke's officers, not against the king-duke himself.[115] Furthermore, he had to counter the claim of the French crown to legislate for the duchy. This had begun in the late thirteenth century, and the edicts were falling thick and fast under Philip the Fair in the early fourteenth century. All that the king-duke had to do was to legislate in the same way – to try to anticipate French edicts, or to follow them immediately with his own.[116] The nearest approach which was made to judicial independence was in 1289, when Edward I enacted that the seneschal of Aquitaine was the principal seneschal set above all the sub-seneschals (of the Agenais, Landes, Quercy, Limousin and so forth). They received their powers not from the king-duke but from the seneschal of Aquitaine, as did the king-duke's proctors in the Paris Parlement.[117] This meant that any Gascon appealing against the verdict of one of the sub-seneschals could not go directly to Paris. The way was barred. The case had first to be heard in the court of the seneschal of Aquitaine, or 'court of Gascony' as it was entitled.[118] If an appeal to France was subsequently made, a system of agreed delays in hearing at Paris, until further action by the ducal courts in Aquitaine had been taken, was instituted.[119] If the proctors who represented the king-duke at Paris also received their authority not from him, but simply from the seneschal of Aquitaine, then Edward I was not personally involved in proceedings in the French court. All this was intended to demonstrate to the king of France that these officials were not the king-duke's accredited representatives, but merely the delegates of his seneschal. So they were appointed under the seal of office of the seneschal, not the great seal of England.[120] If he so wished, Edward I or Edward II could disown the actions of the proctors in the Parlement. He could do what he liked. But none of these legal tricks and fictions could alter one formidable fact: the king of England, as duke of Aquitaine, was technically a vassal of the French crown. All that such devices could ever hope to do was to stave off the exercise of French sovereignty. They could never eliminate it. But that was no mean achievement. It was, however, often in the best interests of the French crown to allow the ducal jurisdiction considerable freedom of action. Direct government of Aquitaine from Paris was out of the question, and the interposition of ducal authority between the Gascons and the Capetian monarchy served to

---

[115] See Chaplais, 'Les appels gascons au roi d'Angleterre sous le règne d'Edouard I (1272–1307)', in *Essays in Medieval Diplomacy*, pt VI, pp. 382–99 for the most authoritative discussion of the question.

[116] Chaplais, 'La souveraineté du roi de France et le pouvoir législatif en Guyenne au début du xive siècle', in *Essays in Medieval Diplomacy*, pt V, pp. 459–64, 466.

[117] BL Cotton MS Julius E 1, fos 155^r–57^v (1289); cf. C 47/29/10 for an assertion by Edward I's lieutenant in the duchy that the Paris Parlement still refused appeals from one seneschal to another (c.1291).

[118] Chaplais, 'The Chancery of Guyenne', p. 67.

[119] AN, J 654, no. 24; Chaplais, 'Les appels gascons', pp. 385–8.

[120] Chaplais, 'The Chancery of Guyenne', pp. 66–7.

relieve the French crown of many tiresome and onerous burdens.[121] To let the Plantagenet administration do the work of government while reserving the right of intervention in the last resort was a sensible and inexpensive use of limited Capetian resources. There was therefore no desire to expropriate the Plantagenets in Aquitaine before 1294.[122]

Yet the judicial and administrative reforms of 1289 in the duchy gave rise to certain anxieties. Edward I was establishing a more powerful regime there and his presence in France was both symbolically and physically more visible.[123] Since the treaty made with Philip III at Amiens in 1279, the Plantagenet presence in France had also increased in territorial scope. In May 1279, Edward I had become count of Ponthieu, as well as duke of Aquitaine. By right of his wife, Eleanor of Castile, he inherited the northern French *comté* through the death of her mother Jeanne on 16 March 1279.[124] In so doing, he secured a foothold on the northern borders of the kingdom of France which brought him important benefits, as well as vexing problems. The *comté* of Ponthieu was a small lordship on the estuary of the Somme, but its urban and rural life was vigorous.[125] Abbeville, Le Crotoy and Montreuil were important centres of cloth production, and the region's agriculture was dominated by the exploitation of its forests for timber. The union of the *comté* to England in 1279 gave Ponthieu an administration in which Englishmen served, as they served in the duchy of Aquitaine. It also gave England useful servants whose careers were advanced through the conduct of Anglo-French diplomacy. Men from Ponthieu were also prominent among those who played a part in the worsening of English relations with the French monarchy in the latter part of Edward II's reign and the early part of Edward III's. The outbreak of the Hundred Years War itself was not unconnected with intrigues on behalf of men, such as Robert of Artois in which northern Frenchmen had important vested interests.[126]

---

[121] See J. Favier, *Philippe le Bel* (Paris, 1980), p. 223: where the idea that to 'unir le duché [d'Aquitaine] au domaine royal eût sans doute procuré des vassaux aussi difficiles à gouverner pour le Capétien qu'ils avaient été pour le Plantagenet' is put forward.

[122] Cf. Le Patourel, 'Origins of the Hundred Years War', p. 46: 'the French, for their part, either could not find the means to throw them [the English] out completely, or . . . took a long time to see that that was the only solution to their problem; for they also stood to benefit from the fact that the King of England was also the duke of Aquitaine – if only he would play their game'. It will be argued later that there were more substantial obstacles to French annexation of Aquitaine than Le Patourel perhaps realized. See below, pp. 185–91.

[123] For a French contemporary's comments see Guillaume Guiart, *Branche des royaux lignages*, ed. J. A. Buchon (Paris, 1828), ll. 3735–37, and for Edward's itinerary in France and Gascony, J.-P. Trabut-Cussac, 'Itinéraire d'Edouard 1er en France, 1286–1289', *BIHR*, xxv (1952), pp. 170–200.

[124] See H. Johnstone, 'The county of Ponthieu, 1279–1307', *EHR*, xxiv (1914), pp. 435–52; *CPR, 1279–81*, p. 306.

[125] Johnstone, 'The county of Ponthieu', pp. 439–40. See Appendix III, Map 2.

[126] See P. Chaplais, 'Un message de Jean de Fiennes à Edouard II et le projet de

The administration of Ponthieu bore some superficial resemblances to that
of Aquitaine. A seneschal, receiver (equivalent to the constable of Bordeaux)
and controller were at the head of the hierarchy. The seneschals tended to be
Englishmen and between 1279 and 1307 Thomas of Sandwich, knight,
Richard of Pevensey, Thomas de Belhus, knight, John Bakewell and John
Clinton of Maxstoke held the office.[127] Thomas of Sandwich subsequently
became mayor of Bordeaux in 1289, and became embroiled in a dispute with
the burgesses which led to an appeal to the Parlement of Paris;[128] his place as
seneschal of Ponthieu was taken by Richard de Pevensey. By March 1289,
however, a new seneschal had been appointed, this time a native of Ponthieu.
Guillaume de Fiennes and Tingry was described by Edward I as his
'kinsman'. Fiennes's sister, Mahaut, had married Humphrey de Bohun, earl
of Hereford and constable of England, and was thus directly related to the
English ruling house.[129] He was not the first of his family to serve the English
crown, because his kinsman, Michel de Fiennes, had acted as chancellor to
the Lord Edward during his stay in Gascony in 1254–5.[130] By 1265, Michel
had become bishop of Thérouanne. The family continued to play a significant part in Anglo-French affairs: in January 1317, Jean, sire de Fiennes,
wrote to Edward II as his loyal vassal in Ponthieu, informing him of a
rumoured scheme for the partition of the kingdom of France on the death of
Louis X. His motive was not entirely altruistic, for Fiennes was a chief ally
and supporter of the rebellious Robert of Artois, and hoped for English aid in
the form of ships with which to enter Calais and St Omer.[131] The English
tenure of Ponthieu, moreover, was a further means whereby vigilance could
be exercised over the affairs of France, and Edward I retained a permanent
staff of lawyers at Paris who dealt with appeals from the *comté* to the
Parlement. It was at Montreuil in Ponthieu that a series of Anglo-French
meetings took place over the issues of sovereignty and homage in 1306.[132] To
discuss such issues outside the Parlement of Paris, in territory which was in
the immediate lordship of the English crown (though held from the crown of
France), represented a concession to English requests for a meeting which
did not take the form of a lawsuit between unequals.[133] Philip the Fair's

---

démembrement du royaume de France (January 1317)', in *Essays in Medieval Diplomacy*, pt X,
pp. 147–8; see below, pp. 259–60.

[127] Johnstone, 'The county of Ponthieu', pp. 443, 446–7, 450–1.

[128] SC 1/23, no. 132 (*c.*1290) where John of Havering referred to certain citizens of Bordeaux
who had appealed against Sandwich as 'sons of iniquity'. See also Trabut-Cussac, *L'Administration anglaise*, pp. 101–2, 104.

[129] Johnstone, 'The county of Ponthieu', pp. 446–7. In November 1290 the *comté* of Ponthieu
passed to Edward of Caernarvon and was held during his minority by Edmund of Lancaster.

[130] G. P. Cuttino, 'A chancellor of the Lord Edward', *BIHR*, 1 (1977–8), pp. 229–32.

[131] Chaplais, 'Un message de Jean de Fiennes', p. 147.

[132] Cuttino, *English Diplomatic Administration*, pp. 49–72; Chaplais, 'Règlement des conflits
franco-anglais', pp. 279–80.

[133] Cuttino, 'The Process of Agen', *Speculum*, xix (1944), pp. 166–70.

government was often (sometimes surprisingly) prepared to compromise during the later stages of his reign, an attitude clearly reflected in the 'process' of Montreuil in Ponthieu.

In Ponthieu the seneschal's functions did not differ substantially from those of the seneschal of Gascony. He was concerned with the sale and exchange of fiefs and the [...] comital domain: there is some [...] 1273–5 in Gascony, measures [...] structure of the *comté* were [...] 5 June 1285 Edward and [...]ville, lord of Mons-Bouberc, in [...] annual rent on his property at [...] lordship of Bouberc, 'in one [...] forbidden.[135] There is more [...] restraint of alienation which [...]*tores* (1290). But there was no [...] England to Ponthieu, just as [...] Unlike Ireland, where English [...]sions of the Plantagenets were [...]d were administered strictly [...]ll have had similar goals for [...] finition of feudal obligations, [...]nd a more precise knowledge [...]ns by which those ends might [...]ent the outbreak of rebellion, [...]n, he was bound to operate [...]nd privileges.[137] A tolerable [...]pts at administration on the [...]ur cost, it was to be another

[...]340 for the higher offices in [...] Englishmen, or at least [...] list of well-known English [...] trained in Gascon affairs in [...]d be long indeed'.[138] The [...] Bordeaux were, on the whole, English-born knights and clerks. The exceptions were the Frenchmen and Savoyards in the service of Henry III, Edward I and Edward II, such as

[134] Johnstone, 'The county of Ponthieu', pp. 433–4.

[135] *RG*, iii, no. 5068 (5 June 1285).

[136] Le Patourel, 'Plantagenet dominions', pp. 304–5.

[137] This practice is exemplified by the endorsements to many Gascon petitions, where the case is referred to a ducal officer in Aquitaine for adjudication or judgement according to the laws and customs of the area.

[138] Powicke, *Thirteenth Century*, p. 276.

Jean de Grilly or Maurice and Amaury de Craon, who served as seneschals; or the Italian creditors of Edward I and Edward II who held the financial office of constable as a means whereby their loans were assigned for repayment from Gascon revenues.[139] The inhabitants of the duchy generally preferred to be governed by a non-Gascon. Soon after 1300 Gascon lieutenants and seneschals of the king-duke became exceptional.[140] Petitions for English (or Angevin, or Savoyard) seneschals were made under Edward II, on the grounds that a Gascon might have vested interests in the politics of the duchy and would be unable to adjudicate disputes with impartiality. A parallel with the *podestà* of an Italian city-state would not be inappropriate.[141] The seneschal or his lieutenant would often act as an arbitrator or third party in conflicts between nobles, or between communes and their neighbouring lords. This was an essential part of their duties in an area in which private war was endemic.[142] Sometimes the choice of non-English knights, without lands in England, might be troublesome – the Savoyard Jean de Grilly, for example, used his position as lieutenant and seneschal in Aquitaine to build up a considerable territorial holding in the Bordelais. His tenure of the seneschalship of Aquitaine was stormy, and his dismissal and replacement by an Englishman in 1287 was applauded by the Gascons.[143] Between 1254 and 1272, moreover, the position had been made more complex by clashes between Henry III and the Lord Edward. There were fourteen changes of seneschal in Gascony during these eighteen years, while under Edward, as king, only six changes took place in the twenty-two years from 1272 to 1294.[144] It has recently been pointed out by Dr J. R. Studd that 'one of [the Lord] Edward's greatest problems was his inability to settle lands from his appanage [of Gascony and the isle of Oléron] on those who gave him loyal service in a traditional way'.[145] Only Jean de Grilly (seneschal 1266–8) and Thomas de Ippegrave, clerk of Edward's household (1268–9), seem to have been the results of Edward's own personal choice. Of Edward's six seneschals during his first twenty-two years as king, however, five were Englishmen[146] and none of them acted as Grilly had done, amassing a

---

[139] See Trabut-Cussac, *L'Administration anglaise*, pp. 371, 373–5; *RG*, iv, pp. xxi–xxii; T. F. Tout, *Chapters in the Administrative History of Medieval England*, vi (Manchester, 1933), pp. 67–8.

[140] See Chaplais, 'The Chancery of Guyenne', p. 74; M. Vale, 'Nobility, bureaucracy and the "state" in English Gascony, 1250–1340: a prosopographical approach', in *Genèse de l'Etat Moderne: prosopographie et histoire*, ed. F. Autrand (Paris, 1985), pp. 309–10.

[141] See D. P. Waley, *The Italian City-republics* (London, 1978), pp. 32–6.

[142] See below, pp. 120–3.

[143] *RG*, iii, pp. xxxiii–xxxvii; Trabut-Cussac, *L'Administration anglaise*, p. 375; *AHG*, xvii, p. 131.

[144] Vale, 'Nobility, bureaucracy and the "state"', p. 309; Trabut-Cussac, *L'Administration anglaise*, pp. 372–5.

[145] Studd, 'The Lord Edward and Henry III', p. 10.

[146] Trabut-Cussac, *L'Administration anglaise*, pp. 373–5.

patrimony for themselves and their heirs in the duchy. This lack of English settlement in Aquitaine struck the first British student of Anglo-Gascon history as notable. Montague Burrows, Chichele Professor of Modern History at Oxford, wrote from an Anglocentric point of view in 1886 that the English imperial administration of India bore certain similarities to that of medieval Aquitaine:

> it would be strange if the reflection did not occur to an Englishman that he is witnessing something with which he is more familiar than he expected to be. Is it medieval Aquitaine or modern India, whose government he is studying? Not, of course, in any sense whatever as to the people governed, but as to the multifarious nature of the administration, the multitude of English families engaged in the process, the interchange of products, the action and reaction of the two countries upon one another in peace and war, and the extremely delicate nature of their mutual relations.[147]

Burrows was no doubt thinking of the commercial contacts between England and Aquitaine, and the way in which at least a crude comparison might be drawn between English dealings with the greater nobility of Aquitaine – the Foix-Béarn, Armagnac, Albret, Comminges and so on – and British policy towards Indian princes. But his main point was that the English did not settle in Gascony: 'no colonial dependency of England', he concluded, 'has ever offered a similar parallel, nor, it may safely be said, ever will. In Aquitaine and in India alike the Englishman was, and is, a foreigner, with a home elsewhere: in our other colonies men, with their families, settle and only now and then return'.[148] The resemblance was quite fortuitous, and the differences outweigh the similarities. Gascony was not a colony in the accepted sense of a conquered territory subject to foreign domination and laws, and exploited by a foreign power. But its governors of the thirteenth and early fourteenth centuries were certainly administrators and soldiers, not settlers, and they returned to their English, French or Savoyard estates. Men such as Roger de Leyburne (see plate 3.1), the Kentish knight, or John of Hastings (from Sussex), gave their names to new settlements in Aquitaine (Libourne and Hastingues) but never themselves settled in the *bastides* which still bear their names.[149] Edward I's workhorses were the knights and clerks of his household. As Professor Michael Prestwich reminds us, men such as Leyburne, Hastings, Odo de Grandson, or Sir John St John served in almost every part of Edward's possessions: England, Aquitaine, Ponthieu, Wales,

---

[147] Burrows, *The family of Brocas of Beaurepaire and Roche Court* (London, 1886), p. 18.

[148] Burrows, *The family of Brocas*, p. 27.

[149] M. W. Beresford, *New Towns of the Middle Ages*, pp. 604, 597. See below, pp. 156–8 and plate 3.1.

3.1 Tomb slab probably commemorating Aliénor de Vipont (d. 1270), wife of Roger de Leyburne, knight, lieutenant of Henry III in Aquitaine (1269–72). The naked figure is partially covered by a shield bearing the arms of her husband, who gave his name to the town of Libourne. (Bordeaux, Musée d'Aquitaine, inv. no. 12.596.)

Ireland.[150] The office of seneschal or king-duke's lieutenant in Aquitaine was therefore not a specialized one, although the tendency for men with legal training to be appointed increased as difficulties over the respective spheres of Capetian and Plantagenet jurisdiction in Aquitaine multiplied in the 1280s and early 1290s.[151] But the need for a military commander certainly did not diminish during Edward's reign – it became increasingly common for a king-duke's lieutenant to be appointed to lead the military forces of the duchy, as well as a seneschal with largely judicial functions. The turning point here was, of course, the war of 1294. At periods of crisis, lieutenancies were held by the greater English magnates – Edmund of Lancaster in 1295–6 or Henry de Lacy, earl of Lincoln, in 1296–9 and 1303–5.[152] But the day-to-day administration of the south-western French possessions of the English crown was in the hands of knightly-seneschals or lawyer-seneschals, aided and abetted by a Gascon council, by their own lieutenants, and (after 1279) by sub-seneschals in the major subdivisions of the duchy.

Most of the sub-seneschals were Gascons, and self-government was allowed to develop in their jurisdictions, intervention by the seneschal of Gascony being largely confined to the adjudication of disputes. Of forty-two sub-seneschals appointed between 1254 and 1317 (of Agenais, Bigorre, Landes, Périgord, Quercy, Limousin and Saintonge) no less than thirty-nine were Gascon nobles, two were English and one was a Savoyard.[153] Again, an analysis of the lesser offices of *bailli*, *prévôt* and constable (of a castle) between 1254 and 1307 reveals that at least sixty-one identifiable Gascon nobles held these offices, as against a mere nineteen English or Anglo-Normans, of whom ten were appointed by Simon de Montfort and the Lord Edward in a single year (1253–4).[154] Apart from that somewhat exceptional period, in which members of these magnates' entourages were rewarded with Gascon positions, the great majority of local offices in the administration were tenaciously held by the Gascon nobility. It was one of the prices of survival for the Plantagenet regime, a price well worth paying at periods of crisis such as the Anglo-French clashes of 1294–1303 and 1323–5.[155] At that level, there can be no doubt of the equation between public office and private interest.

The transfer of one sub-*sénéchaussée* – the Agenais – to Edward I at Amiens in 1279 marked a significant stage in the administrative development

---

[150] M. Prestwich, *War, Politics and Finance under Edward I* (London, 1972), ch. 2; also see J. Prestwich, 'The military household of the Norman kings', *EHR*, xcvi (1981), pp. 1–4. See also plates 6.2 and 6.6.

[151] Chaplais, 'Les appels gascons', pp. 384–8.

[152] See below, pp. 202, 205–6.

[153] These figures are computed from the lists given in Trabut-Cussac, *L'Administration anglaise*, pp. 341–87, and *RG*, iii, pp. xcii–cii; iv, pp. xviii–xxxi.

[154] See Vale, 'Nobility, bureaucracy and the "state"', p. 309.

[155] See below, pp. 217–26.

of Gascony. This sizeable addition to the king-duke's possessions necessitated the subordination of the so-called sub-seneschals to the overall authority of the seneschal of Gascony. He became styled 'seneschal of Aquitaine' in August 1280 (or *senescallus principalis*); his actions were supervised by a small council at Bordeaux, and by what was described as the 'court of Gascony'.[156] The origins and early history of this institution are very obscure, but we know that in 1273 Edward initiated the *Recogniciones feodorum* 'in curie Vasconie', which had assembled at St Sever.[157] This, according to a Gascon petition of 1279, was traditionally composed of the prelates, barons, knights and other nobles of the land and was to adjudge all cases concerning inheritance and other matters relating to the first two estates (clergy and nobility) of the duchy.[158] It was of significance both outside as well as inside the limits of Aquitaine. In their petition, the Gascon clergy and nobility reminded Edward that his predecessors as 'lords' (*domini*) of Aquitaine, and their seneschals, had made full use of this assembly and that it was a valuable weapon in his armoury against the pretensions of the king of France and his officers.

They claimed that Philip III of France, his court and his officers had recently (*a modico tempore*) hindered and troubled them by citing them before other courts – not only the Paris Parlement, but the court of the French seneschal of Périgord. This contravened their ancient privileges, and Edward was requested to restrain Philip III and his agents from this abuse of authority. Most striking is the conclusion of their petition (which was shared by that from the nobles of the Agenais) about the restoration of their court to its ancient status: 'and by this means', they told Edward, 'the appeals which are at the court of France . . . shall cease'.[159] That is, the restoration of the court of Gascony to its former purpose would mean that appeals would not leave the duchy for the Paris Parlement. There is some evidence that Edward acted upon this request: in 1289 a specific judge of appeals (*unus jurisperitus judex appellacionum*) was created to handle cases arising from the court of Gascony, and a number of assemblies took place which gathered together the prelates, barons, knights and other nobles of the duchy, culminating in the great council at which Edward's judicial and administrative ordinance (1289) for the future government of Aquitaine was promulgated.[160] This set the pattern of Anglo-Gascon administration for the rest of the Middle Ages, and there was little departure from its terms before the final *débâcle* of 1453.

---

[156] *RG*, ii, nos 415–16.

[157] Trabut-Cussac, *L'Administration anglaise*, pp. 43–5.

[158] SC 1/38, no. 55 (ii).

[159] SC 1/38, no. 55 (ii); see also Edward I's petition to Philip III for the creation of 'one superior seneschal or judge' in Aquitaine, whereby appeals could be contained within the duchy, in 1279 (C 47/29/2, no. 5).

[160] *Gascon Register A*, p. 209; Chaplais 'Les appels gascons', pp. 385–6.

Yet, however easily accessible or however beneficial the judicial service provided to the king-duke's Gascon subjects was, the possibility of appeal to the crown of France could never be entirely eliminated.[161] This possibility became an actuality when the disaffected, or simply vindictive, wished to achieve their ends. From there, it could be only a short step to Anglo-French war.

---

[161] See C 61/32, m. 5, where Edward II pointed out to Philip V that 'immediate jurisdictio de omnibus et singulis subditis nostris ducatus predicti in eodem ducatu contingentibus ad ministros nostros euisdem ducatus nomine nostre excercenda pertineat, nec debeant huiusmodi ad curiam vestram devolvi, nec in eadem tractari, *nisi per viam resorti*' (my italics). But that *ressort* could be exercised effectively when it was in the interests of the French monarchy and its agents to do so.

4

Politics and Society in Aquitaine – I: The Nobility

4.1 The Structure and Political Behaviour of the Gascon Nobility

This chapter and the next will attempt to examine the political, social and economic characteristics of the duchy of Aquitaine. Divisions are always artificial and often misleading, but the material can be more easily considered if we make a distinction between nobility and townsmen.[1] The Gascon nobility and the clergy (who were often closely related to them) are therefore the subject of this chapter. We saw in previous chapters that Aquitaine was a primary source of Anglo-French tensions. This stemmed partly from the plain fact that the Plantagenet king-duke owed homage to the Capetian crown for his south-western French possessions. But there were also features of the area itself which exacerbated Anglo-French friction and which have not been so closely studied. Among these was the unruliness of the nobility.[2] The structure and behaviour of this group could promote conflict, and the laws and customs of the region did little to avert the outbreak of clashes which could develop into larger quarrels, sometimes of alarming proportions. In a papal register of 1322–3 an Avignonese clerk noted that there were two reasons for the disturbed state of Aquitaine at that time: the existence of laws and customs which were neither written down nor

---

[1] There is no published study of relations between the Gascon nobility, clergy and towns and the king-dukes of Aquitaine during the period 1250–1340. J.-P. Trabut-Cussac intended to conclude his examination of Plantagenet administration between 1254 and 1307 with an account of 'les administrés et . . . leurs rapports avec l'autorité ducale et ses agents' but did not live to undertake this task. See Trabut-Cussac, *L'Administration anglaise en Gascogne sous Henry III et Edouard I de 1254 à 1307* (Geneva, 1972), p. ix.

[2] Adam Limber, constable of Bordeaux, expressed one contemporary view of the Gascon subjects of Edward II when he told the king-duke that he should receive their homages in person 'et vous les averez molt [le] plus enclyns et obeissantz a vous, *car ils [son]t ore touz le plus come sauvages et ne conissent point ce qe seignurie est* a regard de ceo qils feroient apres ce qils vous eussent veu et fait lour homages' (at Blaye, 8 December 1323); *The War of St Sardos 1323–1325. Gascon correspondence and diplomatic documents*, ed. P. Chaplais, Camden Society, 3rd ser., lxxxvii (London, 1954), p. 4 (italics mine).

consistent with justice or reason; and the maintenance of excessively large households and retinues by the nobility.[3] They could not provide for them from their own resources, he alleged, and hence resorted to war, pillage and brigandage in order to sustain their followings. An English memorandum of May 1311 also attributed the difficulties of governance in Aquitaine to the 'arrogant presumption of the nobles and magnates [*potentium*] of the land' which engendered frivolous appeals to the court of France.[4] A turbulent and unruly nobility was not peculiar to south-west France, but the underlying causes of that turbulence warrant investigation.

Among the factors which may have contributed to the disorderly condition of the Gascon nobility was the slackening of the crusading effort against the infidel. Members of that nobility had been prominent in the wars against the Muslims in Spain rather than in *Outremer*, and the decline of military opportunities in the Iberian peninsula after 1264 left aggressive energies untapped.[5] Some Gascon nobles had fought with Simon de Montfort against the Cathars during the Albigensian crusades, but benefited less from them than their northern French contemporaries. The loss of Acre in 1291 had a symbolic significance for all the nobilities of western Europe, but a sense of unfulfilled obligation still lingered on in the testamentary dispositions of Gascon nobles. In his will of May 1300, Pierre-Amanieu, captal de Buch, referred to the crusading vow which he had taken in the company of Edward I, in 1287, 'to go to the aid of the Holy Land in *Outremer*'.[6] Although the vow was only to be accomplished if Edward went in person, Pierre-Amanieu none the less felt sufficiently bound by his oath to leave 500 *livres bordelaises* (*l. b.*) to a knight, chosen by his executors from his 'companhons', who was to serve in his stead in the next 'general passage' to the Holy Land. Similarly, in March 1312, Arnaud-Raymond, *vicomte* of Tartas, ordered his executors to send one man-at-arms to the Holy Land for the sake of his soul and those of his house. The man was to be given 3000 *s. morlaas* and the seneschal of Gascony was to constrain Arnaud-Raymond's heirs to implement his wishes.[7] An identical sum was bequeathed by Margaret, countess of Foix, *vicomtesse* of Béarn and Marsan, in March 1319, to send a Béarnais noble of her family or household to serve in *Outremer*. She desired that the legacy should not be in any way

---

[3] 'Documents pontificaux sur la Gascogne', ed. L. Guerard, in *Archives Historiques de la Gascogne*, 2nd ser., ii (Auch, 1896), p. 215, n. 1, from Arch. Vatican, *Servitia Communia*, 4, fo. 90. His remedies were that customs should be written down and that Edward II should decree that no noble, bourgeois nor any other person should retain any members in his household (*familia*) for whom he was not prepared to be responsible in cases of crime.

[4] SC 1/29, no. 196 (at Bordeaux, 23 May(?) 1311); *RG*, iv, p. 551.

[5] See A. Mackay, *Spain in the Middle Ages. From Frontier to Empire, 1000–1500* (London, 1977), pp. 30–1, 58–65.

[6] APA, E 20, no. 6 (20 May 1300).

[7] APA, E 225, no. 6 (at Tartas, 29 March 1312). He was about to set out on a pilgrimage to St James of Compostella.

altered by the pope nor any other person.[8] The crusading ideal was by no means moribund among the nobility of south-west France, but opportunities for its expression were in decline.[9]

To offer generalizations about the 'Gascon' nobility can pose more problems than it solves. Regional variations abounded and the nobility was not a homogeneous group. 'L'ordre de la noblesse', wrote Boutruche, 'souffre d'une grande confusion intérieure qui se retrouve jusque dans le comportement de ses membres, caracterisé par un étroit particularisme ou une entr'aide provisoire, limitée à la famille et à un petit cercle de vassaux, d'amis et de compagnons'.[10] Unless they were faced with a common enemy, as we shall see, concerted action by the nobility was difficult to achieve.[11] Customs of inheritance differed sharply on a regional basis, and the distribution of wealth, castles, fiefs and allodial holdings was uneven. Impartible and partible inheritance customs co-existed side by side, and marked variations were to be found in the degree to which elder and younger children were favoured or disadvantaged.[12] Disparities between areas of customary law could, however, be exploited by the ducal administration in Aquitaine during lawsuits. In February 1284, Constance de Béarn, *vicomtesse* of Marsan, complained that her claim to the *comté* of Bigorre had been assigned a hearing by Jean de Grilly, seneschal of Gascony, at Langon in the Bazadais because, she alleged, he knew that 'the customs of Bazadais were against her, and that the opposing parties would be aided by those customs'.[13] Yet in most cases regional custom was the surest defence against the aggression of neighbours, immediate lords or sovereigns. In August 1318, Margaret, countess of Foix, was supported by Pope John XXII against the officers of Philip V of France. Their action in confiscating certain lordships from her was not only inherently unjust, wrote the pope, but contrary to the customs of the court of Béarn.[14] This required judgement by two bishops and eleven barons of the

---

[8] APA, E 196, no. 53 (at Orthez, 21 March 1319).

[9] The resurgence of Christian warfare against the Muslims in southern Spain during the early 1340s, however, led directly to the death of Gaston II, count of Foix, at Seville in September 1343. He died from disease contracted at the siege of Algeciras where he was fighting the Moors of Granada and Morocco for Alfonso XI of Castile. See *Chroniques romanes des comtes de Foix composées au xve siècle par Arnaud Esquerrier et Miègeville*, ed. F. Pasquier and H. Courteault (Foix, Paris, Toulouse and Pau, 1895), p. 51; Mackay, *Spain in the Middle Ages*, pp. 65–6; J. Robson, 'The Catalan fleet and Moorish sea-power (1337–1344)', *EHR*, lxxiv (1959), pp. 386–408.

[10] R. Boutruche, *La Crise d'une société: seigneurs et paysans du Bordelais pendant la guerre de Cent Ans* (Paris, 1963), p. 82.

[11] See below, pp. 206, 210–11.

[12] See J. Poumarède, *Les Successions dans le sud-ouest de la France au Moyen Age* (Toulouse, 1972), pp. 238–40, 305–7 and maps. Cases relating to inheritance customs and disputes concerning noble succession were said to be within the judicial competence only of the king-duke of Aquitaine or his seneschal, in consultation with the 'court of Gascony' (SC 1/38, no. 55; *temp.* Edward III).

[13] APA, E 170, no. 6[a], m.l.

[14] 'Documents pontificaux', no. 61 (8 August 1318); *Foedera*, II, i, p. 144.

vicomté, and the French royal courts had no cognisance of such cases. A similar proposition was put forward in a petition from the prelates, barons, knights and other Gascon nobles to Edward III that their ancient liberties, *fors* and customs stipulated that all issues of inheritance and other cases concerning prelates and nobles were to be heard by the king-duke or his seneschal.[15] The court of Gascony, composed of prelates and barons, was to be consulted to this end. An entrenched and intransigent defence of regional customs was a binding force, especially at times of crisis, which could serve to unite a heterogeneous nobility.

A degree of freedom was afforded to the Gascon nobility by the prevalence of allodial tenures, whereby no immediate lord was recognized, in certain parts of the region.[16] Yet the king-duke began to insist from the 1270s onwards that all allods were *sub posse et dominio . . . regis et ducis* ('under the power and dominion of the king-duke').[17] One purpose of Edward I's *Recogniciones feodorum* of 1274–5 was to ascertain the number and nature of allodial tenures in the duchy and there is some evidence for the 'feudaliz-ation' of allods by the king-duke after that date.[18] But the tenurial structure of south-west France remained confused and 'theoretical distinctions be-tween nobles and non-nobles, . . . fiefs and rented holdings, did not corre-spond to reality'.[19] The potential for dispute and conflict over rights of jurisdiction, tolls, *esporles* (entry fines paid on change of lord), and the status of holdings was great. The prevalence of *co-seigneurie*, or lordship shared among two or more lords, in areas such as the Agenais or Bazadais, could promote discord and a number of private wars broke out, as we shall see, between co-seigneurs.[20] Contracts of *paréage*, whereby the rights and profits of a lordship were shared, normally by two lords, sometimes produced conflict between them. In a relatively loosely structured society of this kind, the opportunities for abrasion were many and there was no lack of candidates to indulge in judicial, economic and military conflict. It was often difficult for 'higher' authorities – Plantagenet or Capetian, their identity was in some respects immaterial – to remain uninvolved in, and aloof from, these disputes. A constant underlying tension therefore characterized the socio-political structure of the duchy of Aquitaine.

The Great Families

At the top of this structure stood a small number of great families. The counts of Foix, Armagnac and Comminges, the *vicomtes* of Béarn and the lords of Albret were differentiated from the mass of middling and petty

---

[15] SC 1/38, no. 55.

[16] J. Brutails, 'Les fiefs du roi et les alleux en Guienne', *AM*, xxix (1917), pp. 65–6.

[17] Brutails, 'Les fiefs du roi', p. 65.

[18] See J.-P. Trabut-Cussac, 'La foundation de Sauveterre-de-Guyenne (1281–3)', *Revue Historique de Bordeaux*, n.s., ii (1953), pp. 181–217.

[19] Brutails, 'Les fiefs du roi', p. 83.

[20] See below, pp. 102, 134–9.

nobles by their landed wealth and political power. An early-fourteenth-century description of Gascony listed four counts and fifteen *vicomtes* among the upper nobility, set apart from the *plèbe nobiliaire* beneath them.[21] Descended from the Carolingian counts and *vicomtes*, they possessed and exercised very ancient rights of jurisdiction over their lordships. A tendency to absorb smaller houses and to engage in a conscious policy of territorial expansion appears to have marked their behaviour in the second half of the thirteenth century. With their absorption of the *vicomté* of Béarn through marriage and inheritance in 1290, the counts of Foix became the single most powerful house in the south-west.[22] Detached from the orbit of the old Raymondin counts of Toulouse, they were carving out a quasi-autonomous sphere of influence for themselves along the Pyrenean frontier. Endowed with ancient privileges, ruling 'by the grace of God', the counts of Foix-Béarn continued to absorb lesser lordships and to extend a spider's web of connections among the Gascon nobility through contracts of vassalage and alliance.[23] This brought them into hostile contact with some of their neighbours, especially with the counts of Armagnac. The later thirteenth century witnessed a sudden and rapid expansion of their territorial possessions, and by 1300 their hegemony was established not only over the previously independent *vicomté* of Béarn, but in the *comtés* of Bigorre and Comminges and the *vicomtés* of Nébouzan and Marsan.[24] Before the accession of Roger-Bernard III, count of Foix, to Béarn in 1290, its *vicomtes* had been relatively penurious. Edward I told Gaston VII of Béarn in December 1282 that 'we believe that you do not abound in money', and the depredations and seizures of other people's property carried out by the impecunious Gaston and his allies between 1270 and his death in 1290 tried Edward's patience sorely.[25] The ascendancy of the house of Foix, with its extensive possessions in the central and eastern Pyrenees and in Catalonia, Roussillon and Navarre, brought a political force inclined towards the Capetians rather than the Plantagenets into the arena of Gascon politics at a troubled time.[26] In this

---

[21] *Archives Municipales de Bordeaux, v, Livre des Coutumes*, ed. H. Barckhausen (Bordeaux, 1890), p. 609.

[22] P. Tucoo-Chala, *Gaston Fébus et la vicomté de Béarn (1343–1391)* (Bordeaux, 1959), pp. 37–42.

[23] See *Chroniques romanes des comtes de Foix*, pp. 35–9. There has been no recent study of the house of Foix-Béarn before the accession of Gaston Fébus in 1343.

[24] See *Chroniques romanes des comtres de Foix*, pp. 35–7; C. Higounet, *Le comté de Comminges de ses origines à l'annexation à la couronne* (Toulouse and Paris, 1949), pp. 124–6, 236–9. See below, Appendix III, Map 3.

[25] SC 1/12, no. 45 (22 December 1282); C 47/25/1, no. 4: it was estimated that Gaston VII and his allies had caused 100,000 *l.t.* worth of damage during their *cavalgade* and plundering raids.

[26] Tucoo-Chala, *Gaston Fébus*, pp. 39–41; and his 'La perte par les vicomtes de Béarn de leurs possessions catalanes (fin xive–debut xve siècle)', *Rapports du iiie congrès international des études pyrénennes* (Gerona, 1958), pp. 48–62, and 'Les relations economiques entre le Béarn et les pays de la couronne d'Aragon (du milieu du xiiie au milieu du xve siècle)', *BPH*, 1957 (1958), pp. 115–36.

respect, as in others, the 1290s were to be a period of crisis and change which was to make an impact on Anglo-French relations.

The house of Foix-Béarn extended its influence by methods common to all princely houses of the later Middle Ages. Acquisitiveness was served by marriages, alliances and sheer brute force. Forms of alliance were developed to enlist the service of nobles whose lands lay beyond its own lordships. In a letter of May 1259, Gaston VII of Béarn referred to the lordship which he exercised over Amanieu VI, lord of Albret, and to the 'contracts [*convenz*] that are between us'.[27] Albret held the castle of Casenave from him, and was his vassal, although the centre of Albret power lay well outside the *vicomté* of Béarn. Similarly, in June 1253, Arnaud-Guillaume de Gramont had promised to aid Gaston VII, who would be his 'good lord' from whom he received a rent secured on the *bailliage* of Sauveterre-de-Béarn.[28] Gramont's lands lay on the northern frontier of Béarn, and he, like Albret, was a vassal of the Plantagenet king-duke of Aquitaine. It was by such means − both 'feudal' and non-feudal − that the house of Foix-Béarn exercised some degree of control over those members of the Gascon nobility whose lordships lay outside their own domains. The origins of the *alliance*, cultivated by the great families of the south-west in the later fourteenth and fifteenth centuries, are to be sought in these early contracts.[29] So well known were the acquisitive instincts of Roger-Bernard III, count of Foix, by 1300 that the treason charges made by Philip the Fair's proctors against Bernard Saisset, bishop of Pamiers, included allegations that Saisset had promised to make Foix lord of the *comté* of Toulouse in 1295−7, so that his power would then be feared from Bordeaux to the Pyrenees.[30] Although the collusion of Roger-Bernard in Saisset's alleged fantasies was strenuously denied, the mere existence of the charges suggests that they carried a certain credibility. Given Foix's *Hausmachtpolitik* at this time, a desire to dominate the south-west by annexing further territories was easily attributed to the count. But he chose to do so by exploiting the lieutenancy offered to him by Philip the Fair in 1295, rather than by rebellion against the crown.[31] A memorandum prepared for him, probably in 1297, claimed that he was owed over 50,000 *l.t.* in unpaid wages of war in Gascony by Philip, and that he, like his predecessor Gaston VII of

---

[27] APA, E 22, no. 48 (at Bazas, 4 May 1259). Witnesses included Géraud V, count of Armagnac.

[28] APA, E 288, no. 1 (at Sauveterre-de-Béarn, 1 June 1253).

[29] See below, pp. 122−4, 129−30; P. S. Lewis, 'Decayed and non-feudalism in later medieval France', in *Essays in later medieval French history* (London, 1985), pp. 41−68; M. Vale, *English Gascony, 1399−1453* (Oxford, 1970), pp. 170−9.

[30] P. Dupuy, *Histoire du différend d'entre le pape Boniface VIII et Phillippes le Bel Roy de France* (Paris, 1655), *Preuves*, pp. 632−3, 634, 639.

[31] *Chroniques romanes des comtes de Foix*, p. 39; C. de Vic and J. Vaissete, *Histoire générale de Languedoc, avec des notes et les pièces justificatives* (Toulouse, 1872−1904), x, cc. 334−5.

Béarn, *in presenti multum indiget* ('was at present very hard up').[32] The appetite of the house of Foix-Béarn for income and revenue was insatiable.

Apart from the conclusion of alliances with other nobles, and the exploitation of casual sources of income, a major instrument of expansion was the diplomatic marriage. One of the most important of these marriages was the match contracted in October 1256 between Esquivat, count of Bigorre, and Agnes, daughter of Roger IV, count of Foix (1241–65).[33] It gave the house of Foix some claim to the succession in Bigorre and, when Esquivat died without heirs in 1283, a conflict broke out which was not to be resolved until 1307.[34] It was notoriously difficult to deal with Esquivat. Jean de Grilly, seneschal of Gascony, told Edward I in 1282 that he was quite unable to predict the upshot of negotiations over Bigorre 'not least because of the changeability and inconsistency of the count'.[35] A plethora of words, Grilly claimed, impeded the conclusion of business. The house of Béarn had a strong claim to Bigorre on Esquivat's death, as the much-married Petronilla, countess of Bigorre (1190–1251) had ordained in her will that, should her grandson Esquivat die without heirs, the *comté* was to be held by her daughter Mathe de Bigorre, wife of Gaston VII of Béarn.[36] In the event the union of Foix and Béarn in 1290 effectively solved one aspect of the controversy – Roger-Bernard III, count of Foix and *vicomté* of Béarn, now embodied the claims of both houses to Bigorre. But, as we shall see, the final settlement was by no means so easily achieved, and no less than six claimants submitted their cases to Philip the Fair in 1302.[37] Nevertheless, the house of Foix-Béarn emerged as the neighbouring territorial power with the greatest measure of control over Bigorre and the important Pyrenean passes which lay within its boundaries.

A less stormy sequence of events lay behind the conclusion of an alliance between the houses of Foix-Béarn and L'Isle-Jourdain, lords of the frontier zone which lay between the lands of Armagnac, Foix and the *comté* of Toulouse.[38] The L'Isle-Jourdain were an ancient family, which had produced the twelfth-century bishop of Comminges, St Bertrand, whose cult was

---

[32] APA, E 371 (unnumbered). Roger-Bernard requested that he be paid 10,000 *l.t.* immediately by the treasurer of Carcassonne and by Gérard Baleine, Philip the Fair's treasurer for wars in Aquitaine.

[33] APA, E 369, nos 5, 16.

[34] For a good account see F. M. Powicke, *Henry III and the Lord Edward* (Oxford, 1947), i, pp. 220–6, where Simon de Montfort's defiant behaviour over Bigorre in 1262 is held responsible for its eventual acquisition by the French crown (pp. 225–6).

[35] SC 1/18, no. 58 (19 May 1282).

[36] Powicke, *Henry III and the Lord Edward*, i, p. 226.

[37] See below, pp. 88–90.

[38] There is no general account of the L'Isle-Jourdain family during the thirteenth and fourteenth centuries, and their great cartulary, the *Saume de L'Isle*, remains a largely unexploited source for this period (ATG, A 297).

to be promoted by Pope Clement V between 1290 and 1314.[39] They were a powerful clan, with wide-ranging connections, and the marriage which was contracted in 1291 between Margaret, daughter of Roger-Bernard III of Foix and Bernard-Jourdain, son of Jourdain de L'Isle, secured a valuable ally.[40] Despite disagreements about the payment of her dowry, Margaret's marriage gave rise to a military and diplomatic alliance between the houses of Foix-Béarn and L'Isle-Jourdain, concluded in January 1298, which was to serve the counts well in their quarrel with the house of Armagnac.[41] Jourdain de L'Isle had already renounced an existing alliance with Bernard VI, count of Armagnac, in January 1289. The *pacta, statuta et ordinaciones* agreed between them were revoked, and the L'Isle-Jourdain began to turn away from Armagnac and towards Foix.[42] During the minority of Roger-Bernard III's grandson, Gaston II (1315–23), custody of the *comté* of Foix was granted to Bernard-Jourdain de L'Isle until the count reached the age of fourteen.[43] Despite the flux of political events some alliances of this kind proved surprisingly durable.

Between 1290 and the outbreak of the Anglo-French war of St Sardos in 1324, a growing hostility between the house of Foix-Béarn and the Plantagenet administration in Aquitaine may be detected. The increase in ducal authority which followed upon the transfer of the Agenais and of southern Saintonge to Edward I and the tighter control exercised by the king-duke over his vassals, including some Béarnais nobles, impinged upon the power of the *vicomtes*.[44] Although he received a pension from Edward I after 1280, Gaston VII of Béarn was not the most conspicuously loyal of Edward's vassals, and his successor, Roger-Bernard III, served Philip the Fair during the Anglo-French war of 1294–8.[45] His grandson, Gaston II (1315–43), also supported Charles IV of France during the war of St Sardos.[46] Yet some Béarnais nobles, including the baronial houses of Lescun, Audoins, Gayrosse, Gabaston, Miossens and Gerderest, consistently served the Plantagenet administration against the French.[47] The *vicomtes* of Béarn could not therefore rely on the loyalty of those of their vassals who also held lands,

[39] See Higounet, *Le Comté de Comminges*, pp. 321–8.

[40] ATG, A 297, fos 336ᵛ (29 November 1291), 338ʳ–9ʳ. Arnaud de Gabaston (Piers Gaveston's father), Roger de Montaut and Guillaume-Raymond de Caumont were among the witnesses to the marriage contract.

[41] ATG, A 297, fos 334ᵛ–6ʳ (9 January 1298); 223ᵛ–4ʳ (20 January 1298). See below, pp. 130–1.

[42] ATG, A 297, fos 256ᵛ–7ʳ (23 January 1289). See below, p. 130.

[43] APA, E 402, no. 46.

[44] J. Gardelles, *Les Châteaux du Moyen Age dans la France du Sud-Ouest (1216–1327)* (Geneva, 1972), pp. 22–3; Trabut-Cussac, *L'Administration anglaise*, pp. 59–67.

[45] E 101/152/7, m. 1; see above, n. 31; Devic and Vaissete, *Histoire générale de Languedoc*, x, cc. 289–91.

[46] *St Sardos*, pp. 5, 16–17, 22.

[47] SC 1/50, no. 6 (26 April 1323); E 372/183, m. 59; C 61/36, m. 5ᵛ (24 December 1324).

offices and pensions from the king-dukes when an Anglo-French war erupted in Aquitaine. This was to be characteristic of the Béarnais nobility throughout the Hundred Years War. However, the origins of increasing tension between the *vicomtes* of Béarn and the Plantagenets lie in the consequences of the disputes which developed after 1287 over the succession to Bigorre, Marsan and Béarn. Bigorre, as we have seen, was a Pyrenean lordship of considerable strategic and economic importance. One claimant was Constance, *vicomtesse* of Marsan, daughter of Gaston VII of Béarn.[48] She had been married at Henry III's instigation to Henry, son of Richard of Cornwall, in 1269. Widowed in 1271, Constance's claim was supported by her father, and she laid charges of forcible dispossession from Bigorre against Edward I and his seneschal, Jean de Grilly.[49] She claimed that she had surrendered possession of Bigorre to Edward I in England by word of mouth, but without prejudice to her rights.[50] But her rights had indeed been prejudiced by the manner in which Grilly had behaved, claiming that the *comté* was to be surrendered unconditionally, and acting in a high-handed manner during the ceremony in which the keys of the comital *aula*, or hall, at Tarbes were handed over. Constance had clearly come to hate Jean de Grilly, whom she described as 'so openly contrary and suspect to her, favouring her enemies',[51] that she refused to stand judgement before him unless he was accompanied by the bishop of Aire and abbot of St Maurin in the Agenais. He refused, whereupon she argued that he was impeding and delaying justice by *cavillaciones et diffugia* ('quibbling objections and subterfuges'), and aimed to dispossess her not only of Bigorre, but of her *vicomté* of Marsan as well.[52] The techniques which Grilly was applying seem to have resembled those employed in England by Edward I's treasurer, Walter Langton, in his pursuit of the inheritances of great heiresses such as Isabel de Forz.[53] Gaston VII of Béarn thus cast himself in the role of his daughter's protector against the territorial ambitions of Edward's seneschal, which were soon to lead to Grilly's dismissal from his post.[54]

But old resentments died hard and they reappeared after 1290, when

[48] APA, E 370, nos 6, 6[a], 10; E 382, nos 17, 21. The events concerning Bigorre in 1284 are very well documented in this series of notarial instruments.

[49] APA, E 290, mm. 1–3 (marriage negotiations, 1268); E 370, no. 6[a] (1284).

[50] APA, E 370, no. 10 (at Tarbes, 28 March 1284); *Gascon Register A*, no. 278. Jean de Grilly's account of the surrender of the keys of the comital hall (*aula*) at Tarbes is in a letter to Edward I, dated 'in quindena Pasche' at Lectoure in 1284 (SC 1/47, no. 123).

[51] APA, E 370, no. 6[a], m. 1: she told Grilly that he was 'si aperte et contrarius et suspectus et adversariis suis favens et ipso sue soli ordinacioni et recordo non staret'.

[52] APA, E 170, no. 6[a], m. 2. She claimed that Grilly and other Plantagenet officers had prevented her exercise of jurisdiction over Marsan by 'constructing bastides, arrest of her men,. . . summonses, extortions of money and other things'.

[53] See K. B. McFarlane, 'Had Edward I a "policy" towards the earls?', in *The Nobility of Later Medieval England* (Oxford, 1973), pp. 257–9.

[54] *RG*, iii, pp. xxxiii–xlvii.

Roger-Bernard III of Foix became *vicomte* of Béarn. The judicial squabbling provoked by the succession to Bigorre offered opportunities for intervention to the French crown. Although in 1284 Edward I had considered that 'the *comté* of Bigorre is held freely from . . . the king of England, so that the king of France is not recognised as sovereign there', Philip the Fair's lawyers were not prepared to accept this view.[55] Grilly's attempts to adjudicate the question had failed, and Pierre Flote was deputed to bring the affair to the cognizance of the court of France. By 1292 the *comté* had been sequestrated by Philip, and a series of hearings in the Paris Parlement began.[56] Capetian claims to jurisdiction were therefore certainly experienced in Béarn and Bigorre after 1285, but it cannot be argued that either Gaston VII or Roger-Bernard III were willing instruments of French royal sovereignty. The question of Bigorre was also complicated by the claims of a religious foundation – the bishop and chapter of Le Puy in Velay – to exercise feudal rights over the *comté*.[57] In 1062, Bernard, count of Bigorre, had unwisely granted the bishop and canons a sum of money secured on his *comté* during a pilgrimage to Le Puy. This resulted in a claim of the canons of Le Puy to receive homage from Bigorre, which they allegedly sold in 1253 to Henry III. It was by virtue of this act that Edward I demanded its surrender to him in 1284. But a judgement in favour of Le Puy was given in the Paris Parlement in 1290. This was in fact contested not only by Edward I, but by Roger-Bernard III of Foix, acting as Constance of Marsan's proctor, in October 1292.[58] Roger-Bernard III appealed against execution of the sentence by Eustache of Beaumarchais's lieutenant in the *sénéchaussée* of Toulouse, acting for Philip the Fair. The count alleged that the seneschal's lieutenant entered the hall of the castle at Vic-de-Bigorre with the dean of Le Puy, and treated him in an inexcusably unmannerly fashion by seizing him by his clothing and expelling him and his household *familia* from the place.[59] The lieutenant had then flown the banners of the king of France and the church of Le Puy over the barbican at Vic-de-Bigorre, and had refused to countenance Roger-Bernard's protest on behalf of his sister-in-law. A similar sequence of events had taken place at the castle of Mauvezin in Bigorre and a charge that the lieutenant had far exceeded the limits of his jurisdiction was made.[60] Jean de Grilly's behaviour towards the house of Béarn had been bad enough in 1284, but in the eyes of the count the arrogant and arbitrary actions of Eustache de Beaumarchais's lieutenant in 1292 were even worse. There was little to

---

[55] APA, E 370, no. 6ᵃ, m. 2.

[56] Powicke, *Henry III and the Lord Edward*, i, 226–7; APA, E 371, nos 8, 4 (October 1292); AN, J 294, no. 13 (1294–6).

[57] Trabut-Cussac, *L'Administration anglaise*, pp. 72–7.

[58] APA, E 371, no. 4 (11 October 1292).

[59] APA, E 371, no. 8 (2 October 1292).

[60] APA, E 371, no. 4 where it was claimed that Roger-Bernard merely wished to safeguard Constance's rights as rightful heiress to Petronilla of Bigorre. Witnesses to the proceedings at Mauvezin included Bernard, count of Comminges and Centulle, count of Astarac.

choose between the behaviour of the agents of Plantagenet and Capetian power.[61] Ultimately neither the king-duke nor the count of Foix emerged victorious from the quarrel, because in 1307 the chapter of Le Puy formally surrendered their feudal rights over Bigorre to Philip the Fair. When Constance of Marsan died, the *comté* passed to Jeanne de Navarre, queen of France.[62]

Another diplomatic marriage was that which attempted to bring the house of Foix into a closer relationship with the French crown and with the great families of northern France. In October 1301, Roger-Bernard III's son Gaston, who was to succeed him in 1302, was married to Jeanne d'Artois, sister of Robert II, count of Artois, at the very heart of the Capetian court circle.[63] This was perceived as a threat to the Plantagenets in Aquitaine. A series of monetary gifts from Philip IV followed the marriage, levied on lordships in Bigorre, Marsan, Castelnau-de-Rivière and Gabardan, and Gaston I served both Philip and his son Louis X in war. He performed military service during the king's Flemish campaign of 1315 and died at the abbey of Maubuisson, near Pontoise, on 13 December of that year.[64] But the intrusion of an heiress from a northern French family into the relatively closed circle of Foix-Béarn created tensions within it. Gaston I quarrelled with his mother, Margaret of Béarn (d. 1319) and despite a reconciliation in September 1312, a dispute then broke out over the custody and tutelage of his heir.[65] Gaston II was seven years old at his father's death in 1315 and custody was claimed by his grandmother, against the rival claims of his mother, Jeanne d'Artois. In July 1318, Pope John XXII wrote to Philip V of France informing him that although the king's court had conferred tutelage of Gaston I's children on Jeanne, Margaret of Béarn already had Gaston II in her keeping and was in any case to be preferred as guardian of the young count.[66] Unlike Jeanne d'Artois, whom he judged to be 'prodigal and immoral', the pope thought Margaret well able take the place of a mother and commended her to Philip V.[67] She had in effect governed Béarn, and

---

[61] For complaints against both Capetian and Plantagenet officials in 1293–4, see below, pp. 180–4.

[62] Powicke, *Henry III and the Lord Edward*, i, pp. 225–6. By June 1293, Constance had appointed Roger-Bernard to perform her oath of fealty to the bishop and chapter of Le Puy, on account of her 'infirmity and bodily weakness': APA, E 371, no. 30.

[63] *Chroniques romanes des comtes de Foix*, p. 40; APA, E 399, no. 42; E 401, no. 32.

[64] *Chroniques romanes des comtes de Foix*, pp. 40, 44.

[65] AN, JJ 49, fos 18ᵛ–19ᵛ: peace settlement between Gaston and his mother (21 September 1312). It was arbitrated by the lieutenant of Edward I's *prévôt* of St Sever, at the request of all parties. Arrangements for Gaston II's minority are found in APA, E 402, no. 46 (1315).

[66] 'Documents pontificaux', no. 57 (29 July 1318); Tucoo-Chala, *Gaston Fébus*, p. 49.

[67] 'Documents pontificaux', nos. 57, 69; Tucoo-Chala, *Gaston Fébus*, p. 60. Jeanne was imprisoned by Philip VI in 1331. Charles IV had pardoned her for 'crimes and excesses', including the removal of the royal *pennonceaux* from certain places in Béarn and Bigorre in February 1325 (APA, E 403, no. 38).

governed it well, since Gaston I's death in 1315, but was to die in 1319. Gaston II came of age in 1323, but after the death of Margaret of Béarn his mother's influence played an important part in determining the anti-Plantagenet stance of the house of Foix-Béarn during the war of St Sardos.

The youth and inexperience of Gaston II caused concern to those who worked for peace in south-west France; above all, to the Pope. In May 1323 John XXII told Fulk Lestrange, Edward II's seneschal of Aquitaine, to make peace with Gaston, as he was not responsible for the excesses of his own officers and subjects, who had been provoked and encouraged by his mother.[68] In a further letter, dated 28 June 1323, the pope reminded the bishop of Aire, who was acting as an intermediary between Lestrange and Jeanne d'Artois, that Gaston II was very young, and was surrounded by young men who were easily swayed to unbridled and ill-considered actions.[69] The bishop was requested to advise them *maturo consilio* to restrain their passions and to come to terms with the Plantagenet administration in their quarrel over attacks upon ducal officers and subjects in the *vicomté* of Marsan. In the 1320s the problems of disorder were compounded by the fact that both the leading houses of the region – Foix and Armagnac – were governed by youths who had barely achieved their majority. Jean I of Armagnac (1319–73) was similarly youthful and lacking in political experience, a fact noted by John XXII in April 1322.[70] The prevalence of conflict in Gascony during this period reflects the vulnerability of minors to the political ends of their elders.

Both Foix and Armagnac, however, were anxious to forge links with the papacy, clearly viewing a connection with Avignon as a vital element in their local power. The Gascon origins of both Clement V and John XXII made this much easier, and although the house of Foix-Béarn did not succeed in marrying into the papal clan, a strengthening of bonds with the Duèse family (from Cahors) can be detected in a number of casual, but significant, references.[71] In December 1316, Bertrand de Goth, *vicomte* of Lomagne and Auvillars, acting as Clement V's executor, returned to Margaret of Béarn and the seven-year-old Gaston II a 'certain little knife' (*cultellum*), which Gaston I of Foix had lent to the pope. In 1318, after an attempt to poison him in the previous year, John XXII thanked Margaret for sending him 'a certain knife-handle in serpentine form' which was reputed to detect poison.[72] This may have been the same object as that lent by Gaston I to

---

[68] 'Documents pontificaux', no. 242 (27 May 1323); cf. nos. 239 (25 May 1323), 240–2.

[69] 'Documents pontificaux', no. 249 (28 June 1323). The pope was also in correspondence on the subject with John, bishop of Ely, Edward II's special envoy to Aquitaine: nos. 248, 254.

[70] 'Documents pontificaux', no. 178 (22 April 1322).

[71] For John XXII's background, see N. Valois, 'Jacques Duèse, pape sous le nom de Jean XXII', *Histoire littéraire de la France*, xxxiv, pp. 319–630; E. Albe, *Autour de Jean XXII. Les familles du Quercy* (Rome, 1903–6), p. 1–5, 57–9.

[72] APA, E 403, no. 3 (at Orthez, 21 December 1316); 'Documents pontificaux', no. 3 (8

Clement V. The pope agreed to keep the talisman safely and to excommunicate anyone else who attempted to use it. Perhaps the counts of Foix were
fulfilling a traditional office for the papacy. Whatever the case, the alliance
which they had made with the family of L'Isle-Jourdain (closely related to
the Duèse clan), stood them in good stead with the Avignon papacy until
John XXII's death in 1334.

The tendencies towards territorial and dynastic aggrandisement displayed
by the house of Foix-Béarn were echoed by the counts of Armagnac. Géraud
V of Armagnac (1256–85) had married Mathe of Béarn, daughter of Gaston
VII and sister to both Constance of Marsan and Margaret of Béarn, and
therefore possessed claims through the female line to both Béarn and
Bigorre.[73] Until 1290, the great houses of south-west France – Foix, Béarn
and Armagnac – existed in relative harmony. Géraud V of Armagnac was
apparently on better terms with Edward I than his contemporary Gaston
VII of Béarn. He was constantly harassed by Philip III of France and his
officers as a result of a fine of 15,000 *l.t.* imposed upon him by the French
king's court in 1273.[74] Edward I provided a useful source of potential support
against Capetian bullying, and in 1282 Jean de Grilly wrote to Robert
Burnell and Odo de Grandson, that Armagnac 'is and always remains
faithful to our lord the king'.[75] He was, confided Grilly, one of his 'best
friends' in Gascony, the lord whom he trusted most. Philip III had imprisoned Armagnac at Péronne for non-payment of the fine and Edward I wrote
letters supporting him in September and November 1282.[76] Aid was promised from Edward's advocates at the court of France. Writing from Paris,
Jean de Grilly expressed considerable anxiety over the pressure exerted upon
Armagnac to render homage to Philip III.[77] Armagnac's brother, the archbishop of Auch, had acknowledged that his temporalities were held from the
crown of France, and Capetian lawyers tried to argue that the lordships of
Armagnac and Fézensac were fiefs of the archbishopric and therefore subject
to the superior lordship of the French crown.[78]

By the autumn of 1283 the danger of Armagnac submission to the

---

March 1318). A similar device, reputed to detect the presence of poison in food, was in use at the
court of Burgundy in the later fifteenth century. See Olivier de la Marche, 'Etat de la maison du
duc Charles de Bourgoingne', *Mémoires*, ed. H. Beaune and J. d'Arbaumont (*SHF*, 1886), iv, pp.
22–7, 46. For the attempted poisoning of John XXII in 1317 by Hugues Géraud, bishop of
Cahors, see G. Mollat, *Les Papes d'Avignon, 1305–1376* (Paris, 1949), pp. 42–4.

[73] See above, pp. 86, 88–90.

[74] AN, J 392, nos 13 (at Agen, 28 February 1273), 14 (11 March 1273), 15 (5 March 1273).
The house of Armagnac during this period has not yet found its historian. For a brief survey of
its history see P. Wolff, 'The Armagnacs in southern France (14th–15th centuries)' *BIHR*, xx
(1945), pp. 186–91.

[75] SC I/23, no. 114 (at La Réole, 8 February 1282).

[76] SC I/13, no. 17 (9 September 1282); SC I/12, no. 38 (18 November 1282).

[77] SC 1/18, nos 53 (at Paris, 14 August 1282), 54 (16 August 1282).

[78] SC 1/18, no. 55 (3 February 1283).

immediate lordship of the French crown appeared to have passed, but the behaviour of Philip III's officers, especially his seneschal of Toulouse, had given rise to great concern among Edward I's Gascon council at Bordeaux and among his proctors and advocates at Paris. Writing in June 1283 from Monflanquin, Jean de Grilly informed Edward that Armagnac's proctor had already been sent to deliver the castle and town of Auch to the seneschal of Toulouse, to be held in liege homage from the French crown. The two brothers of Armagnac, count and archbishop, thought Grilly 'are so oppressed . . . that in the end they will be compelled to submit by some contrived method . . . and one cannot believe that they can withstand these afflictions much longer'.[79] Similar techniques were adopted by the French in 1293–4, when Bernard VI of Armagnac (1285–1319) was summoned to perform homage at Paris for the *comtés* of Armagnac and Fezensac, and the *vicomté* of Brulhois.[80] Edward I was also summoned at the same time, as duke of Aquitaine, 'to reply to us concerning the homage of Armagnac and Fézensac', Auvillars, Lomagne and Lectoure, in a peremptory letter from Philip the Fair (December 1293).[81] There was evidently doubt as to the status of the Armagnac lordships and about the nature of the homage to be performed. We know that Edward I's seneschal of Gascony, John of Havering, was prompt to pay Armagnac's pension in January 1294, ordering the constable of Bordeaux to make the payment without delay 'as you esteem the king's honour'.[82] Loyalties as subject to rival pressures as that of Armagnac demanded constant vigilance and reward to keep them fresh and responsive to ducal needs.

The Armagnacs were in a particularly vulnerable position as a result of the geographical location of their lands. Lacking a defensible mountainous region into which, like the counts of Foix, they could retreat, their energies were primarily absorbed in the defence of their territories against their immediate neighbours. As we shall see in the second part of this chapter, their conflict with the house of Foix was to become a dominant theme of the politics of south-west France. Holding lands which lay on the boundaries of Plantagenet Aquitaine, the Capetian *sénéschaussée* of Toulouse, and the lordships of Foix-Béarn, Pardiac, Astarac and L'Isle-Jourdain, they were essentially marcher lords, attempting to enlarge and unite their territories.[83] Their attempts to acquire Bigorre and Comminges were effectively blocked by the

---

[79] SC 1/18, no. 58 (at Monflanquin, 8 June 1283).

[80] AN, J 631, no. 10 (i) (31 December 1293); confirmed by notarial instrument at Auch (4 January 1294).

[81] AN, J 631, no. 10 (ii) (10 December 1293); confirmed on 8 January 1294. Raoul de Nesle, constable of France was, however, prepared to compromise with Armagnac to the extent of permitting his men and subjects not to appear to answer charges in the *bastides* and other places of the king of France until Armagnac or his officers had been informed of the nature of their crimes: ATG, A 237, fo. 126ʳ; at Toulouse, –1293. See below, pp. 183–4.

[82] E 101/152–6, no. 5 (11 January 1294), 6, 7.

[83] Wolff, 'The Armagnacs', pp. 187–8.

counts of Foix, but Bernard VI of Armagnac's inheritance of the town and *comté* of Rodez in 1304 (as a result of his second marriage to Cécile, daughter of Henri, count of Rodez) was a valuable acquisition.[84] Rodez was added to the other Armagnac possessions in the archdiocese of Auch, and Bernard VI and his son Jean I became powerful in the Languedoc as well as in Gascony. They ruled over Rodez as counts *Dei gratia* and claimed the right to wear the iron crown of Rouergue. For the Armagnacs, the acquisition of Rodez was the equivalent of that of Béarn for the counts of Foix.[85]

During the first quarter of the fourteenth century, the Armagnacs also benefited from their close ties with the Avignon papacy. The registers of the Gascon Bertrand de Goth, elected pope as Clement V in 1305, included twenty bulls relating to the family.[86] A dynastic connection was established by the marriage in 1324 of Jean I of Armagnac to Régine de Goth, daughter and heiress of Bertrand de Goth, *vicomte* of Lomagne and Auvillars, nephew of Clement V.[87] By the marriage contract Bertrand was obliged to give 1000 *l.t.* annually to Jean I, as Regine's dowry from lands in the Bordelais and Agenais. These represented a significant addition to the lands of Armagnac because Bertrand instituted Régine, countess of Armagnac, as his sole and universal heir.[88] Lordships in the heart of Plantagenet Aquitaine, as well as in the Agenais and the Gers, were thus held by the short-lived countess of Armagnac until her death in 1325. The *vicomtés* of Lomagne and Auvillars, the castellanries of Duras, Puyguilhem, Alemans and Montségur, the lordships of Veyrines and Blanquefort in the Bordelais, and of Dunes and Donzac in the Agenais, then descended to the young Jean I of Armagnac as his wife's universal heir.[89] Bertrand de Goth had also profited from his favoured position among Clement V's relations to acquire the Italian marquisate of Ancona, as well as land on the other side of the Rhône, including the castle of Monteux in the Comtat Venaissin. He bought the lordship in 1313, granted it to Régine de Goth in his will, and she in turn bequeathed it to Jean I of Armagnac.[90] But the animosity conceived by John

---

[84] ATG, A 24, where the succession to Henri, count of Rodez, was settled and his debts liquidated (1321–2), especially fos 49^v–53^r.

[85] See Wolff, 'The Armagnacs', p. 187; A. Bristow, *Fourteenth-century Rodez* (unpublished Oxford D.Phil. thesis, 1976), pp. 252–78.

[86] J. Bernard, 'Le népotisme de Clément V et ses complaisances pour la Gascogne', *AM*, lxi (1948–9), p. 588.

[87] ATG, A 23, no. 1 (marriage contract of Jean I of Armagnac and Régine de Goth); *St Sardos*, p. 16: Ralph Basset, seneschal of Aquitaine, had attempted to negotiate a marriage between Régine and Edward II's brother, Edmund, earl of Kent, but had failed. He feared the consequences if Armagnac, Bertrand de Goth and Amanieu VII d'Albret acted together 'as one person' (*c.*23 January 1324).

[88] ATG, A 23, no. 2 (undated).

[89] ATG, A 28, no. 2, fos 8^r–11^r (testament, at Lavardans, 12 August 1325). See Appendix III, map 1.

[90] ATG, A 28, no. 1.

XXII against Clement V's kinsmen and women was vented against Bert-rand de Goth's heirs, and Monteux was seized into papal hands in February 1326. It was not restored. The Armagnacs thus lost the foundations of a potential power-base in Provence, but had greatly enhanced their position in the south-west.[91] Despite Edward II's attempt to take the lordships of Blanquefort, Montségur, Lectoure, Dunes and Donzac into his own hands on Régine de Goth's death in September 1325, Armagnac retained his territorial foothold in Plantagenet Aquitaine. The argument of Edward's lawyers that a woman could not succeed to a fief was not upheld by local custom, and so Jean I of Armagnac remained the beneficiary of much of the de Goth inheritance in the duchy.[92] These lordships were, however, to become a source of renewed Anglo-French tension under Edward III.[93] Armagnac's second marriage, to Béatrix de Clermont, tended (like that of Gaston I of Foix-Béarn to Jeanne d'Artois) to incline him towards northern France and the Capetian or Valois court rather than towards an absentee king-duke of Aquitaine. The history of the house of Armagnac at this time is poorly documented, but a greater dependence upon sources of income, power and influence in the gift of the French crown seems evident. Yet the steady accumulation of territories and the regional power which accompanied it was soon to render Armagnac, like Foix-Béarn, one of the most independent of noble houses, especially during the crises of the mid fourteenth century.[94]

Among the old families of Plantagenet Aquitaine there was by the late thirteenth century only one outstanding dynasty. The house of Albret had emerged from obscure origins to become the most important single lineage in the duchy. Stemming from the poor and insignificant Landais lordship of Labrit, they had built up a large territorial holding along the Atlantic coast of Aquitaine. Their lands bordered the lordships of Foix-Béarn on the east, the *vicomté* of Soule and community of Labourt to the south, and the petty lords of the Bordelais and Bazadais to the north.[95] With the exception of some thrusts into the Agenais, the primary sphere of acquisitive activity for the Albret at this time was the Bordelais and Bazadais. Amanieu VII's marriage to Rose de Bourg brought with it important landed possessions around Bourg and Blaye; his daughter Mathe married Renaud de Pons, lord of Bergerac, in 1314, and was to give the Albret a significant foothold on the borders of Périgord; while Amanieu's son, Bérard I (d. 1346) who was lord of Vayres and Vertheuil in the Entre-deux-Mers, acquired the castles and

---

[91] ATG, A 28, no. 2, fos 11^r–12^v (23 August 1325); no. 1, mm. 2^v–3^r.

[92] C 61/38, mm. 8 (23 September 1325); 7 (2 October 1325).

[93] See below, pp. 254–5.

[94] See, for example, H. Morel, 'Jean de Labarthe et la maison d'Armagnac, un épisode de la concentration féodale au xive siècle', *AM*, lxi (1949), pp. 257–311; Wolff, 'The Armagnacs', pp. 187–9.

[95] For the early history of the Albret see J.-B. Marquette, 'Les Albret I. Les origines (xie siècle–1240)', *Cahiers du Bazadais*, xxx, xxxi (1975), pp. 5–107.

lordships of Langoiran and Podensac for his cadet son Amanieu through the latter's marriage to Mabille d'Escossan in 1345.[96] The Podensac, who held a number of strong-points on the Garonne, had married into the bourgeois family of Caillau at Bordeaux in 1293 and thus brought much of their fortune into the Albret inheritance.[97] Bertrand de Podensac was already a client of Amanieu VII d'Albret in 1296 and appointed Albret as 'tutor de . . . ma heretere', with full power to exercise custody over his heiress and her lands until she reached the age of fourteen.[98] Her marriage was to be arranged by Albret and another Bordelais knight, Barrau de Sescas, whom Bertrand appointed as his executors. As a result of two further marriages, an alliance was forged by the Albret with the house of Armagnac. Bernard VI, count of Armagnac, had married Isabelle d'Albret (d. 1294) as his first wife, and Amanieu VII d'Albret's eldest son Bernard-Ezi V (1326–59) was husband to Mathe d'Armagnac, Bernard VI's daughter.[99] A tendency for the two houses to act together in their political connections and allegiances became increasingly notable in the 1340s.[100]

Like the Armagnacs, the Albret profited from the rise of the de Goth family and its branches to a place in the sun under Clement V. Between 1305 and 1314 there are fifty references to Amanieu VII d'Albret in the papal registers: he received appointments as papal vicar in Italy and as a nuncio, although he was a layman, to England.[101] Amanieu VII was an executor of Régine de Goth, countess of Armagnac, in 1325 and his son Bernard-Ezi, who began his career as a clerk, was especially favoured under Clement V.[102] In August 1305, for example, the pope recommended him to the abbot of St Denis and the deans of Bordeaux and Bourges.[103] He was already a canon of Notre-Dame-de-Paris, and was to be given the first vacant prebend at Bordeaux or Bourges by papal provision. Clement also furthered the secular ambitions of the Albret. In August 1306, at the pope's request, Amanieu VII was granted the lordship of Meilhan in the Bazadais by Edward I.[104] The grant was not to prejudice the existing rights of another lord, Auger de Mothe, to levy a lucrative toll or *péage* at Meilhan, but Albret willingly agreed to this because

---

[96] See *Le Trésor des Chartes d'Albret. I. Les Archives de Vayres*, ed. J.-B. Marquette (Paris, 1973), pp. 13–23; see Appendix III, map 3.

[97] *AHG*, xv, p. 191; for the Caillau see Trabut-Cussac in *Histoire de Bordeaux, III*, pp. 72–4, and Y. Renouard, *Etudes d'histoire médiévale* (Paris, 1968), pp. 346–7, 350–2. See below, pp. 146, 160–4.

[98] *Trésor des Chartes d'Albret*, I, no. 52 (pp. 79–81).

[99] See Appendix I, Table 3a.

[100] See below, pp. 254, 263.

[101] Bernard, 'Le népotisme de Clément V', p. 403; B. Guillemain, 'Les recettes et les dépenses de la Chambre Apostolique pour la quatrième année du pontificat de Clément V (1308–9)', *Collections de l'Ecole française de Rome*, xxxix (Rome, 1978), nos 208, 733.

[102] ATG, A 28, no. 2, fo. 11[v].

[103] APA, E 20, no. 7 (29 July 1305).

[104] APA, E 190, no. 5, and unnumbered original letters dated 7 and 14 August 1306.

he and Auger had been 'companions and friends since their youth' (*a suis juventutibus fuerant socii et amici*).[105] The circle of the Albret affinity was wide and included most of the lesser seigneurs of the Bordelais and Bazadais. The list of witnesses to the grant of Meilhan included Arnaud-Garcie de Goth, *vicomte* of Lomagne and Auvillars, the pope's nephew; Arnaud de Caupenne, knight; Amanieu de Sescas, Guillaume-Raymond de Gensac and Bertrand de Sauviac, esquires; and three citizens of Bordeaux. The Sescas family were vassals of the Albret, and Barrau de Sescas, knight and admiral of Bayonne, was described in May 1297 as the 'man' of Amanieu VII in letters of Edward I to Albret, requesting his indulgence towards Barrau, who was detained on the king-duke's business in England through no fault of his own.[106] His son, Guillaume de Sescas, esquire (*douzet*) recognized that he was a liegeman and military tenant of Albret in July 1309, holding land and tithes from him in the Bazadais, and owing him service, counsel and loyalty in perpetuity.[107]

Papal favour was meted out not merely to the senior and cadet branches of the Albret under Clement V but to their more distant kinsmen and clients. In June 1312, Guichard d'Albret, non-resident archdeacon of Canterbury, and Amanieu VII's nephew Guillaume de Brutails both received provisions and dispensations enabling them to draw the fruits of their benefices. Guichard was provided to the rectory of Ightham (dioc. Canterbury) 'which he has already held for three years without ordination and without papal dispensation'.[108] A further three year's non-residence, as well as the revenues of Ightham, were also granted to him by papal indult. There was nothing exceptional about such favours, but the Albret and their connections did especially well out of them. The search for endowments, rents, lordships and revenues was particularly intense among all branches of this prolific family, and their relatively unproductive Landais lordships were a constant spur towards further, more profitable acquisitions. They were prominent beneficiaries of grants from Edward I, and Amanieu VII served the king-duke loyally during the Anglo-French war of 1294–8. He saw service in Scotland in 1300–1, and was celebrated by the anonymous author of the heraldic *Song of Caerlaverock* (1300).[109] With other Gascon nobles, he was partly repaid for his services by the grant of revenues from alien priories, and in June 1300 was acting as

---

[105] APA, E 190, no. 5. For Albret's seigneurial obligations at Meilhan, including the duty of providing seven knights for the king-duke's army, see no. 18; *RG*, iv, nos 629, 633, 634, 690, 700.

[106] *RG*, iii, p. clxxxix, nos 4481, 4483 (7 May 1297).

[107] APA, E 199, no. 3 (3 July 1309).

[108] *Calendar of Entries in the Papal Registers Relating to Great Britain and Ireland. Papal Letters, ii (1305–42)*, ed. W. H. Bliss, pp. 95, 97, 110, 112.

[109] See M. Vale, 'The Gascon nobility and the Anglo-French war, 1294–98', in *War and Government in the Middle Ages*, ed. J. Gillingham and J. C. Holt (Woodbridge and Totowa, 1984), pp. 138–9; *The Siege of Caerlaverock (1300): The Roll of Arms of the Princes, Barons and Knights who Attended King Edward I to the Siege of Caerlaverock in 1300*, ed. T. Wright (London, 1864), p. 11.

'receiver of monies' from the priory of Blyth.[110] But, as we shall see, the death of Edward I led to an increasing alienation of Amanieu VII from the Plantagenet regime, which was to culminate in his desertion of Edward II for Charles IV of France during the War of St Sardos. Piers Gaveston and his Gascon allies were partly instrumental in arousing Albret's hostility and the Despensers did little to achieve a reconciliation.[111] It was left to Edward III to rebuild the amicable relationship between the Plantagenets and their most prominent Gascon vassal.

The Middling and Lesser Nobility

Below the greater families stood a large number of lesser nobles, a few styling themselves 'baron', most content with the title of 'seigneur' or 'sire', often accompanied by a patronymic derived from the name of their principal or original lordship. A marked increase in the numbers of nobles had taken place since the early twelfth century.[112] The Gascon nobility were not exempt from the demographic growth of the period. In the Bordelais, eight castellan families were to be found at the beginning of the twelfth century, but their number had grown to twenty-four by 1294.[113] From about fifty families in c.1150, the nobility of the Bordelais had increased to about 200 by 1300.[114] Among the *noblesse moyenne* a group of men styled 'knight' (*miles*) was emerging, but the rise of knighthood occurred considerably later in Gascony than in other regions, such as Mâconnais or Picardy. Whereas the eleventh and early twelfth centuries witnessed the emergence of knights in greater numbers in northern France, the title was rare in the south-west until the first half of the thirteenth century.[115] The extension of northern French influences from the Languedoc as a result of the Albigensian crusades may have contributed to this tardy development. The first designation of the substantial Agenais family of Durfort as knights, for instance, dates from as late as 1243.[116] They were first styled *nobiles viri* only in 1256, and a tendency towards a late crystallization of a titled *noblesse* at this level is found in much of south-west France, with the possible exception of the *vicomté* of Béarn and

---

[110] E 101/155/15, no. 2 (11 June 1302); E 101/371/21, nos 77, 80, 81 (1300–1).

[111] See below, pp. 166–9.

[112] C. Higounet, 'La société nobiliaire en Bordelais à la fin du xiiie siècle', in *Société et groupes sociaux en Aquitaine et Angleterre* (Bordeaux, 1976), pp. 8–9; *Documents sur la maison de Durfort (xie–xve siècles)*, ed. N. de Peña, i (Bordeaux, 1977), pp. xx–xxi.

[113] Higounet, 'La société nobiliaire', p. 8, and his 'En Bordelais: "Principes castella tenentes"', in *La Noblesse au Moyen Age*, ed. P. Contamine (Paris, 1976), pp. 97–104.

[114] C. Higounet, 'Le groupe aristocratique en Aquitaine et en Gascogne' in *Les Structures sociales de l'Aquitaine, du Languedoc et de l'Espagne au premier age féodal* (Toulouse and Paris, 1969), pp. 221–37. For a rare effigy of a Gascon noble of this period see plate 4.2.

[115] De Peña, *Documents sur la maison de Durfort*, i, p. ix; Higounet, 'La société nobiliaire', pp. 2–3; for the Mâconnais, see G. Duby, *La société aux xie et xiie siècles dans la région mâconnaise* (Paris, 1953), pp. 191–201, 317–36.

[116] *Documents sur la maison de Durfort*, i, pp. viii, ix, xix–xx.

other areas where primogeniture and impartible inheritance were established at an earlier date.[117] Knighthood was not yet a status sought after by the middling and lesser nobility of the south-west, and the rise of 'new men' as *milites* only seems to have begun in the mid-thirteenth century. These were essentially fighting men, or *milites strenui*, making a career of arms and receiving the sword-belt from a superior lord, preferably a king or at least a count.[118] Edward I, as duke of Aquitaine, was particularly sought after by Gascon nobles as a patron of knighthood, prepared to gird them and their sons with the sword which was the symbol of their order.[119] By 1300 there were about eighty men styled 'knight' in the Bordelais from a total group of about 200 nobles. Professor Higounet calculated, largely from the evidence of the *Recogniciones feodorum* of 1273–5, that there were six 'lords' (*domini*), eighty knights, seventy-four *damoiseaux* (esquires), between twenty and forty other heads of families styled 'noble' and about a dozen patrician families of Bordeaux among the Bordelais nobility.[120] But the costs of knighthood were high, and some nobles were unwilling or unable to meet the expenditure which was demanded of them. In 1319, for instance, the wealthy Genoese merchant Antonio di Pessagno, formerly seneschal of Aquitaine, claimed that he had been granted 3000 *l.st.* by Edward II for the expenses of his knighting (*a sa chivalerie*) assigned on Gascon revenues.[121] Others were not so favoured, and were obliged to meet the costs of the knighting ceremony and the provision of horses and equipment themselves. Unless subsidies were forthcoming, it was only great and favoured men such as Jean de Grilly who requested knighthood for their sons from Edward I at their own expense.[122] In relation to the total number of nobles in Gascony, the proportion of knights was therefore relatively small. Among the twenty-three barons of Béarn who agreed to serve Gaston II of Foix-Béarn in war against Edward III in June 1338, only five were knights.[123] As in most Gascon forces of the time, they were surrounded by a mass of *damoiseaux, donzels* or *douzets*, some of whom were not young, inexperienced esquires but veterans of many campaigns and expeditions. The lesser nobility frequented the profession of arms, but few rose into its higher ranks unless they were fortunate enough to be knighted by their lord at a battle or siege and endowed with an income to sustain their estate.

The proliferation of the lesser nobility was accompanied by an increase in

---

[117] *Documents sur la maison de Durfort*, i, no. 40; *Recogniciones feodorum*, p. 335 (for the only reference in the inquiry of 1274–5 to a *homo nobilis*).

[118] Higounet, 'La société nobiliaire', pp. 2–4.

[119] See, for example, SC 1/18, no. 68: petition of Jean de Grilly to Edward I, reminding him of his promise to confer knighthood upon Pierre de Grilly, his son (*c.*1282).

[120] Higounet, 'La société nobiliaire', pp. 2–5.

[121] E 159/93 m. 76^v (1 February 1319).

[122] See above, n. 119.

[123] J. J. Monlezun, *Histoire de la Gascogne depuis les temps les plus reculés jusqu'à nos jours* (Auch, 1850), vi, pp. 188–9; *Chroniques romanes des comtes de Foix*, pp. 48–50.

the number of seigneurial castles in Aquitaine.[124] These multiplied especially along the routes and inland waterways of the region. Many lords profited from the tolls charged on travellers and merchandise, and their castles were often sited at points where roads or rivers met, and where merchants and pilgrims congregated. The pilgrimage route from northern and eastern France to Compostella via Roncevaux and the Basque country passed through the duchy of Aquitaine and its neighbouring lordships, so that the nobility of the region benefited from the *péages* (tolls) levied on these routes.[125] These exactions could lead to quarrels, especially with the Church. Tolls taken by the Durfort in the Agenais hampered the economic development of some Cistercian houses of the region, and the abbeys of Moissac, Belleperche and Grandselve engaged in litigation not only with the Plantagenet king-dukes but with many local seigneurs in defence of their rights and revenues.[126] The value of tolls levied in the duchy was specifically alluded to in a memorandum of 1294: the French had occupied the duchy, had seisin of *péages* and rents in Aquitaine, and therefore controlled most of it.[127] Yet no regime could afford to alienate its supporters, and it was unwise to take too many castles and tolls into royal or ducal possession. By 1294 five-sixths of the castles within the duchy of Aquitaine were held by the nobility: thus, of 130 fortresses in the Agenais, only six were in ducal hands.[128] The price of loyalty was high. A small ducal domain – Edward I held only twenty castles in Aquitaine in the 1290s – ensured the survival of his regime and the Plantagenets consciously and purposefully alienated most of their Gascon assets, with the important exception of the wine customs collected at Bordeaux. The principal beneficiaries of these grants were the middling and lesser nobility.[129]

Similarly, despite the Gregorian reforms of the later eleventh and early twelfth centuries, many Gascon lords held tithes, or a proportion of them, from parishes within their lordships. The appropriation of ecclesiastical revenues by secular lords such as the Durfort during the twelfth century, and the installation of kinsmen in the more lucrative benefices, meant that a greater degree of lay patronage of the Church was exercised by the Gascon nobility than by their northern French contemporaries.[130] Sometimes elder, as well as

---

[124] Gardelles, *Les Châteaux*, pp. 13–15, 17–22. See below, pp. 103–8, 114–18.

[125] Gardelles, *Les Châteaux*, pp. 14–15.

[126] *Documents sur la maison de Durfort*, i, p. xviii–xxii; cf. J. A. Kicklighter, 'Les monastères de Gascogne et le conflit franco-anglais (1270–1327)', *AM*, xci (1979), pp. 121–33.

[127] C 47/29/3, no. 10 (memorandum relating to Edmund of Lancaster's mission to the French court, 1294).

[128] Gardelles, *Les Châteaux*, p. 32.

[129] See Trabut-Cussac, *L'Administration anglaise*, pp. 342–70; M. Vale, 'Nobility, bureaucracy and the "state" in English Gascony, 1250–1340: a prosopographical approach', in *Genèse de l'Etat moderne: prosopographie et histoire*, ed. F. Autrand (Paris, 1985), pp. 308–11.

[130] *Documents sur la maison de Durfort*, i, pp. viii, xvii–xviii; *RG*, iii, p. cxcii (petition of Bertrand de Panissau, knight, to Edward I for grants to his unbeneficed sons; after Easter, 1297).

younger, sons began their careers in the Church and only renounced their unordained clerical status later in life. This was the case with Bernard-Ezi V d'Albret (1326–59) or Gaillard I de Durfort (*c*.1299–1356), who had been a notable canon lawyer, prebendary of Saintes, Agen and York, and archdeacon of Périgueux.[131] Gaillard inherited the Lacour-Durfort lands in 1345, after his marriage to Marguerite de Caumont, and his clerical career was abruptly terminated. The tight grip of the Gascon nobility on the Church served their dynastic interests well. Cathedral chapters and collegiate churches were full of their relatives and exclusive foundations such as Uzeste, Villandraut or St Bertrand-de-Comminges provided subsistence for the younger sons of many families.[132] The sees of the region were also largely occupied by men of noble birth, and papal provision during the early Avignonese period worked in their favour. There were notably few clashes over elections in the south-west. With a de Goth or Canteloupe as archbishop of Bordeaux, and an Armagnac as archbishop of Auch, the alliance of higher clergy and nobility was assured, although family feuds could always spill over into ecclesiastical politics. The regular clergy remained a major source of friction, however, and the claims of Benedictine and Cistercian monasteries and nunneries could often run counter to the interests of secular nobles. But the need to provide for cadet sons and daughters could lead the nobility to compromise with abbots, priors and abbesses.

The formation of senior and cadet branches within many noble families was a marked characteristic of the period *c*.1100–1250. A preference for primogeniture or other forms of impartible inheritance was common among senior branches, such as the Albret or Durfort, and it is arguable that this contributed substantially to their survival.[133] But a family whose lands lay in an area of customary law where partible inheritance was the rule faced considerable problems. In the Bazadais, Bordelais, Agenais, Pays d'Albret, the Landes, Marsan, Gabardan, Tursan, Capbreton, Auribat and the *prevôté* of St Sever, inheritances were divided, sometimes among all heirs, both male

---

[131] For Albret, see Boutruche, *La Crise d'une société*, pp. 379–85; APA, E 20, no. 7 (29 July 1305); for Durfort, see P. Fournier, 'Note complémentaire pour l'histoire des canonistes au xive siècle. III. Gaillard de Durfort, Canoniste et seigneur féodal', *Nouvelle revue du droit français et étranger*, (1920), pp. 516–24; *Documents sur la maison de Durfort*, i, p. xxvii. For the more general context of these movements from ecclesiastical to secular life, see J. Dunbabin, 'From clerk to knight: changing orders', in *The Ideals and Practice of Medieval Knighthood II*, ed. C. Harper-Bill and R. Harvey (Woodbridge, 1988), pp. 26–39.

[132] Bernard, 'Le népotisme de Clément V', pp. 375, 377; G. Lizerand, *Clément V et Philippe IV le Bel* (Paris, 1910) pp. 380–1; *Regestum Clementis papae V*, ed. Benedictines of Monte Cassino (Rome, 1885–92), nos 8124, 3705, 10340. The tombs of the canons preserved in the cloister at St Bertrand-de-Comminges bear the arms of their families. Clement V had, of course, been bishop of Comminges before his elevation to the papacy. See J. Rocadier, *St Bertrand-de-Comminges* (Toulouse, 1987), pp. 93–122 and *Regestum Clementis papae V*, no. 3994 (16 January 1309).

[133] Boutruche, *La Crise d'une société*, pp. 384–8; *Documents sur la maison de Durfort*, i, pp. xxvi, xxxi–xxxii, xl.

and female.[134] Yet the liberty to prefer one heir was generally available and many testators took advantage of this practice in their wills and testaments. To institute a 'universal heir' was increasingly common, and that heir was normally male.[135] But the perennial problem of providing for other children remained. At worst, the cadet and bastard sons sought occupation and profit in brigandage. In 1311–12, for example, the consuls and commune of Montclar-d'Agenais told Edward II that their *bailli* had seized a gang of robbers and murderers, one of whom was 'called *Burd*, natural son of . . . Amanieu de Fossat, knight, lieutenant of the seneschal of Gascony'.[136] They were therefore unable to ensure that justice was duly done because Amanieu de Fossat was protecting him. At best, a delicate balance had to be achieved among the male heirs in a family which might necessitate the sharing of lands and castles. Sometimes two castles would co-exist on the same site; at others, a castle could be shared among co-seigneurs. At Roquetaillade in the Bazadais there were 'old' and 'new' castles, while at Puy-Calvary in the Agenais, the castle was divided by their father between his two sons, Raymond-Guillaume and Guillaume de Palazols.[137] A notarial instrument of April 1288 recorded the agreement specifying the position of the common wall which divided their respective quarters.[138] Raymond-Guillaume was to hold the *salle* (hall with living quarters) while Guillaume held the tower. Neither brother was to molest nor disturb the other by making windows from which the other could be observed, but such arrangements could all too readily generate friction. *Condominium* could be a divisive practice and lead to private war.[139]

A distribution map of Gascon lordships would emphasize the significance or river valleys and of the more fertile regions as areas of seigneurial concentration. The Cernès, Graves and valley of the Ciron in the Bordelais and Bazadais, for instance, were areas of high density, where noble families had benefited from the colonizing efforts of the period 1100–1250 in the duchy of Aquitaine.[140] The relative absence of castles in the Landes is explained by the poor soils and lack of adequate water supply that deter-

---

[134] Poumarède, *Les Successions dans le sud-ouest*, pp. 238–40, 305–7 and see the maps on pp. 238, 306. Poumarède points out that the strictest partible inheritance customs tended to correspond with infertile areas where there was little urban settlement (p. 238).

[135] Good examples are the testament of Margaret, countess of Foix, *vicomtesse* of Béarn and Marsan, where her grandson Gaston II, count of Foix, was instituted as 'universal heir': APA, E 196, no. 53 (April 1319); or that of Jean de Grilly, appointing his grandson, Pierre, as his universal heir: ATG, A297, fos 1060ᵛ–1068ʳ (June 1303). For the practice and its development see Poumarède, *Les Successions dans le sud-ouest*, pp. 208–17. Also APA, E 27, no. 12 (Albret, 1324); E 240, no. 10 (Lamothe, 1292).

[136] SC 1/34, no. 134.

[137] Gardelles, *Les Châteaux*, pp. 208–10 (Roquetaillade); 202 (Puycalvary).

[138] ALG, 6J 43; fonds de Raffin, transcription of lost original (April 1288).

[139] See below, pp. 134–9.

[140] Higounet, 'La société nobiliaire', pp. 7–8; Gardelles, *Les Châteaux*, pp. 13–14.

mined its seigneurial geography.[141] With the exception of a few better-endowed families, the great majority of Gascon nobles were men of very modest means. Valuations of the lands held by dispossessed Gascons during French occupation in 1294–1303 indicate that 300 *l.t.* was at the upper level of annual income amongst Gascon nobles.[142] Pierre de Bordeaux, last surviving representative of the ancient house of Puy-Paulin, outstripped all his peers with an estimated annual income of 1500 *l.t.*, followed by Pons de Castillon and the captal de Buch with 1000 *l.t.*, while most nobles in the list enjoyed landed incomes of between 100 and 250 *l.t.* A fine warhorse could cost 200 *l.t.* at this time.[143] Most nobles were dependent for their livelihood upon the labour of serfs (*questaux*) and the receipt of rents. In *c.*1305, Arnaud-Loup, lord of Estivaux, complained that three of his 'vilains' had appealed from his jurisdiction to the lieutenant of Gascony and had been received into the latter's protection. Arnaud-Loup claimed he had lost his seigneurial dues and that the king-duke's lieutenant 'had never had jurisdiction over them'.[144] The disturbed conditions of wartime and the French occupation of the duchy had enabled the unfree tenants of some lords to escape from their bondage and seek liberty in the towns. Bernard de Blanquefort, lord of Audenge, whose lands were assessed at 250 *l.t.* per annum in 1299, petitioned Edward I in 1305 that many of his *vileyns, serfs et neyfs* had left his service during his absence and had fled to Bordeaux and elsewhere. They claimed to be free 'through their residence there', but he wanted them back as before the war.[145] The seneschal of Gascony was ordered by the king-duke to discover whether the serfs had escaped as a result of their lord's absence in his service and, if so, they were to be returned to Bernard de Blanquefort as his chattels. That the problem was not merely confined to a few individuals is evident from a petition addressed in Edward II's name to Philip the Fair in which it was requested that no *hommes questaux* nor serfs in the duchy were to be received as freemen, *voisins* or burgesses in the *bastides* founded there by the king of France.[146] Despite the greater prevalence of peasant freedom in Aquitaine than elsewhere, the losses sustained by landlords as a result of desertion by their unfree labour force were clearly sufficiently damaging to cause concern at the highest level.[147] The lesser nobility were economically vulnerable.

---

[141] Gardelles, *Les Châteaux*, pp. 15–16, 19.

[142] *RG*, iii, nos. 4529–31 (25 August 1299); C 47/26/6; Vale 'Seigneurial fortification and private war', pp. 135–6.

[143] See Vale, 'Warfare and the life of the nobility', pp. 173–6; see below, pp. 111–12.

[144] SC 8/289. no. 14410.

[145] SC 8/284, no. 14194.

[146] AN, J 654, no. 24 (undated petition of Edward II, as a 'humble son', to Philip the Fair). For the *bastides* and their implications for Anglo-French relations and local conditions, see below, pp. 152–60.

[147] For peasant freedom, see Higounet, *Paysages et villages neufs du Moyen Age* (Bordeaux, 1975), pp. 111–16, 373–97.

Inability to gather the harvest, for example, was deemed to be potentially crippling for a lord. In September (?) 1295, Bertrand d'Escossans, lord of Podensac, wrote to his son from Péronne where he was being held by the French, telling him that he urgently needed money and that all his vines at Podensac should be harvested.[148] His rents and dues (*cens et questas*) were to be collected forthwith, and the money sent to him if he had not already been released. The monetary income derived from vines, corn, cattle and fruit-growing was supplemented by revenues from tolls, tithes and, above all, the seigneurial control of mills. Wind- and water-mills were especially vulnerable in time of war and provided easy targets for enemies whereby seigneurial incomes could be rapidly and effectively damaged.[149] In 1305, for example, Vidau Brane, lord by right of his wife of La Mote de Villeneuve, requested the king-duke's protection during a private war among the nobles of Brassenx.[150] His mills and his men were under attack and he stood to lose all his income from that lordship. The fortified mill as well as the fortified church was not an uncommon feature of the landscape. Owing to the lack of seigneurial accounts, rentals and *terriers* (land surveys) from this period, the component parts of a lord's income are difficult to assess. But inquiries into the value of confiscated lands can provide some information. In February 1299, a French inquest into the value of lands in the Bazadais confiscated from supporters of Edward I revealed that the castellanry of Auros yielded an annual rent from the inhabitants of 25 *l.b.*, high and low justice was estimated at 6 *l.b.* per annum, a toll at 40 *s.b.* per annum, sales of wine at 20 *s.b.*, with rights over vines, meadows, and water-mills bringing the total income up to 711 *l.* 8*s.* 6*d.b.*[151] It was estimated that the vines of Raymond Fort de Lados could be harvested in one day by a workforce of seventy men, while Pierre de Gavarret's holding at Langon included a valuable water-mill on the Garonne. The French seneschal discovered that war damage had drastically reduced the value of these possessions as witnessed by six aged and worthy men of the district who had sworn on the Gospels that these valuations were correct. Warfare of this severity, which spread beyond the frontiers of the duchy, was a very occasional phenomenon but its effects, though short-lived, could be very damaging to a nobility who were so heavily dependent upon landed incomes.

There were a number of methods whereby noble incomes could be both sustained and increased: the creation and exploitation of new settlements

---

[148] *Trésor des Chartes d'Albret*, i, no. 49 (APA, E 172).

[149] C 47/25/2, no. 17; undated petition to Edward II for an inquiry into the value of the king-duke's revenues from 'men and mills' on the Lot in the Agenais; APA, E 22, no. 6: letters of Philip the Fair to his seneschal of Toulouse on assaults against appellants to the French crown in Aquitaine, including destruction of their mills (20 August 1312). For the value of mills to seigneurial incomes see G. Bois, *Crise du féodalisme*, pp. 205–11, 307, 318–20.

[150] SC 8/292, no. 14557.

[151] AN, JJ 38, fos 12^v–13^r (at La Réole, 24 February 1299).

within a lordship; the patronage of a greater family; service to a prince; manipulation and adjustment of inheritance customs; and marriage into patrician or bourgeois families.[152] The foundation and exploitation of new settlements – *castelnaux* and *bastides* – as sources of financial profit by the lesser nobility will be considered in the next chapter. We have already seen the effects of Bertrand de Goth's elevation to the papacy as Clement V in 1305 on some of the greater noble families of south-west France.[153] But the network of the de Goth clan spread over a very large number of middling and lesser nobles who exploited their relationship to good effect. Clement V created five cardinals from among the Bordelais, Agenais and Bazadais nobility.[154] There were few families who did not benefit from the patronage of the Gascon pope and cardinals. Raymond de Durfort (d. 1341) became bishop of Périgueux, and Arnaud de Durfort (d. 1322) married a niece of Gaillard de Goth.[155] It has been calculated (by Professor Jacques Bernard) that of 10,500 bulls issued by Clement V, 2500 concerned south-west France: the diocese of Bazas received 130, Agen 180 and the archdiocese of Bordeaux 220 bulls. Clement's former bishopric of St Bertrand-de-Comminges benefited from over eighty citations and his collegiate foundations at Uzeste and Villandraut received fifteen bulls between them.[156] Bernard concluded that 'plus on se rapproche de la Gascogne proprement dite et du pays natal de Clément V, plus se multiplient les marques de faveur et d'affection'.[157] His ten brothers and sisters, and sixteen nephews and nieces, were especially generously treated, while Arnaud-Garcie de Goth, with his son Bertrand, emerged as the most favoured kinsmen. Arnaud-Garcie had been a very minor figure among the Gascon nobility before 1305, and served Edward I with a single man-at-arms during the Anglo-French war in Aquitaine in 1295–6.[158] His knighting by Philip the Fair, at Clement's request, and the grant to him and his son Bertrand of the lordships of Lomagne and Auvillars

---

[152] See below, pp. 146, 153–6.

[153] See above, pp. 91–2, 94–5, 96–7.

[154] Lizerand, *Clement V et Philippe le Bel*, p. 387; *Le Dossier de l'affaire des Templiers*, ed. G. Lizerand (Paris, 1964), pp. 86, 88. The five cardinals were Raymond de Goth, Raymond de Fargues, Arnaud de Canteloupe, Bernard de Jarre and Arnaud de Pellegrue. For Clement's admission of favours granted to those of 'insufficient merit' by him, which should be revoked, see *Regestum Clementis papae V*, no. 2263 (20 February 1307).

[155] *Documents sur la maison de Durfort*, i, pp. xxv, xxviii.

[156] Bernard, 'Le népotisme de Clément V', pp. 369–70, 375; Lizerand, *Clement V et Philippe le Bel*, pp. 380–1. His liberation of the archdiocese of Bordeaux from subjection to the jurisdiction of the archbishop of Bourges (1305–6) was also a measure which greatly enhanced its wealth and status. See J. de Bascher, 'La chronologie des visites pastorales de Simon de Beaulieu, archevêque de Bourges', *Revue d'Histoire de l'Eglise de France*, lvii (1972), pp. 73–89.

[157] Bernard, 'Le népotisme de Clément V', p. 374.

[158] E 101/152/8, no. 26; 154/12, no. 14. He received payments of his wages at York, Westminster and London (1 September 1302).

during the pope's visit to Lyon for his coronation in December 1305, lay at the root of Arnaud-Garcie's fortune and that of his children.[159] .

Not only did Arnaud-Garcie's sons enjoy papal patronage but the de Goth's rise to power and wealth meant that his daughters and grand-daughters were much in demand on the marriage market. Apart from the Armagnac and Durfort marriages, a third grand-daughter married the influential Sansaner de Pins, who acted as an intermediary with the papacy on behalf of the inhabitants of south-western dioceses such as Auch, Agen and Lectoure.[160] Connections were also established to the benefit of the Lamothe, Budos, Sauviac, Fargues and Preyssac families, all stemming from the Bordelais and Bazadais.[161] The degree of patronage enjoyed by these minor lords was reflected in their castle-building activities. Villandraut, Roquetaillade, Budos, Fargues, Blanquefort, Sauviac and La Trave represent the best concrete examples of Clement V's nepotism. Some of these are sophisticated strongholds, built between 1305 and 1320, taking account of residential as well as military needs.[162] Villandraut (begun in 1306) stands comparison with Caerphilly, Beaumaris and Harlech. The visible influence of Edward I's Welsh castles is clearly pronounced at both Villandraut (see plate 4.1) and the 'new' castle of Roquetaillade, constructed after 1316 by the lords of La Mothe after the elevation of one of their number to the College of Cardinals.[163] Although Roquetaillade still retains a keep, the great cylindrical drum towers, the elaborate gatehouses and extensive curtain walls of these fortresses show affinities with the work of Master James of St George, the Savoyard master-mason employed by Edward I.[164] The services of the Savoyard Grilly and Grandson families to the king-duke in Gascony may have reinforced, perhaps even transmitted, that influence. Master James is known to have been with Edward in Gascony between 1287 and 1289.[165] The heart of Jean de Grilly's son, Pierre, who predeceased his father between

[159] AN, JJ 38, fos 60[r–v] (14 December 1305), 61[r]–2[v] (20 December 1305); APA, E 269, nos 5, 11 (original letters of John de Havering, seneschal of Aquitaine, consenting to the grants in Edward I's name, at Bordeaux, 20 February 1306).

[160] Bernard, 'Le népotisme de Clément V', p. 388; Regestum Clementis papae V, no. 7454.

[161] Bernard, 'Le népotisme de Clément V', pp. 390–3. The Fargues did particularly well, supplying one cardinal and three bishops (of Narbonne, Agen and Toulouse). Their secular kinsmen profited as a result. See Gardelles, Les Châteaux, p. 134.

[162] See L. Drouyn, La Guienne militaire (Bordeaux and Paris, 1865), i, pp. 36–47 (Villandraut); 1–15 (Roquetaillade); ii, pp. 148–58 (Budos); 329–37 (Fargues); 44–68 (Blanquefort); i, pp. lv–lix (Sauviac); 95–102 (La Trave).

[163] Gardelles, Les Châteaux, pp. 71–2, 208–10; L. Cadis, Le Château de Villandraut (Paris, 1942), pp. 16–24; Bernard, 'Lé nepotisme de Clément V', pp. 390–1.

[164] The history of the King's Works, I. The Middle Ages, ed. R. A. Brown, H. M. Colvin and A. J. Taylor (London, 1963), pp. 203–5.

[165] A. J. Taylor, 'Master James of St George', in Studies in Castles and Castle-building (London, 1985), pp. 64–97, esp. p. 73; King's Works, i, p. 204; Trabut-Cussac, 'Itinéraire d'Edouard Ier en France, 1286–1289', BIHR, xxv (1952), pp. 160–203.

4.1 Castle of Villandraut. Begun by Pope Clement V in 1306, it has affinities with Edward I's Welsh castles and is the most elaborate of the fortresses built in Aquitaine by the pope's family.

1301 and 1303, was buried close to Clement V himself in the collegiate church at Uzeste. Jean had stated in his will (June 1303) that he wished his body to be buried, if he were to die in Gascony, 'next to the heart of our most dear son . . . Pierre, which is buried there'.[166] Pierre's tomb survives, with the Grilly arms, differenced by a label, on the effigy's shield. In the event Jean died, and was buried, in Savoy.

Papal favour thus gave certain lesser nobles of the Bordelais and Bazadais a privileged position which was bequeathed to subsequent generations of La Mothes, Montferrands, Grilly (or Grailly as they came to be known) and Durforts. A tangible architectural legacy was left by them and their kinsmen in the duchy. Clement V's cousin, Arnaud, cardinal of Auch, founded and built a collegiate church at La Romieu (Gers) between 1313 and 1318 which was decorated with wall-paintings depicting trumpeting and censer-swinging angels in which Italian influences can be detected.[167] Bertrand de Goth and his heirs decorated their castle at Veyrines, on the outskirts of Bordeaux,

---

[166] ATG, A 297, fo. 1060ᵛ; L. Gardeau and J.-P. Trabut-Cussac, 'Les premiers Grailly et la tombe de Pierre I de Grailly à Uzeste', *BPH* (1960), pp. 713–22, esp. p. 718.

[167] R. Mesuret, *Les Peintures murales du sud-ouest de la France du xiᵉ au xviᵉ siècle* (Paris, 1967), pp. 95–6.

with secular wall-paintings, while the interior decoration of Villandraut must once have been sumptuous.[168] The power and social ascent of the de Goth was reflected in all these enterprises. By October 1315 Bertrand de Goth, *vicomte* of Lomagne and Auvillars, evidently considered himself to be in a strong enough position to refuse a request from Edward II for a loan of 8000 *l.st.* He claimed, improbably, that his means were insufficient, and that he had already lent his available capital to Louis X of France while serving in the Flemish campaign of that year.[169] Like many *nouveaux venus*, his behaviour towards his own subjects and tenants was not exemplary. In 1310, it was reported that the men of Mézin and other places in the Gers would 'rather be subject to the devil' than to the *vicomte* of Lomagne and Auvillars.[170] But his heirs – notably the house of Armagnac – profited substantially from the accumulation of his great fortune and successfully survived the attacks launched by John XXII against Clement V's relatives and their descendants. Clement V had brought solvency not only to the Avignon papacy, leaving 1,040,000 florins in the papal treasury at his death, but to an important section of the Gascon nobility.[171]

In the redistribution of wealth which took place among Gascon nobles during the period 1280–1320, service to the Plantagenet king-dukes must also be accorded a central place. War, administration and diplomacy furnished opportunities to the middling and lesser nobility of the duchy whereby seigneurial incomes were bolstered. Wages for military service and *restaur* (compensation paid for lost horses) accounted for 53 per cent of Edward I's total expenditure on warfare in 1294–8.[172] Feudal services, as set out in the *Recogniciones feodorum* were quite inadequate to meet the king-duke's demands at times of crisis. The stipulated terms of service was often too short for any but the most fleeting of campaigns, for many nobles were bound to serve for a mere fifteen days, within strict territorial limits.[173] The Plantagenet regime thus raised military support by contract in Aquitaine. Stipendiary knights and esquires provided resident garrisons at the castles of Bourg, Blaye, Langoiran and in the many *castelnaux* of eastern Gascony.[174] Younger and bastard sons might garrison their kinsmens' castles, while lesser nobles served in the companies of greater men such as Albret, Foix or Armagnac.[175] There is, moreover, plentiful evidence for service to Edward I

---

[168] Gardelles, *Les Châteaux*, pp. 232, 234–5; Drouyn, *La Guienne militaire*, iii, pp. 313–18.

[169] SC 1/34, no. 111 (7 October 1315); *Foedera*, II, i, p. 259.

[170] E 30/1521, no. 12 (22 April 1310).

[171] Lizerand, *Clément V et Philippe le Bel*, p. 385–7.

[172] This figure is computed from the accounts in E 101/152–5 and E 372/160. See Appendix II.

[173] Brutails, 'Les fiefs du roi', pp. 76–7; *Recogniciones feodorum*, nos 27, 43.

[174] *RG*, iii, no. 4262; Higounet, 'La société nobiliaire', pp. 3–4; B. Cursente, *Les Castelnaux de la Gascogne médiévale* (Bordeaux, 1980), p. 108.

[175] Vale, 'Seigneurial fortification and private war', p. 137; cf. J. Heers, *Le Clan familial au Moyen Age* (Paris, 1974), p. 38.

4.2   One of the very few surviving effigies of a Gascon noble, dating from the late thirteenth or early fourteenth century. It may represent one of the lords of Sadirac. (Sadirac, *dép.* Gironde, château de Tustal.)

and Edward II in Wales and Scotland by Gascon nobles and their retinues from 1282 onwards. Amanieu de Fossat petitioned Edward II in 1318 for a grant of lands in the Agenais and offered his services to the king-duke in Scotland. He asked Edward: 'si par aventure vous mandez nulh homme de par desa pour aler en la terra Descosse ou alhors, mon tres chier Seigneur, encors vous suppliez humblement qe vous me degnetz feire tant doneur qe je, qi sui et serai de cuer joyious tout apparelhie, soie des primies mandez'.[176]

Amanieu was serving at Berwick with a company of Gascons soon afterwards and had been paid 1567 *l.* 13 *s.* 4 *d.* (*l.st.*) in wages by 1323–4.[177] In April and May 1322 Edward had appealed to his Gascon subjects for aid against the Scots, and 200 crossbowmen, with 200 foot soldiers armed with lances under the command of a lesser noble, Raymond de Miossens, were sent by sea to Newcastle upon Tyne.[178] Amanieu de Fossat and nine of his peers were also asked for aid, and in September Edward wrote to Arnaud-Guillaume de Marsan and five other lords thanking them for their offers of

---

[176] SC 1/34. no. 2, and for other examples from 1282 onwards see SC 1/20, no. 199 (1282); E 101/14/10, m. 2 (1297); SC 8/91, no. 14547 (1305); SC 8/285, no. 14239 (1312).

[177] E 372/183, m. 60.

[178] C 61/35, mm. 13, 15 (2 and 6 April 1322).

service against the Scots.[179] By January 1323, a circular letter was dispatched
to 202 Gascon nobles requesting military aid in a forthcoming Scots campaign *in instanti seisona estivali*.[180] But internal disturbances in Aquitaine,
which were to lead to the war of St Sardos, disrupted the king-duke's plan of
action.

It was nevertheless clear that their Gascon possessions offered the Plantagenets a reservoir of men who were both able and willing to serve them in
warfare. The Gascon nobility displayed none of the resistance to 'foreign'
service manifested by their English contemporaries.[181] But they demanded
payment and reward for their service as well as the honour of serving the
king-duke. In January 1316, for example, the nobles of the Agenais agreed to
serve Edward II in Scotland, but at his expense, claiming both wages and
restaur.[182] Some of their peers in the Bordelais and Bazadais asked for the
supply of equipment as well as wages, while others agreed to equip themselves at their own cost, but insisted that they 'should be given wages just as
the rest'.[183] These petty seigneurs were extremely dependent upon such
infusions of liquid capital into their coffers. In 1305, a kinsman of the lord of
Caupenne told Edward I that, during a truce in Aquitaine, the French had
burnt his houses and all his goods, including the documents relating to his
wages of war.[184] He asked that the 'rolls' be searched by the king-duke's
clerks so that payment might be made. John Sandale and Thomas of
Cambridge were accordingly ordered by Edward to 'search their books' and
to certify the amount which was owed to Caupenne. The financial position of
many lesser Gascon nobles was very similar to that found at this time among
other nobilities, such as those of Forez, Alsace or Lorraine.[185] Valuations of
the horses which they brought to war are revealing in this context. A muster
of nobles and their horses from the Landes, Labourt and Soule, dating from
1294–7, demonstrates that of 104 men, 69 brought horses of low value,
valued at 30 *l.t.* or less.[186] A later horse-list, probably drawn up in 1323,
shows that of 37 nobles from the Landes, 25 (including one knight) rode
horses valued at 25 *l.t.* while their richer neighbours possessed *destriers* or

---

[179] C 61/35. m. 15 (15 May 1322).

[180] C 61/35, m. 10 (30 January and 2 February 1323).

[181] See A. Tuck, *Crown and Nobility, 1272–1461* (London, 1985), pp. 35–7, 47–9, 118 for a
recent survey.

[182] *RG*, iv, p. 574. For Edward II's attempted use of his Gascon possessions as sources of
financial aid at this time, see E. A. R. Brown, 'Gascon subsidies and the finances of the English
dominions, 1315–24', in *Studies in Medieval and Renaissance History*, viii (1971), pp. 33–146.

[183] *RG*, iv, p. 574.

[184] SC 8/129, no. 14542.

[185] See E. Perroy, 'Social mobility among the French *noblesse* in the later Middle Ages', *PP*, xxi
(1962) pp. 228–9; M. Parisse, *La Noblesse lorraine, xie-xiiie siècles* (Lille and Paris, 1976),
pp. 354–78; H. Dubled, 'Noblesse et féodalité en Alsace du xie au xiiie siècle', *Tijdschrift voor
Rechtsgeschiednis*, xxviii (1960), pp. 129–80.

[186] E 101/14/4 (undated, headed: 'Rotulus Vasconie de equorum appreciatione').

chargers, worth 100–200 *l.t.*[187] The quality of many of these mounts could not have been high, and some nobles rode horses worth little more than rouncies or plough-horses. Noble penury and its implications is a theme to which we shall return.[188]

In later thirteenth-century France, the expenditure involved in equipping a knight and his immediate retinue was normally equivalent to between six and eight month's wages of war.[189] The cost of knighthood rose with the general inflation of military costs between 1290 and 1330, and many nobles were disinclined to accept its burdens. In south-west France a knight banneret's warhorse alone cost just over two and a half month's wages in 1316, while an esquire could expect to spend about one and a half month's wages on a horse valued at 25 *l.t.*[190] An annual income of at least 200 *l.t.* was the minimum laid down for the upkeep of a brood mare (*jument qui puisse porter faon*) with which to breed warhorses, by knights and *gentils* in Philip III of France's sumptuary *ordonnance* of 1279.[191] But an annual landed income of 200 *l.t.* was not within the grasp of many nobles, especially in the south-west. Unless they were beneficiaries of unforeseen events such as Clement V's election to the papacy, most Gascon petty seigneurs were increasingly forced to depend upon compensation for horses lost in war, and upon wages, pensions, fees, gifts and annuities from princes and greater magnates. Without access to the financial resources of greater lords, they would have been unable to maintain their noble estate. Just as the Church harboured a mass of unordained clerks, so the nobility embraced a large number of *hobéreaux* and rural squires who were quite unable to afford the expenses of knighthood and soldiering without subsidy from richer and more powerful lords. The lifeline at which the Gascon *noblesse* clutched to retain their nobility was not trade, nor the law, but paid service, recompense and plunder in the wars of princes and greater magnates. When the Plantagenets and Capetians were not at war, the opportunities presented by border raids and private wars were eagerly grasped. For the greater part of the period which is our concern, private war, with its skirmishes, mêlées, raids (*cavalcata*), ambushes, arson, cattle-theft and casual brigandage was a dominant characteristic of 'living nobly'. As the following section will attempt to suggest, it was a hallmark of a frontier or marcher society. What made it particularly dangerous in Gascony was the extent to which higher authorities became inextricably involved in the feuds and quarrels of the nobility, so that essentially local conflicts could erupt into more general war. Unless their

---

[187] E 101/17/38 (undated, headed: 'Appreciatio equorum militum Vasconie apud Aques, Sanctum Severium et Bonegarde', probably drawn up between 9 and 24 November 1323).

[188] See below, pp. 116–17, 150–1.

[189] See P. Contamine, *La Guerre au Moyen Age* (Paris, 1980), p. 198.

[190] *RG*, iv, p. 574; Vale, 'Warfare and the life of the nobility', pp. 178–9.

[191] H. Duplès-Agier, 'Ordonnance somptuaire de Philippe le Hardi (1279)', *BEC*, xv (1854), p. 180.

acquisitive demands were met and their quarrels effectively arbitrated, the structure, economic position and political behaviour of the Gascon nobility were not conducive to Anglo-French peace.

4.2   Private War

There was little doubt in contemporary minds that the nobility's assumed right to wage war among themselves contributed substantially to the turbulence of Gascon society. They were not unique in this respect among the nobility of thirteenth- and early fourteenth-century France. Philippe de Beaumanoir was quite clear that 'gentil homme puissent guerroier selonc nostre coustume' in the Beauvaisis, but he was careful to set out the limitations imposed by public justice on the exercise of the *droit de guerre*, that is the right to wage private war.[192] In Gascony, however, private possession of public authority and the very tardy development of Capetian jurisdiction often gave the impression of an unlimited use of the *droit de guerre* and *port d'armes* (carrying of arms against enemies) in the south-west. The Angevin Amaury de Craon, seneschal of Aquitaine, told Edward II in a letter written at Bazas in October 1313 that his Gascon subjects were 'men who neither know nor fear justice', that they needed the rule of law in times past and at the present.[193] He was supported in this view by Pope John XXII, who exhorted Amaury's successor, Fulk Lestrange, lord of Whitchurch (Shropshire) in August 1322 to intervene between warring nobles who were indulging in violence 'as if deprived of a superior lord' (*quasi superiori carentes*).[194] Lestrange's appointment had to some extent been a response by Edward II to previous papal criticism, since John XXII had told him in June 1318 that his duchy of Aquitaine was a place 'where . . . justice is banished, and [the duchy] remains almost without law and without a king'.[195] The pope maintained that the Gascon nobility were responsible for waging private wars in which ecclesiastical persons – such as his legate – and property were attacked, and the appointment of a God-fearing and peace-loving representative of ducal authority was imperative.

Popes might fulminate, kings and magnates might legislate, but the control of private war among the nobility was an exceptionally difficult task at this time. Professor Raymond Cazelles has shown that the Capetian and early Valois ordinances in restraint of private war contained only one coherent and reiterated point: the prohibition of such conflicts when the king

---

[192] Philippe de Rémi, sire de Beaumanoir, *Coutumes de Beauvaisis*, ed. A. Salmon (Paris, 1900, repr. 1970), ii, 1673 (p. 357); and pp. 354–65 for the nobility's right to wage private war in the Beauvaisis.

[193] SC 1/33, no. 115 (2 October 1313).

[194] 'Documents pontificaux', no. 203 (29 August 1322).

[195] 'Documents pontificaux', no. 77 (26 June 1318).

himself was at war.[196] St Louis had tried to prevent them in 1258; Philip the Fair repeated the terms of his saintly predecessor's ordinance in January 1304 when he prohibited all 'wars, homicides, burning of towns or houses, attacks and assaults on fields or ploughs . . . challenges to duels and *gages de bataille* during our wars'.[197] The uncompromising stance adopted at this juncture was soon abandoned: in 1306, trials by combat and duels were again authorized by the king, and in April 1315 Louis X was forced to permit the nobles of Burgundy and Forez to exercise their ancient right whereby they 'puissent et doient user des armes, quant leur pleira et que il puissent guerroier et contregagier'.[198] In February 1339, in a bid for the support of Bernard-Ezi V, lord of Albret, Philip VI confirmed the ancient right of the Gascon nobility to 'declare, pursue and continue' private wars at will after due defiance and serving of notice. The French crown's efforts to exercise some degree of control over private war among provincial nobilities were therefore not glitteringly successful.[199] Ancient unwritten usage proved exceedingly resistant to royal initiatives of this kind.

A long-standing tradition of private war among Gascon nobles stood in the way of any superior authority in its attempts to reduce the duchy of Aquitaine and its neighbouring territories to order. In the disturbed conditions of the 1390s, for example, the right to make war was still publicly defended before the Paris Parlement by Géraud, count of Pardiac, who asserted that 'il loist aux nobles du pays faire guerre les ungs contre les autres, *rege inconsulto*', and in December 1395 it was argued that 'en Gascongne nest point defendu a faire guerre, et s'il nest loisible, toutes fois on en a ainsi usé au pais sans en estre reprins'.[200] Bernard VII, count of Armagnac, told Charles VI that he had exercised the right to make war and defend himself against the count of Pardiac in 1402 because 'les barons de Guienne aient privilege ancien de vos predecessours rois de France de faire guerre l'un a lautre et en aient usé par moult longtemps'.[201] The issue had been debated at some length almost a century earlier, when Edward II's representatives at Paris had complained that, far from acting as impartial judges in such quarrels, Capetian officers had encouraged frivolous appellants to defend themselves by force against ducal officers.[202] This had simply exacerbated

---

[196] R. Cazelles, 'La règlementation royale de la guerre privée de St Louis à Charles V et la precarité des ordonnances', *RHDFE*, xxxviii (1960), p. 545.

[197] *Ordonnances des rois de France de la troisième race*, ed. E. J. de Laurière, i, 390–2; Cazelles, 'La règlementation royale', pp. 539–50.

[198] *Ordonnances*, i, p. 559.

[199] *Ordonnances*, ii, pp. 61–3; Cazelles, 'La règlementation royale', pp. 532–8; APA, E 30, nos 4, 17.

[200] P. Durrieu, 'Documents relatifs à la chute de la maison Armagnac-Fézensaguet et la mort du comte de Pardiac', *Archives Historiques de la Gascogne* (1883), pp. 12, 19.

[201] Durrieu, 'Documents relatifs', p. 83.

[202] SC 1/29, no. 196 (23 May(?) 1311); cf. AN, J 654, no. 24 (undated petition of Edward II to Philip the Fair).

the problems of private war and self-help against private enemies. Homicide, arson, mustering of armed forces, besieging of castles, depopulation and wasting of the *pays* had followed. Recourse to violence was in no way mitigated by such partisan behaviour.

A revealing English conciliar memorandum and draft report of a discussion relating to the issue of private wars in Aquitaine has survived. Addressed to 'reverendissime patre', the document was said to have been drawn up at the instigation of John, bishop of Ely, probably in November 1323.[203] The memorandum referred to the many private wars in Aquitaine which had moved Charles IV of France to attempt to prohibit them. None of the participants in these quarrels had replied to the king's inquiry, except one, who told him that 'he was from Gascony where wars may be waged according to the *fors* and customs of the land' and 'that they [the Gascon nobility] possessed the right to do so'.[204] Their immediate lord, the king-duke of Aquitaine, was bound to observe those customs and the respondent opined that he could not believe that Charles IV would wish to contravene them by forbidding private war. But Edward II's council understood that Charles had replied in person, prohibiting the usage, outside the 'chamber of pleas in the king's chamber' at Paris, but had not summoned the king-duke's proctors. Edward's council and the French were, however, agreed that such customs and usages should be suppressed and their validity denied. Two courses of action were proposed: either Charles should be asked to prohibit private wars in Aquitaine, or he should declare such laws and customs to be perverse (*corruptelas*) and revoke them. In both cases the upshot would be similarly damaging to Edward II's authority as duke of Aquitaine. It was Edward's prerogative to prohibit private war as immediate lord, for his rights and fame (*gloriam*) would be appropriated if Charles IV was to legislate in this way. Secondly, if the French crown was allowed to revoke these evil customs, such exercise of sovereign authority could only lead to further interventions in minor cases of wounding and of bearing arms in the duchy. Hence the French would enjoy many ways of entering the duchy and undermining ducal authority. We do not know the reaction of Edward II and his counsellors to the issues raised by this draft memorandum. But it indicates an additional obstacle to the adjudication and settlement of feuds in the duchy: the conflict of jurisdiction between sovereign and immediate lord.[205]

Insecurity inevitably produced a concern for defence among both nobles and townsmen in the duchy. The proliferation of seigneurial castles has already been noted. By 1337, there were probably about 1000 castles and

---

[203] C 47/29/9, no. 6. John Hotham, bishop of Ely, returned to England from his mission as Edward II's special envoy to Gascony on 15 November 1323 (*St Sardos*, p. 5, n. 2).

[204] C 47/29/9, no. 6. The words may have been those of Jourdain de L'Isle. See *Confessions et jugements de criminels au Parlement de Paris*, ed. M. Langlois and Y. Lanhers (Paris, 1971), p. 39.

[205] See above, pp. 69–70, 78–9.

maisons-fortes in Gascony, if the frontier zone of the Agenais and the *vicomté* of Béarn are included.[206] In the Agenais, where licences from a superior lord to fortify were not customarily required, the number of fortifications had risen dramatically from 80 in 1259 to 130 by 1327.[207] The period of greatest proliferation ran from *c.*1290 to 1337, when castles and other fortifications were created on a scale comparable with that of castle-building in Wales and the Marches after 1282.[208] Gascon castles were concentrated not only on the frontiers of the Plantagenet duchy of Aquitaine – in the Agenais, on the edge of the forest of Périgord and on the borders of Quercy, Marsan and Béarn – but also in the more fertile regions of the duchy. Water supply was crucial, and the relative dearth of castles in the Landes was offset by their high density in the river valleys between the Midouze, the Adour, the Gave de Pau and the Pyrenees. By the outbreak of the Hundred Years War, therefore, Gascony was studded with forts, not only on its borders, but throughout the 'mosaic of frontiers' within the duchy of Aquitaine.[209] The evidence suggests that there was little new castle-building after 1340 because there was no need for it. Adaptation of existing structures to meet new developments in siege-craft and artillery became common, and it cannot be argued that the Hundred Years War had any appreciable impact upon the network of seigneurial fortifications which already covered the region.

The very fact of such proliferation suggests a generally unrestricted use of the power to fortify by middling and lesser nobles. In some areas, such as the Agenais, Astarac, Pardiac and Fézensac, licences to fortify were not required.[210] Despite the attempts made by Edward I, as duke of Aquitaine, to exercise a stricter control over the licensing of fortifications (as did the *vicomtes* of Béarn), there was little that a higher authority could do to prevent the erection of seigneurial castles and *maisons-fortes*.[211] Short of outright demolition, it was extremely difficult for effective sanctions to be taken against contumacious and disaffected vassals who might use their private fortresses to good effect against other lords. But it would be something of a distortion of the Gascon evidence to assert, as had been argued for England, that the granting of licences to fortify was merely 'honorific', automatically obtained and largely meaningless.[212] The surrender clauses, or stipulations

---

[206] Gardelles, *Les Châteaux*, p. 13. There were approximately ninety castles in the Welsh March during the fourteenth century: R. R. Davies, *Lordship and Society in the March of Wales, 1282–1400* (Oxford, 1978), p. 71.

[207] Gardelles, *Les Châteaux*, pp. 18, 32 and Map IX.

[208] Davies, *Lordship and Society*, pp. 70–4; Gardelles, *Les Châteaux*, pp. 13–19.

[209] J.-P. Trabut-Cussac, 'Bastides ou forteresses', *MA*, lx (1954), p. 122. See Appendix III, Map 1.

[210] Cursente, *Les Castelnaux*, p. 31; Gardelles, *Les Châteaux*, pp. 18, 32.

[211] Trabut-Cussac, *L'Administration anglaise*, pp. 212–18; Gardelles, *Les Châteaux*, pp. 23, 31–2.

[212] C. Coulson, 'Structural symbolism in medieval castle architecture', *Journal of the British Archaeological Association*, cxxxii (1979), pp. 78–81; 'Rendability and castellation in medieval France', *Château Gaillard. Etudes de castellogie médiévale*, vi (1972), pp. 59–67.

about 'rendability' upon demand which they contain, deserve to be taken very seriously in this contested area. In 1294, for example, Piers Gaveston's brother, Arnaud-Guillaume de Marsan, temporarily handed over his castle of Roquefort to Edward I's lieutenants, with its garrison of seven men-at-arms and thirty foot-serjeants, on the outbreak of 'public' war between England and France. He then went to serve the Plantagenet cause with distinction during the war with Philip the Fair at St Sever, leaving his castle in the hands of a captain appointed by the Plantagenet administration.[213] In 1318, Raymond-Bernard de Montpezat was ordered to surrender the castle of Montpezat to the seneschal of the Agenais as a punishment for his seizure of the seneschal's serjeants during a raid which he had conducted from that castle. He refused to hand over the keys and was declared a rebel.[214] Similarly, in 1333, Pierre de Grailly, *vicomte* of Bénauges and Castillon, openly resisted an order to surrender his castle of Ste-Bazeille.[215] In some cases, demolition ensued. Amanieu de Fossat, lord of Madaillan, witnessed the partial destruction of his castle in 1327, but was permitted to rebuild it by Edward III in 1331.[216] The 'new castle' of Madaillan, once thought to be a product of the early stages of the Hundred Years War, was in fact an example of the effects of direct action by a higher authority against seigneurial independence.

Among the middle and lesser nobility, some claimed the right to fortify without licence from a superior lord. Those who styled themselves 'baron' certainly did so, and clearly possessed the means to build stone fortresses rather than earthworks with readily inflammable timber palissades.[217] In 1312, Guillaume–Ayquem, lord and baron of Lesparre in the Médoc, claimed that he had spent the very large sum of 10,000 *l.t.* on fortifying his castle there against John Ferrers, seneschal of Gascony (see plate 4.3). The surviving keep at Lesparre probably dates from this period.[218] Although the sums spent by the lords of Albret, the *vicomtes* of Béarn and the counts of Armagnac no doubt exceeded that figure many times over, fortification could certainly absorb a considerable proportion of petty seigneurial income. In 1289, for example, a marriage contract between Isabella, daughter of Alexandre de la Pebrée, knight, and Assaride de Turenne, lady of Aguérac and Gensac (on one side), and Anessans de Caumont, knight (on the other), included the provision of a sum of 300 *l.t.* in Isabelle's dowry for the construction of a *maison-forte* within one of five parishes around Gensac.[219]

---

[213] SC 1/19, no. 103; *RG*, iii, no. 4248 (18 May 1296).

[214] C 47/25/2, no. 24; *St Sardos*, pp. 30–4.

[215] APA, E 18, fos 44^{r-v} (20 July 1333).

[216] SC 8/285, no. 14210; Gardelles, *Les Châteaux*, p. 169; SC 8/284, no. 14152 for a petition from Raymond-Bernard de Marmande to rebuild two castles (*c.*1330).

[217] Coulson, 'Structural symbolism', p. 78, n. 17; and see above nn. 201, 203.

[218] *Olim*, iii, pp. 814–15; APA, E 20, no. 9, mm. 3, 4 (June 1312); Gardelles, *Les Châteaux*, p. 165, figures 88–90. See also plate 4.3.

[219] APA, E 19, no. 15 (6 June 1289); *RG*, ii, no. 1239.

4.3 Keep of the castle at Lesparre (Médoc). This stronghold was among the most important seigneurial fortresses of the region and the keep was rebuilt by Guillaume-Ayquem, lord of Lesparre, after the Anglo-French war of 1294–1303.

Her dowry was fixed at 1000 *l.t.*: 300 *l.t.* would have represented the annual landed income of a noble in the 1290s.

The importance of self-defence against traditional enemies and violent neighbours led both nobles and bourgeois to provide for this need, even in their wills. In his will, made at Bayonne as he lay dying on 15 May 1296, Bertrand de Podensac stipulated that his new parish church at Podensac should be built in such a way that a crossbow bolt could not be shot from it into his castle there.[220] In the aftermath of the Anglo-French war of 1294–8, which had led to violations of rights and the prosecution of private feuds in the disturbed conditions accompanying public war, men such as Bernard de Vignoles, knight, requested licences to fortify from Edward I. Bernard's fears of the lord of Navailles, who had killed his father, and of the lord of Mauléon, induced him to petition for a licence to fortify his *domus* at Vignoles, 'aussi forte cum jeo pourrai'.[221] He was permitted to build a *maison-forte* in 1305 'as shall seem expedient to him', but was to surrender it to the seneschal of

[220] *Trésor des Chartes d'Albret*, i, no. 52 (p. 79).
[221] SC 8/291, no. 14547; *RG*, iii, nos 4684, 4894; SC 8/285, no. 14239. In July 1331, Edward III granted six licences to fortify to Gascons (C 61/43, m. 11).

Aquitaine on demand. Towns were also very vulnerable to the attacks of private enemies and felt the effects of noble feuding directly. It was ordained at Lectoure in 1294 that if there was private war between nobles who held fortresses and towers within the town, they were to be surrendered to the council and *prud'hommes* of the town until peace was made.[222] This was clearly an attempt to prevent quarrels between nobles in the surrounding country-side from spilling over and causing disorder in the town. Conditions were particularly difficult in towns which lay on the frontiers between lordships. The inhabitants of the *bastide* of Hastingues told Edward II that their town was situated in the 'worst march of the duchy', between the lordships of Navarre, Béarn, Albret and Gramont, where 'le plus graunt partie dous bandiz de la duchie de Guienne fuyent et habitent e dilloques enfors guerreyen et dampnagen mout grevement les genz de la dicte basti[d]e pour ceo qe il les deffendent le frontere'.[223]

At Miramont in 1323, St Luc-de-Bigorre in 1326 (on the frontiers of Astarac, Armagnac and Comminges), Terraube in 1308 and Villeneuve-sur-Lot in 1313, petitions for subsidies to fortify and enclose the town were accompanied by similar justifications.[224] At Villeneuve, the consuls told Edward II that their town was 'exposed and enfeebled through lack of an enclosure, and it is sited amongst powerful and ill-disposed [*maliciosos*] neighbours who frequently provoke wars and do not shrink from committing various evil deeds'.[225] Normally the king-duke agreed to provide fortified gates for a town, while the inhabitants enclosed the rest at their own expense. Allowing for the usual exaggeration of petitioners, the evidence points to a level of insecurity determined largely by local feuds and raids demanding a degree of fortification comparable with that found on the Welsh and Scottish Marches.[226]

The study of feuds, vendettas and private vengeance has been undertaken by social anthropologists as well as historians. Apart from some helpful conceptual generalizations, the use of anthropological methods and assumptions is often limited by fundamental differences between the societies studied by anthropologists and historians. Most anthropological work has been devoted to tribally organized lineage societies, rather than kindred based, bilateral societies and direct comparisons between peoples such as the Nuer or Ashanti and the counts of Foix and Armagnac are more likely to distort

---

[222] Monlezun, *Histoire de Gascogne*, vi, p. 79. A parallel with the Italian communes of this period would not be inappropriate.

[223] SC 8/290, no. 14482; for subsequent grants by Edward II and III to Hastingues, see C 61/35, m. 19 (October–November 1321); 40, m. 6 (May 1328); 43, m. 4 (1331); 44, m. 4 (1332).

[224] C 61/35, m. 15 (27 May 1323, Miramont); AN, JJ 64, fo. 104ᵛ (June 1326, St Luc-de-Bigorre); Montlezun, *Histoire de Gascogne*, vi, pp. 266–69 (Terraube, September 1308); *RG*, iv, nos 1030, 1094 (Villeneuve-sur-Lot, June 1313).

[225] *RG*, iv, no. 1030 (29 June 1313).

[226] See, for example, Davies, *Lordship and Society*, pp. 70–6.

than illuminate.[227] But feuding societies often displayed common features – conflicting interests aggravated by physical proximity and inability to move elsewhere; the importance of wounded honour and pride; and the pre-eminent role of arbitration in the settlement and conclusion of feuds. As Charles Petit-Dutaillis pointed out long ago, the *droit de vengeance* was 'une des premières formes organisées de la justice' and took the form of the *Fehde* (licensed private war) in Germany, or the *faide* in the Low Countries during the Middle Ages.[228] Most feuding societies developed means of preventing anarchical behaviour and restraining the parties involved, but the role of public authority varied greatly from region to region. In south-west France, arbitrations, local truces and intervention by superior powers were all deployed, often simultaneously, to halt the violence and reconcile the participants. There was clearly a less crucial part for the extended kin-group to play in these transactions at that time, and a multiplicity of influences operated to exert pressure on the warring groups to reach a settlement. In other words, political and institutional pressures played as significant a part in the course and conclusion of feuds as those stemming from the social and familial structure of kin-groups. The early medieval practice of involving the whole lineage in the operation of the *droit de vengeance* had given way to independent arbitration or adjudication by higher authorities.[229]

Although the *droit de guerre* in south-west France was claimed as an unwritten right, which was not embodied in any formal code, its exercise was so common and customary that formal procedures had been developed to regulate its use and limit its worst excesses. Defiances and challenges appear to have been verbal, conveyed by word of mouth rather than by written instrument, although *lettres de défi* may simply not have survived from this period.[230] We know far more about attempts to resolve disputes by means of arbitration or mediation than about the manner in which they had begun. Notarially attested instruments, papal letters, financial accounts, occasional memoranda and casual references in correspondence form the surviving sources for private war. With the single exception of the vernacular chron-

---

[227] See J. Black-Michaud, *Feuding Societies* (Oxford, 1975), p. xxix; cf. E. E. Evans-Pritchard, *Essays in Social Anthropology* (London, 1962), p. 59; and the essay on 'The peace in the feud' in M. Gluckman, *Custom and Conflict in Africa* (Oxford, 1965), pp. 1–26. For an excellent recent study of compromise and arbitration in the fourteenth century see J. Rogozinski, *Power, Caste and Law. Social Conflict in Fourteenth-century Montpellier* (Cambridge, Mass., 1982), pp. 95–113.

[228] C. Petit-Dutaillis, *Documents nouveaux sur les moeurs populaires et le droit de vengeance dans les Pays-Bas au xve siècle* (Paris, 1908), p. 43.

[229] M. Fourgous, *L'Arbitrage dans le droit français aux xiiie et xive siècles* (Paris, 1906); Petit-Dutaillis, *Documents nouveaux*, pp. 43–4; Black-Michaud, pp. 41–103 for arbitration among the Bedouins, Berbers and Albanians.

[230] For formal letters of defiance see J. Glénisson, 'Notes d'histoire militaire. Quelques lettres de défi du xive siècle', *BEC*, cvii (1947–8), pp. 235–54 drawing upon Italian sources; *Recueil des actes de Jean IV, duc de Bretagne, I, 1357–82*, ed. M. Jones (Paris, 1980), no. 225 (August 1373) for a letter of defiance sent by Jean IV of Brittany to Charles V.

icles of the counts of Foix there are no narrative sources which contain more than the barest and most laconic of references to these feuds.[231] Our picture has to be pieced together from archival and documentary remains and resembles a jigsaw from which many pieces are missing. Yet the very existence of notarial instruments, normally drawn up at the request of both parties to a dispute and agreed by them, means that this fragmented impression is more likely to reflect the actual course of events than a chronicler's inaccurate, biased and sometimes mendacious account.[232] Notarial narrative is generally to be preferred to the imaginative recreation of past events by near-contemporaries.

There were two main sources of arbitration and mediation which could be drawn upon at this period: first, the pope and cardinals; secondly, secular lords, whether sovereign princes or not. There is very little surviving evidence for mediation in cases of private war by secular nobles who were not acting as representatives of a higher authority. An exception was the appointment of Garcie-Arnaud, lord of Séailles, knight, as *arbitrator seu amicabilis compositor* of a dispute between Arnaud-Guillaume, count of Pardiac, and certain nobles of his *comté* in January 1322.[233] The arbitration was awarded in the parish church of Marciac and a penalty of 2000 *l.t.* imposed for its non-observance, but neither Arnaud-Guillaume of Pardiac nor his son were present at this proclamation of 'perpetual peace'. That it may not have been very effective is suggested by a pardon and remission granted by Charles IV of France's lieutenant to Pardiac and his sons in September 1326.[234] They were pardoned for waging private and illicit war against another noble, Gentille de Montesquieu, but the quarrel had been settled by the seneschal of Toulouse. The king's lieutenant therefore remitted all penalties imposed upon them in the expectation that they would serve Charles IV faithfully in the war of St Sardos. A fundamental drawback to the appointment of neighbouring lords as independent arbitrators in conflicts of this kind was not only their susceptibility to pressure and influence, but their inability to impose effective sanctions and enforceable penalties upon the participants in

---

[231] See H. Courteault, 'Un archiviste des comtes de Foix au xve siècle. Le chroniqueur Michel du Bernis', *AM*, vi (1894), pp. 281–300; C. Samaran, 'Un texte historiographe à retrouver: les chroniques de la maison d'Armagnac (xive siècle)', in *Recueil . . . Clovis Brunel*, ii (Paris, 1955), pp. 501–6.

[232] See A. Gouron, 'Les archives notariales des anciens pays de droit écrit au moyen age', *Recueil de mémoires et travaux par la société d'histoire du droit et des institutions des anciens pays de droit écrit*, v (1966), pp. 47–60; R. Aubenas, 'Documents notariés provencaux du xiiie siècle', *Annales de la faculté de droit d'Aix*, xxv (1935), pp. 82–90.

[233] Montlezun, *Histoire de Gascogne*, vi, pp. 49–53. For the use of this formula from canon law, see K. Bader, 'Arbiter, arbitrator et amicabilis compositor: Zur Verbreitung einer kanonistischen Formel in Gebieten nördlich der Alpen', *Zeitschrift der Savigny Stiftung für Rechtesgeschichte, Kanonistische-Abteilung*, xlvi (1960), pp. 239–76; K.-H. Ziegler, 'Arbiter, arbitrator und amicabilis compositor', *Zeitschrift der Savigny Stiftung, Romanische Abteilung*, lxxxiv (1976), pp. 366–81.

[234] AN, JJ 66, fos 9^{r-v} (at Puyguilhem, 17 September 1326).

a feud. Hence the increasingly frequent appearance of popes, sovereigns and immediate lords (or their representatives) in the mediation and settlement of conflicts which could all too readily escalate into 'public' wars embroiling two of the greatest powers in western Christendom.[235]

Boniface VIII, Clement V and John XXII were all concerned to prevent such escalations. John XXII's interventions were especially direct, and he set out the principle of papal mediation on numerous occasions. In 1318 he insisted on the papal right to impose truces upon kings and their subjects, much in the manner of Boniface VIII's assertions of his duty to interfere in the affairs of secular rulers *ratione peccati* ('by reason of sin').[236] He reiterated the words of his predecessor, John XXI, in 1277 when he claimed that he was doing no more than any bishop was entitled to do in his diocese, and had no wish to prejudice the rights either of Philip V or Edward II.[237] There was nothing novel or unprecedented about this behaviour, because Clement V had imposed truces upon Foix, Armagnac and other nobles; John XXII himself had already stopped the wars between Amanieu VII d'Albret and Sansaner de Pins in 1316–17; between Béraud de Mercoeur and Hugues de Châlon; and between certain nobles of the Mâconnais. John XXI had imposed truces upon Philip III of France and the kings of Castile and Léon. Neither Philip V nor Edward II had shown themselves able, or even inclined, to bring Foix and Armagnac to heel, so the pope felt himself bound to intervene.[238] Papal legates were therefore busily occupied in Aquitaine throughout this period. But they themselves, given their southern French origins, could be caught up and implicated in local quarrels. In June 1318, the pope's 'angel of peace' Isnard de Montaut, sent to reconcile the warring houses of Foix and Armagnac, was assaulted at Valence d'Agen by the accomplices of Master Pierre de Galician, canon of Agen.[239] Isnard was guardian of the Franciscans at Agen and Pierre de Galician's attack must have been prompted by personal hostility. The legate and his company had been refused hospitality at Valence and he had excommunicated a chaplain there for his refusal. The local *bailli* supported the malefactors, who had dragged the legate and his companions from their horses, pillaged their belongings and stolen the pope's letters. Edward II's seneschal of Aquitaine had done nothing to prevent this nor to bring the offenders to justice and the pope inveighed against this flagrant breach of safe-conducts accorded to all papal legates and nuncios.[240] But it was not always possible to guarantee their security when they themselves were Gascons already embroiled in the conflicts of the region and

---

[235] See 'Documents pontificaux', no. 77 and pp. lxx–lxxi, lxxv–lxxvi.

[236] 'Documents pontificaux', no. 67, pp. 100–3 (11 September 1318).

[237] For John XXI's letters imposing truces, see *Les Registres de Grégoire X (1272–76) . . . suivis du Registre de Jean XXI (1276–77)*, ed. J. Guiraud and L. Cadier (Paris, 1898), nos 157–8.

[238] 'Documents pontificaux', no. 67, and cf. no. 43 (15 June 1318).

[239] 'Documents pontificaux', no. 50 (19 June 1318).

[240] 'Documents pontificaux', nos 51, 53 (19 and 26 June 1318).

in the faction-fighting of the papal household. Pierre de Galician had formerly been proctor to Bertrand de Goth and had no reason to respect the immunity of John XXII's familiars.[241] The pope in turn had no coercive power other than the over-used and consequently blunted weapon of excommunication.

Secular rulers could employ more effective sanctions if they were so minded. As we have seen, the Plantagenets and their advisers took the view that it was the responsibility and prerogative of an immediate lord to assert his rights over the regulation and adjudication of private wars.[242] As most of the Gascon nobility stood in some kind of dependent or subordinate relationship towards the king-duke it was therefore incumbent upon him to intervene in their quarrels. Thus on 25 July 1303 Henry Lacy, earl of Lincoln, lieutenant of Edward I in Aquitaine, sat in the abbey cloister at St Sever to arbitrate a private war between Bertrand, lord of La Mothe, and Auger de Poudenx on one side, and Arnaud de Marsan, lord of Cauna, and his brother Arnaud-Raymond, on the other.[243] Lacy was acting as *arbitrator vel amicabilis compositor* of the quarrel. All parties agreed to pay a penalty of 3000 silver marks to Edward I if Lacy's arbitration was not observed by any one of them. The seneschal of Gascony was to levy the fine and to compell payment. In the event Lacy ordered the warring groups of *valedors et adherens* to make 'perpetual peace', and the kiss of peace was bestowed by the major protagonists accompanied by an oath on the Gospels. The witness-list was long and impressive.[244] The fact that the agreement was confirmed in 1315 and 1323 suggests that the parties (and their heirs) had to be reminded of its terms. Henry Lacy had acted in this instance not as king-duke's lieutenant in Aquitaine but as an impartial arbitrator freely chosen by both parties to the dispute. Yet his ruling was made effective by the authority of the king-duke's officer – John de Hastings, seneschal of Gascony, who witnessed the agreement – to impose and levy a fine for breach of its terms.

Independent judgement was thus more likely to be given, and accepted, by ducal officers of a status and authority which might command respect. It was thought that foreigners – English or Anglo-French – were better suited to this task than Gascons. In *c.*1310, a report to Edward II on the lawlessness of Aquitaine contained the advice that the seneschals of Gascony, Agenais, Périgord and Saintonge should be 'powerful and noble persons from [England] and should be sent to the duchy immediately'.[245] The duchy, especially

---

[241] *RG*, iv, p. xxix. He was a king's clerk of Edward II, and was appointed treasurer of the Agenais in August 1316 (*RG*, iv, no. 1693).

[242] See above, pp. 113–14.

[243] ADG, I 2248 (Marsan) (25 July 1303), confirmed on 8 April 1315 and 11 August 1323. For a comparable form of arbitration at Montpellier in 1331, see Rogozinski, *Power, Caste and Law*, pp. 97–8, 103–4.

[244] ADG, I 2248: witnesses included John de Hastings, seneschal of Gascony, Amanieu VII d'Albret, Fortaner de Lescun, Arnaud de Caupenne and Barrau de Sescas.

[245] E 30/1557 (*c.*1310).

the Agenais, was said to be in a poor condition 'because of the wars amongst the barons and the robbers, murderers and footpads who . . . are harboured and even sustained by the barons'.[246] Gascon lieutenants of the seneschals, it was argued, did not enjoy the dignity and status which would help to make them obeyed. When a seneschal did pronounce a judgement, however, his ruling could be countermanded by the king-duke as a result of petitions from those who claimed to have been wronged or victimized. Thus in October 1315 a condemnation by Amaury de Craon, allegedly pronounced 'contrary to the *fors* and customs' of the Landes, was to be submitted on Edward II's order to scrutiny by his Gascon council.[247] Arnaud-Guillaume de Casaux, lord of St Martin, and his accomplices had been fined 700 *l.t.* by the seneschal and their lands and possessions had been declared forfeit for a private war against the *vicomte* of Marensin. They had protested to the king-duke, who seems to have been over-suspicious of his own officers. Even without such hindrances the most vigilant and assiduous of seneschals found it difficult to enforce their own edicts. Part of the responsibility must lie with Edward II's frequent changes of seneschal at this time. But the successive assaults by the count of Armagnac's men between 1317 and 1318 against the castle of Bachen and other possessions of Pierre, lord of Castelnau-en-Tursan, despite prohibitions and truces imposed by two successive seneschals, demonstrated how difficult it could be to curb the aggressive behaviour of a great noble, his vassals, *alliés* and clients.[248]

Occasionally the only remedy for such turbulence was felt by the seneschal of Gascony and his council at Bordeaux to lie in punitive expeditions against warring nobles. As we shall see, this was attempted with varying degrees of success in 1305, 1312 and 1323.[249] Fulk Lestrange, seneschal from 1318 to 1323, adopted tough and intransigent measures, and was congratulated by John XXII on his strenuous efforts to restore peace in the duchy.[250] He spent 6995 *l.* 12 *s.* 11 *d.b.* on the wages of an army raised in April and May 1323 to put down private war in Marsan.[251] A siege engine was used to good effect against the rebels during the expedition.[252] Force was countered by force and in some instances order was restored. But the consequences could be damaging to those who assisted the seneschals in their task. Vidal de Poudenx, esquire, had served Lestrange in arms between 1318 and 1323 and had been involved in clashes between the seneschal's forces and those of both Albret

[246] E 30/1557: the need for urgency was stressed, because the insecurity of the roads prevented merchants and bourgeois from venturing out upon them.

[247] *RG*, iv, nos 1467, 1474 (12 and 14 October 1315).

[248] SC 8/284, no. 14517: ADG, E 476 (Castelnau); Gardelles, *Les Châteaux*, p. 89.

[249] See below, pp. 131–9, 167–72, 230–2.

[250] 'Documents pontificaux', nos 109 (25 September 1322), 247 (28 June 1323).

[251] E 372/183, m. 59 (April–May 1323).

[252] E 372/183, m. 60: payment for materials with which to construct 'unum ingenium . . . ad debellandum castra et loca inimicorum Regis et ducis' in Marsan.

and Béarn.[253] Albret's men had been worsted in the fight and had subsequently carried on a vendetta against him, while Raymond-Arnaud, bastard of Béarn, and his men had tried to enter his castle at Poudenx 'sur semblaunce de bien bevaunt et mangeant en le dit lieu'.[254] But they had been driven away and began to kill and rob the inhabitants of the settlement around the castle. This, claimed Vidal, was because of another fight which had arisen between the Béarnais and Lestrange's troops when Vidal was *prévôt* of St Sever. When he saw that the Béarnais were taking prisoners, Vidal and his men had rescued them. He did not dare to journey to Bordeaux, nor leave his castle, for fear of death at the hands of his enemies. In a society where the king-duke's representatives relied on the nobility of the area to provide them with military forces in order to conduct such campaigns, both old and new scores were bound to emerge. Recourse to self-help was not always suppressed by such forceful measures, which could themselves be productive of further feuds and vendettas.

Foix and Armagnac

The great feud between the houses of Foix and Armagnac was thought by some contemporaries to rank highly among the European power-struggles of the age. Philippe de Mézières, in his *Songe du vieil pélerin* (*c.*1389), compared it to the Guelf–Ghibelline conflict, the Anglo-French war and the rivalry between Castile and Portugal.[255] The vernacular *Chronique romane des comtes de Foix* of the Béarnais Arnaud Esquerrier traced its origins to the union between Foix and Béarn in 1289–90, when Gaston VII of Béarn and Mathe de Bigorre 'denied [the succession] to the count and countess of Armagnac, because they had not given them any assistance' against their enemies.[256] On Gaston VII's death on 26 April 1290, Roger-Bernard III, count of Foix (who had married Gaston VII's daughter Marguerite in October 1252), was preferred to the children of his other daughter Mathe, who had married Géraud V, count of Armagnac (d. 1285).[257] Bernard VI of Armagnac (1285–1319) inherited his father's claim to both Béarn and to Bigorre, and attempted to gain possession of both lordships through sequestration by the Capetian monarchy. But, wrote Esquerrier, *no eran de aquela obediensa* (they were not part of Capetian jurisdiction) and thus began the great private war between the two houses.[258] As we have seen, Géraud V of Armagnac had tended to

[253] SC 8/290, no. 14485 (?1323).

[254] SC 8/290, no. 14485; cf. *St Sardos*, pp. 8, 27–38. Vidal de Poudenx was captain of Le Mas-de-Ste-Quitterie for Edward II from December 1324 to July 1325 (*St Sardos*, p. 274).

[255] Philippe de Mézières, *Le Songe du vieil pélerin*, ed. G. W. Coopland, 2 vols, (Cambridge, 1969), i, p. 294. We might see affinities with the rivalry of Percy and Neville in northern England during the fourteenth and fifteenth centuries.

[256] *Chroniques romanes des comtes de Foix*, p. 35, *sub anno* 1286 (for 1289).

[257] Tucoo-Chala, *Gaston Fébus*, p. 40. See Appendix I, tables 3b and 3c, and above, pp. 86–8.

[258] *Chroniques romanes des comtes de Foix*, p. 37. For tension between the 'traditional' interests of Foix and Béarn after the union of 1290, see Tucoo-Chala, *Gaston Fébus*, pp. 49–51.

support Edward I against Gaston VII of Béarn in the succession dispute over Bigorre in 1284, and was in receipt of a pension from Edward.[259] By 1341, Jean I of Armagnac could refer to conflicts between his house and that of Foix which 'had lasted a long time and still existed', and in 1361 declared that the issues in dispute were essentially rooted in 'properties, inheritances, jurisdictions and homages'.[260] Dynastic, judicial and tenurial questions lay at the heart of the quarrel, exacerbated by the expansionist tendencies of both houses. Conflicts over property, inheritance, jurisdiction and homage formed the very stuff of princely and seigneurial politics in medieval Europe: but the Foix–Armagnac conflict was marked by certain characteristics which contributed to its longevity.

The first of these was the existence of a common frontier between lordships held by each house. The Foix-Béarn lands of Marsan and Gabardan had a contiguous boundary with those of Armagnac, such as Rivière-Basse; the *vicomté* of Nébouzan lay alongside the Armagnac lordship of Magnoac, and such tiny enclaves as the Pyrenean valley of Larboust were surrounded by lordships either in Armagnac hands or in their *ambiance*.[261] Attempts by the Foix-Béarn to link and unite their eastern Pyrenean possessions (Foix, Donezan, Andorra) to Béarn on the west were constantly hampered by the blocs of Armagnac territory between them.[262] Seigneurial geography therefore had an important part to play in the Foix–Armagnac feud. Expansion or infiltration by both houses into other regions increased the opportunities for abrasion and friction. Territories such as Marsan or Nébouzan became contested areas, where raids and plundering expeditions took place, often without formal defiance, but with banners unfurled as a sign of war.[263] The position of both nobles and towns located on such boundaries was not always an enviable one. In July 1318 Pierre de Vaux, esquire, told Edward II that he held his patrimonial lordship immediately from the king-duke, but that it lay next to lands dominated by 'certain great magnates' who had conceived an implacable hatred of him. He wished to exchange his lands for others in the diocese of Agen or the surrounding area.[264] The rivalry of Foix and Armagnac was specifically mentioned by Amaury de Craon in a letter to Edward II written in October 1313. The *bastide* of Fleurance had been granted by Edward to Gaston I of Foix, therefore, it was claimed, prejudicing the consuls of the town.[265] Armagnac lordships surrounded the place and all

---

[259] See above, pp. 87–90.

[260] APA, E 31, no. 4 (20 March 1341); E 281, no. 29 (23 February 1361).

[261] APA, E 507, no. 31 (1309); Higounet, *Le Comté de Comminges*, pp. 124–6, 236–9; see Appendix III, map 3.

[262] See Appendix III, map 3. Tucoo-Chala, *Gaston Fébus*, p. 40.

[263] ATG, A 27, no. 1, m. 2 (*c.*1340). For the significance of unfurling banners, see M. H. Keen, *The Laws of War in the Late Middle Ages* (London, 1965), pp. 106–9.

[264] C 61/32, m. 8 (July 1318).

[265] SC 1/33, no. 115 (October 1313).

the greater bourgeois, wrote Amaury, held property from Bernard VI of Armagnac and his brother. If the gift to Foix was implemented, the consuls threatened to appeal to the court of France, citing a privilege obtained from Edward I that they should never be placed under any other jurisdiction but the king-duke's. Amaury de Craon thought the matter to be of considerable gravity, because Fleurance was on the border with the Toulousain and was worth 1500 *l.*(?)*st.* in rent per year. He claimed that this was as much as Bayonne, Dax, Bazas and Condom 'qui sont grosses villes' were worth in revenue to the ducal treasury.[266] Edward II wisely agreed to keep Fleurance in his own hands. Local resistance could provide a further obstacle, especially when protected by a higher authority, to the acquisitive behaviour of the greater nobility.

A second factor which served to make feuds such as that between Foix and Armagnac so long drawn-out was the absence of mechanisms in Gascony which might achieve a lasting settlement. Apart from the negotiation of local truces, there was little that third parties could achieve. This was better than nothing but hardly solved the problem. A society inured to private war and frontier raids was unlikely to respond with alacrity to the imposition of 'perpetual peace' because the nobility had come to regard the *droit de guerre* and its practical expression not only as their inalienable right but as a way of life. It was a ready source of profits, and lands lying on the borders between lordships, like those in the Scots marches, could supply lucrative plunder, booty and ransoms.[267] Attempts to put quarrels to the test of formalized single or group combat also proved unsuccessful. Sovereign and other authorities were not in favour of judicial duels unless they were conducted under the strictest controls. Edward I declined to allow Charles of Anjou, king of Sicily, to fight Pedro of Aragon at Bordeaux in June 1283 with a hundred knights on each side. He would not permit 'si graunte cruaute' to take place before him nor in any place subject to him.[268] Philip the Fair was a little more accommodating towards the counts of Foix and Armagnac in 1293, for he decreed that they might fight together in his presence at Gisors. Armagnac had asserted before Philip that Roger-Bernard III, count of Foix, had falsified Gaston VII of Béarn's testament, and the judicial duel sprang from that dishonourable allegation.[269] But the king stopped the combat and declared it null and void after Armagnac fell from his horse, so that the question of succession to Béarn could not be resolved in this manner.[270] But

[266] *RG*, iv, nos 1145–6 (23 November 1313); SC 1/33, no. 115. The statement was clearly an exaggeration, probably based on the consuls of Fleurance's petition to the seneschal.

[267] Cf. J. Campbell, 'England, Scotland and the Hundred Years War in the fourteenth century', *Europe in the Late Middle Ages*, ed. J. R. Hale, J. R. L. Highfield and B. Smalley (London, 1965), pp. 214–15.

[268] *Foedera*, I, ii, pp. 626–7 (22 and 25 March 1283). See below, pp. 177–8.

[269] *Chroniques romanes des comtes de Foix*, pp. 38–9.

[270] *Grandes Chroniques de France*, ed. J. Viard, viii, pp. 150–1.

all other efforts to bring the conflict between Foix and Armagnac before Capetian judicial machinery were doomed to failure.

The Anglo-French war of 1294 at least brought a temporary halt to the quarrel, and the participation of both houses in Philip the Fair's armies against Edward I prevented further outbreaks of feuding between them.[271] But on 12 January 1298, after the conclusion of a truce between Philip and Edward, the conflict was rekindled.[272] By August 1305, John de Havering, seneschal of Gascony, was disturbed enough by the news that Foix and a 'great company of men-at-arms' had invaded Armagnac's lands and raided areas in Edward I's allegiance, to raise an army of at least 370 Gascon nobles and their retinues to serve in a punitive expedition.[273] A total sum of 304 *l.* 15 *s.st.* was spent by the constable of Bordeaux on their wages. The seneschal's expenditure during his term of office (1303–5) for 'quelling the wars of the magnates in the duchy' cost Edward I well over 10,000 *l.t. in toto.*[274] While Havering and his army tried to subdue the young Gaston I of Foix, the newly elected Clement V inaugurated his career of mediation by intervening in the conflict. Negotiating through Margaret of Foix, Gaston's mother, and Constance de Marsan, his sister, Clement secured an agreement that Foix was to compensate Armagnac for all damages within a time ordained by the pope and John de Havering.[275] But the terms do not appear to have observed by Gaston I, because Clement wrote from Bordeaux in March 1307 that Gaston had been excommunicated and his lands placed under interdict as a result of his wars with Armagnac.[276] His mother had, however, requested an inquiry into the affair because the majority of his vassals in Béarn and elsewhere were neither guilty nor implicated in it. By April 1308 the sentence had been partially lifted, and ecclesiastical burial was again allowed to the 'followers' (*sequaces*) of Gaston I.[277] But the issue had by no means been resolved.

Clement V professed himself ready to absolve Gaston I in January 1309, but only if suitable guarantees and sureties were given by him.[278] If either Foix or Armagnac again tried to invade each other's lands, an interdict would be imposed upon both. Philip the Fair then attempted to apply coercive force to the dispute. At Toulouse on 26 April 1309 he ordered Foix to pay 6000 *l.t.* to Armagnac as damages; decreed that the lands of Gavarret

---

[271] See below, pp. 204–5, 215.

[272] ATG, A 297, fos 223ᵛ–224ʳ; de Vic and Vaissete, *Histoire générale de Languedoc*, ix, pp. 203–4; APA, E 401, no. 34 (1296–1303).

[273] E 101/160/4, m. 2; *RG*, iii, pp. cxcviii–cxcix.

[274] E 101/160/1, m. 1ʳ. The total sum, including the seneschal's fee and wage, was 13,407 *l.* 10 *s.t.*

[275] E 101/160/4, m. 2 (August 1305); *RG*, iii, pp. cxcviii–cxcix. Clement was at Bordeaux during this period.

[276] *Regestum Clementis papae V*, no. 1731 (10 March 1307).

[277] *Regestum Clementis papae V*, no. 2703 (24 April 1308). There was also a threat of private war between Foix and Albret in 1308. See SC 1/33, no. 146; *Foedera*, II, i, p. 60.

[278] *Regestum Clementis papae V*, no. 3674 (6 January 1309).

and Gabardan be surrendered by Foix to Armagnac, and imposed peace on both parties, their 'valedors, amycs, aliats et subjects'.[279] In a series of protests, some made through her proctors and lawyers, Margaret of Foix claimed that both Gavarret and Gabardan were rightfully hers and were therefore part of the lawful inheritance of her son.[280] The rival claim of Armagnac was put forward by the representative of the countess of Armagnac, at Langon in November 1309, when he required Philip IV's ruling to be executed.[281] This had still not been done in 1310 by the Plantagenet officers responsible – John de Hastings, seneschal of Gascony, and his lieutenant Amanieu de Fossat. The Armagnacs accused the king-duke's officers of procrastination and delay, threatening recourse to the French seneschal of Toulouse to obtain enforcement of the royal pronouncement.[282] Even the combined apparatus of papal excommunication and French royal *ordonnance* had failed to achieve a lasting settlement. The lack of effective sanctions, and of a machinery whereby Capetian rulings might be enforced, precluded anything more than the most tenuous control by 'higher' authority over the behaviour of the two feuding houses.

Conflict over Gabardan flared up again in 1318. John XXII was the first to intervene, calling upon third parties such as the archbishop of Auch and the Dominican and Franciscan priors at Agen to mediate between the two sides.[283] Foix and Armagnac had clashed at Laserrade, in Gabardan, and the pope dispatched two legates to Gascony on 25 April 1318.[284] A truce was imposed on the warring houses on 11 May, to last, under penalty of excommunication, until Michaelmas. Bernard IX, count of Comminges, was requested to use his influence with Armagnac to bring about a reconciliation. Armagnac was reminded by the pope that he had already twice offered mediation between him and Foix: although the latter had sent a proctor to Avignon, Armagnac had not done so.[285] The pope then began to build up a case against Armagnac, telling Philip V on 15 June that he had imposed a truce and hoped that papal arbitration would end the conflict. In the meantime, he requested Philip to stay execution of his *arrêt* of 6 June 1317 concerning Gabardan until the papal legates had done their work.[286] Armag-

---

[279] *Chroniques romanes des comtes de Foix*, pp. 42–3; de Vic and Vaissete, *Histoire générale de Languedoc*, x, *Preuves*, cc. 490–6.

[280] E 30/1473 (24 October 1309); APA, E 486 (15 November 1309); E 507, no. 31 (1309).

[281] APA, E 486, m. 2 (15 November 1309).

[282] APA, E 237, fos 85^{r-v} (26 April 1309).

[283] 'Documents pontificaux', nos 5, 8, 9 (21 March and 15 April 1318).

[284] de Vic and Vaissete, *Histoire générale de Languedoc*, x, p. 583 ('Gerrada'); 'Documents pontificaux', nos 10, 13; APA, E 296, no. 33 for fines imposed by Margaret of Foix on sixteen Béarnais nobles who had failed to perform military service to her in 'the army of Lembeye' (*la ost de Lembeye*) in 1318.

[285] 'Documents pontificaux' nos 32, 33, 34 (11 May 1318).

[286] 'Documents pontificaux', no. 43 (15 June 1318); *Actes du Parlement de Paris*, ed. E. Boutaric, ii, nos 4887–8.

nac, claimed the pope, was refusing to end hostilities with Foix until this royal sentence, awarding Gabardan to the Armagnacs, was put into effect. The pope thus defended the rival rights of Margaret of Foix and her son to the lordship, and clearly saw the issue of Gabardan as the crux of the Foix–Armagnac dispute at this juncture, requesting Henri de Sully, Philip V's familiar and *grand bouteiller* of France to persuade the king not to execute his own *arrêt*.[287] Papal intervention had secured a solitary gain by July 1318, when the pope told the bishop of Aire that both Foix and Armagnac had promised to respect the truce but would not swear to observe it. As 'God does not distinguish', he wrote, 'between a simple verbal assurance and an oath', the bishop was to insist that both parties observed the 'simple promise made by them'.[288] But the maximum advantage attained by papal intervention was a further renewal of the truce until Easter 1319.[289] The pope threatened to release all vassals and subjects of Foix and Armagnac from their oaths of allegiance if the truce was broken during this period. But John XXII did not proceed to a formal arbitration of the quarrel at this date and left matters as they were. Philip V's intervention had made matters worse and, once truces had been established, it was best to leave well alone. Popes and kings were no match for great provincial nobles locked in ancestral feuds. Neither possessed sufficient coercive power to enforce their own edicts.

Behind the principal protagonists in these feuds lay coteries or pyramids of support which are often difficult to penetrate during this period – our knowledge of the wider personnel engaged in the Foix–Armagnac feud begins to become fuller and clearer after 1376 when Gaston Fébus of Foix-Béarn mustered his vassals, *alliés* and 'valedors . . . qui no son sous sosmes' ('supporters . . . who are not his subjects') at Morlaas.[290] But the anonymous 'men-at-arms', *valedors* and *adhérens* referred to in our sources must have stemmed from the feudal and non-feudal contracts drawn up between the two houses and lesser nobles of the region. The right to *excercitum et cavalgatum* (military service) was still a common seigneurial prerogative at this time, claimed and evidently exercised by the count of Armagnac over Ste-Gemme in 1275, or by Margaret of Foix over the *vicomté* of Marsan in 1309.[291] It was obviously the first line of defence against private enemies and the primary means of raising a band of mounted men-at-arms for a short-term raid. Vassalage was a force to be reckoned with in the south-west, and the registers of homages compiled at this time (and later) were not simply

[287] 'Document pontificaux', no. 45 (15 June 1318); for his important role in Anglo-French relations at this time see below, pp. 228–9.

[288] 'Documents pontificaux', no. 55 (7 July 1318).

[289] 'Documents pontificaux, nos 62, 63 (17 August 1318). The conflict between the two houses over Gabardan was not resolved until 1379.

[290] 'Rôles . . . de l'armée assemblée à Morlaas par Gaston Phoebus, comte de Foix en 1376', ed. P. Raymond, *AHG*, xii (1870), pp. 141, 167–73.

[291] Monlezun, *Histoire de Gascogne*, vi, p. 282 (May 1275); APA, E 507, no. 31.

records of archaic and fossilized survivals.[292] In his study of the rural and seigneurial origins of the urban family clan of the later Middle Ages, Jacques Heers has emphasized the importance of poorer nobles, acting as 'alliés et . . . clients plus ou moins soumis aux maîtres'.[293] The existence of *valedors* and *adhérens* in Gascony between 1290 and 1340 was undoubtedly part of a development which was to lead to the formal written contracts of *alliance* which survive from 1358 onwards. However, an approach to later contracts is found in an agreement made between Roger-Bernard III, count of Foix, Jourdain de L'Isle, lord of L'Isle-Jourdain, and their sons in January 1298.[294] All parties swore on the Gospels that they would 'lend mutual aid and succour with or without arms, and in good faith, with all the necessary friends [*amicis*] both in and out of court, against . . . the count of Armagnac and his men'. The reference to 'friends . . . both in and out of court' already suggests the recruitment of *alliés*.[295] By this agreement they bound themselves and their successors never to make peace with Armagnac without the express consent of all parties to the *alliance*. Jourdain de L'Isle was already Roger-Bernard III's creditor in January 1298, and he had revoked his previous alliances with Bernard VI of Armagnac in January 1289, countermanding a previous arrangement whereby Armagnac was to be recognized as suzerain of the castle, *fortalicium* and lordship of L'Isle-Jourdain.[296] These measures would have led to conflict (*briga*), especially if Armagnac were to be installed in any part of Jourdain's lands. A shift of alliance towards Foix-Béarn was an obvious next step to meet threats from the neighbouring Armagnacs.[297]

The Foix–Armagnac feud did not create a permanent state of open war in south-west France, and in that sense it cannot be argued that warfare between the two houses was endemic. Long periods of truce punctuated the conflict, such as that negotiated through the arbitration of Philip III of Evreux, king of Navarre (1301–43), at Tarbes in October 1329.[298] By the terms of that agreement Gaston II of Foix was obliged to pay 13,000 *l.t.* to Jean I of Armagnac and Géraud, *vicomte* of Fézensaguet. The absence and capture of Jean I during the Italian campaigns of Jean of Luxembourg, king of Bohemia, in the mid-1330s also contributed to the abatement of the

---

[292] See, for example, the homages to the Armagnacs in ATG, A 24, A 73, A 262, A 264–6, and to Albret in APA, E 199, no. 3 (homage of Guillaume de Sescas, *douzet*, to Amanieu VII d'Albret, July 1309).

[293] Heers, *Le Clan familial*, p. 35.

[294] ATG, A 297, fos 223ᵛ–224ʳ (20 January 1298); cf. the contracts of *alliance* printed in P. S. Lewis, 'Decayed and non-feudalism', *Essays in Later Medieval French History*, pp. 63–8; Vale, *English Gascony*, pp. 170–9. Also see above, pp. 122–3.

[295] ATG, A 297, fo. 224ᵛ.

[296] ATG, A 297, fos 222ʳ⁻ᵛ, 256ᵛ–257ʳ (23 January 1289).

[297] See above, pp. 86–7; below, pp. 138–9.

[298] APA, E 237, fos 80ʳ⁻ᵛ, 87ᵛ (20 October 1329); Tucoo-Chala, *Gaston Fébus*, p. 60.

feud.[299] But it was to reignite in 1339–40 and, as we shall see, was promptly subsumed in the greater conflict between England and France.[300]

Other Conflicts

Besides the Foix–Armagnac dispute, a series of private wars and armed clashes between nobles disturbed the peace of the duchy of Aquitaine between 1305 and 1339. Some were clearly related to the Foix–Armagnac feud and coincided with its outbreaks. A private war 'through which the whole duchy . . . was thrown into disorder' and which also affected Poitou, Saintonge, Périgord, the Toulousain and Comminges erupted between the lords of Albret and Caumont in May–June 1305.[301] Foix and Armagnac were also to be at war by August of that year. John de Havering, Edward I's seneschal, raised and paid a force of knights, esquires and foot-serjeants for periods ranging from fourteen to twenty-six days to pacify those parts of the duchy affected by private wars *vi vel metu*.[302] Pons de Castillon, Amanieu de Curton, Pierre de Castelnau, styled 'baron', Gaillard de Castetpugon, Elie de Caupenne, styled 'baron', and others brought retinues ranging from a mere handful of men to fifty or more combatants.[303] Havering's army marched to La Réole and to the Albret and Caumont strongholds of Casteljaloux and Le Mas, arrested both lords and seized their castles. Albret was detained at Bordeaux; Caumont at La Réole while other malefactors, rebels and disturbers of the peace were arrested in the Agenais and distributed among other strongholds held by the king-duke.[304] Havering also felt it necessary to send messengers to the French seneschals of neighbouring areas asking them to prevent men-at-arms from those regions from converging upon the duchy 'by reason of the aforesaid wars'.[305] Private war was evidently a magnet for the nobility of many areas and allegiances.

The methods applied by the Avignon papacy and the French monarchy to resolve the issues dividing Foix and Armagnac were similarly deployed in their attempts to appease other quarrels. Between September 1316 and April 1322 John XXII tried unsuccessfully to bring about a reconciliation between

---

[299] See below, pp. 253–4.

[300] See below, p. 263.

[301] E 101/160/4, m. 1; *RG*, iii, pp. cxciv–cxcvi.

[302] E 101/160/4, m. 2. Havering had lost a warhorse worth 300 *l.t.* and a palfrey (70 *l.t.*) during the expedition.

[303] E 101/160/4, m. 1: Bernard Trencaléon brought twenty-three esquires and thirty serjeants, Auger de Pouillon thirty-four foot-serjeants, Assieu de Galard eighteen esquires and twenty-five foot-serjeants while Pons de Castillon commanded the force, bringing two knights and twelve esquires with him in his company. Many of these nobles had returned from exile in England to the duchy in March 1303 (E 101/10/23).

[304] E 101/160.4 m. 1: Albret's castle of Casteljaloux and the Caumont stronghold of Le Mas were seized into the king-duke's hands: Gardelles, *Les Châteaux*, pp. 114–15.

[305] E 101/160/4, m. 1; *RG*, iii, pp. cxciv–cxiv.

Amanieu VII d'Albret and his own kinsman Sansaner de Pins, imposing truces, threatening excommunications and dispatching nuncios as he had done to Foix and Armagnac.[306] The private war centred upon the disputed lordship of Nérac (Agenais), claimed by Albret, which was held by the wife of Sansaner de Pins, Jeanne de Périgord, lady of Lavardac.[307] Other members of the kindred were solicited by the pope to intervene in the dispute, including Brunissende de Foix, countess of Périgord, Roger d'Armagnac, bishop of Lavaur and Bertrand de Goth, *vicomte* of Lomagne and Auvillars.[308] A perennial danger of such conflicts was that they could so easily spread to involve much larger groups of nobles. John XXII ordered his envoys in April 1322 to arbitrate urgently between the warring factions, because 'not only do the dissidents [Albret and De Pins] clash in warlike encounters, but almost all the nobles and magnates . . . not simply from those parts but from neighbouring areas, take part in them'.[309] Private war again exerted a powerful attraction over both the greater and lesser nobility of the southwest, eager to profit from the disorder which followed in its wake. The fact that there seem to have been no tournaments among the Gascon nobility at this time may partly be explained by the opportunities for military activity offered to them by private wars. Unless the bans on tournaments decreed by the French crown were strictly observed in Aquitaine (which is most unlikely), this absence of evidence is very telling indeed.[310] The only mêlées documented in the sources took place not at the *tournoi*, as in northern France and the Low Countries, but during local wars.[311]

A second type of skill in arms – single combat – which was tested by the tournament in the form of the joust or hastilude, was confined in Gascony to the judicial duel or *gage de bataille*. Examples can be adduced at random from casual references in a variety of sources: one took place between Bertrand de Godorie, esquire, and Austorge de Soirin before the seneschal of Périgord in May 1318,[312] while a more celebrated combat was arranged at Bordeaux in April 1318 between Alexandre de Caumont and Jourdain de L'Isle.[313] The

[306] 'Documents pontificaux', nos. 1, 15, 16–19; APA, E 240, no. 1 (September 1316–July 1317).

[307] APA, E 618, no. 4 (15 and 30 May 1318).

[308] 'Documents pontificaux', nos 17, 179–81. A petition to Edward II on Gascon affairs expressed the wish that the king-duke quell the war between Albret and Sansaner de Pins, because 'la guerre est perilous pur le heritage le Roi et pur les gentz de la terre' (C 47/25/2, no. 17).

[309] 'Documents pontificaux', nos 174, 176 (11 April 1322).

[310] For tournament bans, see R. Harvey, *Moriz von Crâun and the Chivalric World* (Oxford, 1961), p. 136.

[311] See, for examples, SC 8/290, no. 14485; C 47/25/2, no. 6, m. 2; cf. J. Vale, *Edward III and Chivalry*, pp. 5–6, 12–13, for northern French *tournois* of the later thirteenth century.

[312] C 61/32, m. 6 (27 May 1318).

[313] A detailed record of the events leading to the combat and the abortive duel itself are found in C 47/26/12 (April–September 1318). See below, pp. 135–6; also J. A. Kicklighter, 'The

fact that the duel was proclaimed at all may stem from Philip the Fair's partial revocation of his ordinance issued at Toulouse on 9 January 1304 prohibiting *provocationes . . . ad duellum et gagia duellorum*.[314] In 1306 he issued a great ordinance permitting judicial combat in certain cases, such as homicide, treason and other violent crimes.[315] The form of challenges and protestations was set out in the ordinance and detailed regulations for the conduct of the combatants in the lists drawn up. It could be argued that this more permissive attitude towards trial by battle was in part a concession to the nobility, but it also offered a formal procedure whereby quarrels which often led to private war could be put to the test of arms in the presence of a public authority. If a sovereign or immediate lord could bring the warring parties together and let them fight it out in his or his representative's presence, a minimal degree of control might be exercised over their behaviour.

The L'Isle-Jourdain were noted for their turbulent conduct, although they were not conspicuously more uninhibited than many of their contemporaries, especially among the nobles of the Agenais.[316] In 1298 Bernard-Jourdain and his brother Jourdain de L'Isle were the subject of complaints by Mabille, widow of Jean Colom of Bordeaux, whose property they had stolen, and the two brothers were themselves in conflict over the lordship of St-Sixte-del-Douple and other inheritances between 1307 and 1309.[317] Jourdain de L'Isle, as a younger son, clearly felt himself badly treated by family settlements. But he made a good marriage to Catherine, daughter of Jean de Grilly, in July 1304.[318] His fortunes were apparently set back, however, by a sentence delivered by Bertrand de Goth, *vicomte* of Lomagne and Auvillars, on the division of the L'Isle-Jourdain inheritance in 1309.[319] Bertrand was to be one of the agents of Jourdain's ultimate downfall in 1323. A picture of his career of brigandage, homicide and private war can be pieced together from the fragmentary sources, most of them weighted in favour of his accusers. Seneschals of Gascony, from Guy Ferre to Fulk Lestrange, found themselves involved in his affairs, issuing summonses, passing sentences and granting pardons to him and his accomplices.[320] He was attacking Fortaner de Lescun in 1309, the consuls of the town of Ste-Bazeille in 1314, and pillaged the Cluniac priory of Vienne (dioc. Agen) in the same year.[321] Jourdain was said

nobility of English Gascony: the case of Jourdain de L'Isle', *JMH*, xiii (1987), pp. 327–42 for an account of the affair based on published sources.

[314] *Ordonnances*, i, p. 390 (9 January 1304).

[315] *Ordonnances*, i, pp. 435–41 (1 June 1306).

[316] See above, pp. 112–24.

[317] ATG, A 297, fos 394^v–5^r (1298), 639^v–42^r (1309), 1016^v–18^r (1308), 1025^r–6^v (1309), 1028^v–32^v (1304), 1032^v–7^v (1307).

[318] ATG, A 297, fos 637^v–8^v (11 July 1304); *RG*, iv, no. 1319.

[319] ATG, A 297, fos 956^r–60^v (1309).

[320] *RG*, iv, nos 185, 1306; 1216, 1319; C 61/32, m. 11.

[321] *RG*, iv, no. 185; C 81/61/380 (January 1309); *Confessions et jugements de criminels*, p. 37; *Olim*, iii, pp. 922–3.

to have seized corn, wine and other property from the prior, and although the French seneschal of Périgord had imposed a fine of 1000 *l.t.* upon him, the sum could not be levied *propter rebellionem dicti Jordanis*.[322] In a confession which he made on the scaffold before his execution in Paris in May 1323, he claimed that he had done these things to sustain himself and his men 'de sa guerre et que ainssi le fait len en son pais'.[323] The Paris Parlement had confirmed the penalty in 1314 and ordered the seneschal of Périgord carry it out.[324] But at his juncture Jourdain appeared to be enjoying a certain amount of favour from his immediate lord, Edward II, and benefited from restorations of property and protections against his enemies.[325]

Ducal patronage came to an end in 1317, when Jourdain began a private war with his former accomplice in brigandage, Alexandre de Caumont. The Caumonts were Albret clients and had supported Amanieu VII d'Albret in his appeals against Edward II's officers in the duchy in 1312.[326] They were powerful lords in the Agenais, and Alexandre de Caumont was co-seigneur with Jourdain de L'Isle of the lordship of Ste-Bazeille.[327] By November 1317 friction between the co-seigneurs had flared up into a private war, causing Gilbert Pecche, knight, seneschal of Gascony for Edward II, to set out with an armed force into the Bordelais to appease the conflict.[328] Pecche's successor, the Genoese Antonio di Pessagno, inherited an unpropitious legacy of disorder in the duchy in which the L'Isle-Caumont dispute played a predominant role. Pessagno arrived in Aquitaine on 16 March 1318.[329] His first reaction was not unintelligent. It was to dispatch Jourdain de L'Isle with 200 men-at-arms and 2000 Gascon infantry to serve Edward II in Ireland.[330] But lack of finance kept Jourdain in Gascony, and the expedition never took place. The quarrel had consequently to be contained and adjudicated within the duchy itself, and matters were not helped by John XXII's interventions in Jourdain's favour. The papal family of Duèse was related to the L'Isle-Jourdain and on 7 March 1318 the pope sent a letter of recommendation in Jourdain's favour to Pessagno. It no doubt awaited the new seneschal on his arrival in the duchy and requested that Jourdain be well treated 'through reverence for the apostolic see and for ourself'.[331] The pope's hopes were soon to be dashed.

---

[322] *Olim*, iii, p. 923 (14 May 1314).

[323] *Confessions et jugements de criminels*, p. 39.

[324] *RG*, iv, nos 1306 (24 March 1315); 1216 (8 May 1314); 1319–25 (March 1315).

[325] C 47/26/12, m. 1.

[326] C 47/25/2, no. 6 (30 August 1312). See below, pp.166–8.

[327] 'Documents pontificaux', no. 70 (25 October 1318); APA, E 150, no. 7.

[328] AN, J 633, no. 37 (at Paris, 28 October 1317).

[329] E 368/90, m. 13; see N. Fryde, 'Antonio Pessagno of Genoa, king's merchant of Edward II of England', *Studi in memoria de Federigo Melis*, ii (Naples, 1978), pp. 159–78.

[330] E 159/93, m. 76ʳ (Pessagno's account for 1318–19).

[331] 'Documents pontificaux', no. 26 (7 March 1318).

On 24 April 1318 the pope again wrote to Pessagno, wondering at his hostility towards Jourdain despite his earlier letter.[332] In the meantime, Pessagno had decided to allow the quarrel between Jourdain and Caumont to be put to trial by battle. A detailed notarial record of the preliminaries and course of the procedure survives unnoticed by historians.[333] Both parties appeared before Pessagno and a crowd of witnesses in the market place at La Réole on 3rd April 1318. They were accused of making war illicitly, with banners unfurled, and disturbing the peace of the duchy despite repeated prohibitions issued by the seneschals of Gascony. Jourdain de L'Isle not only denied these charges but insisted that as he was an appellant before the court of France, he was immune from the jurisdiction of his immediate lord, the king-duke of Aquitaine.[334] He claimed that the war between Caumont and himself had been arbitrated by Bertrand de Goth, but the peace had been broken by Caumont and his accomplices who had assaulted, wounded and killed members of Jourdain's *familia* and household on the road between Ste-Bazeille and Marmande. He accused Caumont of being a 'false, perverse traitor' and challenged him to a judicial combat *in campo clauso* to be fought to the death. The challenge was delivered in Gascon, and both nobles threw down gloves before the seneschal as *gages de bataille*. Combat was to be on horseback, with the appropriate weapons. A day was fixed for the inspection by the seneschal of both combatants' arms and equipment on Monday 2 October 1318.

A large gathering of witnesses accordingly met before the gate of Bordeaux castle on the appointed day. Caumont and his pledges presented a schedule itemizing the armour, food and drink that he had brought for the day of the combat. These included a total of seven horses, four maces, five lances, five shields, two bacinets, six swords, two visored helmets, various pieces of mail- and plate-armour, and horse-coverings. He had chosen to ride a black horse with a white face, and the list of equipment which he carried corresponded well to that enumerated in Philip the Fair's ordinance of 1306.[335] As Pessagno was deemed by Jourdain de L'Isle to be *suspectus* and hostile to him, the seneschal appointed Amanieu de Fossat, knight, his lieutenant, to act in his stead. Jourdain de L'Isle had not yet appeared at the view and presentation of arms required of the combatants, and a decision on the case was referred by the seneschal and his lieutenant to a body of 'neutral and non-suspect' nobles and others of the Bordelais and Agenais. Seated in the hall of Bordeaux castle (where pleas were normally heard), this representative tribunal returned the verdict that as Jourdain had not responded to four summonses *alta voce* (three proclaimed inside the hall and one outside the

---

[332] 'Documents pontificaux', no. 29 (24 April 1318).

[333] C 47/26/12 (roll of seven membranes, 3 April–3 October 1318); apparently unknown to Professor Kicklighter. I hope to edit it in due course.

[334] C 47/26/12, m. 1. The following section is based on mm. 2, 3, 5.

[335] *Ordonnances*, ii, pp. 435, 438. For the following passage see C 47/26/12, mm. 5–7.

castle gate) he was to be adjudged in default. The hour was late, the sun was setting in the west and the first stars had appeared in the evening sky. Proceedings were adjourned until the morrow, because the notary who was recording the case could no longer see to write without a candle.

On Tuesday 3 October, Alexandre de Caumont presented himself, ready to do battle in the Roman amphitheatre, or *Palais Gallien*, at Bordeaux. An enclosed area (*campo duellare infra lissas*) for combat had been set up, as was customary in such cases. Caumont waited. The hour of vespers approached and still Jourdain de L'Isle was nowhere to be seen. Pessagno and his lieutenant proclaimed by sound of trumpet, four times, that he was adjudged absent and in default by the tribunal. His failure to appear signified his guilt and Pierre Fulcher, Edward II's proctor, pressed for the death sentence for treason to be passed on him. Caumont was declared innocent of all allegations made against him 'saving the king-duke's right', while Jourdain was to be punished according to the custom of the Bazadais. Unless he could demonstrate extenuating circumstances, as allowed by that custom, he was to put himself and his movable possessions into the hands of the king-duke. A plea for clemency towards Jourdain came from the pope on 25 October 1318. John XXII wrote to Edward II, protesting that Pessagno had compelled Jourdain to challenge Caumont to a duel, then suddenly reassigned the date of the combat, giving only fifteen days' notice to Jourdain.[336] Hence Jourdain had appealed to the court of France. Thomas of Lancaster and Aymer de Valence received papal letters requesting them to exercise their influence on the king-duke in Jourdain's favour.[337] Philip V was also asked to take the case in hand by the pope, before it made a mockery of his sovereignty. Louis d'Evreux, the king's uncle, and Henri de Sully, *grand bouteiller* of France, were solicited to influence the king.[338]

By 20 January 1319, Edward II had written to both parties in the conflict, exhorting them to make peace, as requested by the pope.[339] Pessagno had been recalled from the duchy for suspected forgery and peculation in November 1318, although Edward and his advisers may also have been swayed by papal entreaties to remove the seneschal.[340] But the mere absence of Jourdain de L'Isle's most implacable opponent did not solve the issue. The pope unleashed a further barrage of letters in April 1319. One exhorted Jourdain to renounce his challenge to Caumont, because duels tempted providence and perverted true justice, and begged him to submit to rational judicial process.[341] Others enlisted the support of Bernard-Jourdain de L'Isle, cardinal Gaucelme Duèse, nuncio, who was in Flanders, Henri de Sully and the

---

[336] 'Documents pontificaux', no. 70 (25 October 1318).
[337] 'Documents pontificaux', no. 71 (25 October 1318).
[338] 'Documents pontificaux', no. 75.
[339] C 61/32, m. 11 (20 January 1319).
[340] E 159/93, m. 76ʳ; Fryde, 'Antonio di Pessagno', p. 177.
[341] 'Documents pontificaux', no. 106 (? 29 April 1319).

count of Comminges.[342] Under no circumstances, the pope observed, was a duel to take place. It was perhaps fortunate for all those involved that attention was focused on Philip V's Flemish campaigns, and on the private war between Amanieu VII d'Albret and Sansaner de Pins in Gascony between 1319 and 1321, so that the L'Isle–Caumont quarrel receded from the centre of the stage.[343] But by the summer of 1322 a more serious imbroglio had arisen. Bernard-Jourdain de L'Isle was at war with Amanieu d'Albret and it was likely that if the conflict continued, Edward II's expectations of aid from his Gascon possessions for the Scots war would not be realized.[344] On 29 August 1322, John XXII expressed his surprise to the L'Isle-Jourdain brothers that they had challenged Albret (who was not a young man) to a duel. He told Bernard-Jourdain that he was behaving like a prize-fighter (*velut pugilem te constituens*) and ought to know better. But the odds were building up against Bernard-Jourdain and his brother both in Gascony and at the court of France. Bernard-Jourdain had been summoned to Paris, and the pope gave him avuncular advice on the pitfalls to be avoided at the courts of princes. The voluble Gascon was to hold his tongue, curb his language and assume an air of innocence so that jealous rivals would be unable to harm him.[345]

Nevertheless L'Isle-Jourdain had succeeded in alienating two of the most powerful magnates in the south-west by the winter of 1322: namely Amanieu d'Albret and Bertrand de Goth, *vicomte* of Lomagne and Auvillars, marquis of Ancona. Jourdain completed his collection of challenges with a defiance addressed to Bertrand, ostensibly acting on the pope's behalf. John XXII was anxious to dissociate himself entirely from this rash and ill-considered assault on the most favoured surviving kinsman of Clement V. The pope reiterated his distaste for duels even in defence of papal interests. The provocation of Bertrand de Goth was the beginning of the end for Jourdain de L'Isle. A note of increasing despair at the behaviour of his kinsmen marks the last letters which John XXII wrote in Jourdain's favour to Charles IV of France on 23 and 25 March 1323. Charles was begged not to believe the calumnies uttered in his court against the hapless Jourdain, but was to listen benignly to his excuses, while letters of almost identical wording were received by the major figures at the French court. Such was the lack of success experienced by papal overtures to Charles IV that the pope, in his last letter supporting Jourdain, dated 25 March 1323, expressed his concern that his letters were not reaching the king at all. By 7 May Jourdain was dead, hanged from the gibbet at Paris.

His fate was sealed by the Parlement on the grounds that his persistent

---

[342] 'Documents pontificaux', nos 107–10.

[343] C 47/25/2, no. 17; 'Documents pontificaux', nos 174–8.

[344] SC 1/21, no. 158 (? August 1322).

[345] 'Documents pontificaux', nos 201–2 (29 August 1322), and nos 182, 218, 217, 230, 237 for the following paragraph.

and contumacious insults to Charles IV's sovereignty could no longer go unpunished. Jourdain had recently hanged two appellants to the court of France within his own lordships, and the *Grandes Chroniques* reported that he had killed a royal serjeant with the mace, enamelled with the fleur-de-lis, which he carried.[346] But there can be little doubt that he was also the victim of his enemies' malice. Edward II and his representatives at Paris and in Aquitaine did nothing to aid him. He was an expendable irritant, although the opportunity to be rid of him by ducal initiative in 1318 had been lost. His relationship to the pope could not save him and there were many who relished this display of Avignonese impotence. The *Grandes Chroniques* even alleged that he was drawn and hanged dressed in the pope's livery.[347] His voluntary confession in the Châtelet before execution survives in a register kept by one of the court's notaries.[348] He acknowledged that his men had killed, wounded and burned in Gascony, but said that this was their manner of waging war there. He had unjustly extorted money from his tenants, and his brother was to restore it to them. He said that he deserved to die, but he wanted to take with him to the scaffold 'a little purse, in which there was found a piece of the True Cross, and some relics of St George, as he said, and some writings, that is to say, the names of Our Lord and the Gospels'. They were removed from him by Gautier de Châtillon and he went to his death without the consolation of these talismans.[349]

Jourdain de L'Isle was to some extent unlucky, but he had thrown too many hostages to fortune. It was a measure of the problems faced by higher authorities in their attempts to reduce the nobles of south-west France to order that his career of lawlessness lasted for so long. After his execution his immediate family fell prey to attempts to seize his lands and possessions. In June 1323, supported by John XXII, Bernard-Jourdain complained to John, bishop of Ely, who was acting as Edward II's commissioner to reform affairs in Aquitaine, that Fulk Lestrange and John Felton, seneschal of the Agenais, had sequestered Jourdain's castles of Casaubon, Montgaillard, Puch-de-Gontaud, St-Sixte-del-Douple and other lordships.[350] Bernard-Jourdain claimed to be in possession of these after his brother's death. His case was reiterated by the pope in letters of 12 October to Edward II and his counsellors in England.[351] The L'Isle-Jourdain were to be allowed recourse to proper and impartial justice. The pope renewed his requests on 7 January 1324, in stronger terms, addressing them to the king-duke, Hugh Le Despenser,

---

[346] *Grandes Chroniques*, ix, p. 17; cf. BN, ms. fr. 10132, fo. 405^v for a colourful interpolation in the text of another manuscript which blackened Jourdain's reputation even further.

[347] *Grandes Chroniques*, ix, p. 18.

[348] *Confessions et jugements de criminels*, pp. 38–9.

[349] *Confessions et jugements de criminels*, p. 39.

[350] ATG, A 197, fos 986^v–8^r (21 July 1323), 1007^r–9^r, 1009^r–10^v, 1013^r–16^r.

[351] 'Documents pontificaux', nos 260, 261 (12 October 1323), and nos 268–71, 279 for the next five sentences.

Robert Baldock and Walter Stapleton. But the aftermath of the affair of Jourdain de L'Isle was about to be engulfed in the prelude to the War of St Sardos. On 19 January 1324 the pope wrote to Charles IV, emphasizing the loyalty of Bernard-Jourdain and his ancestors to the French crown, and urging the king to turn a deaf ear towards the vicious lies spread about by jealous rivals (*emulos*), who were secretly trying to poison the king's mind. But an opportunity for restoration to grace was offered to Bernard-Jourdain by Charles IV's arrival at Toulouse to investigate the St Sardos affair, which he and the Duèse *nepotes* took.[352] They met the king there in January 1324, and pledged their loyal services to him. Jourdain's widow, Catherine de Grilly, was the object of attacks by her late husband's enemies, and the pope consistently supported her against his creditors because 'wives should not be molested for their dead husbands' crimes or transactions'.[353] She had a case pending before the Paris Parlement and the pope asked the Chancellor of France to aid her in that suit.[354] In October 1325 he requested Charles IV to grant her a respite in order to pay a 500 *l.t.* fine, because her possessions were in disarray as a result of the Anglo-French war in Aquitaine. But her best hope of defence against her enemies, the pope told her in a letter of 28 October, was to remarry.[355]

Jourdain de L'Isle's condemnation and death on the gallows caused a certain stir among his contemporaries. He was, wrote the author of the *Grandes Chroniques*, 'tres noble de linage, mais très desordené en fais et en meurs'.[356] There were others to whom that description might justly apply. But the outbreak of an Anglo-French war in Gascony in June 1324 swept the problem of private war and its associated evils aside for a time. As we shall see, personal and local scores could be settled during 'public' war, waged on behalf of a higher authority.[357] This was to be a pattern which might determine allegiances and inform the behaviour of Gascon nobles in the greater Anglo-French conflict. The execution of Jourdain de L'Isle solved nothing and set no precedent for the immediate future.[358] Private war in and on the frontiers of Aquitaine could not be eliminated by such tardily applied and occasional punitive acts. But Charles IV's intervention had wider implications. If the French crown was again permitted to impose punitive sanctions in this manner, the king-duke's authority over his duchy of Aquitaine would be further undermined. In the heightening of Anglo-French tension, the affair of Jourdain de L'Isle and the attempted prohibition of private war among the Gascon nobility played a central and fundamental part.

[352] See *St Sardos*, pp. 5, 10–11, 22.

[353] 'Documents pontificaux', no. 286 (9 February 1324).

[354] *St Sardos*, p. 22; 'Documents pontificaux;, no. 312 (4 August 1324).

[355] 'Documents pontificaux', no. 338.

[356] *Grandes Chroniques*, ix, p. 16.

[357] See below, pp. 217–18, 242–4.

[358] The next recorded execution of a Gascon noble for treason took place in 1377 (E 101/181/6); *AHG*, xxvi (1888–9), pp. 149–63.

5

Politics and Society in Aquitaine – II:
Town and Countryside

5.1 Economic Activity and Social Texture

This chapter will attempt to introduce an economic and social dimension to the discussion of issues which have often been treated from a purely political perspective. War, politics and diplomacy are shaped by, and reflective of, impersonal forces as well as the aims and ambitions of rulers and their subjects. In 1897 Frantz Funck-Brentano saw Anglo-French politics and diplomatic activity before the Hundred Years War merely as 'le côté extérieur des événements. On n'y voit jamais les causes efficientes qui sont toujours dans les conditions sociales et économiques des peuples.'[1] Without underrating the significance of the autonomy of politics and diplomacy, the underlying causes of conflict between England and France may be approached from other points of view. Material factors, as well as judicial, ideological and political issues contributed to the outbreak of Anglo-French warfare in 1294, 1324 and 1337. One does not need to be a marxist historian to perceive a relationship between the 'côté extérieur des événements' and the structure and dynamic of the societies in which those events took place. Nor should the historian of war and politics be deterred from embarking upon discussion of the economic and social trends which lay beneath the 'shiftings day by day of the diplomatic game' which, wrote Tout, 'give very little enlightenment as to permanent conditions'.[2] We therefore aim to assess the extent to which changing economic conditions during the period 1250–1330 contributed to a growth of tension in Aquitaine between the Plantagenets and Capetians.

Historians have achieved an unusual degree of consensus in interpreting the thirteenth century as a period of demographic growth. The urban popu-

---

[1] F. Funck-Brentano, 'Les luttes sociales au xive siècle: Jean Colom de Bordeaux', *MA*, x (1897), p. 319. See also the Introduction to his *Les origines de la Guerre de Cent Ans. Philippe le Bel en Flandre* (Paris, 1897), p. iii.

[2] T. F. Tout, *France and England. Their Relations in the Middle Ages and Now* (Manchester, 1922), p. 2.

lation of western Europe grew rapidly and, as Jacques le Goff has written, 'until around 1280 in the greater part of the Christian world the wave of urban prosperity overflowed to the countryside, bringing technical and economic progress, freeing men and urbanizing the rural areas'. After that date (and especially after *c*.1320–30), 'urban civilization was in crisis'.[3] We shall see that urban developments in much of south-west France followed a rather different chronological pattern, and that the 1280s, rather than the earlier part of the century, marked the beginnings of a period of economic growth which was to endure until the 1330s. During that time, the duchy of Aquitaine and its immediate neighbours reached the zenith of their medieval prosperity. In 1317 John XXII created the new diocese of Condom, by dividing that of Agen, remarking that the Almighty had blessed the city and diocese of Agen with a large and fecund population, while Boniface VIII had elevated Pamiers to diocesan status in 1295.[4] By 1316 the duchy of Aquitaine contained an estimated population of 625,000 inhabitants, that is, one-twenty-seventh of the French kingdom's total population or one-seventh of that of England.[5] Bordeaux was 'at one of the peak points in its history', admirably placed to meet the increasing demands for wine of a larger population and a wealthier mercantile class.[6] The Garonne basin, dominated by Bordeaux as an economic as well as a political capital, became a source of considerable revenue to the king-duke and of profit to his subjects.

It followed from this development that both Plantagenets and Capetians found in the duchy a highly desirable source of income. The Capetians, however, were denied direct access to this revenue by the immediate lordship of the king-duke and, in contrast with the *comté* of Flanders (where they intervened to benefit from taxes and from monetary manipulation), were unable to profit from exploitation of the region's resources.[7] This was to provide an important dimension to the Anglo-French war of 1294. In 1308–9 the export of wine from Bordeaux reached its highest recorded figure of 102,000 tuns paying customs duty there. Between 1305 and 1336, an annual average of 83,000 tuns was exported, and the figure on the eve of the Hundred Years War in 1335–6 still stood at 74,000.[8] The subsequent years

[3] J. Le Goff, 'The town as an agent of civilisation', in *The Fontana Economic History of Europe. The Middle Ages*, ed. C. M. Cipolla (London, 1972), p. 93.

[4] J. J. Monlezun, *Histoire de Gascogne depuis les temps les plus reculés jusqu'a nos jours* (Auch, 1850), vi, pp. 393–4; for Pamiers see J.-M. Vidal, *Histoire des Evêques de Pamiers. I. Bernard Saisset (1232–1311)* (Toulouse and Paris, 1926), pp. 39–41.

[5] Y. Renouard, 'Conjectures sur la population du duché d'Aquitaine en 1316', *Etudes d'histoire médiévale*, i (Paris, 1968), p. 169.

[6] E. M. Carus-Wilson and O. Coleman, *England's Export Trade, 1275–1547* (Oxford, 1963), p. 203.

[7] See Funck-Brentano, *Philippe le Bel en Flandre*, pp. 10–11, 101–4, 126–7.

[8] Carus-Wilson and Coleman, *England's Export Trade*, pp. 203–4; M. K. James, 'Fluctuations of the Anglo-Gascon wine trade in the fourteenth century', *EcHR*, 2nd ser., iv (1951), pp. 191–2; J.-P. Trabut-Cussac, 'Les coutumes ou droits de douane perçus à Bordeaux', *AM*, lxii (1950), pp. 135–50.

of war resulted in a drastic decline in the export figures. Commerce on this scale brought rich returns to the English exchequer: a clear receipt of 13,000 *l.st.* was estimated from the duchy in 1324, surpassing the annual revenues from English shires by over 1000 *l.* (11,742 *l.* 12 *s.* 3 *d.*) Aquitaine was therefore worth fighting for in financial terms alone.[9] In 1306–7, ducal revenues had reached 17,000 *l.st.* (84,000 *l.b.*), of which almost half (46.4 per cent) stemmed from Bordeaux and the Bordelais. Of this, in turn, 79.5 per cent came from the customs levied on merchandise, above all on wine, passing through the city's port.[10] A parallel rise in ordinary revenues was discernible at this time, and reforming attempts in 1310–11 and 1319–20 set higher limits on the farming out of *bailliages* and other offices in the ducal administration.[11] Economic gain was an essential objective of administrative reform.

A concrete expression of the duchy's prosperity during this period is to be found in its ecclesiastical and secular architecture. The cathedrals of St André at Bordeaux and Ste-Marie at Bayonne reflected the wealth generated by the economic tendencies of the period 1280–1330. The vast choir of St André, begun in a northern Gothic *rayonnant* style between 1300 and 1305, bore witness not only to Clement V's patronage but also to the wealth of the city's inhabitants, many of whom subscribed to the fabric fund and appropriated chapels for their own use in the choir and aisles. At Bayonne, the dimensions of the cathedral's choir and transepts were similarly impressive and the early fourteenth-century cloister made lavish use of decorated motifs.[12] Mercantile wealth also expressed itself in the public buildings of the period: the *arcades* and *cornières* supporting municipal councillors' meeting places at Agen, Bayonne and elsewhere represented investment in 'civic' amenities shared, on a smaller scale, by the newly founded *bastides* of the south-west. Residences for the seneschals who governed the region, and their lieutenants, began to proliferate, new bridges were built, while the castle-building activities of the nobility have already been described.[13] Surplus capital was clearly available, and the renovations and

---

[9] G. L. Harriss, *King, Parliament and Public Finance in Medieval England to 1369* (Oxford, 1975), p. 523.

[10] E 101/161/16 and 17 (accounts of Richard de Havering, constable of Bordeaux 1306–7); *Gascon Register A (Series of 1318–19)*, ed. G. P. Cuttino and J.-P. Trabut-Cussac, i, no. 11, p. 84; cf. *RG*, iv, pp. 548, 549–51 (1311–12 accounts).

[11] See *Gascon Register A*, i, nos 12–13, 44–5, 51; C 47/25/2, no. 17 (1319–20): a decline was noted in the yields of *bailliages* since the time of Gilbert Pecche, seneschal of Aquitaine. The farm of the *bailliage* of l'Ombrière at Bordeaux was thus to be increased from 120 *l.t.* to 500 per year; the *bailliage* of Puynormand from 400 to 800 *l.t.* per year, and the salt-works of Agen from 900 to 1500 *l.t.* per year.

[12] For the cathedral of Bordeaux, see *Histoire de Bordeaux, III. Bordeaux sous les rois d'Angleterre, 1152–1453*, ed. Y. Renouard (Bordeaux, 1965), pp. 325–32. For Bayonne, *Archives Municipales de Bayonne. Livre des Etablissements*, ed. E. Dulaurens, (Bayonne, 1892), pp. xliv–xlv.

[13] See, for example, the *maison du sénéchal* at Agen, and the *cornières* or arcaded passages around the market places in many Gascon *bastides*, described in M. Beresford, *New Towns of the Middle*

additions made to the ducal castles at Bordeaux and Bayonne between 1320 and 1330 were partly financed from increased revenues in the duchy.[14] By 1313 the income derived from Gascon sources was sufficient for the duchy's revenues to be pledged by Edward II as security for the 25,000 *l.st.* loan obtained by the king-duke from Clement V.[15] Aquitaine was by no means the least valuable part of the Plantagenet dominions.

Economic historians have sometimes emphasized the damaging effects of the great famine of 1315–17, whose effects were felt until 1322, on the northern European economy.[16] Southern Europe appears to have escaped the crisis, and Aquitaine was no exception. Edward II experienced the calamity of Bannockburn shortly before the famine, while Louis X's Flemish campaign of 1315 was wrecked by the torrential rain and epidemics which impeded the progress of his army. Aquitaine therefore became a source of supply for more northerly areas. The chronicler Jean, canon of St Victor-de-Paris, reported in 1315 that wine and victuals were then brought to France from Gascony, and that the Flemings attacked and seized Bayonnais ships taking wine and corn to England. Supplies of foodstuffs for French consumption were, however, exhausted by 1316 and 'the greatest dearth' then afflicted the northern parts of the kingdom and the Low Countries.[17] There is, moreover, plentiful evidence for the export of corn as well as wine from Gascony to England in 1315–17. On 30 May 1316, for instance, the appropriately named William Welyfedd, king's merchant of Melcombe, was licensed to go with his ship to Aquitaine to buy corn for sale in Dorset and Somerset. A month later Guillaume de Balet, canon of Agen, brought corn from Gascony to England 'for the sustenance of himself and his household', while in January and April 1317 two king's merchants and four burgesses of Berwick-upon-Tweed received safe-conducts to journey to Gascony to buy 'corn, wine and other victuals', some destined for the provisioning of Berwick.[18] The high prices which they no doubt paid could only benefit the

---

Ages. Town Plantation in England, Wales and Gascony (London, 1967), pp. 166–7. For castles, see above, pp. 114–18.

[14] See E 30/1579, mm. 2–5: charges against Richard de Elsfield, constable of Bordeaux, relating to seizures and abuses during the construction of a new tower at the castle of l'Ombrière (February 1320); C 61/32, m. 4 (Edward II's order to Elsfield to repair and improve all ducal castles in Aquitaine, 6 December 1318); E 36/78, p. 41 (works at Bayonne castle, 1329–30).

[15] See E. A. R. Brown, 'Gascon subsidies and the finances of the English dominions, 1315–24', *Studies in Medieval and Renaissance History*, viii (1971), pp. 146–53.

[16] H. S. Lucas, 'The great European famine of 1315, 1316 and 1317', *Speculum*, v (1930), pp. 343–8, 364–75; cf. I. Kershaw, 'The great famine and agrarian crisis in England, 1315–1322', *PP*, lix (1973), pp. 3–5, 48–50; J. Day, *The Medieval Market Economy* (Oxford, 1988), pp. 185–90.

[17] Jean de St Victor, *Prima vita Johannis XXII*, in *Vitae Paparum Avenionensium*, ed. S. Baluze, re-ed. G. Mollat, i (Paris, 1914), pp. 114, 115; M.-J. Larenaudie, 'Les famines en Languedoc aux xive et xve siècles', *AM*, lxiv (1952), p. 37; Brown, 'Gascon subsidies', pp. 48, 61–2.

[18] *CPR, 1313–17*, pp. 467, 478, 613, 641.

duchy's inhabitants. Bullion was increasingly drawn from England to Gascony through wine and corn purchases, although some reciprocity of trade was achieved in non-famine years. But Aquitaine's previous position as a net importer of foodstuffs was clearly reversed at this time.

Demographic growth was above all concentrated in both old and new towns within the duchy and on its borders. The foundation of *bastides* will be treated in the following section, but older settlements clearly also witnessed a considerable expansion in their populations. By 1300 Bordeaux was probably at its demographic peak, with an estimated 30,000 inhabitants, equal in size to London at the beginning of the thirteenth century. The construction of a new *enceinte*, or fortified enclosure, at Bordeaux between 1302 and 1327 probably reflects expectations of further population growth.[19] The city was comparable in size with Bruges (about 35,000 inhabitants in 1340), or Toulouse (about 34,000 inhabitants in *c.*1335). Ghent outstripped all other regional capitals with its patrician, mercantile and industrial population of over 60,000 on the eve of the Black Death. The remainder of the towns of south-west France were relatively small, though not unusually so – Bayonne probably had a population of 8000 in 1316, while Agen and Périgueux contained about 6000, leaving Bazas, La Réole, Libourne, Marmande, St Macaire and St Emilion with about 2500 inhabitants each.[20] Renouard estimated that the 'urban' population of Aquitaine stood at about 90,000 inhabitants in 1316, and therefore represented 14.4 per cent of its total population of 625,000. But numbers were overwhelmingly concentrated at Bordeaux, and some areas such as the Landes were very sparsely populated, approaching a near-desert of scrub and wasteland in certain regions.[21] These heathlands, as we shall see, and the densely afforested areas, were ripe for colonization as the population continued to increase.

With 33 per cent of the duchy's urban population gathered within its walls and suburbs, Bordeaux's status as a regional capital was unchallenged. The city was ruled by a mercantile elite of *jurats*, self-perpetuating and inter-related by kinship and marriage, and there was little corporate organization of the artisan class into *métiers* or guilds on the Flemish pattern.[22] There was little manufacturing industry in the city, and its 'proletariat' consisted largely of those who serviced the needs of the port and supplied the population with food. A large group of dockers and bargees (*gabarriers*) represented the only section of the population who, together with the butchers, might be incited to rise on behalf of a faction in the confused internal politics

---

[19] L. Genicot, 'Les grandes villes de l'Occident en 1300', in *Economies et sociétiés au Moyen Age. Mélanges offerts à Edouard Perroy* (Paris, 1973), p. 208; *Histoire de Bordeaux, III*, pp. 224–9.

[20] Genicot, 'Les grandes villes de l'Occident', pp. 209, 211, 217; Renouard, 'Conjectures sur la population', pp. 168–9.

[21] Renouard, 'Conjectures sur la population', pp. 169–70.

[22] *Histoire de Bordeaux, III*, pp. 347–9.

of the city.[23] Bordeaux's ruling class, from whom its mayors and *jurats* were recruited, displayed an ambivalent attitude towards the trade and commerce which was the source of their enrichment. Land-hunger had prevailed over sea-fever among them, for the pull towards landed wealth was strong. The old patrician families – the Rostain, Monadey, Béguey, Lambert and d'Ailhan – tended to marry into the local nobility of the Bordelais, and their landed connections were both ramified and extensive. They have been described as an essentially 'rural, land-hungry stock', and their lack of interest and involvement in 'venturing' and the construction or fitting-out of ships reflected this preoccupation with land, privilege and security.[24] Most of them possessed vineyards and marketed their wine. Yet, as has already been argued, the rise of newer, commercial families in the early thirteenth century began to change the dominant character of Bordeaux's elite. The Colom, Soler and Caillau owed much of their fortune to trade and commerce, particularly with England, and the establishment of a powerful and privileged body of Gascon vintners in London expressed the strength of this relationship. By 1302 a series of privileges had been confirmed, enjoyed by the Gascon residents in Vintry ward, with great warehouses such as the establishment known as 'La Réole' or Tower Royal to which the winecasks were brought up from the Thames. They were an important and, their English rivals claimed, an excessively privileged group among London's commercial population.[25]

The bourgeois of Bordeaux enjoyed specific legal and economic benefits as a result of their membership of that body of enfranchised citizens, providing the *jurade* of twenty-four councillors and the members of the rarely convoked council of Three Hundred. They gained exemption from payment of customs on their wine and enjoyed the right to sell their own wine before that of the hinterland (*haut pays*) which was withheld from sale until the Bordeaux vintage had been bought. Given the profits made by the Plantagenet regime from the 'great custom' at Bordeaux, (between 6 and 10 per cent of the price of the wine), it was clearly to the king-duke's advantage to limit entry into the city's bourgeoisie. In 1261 a statute, confirmed in 1331, confined the status of bourgeoisie to those who fulfilled two criteria: they had to reside permanently at Bordeaux, and should not be members of the nobility.[26]

[23] See C. Bémont, 'Les factions et les troubles à Bordeaux de 1300 à 1330 environ. Documents inédits', *BPH* (1916), pp. 121–80, esp. p. 168; Funck-Brentano, 'Les luttes sociales au xive siècle', pp. 313, 317–18.

[24] J. Bernard, *Navires et gens de mer à Bordeaux (vers 1400–vers 1550)*, i (Paris, 1968), pp. 17–21.

[25] See above, pp. 19–20; G. A. Williams, *Medieval London. From Commune to Capital* (London, 1963), pp. 109–10, 117–18; M. K. James, 'Les activités commerciales des negociants en vins gascons en Angleterre à la fin du Moyen Age', *AM*, lxv (1953), pp. 39–42, 45–7.

[26] P. Chaplais, 'A propos de l'ordonnance de 1375 sur la bourgeoisie et la jurade de Bordeaux', in *Essays in Medieval Diplomacy and Administration* (London, 1981), pt XI, pp. 113–14; *AMB. Livre des Bouillons*, p. 380.

Henry III had no wish to see an increase in a class which paid no taxes on wine, and it was argued that if nobles were freely admitted to the bourgeoisie they might play a preponderant role in the city's affairs, contrary to the interests of both king-duke and bourgeois. But the king-duke reserved the power to grant letters of bourgeoisie to nobles of the Bordelais and exercised this right until 1375.[27] The existing connections between the nobility and bourgeoisie were thus maintained, but the conditions under which new bourgeois were created underwent some change.

It would be a distortion of the evidence to draw sharp distinctions between 'nobles', 'patricians' and bourgeois at Bordeaux during this period. Even the so-called 'new' families of Soler, Colom and Caillau soon forged links with the rural nobility through marriage. It has been rightly said that medieval urban conflicts are resistant to analysis along 'class' lines, for 'landed nobles and bourgeois traders' did not 'constitute mutually exclusive groups whose economic interests were straightforwardly aligned against each other and the same goes for merchants and artisans'.[28] At Bordeaux the most ancient family was that of Puy-Paulin, who held the title of Captaux de Buch. They resided at the urban palace of Puy-Paulin, reconstructed in c.1230, but became extinct in the direct male line by 1300. The ubiquitous Grilly family absorbed this ancient line and added the Captalat de Buch to their other lordships in the early fourteenth century. With the death of Pierre 'lo Massip', lord of Puy-Paulin and captal de Buch, and his wife Jeanne de Périgord in May 1309, the way lay open for Pierre II de Grilly (husband of Assalhide de Bordeaux, lady of Puy-Paulin) to claim their inheritance.[29] Other bourgeois families sought unions with the local nobility – the Lambert's daughters married into the Tartas and de Goth families; the Caillau into the Podensac; the Soler to the vicomtes of Fronsac and Tartas; the Colom into the Escoussan and Montferrand.[30] The Soler had been lords of Belin since the 1230s, but resided at their urban *oustau* in the Faubourg St-Eloi at Bordeaux. The Colom took up residence in the commercial quarter known as La Rousselle and, as we shall see, the factional politics of the city began to assume a topographical character. A passion for land and office consumed these family clans, and they sought support from outside the city, partly as a result of marriages with the rural nobility.[31]

Bordeaux's relationship with the countryside of the Garonne basin was, at first sight, a dominant one: Marx's observation that 'the bourgeoisie has enslaved the countryside to the town' might seem to be borne out by the

[27] Chaplais, 'A propos de l'ordonnance de 1375', pp. 114–16.

[28] S. Reynolds, *Kingdoms and Communities in Western Europe, 900–1300* (Oxford, 1984), p. 203.

[29] *Histoire de Bordeaux, III*, pp. 69–72.

[30] *Histoire de Bordeaux, III*, pp. 72, 78, 80–1.

[31] J. Bernard, 'Trade and finance in the Middle Ages', in *Fontana Economic History of Europe*, pp. 308–9; *Histoire de Bordeaux, III*, pp. 80–1.

history of Bordeaux between 1250 and 1330.[32] Smaller towns such as St Emilion, Langon, St Macaire, Penne d'Agenais, La Réole or Agen were to some extent dependent upon Bordeaux as both a market and outlet for their produce. These places, however, despite Bordelais opposition, still managed to gain preferential tariffs on their goods sold within the city. Signs of the emergence of Bordeaux as an incipient city-state or republic have been discerned by 1300. A large autonomous city with its surrounding *contado*, on the Italian or Flemish pattern, might indeed have developed, but such tendencies were largely cut short by political factors: principally the outbreak of Anglo-French war in 1294 and the practice whereby a mayor was chosen for Bordeaux by the king-duke of Aquitaine. As Renouard concluded, 'il n'y a place pour une république urbaine entre les rois de France et d'Angleterre' in the early fourteenth century.[33] Bordeaux's close external relations with higher authorities, both Plantagenet and Capetian, and the nature of its internal politics conspired to prevent the emergence of a quasi-independent city-state in south-west France.

Bordeaux was in fact as dependent upon its hinterland for its life-blood as the latter was dependent upon the city as an *entrepôt*, port and regional market. Since the loss of Poitou and La Rochelle by the Plantagenets between 1224 and 1242, England's wine consumption and import trade became exclusively concentrated upon Aquitaine.[34] Demand could not be met solely from the produce of areas within the Plantagenet duchy, and a considerable proportion of the wine brought to Bordeaux in the early fourteenth century originated in the *haut pays* of the Dordogne, Garonne and the Languedoc. About 50 per cent of wine exported from Bordeaux between 1305 and 1320 derived from market towns as distant as Albi, Pamiers, Montréjeau or Souillac, linked to the city by a network of waterways stemming from the Garonne and Dordogne. The region irrigated by the Lot, Tarn and Garonne was economically orientated towards the west, for the 'natural direction of river traffic was towards Bordeaux rather than towards the Mediterranean'.[35] As a means of communication and supply, the river-system of the south-west and the Languedoc greatly assisted the wine trade, for overland routes were slow and difficult. Bordeaux's geographical position as an outlet to the Atlantic and thence to north-west Europe conferred a commercial monopoly which was to survive the outbreak of Anglo-French war in 1337. But the volume of its export trade fell dramatically as the *haut pays* became the *pays rebelle*, a hostile territory in enemy hands. Although

---

[32] Quoted by Le Goff, 'The town as an agent of civilisation', p. 92.

[33] *Histoire de Bordeaux, III*, p. 563; cf. B. Guenée, *States and Rulers in later Medieval Europe*, tr. J. Vale (Oxford, 1985), p. 164.

[34] Y. Renouard, 'Le grand commerce des vins de Gascogne au Moyen Age', *RH*, ccxxi (1959), pp. 261–304; 'Vignobles, vignes et vins de France au Moyen Age', *MA*, lxvi (1960), pp. 342–4.

[35] Beresford, *New Towns of the Middle Ages*, p. 364; E 101/161/17, mm. 2^r–6^v (customs accounts at Bordeaux, 1306–7).

licences were issued for the sale of *haut pays* wines at Bordeaux, by 1350 the average annual export of wine had fallen to 8000 tuns.[36] But it would be erroneous to see the city as the centre of an export trade confined solely to the products of viticulture. It has been concluded that 'the development of the wine industry and its large-scale export never completely superseded the cornfields and meadows, orchards and woodlands, freshwater fishing, and the complex of local exchanges which for a long time guaranteed the stability of the local and regional economy'.[37] Bordeaux therefore served as an important local market, and some of its merchants traded exclusively with the hinterland of the Garonne basin, supplying freshwater and salt-fish, cloth, furs, wood and many other commodities to the Bordelais and *haut pays*. Even as an exporter Bordeaux's activities were not restricted to the wine trade. Grain, woad – the blue dye from the Toulousain and Albigeois used by the cloth industry – resins, honey and the wood from which textile combs were made supplemented the cargoes of the wine fleets.[38]

There was thus a close interrelationship between Bordeaux's external trade and its economic connections with inland regions. The ambivalent attitude displayed towards trade and commerce by its ruling class was to some extent reflected in the city's political allegiances. Within the city, factions grew whose loyalties were in part determined by economic consider-ations. Trade with England or closer contacts with those parts of its hinter-land held directly by the Capetians could appear as mutually exclusive aims in the factional struggles of this period. An increasingly commercial upper bourgeoisie was, however, anxious to ensure the survival of a status quo which was very much to its advantage. Allegiance to the Plantagenet king-dukes was cemented by economic benefits, privileges and monopolies. In the midst of intense factional strife, there remained a fundamental loyalty to the Plantagenet regime which was to survive until the mid fifteenth century. When the *jurats* of the city wrote to John Salmon, bishop of Norwich, requesting him to intercede for them with Edward II over the appointment of a mayor who would restore peace and stability in 1310–11, they warned him that 'unless our lord the king urgently interposes [good] counsel, the power of the French will put down its ineradicable roots [*radices suas inextirpabiles*], but may Almighty God prevent that'.[39] There could be no clearer statement of the preferred allegiance of the *jurade* to their natural lord, the king-duke of Aquitaine.

[36] Carus-Wilson and Coleman, *England's Export Trade*, p. 202; M. K. James, *The Non-sweet Wine Trade of England in the Fourteenth and Fifteenth Centuries* (unpublished Oxford D. Phil. thesis, 1952), pp. 48–50.

[37] Bernard, 'Trade and finance in the Middle Ages', p. 305.

[38] James, *The Non-sweet Wine Trade*, pp. 273–80; Bernard, 'Trade and finance in the Middle Ages', p. 282.

[39] E 101/161/25, no. 40: 'nisi dominus noster Rex inibi breviter consilium interponet, Guallicorum potestas radices suas inextirpabiles radicabit, sed Deus omnipotens hoc advertat'.

Unlike Bordeaux, the town of Bayonne lived largely from and by sea-faring. Its population consisted of shipbuilders, shipmasters, sailors and craftsmen engaged in the construction and equipping of vessels. It was a fitting-out port and, although its position on the estuary of the Adour gave it a fertile hinterland, Bayonne never achieved Bordeaux's rôle as a great trading-centre which provided both capital and freight for maritime enterprises.[40] Bayonnais merchants were adventurous; Bayonnais shipmasters and sailors were renowned for their aggressive and piratical tendencies. High profits – of 30–40 per cent – could be won from adventurous trading, but the risks were commensurately great. The Bayonnais provided ships for the external maritime trade of Bordeaux and were among the most prominent carriers of north-west Europe. The town's function was similar to that of the south-western ports of the English coast, and to the Cinque Ports. Bayonne's role was to provide Bordeaux with ships and crews who ventured beyond the treacherous sandbanks into the Bay of Biscay and the Atlantic. In 1303–4, they supplied 86 out of the 464 ships loading cargoes at Bordeaux, but were in fierce competition with Breton, Spanish and Norman shipowners. No less than 119 Breton ships were at Bordeaux in 1303–4, while the Normans were represented by 59 vessels.[41] This inevitably resulted in friction and conflict, and Bayonnais encounters at sea with their commercial rivals were to contribute substantially to the escalation of Anglo-French tensions.[42] In 1308 they refused to allow Edward II's seneschal of Aquitaine to appease their conflict with Spanish mariners and, although they were theoretically subject to the jurisdiction of the *Rôles d'Oléron* and the *prévôt* of the Ombrière at Bordeaux, the laws of the sea sat lightly upon them.[43] They were too useful and valuable an interest-group for the king-dukes and their officers to alienate.

Apart from their apparently spontaneous and complementary partnership with Bordeaux, the mariners of Bayonne formed part of a maritime union which linked them with English ports from Bristol to Berwick. Bayonne was in a sense the sixth Cinque Port. The Bayonnais generally made common cause with English sailors against the Normans and other subjects of the French crown. They were included in maritime truces together with the men of King's Lynn, Yarmouth, the Cinque Ports and their Gascon compatriots at Blaye and Bourg in 1298 and in the 1330s.[44] In 1302 a deputation from the shipmasters and mariners of 'the ports of the English kingdom and other lands annexed to the English crown', including the Bayonnais, put certain

---

[40] J. Bernard, 'Les types de navires ibériques et leur influence sur la construction navale dans les ports du sud-ouest de la France (xve–xvie siècles)', *Les Aspects internationaux de la découverte océanique aux xve et xvie siècles*, ed. M. Mollat and P. Adam (Paris, 1966), pp. 196–7, 201.

[41] *Histoire de Bordeaux, III*, pp. 242, 283–5; cf. E 101/163/2 (1308–10).

[42] See below, pp. 183–5.

[43] SC 1/33, no. 146; *Foedera*, II, i, p. 60.

[44] *CPR, 1281–92*, p. 520; C 47/29/4, nos 23, 26(b); *Foedera*, II, ii, p. 963 (20 March 1337).

articles of complaint against Philip the Fair before a sympathetic Boniface VIII.[45] Unlike their Bordelais partners, they had developed a collective organization known as the *Societas navium baionensium*, which originated in 1206 as guild of merchants, shipowners, shipmasters and sailors. It was a powerful confraternity, and its badge can still be seen on the roof-bosses of Bayonne cathedral. There was safety in numbers at sea, and the *societas* provided ships for the convoys which plied between Bordeaux and Bristol, London, the ports of south-west England and East Anglia.[46] Bayonne was formally annexed to the English crown, as part of its Angevin inheritance, and a memorandum of Edward III's reign stated that the town was 'forever joined to the English crown without intermediate [lord], and incorporated into the patrimony of the kings of England without ever being . . . severed from the aforesaid crown'.[47] The power of the ruling class was exemplified in 1324 when Bernard de Vielle, Bayonne's protocor, told Edward II that he should not change his seneschals so frequently in Aquitaine, to which the king-duke agreed. The composition of the ducal council was also criticized by the Bayonnais, and Edward similarly accepted their recommendation.[48] Although it was in effect a relatively small coastal harbour, Bayonne clearly possessed considerable political as well as economic influence. This was to have an important effect upon Anglo-French relations at periods of crisis.

Although they tended to be dependent in varying degrees upon Bordeaux for access to wider markets, the remaining towns of the duchy enjoyed some independence of activity and association. Agen was a small regional capital of some 6000 inhabitants which grew rapidly during this period, well placed as a result of its situation close to the confluence of the Garonne and the Lot. In 1319, the merchants of Agen, Cahors and Albi were in conflict with the mayor and *jurats* of Bordeaux over a custom on wines brought to Bordeaux imposed by Philip the Fair during the French occupation of the duchy between 1294 and 1303. Although the ducal court had abolished the custom *cessante causa*, the case had gone to the Paris Parlement and sentence had been delivered against Bordeaux.[49] Towns such as Agen, Penne d'Agenais, Villeneuve-sur-Lot and others in the Toulousain and Albigeois were in fact privileged by the Plantagenets through the concession of franchises allowing them to pay customs on their wine at preferential rates. Such rights were confined to their bourgeois, and specifically excluded the nobles, as Gérard

[45] C 47/27/3, no. 34.

[46] See J. Balasque and E. Dulaurens, *Etudes historiques sur la ville de Bayonne*, i (Bayonne, 1862), pp. 54–72; Bernard, 'Trade and finance in the Middle Ages', p. 320.

[47] C 47/28/5, no. 52. The memorandum also set out regulations and privileges relating to the taking of prizes, letters of marque, and the hearing of maritime and other cases according to the Gascon 'marcher law' (*loi de marche*) or the laws of Oléron.

[48] C 47/24/3, no. 15: 'Les poinz de la creance Bernard de Vile et tout le lignage de vile de Bayon'.

[49] C 61/32, mm. 11, 13 (1 March and 20 April 1319).

de Poujols, *bacheler*, resident at Penne, pointed out in *c*.1327.[50] The bourgeois of these towns levied tallages, *questes* and other impositions on all inhabitants, including nobles, and Gérard complained to Edward II that he should be free from such taxes and 'in no way comparable with the peasants of the countryside'. Towns exercised quasi-seigneurial privileges and their exactions and exemptions could give rise, as we shall see, to opposition from the nobility. Social tensions were generated by such issues, especially in the Agenais. In 1292, the consuls of Agen and Condom petitioned Edward I that the barons, prelates and nobles of the region intended to obtain from him certain concessions which would redound to the detriment of the public good of towns in the Agenais. These probably concerned fiscal and judicial immunities, and in May 1294 (on the eve of the Anglo-French war) both Agen and Condom agreed to share the costs of a delegation to England in proportion to the number of hearths (*feux*) in each town.[51] Mutual association between the consuls or *jurats* of south-western French towns was not an infrequent event at this time.

One price of urban loyalty to the king-dukes was the grant of aids and subventions for projects of public works. Of these, bridge-building was among the most significant in this country of rivers and waterways. The saga of the bridge over the Garonne at Agen, which was subject to heavy flooding, was a protracted one, beginning in 1280 and ending with a dispute between the consuls and the Cahorsin mason employed by them in 1298. This was a period of widespread bridge-building in south-west France, where new fortified bridges of stone or brick were constructed at Montauban (1303–16), Cahors (1308–10) and Agen. In 1280 the consuls of Agen received a gift of 8000 *s.b.* from certain inhabitants of Montauban in remission of crimes committed against them, and between 1282 and 1287 Edward I and his seneschals made a series of grants to enable the uncompleted bridge to be properly constructed. An attempt to finish the edifice was thwarted by flooding in 1286, which broke the existing structure 'to the great damage of the town . . . and surrounding regions', and Edward I granted the consuls the right to levy a special toll on all traffic crossing the river. Agen was situated on a pilgrimage-route to Compostella, which gave additional weight to pleas for aid in 1287.[52] Further troubles were experienced in August 1298, when the newly completed bridge apparently showed signs of cracks, and Bernard Tixier of Cahors was accused by the consuls of inferior workmanship. The emplacements for crossbows were also considered to be inadequate, but the dispute was resolved before the bishop's seneschal and the *bailli*, apparently to the satisfaction of all parties. A bridge was a vital part of

---

[50] SC 8/289, no. 14426.

[51] SC 1/14, no. 145; 16, no. 61; *AM Agen. Chartes (1189–1328)*, ed. A. Magen and G. Tholin (Villeneuve-sur-Lot, 1876), nos 88–9.

[52] See *AM Agen. Chartes*, nos 61, 78, 111.

a town's resources, often providing a source of both road and river tolls as well as easing the passage of merchants, pilgrims and merchandise. As the Pont Valentré at Cahors still demonstrates, it could also be an important part of a town's defensive apparatus whereby a meandering river could serve as a moat, and a bridge as a barbican. But without external assistance from a prince or great lord, few towns could finance such enterprises.

A further price of urban loyalty was the privilege of summons only to courts lying within a town's immediate area. In October 1300 the men of Agen were confirmed in their refusal to appear before the seneschal of Périgord by Philip the Fair, because they were not to be summoned outside the *sénéchaussées* of the Agenais or (so the royal lawyers argued) Toulouse.[53] A similar case arose in 1312, when the mayor, *jurats* and commune of Dax complained to Edward II that the French seneschal of Périgord had cited them to appear at Paris, Périgueux and elsewhere outside their own *banlieu* and the king-dukes' jurisdiction. A plethora of appellants to the French crown had plagued them, and they accordingly drew up two ordinances to prevent the evil consequences of such actions both for Edward II's lordship and for their own *fors*, customs and privileges. They reported that the entire commune had sworn on the altar of Notre-Dame at Dax to obey only the king-duke or his seneschal, with the exception of eight craven burgesses who feared the wrath of the French.[54] The costs, difficulties and delays of Capetian justice were often sufficient disincentives to potential appellants against ducal jurisdiction and the evidence from Gascon towns at this date suggests that too much importance may have been attached in the past to the problem of appeals. A fundamental loyalty to the king-dukes, sustained and nourished by privileges, was to survive in the longer term through the many vicissitudes of Anglo-French relations. Short-term changes nevertheless had important effects. The following section will consider the urban developments of the period from 1250 to 1340 and assess the changes which new town foundation brought to the political, economic and social structure of the duchy of Aquitaine.

5.2   New Settlements

The creation of new settlements in south-west France between 1250 and 1330 was a reflection of a more general European phenomenon. Whether these were described as *bastides*, *sauvetés*, *castelnaux*, *bourgs castraux* or *castra populata*, their foundation represented 'l'aspect régional d'un phenomène d'ampleur européenne'.[55] The chronology of town plantation in southern France during

---

[53] *AM Agen. Chartes*, no. 122 (6 October 1300). In November 1312 the *jurats* of Bordeaux argued that they were not obliged to plead in any court outside the city or diocese of Bordeaux, least of all in the seneschal's court at Toulouse which was four days' journey and more from Bordeaux: APA, E 22, no. 9, m. 5.

[54] SC 8/290, no. 14468.

[55] B. Cursente, *Les Castelnaux de la Gascogne médiévale* (Bordeaux, 1980), p. 94.

the thirteenth century, however, did not proceed at a uniform pace. In the lands of Alphonse de Poitiers, *bastide* foundation began in 1246 and reached a peak in the 1260s.[56] The first of the new settlements in Plantagenet Aquitaine was the *bastide* at Monségur in 1263, with further periods of concentrated activity in 1280–92 and 1308–20.[57] There was therefore some retardation in the process of town creation within the duchy of Aquitaine. This was probably less the result of the preoccupation of the king-dukes with their English kingdom than of the effects of political turbulence in Gascony during the 1240s and 1250s. The uncertain status of the duchy before 1259 did not increase its security and it was only after the acquisition of the Agenais by Edward I in 1279 that newly planted towns began to proliferate in his domains.[58] It could also be argued that the loss of Poitou by Henry III between 1224 and 1242 provided an incentive to concentrate resources primarily upon Bordeaux and its defence as the capital of the Plantagenet dominions. Simon de Montfort's subsequent government in Aquitaine did not create conditions in which new foundations might easily be undertaken and, with the exception of Libourne (1270), Beaumont-de-Périgord (1272) and Pellegrue (1272), the first spate of *bastides* in ducal Aquitaine dated from Jean de Grilly's tenure of the *sénéchaussée* between 1278 and his dismissal in 1287.[59] The creation of Valence d'Agen in 1279, named after William de Valence, who had negotiated the transfer of the Agenais to Edward I, probably marked a turning-point. On 15 November 1279 Edward I commissioned Grilly, as seneschal of Gascony and the Agenais, to construct *bastides* in those regions and to grant them liberties and franchises. The king-duke agreed to confirm all such concessions.[60] Grilly fulfilled the terms of his commission, and at least twenty-four *bastides* were founded during his term of office. The course of foundation was to be interrupted only by the Anglo-French war of 1294–1303.

The creation of new settlements, whether imposed upon existing centres of population or reclaimed from wasteland, obviously conferred benefits on those who founded them. But they could be the cause of problems. The effects of newly planted *bastides* or *novae populaciones* on local conditions could be disruptive, and existing economic and social patterns could be disturbed and threatened by them. When established in contested territory, their foundation had political as well as economic implications.[61] The context in which new plantations must be seen was one of reclamation and colonization.

---

[56] See Beresford, *New Towns of the Middle Ages*, pp. 352–63, figure 61; C 47/29/1/10 for a list of his and his seneschals' foundations.

[57] Beresford, *New Towns of the Middle Ages*, tables XXII.1, XIII.3 on pp. 353, 357–8.

[58] J.-P. Trabut-Cussac, 'Bastides ou forteresses', *MA*, lx (1954), pp. 122–4, 125; Beresford, *New Towns of the Middle Ages*, table XXIII.3.

[59] Trabut-Cussac, *L'Administration anglaise en Gascogne sous Henry III et Edouard I de 1254 à 1307* (Geneva, 1972), pp. 58–64, 98.

[60] *RG*, ii, no. 259; Trabut-Cussac, *L'Administration anglaise*, pp. 64–5.

[61] Trabut-Cussac, 'Bastides ou forteresses', p. 126.

Bastides possessed no evident military function, and their primary purpose was colonization and exploitation.[62] In the thirteenth century, south-west France was covered by vast areas of uncultivated woodland, scrubland and marshes, to which settlers could be attracted only by the grant of extensive liberties and privileges. *Bastides* such as Baa, founded in 1287 and named after Robert Burnell, bishop of Bath and Wells, were created to recover cultivable land from waste and forest and these settlements resembled the earlier *sauvetés*, founded by religious houses on inferior or marginal lands.[63] The Cistercians possessed large estates in the region, and new settlements often correspond with their granges. The order founded forty-four *bastides*, twenty-eight as the result of contracts of *paréage* with Alphonse de Poitiers, Eustache du Beaumarchais and other seneschals of the French crown. Yet none of the planted towns of this period appear to have been fortified from their inception.[64] No document demonstrates the king-duke of Aquitaine's initiative, for example, behind the fortification of Gascon *bastides*. They did not defend frontiers in a military sense, but could serve to demarcate judicial and administrative boundaries and spheres of influence, especially when created in contested territories. New settlements lying on the marches of the duchy could form part of a zone (or *champ limitrophe*) while others were enclaves within the jurisdictions of other lords. The *bastides* created frontiers rather than defended them. In 1305, Arnaud-Loup, lord of Estivaux, proposed an alliance or *paréage* with Edward I in order to construct a new *bastide* on his land at Ozourt (Landes) where Arnaud-Loup's enemy, the lord of Navailles, had committed various outrages. There was, he stated, sufficient land and wood to support over 2000 inhabitants, and there was little doubt that this act of demarcation and exploitation might prove mutually beneficial.[65]

Bastide foundation, like that of *castelnaux* or new fortified villages, must therefore be related to demographic growth, seigneurial profit and the desire to colonize and reclaim. The example of Alphonse de Poitiers was undoubtedly influential. In his *comté* of Toulouse, he and his seneschals had created thirty-eight bastides between 1249 and 1272, which each yielded an annual revenue of more than 1000 *livres tournois* (*l.t.*) at his death. They were intended to 'establish his authority in frontier areas while attracting to himself the men of neighbouring lordships'.[66] The Plantagenet regime followed suit, slowly after 1263, more rapidly after 1279, and its *bastides* served

[62] O. de St-Blanquat, 'Comment se sont créeés les bastides du sud-ouest de la France?', *Annales*, iv (1949), p. 278.

[63] J.-P. Trabut-Cussac, 'Date, fondation et identification de la bastide de Baa', *RHB* n.s., x (1961), pp. 133–44. The *bastide*, which was intended as a means of forest clearance around Bordeaux, failed, as did the nearly contemporary *Burgus Regine*. For Cistercian foundations and *paréages* see C. Higounet, 'Cisterciens et bastides', *MA*, lvi (1950), pp. 69–84.

[64] See Trabut-Cussac, 'Bastides ou forteresses', pp. 94–121, for detailed discussion of this point and a demonstration that bastides did not conform to any identifiable 'line of defence'.

[65] SC 8/29, nos 14543, 2943; Beresford, *New Towns of the Middle Ages*, p. 607.

[66] St-Blanquat, 'Comment se sont créeés les bastides?', p. 282.

as active agents of ducal authority, normally shared with local lords. Many of Edward I's *bastides* were built on the edge of afforested land, and assarting or clearing woodland was inevitably a major occupation of their earliest settlers. Sauveterre-de-Guyenne, founded in 1281, chartered in 1283 on the model of Monségur (1263) was the product of an essentially local initiative.[67] The abbot of Blasimont and Jourdain de Puch, esquire, entered into a contract with Edward I to exploit their land there more effectively by establishing a *nova populacio* at Sauveterre. Each inhabitant was to have as much land as he could work with two oxen, a garden, a vine, and a plot in the grid-pattern of the new settlement on which to build a dwelling. The *bastides* were thus primarily units of collective agricultural exploitation, in which colonies of free labourers clustered. Their mode of foundation was comparable with the allotment of uncultivated lands to individual settlers by the seneschals of Aquitaine, whereby *possessiones steriles . . . vel quasi steriles* were brought into cultivation.[68] There can be no doubt that the primary motive for the creation of *bastides* was economic.

The benefits to be derived by the founders of a *bastide* were clearly set out in a contract of *paréage* agreed in the castle chapel at St Gein-en-Marsan on 10 September 1284 by Raymond de Mirailh, constable of Bordeaux acting for Edward I, and Sanche-Loup, Lord of Castandet.[69] The latter agreed to surrender one-half of his lands there to the king-duke, retaining the *motte* or fort which served as a barbican to the castle at St Gein. Edward was to build two mills there at his own expense, and maintain the castle; both parties were to appoint a *bailli* or *prévôt*, dividing the fines of justice between themselves in equal shares. Various penalties were devised for non-fulfilment of the contract's terms, because Sanche-Loup had entered upon it in the hope that his lands might be improved and hence qualified for compensation. The *bastide* was duly established, the *paréage* renewed and confirmed in 1304, 1316 and 1321. Numerous examples of such agreements could be cited. *Bastides* were often founded by minor lords subject to the hostile incursions of their neighbours. Such was Pierre, lord of Castelnau-en-Tursan, who agreed to construct the aptly named settlement of Geaune (Genoa) through a *paréage* concluded with the Genoese seneschal of Aquitaine, Antonio di Pessagno, on 17 November 1318.[70] In a later petition, Pierre de Castelnau claimed that there were already more than 1000 houses in the new settlement, half of which was held by himself and the other half by Edward II. A confirmation

---

[67] J.-P. Trabut-Cussac, 'La fondation de Sauveterre-de-Guyenne (1281–3)', *RHB*, n.s., ii (1953), pp. 181–217.

[68] See P. Chaplais, 'The Chancery of Guyenne', in *Essays in Medieval Diplomacy*, pt VIII, pp. 72–3, esp. p. 73, n. 6 (12 March 1308).

[69] A. D. Gers, E 847 (confirmation of the *paréage* of 10 September 1284 by Thomas Felton, knight, lieutenant and seneschal of Aquitaine for Edward III, at Bordeaux, 21 January 1376); Beresford, *New Towns of the Middle Ages*, p. 609.

[70] A. D. Gers, E 476; APA, E 511 (confirmation of the *paréage* by Fulk Lestrange, 2 January 1319).

of the *paréage* by the seneschal of the Landes, holding his court in the refectory of the monastery at St Sever in 1322, spoke of Pierre's wish to put himself, his heirs and his subjects under the king-duke's protection. The *bastide* was henceforth to include an enclosure for a ducal castle (or *maison-forte*) to defend the place.[71] Increased seigneurial incomes undoubtedly resulted from the construction of both *bastides* and *castelnaux*, and it has recently been concluded that the latter offered a remedy for the chronically low level of seigneurial incomes.[72] The new castellated villages also permitted lords to retain larger military followings without the granting out of fiefs and, by concentrating seigneurial revenues, arrested their tendency towards fragmentation at this period. There were therefore irresistible financial motives behind regroupings of agricultural labour in the *bourgs* or *castelnaux* of eastern Gascony.[73]

The appearance of new, privileged settlements posed a threat to the lords and inhabitants of older-established towns and villages. Personal freedom was granted to the first settlers, and this proved attractive to surrounding populations. In 1278 and 1289, Edward I's lieutenants promised the nobility of the Bazadais not to create *bastides* on their lands without prior consent, and in the Agenais and Béarn agreements were made whereby serfs from neighbouring lordships were not to be received into new *bastides*.[74] The liberties granted to settlements such as Montclar (1256), Monflanquin (1270) and Monségur (1263) provided models which were followed by other *bastides*.[75] Their inhabitants were exempt from taxation, and had the right to marry freely and draw up testaments. *Bastides* were granted fairs and markets which tended to be held more frequently than in existing settlements, and many of the new foundations became important centres of local administration, trade and exchange. At Créon, founded in 1315 by Amaury de Craon, the popularity of its market aroused the hostility of the nearby abbot and monks of La Sauve-Majeure, whose income from local commerce at La Sauve was threatened. They appealed to the Paris Parlement in 1320–1 and the *bastide* was confiscated by the French.[76] Créon also had its fairs, as well as a weekly market, and six of these took place every year. The conflicts

[71] SC 8/284, no. 14157; A. D. Gers, E 476. Pierre de Castelnau served as captain of Pimbo, Miramont and Geaune in 1323 (E 101/164/16, no. 17), and during the War of St. Sardos (*St. Sardos*, p. 273).

[72] Cursente, *Les Castelnaux*, p. 108.

[73] B. Cursente, 'Les habitats villageois fortifiés en Gascogne: une mise à jour', in *Habitats fortifiés et organisation de l'espace en Méditerranée médiévale*, ed. A. Bazzana, P. Guichard and J. M. Poisson (Lyon, 1983), pp. 57–61.

[74] St-Blanquat, 'Comment se sont créés les bastides?' p. 284.

[75] Trabut-Cussac, 'La fondation de Sauveterre-de-Guyenne', p. 186. It was a common twelfth- and thirteenth-century practice for both towns and village communities to adopt the customs of existing settlements. See Reynolds, *Kingdoms and Communities*, pp. 131–2.

[76] J.-P. Trabut-Cussac, 'Créon, bastide administrative', *AM*, lxvi (1954), pp. 345–7; G. Loirette, 'La charte de coutumes de la bastide de Créon (1315)', *AM*, lxiv (1952), pp. 283–95.

generated by the *bastide* at Hastingues, near the confluence of the Adour and the Gave de Pau, typified the problems associated with town plantation. Founded on the site of an earlier proposed *bastide* of 1289 by John de Hastings (seneschal of Aquitaine, 1302–4), Hastingues provoked opposition from the mayor and *jurats* of Bayonne and from the inhabitants of Sorde-l'Abbaye, situated on the opposite bank of the Gave de Pau. According to the proctor of Sorde, John de Hastings had ordered the *bailli* of the area that all boats which were wont to sail on the river between Bayonne and Sorde 'since time immemorial' were now to discharge their cargoes at Hastingues. This gravely damaged the interests of the inhabitants of Sorde, for they had to collect all merchandise from Hastingues and buy goods in the market there.[77] The Bayonnais were similarly incensed by the right granted to the consuls of Hastingues to levy a toll on all river traffic so that a bridge might be built and the *bastide* enclosed with walls, against the wishes of the men of Bayonne. They complained to Edward II that the river was in fact blocked by this measure and petitioned for the free passage of merchandise and exemption from any tolls to be levied on the bridge at Hastigues. Edward acceded to their request.[78]

The men of Hastingues set out their own case in a long petition addressed to Edward II, probably in 1321.[79] They emphasized their insecure position on the marches of the duchy and claimed that John de Hastings, 'fundedor du dit leu', had promised that the place would be enclosed with stone walls and other fortifications and that a bridge would be built. A toll had been granted to them for ten years, but war in the duchy had drastically reduced its value. A further list of requests followed, including the levy of a new toll, the right to bear arms throughout the duchy, the creation of a fair and market, and settlement of a claim they had to lands allegedly granted them by the Abbot of Arthus at the time of the *bastide's* foundation. This lack of available land had led to difficulties in populating the settlement adequately. It was left to Edward III, in May 1328, to grant them a new *péage* (toll) and a licence to fortify against their enemies.[80] Threats to commercial prosperity were paralleled by anxieties about depopulation among the ruling groups of older settlements. A *paréage* which created the *bastide* of Marciac in the *comté* of Pardiac contained a prohibition of migration from nearby settlements for six years, and these terms were echoed at Gimont and Mirande.[81] *Bastides* could be destructive of small castles and the populations which clustered around them, and the scattered inhabitants of hamlets and isolated farm-

---

[77] SC 8/291, no. 14522; Beresford, *New Towns of the Middle Ages*, p. 604.

[78] SC 8/290, no. 14460.

[79] SC 8/290, no. 14482; C 61/35, m. 19 (25 October and 12 November 1321).

[80] C 61/40, m. 6 (20 May 1328).

[81] Cursente, *Les Castelnaux*, pp. 84–5; Monlezun, *Histoire de Gascogne*, vi, pp. 8–9 (customs of Fézensac). In July 1275, Philip III promised to found no *bastide* or new town in Pardiac without the count's consent and his letters were confirmed by Philip VI in July 1329 (AN, JJ 66, fo. 9ʳ).

steads were naturally drawn towards them. Much of their population was recruited from migrants and they became 'isolated and inorganic communities', poorly integrated into the rural world around them.[82] They could fracture a cohesive rural society, disrupt networks of local trade and increase the incomes and authority of the 'middling' nobility at the expense of other lords.

By introducing new tensions and conflicts into rural society, *bastide* foundations, however profitable in the short term, was a mixed blessing. The attractiveness of contracts of *paréage* induced some ecclesiastical and secular lords with lands located in sensitive areas to found *bastides* in partnership with other lords in the immediate lordship of the French crown. Even in the heart of Plantagenet Aquitaine, opportunities for appeal to sources of justice outside the ducal administration were offered to lords and communities locked in conflict over the real or imagined losses and disadvantages sustained by them as a result of *bastide* foundation. They could exacerbate existing political and judicial squabbles. In 1313 Margaret of Béarn, countess of Foix, claimed that her own jurisdiction and income had been usurped when Odo de Lados, Edward II's *bailli* of St Gein-en-Marsan, levied a new *péage* or toll at that *bastide*.[83] As we shall see, the damage inflicted on local interests by a proposed *bastide* at St Sardos in the Agenais was to lead to the Anglo-French war of 1324–5.[84] But the circumstances which occasioned that conflict were not in themselves dissimilar to those which characterized the relations between other lords and communities during the previous forty or so years.

The foundation of the *bastide* at Sauveterre-de-Guyenne between 1281 and 1282 was, for example, indicative of the problems encountered by other proposed settlements.[85] Claims were made against the rights of the parties involved in a proposed *paréage* by neighbouring lords, amongst them Jean de Grilly as lord of Bergerac, and Alexandre de la Pebrée, lord of Gensac. Edward I then ordered an inquiry, as a result of which he commanded that the building of Sauveterre – halted by the dispute – should recommence.[86] Although the new *bastide* had been granted his protection, continuing conflicts over boundaries, and over the right to hold a fair, plagued the settlement's early years. In 1284 the serjeants and heralds who proclaimed the fair at Sauveterre were assaulted by Grilly's men, and the heralds' trumpets were broken. The vines owned by one party to the foundation charter were destroyed, letters from Edward I to the *nova populatio* were torn up, and difficulties were experienced in populating the *bastide*. Trabut-Cussac concluded that 'le voisinage de seigneurs plus puissants etait aussi néfaste aux

---

[82] Cursente, *Les Castelnaux*, pp. 83–5, 116–18.

[83] APA, E 507, no. 31, m. 2.

[84] See below, pp. 233–5.

[85] Trabut-Cussac, 'La fondation de Sauveterre-de-Guyenne', pp. 181–6.

[86] C 47/26/3; Beresford, *New Towns of the Middle Ages*, p. 600.

alleux qu'aux jeunes *bastides* et les féodaux prisaient mal une indépendance qui tout a fois les choquait et les humiliait'.[87] Despite such vicissitudes, the new *bastide* began to prosper, and its *baillie* was yielding 240 *l.b.* annually by 1306–7. The quarrels between its first ducal *baillis* and the neighbouring lords reflected a sudden extension of the ducal domain and a consequent rise in ducal revenues. Edward I's relatively firm hand and the conduct of a proper inquiry into seigneurial rights in 1282 contributed to the successful outcome. Anglo-French issues did not come into play, as they did at St Sardos in 1323. Jean de Grilly and Alexandre de la Pebrée were both loyal subjects of the king-duke, who owed more to his favour than any profit which they might derive from a protracted dispute over seigneurial privileges, and they made their peace with the new *bastide* at Sauveterre.[88]

There were nevertheless disturbing signs that *bastide* foundations in certain regions, such as the Agenais and the Gers, could generate friction which tended to widen the potential dimensions of Anglo-French conflict. A complaint to Edward I concerning damages sustained from the actions of Capetian officers in the diocese of Lectoure (*c.*1290–4) emphasized the usurpations of the king-duke's jurisdiction committed by Jean Archier, knight, *bailli* of the new French *bastide* of Grenade. He had summoned the king-duke's subjects before him and had attempted to hear cases concerning contracts and crimes which lay within Edward I's judicial competence.[89] A petition of Edward II to Philip the Fair requested that all *bastides* founded by the French crown and its officers were to be subject to the law (*comun droit*) observed in existing towns within his jurisdiction, 'ostees et abatues toutes mauvaises franchises'.[90] Of the Gascon cases pending before the Paris Parlement in March 1324 on the eve of the War of St Sardos, at least five concerned *bastides*, including two brought by local lords against the building of Créon.[91] But despite such conflicts, *bastides* remained a source of badly needed income to both Edward I and Edward II. For Edward I, the creation of new settlements in Aquitaine depended less upon 'his appreciation of the political support that newly founded towns could give him against the notoriously fractious Gascon vassals' than upon the revenues which accrued from them.[92] These were shared with Gascon vassals and provided another means whereby existing loyalties were strengthened and secured. In 1306–7, the *bastides* of the Agenais contributed 70 per cent of its farmed *bailliage* revenues, while 50 per cent stemmed from *bastides* in Limousin, Quercy and

---

[87] Trabut-Cussac, 'La fondation de Sauveterre-de-Guyenne', p. 210, and pp. 216–17 for the following sentences.

[88] *Gascon Register A*, i, no. 11, p. 86 for its value in 1306–7. For other manifestations of local resistance to Sauveterre, see *RG*, ii, nos 1378, 1412, 1619.

[89] C 47/29/3, fos 9[r–v].

[90] AN, J 654, no. 24.

[91] E 30/1601; *St Sardos*, pp. 38–9; AN, J 634, no. 1 (28 July 1322).

[92] Beresford, *New Towns of the Middle Ages*, p. 360.

Périgord.[93] It was to the mutual advantage of both the king-dukes and local seigneurs to engage as partners in *bastide* foundation when and where human and material resources were available. Considerations of honour, status and material need combined to promote new settlements during a period of demographic growth and relative economic prosperity. But the history of *bastide* foundation in the duchy of Aquitaine was virtually at an end by 1324.[94] The political crisis of that year, the War of St Sardos, and the eruptions of Anglo-French conflict which followed it into the reign of Edward III, did not engender a climate favourable to further settlements. Financial and economic gain had been to some extent achieved at the expense of political stability.

5.3   Faction and Conflict

Factional strife was commonplace in the political life of medieval towns. The most densely urbanized regions of western Europe – northern Italy and the Low Countries – witnessed long-standing conflicts between opposing groups organized into parties, factions and clans throughout the later Middle Ages. Faction was particularly prominent in towns which, as Jacques Heers has remarked, 'échappent à la dure tutelle d'un état princier'.[95] Even in areas subject to princely rule, however, factional warfare was rife, and the prince's authority was expressed largely through the arbitration of disputes. A town might be divided into areas or *quartiers* with opposing factional loyalties or even into two discrete blocs. At Louvain, the feud between the Van den Blankharden and the Van den Cok split the town into two identifiable districts after 1265.[96] At Bordeaux, geographical power-bases began to emerge in the thirteenth century as the major families who dominated the *jurade* and vied for the mayoralty settled in clearly defined parts of the city. The Colom had their stronghold at La Rousselle, the Caillau in the Rue-Neuve, the Soler in the Fauborg St-Eloi, but members and allies of all the major families seem also to have resided in the Rue-Neuve.[97] Communal politics became polarized, often leaving a third party of townsmen wearied by factional strife who might seek a resolution of internal struggles through the intervention of an external authority. Whether that authority was the king-duke of Aquitaine or the king of France depended upon uncertain and incalculable factors which did not contribute to the political stability of the region.

---

[93] E 101/161/16 (1306–7 accounts); *Gascon Register A*, i, no. 11, pp. 87–8.

[94] See table XIII.3 in Beresford, *New Towns of the Middle Ages*, p. 358.

[95] J. Heers, *Le Clan familial au Moyen Age* (Paris, 1974), pp. 116, 113–20; also Reynolds, *Kingdoms and Communities*, pp. 203–14.

[96] Heers, *Le Clan familial*, p. 55.

[97] *Histoire de Bordeaux, III*, pp. 72, 74, 78, 346. La Rousselle was the quarter most densely populated by the mercantile and commercially active families of the city.

One hallmark of urban politics at this time was the tendency among upper bourgeois families, linked by marriage to the nobility, to gather retinues or *mesnies* of armed followers around them. These bands were liveried, paid and fed by the participants in urban faction-fights, and they proliferated especially after the French occupation of Bordeaux between 1294 and 1303. Just as the retainers of English magnates were given robes and fees so, for example, were Arnaud Caillau and others described as being of the 'ostel, robes et maynée' of Jean Colom of Bordeaux in the 1310s and 1320s.[98] It cannot be argued convincingly that the troubles experienced at Bordeaux were related to 'inherent conflicts of interest between the "patrician oligarchies" who ruled the towns and those whom they ruled'.[99] The excluded wage-earning classes at Bordeaux rarely, if ever, made common cause and there was no large industrial proletariat on the Flemish pattern. Guild organization barely existed, and Funck-Brentano's contention that southwest France saw the outbreak of conflict between merchant-patricians and artisans, represented by fraternities, cannot be sustained during this period.[100] Nor can a political dimension be added to the internal conflicts of Bordeaux which sees 'pro-French' and 'anti-English' forces at work to determine the alignments of groups and factions.[101] The Soler were never consistently opposed to the Plantagenet regime, nor were the Colom its consistent supporters.

In origin, the conflict between the Soler and Colom appears to have stemmed from the so-called 'sedition' at Bordeaux of 1228–9.[102] Amanieu Colom was mayor in 1228, but was replaced by Alexandre de Cambes (a protégé of the Soler) with the support of Henry III's seneschal of Gascony. The Colom rebelled against the seneschal, who was seen as an instrument of the Soler and their clients among the city's ruling elite, including the Lambert, Rostaing, Béguey and D'Ailhan, all ancient dynasties ranged against the 'new' families led by the Colom. Thus the rebellion reflected internal divisions which were beginning to tear the city apart, rather than loyalties or antipathies towards a superior lord.[103] Indeed, the Colom were

---

[98] Funck-Brentano, 'Les luttes sociales au xive siècle', p. 296; Bémont, 'Les factions et les troubles à Bordeaux', p. 169 (art. 78 of complaints against Jean Colom); Heers, *Le Clan familial*, pp. 108–9, 184.

[99] Reynolds, *Kingdoms and Communities*, p. 203.

[100] Funck-Brentano, 'Les luttes sociales au xive siècle', pp. 291, 296; cf. Heers, *Le Clan familial*, pp. 122–6.

[101] See below, pp. 173–4. For a contrary view see J. A. Kicklighter, 'English Bordeaux in conflict: the execution of Pierre Vigier (sic) de la Rousselle and its aftermath 1312–24', *JMH*, ix (1983), pp. 1–14 where it is argued that a 'Francophile faction . . . dedicated to the destruction of ducal authority there' existed (p. 6). See also his 'French jurisdictional supremacy in Gascony: one aspect of the ducal government's response', *JMH*, v (1979), pp. 127–34.

[102] F. B. Marsh, *English Rule in Gascony, 1199–1259* (Michigan, 1912), pp. 153–4; *Histoire de Bordeaux, III*, pp. 46–7.

[103] *Histoire de Bordeaux, III*, p. 47.

probably the leading creditors of Henry III and his lieutenants in Gascony, advancing huge sums to them in 1225 and in 1242–3 during years of political crisis. By 1249 the tables were turned, and Simon de Montfort, as Henry III's representative in Gascony, supported the Colom against the Soler during pre-election riots and disturbances at Bordeaux in June 1249. The deaths, woundings and demolition of Rostand del Soler's urban fortress in that year marked the formal outbreak of the feud between the two families.[104] In October 1254 Henry III himself arbitrated the conflict and it was the deadlock which subsequently resulted that led the Lord Edward to take the right to choose a mayor into the hands of the king-duke or his representative in 1261.[105] The exercise of that prerogative may have saved Bordeaux from becoming an entirely faction-ridden city on the Flemish or north Italian pattern, in which urban politics were dominated by riots, confiscations of property and the banishment of political opponents.

The events of 1249 and of 1277–87, when the right to elect their mayor had been restored to the *jurade*, did not induce optimism as to the city's ability to choose its leading representative without violence and disorder.[106] Conflicts over the mayoralty and the membership of the *jurade* were generally unrelated to broader political issues. Attempts to involve the representatives of higher authorities were dictated by the self-interest of the rival factions, such as the appeals engineered by the Colom to Philip the Fair in 1290–1.[107] One decisive piece of evidence supporting the view that such appeals to the Paris Parlement were essentially an instrument of factional strife, with little or no grounds in law, was the rejection of the Coloms' case by the Parlement in 1291.[108] The mayoralty was again surrendered to the king-duke, and the dominant issue which had provoked the crises of 1228–9, 1248–9 and 1287–90 was again resolved until the middle years of Edward II's reign. In 1291, the Colom may well have wished to recover their former authority and possession of the mayoralty by surrendering Bordeaux to Philip the Fair, an event in which they were quite prepared to acquiesce in 1294.[109] They were to be disappointed and deceived by the results. Appeals were clearly tactically motivated, and appear to have been a means of delaying the exercise of justice in Aquitaine and of putting pressure upon the king-duke and his officers. In the towns, as in the countryside, frivolous appeals abounded and

---

[104] For the Colom's support of Henry III see above, pp. 19–20; *Histoire de Bordeaux, III*, pp. 47, 72; *CPR, 1247–56*, p. 23 for the first recorded peace treaty between the Soler and Colom. For the most recent account of Henry III's dealings with Bordeaux and other Gascon towns between 1224 and 1242 see R. C. Stacey, *Politics, Policy and Finance under Henry III, 1216–45* (Oxford, 1987), pp. 166–80, 197–200.

[105] See above, pp. 18–19; *Histoire de Bordeaux, III*, pp. 103–12.

[106] *AMB Livre des Coutumes*, pp. 405–6, 343; *RG*, ii, no. 1021.

[107] *Histoire de Bordeaux, III*, pp. 122–4; SC 1/23, no. 132; 24, nos 105–6.

[108] *Histoire de Bordeaux, III*, p. 125.

[109] See below, pp. 221–3.

appellants similarly took advantage of their privileged and protected status to evade ducal jurisdiction. Others had more genuine grounds for their appeals, which generally resulted from abuse of authority or denial of justice by a ducal officer. In 1319, therefore, Arnaud-Sanche de Luc, 'one of the most important [*magnatibus*] burgesses of Bayonne', had good reason to complain about the behaviour of Richard de Elsfield, constable of Bordeaux, who had seized a consignment of 14,300 herrings from his warehouse at La Rousselle in Bordeaux and taken them to the castle of the Ombrière.[110] Isolated appellants might be contained, but appeals stemming from groups and factions were more difficult to prevent or disarm. Faction was to return to the stage between 1308 and 1313 when Edward II's grip upon Gascon affairs slackened and the Plantagenet regime became overtly partisan.

The recrudescence of faction-fighting after the French occupation of Bordeaux (1294–1303) partly resulted from the rise of the Caillau family to political dominance in the city. The family was internally divided between members supporting the Colom and the Soler.[111] In January 1303 Arnaud Caillau III had exploited the widespread dissatisfaction within the city at the harshness of the French occupation and brought the mayoralty and *jurade* under the control of the Colom until 1308.[112] In that year, his cousin Pierre Caillau IV seized the mayoralty in the Solers' name and gained a majority for them in the *jurade* which then co-opted clients of the Soler and perpetuated their hegemony. In 1310, Edward II intervened through commissioners appointed to reform the city. The commissioners, relying upon the support of the neutral third party, or 'commune', appointed a mayor unrelated to the Soler, Colom or Caillau. This was the minor noble Odo de Lados, from the Bazadais, who was said by the 'commune' on 2 March 1311 to have kept the peace and successfully put down Pierre Caillau and his associates' rebellion against ducal authority.[113] But Edward II then allowed the situation to deteriorate by replacing Lados with the pro-Soler Amanieu de Fossat, knight; whether by accident or design is unclear. The 'commune' wrote to the king-duke on 17 March and 10 May 1311 protesting at this appointment, and claimed that it would not only wreck the reforms which they intended to effect, but had encouraged Arnaud Caillau and the Colom to pursue their appeal to the court of France, or the French seneschal of Périgord, against Edward's authority.[114] The king-duke replied, in his usual tardy fashion, only on 8 October 1311, reinstating Odo de Lados in the office

---

[110] E 30/1579, m. 2 (February 1320). For appeals which were related to faction-fights at Bayonne in 1312–13, see A. Giry, Les *Etablissements de Rouen* (Paris, 1885), i, pp. 124–7; *Registres du Trésor des Chartes*, i, nos 2019, 2020; AN, JJ 49, fo. 43^v (July 1313).

[111] *Histoire de Bordeaux, III*, pp. 72–4.

[112] Bémont, 'Les factions et les troubles à Bordeaux', pp. 122–6.

[113] Bémont, 'Les factions et les troubles à Bordeaux', pp. 137–8; *RG*, iv, no. 542; *Histoire de Bordeaux, III*, pp. 351–2; E 101/161/25, no. 40.

[114] Bémont, 'Les factions et les troubles à Bordeaux', pp. 137–42; *RG*, iv, nos 502, 503.

of mayor until a seneschal of Gascony had been appointed and had arrived in the duchy.[115] Into this disturbed situation, with Bordeaux in political turmoil and appeals from Jean Colom, Arnaud and Pierre Caillau and Edward II's leading Gascon vassal, Amanieu VII of Albret, pending before the Paris Parlement, came John Ferrers of Chartley, knight, seneschal of Gascony. His tenure of the office and its aftermath deserve detailed consideration.

John Ferrers and the Crisis of 1312

John Ferrers, lord of Chartley, was murdered in Aquitaine at some time between 27 August and 9 October 1312. Matthew of Westminster wrote in the *Flores Historiarum* for that year:

> In the course of the present year the Gascons, those most vile betrayers and traitors, wickedly murdered with noxious poison Lord John de Ferrers, that matchless flower of knighthood and seamanship, the invincible seneschal of Gascony, whom the king had appointed to that place in order to curb them, because he had been unable of his own authority to control that detestable rabble.[116]

These were strong words, which were perhaps intended by the author as a salutary warning to those who, like Edward II, had recently put their trust in a Gascon. It was not a normal practice, however, for the inhabitants of the duchy of Aquitaine to murder the king-duke's seneschal. Plantagenet officers in the duchy could be highly unpopular, and some were dismissed from office, but they were not victims of homicide. Ferrers's death was part of a complex sequence of events both in England and abroad, in which the interplay of domestic and external politics must be taken into account.

John Ferrers (b. 1271) was lawful heir to the earldom of Derby, but had been in effect deprived of his inheritance by Edward I, who had given it in 1269 to his own brother, Edmund of Lancaster.[117] Ferrers opposed the king during the crisis of 1297–8 and was the only magnate besides Bohun and Bigod to be specifically named in the *Articuli super Cartas* and *De Tallagio non concedendo*. Ferrers had 'a clear private motive for opposing the king', and his animosity spread to embrace Edward's treasurer Walter Langton, bishop of Coventry and Lichfield, within whose diocese he held lands.[118] Ferrers was

---

[115] *RG*, iv, no. 551; Bémont, 'Les factions et les troubles à Bordeaux', pp. 145–6.

[116] *Flores Historiarum*, ed. H. R. Luard, iii (RS, London, 1890), p. 153. The passage follows immediately after the account of Piers Gaveston's death.

[117] For a biography, see *Complete Peerage*, v, pp. 305–10; K. B. McFarlane, 'Had Edward I a "policy" towards the earls?', in *The Nobility of Later Medieval England* (Oxford, 1973), pp. 254–6 for an account of the grievances against Edward I of the house of Ferrers.

[118] See *Documents Illustrating the Crisis of 1297–8 in England*, ed. M. Prestwich, Camden Society, 4th ser., xxiv (London, 1980), pp. 14, 154–6; *Records of the Trial of Walter Langton . . . 1307–12*, ed. A. Beardwood, Camden Society, 4th ser., vi (1969), pp. 283–90.

engaged in litigation with Langton in 1301 and 1307–8, but served in the Scots wars between 1298 and 1303, becoming constable of the king's army in Scotland in 1306. He was appointed keeper of Gloucester castle in September 1311, his last office before he became seneschal of Gascony.[119] Unlike his immediate predecessors as seneschal, he had no experience of Anglo-French affairs and no foreign service of any significance. His appointment may have been made on the strength of his military career and proven qualities as a soldier, but there were other considerations behind the decision to dispatch him to Aquitaine.

In October 1311, the disgraced Walter Langton, deposed on Edward I's death, was freed from arrest and restored to the king's council. On 23 January 1312 Edward II confirmed him in possession of his lands and wrote to Clement V telling the pope of Langton's 'patiently-suffered persecutions and tribulations' and of his restoration to grace because he was 'wise, discreet and useful' to the king. He was created treasurer on the same day and Ferrers's appointment as seneschal of Gascony followed forthwith, on 24 January 1312.[120] It was no doubt beneficial to Langton's position that Ferrers should be out of England – there would then be less chance that he might resume the litigation and personal attacks which had characterized Langton's previous tenure of the treasurership. After Gaveston, Langton was now 'the closest' of Edward II's advisers, and he soon began to use his newly found influence to ensure Ferrers's discomfiture.[121] On 14 February 1312 he was instrumental in charging the repayment of a large royal debt to Gascon vintners on the duchy's revenues and thereby effectively depriving Ferrers of a substantial portion of his annual fee as seneschal.[122] On 15 February, Ferrers received letters of protection for two years, implying that he was to stay abroad for that period of time. A reforming brief was worked out for him in the duchy and he was empowered to defend the king-duke's rights there, at the Paris Parlement and elsewhere.[123] He was allowed respite of his debts at the Exchequer on 12 February 'on the information of Walter, bishop of Coventry and Lichfield'.[124] Langton was no doubt attempting to hasten his departure. Ferrers's mission was also to take him to Paris and Avignon before his arrival in the duchy, and on 16 February letters of credence were

---

[119] See *Complete Peerage*, v, pp. 307–8. He was at the Dunstable tournament of 1309 in the retinue of the earl of Hereford: *Collectanea Topographica et Genealogica*, iv (London, 1837), p. 65; A. Tomkinson, 'Retinues at the tournament at Dunstable, 1309', *EHR*, lxxiv (1959), pp. 73, 74.

[120] A. Beardwood, 'The trial of Walter Langton, bishop of Coventry and Lichfield', *Transactions of the American Philosophical Society*, n.s., liv (1964), p. 10; *CCR, 1307–13*, pp. 395–6; *Foedera*, II, i, p. 154; *Flores Historiarum*, p. 148; *RG*, iv, nos 601–2 (24 January 1312). Ferrers was ordered to restore certain of Langton's lands which he was holding (*CCR, 1307–13*, p. 396).

[121] J. R. Maddicott, *Thomas of Lancaster, 1307–22* (Oxford, 1970), p. 122.

[122] *RG*, iv, no. 623 (14 February 1312, endorsed *per ipsum Regem, nunciante W. Coventr. et Lich. episcopo*).

[123] *RG*, iv, xx–xxi; no. 619.

[124] *CCR, 1307–13*, p. 401; *CPR, 1307–13*, pp. 430, 441; *RG*, iv, nos 615, 621, 622.

issued introducing him to Philip the Fair. He probably left England in March, when he appointed attorneys to act for him during his absence.

Ferrers was not given an easy task. In 1312 the duchy had still not recovered from the war and occupation of 1294–1303 which had left ducal rights and revenues usurped, ducal archives in disarray, and a legacy of litigation and appeals over forfeited, confiscated and despoiled lands. Ducal finances were in the hands of the Frescobaldi, the king-duke's Florentine creditors and agents until, under the terms of the baronial ordinances of September 1311, they were expelled from both England and Aquitaine.[125] Worse still, Edward I's loyal Gascon vassal Amanieu VII d'Albret had appealed to Philip the Fair in January 1310, claiming that he had been evicted from his lordship of Nérac by the seneschal of the Agenais. This was Piers Gaveston's brother, Arnaud-Guillaume de Marsan. Gaveston had come to England in 1296, with his Béarnais father Arnaud, lord of Gabaston, exiled from the duchy of Aquitaine by the French.[126] By 1297 Gaveston was receiving fees and robes as an esquire of the king's household, where he must have attracted the attention of Edward, prince of Wales. Albret clearly regarded Gaveston with contempt and a dangerous estrangement from Edward began.[127] In his appeal Albret claimed that Gaveston and Arnaud-Guillaume de Marsan were conspiring to prejudice Edward II's honour and authority by giving away Gascon lands and offices to unsuitable candidates. Arnaud-Guillaume was declared to be 'suspicius et inimicus' to Albret. Albret evidently detested Gaveston, his social inferior from the middling nobility, and resented the favourite's access to power and influence with the king.[128] Although he subsequently renounced his appeal, Albret was in league with Philip the Fair, who also hated Gaveston, intriguing to oust him from his position. Gaveston's influence was not therefore confined to English politics, and Ferrers was sent into one of the stormiest political seas of the time.

Albret's dominant position among Edward II's Gascon vassals was, however, recognized in a letter which the king-duke wrote to him on 14 April 1312.[129] Edward told Amanieu VII that Ferrers had been empowered to act upon his advice and that of other members of the ducal council in Aquitaine. Ferrers was to remove unsuitable and corrupt officers and to conclude *paréages* with local nobles to the king-duke's profit. Most pressing of all, however, was the urgent need to appease and quell the disputes between the mayor and *jurats* of Bordeaux and Edward's officers in the duchy – a

---

[125] A. Sapori, *La compagnia dei Frescobaldi in Inghliterra* (Florence, 1947), pp. 66–7, 73, 119–20.

[126] APA, E 20, no. 1 (12 January 1310); H. Johnstone, *Edward of Caernarvon* (Manchester, 1946), pp. 42–3.

[127] See below, pp. 169–70.

[128] APA, E. 20, no. 1: Albret asserted that 'donaciones terrarum et officiarum factas dicto senescallo et domino Petro de Gavastone fratri eius michi displicant'.

[129] *RG*, iv, no. 660.

concealed reference to the trouble associated with Jean Colom's and Pierre Caillau's appeal and the appointment of Odo de Lados to the mayoralty.[130] But the month of April 1312 witnessed one of those sudden reversals of personal fortune that characterized Edward II's reign when Walter Langton was ousted by baronial conspiracy from the treasurership he had enjoyed for only three months. Edward tried unsuccessfully to reistate him but by 1 May had conceded defeat, when he wrote to the acting constable of Bordeaux that Langton was about to leave England for Avignon on business of his own. But the king-duke announced that, as a special favour, Langton was to be lent up to 1000 marks (666 *l*. 13 *s*. 4 *d.st*.) from Gascon revenues.[131] Ferrers's stipend as seneschal was 500 *l.st*. per year. The ducal treasury at Bordeaux was to bear part of the cost of Langton's enforced exile – a prospect which must have been greeted with little enthusiasm by Ferrers and his subordinates in the duchy.

On 25 May 1312 Amanieu d'Albret drew up the appeal which was ultimately to bring down Ferrers and which nearly provoked an Anglo-French war.[132] Albret's grievances against the seneschal were essentially threefold: firstly, Ferrers had (he claimed) cruelly seized, mutilated and even killed his kinsmen and friends without good cause. Secondly, he had appointed Odo de Lados, mayor of Bordeaux and Albret's 'capital enemy', to the seneschalship of the Landes, where Albret's land, vassals and clients were primarily located. Thirdly, Ferrers had indiscriminately arrested certain of Albret's kinsmen and allies, such as Guillaume-Ayquem, lord of Lesparre. Albret feared for his own safety and refused to appear before Ferrers because he was fearful of the seneschal's violent behaviour. His appeal was endorsed by twenty-five witnesses at his castle of Casteljaloux, and Philip the Fair promptly appointed commissioners, headed by Master Yves de Landévennec, to hear the case. The first hearing, before Master Hugues de Carolles, Landévennec's deputy, took place at Libourne on 19 June 1312.[133] Albret submitted a second notarial instrument to the court, in which his charges against Ferrers were expounded with colourful detail. The seneschal, claimed Albret, had scorned the ancient rights and customs of the duchy, treated its inhabitants ferociously and

gathering a large force of both horse and foot, advanced through Gascony and the Agenais, threatening the [king-duke's] subjects . . . that he would oppress, harm and kill them unless they did what he wanted, . . . thereby breaking his own oath as seneschal, when he promised . . . to observe the laws and liberties of the land.[134]

---

[130] *RG*, iv, no. 670. See above, pp. 163–4.

[131] Beardwood, 'Walter Langton', pp. 10–11; C. 81/83, no. 2537; *CPR, 1307–13*, p. 458; *RG*, iv, no. 683 (endorsed *per ipsum Regem*).

[132] APA, E 20, no. 9. The records of the case have so far been very largely neglected.

[133] APA, E 20, no. 9, mm. 3–5.

[134] APA, E 20, no. 9, m. 3. Ferrers's punitive measures were borne out by the compensations

The hand of the dissident Jean Colom of Bordeaux was said by the authors of a later complaint against him (post-1326) to be behind these events. He had allegedly sown dissension between Ferrers and the 'jurez' and 'commune' of Bordeaux in order to achieve his own end – domination of the city. Colom was also said to have engineered the conflict between Albret and Ferrers so that the seneschal might be brought down.[135] Charges of terrorizing appellants were made by Albret against Ferrers, who was then said to have abused and insulted Philip the Fair's authority through assaults upon his serjeants and notaries. A scandalous incident had taken place in the seneschal's residence at Langon. At some date in April or May 1312, Guillaume Roussel, serjeant of the French royal seneschal of Périgord, came with a notary to serve a summons upon Ferrers charging him with intimidation of Gascon appellants.[136] Ferrers was in the company of Arnaud Caillau at the time. According to one report of the incident, Caillau asked Ferrers: 'Are you going to let these Frenchmen come and summon you like this?' Ferrers allegedly replied: 'What shall we do about it?' 'Well', said Caillau, 'let us fire him from a catapult' (*faites le geter en trebucher*). So they took a table and put one end out of a window, made the serjeant walk along it and then let him fall into the street. He sustained a broken arm and leg and another record tells us that his wand of office, the *baculum* or *bâton* painted with the fleurs-de-lis, was hurled into the Garonne. The royal notary fled from the scene before he suffered the same fate. This, as a subsequent notarial instrument put it, was in contempt of God, reason and royal majesty.[137] Offences of this kind were not uncommon in Aquitaine, but when they were done with the knowledge and connivance of the king-duke's representative, the matter was of more serious consequence.

A further charge laid by Albret against Ferrers was an assault upon Guillaume-Ayquem, lord of Lesparre in the Médoc. As a result of the unions between the upper bourgeoisie and nobility of the Bordelais, Lesparre was a nephew of Pierre Béguey (Viguier) de la Rousselle, citizen of Bordeaux.[138] Pierre Béguey had been arrested and condemned to death by Ferrers, and Lesparre appealed to Philip the Fair against the seneschal's sentence. Ferrers then seized Lesparre 'with his own hands' and thrust him into the condemned cell at the castle of L'Ombrière so that he was forced to renounce his appeal. Pierre Béguey was then executed by the seneschal, on the advice of Raymond de Limoges, a fellow-citizen of Bordeaux, and by verdict of the

---

and pardons for debt granted to Gascons who had served him *cum equis et armis* to suppress dissensions within the duchy; *RG*, iv, nos 1257, 1383; SC 1/55, no. 35; C 47/25/2, nos 6–7, 36.

[135] Bémont, 'Les factions et les troubles à Bordeaux', pp. 161–2 (arts 42–3 from C 47/26/18).

[136] APA, E 20, no. 9, m. 4.

[137] Bémont, 'Les factions et les troubles à Bordeaux', p. 150 (art. 5); APA, E 20, no. 9, m. 4: 'per quandam fenestram altissimam hospicii ipsius senescalli, ad terram projesserunt'.

[138] See above, pp. 145–6; *Histoire de Bordeaux, III*, pp. 79–81; Kicklighter, 'English Bordeaux in conflict', pp. 4–8; *Olim*, iii, p. 814–15; APA, E 20, no. 9, m. 4; E 22, no. 9, m. 3.

'court of Gascony'.[139] His sons petitioned the Parlement of Paris for redress and compensation, claiming that their father's judicial murder had been engineered by Odo de Lados, Aubert Mège, constable of Bordeaux, and other Bordelais. Raymond de Limoges was, however, pardoned for his part in Béguey's death by Philip the Fair in July 1313, and although Edward II was required to compensate Lesparre for damages received by him, the court of France remitted 6000 *l.t.* of the 12,000 *l.t.* fine originally imposed.[140] Pierre Béguey's sons failed to win their case before the Parlement and the affair petered out, to the benefit only of the lawyers concerned.[141] Ferrers had clearly become embroiled in existing feuds and faction-fights among the upper bourgeois of Bordeaux, and his apparent inability to maintain an impartial and independent stance may ultimately have led to his downfall.

Yet there was another dimension to the affair. Unlike his immediate predecessors as seneschal – John de Hastings, John de Havering or Guy Ferre – Ferrers was in no sense a 'king's man', either of Edward I or his son. It was hardly surprising that he was soon to be succeeded by Amaury de Craon, acceptable to both Philip the Fair and Edward II.[142] Ferrers may well have been the victim of intrigue and manipulation by Jean Colom, Arnaud Caillau and their associates at Bordeaux, but common rumour in the summer of 1312 was apparently insinuating that Ferrers himself actively sought to provoke Anglo-French tension by stirring up conflict in Aquitaine. A letter of 20 August 1312 from Philip the Fair to his seneschal of Toulouse spoke of Ferrer's terrorization of appellants in exactly similar terms to those of Albret's appeal against him. Philip claimed that, in league with Odo de Lados, Arnaud de Castelnau, *prévôt* of St Sever, Arnaud de Barbarès, *prévôt* of Dax, and Jourdain Morant, constable of Bordeaux, Ferrers had attacked appellants and committed *lèse majesté* against both himself and Edward.[143] But the king went further than Albret in his charges: Ferrers, he alleged, had actively sought to promote discord between Philip and his son-in-law. The king's letter claimed that:

our son [Edward II] is at present, as you know, absorbed by great matters elsewhere in his lands . . . and the said John [de Ferrers], we learn, behaves thus because . . . just as the late king of England [Edward I] disinherited the said

---

[139] *RG*, iv, no. 1102; Richard de Bury, *Liber Epistolaris*, nos 299, 302 for transcripts of Edward II's letters concerning the case.

[140] AN, JJ 49, fo. 43[v] (2 July 1313); *Olim*, iii, pp. 814–15; C. V. Langlois, 'Rouleaux d'arrêts . . .', *BEC*, 1 (1889), pp. 64–5.

[141] AN, X[2a] 2, fos 12[r-v]; *Actes du Parlement*, nos 5537, 5556, 5564; C 61/32, mm. 4, 13 (15 and 19 March 1318); Kicklighter, 'English Bordeaux in conflict', pp. 11–12.

[142] See above, pp. 33–4; *RG*, iv, no. 969. Etienne Ferréol, lord of Tonneins was appointed interim seneschal.

[143] APA, E 22, no. 6 (20 August 1312). A similar charge was made by Guillaume de Aqua, 'guardian' of Gascon appellants for Philip the Fair, during proceedings of 9 October 1312 against Guy Ferre, as Edward II's lieutenant: APA, E 22, no. 9, m. 4.

John's father, so he [Ferrers] wishes to disinherit his and our son [Edward II],
but may this enterprise, with God's help, not succeed; but if it is true, let him
perish in his iniquity.[144]

An order to all the duchy's inhabitants not to obey Ferrers and his agents
followed. These were grave and not entirely implausible charges. Ferrers
never forgot that he was the rightful heir to the earldom of Derby of which he
had been deprived. Events in England made his actions more dangerous.
The summary execution of Piers Gaveston took place near Warwick, at the
very moment when Albret's appeal was heard at Libourne, on 19 June
1312.[145] Philip the Fair was delighted at the news of Gaveston's death and a
distinct improvement took place in relations between the courts of England
and France. From that moment the prospects for greater Anglo-French
concord, strengthened by the mediating talents of Aymer de Valence,
Clement V and Enguerrand de Marigny, seemed good.[146] By 5 August 1312,
however, this cordiality was put in jeopardy. Edward II was desperately
anxious to remain on the best of terms with both Philip and the pope –
Philip's political support against the English magnates and Clement's financial backing were essential weapons in his armoury. A great loan from the
pope, secured upon the duchy of Aquitaine, was under negotiation in August
1312. According to the *Vita Edwardi Secundi*, Edward was so besotted with
Gaveston that he would have given Aquitaine in fee to Philip and Clement, if
their intervention in return saved his favourite's life.[147] With Gaveston dead,
Edward was thrown back upon their aid. Ferrers's behaviour in Aquitaine
threatened to undermine his position. Albret was closely related to the pope,
Clement was anxious to secure Anglo-French harmony during the Council of
Vienne and the dissolution of the Templars, while the duchy was in turmoil.

Edward's first reaction to the news of Ferrer's quarrel with Albret was to
appoint reforming commissioners in Aquitaine. These were Guy Ferre,
William Inge and Thomas of Cambridge, king's clerk, all well versed and
experienced in Gascon and Anglo-French affairs.[148] On 5 August Ferrers and
Albret were ordered to appear before them, and Ferrers was commanded to

---

[144] APA, E 22, no. 6. The letter accused Ferrers of aiming to 'break the bond of peace and
charity between us and our son [Edward II]'. It echoed the sentiments expressed in Enguerrand
de Marigny's speech to an assembly of the Flemish towns at Tournai on 15 October 1311, which
emphasized the sovereignty and supreme appellate jurisdiction of the French crown. See J. R.
Strayer, *The Reign of Philip the Fair* (Princeton, 1980), pp. 603–4; Funck-Brentano, *Philippe le Bel
en Flandre*, pp. 602–4.

[145] Maddicott, *Thomas of Lancaster*, pp. 126–30; J. R. S. Phillips, *Aymer de Valence, Earl of
Pembroke, 1308–24. Baronial Politics in the Reign of Edward II* (Oxford, 1972), p. 35.

[146] See above, pp. 27–30; Phillips, *Aymer de Valence*, pp. 35–40; Maddicott, *Thomas Lancaster*,
pp. 136–7, 149–52.

[147] *Vita Edwardi Secundi*, p. 24; Phillips, *Aymer de Valence*, pp. 40–1.

[148] *RG*, iv, no. 713 (5 August 1312). They were to promote 'love and concord' between Ferrers
and Albret.

cease his tumultous behaviour.[149] Before 16 August Edward wrote to Albret who, he claimed, enjoyed his 'special affection' which he had shown *viscerali-ter* for a long time. Such was the gravity of the affair that a personal interview between the king-duke and Albret was deemed necessary and he was requested to come to Edward in England to make peace. Three days later Ferrers was peremptorily told to be before the king at the same time.[150] A second letter followed on 22 August, demanding that 1000 tuns of good wine be immediately bought, paid for from ducal revenues, and sent to Westminster before Christmas.[151] Edward was clearly both angry about Ferrers's actions and apprehensive of their consequences. He was not alone in his anxieties. On 11 August, Clement V personally intervened in the dispute and appointed two papal chaplains to arbitrate the conflict between Ferrers and Albret.[152] Clement had no wish for a heightening of Anglo-French tension at the very time when the resolution of the Templar affair was already taxing his limited resources. A second Anglo-French war over Aquitaine was the last thing that the pope desired, and harmony between the courts of England and France could not be sacrificed to the unpredictable course of events in the duchy.

Neither Ferrers nor Albret, however, appear to have obeyed Edward II's summons to his presence. The seneschal pursued his business with vigour in the duchy while Albret must have replied to Edward's letter, for a messenger from him was given a gift by the king-duke on 5 September 1312.[153] Ferrer's activities in the last months of his life fall into two categories: firstly, his relations with the nobles of the duchy and on its frontiers; secondly, his dealings with the bourgeois of some towns of the region, many of which reflected his increasing financial difficulties. Ferrers alienated other Gascon nobles besides Albret and his clients: Arnaud-Raymond, *vicomte* of Orthe, Garcie-Arnaud, *vicomte* of Marsan, and Guillaume-Ayquem, lord of Lesparre.[154] The summer of 1312 witnessed what was in effect a private war in the duchy. Ferrers was not alone in his opposition to Albret and a sentence of banishment pronounced at Agen by Philip the Fair's officers in January 1313 named no less than fifty Gascons, both noble and non-noble, who had conspired against Albret and his supporters.[155] Nobles and townsmen of Béarn, Marsan and the Gers were particularly well represented. Ferrers's alliance against Albret was of motley complexion, headed by Margaret of Béarn, Viscountess of Foix, who aided him 'de force et d'armes', in order –

---

[149] *RG*, iv, nos 715, 716.

[150] *RG*, iv, nos 734, 735.

[151] *RG*, iv, nos 736, 745–6.

[152] APA, E 22, no. 12 (11 August 1312); *Foedera*, II, i, pp. 176–7.

[153] E 101/375/81, fo. 28ᵛ (gift to Guillaume le Poitevin, Albret's *nuncius*).

[154] APA, E 22, no. 9, m. 2; for Lesparre, see above pp. 168–9.

[155] APA, E 22, no. 14 (damaged, 4 January 1313). They included Arnaud de Castelnau, *prévôt* of St Sever, Odo de Lados, Arnaud-Guillaume de Marsan, Loup Bergonde of Bordeaux and Guillaume-Arnaud de Sescas.

she later claimed – to 'maintain, safeguard and protect' Edward II's rights in the duchy. But she also complained that Ferrers had done nothing to defend her against illegal summonses by Capetian officers to appear before them, despite a letter of guarantee under the seneschal's seal that he had given her.[156] Edward's council advised the king-duke to tell Ferrers of his amazement that the seneschal had acted without orders in so irresponsible a manner. But arbitrary exactions from townsmen in the duchy continued. Ferrers was starved of ready money and was thus dependent upon substantial loans from towns such as Bayonne and Dax, and from wealthy individuals among the factional groups at Bordeaux and elsewhere.[157] On the death of Master Pierre-Arnaud de Vic, king's clerk, at Bayonne, for example, Ferrers extracted his silver plate and money from the Franciscan convent there where they were being kept 'for the great necessity of the king-duke's needs and to preserve [his] honour'.[158] Ferrers's last surviving act was the giving of a quittance to Pierre-Arnaud's executors at La Réole on 27 August 1312.[159] He also pillaged the worldly goods of a rich Bordeaux merchant, Robert de Francs, claiming that he had died intestate and without heirs. The claim was untrue, and Amaury de Craon was left to settle the affair which was in danger of generating further appeals to the court of France.[160]

In 1312 there was no Anglo-French war. The peace was kept, but only as a result of intensive diplomatic activity and the murder of Ferrers. Aymer de Valence secured an agreement on 14 March 1313 that Edward II, Queen Isabella and Philip the Fair were to meet to discuss Anglo-French difficulties.[161] The death of Ferrers by 9 October 1312 had certainly helped to prevent a worsening of relations, but one can only speculate about his murderers' identity. Perhaps he had become, like Jourdain de L'Isle, an expendable irritant whose demise was to the advantage of many interested parties.[162] Even in death, Ferrers provoked conflict, and Guy Ferre was accused of disobeying a French serjeant-at-arms who had ordered him neither to move nor bury Ferrers's body until Philip the Fair's wishes were known.[163] This may have been an attempt to ensure that a proper inquest was conducted into the manner and circumstances of Ferrers's death under royal, not ducal, aegis. If so, it failed and nothing more was heard of the

---

[156] SC 8/286, no. 14290; C 47/27/8, no. 26; see above, pp. 90–1.

[157] SC 8/286, no. 14292 (Bayonne); *RG*, iv, p. 572 (Dax); *RG*, iv, no. 947 (Bayonne).

[158] SC 8/282, no. 106; *RG*, iv, no. 906 (27 April 1313).

[159] C 47/24/3, no. 6 (under the seal of the court of Gascony, 27 August 1312).

[160] E 101/164/6: a consignment of Franc's wine had been seized at Marmande, and goods bequeathed by him to 'les povres nostre Seigneur Yhesu Crist' confiscated (30 June 1314). Amaury de Craon feared that delay and denial of justice would lead Franc's executors to 'have recourse elsewhere', as many others had recently done as a result of Edward II's inordinate delay in replying to such requests: SC 1/55, no. 43 (18 December 1315).

[161] Phillips, *Aymer de Valence*, pp. 60–2.

[162] See above, pp. 138–9.

[163] APA, E 22, no. 9, m. 4. The document contains very detailed information about alleged insults to French royal sovereignty in Aquitaine after Ferrers's death.

matter. Petty judicial squabbling was subsumed beneath the atmosphere of Anglo-French goodwill generated by the meetings between Edward II and Philip the Fair at Paris and Poissy in July 1313. The fines totalling over 70,000 *l.t.* imposed by Philip upon both individuals and communities in the duchy as a result of Ferrers's short but damaging career as seneschal were remitted and pardons issued to the banished and exiled for their part in his excesses.[164] The gathering of the Anglo-French family circle restored the status quo ante. The true beneficiary of the whole affair was probably Amanieu d'Albret. He emerged in July 1313 with a grant of 20,000 *l.t.* from Edward II, made at the request of Philip the Fair, on condition that he renounced his appeals to the court of France.[165] It was an example of the manner in which a powerful individual might profit from the disturbed conditions which faction and conflict brought to the duchy. But in the process Edward had forfeited Albret's support.

Edward II's reign had seen the emergence of 'over-mighty' subjects in the English kingdom; they emerged elsewhere. In Aquitaine the behaviour of great nobles such as Amanieu d'Albret, and of urban factional leaders such as Jean Colom or Pierre and Arnaud Caillau posed similar threats to the king-duke's authority. Methods of retaining and sustaining a following in both England and Aquitaine were comparable, and the problem of their control became increasingly acute. In a post-1326 complaint against Jean Colom of Bordeaux, it was reported that Colom had 'provoked all the ill-will there was between the said seneschal [John Ferrers] and the lord of Albret . . . and all the discord between them; by means of which ill-will and discord all the wars in Gascony ensued'.[166] Whether true or not, the allegation is revealing. The alienation of Albret from the Plantagenet regime was to inform his and his allies' behaviour during the War of St Sardos, while the Colom rallied to Edward II's cause. The 'greatest threat of all to the survival of English rule' in Aquitaine was not the 'active intervention of Capetian officials in the duchy'.[167] If the Plantagenet regime *was* gravely threatened, a greater danger was posed by the over-mighty subjects of an insecure and episodically arbitrary ruler such as Edward II. Although appeals to the court of France might be exploited by such disaffected individuals, the evidence offers little room for doubt that direct Capetian lordship in Aquitaine was unwelcome to a majority of the duchy's inhabitants.[168] But the Ferrers affair resulted in a shift in the allegiance of Amanieu d'Albret and his supporters

---

[164] See *Registres du Trésor des Chartes*, i, nos 1970–2, 2003, 2005–9, 2020, 2026–8.

[165] AN, JJ 49, fo. 49, no. 115 (2 July 1313).

[166] Bémont, 'Les factions et les troubles à Bordeaux', p. 162, art. 45 (C 47/26/18, m. 4): 'Item, qe ledit Jehan Colom mist tout le mal qi estoyt entre ledit seneschal et le sire de Le Bret, qe Dieux absolhe, et toute le discorde qi fut entre eus, par qelle mal et discorde toutes les guerres de Gascoigne soy sont ensuies.'

[167] Kicklighter, 'English Bordeaux in conflict', p. 12.

[168] See below, pp. 221–3, for the harsh treatment meted out to hostages taken from Bordeaux during the French occupation, and for the rising against the French in 1303.

away from the Plantagenets. This had very important implications for the balance of power in south-west France, especially in any overt Anglo-French conflict. Albret had been one of Edward I's most loyal companions-in-arms. The events of Edward II's reign transformed him and his house into enemies of the Plantagenet regime.

6

Anglo-French Conflict

6.1   The Causes of War in 1294

Between 20 June 1294 and 24 March 1298 England and France were
formally and publicly at war. Historians have been more than usually
censorious about the nature and upshot of this war. It was 'one of those wars
that accomplish nothing and should never have occurred'; 'a complicated
and ultimately futile conflict'; 'a prolonged but singularly inconclusive
incident'; and 'a non-existent war from the military historian's point of
view'.[1] Such verdicts rest largely upon analysis of the damaging financial
consequences of the conflict and its apparent lack of tactical and strategic
interest. Yet lessons were learned from it by both sides which will be
considered later in this chapter. To describe a conflict as 'futile' or 'useless'
may be to place too high a value upon the efficacy of war as a solvent of
political problems. Medieval wars were not fought solely for political, economic or material gain. A society which set a high value upon lavish gift-giving
and exchange, and upon what later generations have seen as 'conspicuous
waste' and conscious dissipation of resources, was unlikely to have much
room for more recent notions of both political and economic gain.[2] Warfare
commenced when diplomacy failed. Diplomacy was conducted in a highly
legalistic manner, and the points at issue in this extended lawsuit tended to
focus upon rights and status as well as incomes and revenues. We should not
underestimate the defence of honour or the realization of claims to certain
titles, rights and privileges as motivating factors leading to the outbreak of
open and public war during this period. Warfare was both a demonstration
of right and a gesture, symptomatic of more general tendencies within later
medieval society. However misguided and deluded we may believe the rulers
of this period and their advisers to have been in seeking to resolve conflicts by
force of arms, the relative weakness of diplomatic alternatives must always
be borne in mind. Princes were conditioned to believe in the justificatory,

---

[1] J. R. Strayer, 'The costs and profits of war: the Anglo-French conflict of 1294–1303', in *The
Medieval City*, ed. H. A. Miskimin, D. Herlihy and A. L. Udovitch (Yale, 1977), p. 370; M.
Prestwich, *Edward I* (London, 1988), p. 381; M. W. Labarge, *Gascony. England's First Colony*
(London, 1980), pp. 75–6.

[2] See K. B. McFarlane, *The Nobility of later Medieval England* (Oxford, 1973), p. 96.

and even cathartic nature of war as a positive force in human affairs. It was for the *gens des comptes* and the Exchequer or Wardrobe clerks to count the cost, and we might seek analogies between the behaviour of later medieval rulers and that of oriental and African potentates rather than with the 'constitutional' monarchs of later epochs.[3] But there were many things which both the Plantagenets and Capetians had more will than strength to do. The conduct of successful war, as the French learned in Aragon and Flanders, the English in Scotland, and both discovered in Aquitaine, demanded resources in money, manpower and supplies which ultimately lay beyond their available means. If the Anglo-French war of 1294–8 proved anything, it was that neither side could hope to emerge victorious from a conflict fought exclusively in the duchy of Aquitaine. That in itself was a salutary lesson.

It has been observed that there is little evidence that Anglo-French tension 'was any more unbearable in 1293 than it had been earlier'.[4] Until 1290 or so it could, on the contrary, be argued that relations between the two kingdoms were relatively harmonious. From the peace-making and arbitration of the period before 1294, however, a transition to episodic warfare took place. Before that date we are presented with the image of a peace-loving Edward I, seeking to establish concord among the princes of Europe, moved by the interests of Holy Church and the promptings of a crusader's conscience.[5] In November 1294, as war with Philip the Fair of France loomed, Edward was seeking the prayers of the Franciscan chapter-general assembled at Assisi that 'the present tempestuous time be succeeded by a more tranquil one'.[6] As a peace-maker Edward's reputation between his accession and 1294 was high and he spent much time and energy on attempting to reconcile his warring kinsmen abroad.[7] In Sir Maurice Powicke's account, Edward assumes the role of a benevolent uncle, striving (often vainly) to reconcile and placate a fractious group of squabbling children. His own cosmopolitan background and pedigree placed him in an ideal position for such a task. Close relationships between the courts of England, Savoy, Bar, Champagne, Brabant, Aragon, Castile, Navarre and Provence enabled him to act upon requests to arbitrate disputes with some confidence. Most analyses leave no room for aggression on Edward's part – he had no wish to use his extensive continental connections against France, and he had no 'policy of encirclement' which sought to isolate and surround the French kingdom, depriving it of allies in the Low Countries, Burgundy and Savoy.[8] This may well be true of the first decades of his reign, but it could not be said of the years after 1294.

---

[3] See, for example E. E. Evans-Pritchard, 'Zande kings and princes' in his *Essays in Social Anthropology* (London, 1969), pp. 87–116.

[4] J. R. Strayer, *The Reign of Philip the Fair* (Princeton, 1980), p. 317.

[5] *CPR, 1281–92*, 419; *Foedera*, I. ii, p. 815.

[6] *Foedera*, I, ii, p. 815 (23 November 1294).

[7] F. M. Powicke, *The Thirteenth Century* (Oxford, 1954), pp. 245–6.

[8] Powicke, *Thirteenth Century*, p. 246.

However, there is some evidence for increased tension before 1294 between Edward's role as diplomatic arbiter and his vassalic status as liegeman of the French crown. This is seen most clearly in the Gascon problem. But there was a sense in which Edward's reputation as, for want of a better word, a statesman and as the foremost representative of western knighthood, served to challenge and threaten the Capetian monarchy of France. His personal role as arbitrator of disputes, for example, between the houses of Aragon and Anjou, acting from his own duchy of Aquitaine between 1286 and 1289, hardly enhanced the status of Louis IX's heirs.[9] Knighthood at his hands was actively sought and highly prized, a further reflection of his reputation as knight and crusader. There was, crucially, an unspoken expectation among English diplomatic envoys that both Philip III and his son would behave according to the accepted code of kingly honour in their dealings with Edward and his subjects, rather than as liege lord to vassal. But parity of status between the two kings could be difficult to achieve in this context. On the Plantagenet side, Edward barely concealed his assertion of equality, as king of England, with the house of France in some of their exchanges and Edmund of Lancaster assumed in 1294 that Philip the Fair would act as 'loiaux Roy'.[10] Philip did not fulfil their expectations and the easy harmony of the Anglo-French circle was broken.

By the early 1290s, Edward I's international reputation as a just ruler, who was prepared to implement justice – as he perceived it – by force of arms if necessary, was well known. If the Maccabean victories depicted on the walls of the Painted Chamber at Westminster date from a campaign of works undertaken between 1292 and 1297, then they are uniquely relevant as a reflection of Edward's preoccupation with the justice of his cause – in Scotland and, after 1294, in Aquitaine – at this time.[11] The paintings were described in 1323, very inaccurately, as showing 'all the warlike stories of the whole Bible', and their predominantly martial character may tell us something about the ethos of Edward's household in the 1290s.[12] As we have seen, reassertion of identification with the Plantagenet past also took place at this time. His progress of 1286–9 through France and Gascony had been an opportunity to renew existing associations and establish new ones, and Edward's liberality towards religious houses and shrines, and the splendour of his entourage, did not pass unnoticed. He fulfilled expectations in an appropriately regal manner.[13] In his *Branche des royaux lignages* the otherwise

[9] *Foedera*, I, ii, p. 679, 690; see below, pp. 178–9.

[10] *Foedera*, I, ii, p. 794.

[11] P. Binski, *The Painted Chamber at Westminster*, Society of Antiquaries Occasional Paper, n.s., ix (London, 1986), pp. 19–21, 71–80, 82: Edward's court 'resonated as a source of new imagery, particularly the new secular imagery of romance and chivalry'.

[12] Binski, *Painted Chamber*, pp. 1, 96–103.

[13] J.-P. Trabut-Cussac, 'Itinéraire d'Edouard Ier en France, 1286–1289', *BIHR*, xxv (1952), pp. 168, 173–4, 175, 184 for some of Edward's oblations; also PRO, E 36/201, pp. 93–4; Guillaume Guiart, *Branche des royaux lignages*, ed. J. A. Buchon (Paris, 1828), ii, ll. 3732–43. Also see above, pp. 66–7.

robustly pro-Capetian Guillaume Guiart left his French audience in no doubt of the quality of Edward's warhorses and the largesse which he distributed.[14] The young Philip the Fair was to some extent upstaged by Edward, as elder statesman, who took the cross during the chapter-general of the Dominicans at Bordeaux in May 1287, preoccupied all the while with the search for peace between Aragon and Anjou as a necessary condition for the Crusade.[15] This concern was apparently on Edward's mind throughout this period and was in part to determine his behaviour towards the French.

Why, if Edward I consistently sought peace, did Anglo-French relations degenerate from relative harmony into outright hostility in 1294? The answer to that question lies in a series of closely interrelated problems which are difficult to disentangle. Many were related to the search for a settlement of the Angevin–Aragonese conflict which erupted from the war of the Sicilian Vespers in 1284. Edward's dealings with the crown of Aragon in its war with the house of Anjou for the kingdom of Naples and Sicily should be assessed in the light of French humiliation after the disastrous 'Aragonese crusade' of 1285 when a French invading army was overwhelmingly defeated.[16] By negotiating a truce between Philip the Fair and Alfonso of Aragon at Oloron-Ste-Marie in July 1287, followed by the release of Charles of Salerno (son of Charles of Anjou, titular king of Sicily) under the terms of the treaty of Canfranc in October 1288, Edward reversed the previous role of the French and English monarchies in diplomatic arbitration.[17] The treaties of Oloron and Canfranc were perhaps not quite the equivalent of St Louis's Mise of Amiens or his other arbitrations, but the fact that one who was technically a vassal of the French crown was intervening in this manner in Philip IV's affairs could not pass disregarded by the French. Moreover, Edward was undeniably popular with at least some of the Aragonese nobility. Celebrated in troubadour poetry as 'the best lance in the world', and as Christendom's best defender against the heathen, Edward's reputation seems borne out by the eagerness of Catalan nobles to serve him in war.[18] In April 1294, Artoldo de Alagone said that he had been in Edward's company at Oloron in 1287 during the arbitration proceedings, and mentioned the king's great generosity towards him then.[19] The Catalans were to have a significant role in the events which led to the onset of Anglo-French war in 1293–4.

---

[14] Guiart, *Branche des royaux lignages*, ll. 3735–7; M. Vale 'The Gascon nobility and the Anglo-French war, 1294–98', in *War and Government in the Middle Ages, Essays in Honour of J. O. Prestwich*, ed. J. Gillingham and J. C. Holt (Woodbridge and Totowa, 1984), pp. 144–5.

[15] Powicke, *Thirteenth Century*, pp. 251–2; J.-P. Trabut-Cussac, *L'Administration anglaise en Gascogne sous Henry III et Edouard I de 1254 à 1307* (Geneva, 1972), pp. 83–92.

[16] Strayer, *Reign of Philip the Fair*, pp. 368–70; J. Petit, *Charles de Valois, 1270–1325* (Paris, 1900), pp. 9–11.

[17] *Foedera*, I, ii, pp. 679, 690; Trabut-Cussac, *L'Administration anglaise*, pp. 81–92.

[18] F. M. Powicke, *Henry III and the Lord Edward* (Oxford 1947), p. 688.

[19] *Foedera*, I, ii, p. 797; and below, pp. 199, 202–3.

By 1290 the problems associated with Edward's authority and status in the duchy of Aquitaine were becoming more acute. In the past it has often been argued that Edward was content to work within the limits set upon him by his father's treaty of 1259 with Louis IX.[20] His evasive actions in 1282 and 1285, when he gave military aid to neither side in the Franco-Aragonese war, might appear to support this, but it could be argued that Edward's aim was to limit, if not to undo, the more damaging effects of a treaty which, at least initially, he had vigorously opposed. He performed only a conditional form of homage to Philip the Fair in July 1286 and it was dependent upon French implementation of their part of the treaty of Paris.[21] Edward's acquisition of the Agenais and the *comté* of Ponthieu at Amiens in 1279 and of southern Saintonge in 1286 had substantially extended his power-base, while his brother Edmund's marriage to Blanche of Artois in 1275 had given him a further northern French foothold in Champagne. This had been lost as a result of Jeanne of Navarre's marriage to Philip the Fair in 1284.[22]

In addition to the growing threat posed to Philip by Edward's individual reputation and his substantially increased territorial possessions on the continent, Capetian prestige and authority appeared to be further undermined by his administrative and judicial actions in Aquitaine. Edward's perambulation of his French lands in 1286–9 had produced administrative reforms and ordinances for the government of Gascony. As we have seen, the creation of a new appellate jurisdiction within the duchy of Aquitaine, which attempted to bypass the Paris Parlement and the court of the French seneschal of Périgord entirely, could only have been considered as a threat by the French.[23] By June 1293, for example, two Gascon lords promised, on pain of forfeiting all their possessions, to obey his will without challenge or appeal in a case of robbery with violence. There were also signs of greater friction over the question of Edward's homage to Philip the Fair for Aquitaine and Ponthieu in July 1286. Robert Burnell's speech to the French court at Paris on that occasion was in effect a warning: he told them that many of Edward's counsellors had advised him to dispute (*debatre*) the terms of his homage, because the 1259 treaty had not been fulfilled and because certain assaults (*supprises*) had been effected by the French in his lands. Edward was not yet prepared to act on that advice, awaiting Philip the Fair's action in remedying these abuses.[24] But the note of defiance had been sounded.

[20] Powicke, *Thirteenth Century*, p. 271.

[21] *Foedera*, I, ii, p. 665; P. Chaplais, 'Le duché-paire de Guyenne: l'hommage et les services féodaux de 1259 à 1303', in *Essays in Medieval Diplomacy and Administration* (London, 1981), pt III, pp. 24–5.

[22] Powicke, *Thirteenth Century*, pp. 239, 241–4.

[23] Trabut-Cussac *L'Administration anglaise*, pp. 275–80; P. Chaplais, 'Les appels gascons au roi d'Angleterre sous le règne d'Edouard Ier (1272–1307)', in *Essays in Medieval Diplomacy*, pt VI, pp. 382–8; see above, pp. 77–8.

[24] *Gascon Register A* (*Series of 1318–19*), ed. G. P. Cuttino and J.-P. Trabut-Cussac, ii, no. 193 (pp. 533–4); *Foedera* I, ii, p. 665.

The war of 1294–8 was to break out over almost exclusively Gascon issues. These, as Renouard noted, possessed a depth and intensity which can all too easily be underrated, as they were by some contemporaries.[25] Paramount was the question of Gascon appeals and the judicial issues which they raised. Strayer has observed that almost all the appeal cases concerning Flanders and Aquitaine before the Paris Parlement 'came in the years just before the wars in these provinces'.[26] The coincidence is unsurprising. Assertion of Capetian supremacy was very largely confined to the hearing of such appeals and their concentration at these moments of impending crisis is revealing. Pressure from appellants, whether genuine, solicited or feigned, could be exploited by the Capetian monarchy to exert its claims to sovereignty over wayward, defaulting or over-mighty vassals. A cluster of appellants had gathered before the Parlement in 1291–3. On 27 October 1293, Philip the Fair summoned Edward I before his court of Parlement to answer certain charges laid against his officers in Aquitaine.[27] The citation included a list of appellants who had allegedly been denied justice by the king-duke, and whose French royal protections had been infringed. Among them were Bernard de Ravignan, co-seigneur of the castle of Buzet in the Agenais, and Gombaud de Tiran, lord of St-Médard-en-Jalle in the Bordelais.[28] These cases deserve closer examination for what they reveal about the identity of those whose causes were taken up by the French crown.

Bernard de Ravignan's problem was that he could live peaceably neither with the consuls of Agen nor with the clergy: in the Gascon Calendar, compiled by Master Henry of Canterbury in 1322, no less than thirty items are listed concerning his misdeeds against the Church.[29] These dated from 1281 to 1290, ending with a dossier relating to his appeals before the Paris Parlement. He had begun his litigious career at the court of France soon after the cession of the Agenais to Edward I in 1279. By 1281 he was already contesting the right of Edward's seneschal to build a house (*domus*) in a place over which Bernard claimed jurisdiction, and to establish a new *bastide* there. His immediate response to the seneschal's action was to claim denial of justice and appeal directly to the Parlement, bypassing the ducal courts of the Agenais. The Parlement, however, decided that the case should be referred back, and his plea was not heard there in 1281 because in his appeal 'there was no mention made of an appeal from an actual judgement or denial of justice'.[30] Bernard de Ravignan was all too ready to seek redress at Paris but in 1281 the court was not moved by his plea. Its attitude – or rather, the

[25] Y. Renouard, 'Le pape et le conflit franco-anglais en Aquitaine de 1259 à 1337', *Mélanges d'Archéologie et d'Histoire . . . par l'Ecole française de Rome*, li (1934), p. 266.

[26] Strayer, *Reign of Philip the Fair*, p. 201.

[27] *Foedera*, I, ii p. 793; *Olim*, ii, pp. 108.

[28] *Olim*, ii, pp. 5–6.

[29] *Gascon Calendar*, nos 1419–48 (pp. 123–4).

[30] *BEC*, xlviii (1887), pp. 547–55; C 47/29/1/14; *RG* ii, nos 975, 979.

French crown's desire to take up and exploit his case – was, however, to change by 1290. In the meantime Bernard had clashed with the clergy of his region. The dossiers listed in the Gascon Calendar included lawsuits with the Benedictine monks of St Sever, the prior of Buzet and no less than ten documents stemming from his violent feud with the rector and chaplain of the church at Ambrus (Lot-et-Garonne, *arr.* Nérac, *cant.* Damazan), very close to his castle of Buzet.[31] The feud was already in full spate in 1281. Bernard was already the subject of an inquiry before the seneschal of Agenais at the request of the rector of Ambrus in that year. By 1288 he had been condemned by the seneschal to pay a fine of 600 *l.* of Agen (*arnaldenses*) for his breach of a safeguard under which the chaplain there had been placed by the court of the Agenais. Not content with assault upon the church at Ambrus, he turned his attentions to the priory of Buzet itself, a dependent house of the great Benedictine monastery at St Sever. One day, as the aged prior of Buzet lay dying in his chamber, Bernard de Ravignan and his accomplices broke into the room, seized the prior (already *in extremis*), dragged him into the fortified church of the place (where he promptly died), and then proceeded to lay hands on his temporal possessions. This was in manifest contempt of the king-duke's justice, and of the rights of the abbey at St Sever. Bernard agreed to pay his 600 *l.arn.* fine by August 1289, and was granted a pardon by Edward I, a further 500 *l.arn.* penalty being remitted.[32] These were generous terms, but they did not halt this turbulent character in his law-breaking career.

As the price of his remission Bernard was still required to reply before John de Havering, as lieutenant of the seneschal of Aquitaine, to other charges made against him. He was given generous terms of payment by instalment. Not content with this, he again appealed to the Paris Parlement, where an inquiry was set in motion into his 'misdeeds and murders'.[33] In Philip IV's summons to Edward I of 1293, however, Bernard appeared as a wronged party in the dispute, his castle of Buzet taken by armed force, wasted and burnt by the men of the duke of Aquitaine although it was placed under French royal safeguard.[34] If anyone tried the patience of Edward I's officers in Aquitaine, it must have been Bernard de Ravignan. He and his accomplices had also clashed with the citizens of Agen, who drew up a series of complaints about his violent behaviour between January 1294 and October 1300. By March 1299 an appeal by the consuls of Agen against him was lodged at the Parlement.[35] The twenty-four-year story ended on 30 March 1305 when, two years after the conclusion of peace with France, Edward

[31] *The Gascon Calendar of 1322*, ed. G. P. Cuttino, nos 1419, 1421–4, 1427, 1436–7, 1440, 1446.

[32] *RG*, ii, nos 1166, 1201.

[33] *Gascon Calendar*, no. 1445.

[34] *Olim*, ii, pp. 5, 7.

[35] *AM Agen*, nos lxxxvi, lxxxvii (pp. 142–9); cxi (pp. 183–7); cxiii (pp. 190–1); cxx (pp. 203–4), cxxii (pp. 206–7).

ordered his agents never again to molest Bernard, because all rancours and hatred, crimes and excesses had been pardoned him.[36] When the cumulative appeals of such individuals were annexed to a desire in the minds of Philip the Fair and his advisers to make war in Aquitaine, Anglo-French relations degenerated into open conflict.

Bernard de Ravignan was not the only appellant who was mentioned by Philip in 1293. An even longer-standing thorn in Edward I's side was Gombaud de Tiran, esquire, whose case dragged on seemingly incessantly for twenty-two years from 1272 until the outbreak of war in 1294.[37] Gombaud was lord of St-Médard-en-Jalle in the Bordelais, and his case had also reached the Parlement by 1281. Ten years later, an *arrêt* of the Parlement condemned Edward I and his seneschal to pay 2000 *l.t.* fine for disobedience to Philip IV's officers in the affair. Gombaud's lordship, confiscated by the king-duke, was to be restored to him and Edward accepted the Parlement's decision. Yet Gombaud was still listed as a wronged appellant in the citation of 1293. What were his grievances against the Plantagenet regime? In 1281–2 he listed them as follows: the king-duke's men had levied a hearth-tax on his tenants; none of its proceeds had been restored to him and they had arrested some of his men. This was apparently done with good cause: Gombaud and his band had broken into houses in the nearby castellanry of Blanquefort and ransacked them. This led to their banishment from the duchy and the king-duke's proctors rightly claimed that no one condemned to banishment could claim the protection of the crown of France. The Capetian seneschal of Périgord said in court that 'the men of the king of England bear no ill-will towards the said Gombaud', but the Parisian abbot of St Denis, for the French crown, replied: 'what cannot be done directly can be done obliquely, that is to say, by threatening appellants through the persons and goods of their tenants'.[38] But the court agreed to allow the seneschal of Périgord to inquire into the affair. This kind of legal shadow-boxing could go on for ever, to the benefit of no one but the advocates and of the appellant who thereby staved off judgement. It was the normal accompaniment of the tenurial position created by the treaty of 1259. But, at periods of acute Anglo-French tensions, it was all too easy for the issue of appeals and allegations of denial of justice to fan the flames of bellicosity. However just or unjust, serious or frivolous, the appeal might be, the very existence of appellants could be exploited and encouraged by the servants and agents of the crown of France as it could be in the lands of other great magnates. When that crown was worn by a monarch for whom military success had not yet materialized, and who was advised by men of the stamp

[36] *RG*, iii, no. 4328. A Bernard de Ravignan, knight banneret, was found serving in the French garrison at Bordeaux in 1298–9: *CR*, ii, no. 25489.

[37] *Gascon Calendar*, nos 1521–40.

[38] *BEC*, l (1889), pp. 47–52; xlviii (1887), pp. 547–55, 555–63; *Actes du Parlement*, ed. E. Boutaric (Paris, 1863–7), i, nos 2421, 2519, 2738, 3892, and appendix, no. 766.

of Charles of Valois, Robert of Artois and Pierre Flote (all three considered hostile to English and Gascon interests by contemporaries), apparently minor issues such as appeals and maritime clashes could all too readily lead to Anglo-French war.

The immediate causes of the outbreak of Anglo-French war in June 1294 are well known and I do not intend to retrace the steps of Sir Maurice Powicke, Professor J. R. Strayer and Professor Michael Prestwich.[39] A dispute between Gascon and Norman sailors and shipowners, which flared up into open war on the seas, leading to the sack of La Rochelle by the men of Bayonne in May 1293, has usually been given a paramount place (which it deserves) in the series of events which led to the first confiscation of Aquitaine by Philip the Fair. In his letter citing Edward I (as immediate lord of the Bayonnais) to reply to certain grave charges, Philip certainly spoke of the maritime dispute as of paramount importance. French sources also spoke of a desire to recover Normandy from the French as a motive for Anglo-Gascon aggression on the seas, but Edward's concern for former Norman and Plantagenet dominions seems confined to a somewhat vague assertion in his alliance with Adolf of Nassau in October 1294 that Philip and his ancestors had unjustly occupied 'our goods, lands and fiefs and those of our predecessors *a multo tempore*'.[40] Philip's citation of 27 October 1293 insisted that hostages be taken from Bayonne and imprisoned at Périgueux, and that Bordeaux, the Agenais and 'all that other land which your men hold in your name within the limits of our *sénéchaussée* of Périgord and in the three dioceses of Périgueux, Cahors and Limoges' were to be taken into French hands and placed under French royal protection.[41] A total of twenty hostages was required from among Edward's officers in the duchy who, it was claimed, had insulted the crown of France and assaulted its agents. Edward's Gascon subjects had, alleged Philip, killed 'certain Normans' who had lived peaceably at Bourg and Bordeaux for ten or more years, 'simply because they spoke the French language' (*lingua gallica*), and had thrown their dismembered corpses into the river. A royal serjeant, sent to the *bastide* of Villeréal, had had his hand cut off; four royal customs collectors at Fronsac had been killed and beheaded, while their murderers allegedly cried: 'We're doing this to spite the king of France and his brother Charles' (that is, Charles of Valois). A long list of further excesses followed.

It is extremely difficult to sift fact from fiction among these charges. There was undoubtedly friction between Plantagenet and Capetian officers in Aquitaine, and assaults on French royal serjeants, notaries and other officials from the *sénéchaussées* of Périgord and Toulouse were not a novel phenomenon. The historian's task is made more difficult by the absence of a Gascon

---

[39] Powicke, *Thirteenth Century*, pp. 644–719; Strayer, *Reign of Philip the Fair*, pp. 317–20; Prestwich, *Edward I*, pp. 376–81.

[40] *Treaty Rolls, i, 1234–1325*, ed. P. Chaplais (London, 1955), no. 231.

[41] *Olim*, ii, pp. 2–3.

Roll for 1293–4. Allowance for a degree of propaganda, leading to distortion and exaggeration of the facts, must be made in the analysis of Philip's citation of 27 October 1293. Before the summons was issued, Capetian officers had already begun to intervene in the duchy, apparently in the aftermath of the Bayonnais's sack of La Rochelle. The French had already begun to reinforce garrisons, repair and restock castles in Poitou and Saintonge by July 1293. At La Rochelle itself the garrison received an additional fifty crossbowmen, who came from Paris on 4 July, and a further seventy armed men were brought by Pierre de Bailleul, seneschal of Saintonge 'on account of the assault made upon the town by the Bayonnais'.[42] The appearance of Pierre Flote, king's knight and counsellor, in Saintonge at this time brought a champion of Capetian supremacy (his worth already proved in the Bigorre affair) into a highly sensitive area. His presence was of the highest significance. Flote was overseeing repairs to the walls, ditches and bridge at the castle of Benon and ordering payment to the augmented garrison at La Rochelle in September–October 1293. Shortly afterwards, he arrived at Blaye, one of the Plantagenet strongpoints guarding the northern approaches to the duchy of Aquitaine. The seneschal of Saintonge's account tells us that he and Flote came to Blaye with five soldiers who were paid from 28 September to 13 December, and that Flote ordered a payment of 100 *l.t.* to the castellan there.[43] Flote's role in the preliminaries to the Anglo-French war of 1294–8 was a crucial one which demands further analysis.

Although less notorious amongst Philip the Fair's advisers than his successor Guillaume de Nogaret, Flote was a zealous executive of, and then a major formative influence upon Capetian policy from 1291 until his death at the battle of Courtrai in July 1302. He was a standing contradiction of the modern popular view of Philip's counsellors as bourgeois anti-clericals. The cadet son of a noble family from the Dauphiné, he rose as a lawyer in the service of the Dauphin Humbert of Vienne, and was recruited to royal service in 1289.[44] Connected to the Aicelin family, he probably owed his advancement to Gilles Aicelin, archbishop of Narbonne. Flote used his annual pension (granted to him by Philip the Fair in 1289) to buy the lordship of Ravel in Auvergne, which he secured for himself and his heirs. By 1291 he was actively engaged in the defence of royal rights in the Parlement of Toulouse, and proved himself an adept, tenacious and successful promoter, with Aicelin, of Philip's authority in the affair of Bigorre. Boniface VIII described him as a 'devil' during Philip's subsequent conflict with the papacy.[45] His prominence in the events which preceded the outbreak of

---

[42] *CR*, i, nos 7691, 7697.

[43] *CR*, i, nos 7681, 7700, 7699, 7732, 7730–2. For the affair of Bigorre see above, pp. 88–90.

[44] F. J. Pegues, *The Lawyers of the Last Capetians* (Princeton, 1962), pp. 88–9; *CR*, iii, nos 28723, 28779.

[45] See J. G. Black, 'Edward I and Gascony in 1300', *EHR*, xvii (1902), pp. 518–27; T. S. R. Boase, *Boniface VIII* (London, 1933), pp. 297–9, 316.

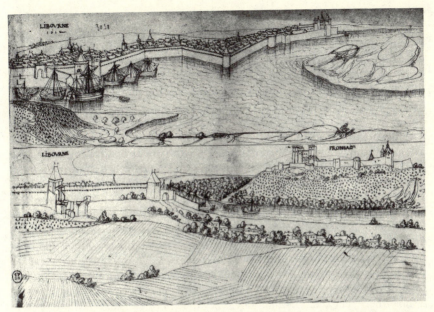

6.1   Views of Libourne and Fronsac by Du Wiert (1612). Libourne is shown with its walls (now destroyed) and the ships moored on the Dordogne indicate the navigability of the river. The size and commanding position of Fronsac castle (also destroyed) is apparent. (Paris, BN, Cabinet des Etampes, Vv 23, for. 5, fo. 56.)

Anglo-French war in 1294 was attested by his presence, with Gui de Nanteuil, king's knight, and Jean d'Arrablaye, seneschal of Périgord, as a leading member of the group of Capetian officers who proclaimed Philip's citation of Edward I at certain towns in Aquitaine in December 1293.[46] The arrogant style, tone and content of that summons has the ring of his influence, if not his authorship.

The Capetian delegation was at Agen on 1 December 1293, reaching Libourne on 12 December, where entry to the town was denied them. Jean d'Arrablaye reported that six ships had come to Libourne (supposedly on the orders of Sir John St John, Edward I's lieutenant in the duchy), manned by Englishmen and Bayonnais who proceeded to prevent all French-speaking subjects of Philip the Fair from sailing on the Dordogne towards Bordeaux or elsewhere. They had attempted to attack the nearby castles of Blaye and Fronsac but had been repulsed by the French garrisons installed there.[47] Financial documents confirm that the castle of Fronsac, as well as Blaye, received French troops at this time (see plate 6.1).[48] Another side to the

[46] *Olim*, ii, pp. 13–21.
[47] *Olim*, ii, pp. 6, 15, 20. For Fronsac see plate 6.1.
[48] *CR*, i, nos 7972–4, 8056, 8064.

story, however, emerges from an undated petition addressed to Edward I by a certain Thomas de Lancastre in which he described himself as 'the man who first sustained damage and performed a deed of arms in Gascony for . . . the king . . . before the beginning of the war'.[49] Thomas claimed that Raymond, *vicomte* of Fronsac, had surrendered his castle to Philip the Fair 'so that he might make war upon the king of England'. This was at least partially true, for Raymond of Fronsac was certainly to serve on Philip's side during the Anglo-French conflict.[50] Thomas de Lancastre claimed that he had loaded a boat with a cargo of herrings at Bordeaux and was taking it to Libourne when he was robbed of it on the Dordogne beneath Fronsac by 'the malefactors who were at that time in the said castle on behalf of the king of France'.[51] He was rewarded for his subsequent services by Edward I on 1 April 1305.[52] Taken with evidence from French royal accounts which reveals that the 'token' forces introduced by the French into Gascon castles were in fact sizeable – eighty serjeants at Blaye, thirty at Fronsac – Thomas de Lancastre's petition suggests that there was aggressive intent on both sides during the autumn and winter of 1293–4.[53]

This was also apparent in the Agenais, Landes and Gers. John St John and John de Havering, seneschal of Gascony, were already gathering and paying troops there between December 1293 and January 1294. A number of Gascon nobles were retained for military service 'cum equis et armis' at Bonnegarde, Puyguilhem, Castelnau-de-Rivière, Lectoure and Mauléon.[54] The consuls of Agen raised fifty armed serjeants for Raymond de Campagne, Edward I's seneschal of the Agenais, who gathered a force of nobles and their companies in January 1294 ostensibly to 'guard the roads and highways against robbers and malefactors'.[55] The lieutenant and seneschal were evidently preparing for every eventuality and resistance to French incursions was clearly a primary aim. Events such as those described by Jean d'Arrablaye, French seneschal of Périgord, thus formed part of a more widespread and general reaction to the infiltration and intervention of Capetian officials and garrisons in the duchy.

The distinctly unenthusiastic attitude displayed by the Gascons towards Philip the Fair and his officers was exemplified by the reception of his envoys at Libourne and St Emilion. As we have seen, Jean d'Arrablaye and his delegation were unable to enter Libourne on 12 December 1293, but he summoned the mayor and *jurats* to meet him outside the town gates. Philip's

---

[49] SC 8/291, no. 14521.

[50] AMB, MS 211, no. 60 (5 May 1309).

[51] SC 8/291, no. 14521.

[52] *RG*, iii, no. 4680 (1 April 1305). The grant was unspecific about his services.

[53] *CR*, i, nos 7972–4, 8056.

[54] E 101/152/6, nos 1–4, 8; 208/1A, no. 8; 1B, nos 1, 8; E 372/160, m. 41r for payments to certain Gascon nobles 'ante guerram predictam'.

[55] *AM Agen*, no. lxxxvi (pp. 142–3). The seneschal's recognizance of the levy was dated at Agen, 13 January 1294; Trabut-Cussac, *L'Administration anglaise*, pp. 107, 109, n. 393.

citation of Edward I was read aloud, but the townsmen refused to accept a copy, which was then nailed to one of the town gates, sealed with the seneschal's seal.[56] At St Emilion an even less ecstatic welcome awaited him. Arriving there on market day, he summoned the captain, mayor and *jurats* from a safe distance, taking up his position beneath an elm-tree outside the town. The mayor's lieutenant and other *jurats* appeared but, like the citizens of Libourne, refused to accept a copy of Philip the Fair's citation. Eble de Puyguilhem, who was captain of the place for Edward I, then presented himself but also refused to accept the offensive document and, according to the seneschal's report, gathered a force of foot-serjeants armed with cross-bows, shields and lances just inside the town gate adjoining the Dominican convent.[57] The town's bell was rung, the populace gathered, but the sum-mons was proclaimed outside the town walls because the seneschal feared an outbreak of violence. A notary, who had been ordered to fix a copy to the gate, was prevented from doing so by Eble de Puyguilhem's armed men. Eble was a member of Edward I's household and was to serve the king-duke throughout the war of 1294–8.[58] He and other members of the Gascon nobility clearly viewed Philip's summons as unfounded and improper.

Strength of feeling was also to be found on the Capetian side. According to Jean d'Arrablaye's report to Philip the Fair, written from the safety of Cahors on 20 December 1293, Pierre Flote had been the guiding spirit behind his mission to proclaim the royal summons.[59] Flote had not only advised him on the defence and war-readiness (*municionem et apparatum*) of his *sénéchaussée* of Périgord, but 'fervently and tirelessly' exerted himself in the defence of Philip's honour and profit. If Flote was a fanatical exponent of the 'religion of monarchy', as he has sometimes been seen, his role in the prelude to the Anglo-French war provides further evidence to endorse that view.[60] With garrisons in both Capetian and Plantagenet territory placed on a war footing by January 1294, if not earlier, the likelihood of armed conflict loomed dangerously close.

The situation was to some extent calmed by the action of Edward I and his diplomatic envoys to Paris, above all Edmund of Lancaster. Edward's brother and his diplomatic advisers have often been censured as the ar-chitects of a humiliating episode in Anglo-French relations.[61] This may misunderstand the situation in which they found themselves. The war of 1294 was not of Edward's choosing and his envoys were instructed to treat for peace with France. Edmund of Lancaster could tell him in late February

[56] *Olim*, ii, pp. 15–16.

[57] *Olim*, ii, pp. 16–17.

[58] E 101/351/25, 26; Trabut-Cussac, *L'Administration anglaise*, p. 79, n. 211; E 101/154/12, no. 37 (18 March 1298); *RG*, iii, nos 4529–31.

[59] *Olim*, ii, p. 21.

[60] Strayer, *Philip the Fair*, pp. 13–16, 34–5.

[61] Prestwich, *Edward I*, p. 380.

or March 1294 that his (previously hostile) officers and subjects in the duchy were now preparing to carry out what was required of them by Philip the Fair's lieutenant, Raoul de Clermont-Nesle, constable of France.[62] Gascon hostages were to be given up, castles surrendered and the temporary occupation of the duchy by the French was under way. It was the price to be paid for the preservation of peace in Christendom and the furtherance of a crusade to recover Acre. The papacy was, moreover, vacant from April 1292 until July 1294 and there was no hope of papal mediation while the college of cardinals was locked in electoral conflict. Edward I was therefore prepared to come to terms with the French and temporarily surrendered Aquitaine to them. The relative ease with which the surrender was accomplished – and which would have been inconceivable a few months earlier – was due to an agreement made by Edmund of Lancaster in Paris in February 1294. This was the so-called 'secret treaty' between Philip and Edward I, negotiated through the mediation of Edward's female relatives at the French court.[63] The treaty was never sealed, although the original French version in the Archives Nationales has holes for sealing cords but no clause of attestation. It bears the endorsement *Non est ibi sigillum* and the words (in a later hand): 'Certain conventions [*convenciones*] which the king of England's men requested . . . before the war, but the lord king [Philip] refused to consent to them.'[64] It is not difficult to see why the terms were opposed. If implemented, the agreement would have effectively created a quasi-independent hereditary principality (or apanage) of Aquitaine, to be held by the children of a proposed marriage between Edward I and Philip's sister, Margaret of France. The thorny issue of Gascon appeals was to be settled in Edward's favour by the removal of those exemptions from ducal jurisdiction which had previously been granted to Gascon appellants. The French royal *pennonceaux*, symbolic of Capetian protection and safeguard, would no longer fly over appellants' castles, town houses or *maison-fortes*.[65] A major cause of Anglo-French tension would be removed at a stroke. Should an appeal against

---

[62] *Foedera*, I, ii, pp. 793–4. The events surrounding the surrender of the duchy are described in P. Chaplais, *English Medieval Diplomatic Practice*, ii (London, 1980), pp. 418–27.

[63] *Foedera*, I, ii, pp. 795–6; AN, J 631, no. 7; C 47/27/4 (manuscript book concerning events surrounding the negotiation of the agreement).

[64] AN, J 631, no. 7; Chaplais, *English Medieval Diplomatic Practice*, ii, pp. 418–20.

[65] *Foedera*, I, ii, pp. 795–6 (cl. XVI). Fawtier believed that the 'royal arms and banner' which Guillaume de Nogaret took with him to Anagni in September 1303 may have been *pennonceaux* of the kind normally used to signify royal protection. William Hundleby's report from Rome to John Dalderby, bishop of Lincoln, stated that Sciarra Colonna carried the 'royal arms and banner of France' which were to be placed on the papal palace at Anagni as a sign of royal protection until Boniface VIII was tried. Dante's allusion (*Purg.*, xx, 86–90) to the fleurs-de-lis flying above the papal palace may have been grounded in fact. See R. Fawtier, 'L'attentat d'Anagni', *Mélanges d'Archéologie et d'Histoire de l'Ecole française de Rome*, lx (1948), p. 171; H. G. J. Beck, 'William Hundleby's account of the Anagni outrage', *Catholic Historical Review*, xxxii (1946–7), p. 200. Professor J. A. Watt kindly drew my attention to this allusion.

Edward or his heirs' justice succeed, there must be no dispossession of the king-duke. Should the impending marriage prove childless, all these concessions were to apply after his father's death to Edward, prince of Wales, as heir to Aquitaine, during his lifetime. By creating a new line of future dukes of Aquitaine, who were to perform an oath of fealty to the king of England while remaining peers of France, the 'secret treaty' tried to grasp the nettle sown by the peace of 1259.[66] Aquitaine would be held at one remove, as it were, from the reigning English monarch, whose majesty would in no way be offended or embarrassed by vassalic status or by the homage ceremony. Anglo-French relations might then be conducted on a basis of equality.

These negotiations ultimately failed and the 'secret treaty' was never honoured. With some justification Edmund of Lancaster believed himself misled and duped by the French. He had perhaps relied too much upon his own connections at the court of France, upon those 'mutual friends' (*amici communes*) to whom a subsequent statement on Edward I's behalf for submission to Boniface VIII referred.[67] Although Philip had twice been requested by Edmund and once by 'certain peers of France and other great lords' that Aquitaine be returned and the hostages released, this was not done.[68] John St John's resistance, as Edward's lieutenant, to Capetian attempts publicly to proclaim Philip's summons of Edward to the Parlement, and then to the demand that the duchy of Aquitaine be surrendered under the terms of the *convenances* agreed by Edmund of Lancaster, was determined by a well-intentioned aim to defend Edward's inheritance. St John still refused to implement Raoul de Clermont-Nesle's orders for the surrender of the duchy on Saturday 20 February 1294, when the Cistercian abbots of Belleperche and Grandselve, with other French commissioners, arrived outside the castle at St Macaire.[69] According to the notarial record of the event, the gates were shut firmly against them, but were eventually opened to admit the French envoys (*nuncii*) but not the notaries who accompanied them. The gate was slammed in their faces, although two notaries were ultimately smuggled into the hall of the castle. There John St John's clerk asked the *nuncii* what their business was, whose letter they carried and whether they were envoys or *executores* of Philip the Fair. The abbot of

---

[66] *Foedera* I, ii, p. 796 (cl. XXIII). See above, pp. 67–9.

[67] Chaplais, *English Medieval Diplomatic Practice*, ii, no. 237 (cl. 12); see above, pp. 187–8.

[68] C 47/30/6/10 (20 June 1294); Chaplais, *English Medieval Diplomatic Practice*, ii, p. 418. This obliged Edward to renounce his homage for Aquitaine, because it was apparent that 'the king of France did not consider him his man, nor did the king of England intend to be his man' (C 47/27.4, fo. 5ᵛ).

[69] AN, J 631, no. 9. This notarial instrument contains a full and detailed record, drawn up by Vital Aicard, notary of the *sénéchaussée* of Toulouse, of the proceedings at St Macaire (20–22 February 1294). See also Chaplais, *English Medieval Diplomatic Practice*, ii. p. 428, n. 44. The use of Cistercians may be paralleled by Edward I's use of friars to act as envoys for him when he renounced his homage for Aquitaine in June 1294. They were technically protected from arrest and assault by their clerical status. For St John's seal see plate 6.2.

Belleperche replied that they were both, bearing a letter from the constable of France, representing the king in the duchy. He was ready to show the letter to John St John in the form of a transcript under the seal of the seneschal and *viguier* of Toulouse. After a long delay, the envoys were ushered into a chamber where John St John received them. The constable's letter was translated and read aloud to him in French (*in romano*) by Sicard de Vaur, one of the envoys. A day of further discussions and exposition of the text followed, until on Monday 22 February the abbot of Belleperche himself expounded the constable's letter, requiring Edward I's lieutenant to surrender the duchy 'as a subject of the king of France' and to remove all garrisons from it. This John St John rightly refused to do. His clerk replied, in his presence, that the powers of the envoys to receive the duchy were invalid and unacceptable until an adequate mandate was shown 'as is the tradition in the duchy of Aquitaine'. The abbot insisted, the king-duke's lieutenant again refused, and his clerk tartly observed that he could certainly see that the letter had a seal but he did not recognize it. A transcript under the seal of the seneschal and *viguier* of Toulouse had no currency in Plantagenet Aquitaine. The constable of France's deputation were sent packing back to their master because there was nothing else that they could do. But John St John had not yet received Edward I's order to surrender the duchy.

The first French attempt to confiscate the duchy of Aquitaine by judicial means ran into deep and troubled waters because of procedural incompetence, or perhaps arrogance. The act was unprecedented. It was unwise, to say the least, to initiate the duchy's surrender on the basis of a mandate which had no more binding force than, for example, a photocopy of a legal document would have today. Capetian over-confidence was perhaps to blame. But the scene which took place in the castle at St Macaire was not to be repeated elsewhere in the duchy. John St John must have received Edward I's order, transmitted by Edmund of Lancaster, requiring him and other ducal officers in Aquitaine to surrender the duchy and the hostages, soon after the abbot of Belleperche's unwelcome visitation. He had certainly received the order by 3 March.[70] He was bound to obey that mandate, and Edmund told Edward I that local resistance to the surrender was overcome by the knowledge that an acceptable, though secret, Anglo-French settlement had been negotiated at Paris.[71] Edward's desire for peace, and his brother's trust in the integrity of Philip the Fair's assurances that the duchy would be returned to the king-duke within three months, overrode the

---

[70] *AM Agen*, no. lxxxv (pp. 139–42). John St John was at Agen on 3 March, where he ordered Raymond de Campagne, seneschal of the Agenais, to obey the French envoys and surrender the *sénéchaussée* because he had received Edward I's mandate. Edmund of Lancaster had issued the order to surrender the duchy at Paris on 3 February 1294 (*Foedera*, I, ii, p. 794).

[71] *Foedera*, I, ii, p. 794: 'noz gentz ne voleient escraier contre lui [Raoul de Clermont-Nesle] pour ceo quil penserent qe ce serroit bien amende solonc les covenaunces que furent faites'. See also C 47/29/3/10 and 14.

6.2 Seal and counterseal of John de St John, knight, of Halnaker, Sussex (1301). His equestrian figure wears a helm with visor down and a crest of a lion between two palm branches. He was with Edward I in Aquitaine (1286–9), served as lieutenant and seneschal there (1293–7) and was captured by the French. He died during Edward's Scots campaign of 1302. (London, Public Record Office.)

valid, if intransigent, stance assumed by his lieutenant in Aquitaine. Edmund of Lancaster recorded that Edward

> for the peace of Christendom, and the furtherance of the Crusade, granted all these things, in order to save the French king's honour, to satisfy those of his council and, to keep the private agreements more secret, . . . wished that a letter patent be issued [stating that] all the land of Gascony should be surrendered to the king of France.[72]

Broader horizons – the Crusade and the peace of Europe – were undoubtedly uppermost in Edward I's mind, but his reasons for the surrender of Aquitaine were also clearly related to the state of affairs at the French court.

To save Philip's honour, satisfy certain members of his council and 'keep the private agreements more secret', Edward was prepared to make a token submission to a token confiscation. The young Philip had personally told Edmund of Lancaster, in the presence of witnesses, that he should not feel injured by the 'harsh reply' which would be given him by his counsellors because 'after certain of them had departed who were opposed to the . . . agreement', he would countermand the surrender.[73] There was clearly an anti-Plantagenet group or faction within Philip's council which had become dominant in the early 1290s. It included assertive royal lawyers and great magnates, self-interested and under-occupied. How far Philip was able or indeed willing to control that faction remains unclear. The admittedly self-justifying evidence presented to Edward I by Edmund of Lancaster suggests that he was not. Like Philip VI of Valois in the early 1330s, Philip the Fair had only tenuous control of his own counsellors.[74] Their assertive advocacy of Capetian supremacy was not wholly confined to the sphere of theory, propaganda and polemic. The ideology which moulded and shaped the thought and behaviour of men such as Pierre Flote was well set out both in the documents emanating from Philip's Chancery at this time and in propagandist tracts such as *Antequam essent clerici*. The play of ideas cannot be divorced from the world of pragmatic politics at this time. Paris theology met Bologna (or Montpellier) law in the circle of advisers around Philip the Fair. Royal clerks had been permitted to attend the University of Paris since 1282 while the lay status and legal training of Flote and other 'king's knights' made them adept at formulating notions of royal authority derived from both feudal and Roman Law.[75] Some of these ideas were exemplified in *Antequam*

---

[72] *Foedera*, I, ii, p. 794; C 47/27/4 fos 4ʳ–5ʳ.

[73] *Foedera*, I, ii, p. 794; 'pour ce que, apres le partir des ascuns de eux, que furent contrairez en fait avant dit, il freit garder et accomplir tout ceo que fuit ordenez'. The terms of surrender were set out in a credence to Master John de Lacy, printed by M. Champollion-Figeac, *Lettres des rois*, i, pp. 406–8.

[74] See below, pp. 250–1.

[75] See *The Cambridge History of Medieval Political Thought*, ed. J. H. Burns (Cambridge, 1988),

essent clerici, and vulgarized for a wider audience in vernacular writings such as Guillaume Guiart's *Branche des royaux lignages*.

Although the anonymous tract known as *Antequam essent clerici* was largely a retort to Boniface VIII's bulls *Clericis laicos* and *Ineffabilis amor* (1296), it embraced views of secular power and of the relationship between king and magnates.[76] Boniface had upheld the justice of Edward I's conduct and position in *Ineffabilis amor* (21 September 1296), but *Antequam* contained a denunciation of the king-duke of Aquitaine in terms similar to the formal instruments emanating from Philip's chancery in 1293–4.[77] Edward's alleged refusal to obey Philip's summons was considered sufficient cause for confiscation of the duchy and consequent warfare. Edward had renounced his homage; therefore his lands held 'by homage and fealty' were forfeit and, owing to his contumacy, had necessarily to be sequestrated by force of arms. The author of *Antequam* opined that both Edward and the King of the Romans 'unjustly and without reasonable cause attacked us' and hence defensive war and the taxation to pay for it were both justified.[78] In Guillaume Guiart's verse chronicle the emphasis was placed firmly upon Plantagenet aggression: Edward I declared war, assembled a great army and aimed to recover Normandy.[79] His verses read like a parody of Philip's citation of October 1293, accusing Edward of collusion with the Bayonnais, feigning an expedition to the Holy Land and refusing to appear before the 'masters' of the Paris Parlement. Guiart omitted to note that a safe-conduct had been denied him by Philip the Fair for his passage to France. The myth-making of *Antequam essent clerici* was echoed by the far more emotive propaganda of Guillaume Guiart.

Guiart's stress upon the maritime dispute which brought war in its wake merely reflected contemporary opinion. The events at sea of April–May 1293 were not interpreted in pro-Capetian sources merely as an episode in a private war conducted by some of Edward I's subjects against their Norman and Breton rivals.[80] The Bayonnais, as subjects of the king-duke of Aquitaine, were thought to be primarily responsible for the conflict, and Edward's efforts to discipline and punish them were considered both ineffectual and insincere. It was evidently by means of the Bayonnais that conflict spread

---

pp. 92–5; J. Favier, 'Les légistes et le gouvernement de Philippe le Bel', *Journal des Savants* (1969), pp. 92–108; Pegues, *Lawyers of the Last Capetians*, pp. 124–37.

[76] It is printed in P. Dupuy, *Histoire du différend d'entre le pape Boniface VIII et Philippes le Bel Roy de France. Preuves* (Paris, 1655), pp. 21–3.

[77] Dupuy, *Preuves*, pp. 18, 22–3.

[78] Dupuy, *Preuves*, p. 23: 'predicti reges injuste, et sine causa rationabili, nos impugnant'.

[79] Guiart, *Branche des royaux lignages*, ll. 202–8, 244–7, 1436–43. Guiart wrote his *romanz* in 1304–6 after he had been wounded during the Flemish war in which he had served as a serjeant for Philip the Fair.

[80] Prestwich, *Edward I*, p. 377. Events on the seas at this period are summarized in C. de la Roncière, 'Le blocus continental de l'Angleterre sous Philippe le Bel', *RQH*, lx (1896), pp. 401–41.

from the seas to the mainland – they had sacked La Rochelle, allegedly attacked the French on the Dordogne, and hence were to provide hostages and prisoners detained in French-occupied areas of the south-west. But the interests of Bayonne could not be ignored by Edward. As we have seen, Bayonne and its shipping was vital to English commercial and maritime interests.[81] The Bayonnais were important enough to be treated as a maritime power in their own right in mercantile treaties made by the Plantagenets with other rulers and their subjects. They were the Genoese of the northern seas. Bayonne was a wealthy community: its citizens offered large loans to the embattled Plantagenet regime in Gascony between 1296 and 1298, and it provided the king-duke with manpower as well as money.[82] The Bayonnais were conspicuously loyal among Edward's Gascon subjects. In 1287–8, eight of the twenty-seven hostages whom he offered as sureties for the execution of the Oloron and Canfranc treaties with Aragon were citizens of Bayonne.[83] When some of its leading citizens were imprisoned by the French in 1293–4, Edward particularly desired them to be well treated, held in 'nette et courte prison' and not delivered to French officers such as Jean d'Arrablaye, seneschal of Périgord, or Etienne de Beaumarchais, seneschal of Toulouse, who were known to be malevolent towards them. Edward's fear that his subjects would be ill-treated was founded partly on the belief that the count of Foix had once been held in prison by the French for one and a half years, well beyond the term specified on his surrender to Philip III.[84] His suspicions were to some degree justified. The French seneschal of Poitou and Limousin accounted for the cost of shackles in which to keep thirty Bayonnais prisoners at Poitiers and Niort in April and May 1294 on the constable of France's orders.[85] Bayonne's inhabitants bore the brunt of the Plantagenet war effort in Aquitaine after 1294 and Edward's sense of honourable obligation towards them was expressed by the repayment of their 50,000 *l.st.* loan to him.[86] It was one of the few sums that he seems ever to have fully repaid during his lifetime.

It is clear, however, that the maritime conflict between the Bayonnais and their rivals formed only one link in the chain of events which led to the Anglo-French war of 1294. The evidence suggests that complete dispossession of Edward as duke of Aquitaine was a major objective of French activity from the outset. Historians such as Strayer believed that Philip IV

---

[81] See above, pp. 149–50. For Bayonne's situation see plate 6.3

[82] *CPR, 1281–92*, pp. 58, 59, 64; C 47/29/4, no. 26(b); and the numerous receipts and quittances for loans from the Bayonnais in E 101/152–5.

[83] *Foedera*, I, iii, p. 690; see above, pp. 177–8.

[84] *Olim*, ii, p. 9; C 47/29/3, no. 10; *RG*, iii, no. 4508. Champollion-Figeac, *Lettres des rois*, pp. 407–8. All Gascon hostages were to be treated 'cortoisement, nettement et onestement, e santz fers'.

[85] *CR*, i, nos 7540–1.

[86] M. Prestwich, *War, Politics and Finance under Edward I* (London, 1972), p. 213; Vale, 'The Gascon nobility and the Anglo-French war', pp. 134–5; SC 8/291, no. 14538.

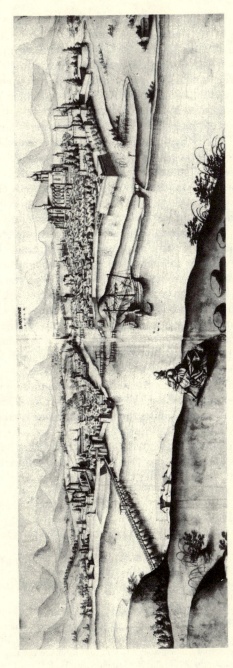

6.3 View of Bayonne by Du Wiert (1612). The castle and cathedral can be seen to the right and the strategic importance of the town and port, at the confluence of the Adour and the Nive, can be appreciated. (Paris, BN, Cabinet des Estampes, Vx 22, gr.fol., fo. 157.)

'began to develop a policy of his own during the early 1290s: a policy of strongly asserting royal rights against the Church and his greatest vassals, the King of England and Count of Flanders'.[87] There is indeed evidence for the strenuous assertion of royal rights at this time, but Philip's own part in this policy remains unclear. As we saw earlier, French incursions into Bigorre, Saintonge, the lands of Armagnac and elsewhere in the south-west in the early 1290s formed a prelude to the occupation in 1294 of the greater part of the duchy of Aquitaine.[88] Philip IV was treating Bordeaux as his own town by August 1294, when he annexed it directly to the French crown and awarded it privileges.[89] Bayonne, if it had not held out for Edward, would undoubtedly have been treated in a similar manner. Philip had omitted, moreover, to address Edward as duke of Aquitaine in his citation before the Parlement in October 1293 and was to refer to him subsequently merely as *tenens ducatum Aquitanie*. Pierre Flote was especially adamant that the title 'duke' should not be attributed to him.[90] This makes the terms of the 'secret treaty' of February 1294 all the more puzzling. A public stance of aggressive denial of right and status supposedly masked a private readiness to compromise and concede on Philip's part.[91] The personal political role of Philip the Fair has always been an historical enigma. But, even if we are sceptical (with Favier and Bautier) of the king's capacity and willingness to formulate and initiate policy, a pertinent question remains: who, if anyone, stood to gain from an Anglo-French war over Aquitaine in 1293–4? Who, if anyone, among the politically powerful in France was especially hostile to Edward I and his subjects?

At least two of the princes of the blood were antagonistic towards the Plantagenets. The first was Charles of Valois, Philip IV's brother; the second Robert II, count of Artois. The English chroniclers accused Charles of Valois of stirring up hostility towards England in 1293–4: the *Annales of Dunstable* claimed that 'he pursued the English with an inveterate hatred', while both Walter of Hemingburgh and the *Annales* of London reported that he was the instigator of the naval battles between the Normans and Anglo-Gascons.[92]

---

[87] Strayer, *Philip the Fair*, pp. 49–50.

[88] AN, J 631, no. 10 (Bigorre); E 101/152/6 (Armagnac); AN, J 294, no. 13 (Bigorre); APA, E 371, nos 4, 8, (Bigorre). See above, pp. 88–90, 183–4.

[89] C 47/27/3, no. 7; AN, J 631, no. 20. In future the Bordelais 'regni Francie imperpetuum adhereant corone, et eidem subsint immediate'.

[90] Chaplais, *English Medieval Diplomatic Practice*, ii, p. 427; C 47/27/4, fo. 5ᵛ; AN, J 632, no. 36 (3 August 1299); J 633, no. 4 (19 April 1301).

[91] *Foedera*, I, ii, p. 794. For what follows, see J. Favier, *Philippe le Bel* (Paris, 1980), pp. 2–5; R.-H. Bautier, 'Diplomatique et histoire politique: ce que la critique diplomatique nous apprend sur la personnalité de Philippe le Bel', *RH*, dcxxv (1978), pp. 3–27; cf. Strayer, *Philip the Fair*, pp. x–xi, 31–2: 'Philip . . . had many able advisers, but he made the final decisions'.

[92] Petit, *Charles de Valois*, pp. 27–8; *Annales Monastici*, ed. H. R. Luard (RS, London, 1865–9), iii, p. 385; Walter of Hemingburgh, *Chronicon*, ed. H. C. Hamilton (London, 1849), ii, pp. 42–5; *Chronicles of the Reigns of Edward I and II*, ed. W. Stubbs (RS, London, 1882–3), ii, p. 101.

The *Lanercost Chronicle* even alleged that he desired to supplant his brother as king of France, and hated the English because Edward I supported Philip.[93] His anti-English sentiments were confirmed by the subsequent marriage of his daughter to Edward Balliol, eldest son of the king of Scotland, in October 1295.[94] Chronicler's rumour-mongering apart, why should Charles of Valois seek to exacerbate Anglo-French tension? Strayer observed that 'it is difficult to see what [he] . . . had to gain from war and he was not one of Philip's most influential counsellors'.[95] Favier takes an opposing view: 'au Conseil, le comte de Valois parle le premier, et il parle haut'.[96] His political importance was in effect sustained by the fact that he was Philip IV's sole surviving brother by Philip III's first wife, Isabella of Aragon, and thus had a special place in Philip's affections. But he had also been invested with the kingdom of Aragon by the papacy in 1283. Strayer comments that 'he had been addressed as a king during his teens, and had never quite recovered from the experience'.[97] The French war with Aragon of 1284–5 was conducted in his name and on his behalf by his father Philip III. Moreover, his title to Aragon was not formally renounced until 20 June 1295, one year after the French occupation of Aquitaine.[98] Charles had good reason for resenting the role that Edward I had played in the Aragonese war, declared in February 1284, for Edward had contracted a marriage between his daughter and Alfonso of Aragon. Edward's consequent arbitration of the Angevin-Aragonese dispute effectively deprived Charles of Valois of his Aragonese title and the ignominous end to the war left him (as Italian chroniclers were pleased to point out) 'Carlo senza Terra' – Charles the Landless.[99] No doubt the counties of Maine, Anjou, Alençon and Chartres granted to him by his brother between 1290 and 1293, and his place in the sun at the French court were some compensation, but he did not wear a crown.[100]

If Charles of Valois's claims to Aragon still held good 1293–4, then he had a specific interest in the affairs of south-west France. The previous French campaign in Aragon of 1284–5 had foundered on poor communications and supply lines, partly because they had lost control of the sea.[101] Gascony was an alternative point of entry into Aragon, and Bayonne might serve as a port through which supplies could be channelled via Béarn or Navarre. The

---

[93] *Chronicon de Lanercost*, ed. J. Stevenson (Edinburgh, 1839), pp. 150–1.

[94] *Foedera*, I, ii, p. 831.

[95] Strayer, *Philip the Fair*, p. 318.

[96] Favier, *Philippe le Bel*, p. 14.

[97] Strayer, *Philip the Fair*, p. 369.

[98] Petit, *Charles de Valois*, p. 22; J. N. Hillgarth, *The Spanish Kingdoms, 1250–1516* (Oxford, 1976), i, p. 264.

[99] Petit, *Charles de Valois*, p. 23; *Foedera*, I, ii, pp. 227–8.

[100] Petit, *Charles de Valois*, pp. 19, 24–5.

[101] J. R. Strayer, 'The Crusade against Aragon', in *Medieval Statecraft and the Perspectives of History, Essays by Joseph R. Strayer*, ed. J. F. Benton and T. N. Bisson (Princeton, 1971), pp. 107–22.

Lanercost Chronicle emphasized Philip IV's action in entrusting the custody and defence of Gascony in 1295 to Charles of Valois, who led the campaign there against Anglo-Gascon resistance.[102] In the early 1300s the French were still very nervous about Aragon, accusing Bernard Saisset, bishop of Pamiers, of attempting to arrange a marriage in 1295–6 between Roger-Bernard, the count of Foix's son, and a daughter of the king of Aragon, against French interests in the Languedoc.[103] Charles nearly realized one of his aims but, with Bayonne firmly holding out for Edward I, his army was stricken with an epidemic while besieging St Sever – the key to the southernmost reaches of the duchy – in May–June 1295, and his ambitions were once again thwarted.[104] With Raoul de Clermont-Nesle, constable of France, Flote, Charles of Valois, and as we shall see, Robert of Artois opposed to a settlement with Edward, the royal will (if Philip ever really intended to implement the 'secret treaty') was in a decidedly weak position. If Charles of Valois had the upper hand in French policy at this date, some puzzling aspects of Anglo-French affairs are perhaps resolved. In a contemporary poem on the treason of Thomas Turberville, an English knight captured (with others) by Charles of Valois at Rions in Aquitaine on 7 April 1295, there are constant references to 'messire Charles', 'le bon chevalier', as if he were in fact king of France.[105] Sir Goronwy Edwards was perplexed by the fact that the poem's author did not seem to know that Philip IV was on the French throne. Such allusions would be rendered comprehensible if they in fact referred not to Philip but to his brother Charles. An intercepted letter written by Turberville to Guillaume de Hangest, *prévôt* of Paris, probably in August 1295, giving classified information about Edward I's plans and movements to the French, speaks of 'le haut seigneur'.[106] Historians have normally assumed that this refers to Philip IV, but Turberville was Charles of Valois's prisoner, and his anxiety about the welfare of his sons, held hostage in France while he spied in England, might make more sense if Charles was his (and their) captor.[107] Charles's brutal treatment of the Gascon members of the garrison at Rions, whom he executed, did not bode well for the safety of Turberville's children.[108]

Active intervention in Anglo-French issues by supporters of Valois interests at the court of France brought war nearer. It is likely that Charles of Valois

---

[102] *Chronicon de Lanercost*, p. 156; Petit, *Charles de Valois*, pp. 28–31; AN, J 164[B], no. 58[bis].

[103] Dupuy, *Preuves*, pp. 632–3, 634, 646, 653–6.

[104] Petit, *Charles de Valois*, pp. 29–31.

[105] *Chronicon de Lanercost*, pp. 484–7 (from BL, Cotton MS Calig. A. XVIII, fo. 21).

[106] J. G. Edwards, 'The treason of Thomas Turberville, 1295', *Studies in Medieval History Presented to F. M. Powicke*, ed. R. W. Hunt, W. A. Pantin and R. W. Southern (Oxford, 1948), pp. 296–309, esp. p. 296, n. 4. The letter is printed on pp. 298–9 from Bartholomew Cotton's *Historia Anglicana*, ed. H. Luard (RS, London 1859), pp. 304–6. For Guillaume de Hangest as *prévôt* of Paris in 1295, see ADPC, A 38, no. 12[b].

[107] Edwards, 'Treason of Thomas Turberville', pp. 299, 300.

[108] Petit, *Charles de Valois*, pp. 28, 29.

was partly responsible for provoking the war of 1294, and the accusation levelled by the French against certain Gascon subjects of Edward I, who were alleged to have killed some Normans and French customs collectors in the duchy 'to spite the King of France and his brother Charles' sounds plausible.[109] French infiltration into Aquitaine and on its frontiers was not the result of accident or the fortuitous ebb and flow of events. Some Catalan nobles, for example, professed themselves disappointed that war had not broken out between Philip and Edward by December 1293, as they had anticipated.[110] The strong anti-French sentiments of the count of Urgel, of Artoldo de Alagone and other Aragonese nobles were no doubt fuelled by memories of the French invasion of 1284–5, and Edward received at least thirteen offers of military service from them, with men-at-arms and foot-serjeants, in March and April 1294.[111] One of them said he would serve Edward against the French 'to the death' (*usque ad mortem*), while others appear to have been offering simultaneous service in a French war or a crusade under Edward's leadership.[112] Events in the *pays d'Armagnac* and the Agenais during 1293 had evidently led to rumours of an Anglo-French war, as Sir John St John mobilized forces, bribed the count of Armagnac and, as we have seen, resisted all French efforts to exercise sovereignty over Aquitaine.[113] It seems that Edward I's *de facto* sovereignty over Aquitaine was a standing provocation in the eyes of an influential party within the French royal council, especially when it stood in the way of Valois ambitions. As subsequent events were to show, there were also strong acquisitive instincts at work among the vassals, clients, allies and dependents of French magnates which were met by the grant to them of lands, rents and offices in Aquitaine during the French occupation of 1294–1303.[114]

One of these magnates was Robert II, count of Artois. He was, as we shall see, to play an important part in the reduction and occupation of Aquitaine. Suspicious of Edward I's intentions since 1275, hostile to the extension of Plantagenet interests in France, and especially vulnerable to English aggression on the seas through his possession of Calais and St Omer,

[109] *Olim*, ii, pp. 7, 15, 19–20; see above, pp. 182–3.

[110] See above, nn. 18 and 19; Trabut-Cussac, *L'Administration anglaise*, pp. 107–9; *Foedera*, I, ii, pp. 797–8, 807.

[111] SC I/14, no. 147; 16, nos 17–19; 20, no. 5; *Foedera*, I, ii, pp. 797–8.

[112] *Foedera*, I, ii, p. 797; and 787, 793, 798 for offers of service in a Crusade. For payments of war wages to these Aragonese nobles for military service against the French in 1295–8 see PRO, E 101/152/8, no. 36; 153/1, no. 23; *RG*, iii, pp. clxxxiv–clxxxv, clxxxviii; nos 4478, 4479, 4486.

[113] Trabut-Cussac, *L'Administration anglaise*, p. 109; PRO, E 101/152/6, nos 1, 2, 4; nos B1, A8. See also AN, J 631, nos 10(1) and (2) for the French summons to the count of Armagnac to perform homage at Paris (December 1293), and above, pp. 189–90.

[114] *RG*, iii, pp. clxv–clxxxii, xcx; AN, J 78, fos 12ᵛ–13ᵛ, and below, pp. 215–19. Boniface VIII's remarks about French avarice and covetousness could be noted in this context. See *EHR*, xvii (1902), p. 523.

Robert of Artois replaced Charles of Valois as Philip IV's lieutenant in the south-west in 1296.[115] Yet his part in the preliminaries to war cannot be overlooked. The volume of expenditure which he incurred on the Calais garrison between August 1293 and March 1294 was unusual, and suggests that it had already been put on a war footing.[116] On 29 June 1294 payments are already found in the Artois accounts for war service at Calais against Edward, 'segneur des Engles'.[117] Edward had renounced his homage to Philip IV in letters dated 20 June.[118] Early in 1294 Robert of Artois had received most of the French court at Hesdin and Creil, where the future Charles IV was baptized.[119] Charles of Valois was there, and we might speculate whether the plan to deceive Edmund of Lancaster and dispossess Edward I of Aquitaine was conceived on that occasion. The unsealed secret treaty was drawn up by 3 February 1294, immediately after the visit of Charles of Valois and other counsellors to Robert of Artois. We know that Robert held an influential place among Philip's advisers. The *Grandes Chroniques* reported that in November 1294 the French reply to Edward I's ally, Adolf of Nassau, took the form of a blank parchment on which were written two words: 'Troup Alemant'. This was said to be the work of Robert of Artois, as contemptuous of a German princeling as he was hostile to a Plantagenet rival to the sovereignty of France.[120]

6.2   War, Finance and Military Organization

'From the purely military point of view', observed Professor Strayer, 'the war of Aquitaine hardly deserves notice'.[121] His interest focused on the financial aspects of the conflict. In the growth of public fiscality and national taxation, the war of 1294–8 was certainly a watershed. Politically, it had very wide implications indeed: 'tous les princes chrétiens de la Norvège à Majorque étant imbriqués dans un complexe réseau d'alliances avec l'un ou l'autre des adversaires'.[122] Historians have therefore concentrated more upon the indirect effects of the war on finance and politics than upon its course.

[115] Powicke, *Thirteenth Century*, p. 239; ADPC, A 41, nos 12–18 for Philip the Fair's letters appointing him to the lieutenancy of Gascony and the duchy of Aquitaine (15–16 April 1296). See below, pp. 208–9.

[116] ADPC, A 38, nos 72, 74, 78; A 40, no. 23; A 136, nos 162–4 (August 1293–March 1294).

[117] ADPC, A 39, no. 28.

[118] *Foedera*, I, ii, p. 807; Chaplais, *English Medieval Diplomatic Practice*, ii, p. 418.

[119] ADPC, A 134, no. 19; A 135, nos 18–20; Petit, *Charles de Valois*, p. 26.

[120] R. Fawtier, 'Un incident diplomatique franco-allemand au temps de Philippe le Bel', *Annuaire-Bulletin de la Société de l'Histoire de France* (1946–7), pp. 27–38. The reply is very reminiscent of Louis VI of France's retort to the Emperor: 'Tpuwrut Aleman' as reported by Walter Map, *De Nugis Curialium*, ed. M. R. James (Oxford 1914), pp. 228–9.

[121] Strayer, 'The costs and profits of war', p. 271.

[122] R. H. Bautier, 'Le jubilé romain de 1300 et l'alliance franco-pontificale au temps de Philippe le Bel et de Boniface VIII', *MA*, lxxxvi (1980), p. 795.

Bémont's narrative of events remains the standard detailed account since it was written eighty years ago.[123] But the conflict taught military and logistical lessons to both sides which demonstrated the problems and difficulties encountered in a war confined to Aquitaine. The widening of the theatre of warfare to embrace Flanders in 1297 was partly an admission that neither side could win a war fought exclusively in south-west France. This lesson, and the precedents of Philip Augustus's reign, combined to shift active warfare towards northern France and the Low Countries. Militarily, the Anglo-French war for Aquitaine may have established guidelines for future strategy at the beginning of the Hundred Years War.

The war effort was sustained by both Capetians and Plantagenets for four years before they were enervated by financial exhaustion and military stalemate. Philip the Fair's assembly of naval forces between 1292 and 1294, his purchase of galleys from Genoa and Provence and his abortive plan to invade England in 1295 failed to bring the conflict to a speedy and decisive conclusion. The Channel and the western approaches did not become an important theatre of war. Concentration of Capetian effort and resources was increasingly centred upon the Languedoc, from which Aquitaine could be attacked. On 21 September 1293, while Flote and his associates were proclaiming Philip's summons to Edward I in Aquitaine, the *arrière-vassaux* of the Languedoc had already been convoked for a Gascon campaign.[124] The inhabitants of Narbonne petitioned for a delay in their service on 20 October, so that they might complete the grape harvest, and in March 1294 refused to contribute to a tax levied upon them to pay for a campaign in Aquitaine.[125] Further north, recruitment of nobles to fight against Edward I and his allies for wages and *restaur* of horses proceeded apace. Thus, for example, Philippe de Vienne, Lord of Penguy in Burgundy, promised to serve Philip at Gisors in August 1294 with forty men-at-arms whenever he was requested, while Robert of Artois had put the castle and garrison at Calais in a state of readiness between August and November 1293.[126] Over and above the normal wages of the garrison, additional costs had been sustained in providing saltfish, shields, *pavais* for archers, lances and other weapons, helmets, crossbow strings and bolts, while an extensive operation to clear the castle's ditches had been mounted. The nobility of Artois were already engaged in war service against Edward I in June 1294, and many of them, as we shall see, were to become closely involved in the Gascon war.

---

[123] *RG*, iii, pp. cxxiv–clxxxii. For a more recent narrative, based upon Bémont's, see Prestwich, *Edward I*, pp. 376–86, 398–9. Events in Flanders and diplomatic alliances with the Empire and imperial vassals are recounted on pp. 387–98.

[124] C. de la Roncière, 'Le blocus continental de l'Angleterre', pp. 401–2, 407–9; A. Z. Freeman, 'A Moat Defensive: the coast defense scheme of 1295', *Speculum*, xlii (1967), pp. 446–8.

[125] C. de Vic and J. Vaissete, *Histoire générale de Languedoc, avec des notes et les pièces justificatives* (Toulouse, 1872–1904) ix, pp. 172, 173–4.

[126] AN, J 620, no. 20 (23 August 1294); ADPC, A 38, nos 72, 74 (21 December 1293); see above, p. 200.

Communications and supplies posed a major problem for the French when campaigning in the south-west. It was essential for sources of war material, provisions and manpower to be established in southern France. Toulouse, Narbonne, Carcassonne and Montpellier therefore supplied victuals and munitions for Philip's armies in Aquitaine. In 1295, moreover, Toulouse acted as a point of collection for 2000 crossbows, 3000 gorgets and 3000 bacinets, presumably for foot-soldiers, which were carried overland to Paris and Rouen.[127] Some of these were no doubt intended for the seaborne army gathering in the Norman ports, others for Charles of Valois's expeditionary force to Aquitaine. Besides the mounted men-at-arms brought by the nobility, large numbers of foot-serjeants were recruited by both sides.[128] The war in Aquitaine was to be primarily a war of sieges, skirmishes and counter-sieges, in which infantry and siege equipment had an important part to play.

The professionalism and quality of some of these troops cannot have been high. Edward I was recruiting pardoned criminals and outlaws, at least 300 of whom were drafted into the first expeditionary force which sailed from Portsmouth in October 1294.[129] Further forces of 13,000, 10,000 and 17,000 infantry were levied in the English shires in 1295 for service in Aquitaine. Some of these were archers and crossbowmen, supplemented by Gascon and Catalan foot-serjeants; this mixture was to be characteristic of Anglo-Gascon forces throughout the war.[130] In a horse-valuation dated c.1297, for example, Auger de Mauleon, esquire, brought eleven mounted men-at-arms (socii) and 140 foot-serjeants to a muster, while Garcie-Arnaud, lord of Navailles had sixteen men-at-arms and 111 serjeants in his company.[131] The latter were recruited locally, and evidence from 1297–8 demonstrates that most of them came from St Sever, Pontonx, Bayonne and other towns in Chalosse and along the southernmost borders of the duchy.[132] Pascau Valentin, knight banneret, called the 'Adaliz' of Aragon, also offered his services to Edward I in 1297 and said that he would contract with 200 or 300 foot soldiers to swell his company's numbers. Edward professed himself content with his present *magnam societatem*, and Valentin was paid for his services by Henry Lacy, earl of Lincoln, at Peyrehorade in September 1297. With his brother Sancho, Valentin was also to serve in Edward's Scots wars.[133] There was no lack of

---

[127] *CR*, ii, nos 25020–309; 26044–363.

[128] *CR*, iii, nos 26364–567. The total cost of foot-serjeants from Toulouse in 1300 for the garrisons of occupied Aquitaine was 27,366 *l.* 10 *s.* 9 *d.t.* See also Strayer, *Philip the Fair*, pp. 374–6.

[129] *RG*, iii, pp. cxxxviii–cxxxix; Prestwich, *Edward I*, p. 381.

[130] *RG*, iii, pp. cxlix–cl; E 101/154/11, no. 12.

[131] E 101/14/4, mm. 1ᵛ.

[132] E 101/154/11, no. 12; 15, nos 16, 33–5.

[133] *RG*, iii, pp. clxxxiv–clxxxv, clxxxviii; nos 4478–9, 4486; E 101/161/25, no. 35; 371/21, no. 37.

willing recruits among certain sections of the Gascon and Catalan nobility who were able to act as military contractors to provide both cavalry and infantry companies.

Two major features of the war in Aquitaine should be emphasized: the significance of sieges and siegecraft, and the importance of sea power, especially in the earlier stages. The sieges of Rions (1295), St Sever (1295), Dax (1296) and St Macaire (1296), together with the ability of Bourg and Blaye to hold out against the French, demonstrated the primacy of fortified towns in the duchy's defences.[134] Some contemporary writers and theorists were well aware of the paramount importance of siegecraft. In his *Summaria Brevis* of *c.*1300, Pierre Dubois drew Philip the Fair's attention to the prevalence of long sieges in the reduction of an area to obedience.[135] A prince, he asserted, often spent more of his and his subject's wealth and resources on sieges than the conquered area was worth. Fortifications and their upkeep, siege engines, miners, pioneers, horses and victualling all cost considerably more in the 1290s than previously and monetary devaluation did not help. Prices were sometimes artificially inflated when a campaign was proclaimed, as suppliers and contractors sought to profit from the demand created by the war.[136] Between 1294 and 1297 Philip's government spent at least 61.5 per cent of its annual income on the costs of war, and the subsequent garrisoning of occupied Aquitaine tied up some thousands of very well-paid and expensive troops.[137] At Bordeaux, for example, the French garrison under the Flemish knight, Robert de Wavrin, lord of St Venant, cost the enormous sum of 20,550 *l.t.* during the six months from September 1298 to April 1299. Of this, 17,820 *l.t.* (86.7 per cent) were spent on their wages alone.[138] A protracted siege could, moreover, immobilize a force for many weeks and add significantly to the wages bill. In the summer of 1295 Charles of Valois spent thirteen weeks besieging St Sever, but his army was decimated by disease and he was forced to leave the town inadequately garrisoned on his recall to Paris.[139] It fell to an Anglo-Gascon force soon afterwards. Sieges demanded increasingly complicated and sophisticated equipment – an English account for the costs of the Gascon war included payments for 'machines, springals, *garottes*, *super-castra*, belfries and other . . . engines' with bolts, quarrels and round stones for them. The war on land was fought around a number of strongpoints which, with the exception of Bourg, Blaye, Bordeaux and Bayonne, changed hands with

---

[134] *The Chronicle of Walter of Guisborough*, ed. H. Rothwell, Camden Society, 3rd ser., lxxxix (London, 1957), pp. 261–2.

[135] P. Dubois, *Summaria brevis et compendiosa doctrina felicis expedicionis et abbrevacionis guerrarum ac litium regni Francorum*, ed. H. Kampf (Berlin and Leipzig, 1936), pp. 2–3.

[136] P. Contamine, *La Guerre au Moyen Age* (Paris, 1980), p. 200.

[137] See Appendix II; Strayer, 'The costs and profits of war', pp. 272–3.

[138] *CR*, ii, nos 25450–507.

[139] Petit, *Charles de Valois*, pp. 30–2.

confusing frequency.[140] This was to become the pattern of warfare in Aquitaine throughout the Hundred Years War.

The second characteristic of what Strayer has called 'this war that was no
war' was the important part played in it by sea power and the control of
inland waterways. The relative speed with which the English expeditionary
force under Jean of Brittany and Sir John St John gained possession of
Castillon-de-Médoc, Macau, Bourg, Blaye, Virelade and Podensac in
October–November 1294 was entirely due to exploitation of the navigable rivers
of the region. By the time the force reached Rions it had spent almost seventeen weeks afloat.[141] At Bayonne, where the town welcomed the Anglo-Gascon
army under John St John in January 1295, the French garrison was
in effect blockaded in the castle by English and Bayonnais ships which cut off
the estuary of the Adour.[142] Hence the vital role of Bayonne in these
campaigns: mastery of the sea remained firmly in Anglo-Gascon hands at
this stage in the war and the appointment of Bayonne's 'captain and admiral'
Barrau de Sescas, knight, to marshall the combined maritime resources of
England and Aquitaine in 1295 and 1297 was one of Edward I and Jean of
Brittany's wisest acts.[143] The defence of Bourg and Blaye throughout the war
clearly owed much to his service there in preventing French occupation of
these two fortified enclaves. It was a remarkable testimony to the effective-
ness of English and Bayonnais seamanship that the supply lines to Bourg and
Blaye from England and Ireland remained open for the duration of hostilities.

Neither side could have sustained a war in Aquitaine for very long without
the support of members of the Gascon nobility and their neighbours in the
Languedoc. A previous study has shown that the great majority of the
duchy's nobles remained loyal to Edward I and his lieutenants throughout
the war.[144] Philip the Fair relied for support upon the nobles and towns of the
Toulousain, Albigeois, lower Languedoc and the lands of the count of Foix.
Roger-Bernard III, count of Foix, served the king during the war, but his
price was high. Grants of confiscated lordships and the lieutenancy in
Aquitaine and Languedoc brought him substantial returns, but he was still
owed 48,000 *l.t.* for the wages of himself and his retinue in March 1297.[145]

---

[140] E 372/160, m. 41^r; E 101/154/15, nos 23, 42 for payments by Henry Lacy, earl of Lincoln, to Master Thomas de la Réole 'fossator' and Master Bernard 'carpentarius bridarum'
(23 March 1294); *RG*, iii, pp. cxlviii–cxlix, clii–clxii.

[141] *RG*, iii, p. cxlvii.

[142] *Chronicle of Walter of Guisborough*, p. 245. Two large French galleys were captured off
Bayonne by Anglo-Gascon forces and immediately requisitioned for their own purposes:
E 372/160, m. 41^r.

[143] *RG*, iii, nos 3883, 4134; 4477; p. clxxxix. He served alongside the English admirals William
Leyburne and John Botetourt, and was appointed lieutenant in Aquitaine by Edward I in 1299
(E 30/1654), an office which he held for three years.

[144] Vale, 'The Gascon nobility and the Anglo-French war', pp. 135–46.

[145] De Vic and Vaissete, *Histoire générale de Languedoc*, ix, pp. 183–93; x, cc. 335, 338–40.

He protested against every attempt by royal officers to levy subsidies within his lordships and openly refused to contribute to hearth-taxes. His service to the Capetian cause was counterpointed by a campaign of resistance to the enforcement of royal edicts on taxation, the treatment of the possessions of condemned heretics and other litigious matters within his own domains. He estimated his unpaid wages at over 50,000 *l.t.* in 1298 and demanded immediate payment by instalments.[146] Foix was a valuable ally for Philip the Fair, but an inordinately expensive one.

Lesser nobles from the Languedoc were also recruited to serve in arms by the French. Men such as Robert de Lévis-Mirepoix and Odo de Montaut joined Robert of Artois's army in Aquitaine during May and June 1296. In July, the count sent messengers to raise reinforcements as rapidly as possible in the *sénéchaussées* of Saintonge, Poitou, Quercy, Périgord, Toulouse, Carcassonne and elsewhere in order to raise the siege of Dax.[147] The old and infirm Constance, *vicomtesse* of Marsan, was given a furred gown and hood in December 1296 by him, for the occupation of her town of Mont-de-Marsan was of considerable strategic value to the French army. After her death in August 1299 Edward I confiscated her English lands and granted them to Amanieu VII d'Albret. Her disseisin from Bigorre by Edward in the 1280s had not redounded to his advantage in the Anglo-French war of the following decade.[148] Elsewhere, nobles and commoners aided the French expeditionary forces with varying degrees of commitment. At Agen, the consuls were ordered by Robert of Artois on 5 May 1296 to send him 200 foot-serjeants, of whom 100 were to be crossbowmen, to muster at Mont-de-Marsan.[149] The king would pay their wages, although the consuls were required to pay the cost of their journey to Mont-de-Marsan. This would be reimbursed from royal funds. On 21 May the count wrote from his camp before Mont-de-Marsan, ordering the seneschal and *bailli* of Agen to forbid seizure of the inhabitants' wine and victuals without payment. As we shall see, war brought dislocation and damage in its wake for which both sides in the conflict were responsible. The evidence from English exchequer sources suggests that payment was generally promised by sealed bonds to merchant creditors and suppliers but was only made in arrears at Westminster or assigned on Gascon revenues. Purchases of cloth and other 'merceries' were made in this way by Henry Lacy, earl of Lincoln, in a series of obligatory bonds in June 1297.[150] Just as Gascon nobles waited for the dis-

---

[146] APA, E 371, unnumbered; De Vic and Vaissete, *Histoire générale de Languedoc*, x, cc. 265–6, 285–7, 289–91.

[147] ADPC, A. 144, no. 1, m. 1; *CR*, ii, nos 30275, 30278.

[148] *CR*, iii, no. 30308; *CPR, 1292–1301*, p. 433; see above, pp. 88–90 for her dispossession from Bigorre.

[149] *AM Agen*, no. xcviii.

[150] See E 101/152/10, nos 7, 13; 153/2, no. 15; 154/3, no. 13: for 'pannis et aliis mercimoniis' (June 1297).

charge of debts to them for unpaid wages and *restaur* of horses, so their bourgeois compatriots were constrained to accept payment for military service, provisions and munitions only after long delays and by assignment on the duchy's revenues.[151] But both Edmund of Lancaster and Henry of Lincoln bound themselves upon solemn oath to discharge their obligations in Edward I's name.

The costs of war to Edward I's government cannot be precisely calculated. A total figure of about 400,000 *l.st.* would probably reflect expenditure quite accurately. The two king's clerks responsible for financing the war, John de Sandale and Thomas of Cambridge, listed their total expenses as 359,288 *l.* 0 *s.* 5 *d.st.*, including the high figure of 154,570 *l.* 4 *s.* $4\frac{1}{2}$ *d.st.* computed from the letters of obligation issued by the captains of Edward's armies in Aquitaine.[152] The total receipts had been just over 300,000 *l.st.* and as their expenses totalled almost 360,000 a sum of almost 60,000 remained outstanding. These figures covered only the years of war and truce from 29 September 1293 until 14 August 1299. The subsequent holding operation in Aquitaine until May 1303 was not accounted for and was separately treated. It can be estimated that average annual war expenditure between 1294 and 1299 consumed Edward I's total annual income, including the *maltolte* and customs. Of that expenditure, almost 60 per cent was spent on wages to Gascon cavalry and infantry, while English troops accounted for only 10 per cent of the budget.[153] It would, however, be unjustified to conclude that 'England was pouring huge sums of money into Gascony – and getting nothing in return.'[154] Apart from the retention and defence of Bayonne and its hinterland, and the support of garrisons at Bourg and Blaye, the 'return' from this vast expenditure was the preservation of the politico-economic union between England and Aquitaine. Gascon creditors were not slow to advance money to Edward's lieutenants and Bémont rightly concluded that the Bayonnais 'ont été sans contredit le principal instrument et sans doute le plus efficace de la reprise de la Gascogne par les Anglais'.[155] To them may be added the towns of Chalosse, the Landes and the Pyrenean frontier, as well as the mass of middling and petty nobles who rallied to the Plantagenet cause. The Plantagenet presence in Aquitaine during the war may well have been precarious, and its foothold could be shaken by defeats such as that sustained by Henry Lacy and John St John near Bonnegarde on 2 February 1297 when the supply-train and escort which they were leading from Bayonne

---

[151] *RG*, iii, pp. clxx–clxxi; E 101/154/1, nos 3, 4; 154/2, no. 11; 154/3, no. 17; 154/11, no. 3; 152/9, no. 39; 153/1, nos 3, 6; 154/12, nos 17, 39; 154/15, nos 4, 14, 15 (war service by bourgeois of St Sever, Bonnegarde and Ste-Quitterie, March 1298).

[152] E 372/160, m. 41ᵛ: their expenses included payments made to 'certain *stipendiarii* of the king of France's obedience who came into the pay of the king of England'.

[153] See Appendix II; *RG*, iii, pp. clxviii–clxix.

[154] Strayer, 'The costs and profits of war', p. 290.

[155] *RG*, iii, p. clxiii. See above, pp. 193–4.

was ambushed by Robert of Artois's troops.[156] But the war effort did not collapse and financial stringency apparently had little effect upon the determination of many Gascons to support the Plantagenets to the bitter end. Many of them – especially, as we shall see, the dispossessed and disinherited nobles – had nothing more to lose. England certainly spent large sums of money on Gascony, but many of the duchy's inhabitants abandoned their lands and possessions, endured imprisonment and underwent exile in return.

The French also spent very large sums of money on the war. An estimated total expenditure of 1,730,000 *l.t.* (432,500 *l.st.*) between 1294 and 1299 probably falls short of the actual sum spent, but French financial sources are far less complete than English at this time.[157] Of this sum, 76.5 per cent was contributed by townsmen and merchants, and an average annual expenditure of 346,000 *l.t.* represented 61.5 per cent of total estimated annual income. But this figure is unrealistic because Philip the Fair had no recurrent income from customs or other forms of indirect taxation and his government's costs were undoubtedly higher than 1,730,000 *l.t.* The French also incurred extremely heavy expenses during their occupation of Aquitaine. As we have seen, the garrison at Bordeaux consumed a vast sum of money in wages alone. A total of 390 men were retained in the *stabilitas* at Bordeaux for varying periods during March and April 1299, of whom 29 were knights, 196 esquires, and 168 foot-serjeants.[158] To pay for such large contingents all possible sources of revenue were exploited, from the confiscated deposit which Bernard Saisset, bishop of Pamiers, had left with the nuns of Notre-Dame at Prouille in return for royal protection in 1302 to the proceeds of currency manipulation and seizures from the Jews.[159] Fines levied by royal commissioners sent to the *sénéchaussée* of Toulouse in 1298 to investigate certain crimes brought in 1912 *l.t.*, including two large sums of 500 *l.t.* imposed on Raymond Martin de Vaur and Odo de Montaut, knight, for the *port d'armes* and violence against their private enemies.[160] Attacks on royal *baillis*, serjeants and notaries were by no means confined to Plantagenet Aquitaine and the treasurer of Toulouse's account provides a valuable insight into the behaviour of the inhabitants of a southern *sénéchaussée* towards Capetian officials during a period of war. One man was fined for releasing without licence an 'Englishwoman' who had insulted Philip the Fair, others for wounding the *bailli* of Vaur; the *bailli* of Gavre for releasing men who refused to serve in the king's army; and the preceptor of the Templars at

---

[156] *Chronicle of Walter of Guisborough*, p. 263–4; *RG*, iii, pp. clxiv–clxv; Guiart, *Branche des royaux lignages*, ll. 4374–4701. The French were divided into three contingents under Thibaut de Cépoy, the count of Foix and Robert of Artois.

[157] Strayer, 'The costs and profits of war', pp. 272–3, 276.

[158] *CR*, ii, nos 25489–507.

[159] J.-M. Vidal, *Histoire des Evêques de Pamiers. I. Bernard Saisset (1232–1311)* (Toulouse and Paris, 1920), i, p. 97; AMB, MS 207, nos 13, 25, 27, 57.

[160] *CR*, ii, nos 25992, 26036.

Vaur for the *port d'armes*.[161] All these offences helped to swell the coffers of the *sénéchaussée* of Toulouse but did not reflect a high degree of public order in the area at any level of society.

The financial and other difficulties encountered by French forces in Aquitaine were well illustrated by the course and fortunes of Robert of Artois's expedition to the duchy in 1296–7. Robert II was appointed lieutenant in Gascony and the duchy of Aquitaine in April 1296. He was given extensive powers by Philip the Fair to act 'as if the king were personally present'.[162] He was to issue pardons, negotiate alliances and truces, conclude *paréages*, inspect garrisons and fortresses, instigate inquiries into the crimes of royal officials and confer knighthood. Robert was to take homages, fealties and oaths from all those living in the lands 'which the king of England was wont to hold within our kingdom'. His powers extended to the neighbouring *sénéchaussées* of Toulouse, Périgord, Quercy, Rouergue, Carcassonne and Saintonge, giving him viceregal authority throughout most of southern France. He lost little time in making ready for his campaign and had already ordered cloth, saddles and other equipment from Salomon Boinebroke, merchant of Douai, on 10 April, all of which were to be sent to him in Aquitaine.[163] The march southwards took him through Auvergne into Poitou, Limousin and Angoumois, reaching Angoulême on 28 April.[164] Nobles of the surrounding region were then retained for two months' service in the host, supplementing his own contingent of Artesian and other northern French troops. By 3 May, the army was at the *bastide* of Eymet in Périgord, where a further group of local nobles and their companions were recruited. His force included Pierre de Bailleul, seneschal of Saintonge, Jean d'Archevêque, *viguier* of Toulouse, Jean de Maignelay, seneschal of Agenais, Gui de Cabrières, seneschal of Rouergue, his own vassals Thibaut de Cépoy, previously captain of St Omer, and Robert de Verlinghem from Artois.[165] Southern nobles such as Alain de Montendre and Odo de Montaut were soon to join the army as it progressed southward towards Langon and St Macaire. While Thibaut de Cépoy held St Macaire against Anglo-Gascon attacks, the count and other captains journeyed to Mont-de-Marsan and Tartas by 25 May, moved back to Mont-de-Marsan by 12 June and then progressed north-westwards to Montségur (25 June), Ste-Foy-la-Grande (26 June), St Emilion (3 July) and Fronsac (11 July). From this strongpoint the beleaguered Anglo-Gascon garrisons at Bourg and Blaye could be harrassed and attacked.[166]

---

[161] *CR*, ii, nos 26014, 26017, 26037, 26034, 26040. It is not clear whether the *mulierem anglicam* was a native Englishwoman or a French supporter of Edward I.

[162] ADPC, A 41, nos 12–18. He knighted the count of Auge outside Bourg on 15 July 1296: ADPC, A 144, m. 4.

[163] ADPC, A 140, nos 30, 40 (10 April and 15 May 1296).

[164] ADPC, A 144, no. 1, m. 1ʳ; A 41, no. 19; A 140, no. 37 (28 April 1296).

[165] ADPC, A 144, no. 1, m. 1ᵛ. For Thibaut de Cépoy see above n. 156, and J. Petit, 'Un capitaine du règne de Philippe le Bel', *MA*, 2nd ser., i, (1897), pp. 224–39.

[166] ADPC, A 144, no. 1, mm. 2ʳ–4ʳ; *AM Agen*, pp. 165–6; Petit 'Un capitaine du règne de Philippe le Bel', pp. 225–6.

It proved impossible for Robert of Artois's force to take Bourg. Its garrison, composed of both English and Gascon men-at-arms, was congratulated by Edward I on its successful defence of the place on 9 December 1296, when the French army was at Marmande, having abandoned its siege.[167] The siege engines for which stones were purchased from stone-cutters earlier in the campaign had evidently failed to reduce the fortress.[168] Supplies of corn, hay, beans, bacon and other victuals continued to reach Bourg from England, for the French blockade of the Gironde, on which 23,141 *l.t.* was spent in 1296, appears to have been ineffective in this respect.[169] Robert of Artois's host was obliged to retrace its steps to recover Tartas in August 1296, which had fallen back into Anglo-Gascon hands and, with the onset of winter, active campaigning gradually came to a halt.[170] The count established himself at La Réole and Bordeaux, while a truce was agreed between the two sides on 12 February 1297.[171] This enabled Edward I and his lieutenants, after the surprise attack on John St John's convoy of supplies for Bonnegarde on 2 February, greater security in which to provide larger consignments of victuals and munitions for embattled garrisons in the duchy. Early in April, corn was taken on board a ship called the *Hulk of St John of Sandwich* to be carried to Bourg 'as soon as God shall grant time for a ship to sail there, under the king's standard'. This was delivered to the ship's owner and master by Adam Wibert of Sandwich and Sir William Trussel, sheriff of Kent.[172] Further transports were requisitioned to carry corn and 'Aberdeen stockfish' to Bourg on 12 and 16 April to feed the garrison. By 25 April a fleet of ships from Looe, Southampton, Fowey, Shoreham, Dartmouth, Weymouth, Winchelsea and other ports was assembled to convey provisions and munitions to Bourg. This was at Edward I's expense and Henry Lacy, earl of Lincoln, was told not to burden himself, as the king-duke's lieutenant at Bayonne, with such a duty.[173] Nor was he to concern himself with the victualling of Blaye, but was to take counsel as necessary in order to prevent a surprise attack by the French on either place. A detailed list of cargo taken to Bourg by William Kingson, master of *La Plenté* of Winchelsea, reveals the kind of demands made upon English resources by the retention of Bourg and other strongpoints at this time.[174] He received 385 quarters of corn and 20 tons of wheat; three springals; forty-eight crossbows, of which twelve were 'great crossbows' with winding mechanisms; thirty-six 'buckets' full of crossbow bolts, each containing 1000 bolts; a further twenty-

---

[167] *RG*, iii, nos 4262, 4368.

[168] ADPC, A 144, m.² (payments for stones and for a siege engine sited *ante tentorum marescalli* at the siege of Bourg).

[169] *RG*, iii, no. 4262, (9 December 1296); Strayer, 'The costs and profits of war', p. 284.

[170] ADPC, A 1015, fos 37ʳ–38ʳ.

[171] ADPC, A 42, no. 4; A 1015, fo. 38ʳ; AN, J 631, no. 17; de Vic and Vaissete, *Histoire générale de Languedoc*, ix, pp. 203–4.

[172] E 101/6/20, no. 19 (8 April 1297).

[173] E 101/6/20, nos 25–9; 1–14.

[174] E 101/6/20, no. 14.

four 'buckets', each containing 500 bolts; four coffers holding 4000 bolts with brass flights; one coffer containing sixty bows and bowstrings; 500 bolts for the springals and further consignments of cereals. He was to sail from the Thames estuary to Bourg, given an estimated sailing time of ten days, and was to return to the king's household.

If a French army, established in garrisons throughout the hinterland of Bordeaux, could cut off supplies from the area immediately surrounding fortresses such as Bourg and Blaye, the only alternative was to stock them with victuals and munitions from England. This was a lesson which was to be learned time and time again during the Hundred Years War. Control of the seas was imperative if supply lines were to be kept open. Further south, opportunities for the acquisition of food, drink and plunder were offered to the Anglo-Gascon forces quartered at Bayonne and elsewhere. Raids into territory occupied by the French were entirely legitimized by the declaration of public war and attacks upon those who claimed to support Philip the Fair's authority were given additional justification. Walter of Guisborough tells us that a major activity of the Anglo-Gascon troops at Bayonne during Robert of Artois's campaign of 1296–7, and later, was the launching of plundering raids into the Toulousain. They returned to Bayonne at the onset of winter in 1296 'with great booty'.[175] For both English and Gascons this form of living off the country may have partially compensated for the non-payment of their wages. Their presence in the Toulousain may be detected in the accounts of the receiver in the *sénéchaussée* of Toulouse for 1298–9. He rendered account for the cost of keeping twenty-one 'English' prisoners at Vaur and Toulouse for one year from 24 June 1297, namely the princely sum of 2 *d.t.* a day for bread and water.[176] Their ravages may have accounted for the exemption from war taxes granted by Philip the Fair's officers in October 1297 to some inhabitants of the Languedoc who had been harmed by the war 'in manifold and intolerable ways'.[177] The deeds of Edmund of Lancaster's and Henry de Lacy's men at St Macaire in April 1296 were comparable and doubtless served to weaken that commune's collective resolve to resist Robert of Artois's besieging force, which retook the place shortly afterwards.[178] Gascon troops under Pierre-Amanieu, captal de Buch, Eble de Puyguilhem and Pons de Castillon pillaged the inhabitants after their entry into the town: wine, oats, corn, hay, bread and other victuals were forcibly removed from the unfortunate burgesses.[179] One of them,

---

[175] *Chronicle of Walter of Guisborough*, p. 262.

[176] *CR*, i, nos 12139, 12152–3.

[177] De Vic and Vaissete, *Histoire générale de Languedoc*, x, c. 345. The collectors of subsidies in the *sénéchaussées* of Carcassonne, Beaucaire and Rodez were told that no precedents were to be set by the levy of subsidies or *fouages* in the Languedoc (8 October 1297).

[178] *RG*, iii, pp. clii–cliii.

[179] C 47/25/1, no. 19: petition to Thomas of Cambridge, king's clerk and commissioner in Aquitaine, from the inhabitants of St Macaire. English captains involved included Roger Mortimer, Hugh and Thomas de Veer, Thomas Paynel and John St John.

Gaillard Ayquem, who was at that time imprisoned as a hostage by the French at Agen, complained that his property had been ransacked: four coffers had been broken open, six feather pillows and eight sheets removed, two cloaks and many bedcovers and hangings looted, grain taken from his storehouse, while his servant had even been stripped of his shirt and held prisoner for at least three days. The habits of men-at-arms which were to be cultivated during the Hundred Years War were already well developed in Aquitaine. Evidence of plundering raids from Bayonne in 1296–7 suggests that techniques acquired during private wars in the duchy were simply applied during 'public' war.[180] The French war of Edward I might be taken as one of the origins of the English *chevauchée* which was developed into a tactical weapon during the Hundred Years War.

One of the hazards of campaigning in Aquitaine, especially during the summer months, was the prevalence of disease in an army. Robert of Artois's progress through the duchy was held up by outbreaks of illness. As early as 28 April 1296, when the count was still at Angoulême, his physician Master Palmier remained behind with Renaud Coignet and other members of his household who were stricken with disease.[181] Camp fever and dysentery were probably the chief ailments, and the recurrent provision of electuaries, syrups and cordials suggests that the count and his men were constantly victims of such perennial accompaniments to campaigning. Cases of illness were recorded at La Réole on 8 May; Bazas on 16 May; Tartas on 25 May; Mont-de-Marsan on 15 and 18 June; St Macaire on 25 June, where the count's chaplain and two others were immobilized for 30 days, and at Ste Foy on 26 June and 2 July, where Robert of Artois himself was ill. Medicines were bought and prepared in large quantities for him – he had already been given *citrongnac*, probably a cordial, by his doctor on 15 June and by 2 July potions made from herbs and 'beavers' testicles' (*testiculis castorum*) were administered to him.[182] Some of these electuaries and cures sound very like the medicaments prescribed for Edward I during his final illness on the campaign which killed him on 7 July 1307.[183] Rose-water, pomegranates, camomile and other herbs were bought for Robert of Artois at Bordeaux and Bergerac in July 1296, while he was besieging Bourg. At Bazas and Mont-de-Marsan, as the August heat no doubt bore down on the army, powders and beverages were made up for him, while crystallized rose-petals and violets, Damascus rose-water and fifty pomegranates were received from

---

[180] *Chronicle of Walter of Guisborough*, pp. 262, 264; Vale, 'The Gascon nobility and the Anglo-French war', p. 141; see above, p. 210.

[181] ADPC, A 144, m. 2; *CR*, iii, no. 30184.

[182] ADPC, A 144, mm. 3–4; *CR*, iii, nos 30196, 30203–4, 30213, 30233, 30238, 30246–7; also A 2, fo. 21ʳ for payment to Master Bienvenue, the count's physician, for *restaur* of horses lost in Aquitaine (8 November 1298); and A 145, nos 23, 38 (8 November and 30 December 1298); *CR*, iii, nos 30234, 30255.

[183] Prestwich, *Edward I*, p. 556.

Bordeaux on 23 August.[184] These were the normal accompaniments of aristocratic life, together with the comital fool and female dwarf who journeyed with the count in his itinerant and makeshift court. At Bayonne, Edmund of Lancaster was also struck down by illness, from which he was to die on 5 June 1296 (see plates 6.4 and 6.5).[185] Both Capetian and Plantagenet commanders were therefore incapacitated by illness at the height of the campaign.

If the Plantagenet war effort in Aquitaine was plagued by inadequate finance, the plight of the Capetian cause was just as serious. Between 10 April and 26 July 1296 Robert of Artois received (and promptly spent) 68,538 *l*. 8 *s*. 8 *d.t*, according to the accounts of his clerk, Master Thierry d'Hérisson, later bishop of Arras.[186] Expenditure on this scale, running at a monthly average of about 29,500 *l.t.* could not be sustained for very long. Thierry's subsequent accounts for the remainder of the campaign survive only in fragmentary form, so complete figures cannot be drawn up. But in July 1298 he acknowledged that only 8000 *l.t.* had been received from the king's treasurer at Paris for large unpaid debts from the Gascon war.[187] Merchants of Toulouse, Montauban, Marmande and Moissac were being paid off in May 1298 for provisions taken from them two years earlier, but the comital debt was substantially increased by loans contracted with the Italian banking house of Scotti and with one Gautier de Bruxelles on the count's return from Aquitaine.[188] Robert of Artois had often relied upon the Crespin of Arras for funds and Guillaume Crespin loaned 1200 *l.t.* for war expenses in July 1296.[189] In June, the *échevins* of Arras had demonstrated their loyalty to their count by granting him a loan of 5000 *livres parisis* which they had initially made to Philip the Fair, and this may have improved the financial situation a little at the height of the Gascon campaign.[190] But there was still an urgent need for money on 12 July, when a messenger was sent post-haste towards Limoges in order to hasten the arrival of coin from France which was desperately required for the siege of Bourg. On 24 July, the count's treasurer was still awaiting 'the money which we hope will come from France'. In the event, a mere 3500 *l.t.* were received on that day from Pierre de Molet, receiver of Poitou.[191] War did not wait for funds to arrive from Artois or Paris, and chronic deficit finance was a permanent feature of the French war effort at this time.

[184] ADPC, A 144, mm. 4–5; A 1015, fo. 37ʳ; *CR*, iii, nos 30264, 30270, 30294–7.

[185] *Chronicle of Walter of Guisborough*, p. 262. For his tomb at Westminster see plates 6.4, 6.5.

[186] The accounts in ADPC, A 144 and A 1015 are printed in *CR*, iii, pp. 101–15. I have, however, also cited the original documents because errors in transcription make the published edition unsatisfactory to use. For the sum spent see ADPC, A 144, m. 5 and *CR*, iii, no. 30287 where '78, 538 *l*. 8 *s*. 8 *d.t*.' should read '68, 538 *l*. 8 *s*. 8 *d.t*.'

[187] ADPC, A 2, fos 7ʳ, 16ʳ, 25.

[188] ADPC, A 181, no. 2, m. 5.

[189] ADPC, A 1015, fo. 34ʳ; *CR*, iii, no. 30325.

[190] ADPC, A 41, no. 20 (7 June 1296).

[191] ADPC, A 144, mm. 1, 4–5; *CR*, iii, nos 30263, 30281, 30110.

6.4 Monument to Edmund of Lancaster (Crouchback) (d. 1296). Edmund was a lieutenant of his brother Edward I in Aquitaine (1295–6) and died at Bayonne. His tomb is French in style. (London, Westminster Abbey.)

6.5   Effigy of Edmund of Lancaster on his tomb (London, Westminster Abbey.)

The progress of armies at this period attracted a swarm of hangers-on, camp-followers, paupers and beggars. These could be a burden upon the purses of the commanders and an impediment to rapid movement. In Robert of Artois's case, there were perhaps additional reasons for the presence of the mendicant poor and infirm at the rear of his army. He was a great and wealthy prince of the blood. He was to be granted a papal indulgence by Boniface VIII's nuncios on 29 April 1297 whereby he was permitted to commute a vow which he had previously made to visit the churches of Rocamadour, Vauvert and St Gilles in the provinces of Cahors and Nîmes into the feeding of thirteen paupers at his own expense in his household.[192] The wars in the kingdom of France and the danger to which his person would be exposed on such a pilgrimage justified the indulgence. On 12 June 1296 a payment was made by Thierry d'Hérisson to the 'paupers and invalids following the army', but on 18, 20, 21 and 25 June the infirm poor were installed in hospitals at Mont-de-Marsan and Monségur and the masters were paid for their upkeep. When the army was at Ste-Foy on 2 July, further infirm paupers were left in the hospital there.[193] Robert of Artois was known to be a generous alms-giver and the accounts for his Gascon campaign are punctuated by regular gifts to recluses, poor children, women and paupers who had escaped from the hands of the enemy.[194] His maintenance of

---

[192] ADPC, A 42, no. 10. Powers to commute vows into other pious works were originally granted to the papal nuncios in France by Boniface VIII on 18 February 1295. Simon, bishop of Palestrina, thus exercised this power in Robert of Artois's favour in April 1297.

[193] ADPC, A 144, mm. 3–4; *CR*, iii, nos 30229, 30239–40, 30241, 30245.

[194] ADPC, A 144, mm. 3–5 (5, 14 June, 3 July); *CR*, iii, nos 30222, 30231, 30257.

paupers was soon to be formalized by the papal nuncios. Expenditure on alms was, however, offset by lavish outlay on horses, falcons, dogs, jesters and a 'king of ribalds' which enabled Robert of Artois to maintain an appropriately princely state in mid-campaign.[195] It was a pattern of campaigning that French armies were to perpetuate during the Hundred Years War.[196]

To maintain effective communications and to receive news of the enemy's movements and intentions, an intelligence and messenger service was imperative. From the beginning of his campaign, Robert of Artois gained information from the counts of Foix, Armagnac and Comminges (18 April and 14 May 1296) and constantly dispatched both messengers and spies to deliver and collect information.[197] He employed the abbot of Sorde, a number of friars, a woman spy and an *insidiator* (plotter) who was sent to stir up the citizens of Bayonne on 5 June.[198] The ambush of the Anglo-Gascon convoy near Bonnegarde in February 1297 was probably due to the activity of spies working on behalf of the French. But the army had also to eat, and foodstuffs could not easily be transported overland from northern France to feed troops fighting in Aquitaine. Local sources were therefore drawn upon, and the Languedoc provided much of the victualling for the host. But cornfields and orchards which lay in an army's path were often laid waste: on 11 June 1296, corn and fruit at Saubrusse (*Saubrosam*) was cut and picked for the troops, and wheatfields were devastated at Captieux (*Capse*) on 17 May, for which the men of the *pays* were paid compensation.[199] There was little difference in this respect between the behaviour of French and Anglo-Gascon armies.

6.3   The Aftermath of War

On 9 October 1297, a truce was agreed at Vye-St-Bavon in Flanders between English and French envoys. This was to last until 6 January 1298 in Aquitaine.[200] The war effort had begun to shift towards Flanders by the spring of 1297 and a stalemate existed in the south-west which was to continue until the restoration of the duchy to Edward I in May 1303.[201] During this time much of the duchy was occupied by French forces, under northern French and Languedocian captains who also received grants of confiscated lands, goods and lordships. The *sénéchaussées* of Aquitaine and its

---

[195] ADPC, A 144, *passim*; *CR*, iii, nos 30195, 30201, 30210, 30267, 30282, 30292–3, 30300.

[196] See, for instance, H. J. Hewitt, *The Black Prince's Expedition of 1355–57* (Manchester 1958), pp. 134–5.

[197] A 144, m. 3; *CR*, iii, nos 30178, 30198.

[198] A 144, mm. 3–4 (5, 16 June); *CR*, iii, nos 30217–18, 30223.

[199] A 144, mm. 3–4; *CR*, iii, nos 30226, 30207.

[200] *RG*, iii, pp. clxv–clxvi.

[201] F. Funck-Brentano, *Les Origines de la Guerre de Cent Ans. Philippe le Bel en Flandre* (Paris, 1897), pp. 267–70, 292–304; Strayer, *Philip the Fair*, pp. 330–32.

neighbouring provinces were granted to vassals and clients of Robert of
Artois, such as Robert de Wavrin or Thibaut de Cépoy, who was appointed
seneschal of the Agenais in November 1298.[202] There is little doubt about the
origins of Adam d'Abbeville, captain of Podensac, Guillaume de Gisors,
castellan of Tournon, Guillaume de Charenton, castellan of Sauveterre,
Béguin and Huard de Dune, *baillis* of Porte-St-Marie and Damazan, or
Guillaume de Cambrai, *bailli* of Agen.[203] They were self-evidently northern
Frenchmen benefiting from the fruits of the occupation. Some still retained
their offices for some months after the restoration of Aquitaine in 1303, and
were obliged to render account for them to Edward I's constable of Bordeaux.
Raymond Balanger, king's knight of Philip the Fair, occupied the *prévôté* of
Bazas from 20 May until 28 September 1303; Gérard Baleine,
Philip's treasurer for war in Aquitaine, received the revenues of the *prévôté* of
Monségur, which had been given him by the king, until 23 December.[204] The
dislodging of Plantagenet officers (who were often the dispossessed nobles of
the area) proved disruptive to the administration of such offices and the
unfamiliarity of Philip's appointees and their lieutenants with local customs
and practices did not contribute to the success of the operation.

The displacement of the records of the Plantagenet administration from
Bordeaux in March 1294, and their subsequent dumping by unpaid sailors
(taking them to England) in the house of the White Friars on the Isle
d'Oléron, did not help the French in their task. Although the documents
were apparently captured by the French, at least some of them seem to have
remained at Oléron.[205] Whatever the case, a report submitted by English
commissioners before the process of Périgueux in 1310 revealed the paucity
of the archives at the castle of L'Ombrière.[206] Complaints against French
royal officers began to be voiced soon after the occupation began. The men of
Agen received assurances of the king's protection in September 1295 after
they had complained about his serjeants' and other officers' behaviour. They
had in effect been pillaged by them.[207] Pons de Monlaur, knight, the
seneschal of the Agenais in 1296–7, owed them substantial sums and the
consuls were still attempting to recover these debts in August 1300.[208] A

---

[202] *AM Agen*, no. xcii; Petit, 'Un capitaine du règne de Philippe le Bel', pp. 227–30 (Cépoy);
Funck-Brentano, *Philippe le Bel en Flandre*, pp. 262–63; *CR*, ii, nos 25450–507 (Wavrin). Both
Cépoy and Wavrin served the king in Flanders after 1303.

[203] *CR*, ii, nos 17820, 17825–27, 17852; *Trésor des Chartes d'Albret*, i, nos 143–44.

[204] E 101/159/4, m. 2ᵛ. For Gérard Baleine's career see Strayer, *Philip the Fair*, pp. 117–18,
165–6. He was from Figeac in Quercy, and was partially disgraced in 1306.

[205] C 47/27/14, fo. 3ᵛ; V. H. Galbraith, 'The Tower as an Exchequer Record Office in the
reign of Edward II', in *Essays in Medieval History Presented to T. F. Tout* (Manchester, 1925),
p. 234; E 101/160/1, m. 3.

[206] *Gascon Register A*, no. 42.

[207] *AM Agen*, nos cxv, xcix.

[208] *AM Agen*, nos cvi, cxxi. For Pons de Monlaur see *CR*, ii, nos 14599, 15019, 15090,
17674–884 (account of the receiver of Agen, 1296–7).

dispute over the form of oaths exchanged between the seneschal and the bishop of Agen arose in May 1299 when the bishop refused to perform fealty to the seneschal, as 'one of the barons and nobles of the Agenais'. He was, he declared, not bound to swear any such oath to the seneschal, only to his lord, who in this case was the constable of France. The oath was to be taken at change of lord, not of seneschal and he cited one of Boniface VIII's rulings on the subject. As a result, Blaise de Loup, the seneschal, was obliged to swear an oath which stated that he did not intend to introduce any new usage into the bishop's tenurial position, and solemnly promised to defend the Church.[209] Ignorance, wilful or otherwise, of existing laws and customs amongst those governing the duchy of Aquitaine for Philip the Fair hardly contributed to the establishment of harmonious relations with its inhabitants.

The extent of dispossession and disinheritance amongst the duchy's propertied classes during the French occupation of 1294–1303 should not be lightly dismissed nor underestimated. Many of them lost all their Gascon lands and movable possessions. In August 1299 Edward I set about the difficult and arduous task of compensating them until their possessions could be restored. Over 450 named Gascons were granted sums ranging from 40 s. to 1500 *livres chipotenses* drawn upon confiscated alien property in England.[210] Unpaid wages for military service were assigned to many of them over and above these grants, but payment was invariably partial and dilatory. As we have seen, some Gascon nobles served Edward in his Scots campaigns and were sometimes paid arrears of their wages from the Anglo-French war in person at Westminster or York.[211] Dispossession imposed strains upon the social order in Aquitaine. The French could be ruthless and uncompromising in their disseisin of men such as Odo de Casenave in the Agenais, while the property of Baudouin d'Auros, Raymond Fort de Lados, Pierre de Gavarret and Doat de Pins 'beyond the river Garonne' was enjoyed by Odo de Montaut, knight, as a reward for his services to Robert of Artois.[212] Defections from one side to another could split a family, and disputes which were not easily quelled broke out between brothers, nephews and cousins. These were not dissimilar to the divisions created between kinsmen during the

---

[209] *AM Agen*, no. xcii (pp. 157–9). The notarial instrument recording the form of the oaths and bishop's position was drawn up on 6 May 1299, witnessed by the seneschal's lieutenant, the *juge-mage* of the Agenais, the *bailli* of Agen and the canons of the cathedral chapter of St Caprais.

[210] *RG*, iii, nos 4528–31 (25 August 1299); C 47/27/6, 7 for valuation of their lands and tenements.

[211] See above, pp. 108–9; also E 101/153/1, no. 11; 154/11, nos 16–18, 23, 24–5; 154/12, nos 19, 24, 25, 35; 155/15, no. 2; Vale, 'The Gascon nobility and the Anglo-French war', pp. 138–9.

[212] See, for a few examples among many, *CR*, ii, nos 17883 (Isarn de Balenx's mills at Soubirons), 17884 (Odo de Casenave's mills at Castelnau-de-Loubès-Bernac); AN, JJ 38, fos 12ᵛ–13ʳ (grants of confiscations to Odo de Montaut, 4 August 1298 and 24 February 1299). For his service to Robert of Artois in 1296–7, see ADPC, A 144, m. 2; *CR*, iii, nos 30168, 30334.

Hundred Years War.[213] The Gascons experienced a foretaste of the effects of disinheritance, confiscation and dispossession at this earlier date. The aftermath of war and occupation between 1294 and 1303 continued to bedevil Anglo-French relations, and much of the business at the subsequent processes of Montreuil, Périgueux and Agen was devoted to issues of compensation for losses and restoration of property confiscated during the war.[214]

Not only did the nobility feel the effects of war, but also the clergy. Guillaume de Seguin d'Escossan, canon of St Seurin at Bordeaux, claimed that he had been deprived of his canonry and other benefices during the war, and the fact that he had carried letters and messages for Edmund of Lancaster meant that he dared not remain in Aquitaine. He wished to attend a university, but was unable to do so. Edward I ordered that he was to be compensated.[215] In another petition, received by Edward after 14 April 1297, the prior of Pontonx-sur-l'Adour in the Landes told the king-duke that the French held all the priory's revenues and had given them 'to a certain monk from Picardy'.[216] He would have to sell his books, declared the prior, unless he was compensated with the revenues of an alien priory in England such as that at Ware (Herts). Edward promised to provide for him when next in London, but he had determined not to compensate any Gascons except nobles and men-at-arms for the time being.[217] The holding operation at Bourg, Blaye and Bayonne clearly outweighed any other consideration. So did provision for the large number of Gascon nobles who had sought refuge from the French occupation in England. In March 1303, as the tide turned against the French in Aquitaine, no less than 112 of them returned from exile to the duchy, sailing from Portsmouth at the king-duke's expense.[218]

Edward I cannot be accused of a lack of generosity towards his Gascon subjects. On 16 October 1297, he wrote from Ghent of his debts to the men of Bayonne as the most urgent and pressing call upon his resources, telling the treasurer and barons of the exchequer that:

> we wish that you should always have such concern for the needs of Gascony that our men who are there shall be relieved and aided as far as possible in the best manner. ... For our honour or dishonour lies in this business, and that of all

---

[213] See A. Bossuat, 'The re-establishment of peace in society during the reign of Charles VII', in *The Recovery of France in the Fifteenth Century*, ed. P. S. Lewis (London, 1971), pp. 60–81.

[214] See G. C. Cuttino, *English Diplomatic Administration, 1259–1339* (Oxford, 1971), pp. 62–111.

[215] SC 8/291, no. 14513. He was a kinsman of Guillaume V Seguin d' Escossan, lord of Rions (*RG*, iii, nos 4529, 4073). He received 60 *l.ch.* from Edward I on 25 August 1299.

[216] *RG*, iii, p. cxc. The priory was recaptured from the French by August 1299, and the prior received 100 *l.ch.* on 25 August: *RG*, iii, nos 4517, 4529, 4985.

[217] *RG*, iii, pp. cxc, cxcii.

[218] E 101/10/23 (March 1303). They included Jean and Guillaume-Raymond Colom, Pons de Castillon, Arnaud de Caupenne, Gaillard de Castetpugon, Eble de Puyguilhem, Isarn de Balenx, Montassieu de Navailles and their companies.

those who love us, and especially those responsible for our affairs in the places where you are at present.[219]

Edward was determined to discharge his debts and obligations towards his loyal vassals and the grant of compensations and reparations to them exercised all the ingenuity and patience of his officials. The list was long indeed, headed by great lords such as Amanieu VII d'Albret, Pierre de Bordeaux and Pons de Castillon.[220] The dispossessed seneschal of the Agenais, Raymond de Campagne, knight, for instance, had been imprisoned by the French, and Edward replied to his petition for assistance in May 1297 with an assurance that he would not merely be repaid all sums owing to him but properly remunerated for his services 'when God granted a more favourable situation'.[221] Arnaud de Caupenne, whose brother Elie had been in prison as a hostage since the beginning of the war, was also very favourably treated, and was appointed seneschal of Périgord, Limousin and Quercy by Henry Lacy, earl of Lincoln, and Odo de Grandson in October 1303.[222] But the damage and disruption occasioned by war and dispossession was not easily remedied and its echoes reverberated until the outbreak of the war of St Sardos in 1324.

The French occupation of Aquitaine was brought to an end by three main developments: a rising tide of local discontent; the outbreak of Philip the Fair's second conflict with Boniface VIII; and the effects of Robert of Artois's defeat and death at the hands of the Flemings at Courtrai in July 1302. Local resistance to the French regime grew partly as a consequence of the conflict between Philip and the papacy. Boniface's fulminations against Philip and Flote, and his dispatch of legates to intervene in the affairs of the French kingdom *ratione peccati* to some degree aroused and legitimized Gascon disaffection.[223] On 10 December 1301 the king wrote to the consuls of Agen,

---

[219] *Documents Illustrating the Crisis of 1297–98 in England*, ed. M. Prestwich, Camden Society, 4th ser., xxiv (London, 1980), p. 163.

[220] *RG*, iii, nos 4419, 4528–31; E 101/154/11, 12, 15; *CPR, 1292–1301*, p. 433; E 101/371/21, nos. 77, 80, 81.

[221] *RG*, iii, no. 4474, pp. clxxxvi–clxxxvii; Trabut-Cussac, *L'Administration anglaise*, p. 381. He was seneschal of the Agenais for Edward I from 12 November 1286 to 3 March 1294, when the *sénéchaussée* was surrendered to Raoul de Clermont-Nesle. See above, pp. 185–6 and *AM Agen*, no. lxxxv (3 and 5 March 1294).

[222] Arnaud was paid 25 *l.st.* to meet his brother's expenses as a prisoner on 18 December 1294. See E 101/152/14, no. 3; also 152/8, no. 5; 154/11, nos 24–5 for wages and *restaur* paid to Arnaud and his company at Bayonne in March 1298. Elie was a household knight of Edward I: Trabut-Cussac, *L'Administration anglaise*, pp. 79, n. 211; 382 for his tenure of the *sénéchaussée* of Périgord-Limousin-Quercy from 1287 to 1294. Further cases of dispossession and subsequent compensation are found in SC 8/287, no. 173, SC 8/291, nos 14525, 14546; SC 8/283, no. 14141.

[223] See Boase, *Boniface VIII*, pp. 60–4, 203–7, 336–7. Boniface was about to excommunicate Philip and release his subjects from their oaths of allegiance to him by the bull *Super Petri solio* in September 1303, but the Anagni outrage supervened. Innocent III had formulated the theory of papal intervention *ratione peccati*.

telling them that he was astounded that Boniface's legate, the bishop of Spoleto, had been sent 'to the parts of Gascony' without his knowledge or licence and had convoked general assemblies of townsmen.[224] The legate had recited extracts from Boniface's letters to Philip from memory in these public gatherings. This redounded to Philip's dishonour and roused the people against him. The consuls were not to believe anything that the legate asserted and were to rest assured that the king would respect their liberties, privileges and franchises. Philip's letter was read out to the consuls of Agen on 14 January 1302. The accusation that pro-papal clergy were stirring up disaffection and plotting against the king in the Languedoc had already been part of the charges levelled against Bernard Saisset, bishop of Pamiers, in May and July 1301.[225] Saisset's alleged boast about the expulsion of the French from the Toulousain and Languedoc, because 'the men of the country do not like the king nor the French, because [they] . . . never did any good to [them], but only evil' can be read in this context.[226] Flote alleged that Saisset

> thought, spoke, negotiated and, as far as he was able, acted during the Gascon war between the . . . kings of France and . . . England, to the end that . . . men might be sooner incited to treason, and aroused against the . . . king of France, and to subvert the whole Kingdom.[227]

This was no doubt wildly exaggerated, but it reflected rumours and information reaching the French court from the south. Philip's choice of the Saisset affair as a trial of strength with Boniface VIII may have been based upon firmer foundations than has often been believed. For the Gascons, many of whom had not welcomed the French into the duchy of Aquitaine, papal resistance to Philip and his agents served both to justify and encourage their own dissension from the occupation of the duchy. It was perhaps unsurprising that a council of the French clergy, convened at Rome by the pope in October 1302, was attended by only thirty-six of the seventy-eight archbishops and bishops summoned.[228] But the archdioceses of Bordeaux and Auch were represented by three and eight bishops respectively, while Narbonne also sent five representatives. Many northern French bishops were conspicuous by their absence. The council was to culminate in the posthumous condemnation of Flote and the issue of the bull *Unam Sanctam*.[229] Philip's government was meanwhile fully absorbed by the Flemish campaign and the truces with England were extended in April, although Edward I emphasized that he did not intend his Scots enemies to be included in them as allies of the

---

[224] *AM Agen*, no. cxxiii. Philip's letter was recited to the inhabitants of Agen on 14 January 1302 by Jourdain, lord of L'Isle-Jourdain and Sicard de Vaur, king's clerk.

[225] Dupuy, *Preuves*, pp. 627, 633, 634, 641–2, 646.

[226] Dupuy, *Preuves*, p. 634 (deposition of Roger-Bernard, count of Foix).

[227] Dupuy, *Preuves*, p. 656.

[228] Boase, *Boniface VIII*, p. 316; Dupuy, *Preuves*, pp. 85–6.

[229] Dupuy, *Preuves*, pp. 53–6.

French.[230] He had agreed to their original inclusion to further the cause of Anglo-French peace, but they had subsequently invaded his subjects' lands and were now to be treated as his enemies. In August, when the French were still recovering from the shock of Courtrai, Edward appointed John de Hastings as his lieutenant and seneschal in Gascony (see plate 6.6).[231] The tide was turning in his favour.

During the occupation of 1294–1303 the French had relied heavily upon their hold on Bordeaux. The city was a political and economic capital from which, with Agen, the northerly parts of the duchy could be administered. But the faction-ridden city, like the Genoa of Simon Boccanegra, was politically volatile and subject to abrupt changes of fortune among the ruling groups. The practice of taking hostages as sureties for good behaviour from the city meant that Bordeaux was held to obedience to the French regime under duress. Although some elements within the city – such as the Colom – initially welcomed the French, the fate and treatment of the hostages did nothing to promote loyalty to the regime. Of 165 citizens held hostage by the French, 29 died in captivity.[232] Originally, only eight notables of the city were taken on 23 October 1294 and imprisoned at Marmande. By April 1299, 110 hostages were held by the French in 'the king's hall' at Toulouse, where they were joined by others from Dax.[233] Other Bordeaux citizens were held at Carcassonne and La Réole, including Jean Colom, the former mayor, who died at Carcassonne in 1296. In November 1297 the mayor and *jurats* of the city addressed a humble supplication to Philip the Fair, in which they pleaded that all the Bordelais held as hostages at Toulouse and elsewhere 'in such poverty and misery' that they could scarcely keep alive, be returned to their homes, wives and families. A threat of defection from the king's obedience was made but not acted upon until 1302.[234] It has been suggested that by taking hostages from the city 'the French may have been able to remove the most anglophile of the inhabitants' but it seems that the selection was indiscriminate and included members of all the leading families – the Soler, Colom, Béguey, Rostanh, Monadey and many others.[235]

Bordeaux's rising against the French was planned by Arnaud Caillau late in 1302 and took place in January 1303. By 15 January Caillau was installed as mayor, and the city experienced a brief period of municipal republicanism

[230] C 47/29 5, no. 1 (30 April 1302); cf. *Foedera* I, ii, pp. 955–6.

[231] E 101/68/1/25 (26 August 1302). Hastings was to serve with thirty men-at-arms, including three bannerets and six knights. He arrived in the duchy on 30 November (E 30/1654). For Hastings' seal see plate 6.6.

[232] *AMB Livre des Coutumes*, pp. 407–13, 538.

[233] *CR*, i, nos 11621, 11635, 12028–31, 12032–4.

[234] AN, J 631, no. 20 (21 November 1297). The communal seal attached to their petition displayed the fleur-de-lisé coat of arms of France on the obverse and the Grosse Cloche (bell-tower) surmounted by a fleur-de-lis on its reverse.

[235] Prestwich, *Edward I*, p. 386; cf. *Histoire de Bordeaux, III*, pp. 210–11.

6.6 Seal of John de Hastings, lord Abergavenny (1301). Hastings served Edward I and Edward II as lieutenant and seneschal of Aquitaine (1302–5, 1309–11). He was brother-in-law to Aymer de Valence. (London, Public Record Office.)

on the Flemish or north Italian pattern until Plantagenet authority was re-established.[236] Caillau clearly used the rebellion to further his own ends against his rivals and behaved in a ruthless and brutal fashion towards Frenchmen in the city. But negotiations were already in progress with Edward I: a Bordelais deputation led by Jean Colom was at Portsmouth early in March 1303, and on 5 March an agreement was reached at Paris between English and French envoys whereby the citizens of Bordeaux were not to be harmed by either side.[237] The rising may well have been planned in conjunction with John de Hastings' Plantagenet regime at Bayonne and with the Bordelais exiles in England. Bernard Cliquat, a bourgeois who had advanced money in order to provide for the city's security during the rising and its aftermath, was reimbursed from the customs at Bordeaux, of which he was appointed receiver.[238] Bordeaux's commerce was in a state of crisis during the period of warfare, as the rivers were blocked by the Anglo-Gascon garrisons at Bourg and Blaye, shipping was commandeered for military uses and the Gironde infested with hostile vessels. Only in 1303 did the city's export trade begin to recover.[239] The French occupation had brought economic as well as social and personal hardships to the Bordelais. The experience was not to be repeated during the next Anglo-French war in Aquitaine, when Bordeaux held out for Edward II.[240] A legacy of ill will between the French and the Bordelais was apparent in July 1305, when the Plantagenet regime was obliged to protect Philip the Fair's envoys who had come to the city to greet the newly elected Clement V.[241] These included such veterans of Anglo-French conflict as Gilles Aicelin, archbishop of Narbonne, Master Pierre de Belleperche and Charles of Valois at whose arrival many of the citizens were 'disturbed because of the malevolence shown towards them' in the recent war and occupation. John de Havering, Edward I's seneschal, mustered seven Gascon nobles and their retinues to protect the envoys while Clement V resided at Bordeaux. Philip the Fair did not formally pardon the Bordelais until, at Clement's request, he issued letters of remission to them on 18 July 1308.[242]

---

[236] Bémont, 'Factions et troubles à Bordeaux', pp. 146–50; E 101/158/10. One Raymond de Le[un], citizen of Bordeaux, claimed that he had brought 'the good news that the town . . . had returned to him' to Edward I. See SC 8/291, no. 14537; *RG*, iii, no. 4534.

[237] AN, J 633, nos 8, 9 (5 March 1303).

[238] E 101/158/10; *Histoire de Bordeaux, III*, pp. 207, 211.

[239] Renouard, 'Le grand commerce des vins de Gascogne', pp. 284, 288; M. K. James, 'Fluctuations of the Anglo-Gascon wine trade in the fourteenth century', *EcHR*, 2nd ser., iv (1951), pp. 170–82.

[240] See below, pp. 238–9.

[241] E 101/160/4, m. 2; partially printed in *RG*, iii, pp. cxcix–cc. Another copy of John de Havering's account for this expenditure is in E 101/160/6. Gifts were presented to the French envoys, and the new pope received presents including a gold cross with a gilded crystal image upon it for his chapel and, at his point of departure from the duchy on his journey to Lyon, two *barellis de cristallo deauratis*, as well as two dolphins, six bitterns and eight herons at Bazas.

[242] *AMB Livre des Coutumes*, p. 540.

The restitution of the duchy of Aquitaine to Edward I's lieutenants, Henry Lacy and Odo de Grandson, took place at a solemn ceremony in the collegiate church at St Emilion in June 1303.[243] All rancours occasioned by the war were to be pardoned and forgiven and Edward I's vassals and subjects were ordered by Richard Leneveu, archdeacon of Auge in the diocese of Lisieux, to renew their accustomed oaths of homage and fealty to their lord. The list of witnesses present included men well versed in recent events in Aquitaine such as Gérard Baleine, Philip the Fair's treasurer of wars, Bernard Pelet, prior of Le Mas d'Agenais, counsellor to Edward I, and the lawyers Yves de Landévennec and Garcie-Arnaud de Caupenne. Agreements to restore the duchy had been concluded at Paris on 20 May and Henry Lacy told Edward that he had performed an oath of *féauté* to Philip the Fair in the king-duke's name, 'purement, simplement et sanz condicion'.[244] A treaty of friendship and alliance was also drawn up between the two rulers, in which both promised not to aid nor harbour each others' enemies. This was to be a significant source of tension at a later date.[245] By 10 July 1303, Edward had confirmed the 'perpetual peace' of England and France. Finally, the king-duke confirmed on 31 July that all bonds and instruments concerning the taking of hostages, and all letters relating to the surrender of Aquitaine, were declared null and void for ever.[246] The status quo ante was to be restored.

It was in the nature of things that this could never be achieved. The disturbed conditions of war and occupation left a legacy of usurped and violated rights, physical damage and, above all, financial deficit. A degree of ill will smouldered in the duchy between Gascons and Frenchmen which the years of war and occupation had only exacerbated. Among the duchy's inhabitants themselves, disputes over dispossessions lingered on after the peace settlement. Ducal rights had been usurped and infringed, and were still subject to inquiries in 1310–11.[247] Seigneurial tolls had been imposed during the war years, rights of justice usurped and unlicensed fortifications erected. A series of *per quod warrantum* (by what right) inquiries were instigated by the Plantagenet administration into ducal rights, revenues and privileges assumed in the aftermath of the war. In 1305, for example, Arnaud de Castelnau, esquire, was required to show by what warrant he held the

---

[243] AN, J 633, no. 22.

[244] AN, J 633, nos 20, 21 (at Paris, 20 May 1303). The betrothal of Isabella and Edward of Caernarvon was agreed on the same day: *Foedera*, I, ii, p. 954.

[245] AN, J 633, no. 15; *Foedera*, I, ii, pp. 952–4. See below, pp. 259–60.

[246] AN, J 633, no. 23; *Foedera*, I, ii, p. 959 for Philip the Fair's letters concerning bonds and hostages (27 August 1303).

[247] *RG*, iii, pp. clxxviii–clxxxi; Trabut-Cussac, *L'Administration anglaise*, pp. 111–13; *Gascon Register A*, no. 45: many places, forests and other ducal possessions occupied unjustly during the war still remained in their usurpers' hands in 1311. The counts of Foix and Armagnac, Constance of Béarn and the lord of Navailles were conspicuous offenders in the Landes and Gers at this time.

bailliage of Castillonès during the first year after the restoration of the duchy (1303–4).[248] He also claimed to have been granted half the revenues of Miramont and Pimbo castles *a tempore guerre* and was ordered to show Henry Lacy's letters which he claimed to possess as warranty for his grant. Sansaner de Poudenx, esquire, was summoned to demonstrate by what warrant he held the *bailliage* of Bonnegarde between May 1303 and May 1304; while Amanieu de Fossat was to account for his tenure of Castelsarrasin in the Agenais which had previously been a den of robbers, held by its lord Auger de Mauléon, between August 1304 and June 1305. Fortaner de Lescun had apparently usurped the king-duke's rights at Lobinger, Hagetmau and elsewhere, but was able to show sufficient title to these places. Auger de Mauléon's right to the revenues of the castle and *prévôté* at Dax between May 1303 and March 1304 was still unresolved in March 1311.[249] It was unrealistic to believe that the status quo ante, assisted by the operation of collective amnesia, could be re-established in Aquitaine. Memories were long in this area and rights were all too easily contested. The war that erupted in 1294 not only changed and disturbed existing patterns, but reinforced tendencies towards the use of violence and self-help in the prosecution of quarrels.

Both Plantagenet and Capetian governments found themselves burdened with enormous debts as a result of the war. In some cases repayment was not made for decades after 1303. Edward II was paying off residual Gascon creditors in the 1320s and representatives of the townsmen of Ste-Quitterie, Bonnegarde, Labatut, Peyrehorade, Pouillon and Huire assembled in the Franciscan chapter house at Bordeaux on 7 March 1330 to claim recompense for the money and victuals which they had supplied to Henry Lacy during the Gascon war.[250] Edward III was to be liable for his grandfather's debts as well as his own. Philip the Fair's financial officials were still paying nobles and merchants for their services in the war in 1310, some from the proceeds of confiscations from the Jews. Although the Quercynois Bernard de Caudaresse, 'baron', had been promised payment of his wages by Gérard Baleine for service in the count of Fox's company under Robert of Artois in November 1297, his executors were still owed precisely the same sum (1177 *l.* 12 *s.t.*) in September 1310.[251] Bernard died in November 1300 and his executors, who included his kinsman Raymond-Arnaud de Caudaresse, bishop of Cahors, certified that he had requested them to recover that sum, so that his own debts for horses, corn, equipment and so forth might be discharged. The list of unpaid creditors who had supplied the French forces in Aquitaine was long and they were treated no differently from those who had sustained

[248] E 101/159/4, m. 2^r; *Gascon Calendar A*, no. 10 (p. 83).

[249] E 101/159/4, m. 2^{r-v}; SC 8/291, no. 14546.

[250] C 61/33, m. 11 (28 February 1320); E 372/183, m. 60; E 101/208/1, B4 (7 March 1330); SC 8/290, no. 14465; C 61/44, m. 8 (26 April 1332).

[251] AMB, MS 207, nos 13, 20, 25, 27.

Edward I's war effort.[252] The Gascon war had shown that, with the exception of Edward's favourable treatment of Bayonne, princes did not possess the financial resources to honour their debts and repay their creditors. There were no *tailles*, *aides* or *gabelles* in the kingdom of France at this period, and *fouages* (hearth-taxes) were still in their infancy. The fiscal expedients and regular taxes with which the French monarchy fought the Hundred Years War barely existed under Philip the Fair. His government was forced to fall back upon loans, monetary debasement, confiscations from Jews and Lombards and the dispossession of the Templars. Parliamentary grants to Edward I and the levy of taxes upon movable goods were likewise insufficient to meet the demands of war on this scale. Both monarchies were thus to a large extent dependent upon credit and this was to be a dominant characteristic of war finance until 1340.[253] War was a highly expensive undertaking, profitable to governments only if it could pay for itself. But princes took a long time to learn that lesson.

Above all else the events of 1294 and the succeeding years demonstrated that when put to the test the loyalties of most of Edward I's subjects in what remained of the Plantagenet dominions were not in doubt. The years of war and occupation in Aquitaine also revealed the fragile authority of the French crown over this remote and turbulent region.

---

[252] See above, pp. 206–7.

[253] See E. B. Fryde, 'The financial policies of the royal governments and popular resistance to them in France and England, *c*.1270–1420', in his *Studies in Medieval Trade and Finance* (London, 1983), pt I, pp. 831–40, and 'Loans to the English crown, 1328–31', pt IV, pp. 198–211.

7

The Coming of the Hundred Years War

7.1 The War of St Sardos and its Consequences

The Anglo-French war of 1294–8 marked a watershed in relations between the two powers. Although the family relationship between the ruling houses was renewed, trust and cordiality were never fully re-established. The unforeseen aftermath of Edward I's arbitration of Angevin–Aragonese affairs had proved destructive of Anglo-French peace. Great magnates such as Charles of Valois and Robert of Artois pursued their particularist ambitions to the detriment of Anglo-French relations. French marriages were arranged for both Edward and his son, but these did not lead to a full and complete reconciliation after 1303. Isabella's union with Edward II was to prove disastrous. The note of impatience and irritation found in Edward I's letter of September 1302 to Henry Lacy, earl of Lincoln, and Amadeus, count of Savoy, his envoys to France, is striking.[1] The king of France, he said, had already put off the day of agreement to terms of peace 'seven or eight times' and Edward could wait no longer. He had summoned Parliament and could not tolerate any further delays in French deliberations at Hesdin. With Scottish affairs still unresolved, an *entente* with France was unlikely to prove lasting. It was the election of Clement V in 1305 which partly ensured that there was peace between England and France until 1324.[2] Mediation by Gascon popes from Avignon succeeded where Celestine V and Boniface VIII had failed. Robert of Artois, Raoul de Clermont-Nesle and Pierre Flote met their deaths at Courtrai in July 1302, while Charles of Valois unsuccessfully sought a crown in Italy and the Empire. Philip the Fair's attention turned towards increased religiosity, Flanders and the destruction of the Templars. The passing of the dramatis personae of the early 1290s may have helped to guarantee some measure of peace between England and France. Former rivalries remained, but were less envenomed by individual antipathy, grounded in the pursuit of self-interest. Yet the origins of Valois hostility to England, and of the rival claims of Plantagenet and Valois to the French

---

[1] SC 1/13, no. 109 (16 September 1302).
[2] See above, pp. 106–8.

crown, may be sought between 1285 and 1307. The French occupation of the
duchy of Aquitaine (1294–1303) left a tenurial disarray that was never
properly resolved and which contributed to Anglo-French tensions. The war
of St Sardos (1324–6) was to bring greater disturbance to conditions in the
duchy and further exacerbate those tensions.

Reparations, compensations and restitution of lands and possessions lost
on both sides during the war of 1294–8 continued to concern the Anglo-
French negotiators during the 'processes' of Montreuil (1306) and Périgueux
(1311).[3] More fruitful were the personal meetings and diplomatic encounters
of the Plantagenets and Capetians at Paris and Poissy in the summer of 1313.
There was greater pretence of equality between the two parties upon such
occasions, while the failure of their lawyers and diplomatic representatives to
reach a settlement of Gascon issues partly stemmed from the tendency of the
French to conduct their meetings as if they were part of a lawsuit between
unequals rather than between two sovereigns of equal authority. At Montreuil, Périgueux and, later, at Agen it was apparent that the crown of France
was disposed to act as both accuser and judge in the matter of Aquitaine.[4]
When negotiation of the kind that succeeded in 1313 failed, the deadlock
could only be broken by force. Force of arms was not resorted to again until
June 1324, because Anglo-French relations under Louis X (1314–16) and
Philip V (1316–22) possessed many of the characteristics of *détente*. Flemish
campaigns and crises also preoccupied the last Capetians between 1315 and
1317, so that armed intervention in Aquitaine lay beyond their available
resources. A war on two fronts, at the extremities of the kingdom, was not
deemed to be feasible at this time. In 1320 a *rapprochement* between England
and France produced compromise over the issue of homage for Aquitaine.
Edward II staved off the performance of homage until that year, pleading
domestic preoccupations, above all the Scots war. Louis X and Philip V proved
to be very accommodating towards their Plantagenet kinsman and vassal.[5]

It was not until Charles IV succeeded to the French throne in 1322 that
the deterioration in relations that was to lead to an Anglo-French war set in.
The new reign began with the displacement of Philip V's counsellors from
favour, including Henri de Sully, butler of France, who, as we have seen, had
acted as an intermediary between the courts of France and England.[6] A new

---

[3] G. C. Cuttino, *English Diplomatic Administration, 1259–1339* (Oxford, 1971), pp. 62–111 for the
most recent account of the three processes; also his 'The process of Agen', *Speculum*, xix (1944),
pp. 161–78; and C 47/29/7, nos 9, 10, 13 for the process of Périgueux.

[4] See P. Chaplais, 'Règlement des conflits internationaux franco-anglais au xive siècle
(1293–1377)', in *Essays in Medieval Diplomacy and Administration*, (London, 1981), pt IX, pp.
269–86.

[5] P. Chaplais, 'Le duché-pairie de Guyenne: l'hommage et les services féodaux de 1303 à
1337', in *Essays in Medieval Diplomacy*, pt IV, pp. 144–54.

[6] N. Fryde, *The Tyranny and Fall of Edward II, 1321–1326* (Cambridge, 1979), pp. 134, 139; and
for Sully's career in Edward II's service, including his capture by the Scots in October 1322, *St
Sardos*, pp. 56–8. See above, pp. 129, 136.

body of advisers formed around Charles IV, among whom his uncle Charles of Valois was pre-eminent. With Charles once more wielding influence at court, the prospects for Anglo-French harmony were not propitious. Since his humiliation at the hands of Edward I and the failure of his Gascon campaign of 1295, he had harboured resentments against the Plantagenets which came to the fore again in 1322. Diplomatic measures were eclipsed by a renewed phase of Capetian aggression and 'in the event, it was the brute force of Charles of Valois rather than negotiations of English ambassadors which settled the issue'.[7] The death of Aymer de Valence on 23 June 1324, on his way to negotiate Anglo-French differences, was to remove another valuable intermediary from the scene.[8] Diplomatic means proved insufficient to contain Anglo-French tension on the eve of the war of St Sardos. Charles of Valois might be seen as seeking a late revenge for his discomfiture at Plantagenet hands in the 1290s. By September 1323, John XXII was writing letters concerning Anglo-French relations to Charles of Valois as well as to Charles IV, and in December he wrote to Gaston II, count of Foix, assuring him that he would support and further Gaston's interests with Charles of Valois. On 19 January 1324 the Pope told Charles that he would guarantee Gaston's loyalty to the house of France, strengthened by his kinship with the royal family through his mother, Jeanne d'Artois.[9] The extent of Sully's fall from favour was evident in September 1324 when, although he was Charles IV's own vassal, he was sent away from the king's presence without a hearing.[10]

The number of Gascon causes pending before the Parlement of Paris in 1323–4 was high. At least thirty-seven cases of appeal were recorded in March 1324 and Master Austence Jourdain was busy pleading the king-duke's cause at Paris.[11] He was also commissioned to give gifts and drinks to the advocates there, while in the duchy itself officers of the French seneschal of Périgord were bribed by Fulk Lestrange, Edward II's seneschal. Bernard Gervais, Charles IV's judge in the *sénéchaussée* of Perigord, was given 100 livres tournois (*l.t.*), so that he might 'more usefully' deal with matters concerning the king-duke and keep his rights intact. Elie de Urdinale, keeper of the French royal seal in Périgord, was also offered 25 *l.t.* to stay his hand in the execution of one of Charles IV's mandates against Edward II in Aquitaine.[12] Both central and local officials of the Capetian crown were

---

[7] Fryde, *Tyranny and Fall*, p. 137; J. Petit, *Charles de Valois, 1270–1435* (Paris, 1900), pp. 206–8; see above, pp. 196–9.

[8] See above, pp. 27–30; *The War of St Sardos*, p. 189.

[9] 'Documents pontificaux sur la Gascogne', ed. L. Guerard, nos 258–9, 267, 275–6. For the Foix-Béarn at this period, see above, pp. 90–1.

[10] Fryde, *Tyranny and Fall*, p. 143; *St Sardos*, pp. 56–7 (letter of Sully to Hugh le Despenser, 7 September 1324); *CPR, 1324–27*, p. 3.

[11] *St Sardos*, pp. 38–9; E 101/164/15; 165/6, D no. 39.

[12] E 372/182, m. 59.

clearly bribable and Lestrange evidently considered such money well spent
at times of tension. The volume of appeals reflected disturbances within the
duchy and on its borders during the previous few years. The affair of
Jourdain de l'Isle and its ramifications, and conflict in the *vicomté* of Marsan,
reached their pitch in 1322–3.[13] Repairs to ducal fortifications and the
construction of new fortified places were common at this time. A survey of
ducal castles in the duchy was undertaken in August 1320, and ordinances
made for the safe-keeping of Saintes, Blaye, La Réole, St Macaire, Marmande, Penne d'Agenais, Tournon, Sempuy, Sauveterre and Mauléon.[14] In
May 1323, as war broke out in Marsan, Edward II ordered his officers in
Aquitaine to supply and garrison all ducal castles so that hostile incursions
might be resisted. Licences to fortify were granted to the *bastides* of Miramont, Frondeboeuf and St Edward near Montfort in 1323–4 and Edward II
spent 8000 *l.t.* in buying out all claimants to the castle and castellany of
Blaye.[15] Its value as a defensive stronghold had been demonstrated during
the previous Anglo-French war and the security of the duchy's northern
frontier was less endangered if Blaye was a ducal castle, garrisoned by the
king-duke's seneschal.

We have already seen the extent to which the duchy was subject to private
wars and feuds in the 1320s.[16] The first outbreak of conflict which was to
involve the Plantagenet regime actively in hostilities came in April 1323,
when the southern parts of the duchy felt the effects of attacks on ducal lands
and officers in the *vicomté* of Marsan. These were perpetrated by the men of
Gaston II, count of Foix, acting at the instigation of his mother Jeanne
d'Artois.[17] Whether the attacks were encouraged by Charles of Valois and
other counsellors of Charles IV we shall probably never know. The Pope
wrote to both Gaston II and his mother on 25 May 1323 urging them to
desist from their aggressive acts towards the seneschal of Aquitaine, while
the bishops of Ely and Aire-sur-l'Adour were also requested to act as
intermediaries between the two sides *super sedando scandalo*.[18] Fulk Lestrange
took military action against Foix in April 1323, leading a force of at least fifty
men-at-arms and 320 foot-serjeants to take possession of Roquefort-de-
Marsan, Captieux, Hontonx and other places belonging to him. His army
included nobles of Béarn, such as Arnaud-Guillaume, lord of Lescun, and
Guillaume, lord of Audoin, who adhered to the king-duke against their

[13] See above, pp. 132–9.

[14] C 61/33, m. 5 (9 August 1320).

[15] C 61/35, m. 15 (10 and 27 May 1323); E 372/183, mm. 58, 59, 80. The Colom family were
the major recipients of this expenditure, and received letters of protection soon afterwards:
C 61/35, mm. 9–10.

[16] See above, pp. 131–9.

[17] Documents pontificaux', nos 239–42, 246; see above, pp. 90–1.

[18] Documents pontificaux', nos 239–42, 249, 254, 256; E 372/183, m. 54 for a gift of 100 *l.t.* for
his labours to Bernard, bishop of Aire.

immediate lord, the countess of Foix, and were paid 1000 *l.t.* for their loyalty.[19] Arnaud-Guillaume de Marsan, lord of Roquefort, also aided the Plantagenets and received 400 *l.t.* for his services from the constable of Bordeaux in the punishment of the countess's 'malice and iniquity'.[20] The *bastide* and castle of St Gein was taken by Lestrange's troops and the seneschal spent almost 7000 *livres bordelais* (*l.b.*) on the expedition.[21] Money raised in subsidies for Edward II's Scottish war was apparently diverted to pay for the 'army of Marsan' and the king-duke's hopes of Gascon military support for a Scots campaign were dashed by the disturbances within the duchy. It was perhaps no coincidence that the outbreak of conflict with Foix followed very shortly after Edward II's announcement to Charles IV on 2 February 1323 that he had summoned a large force of Gascon nobles and others to serve in the Scots war that summer, and requested that Charles grant them safe-conduct through his lands, even though some had been banished from his kingdom.[22] Expecting the duchy to be partially denuded of troops, the French may have seen an opportunity for aggression which was taken by Jeanne d'Artois and her supporters in April and May. By 3 July 1323, Edward simply wrote to all the towns of the duchy thanking them for their previous loyalty and exhorting them to continue in their allegiances.[23] Nothing more was heard of the summons to at least 202 Gascon nobles and their retinues to make war against the Scots. Their services were required by Fulk Lestrange in Marsan, Tursan and in the Landes.[24] The Marsan 'war' was a relatively minor affair, but it was not without consequences nor casualties, including Guillaume de St-Fort, seneschal of the Landes, who was fatally wounded. Most of the southern parts of the duchy experienced its effects and strongholds such as Pimbo, Miramont, Geaune, Montguilhem, Meurin, Sorde-l'Abbaye, St Sever and Sauveterre-de-Béarn were garrisoned by men-at-arms and large numbers of foot-serjeants against the incursions of Foix.[25] It was the prelude to a war of larger proportions and more general implications.

The Marsan war ended in a truce, made through the mediation of the

---

[19] Quittances and warrants for their military service are in E 101/164/16 and 17 (April–June 1323); and accounts for the war in E 372/183, mm. 59–60. For Béarnais nobles in Lestrange's service see SC 1/50, no. 6 (26 April 1323); E 372/183, m. 59.

[20] E 101/164/171 no. 1 (20 August 1323); E 372/183, m. 59. He surrendered his castle of Roquefort to the seneschal under a 'rendability' agreement made with the king-duke.

[21] E 372/183, mm. 59, 60. A total disbursement of 6995 *l.* 12 *s.* 11 *d.b.* was recorded.

[22] C 61/35, m. 10 (at Newark, 2 February 1323); and mm. 6, 13 and 15 for previous requests for money and service from the Gascons; also E. A. R. Brown, 'Gascon subsidies and the finances of the English dominions, 1315–24', *Studies in Medieval and Renaissance History*, viii (1971), pp. 48–50, 142–5.

[23] C 61/35, m. 11 (at York, 3 July 1323); Fryde, *Tyranny and Fall*, pp. 128–33.

[24] E 372/183, mm. 58, 59.

[25] E 372/183, m. 59; E 101/164/16, nos 4, 5, 12, 14, 17. At least thirty-four men-at-arms and 180 foot–serjeants were assigned to these places in May–June 1323.

bishops of Ely and Aire, in June 1323. The pope thanked Lestrange for his prompt response to papal peace-making efforts. John XXII told Ely and Lestrange in September 1323 that they should placate Gaston II, who was very young and had been under his mother's tutelage, so that peace might reign between the Plantagenet regime and the count of Foix. The restoration of one small castle (*castrunculum*), in return for Gaston's acknowledgment of his homage for Marsan and Tursan, would set matters right.[26] But the peace of the duchy was to be shattered again a month later, and the efforts of intermediaries were to prove fruitless on this occasion. In the autumn of 1323, the tension between Edward II and Charles IV over the former's postponements of his homage for Aquitaine and Ponthieu was intensified by events in the duchy. Not only did conflict break out in Marsan, but the French also invaded and occupied the isle of Oléron early in October. Edward II's Gascon council, including Adam Limber, constable of Bordeaux, Robert de Shirland, mayor of Bordeaux, and Masters Austence Jourdain and Henry of Canterbury, met near the high altar in Bazas cathedral on 5 October to hear a report of the incident.[27] The keeper of the isle's lieutenant spoke of a large force of French troops who had occupied the priory of St Denis there, in violation of all Anglo-French peace treaties. There was no fortified place on the island, and it was very difficult to defend. If men-at-arms were sent there, it was feared that the men of La Rochelle would descend and destroy the island. Saintonge was also endangered, and a new seneschal and keeper of the castle at Saintes was appointed, while his brother was to have custody of Oléron and call upon him if necessary. While Edward II pleaded disturbances in England and the recent disastrous Scots campaign as reasons for further postponements of homage to the recently enthroned Charles IV, the situation in Aquitaine deteriorated.[28] French invasions may have been designed as threats so that the homage was performed. Whatever the truth, Edward II and the Despensers were pursuing a dangerous policy. There was always the risk, as Dr Pierre Chaplais has remarked, 'that the king of France might rightly interpret [postponements] as a disguised refusal to pay homage, and decide in consequence to seize his vassal's fief'.[29] He was entitled to do this, or so his advisers counselled him, if he so wished. The situation was then inflamed by an incident which took place on the night of Saturday 15 October 1323 at St Sardos in the Agenais.

The so-called 'War of St Sardos' is to be the subject of a more detailed study by Dr Chaplais, but a general outline of the conflict and its consequences will be attempted here. St Sardos was the site of a Benedictine

---

[26] 'Documents pontificaux', nos 247, 248–9, 253. John Hotham, bishop of Ely was given a reforming commission in Aquitaine by Edward II and returned to England on 15 November 1323 (*St Sardos*, p. 5, n. 2).

[27] E 30/1610 (5 October 1323).

[28] Fryde, *Tyranny and Fall*, pp. 140–1; *St Sardos*, p. ix.

[29] *St Sardos*, p. ix. My debt to the documents printed in this volume will be obvious.

priory, a sub-house of the monastery at Sarlat.[30] The Agenais, in which it stood, had of course been awarded to Edward I as a result of the treaty made at Amiens in May 1279. But the abbot of Sarlat claimed that he possessed a privilege from the king of France whereby the monastery and its dependencies were to be inseparably bound to the French crown. Like the other *privilegiati* – ecclesiastical and secular – of the three dioceses of Limoges, Cahors and Périgueux after 1259, the house and its appendages could not be transferred against the will of the abbot and monks to direct Plantagenet lordship. The abbot was adamant on the issue in 1311: what applied to the mother-house at Sarlat, under the direct lordship of the French crown because it lay within the diocese of Périgueux, must apply to its dependencies. The abbot used a scholastic tag to reinforce his point that 'the members ought to follow the head'.[31] This anthropomorphic analogy was in widespread use but was insufficient to resolve the case before the Parlement of Paris. In 1317 a new element was introduced into the situation. The abbot of Sarlat decided to create a *bastide* or *nova populacio* at St Sardos. Like many other lords, as we have seen, he agreed to offer Philip V of France a share of its lordship through a contract of *paréage*.[32] The proposal was made potentially more difficult by the fact that St Sardos lay in the Agenais, then under Edward II's immediate lordship. If the new, unfortified *bastide* were established outside the priory gate, it would form an enclave within an area of Plantagenet allegiance. There were also local interests which opposed its foundation: the consuls and inhabitants of Agen, and the secular lord of the area, Raymond-Bernard, lord of Montpezat.

Raymond-Bernard de Montpezat was Edward II's vassal for his castle and lands at Montpezat, a few miles from St Sardos. He was not an exemplary subject. In May 1318 he was ordered to surrender the keys of the castle to Achard de Montguidon, seneschal of the Agenais, as a punishment for his seizure of the seneschal's serjeants during a raid which he had conducted from that castle.[33] He had set out with eleven accomplices from Montpezat on the pretext of inviting certain of the seneschal's officers to eat and drink with him. He clearly had a personal feud with the seneschal, and objected to the manner in which his serjeants were executing their orders. He therefore attacked them and brought them back wounded to Montpezat, where they were thrown into prison at the bottom of the keep. Raymond-Bernard claimed that he was prevented from bearing arms for his own protection in areas subject to the king-duke and had accordingly taken the

---

[30] *The Gascon Calendar of 1322*, ed. G. P. Cuttino, no. 1893.

[31] *Gascon Register A (Series of 1318–19)*, ed. G. P. Cuttino and J.-P. Trabut-Cussac, no. 54 (pp. 324–5); *St Sardos*, p. x. The abbot of Sarlat was listed among the *privilegiati*, 'tam in capite quam in menbris' (1310–11).

[32] See above, pp. 154–5.

[33] C 47/25/2 no. 24; *St Sardos*, pp. 30–4.

law into his own hands.[34] Shortly after this incident, he made common cause with the townsmen of Agen when they complained to Edward II that:

> the people of the king of France insist upon founding a new settlement at the place of St Sardos, lying in the middle of the land of Agenais . . . which is under the . . . jurisdiction of the seneschal of the Agenais. . . . Hence, if this (new) population is established in the said place, the land of Agenais will be lost, because almost all the people of this land will flock there on account of the privileges which have been granted to the inhabitants by the King of France.[35]

Raymond-Bernard de Montpezat shared these fears, anticipating the loss of revenues from tolls, fairs and markets which often followed the creation of a *bastide*. A final *arrêt* of the Paris Parlement in December 1322 clinched the issue. The projected settlement was to go forward, despite objections, and all arguments to the contrary were overruled. The French seneschal of Périgord, in whose jurisdiction the monastery at Sarlat lay, then proclaimed a date for the formal ceremony of foundation. This was to be 16 October 1323, the Sunday before the feast of St Luke.[36] A stake bearing the fleurs-de-lis was to be driven into the ground by the French royal serjeant deputed to proclaim the new settlement's existence. From that moment settlers could take up their building plots. The stake was duly implanted in readiness for the ceremony on the, evening of 15 October. But during the night a band of armed men came to St Sardos, set fire to some of the priory buildings, and shouting 'Guyenne!' proceeded to hang the French serjeant from his own stake which bore his master's arms.[37] This was not a unique, nor even an uncommon, event but in the political conditions of October 1323 it was to prove destructive of Anglo-French concord. Those responsible for this insult to Charles IV's sovereignty were thought to be in the pay of Raymond-Bernard de Montpezat. He had been at Agen three days previously, where he took his oath of obedience to the new seneschal of Aquitaine, Ralph Basset of Drayton, who was progressing through the duchy.[38] It was a most unfortunate coincidence, because suspicions of collusion between Basset and Montpezat were soon in the air. Basset heard the news of the outrage very soon indeed after its occurrence, for he was only a few miles from St Sardos on 16 October.[39] To make matters worse, he left his sub-seneschal of the

---

[34] C 47/25/2, no. 24; cf. SC 8/290, no. 14485 for a comparable ruse by Raymond-Arnaud de Béarn against Auger de Poudenx in 1322.

[35] SC 8/287, no. 13303.

[36] *Actes du Parlement de Paris*, ed. E. Boutaric, ii, nos 5466, 6498, 6980; *St Sardos*, p. 256 (from C 47/29/22).

[37] *St Sardos*, pp. 8–9, 186; Fryde, *Tyranny and Fall*, pp. 141–2.

[38] C 47/26/17. Raymond-Bernard de Montpezat took his oath to Basset at Agen on 13 October.

[39] He was at Bouglon in the Agenais on 15 October (E 368/109, m. 32).

Agenais to enquire into the incident and continued his oath-taking tour of the duchy. To the French, his guilt by association was clear and accusations of collusion were soon made. On 3 February 1324 Basset certainly felt it necessary to instruct the mayors and *jurats* of Bordeaux, Bayonne, Dax and St Sever to send copies of identical letters which he had drafted to Charles IV under their communal seals in order to clear his name and those of his officers.[40]

In the event, this proved futile, and both Basset and Montpezat were banished from the kingdom of France by *arrêt* of the Parlement in February 1324.[41] War did not, however, break out for another four months. The slow fuse which burned for eight months after the incident at St Sardos was an example of the extent to which efforts might still be made to resolve Anglo-French difficulties by diplomatic means. The French confiscated the castle of Montpezat, but it was garrisoned by Anglo-Gascon troops who refused to surrender it to the French seneschals of Périgord and Toulouse. Basset's complicity in this refusal was made clear by his payment of gifts, wages of war and *restaur* of lost horses to members of the garrison there between 29 September 1323 and 22 June 1324.[42] Seignoran de Labarthe and Odo, lord of Doazit, were given 140 *l.t.* as a gift over and above their wages at Montpezat owing to a dearth of victuals; Hugh de St Edmund was paid for his custody of victualling there between 1 March and 22 June, while Peregrin de Vaquarissa and Richard 'the siege engineer' were given their wages for going to Montpezat on Basset's orders to supervise its defensive equipment and to repair the crossbows and other 'engines' there. Most damaging of all was Basset's payment of a prest or advance of 160 *l.t.* to Raymond-Bernard de Montpezat himself, for unspecified reasons.[43]

War might still have been avoided but for the indecisive behaviour of Edward II's envoys at Paris, the determination of Charles IV and Charles of Valois to exploit the incident and the lack of credible intermediaries who held the confidence of both sides. Edward's proctors at the Parlement first agreed to surrender Montpezat castle, then changed their minds and asked for a further postponement of homage for Aquitaine.[44] Charles IV had decided to intervene personally in the affair and journeyed to Toulouse in

[40] See *AMB Livre des Etablissements*, ed. E. Dulaurens (Bayonne, 1892), no. 17 (pp. 34–5); *St Sardos*, pp. 11–20 for the letter which the mayor and *jurats* sent to Charles IV on 6 February 1324. The integrity of Edward II's seneschals and the clerical status of the constable of Bordeaux (Adam Limber) was stressed in these letters.

[41] *St Sardos*, pp. 40–1. Edward II continued to put his trust in Basset, for he charged him with 'certain secret matters' and appeared to set him above his own lieutenant Edmund, earl of Kent, in January 1325 (C 61/36, m. 7).

[42] E 372/183, m. 60; *St Sardos*, pp. xii–xiii, 22–4, 25–6.

[43] E 101/164/16, no. 14 for Labarthe's previous service in the Marsan war; E 372/183, m. 60 for Montpezat.

[44] *St Sardos*, pp. xii–xiii, 27–38, 182–4.

January 1324 to oversee the business.[45] This was an exceptional measure, for the Capetians rarely visited their southern lands. Basset had defaulted on a summons before the seneschal of Périgord in December 1323, feigning illness, and was accordingly summoned, with Raymond-Bernard de Montpezat, to be before Charles IV at Toulouse on 23 January. Both defaulted and, after a second non-appearance, both were condemned to banishment from the realm of France.[46] The loyal nobility of Languedoc and the south-west were gathering around Charles IV at Toulouse, including the counts of Périgord, Foix, Comminges and Bernard-Jourdain de L'Isle-Jourdain.[47] War might still have been averted if Edward II and his representatives had shown more sagacity. The pope wrote to Charles IV on 6 April urging him not to 'pursue two hares at the same time', referring to the concurrent problems of both Aquitaine and Flanders. He was to reflect upon the consequences of declaring war merely as revenge for the incident at St Sardos, about which the pope had written to Edward II exhorting him to perform homage for Aquitaine.[48] A negotiated reconciliation was still possible, but that was dashed by Edward II's instructions to his envoys to attempt a further prorogation of the personal meeting and homage ceremony which was to take place, at the very earliest, in October 1324.[49] But the envoys refused to honour the agreement made with the French over the castle of Montpezat and on 10 June 1324 a general proclamation and summons to arms was made in the realm of France.[50] England and France were once again at war.

The conflict which ensued was a desultory affair. Expenditure of 65,000 *l.st.* has been estimated as the cost of the war to Edward II's government. As such, it was far less costly than the war of 1294–8 upon which about 72,000 *l.st.* per year was spent.[51] Edward II's financial position in 1323 was much superior to that of his father in 1294. He possessed 'ample financial resources', but these were mobilized too late to be really effective.[52] The constable of Bordeaux only received the greater part of money from England in May 1325, when 20,441 *l.st.* arrived in the duchy, while Edward still relied

---

[45] *St Sardos*, p. xii. Edward II's proctor at the Paris Parlement, Master Pons de Tournemire, was arrested and thrown into prison at the Châtelet on 21 December 1323. See E 372/143, m. 60 for payments to him for his costs, damages and release from prison, by Basset.

[46] *St Sardos*, pp. 10–11, 15–17, 40–1. Basset claimed that he could only be summoned, as Edward's seneschal of Gascony, before the Parlement 'en la graunt chaumbre de Parys' (p. 15). He also feared for his personal safety if he obeyed the summons to Toulouse. Pons de Tournemire was brought from Paris to Toulouse as a prisoner in chains (E 372/183, m. 60).

[47] 'Documents pontificaux', nos 272–4; Master Robert de Redmere was sent on Edward II's business to Toulouse at this time (E 372/183, m. 60).

[48] 'Documents pontificaux', nos 302, 308.

[49] *St Sardos*, pp. 182–4.

[50] *St Sardos*, pp. 186–7; Fryde, *Tyranny and Fall*, pp. 142–3.

[51] See BL, Add. MS 7967, fos 4[r], 7[v] (account of Nicholas Hugate, treasurer for the war in Aquitaine, 1324–6). For Edward I's expenditure in 1294–8 see above, p. 206 and Appendix II.

[52] Fryde, *Tyranny and Fall*, p. 145.

upon Italian banking houses to provide him with liquid capital. In July 1324, John Travers, constable of Bordeaux, received 3951 gold florins of Florence from the Peruzzi.[53] It was proposed that the war be fought largely by mercenaries recruited from Aragon, Castile and Portugal. Money was amassed to meet such costs, and Walter Stapleton found 12,000 *l.st.* in the treasury upon his appointment as treasurer in 1326. Some Aragonese nobles served in the war, and were finally paid in July 1327, but their service does not appear to have been on the scale of that offered to Edward I.[54] The war of St Sardos was fought largely by Anglo-Gascon forces, which included the retinues of over one hundred Gascon nobles.[55] The English forces under Edmund, earl of Kent, like those raised earlier by Edward I, included criminals and outlaws in large numbers as infantry and hobelars, pardoned for their crimes and recruited through writs to the sheriffs of England between February and June 1325.[56] Edward II was not prepared to spend as much money as his father on a war in Aquitaine and he did not perhaps need to do so, given the relatively short duration of active hostilities. He relied on 'gifts' from his subjects to meet the demands of war, such as the sixty oaks and sixty ash trees which he demanded in aid from the abbots of Westminster and Waltham in January 1325. These were to be used in the construction of siege engines, springals, lances, crossbow bolts and other war material for the defence of 'our inheritance and rights' in the duchy.[57]

The war revolved primarily around the retention by Edward II of the Agenais and Saintonge. The main theatre of war lay in the Agenais, which had already been afflicted with previous disorders for which remedies were prescribed in ordinances drawn up in August 1320.[58] Breaches of the peace were manifold there, and matters had not been improved by demands for subsidies and troops from Agen by Edward II to fight the Scots war in March 1323.[59] Most of the rebel nobles pardoned by Edward in December 1325 were from the Agenais, and confiscations of the persons and goods of the men of Agen, Port-Ste-Marie, Tonneins, Marmande and other towns of the Agenais if found in England were ordered on 28 September 1324.[60] Agen surrendered to Charles of Valois's troops early in the war, and the conflict

---

[53] BL, Add. MS 7967, fo. 4ʳ; E 101/164/18 (receipt at Bordeaux, 6 July 1324).

[54] See M. Buck, *Politics, Finance and the Church in the Reign of Edward II* (Cambridge, 1983), pp. 171–2; *St Sardos*, pp. 140–2; C 61/36 m. 10ᵛ; E 101/165/6, D nos 42, 44, for quittances of Aragonese nobles, 43 and 45 for warrants (10–27 July 1327).

[55] For quittances and warrants for wages see E 101/165/5–10. Payments were made between May 1327 and September 1329.

[56] C 61/38, mm. 1–12 (February–June 1325).

[57] C 61/36, m. 7ᵛ (2 January 1325). The timber was to be felled at Great Amwell (Herts) and Stansted (Essex).

[58] C 61/33, m. 6 (7 August 1320).

[59] *AM Agen*, no. cliii (13 March 1323); Brown, 'Gascon subsidies', pp. 142–9. See above, p. 231.

[60] C 61/36, m. 16 (28 December 1325) for pardons to thirty-two nobles; m. 25 for the arrests.

soon centred upon the siege of La Réole by his army.[61] Edmund, earl of Kent, was shut up inside the castle there for five weeks, holding out until 22 September. The siege was protracted by outbreaks of internal dissension within the French army and by casualties among them caused both by military activity and by disease. There was a dearth of victuals among the besiegers, they ate bad meat (when they could obtain it) and many died of dysentery as a result of drinking contaminated water.[62] In early September the French had most of the Agenais in their hands and much of Saintonge, except for the castle at Saintes, but the greater part of the duchy held out for Edward II and supported him for the rest of the conflict. Charles of Valois was careful to confirm all the privileges of both Agen and La Réole as a guarantee of their loyalty, although he required the services of miners from Rouergue to undermine the castle at La Réole on 3 September 1324.[63]

A striking feature of the war of St Sardos was the loyalty of Bordeaux to the Plantagenets. Unlike their behaviour in 1294, the great majority of the city's ruling class (including the Colom) remained firmly in Edward II's allegiance.[64] Bordeaux did not wish to repeat the experience of 1294–1303. The Plantagenet administration at least did its best to provide for the city's defence against the French. Adam Limber, constable of Bordeaux, spent 4884 *l.* 9 *s.* 4 *d. l.t.* on war material for Bordeaux, Blaye and Montpezat between 29 September 1323 and 30 September 1324, including 347 cross-bows, 200 shields of the king-duke's arms, 4000 crossbow bolts and 2202 bolt heads.[65] William de Martheleye, clerk, and Master Thomas, the siege engineer, supervised the work of carpenters and other artisans on the construction of defensive 'engines' at Bordeaux between November 1324 and July 1325. These were catapults called *brides*, mangonels and trebuchets, made from timber bought from Bordelais merchants and nobles, transported by water to Bordeaux.[66] A 'great engine' was constructed and mounted at the porte de Caillau, erected by fifty mariners from a Bristol ship with seven great hawsers 'to save expense'. Another hawser was requisitioned from Robert Stud, master of a Hull vessel, 'to raise the belfry' (*berfrei*), while sixty sailors and carpenters worked all day to put up the 'great engine' when its 'forks' (*furcas*) were put in place and received 5 *s.t.* worth of wine for their refreshment. Other engines were made from timber and treated with resin

---

[61] Fryde, *Tyranny and Fall*, p. 143; *St Sardos*, p. 50; Petit, *Charles de Valois*, pp. 211–14.

[62] *St Sardos*, p. 50 where many deaths were reported by John Travers 'des grapes et par boyr del ewe' (1 September 1324); AN, JJ 62, fos 262^v–3^r, 269^v for fights among members of Charles of Valois's army. Further details of the siege are in APA, E 350, no. 6.

[63] *AM Agen*, no. cliv (30 September 1324); AN, JJ 64, fo. 399^r (28 September 1324); K. 41, no. 10 (3 September 1324). The miners were provided with clothing, pick-axes and 'a banner of the king's arms' by the treasurer of Rouergue. The operation cost 320 *l.* 5 *s.* 2 *d.t.*

[64] See above, pp. 221–3; *Histoire de Bordeaux*, III, pp. 352–4.

[65] E 372/183, m. 60.

[66] E 101/165/2, fos 1^r, 9^r (9 November 1324–10 July 1325).

brought into the city by the peasants of Bègles and Talence, with their teams of oxen. A serjeant was sent to the loyal *bastide* of Créon to compel forty-five men of the Entre-deux-Mers to carry timber for engines for five days from the forests there to Bordeaux.[67]

The purpose of these measures was to keep the enemy at a distance and to harm their shipping in the Garonne by hurling projectiles at them from these catapaults. Attempts were also made to block the river between St Macaire and Langon so that the French could neither bring men and munitions down the Garonne to Bordeaux nor establish communications by water with La Réole. Jean de Bagnières, a siege engineer, went to St Macaire in November 1324 to find ways of preventing the French from descending in boats and besieging the town.[68] In the event, a pontoon bridge of boats was constructed there which not only blocked the river but allowed Anglo-Gascon troops to be moved rapidly from St Macaire towards Langon. Etienne Seguin, the owner of one of the vessels used to construct the bridge, was compensated for its loss during a storm which struck and sank it.[69] The French had already destroyed a bridge over the Garonne between St Macaire and La Réole, and the maintenance of river communications was of paramount importance. Bordeaux was defended by a large garrison, and a barrier of piles or stakes was driven into the river-bed to prevent a French approach by water. Bourg, Blaye, St Emilion, Libourne, Dax, Condom, St Sever, Mont-de-Marsan and Bayonne remained in Plantagenet hands and, in contrast with 1294–8, did not slip from them.[70] This was partly the result of service by members of the Gascon nobility, including nobles from Béarn, who ensured the survival of the Plantagenet regime. Over one hundred nobles and their companies were paid or owed substantial sums as wages of war. Among those who brought large companies of mounted men-at-arms and foot-serjeants to the king-duke's service were Guillaume de Garland, baron, Guillaume-Raymond de Caumont, Arnaud-Guillaume de Béarn, lord of Lescun, who had already served in the Marsan war, Bernard de Béarn, lord of Arrudy, and Pons de Castillon, all paid between 1000 and 5000 *l.t.*[71] Companies of infantry were raised by captains or 'procurators', themselves foot-soldiers, while bourgeois of Penne d'Agenais, Langon and St Macaire served as both mounted men-at-arms and foot-serjeants. Arnaud de las Salas, for example, bourgeois of St Macaire, acted as procurator for twenty-four other unmounted men-at-arms, all of them bourgeois of the town, and received wages for its defence in July 1327. Similarly, Jean Merle, bourgeois of Penne, served as a mounted trooper, commanding another man-at-arms and four foot-serjeants in his

[67] E 101/165/2. fos 19ᵛ, 20ᵛ, 22ʳ.

[68] BL, Add. MS 7967, fo. 9ᵛ (November 1324).

[69] E 372/185, m. 2ʳ. He received 70 *l.t.* in compensation, and was receiver of a toll at St Macaire in September 1327 (E 101/165/8, I, no. 39).

[70] See above, pp. 200–15; *St Sardos*, p. 53.

[71] E 101/165/5, E no. 4; 0, nos 9, 17, 22; F, nos 19, 20.

tiny retinue.[72] Nobles and townsmen therefore served side by side in this second war of resistance against Charles of Valois.

A conspicuous exception to this support for the Plantagenets was provided by Amanieu VII d'Albret. Albret had been one of Edward I's most consistently loyal supporters against the French during his Gascon war, but the events of Edward II's reign cost the king-duke his loyalty.[73] The behaviour of Gaveston and his Gascon kinsmen had been partly responsible for the appeals of Albret to the French crown in 1309 and 1312, and the crisis of the latter year was thought by some contemporaries to have been the seed-bed of all subsequent Anglo-French conflicts.[74] Attempts by Edward II's seneschals to intervene in Albret's private wars proved irritating and ultimately intolerable to him and in 1324 he rebelled against his immediate lord in favour of his sovereign, Charles IV. He was granted special protection by the king in June, and Charles of Valois (as the king's lieutenant in Languedoc) ordered an inquiry into the many losses and damages which Albret had already sustained in September 1324.[75] As Gascon correspondents to Edward II and Hugh le Despenser were quick to observe, Albret's local authority and knowledge of the terrain was of considerable value to the French invaders, especially in the Landes and Bazadais.[76] His cadet son, Bérard, chose the opposing side and, as lord of Rions and Vayres, served Kent and his seneschal Oliver Ingham. In a testament dated 11 July 1324, Amanieu d'Albret disinherited Bérard, citing the 'custom of Casteljaloux' whereby the liberty to dispose of goods was granted to a testator. Bérard had refused to serve with his father against Edward II and his castles of Gironde and Vayres had thus been seized.[77] Amanieu's 'universal heir', Bernard-Ezi, witnessed the testament and clearly had no interest in opposing its terms. Bérard was knighted by Edward II and made a banneret in July 1326 as a reward for his services.[78] Divided allegiances within a family were to become a common feature of the Gascon nobility during the Hundred Years War. But the restoration of Amanieu d'Albret to Edward II's grace in June 1326 annulled the disinheritance of his youngest son. His choice of allegiance to the French in 1324 represented the result of a long-standing dissatisfaction, and also served to legitimize Amanieu's private feuds in the duchy. On 4 January 1325, Charles IV pardoned him for his violent attacks against Arnaud de Durfort and his family. Durfort and his children had rebelled

---

[72] E 101/165/5, G nos 21, 24; 165/8, E, unnumbered and G, unnumbered (Merle); 165/8, J, nos 27, 28, 42; 165/10, N, no. 41 (616 foot-serjeants retained at Bourg).

[73] See above, pp. 173–4.

[74] C. Bémont, 'Les factions et les troubles à Bordeaux de 1300 à 1330 environ. Documents inédits', *BPH* (1916), art. 45 where Jean Colom was accused of having sown discord between Amanieu d' Albret and John Ferrers, seneschal of Aquitaine, in 1312; see above, pp. 172–3.

[75] APA, E 27, nos 21 (30 June 1324), 24 (30 September 1324).

[76] See, for instance, *St Sardos*, pp. 50–2, 128.

[77] *St Sardos*, pp. 229–30; APA, E 27, no. 12 (11 July 1324).

[78] E 101/382/7, m. 1 (July 1326).

against the French crown and opposed Charles's Gascon expedition. Incursions by both Albret and Armagnac into Durfort's lands were thus legitimized.[79]

A partial reconciliation between Albret and Edward II was negotiated by Ingham, Amanieu de Fossat and Arnaud-Guillaume, lord of Lescun, in June 1326.[80] The war of St Sardos had petered out. On 24 September 1325, homage was performed at Paris for Aquitaine and Ponthieu by Edward, earl of Chester (the future Edward III), who had recently been created duke of Aquitaine by Edward II. Although his son was a minor, Aquitaine had been bestowed upon him and, accompanied by his mother, he thereby performed homage in his father's stead. Charles IV was asked to receive his homage and this was done, although the French council stated that the act was in no way to prejudice Charles IV's rights to Gascon lands surrendered in any peace agreement with Edward II.[81] Edward's request was made through Master Guillaume de Breuil, one of the leading advocates of the Paris Parlement, of whom more will be heard.[82] The grant of Aquitaine to his son by Edward II had partly been motivated by the Despensers' fear that that king's absence from England in 1325 would undermine their own position, and the homage had therefore to be performed by proxy. As it happened this was a grave political miscalculation which enabled Edward's mother to plot her husband's downfall in France and Hainault, refusing to return to England until the Despensers' regime was overthrown.[83] The control of Anglo-French relations began to slip from Edward II's grasp at this juncture, and his impotence in the face of the Despensers, on the one side, and Isabella, on the other, was to become increasingly evident in his letters on Gascon affairs.

A form of peace was agreed upon during the summer and autumn of 1325 and on 14 August a public peace was proclaimed.[84] But peace did not bring harmony and tranquillity to the duchy of Aquitaine. The aftermath of war produced a plethora of pleas and appeals for restitution and compensation, not least concerning the manner and extent of the duchy's restoration to the thirteen-year-old boy who stood in his father's place as duke of Aquitaine. A long list of castles and places seized by the French and their supporters in the duchy was compiled before 6 October 1327 and presented to Charles IV's counsellors.[85] Some places were already illicitly occupied as a result of what was termed the 'first' Gascon war or *commotio* in 1324–5; others had been

[79] APA, E 27, no. 10 (4 January 1325); AN, JJ 62, fo. 129ᵛ; C 61/38, mm. 2, 3 for Edward II's pardons to him and his kinsmen (24 and 25 June 1326).

[80] C 61/38, m. 3 (24 June 1326).

[81] AN, J 634, no. 14 (24 September 1325); Fryde, *Tyranny and Fall*, p. 148; *St Sardos*, pp. 243–5.

[82] AN, J 64, no. 14; C 61/33, m. 5 for a payment by Edward II of 100 *l.t.* to him for his good services as 'our advocate in the court of France' (9 August 1320). See also below, pp. 251–2.

[83] Fryde, *Tyranny and Fall*, pp. 176–85; Buck, *Politics, Finance and the Church*, pp. 161–2.

[84] *Foedera*, II, ii, pp. 599–601.

[85] AN, J 654, no. 10, mm. 1–6; *St Sardos*, pp. 257–66.

'French' in the first and 'English' in a second war which broke out in 1326, or vice versa; others had 'always been English', but were seized during the first war – while Charles of Valois's incursions in 1324 merely made a complicated problem even less easy to resolve. Truce-breaking had led to further seizures, and it was noted that the men of the count of Armagnac and the *vicomte* of Tartas had profited from the disturbed conditions of warfare to raid towns such as Le Mas-Ste-Quitterie or Dax 'under cover of the war between the two kings'.[86] Vines, trees, oxen, cows, horses and corn had been lost and there had been casualties among the inhabitants. The loyal bourgeois of Blaye told Edward II that they had twice suffered severely from the ravages of war within the last thirty years, especially during 'le grant autre guerre' (of 1294–1303) and needed the proceeds of a custom upon wine brought to Blaye from the *haut pays* to repave their streets, repair their fountains and drains and generally renovate the battered town.[87] The quartering of troops and the passage of armies through the duchy hardly improved civic amenities.

Such claims could be met with grants of money, although Edward II's reactions to some of these petitions seem to have been excessively mean-spirited and parsimonious.[88] His son and his own officers in the duchy were generally more sympathetic and generous (as far as they could be) towards the victims of front-line warfare. But major problems were posed by claims to the restitution of lands and revenues from members of the Gascon nobility. A barrage of petitions for restoration of lands and compensation for losses was addressed to Edward II, his council and the young Edward III.[89] On 4 April 1326, Edward II agreed to confirm all grants of compensation made by Edmund, earl of Kent, as his lieutenant in Aquitaine. If the value of lands assigned exceeded that of those lost, the residue was to be accounted for before the constable of Bordeaux. If, on the contrary, lands assigned as compensation proved insufficient, the residue was to be made up by the hapless constable.[90] Sir Oliver Ingham, a client of the Despensers and evidently much trusted by the king-duke, had been appointed seneschal of Aquitaine on 7 October 1325, and in April 1326 extensive powers were granted to him over the financial administration of the duchy and the spending of its resources.[91] These included the power to raise loans up to a total sum of 10,000 *l.st.* on security of ducal revenues. In May a suspicious Edward II, residing at Hailes abbey, ordered Ingham to proceed ex-

---

[86] AN, J 654, no. 10, m. 6: 'sub umbra guerre dictorum regum'; see also C 61/35, m. 6.

[87] SC 8/290, no. 14454. For losses at Bourg, especially of tolls from merchants and pilgrims in time of war, see E 36/78, fo. 5ʳ (1325–6).

[88] C 61/38, m. 4 (24 March and 4 April 1326).

[89] See, for example, SC 8/183, no. 14132; 285, no. 14208; 287, nos 14330–1; 283, nos 14103, 14120; 286, no. 14291.

[90] C 61/38, m. 4 (4 April 1326).

[91] C 61/38, mm. 4, 5 (19 March, 4 April 1326); St Sardos, p. 271. For his tomb effigy see plate 7.1.

7.1 Tomb effigy of Oliver Ingham, knight (Ingham, Norfolk, c.1340). Ingham was seneschal of Aquitaine for Edward II and Edward III (1325–7, 1331–43). He lies in full armour on a bed of stones, ready to rise as if from sleep. (From C. A. Stothard, *The Monumental Effigies of Great Britain*, 1817, plate 67.)

peditiously against all those who were said to be plotting and machinating against the king-duke by arresting them and seizing their possessions.[92] The Gascon nobility were requested to give credence to Ingham and obey him so that he might report favourably upon their conduct. It appeared that the king-duke was prepared to accept Ingham's testimony to their 'strenuous actions and praiseworthy deeds', which Edward himself would personally assess and consider. They would then be appropriately compensated and rewarded. It was perhaps to Ingham's credit that he must have given accounts satisfactory to the nobles themselves, for his subsequent long career in Aquitaine was, as we shall see, a relatively successful one in which he commanded their support (see plate 7.1).[93] But a settlement of so many outstanding claims was beyond the powers and abilities of one man, and was to defeat those who negotiated between the two sides after Edward II's death. The business of compensation was not aided by the loss of the Agenais and – more seriously still – part of the Bazadais to the French. As Raymond-Bernard de Marmande, esquire, complained in a petition to Edward III in *c*.1330, he had served in the war of St Sardos with ten

[92] C 61/38, m. 4 (1 May 1326).
[93] See below, pp. 245–7, 253, 260–2.

men-at-arms and thirty-three foot-serjeants, losing lands worth over 1000 *l.t.* a year.[94] Two of his castles had been demolished by the French. Ingham had given him rebel lands in the Bazadais with an annual rental value of 1000 *l.t.* which the seneschal and his troops had recovered by force of arms. But the restoration to the French of lands in the Bazadais taken by force left him without any source of compensation and he had been forced to sell his war-horses, armour and harness. Such complaints were legion in the aftermath of war.[95] It would be the task of Edward III and his officers to reward Gascon loyalty from depleted territorial resources and thereby retain the Plantagenet inheritance. The defence of Aquitaine was to assume a more significant place in the new king-duke's strategies and calculations than has often been supposed. Edward III's attitude towards his remaining continental possessions before the Hundred Years War demands fresh consideration.

## 7.2	The Defence of Aquitaine, 1326–1340

Historians have been in more or less general agreement that Gascon issues lay at the heart of Anglo-French conflict during the fourteenth century. 'Throughout Edward III's reign', writes one authority, 'the French insisted that the problem of Gascony was at the root of their dispute with the English.'[96] Other historians of the Hundred Years War, from Déprez and Tout to Perroy and MacIsack, pointed to the 'impossible position' in which Edward III found himself as a vassal of the French crown.[97] War, they argued, was becoming inevitable, and the war of St Sardos has been seen as the beginning of a 'cold war' between England and France which led directly to the Hundred Years War.[98] Much has been made by historians of Edward III's aggressive intentions towards France, and Déprez argued that he was 'preparing for war with constant care' from the outset of his reign.[99] Whether that war was to be defensive rather than offensive depended upon many issues, but a war for the defence of Aquitaine was increasingly likely in the 1330s. If the war could pay for itself, so much the better, and a conflict

---

[94] SC 8/284, no. 14152.

[95] Not only did nobles sustain losses but merchants such as Etienne Maynhau, bourgeois of Penne d'Agenais, who lost wine at St Livrade was imprisoned, ransomed and, he claimed, reduced to poverty. He dared not travel in areas subject to the French crown because he had trafficked with Edward II's subjects during the wars; SC 8/28, no. 14114; cf. *St Sardos*, pp. 106, 212.

[96] M. Prestwich, *The Three Edwards. War and State in England, 1272–1377* (London, 1980), p. 166.

[97] E. Déprez, *Les Préliminaires de la guerre de Cent Ans (1328–42)* (Paris, 1902), pp. 400, 403–6; T. F. Tout, *France and England: Their Relations in the Middle Ages and Now* (Manchester, 1922), pp. 114–15; E. Perroy, *The Hundred Years War*, trans. W. B. Wells (London, 1945), pp. 60–4; M. McIsack, *The Fourteenth Century*, (Oxford, 1959), pp. 105–8.

[98] J. Maddicott, 'The origins of the Hundred Years War', *HT*, xxxvi (1986), p. 35.

[99] Déprez, *Les Préliminaires*, p. 405.

funded by Gascon revenues and the profits of raiding and ransoming offered a potentially attractive prospect to Edward and his companions-in-arms. Military activity in Aquitaine therefore became more intensive during this period of 'cold war' between England and France. Déprez concluded that 'l'interêt capital de la guerre de Cent Ans à ses débuts, réside dans les négociations diplomatiques'. There was, he argued no 'grande guerre' until Crécy and the siege of Calais in 1346–7. But medieval land warfare did not favour the 'decisive' battles beloved of military historians – as we have seen, it followed a pattern of sieges and skirmishes.[100] Between 1326 and 1340, Anglo-French war in Aquitaine was of that nature, punctuated by truces and peace treaties, all destined to be broken.

A primary concern of the Plantagenet administration in the duchy remained the defence of Bordeaux. In April 1326 Edward II ordered the mayor and *jurats* to proceed with the utmost haste to complete the new *enceinte*, or ring of walls, around the city, as the king-duke had lent them money to do so.[101] The exposed island of Oléron, prone to French raids and surprise attacks, was also a source of anxiety and Gaillard de Fargues, esquire, was retained with men-at-arms, sailors and 145 foot-serjeants who served aboard galleys to defend the isle between March 1326 and March 1327.[102] There were also problems of treason and disaffection to be resolved in the wake of the St Sardos war. In March 1326 Oliver Ingham was empowered as seneschal to receive all former rebels and contrariants into the king-duke's grace and to pardon them, but was to be vigilant in the detection and seizure of traitors and conspirators.[103] Edward II's suspicions were not wholly unfounded, for war broke out again in the duchy between June and August 1326, and the seizure of all Frenchmen and their goods was ordered within his lands. Charles IV retaliated on 16 August.[104] By this time Edward's own regime in England was endangered, largely by the invasion planned by Isabella and her allies, which was feared to be a much larger venture than in fact materialized in September 1326. In Aquitaine, Ingham was gathering the nobility of the duchy against French aggressions there and Edward granted pardons to eleven nobles (mainly from the Agenais) for their former service to Charles IV in late August and early September. He referred to the 'detention' of Isabella and the young Edward in France and enjoined resistance on Guillaume, lord of Caumont, and other nobles *viriliter et animose*.[105] Confusion was caused by Isabella's behaviour, and a number of Gascon nobles and townsmen were warned by Edward that they should ignore letters from her because they 'contained certain things contrary to our

---

[100]See above, pp. 200–15, 236–42.
[101]C 61/38, m. 3ᵛ (4 April 1326); *Histoire de Bordeaux, III*, p. 225.
[102]E 36/78, p. 36. He was paid 4797 *l. 7 s ½ d.t.* for their services.
[103]C 61/38, m. 5 (March 1326).
[104]Fryde, *Tyranny and Fall*, p. 182.
[105]C 61/38, m. 5ᵛ (29 August 1326).

will'.[106] In a letter to his loyal towns dated 27 June 1326 the king-duke ordered them to obey only Ingham as his true representative, stressed his son's tender age and virtual captivity and, so that they might be sure that his present letters were authentic, sent them a French version under the privy seal as well as a Latin text under the great seal.[107] These cumbersome exercises in diplomatic were no doubt necessary, but hardly reflected much control by Edward over his wife, son and their counsellors. The basis of Edward's power was narrowing dangerously, but he hoped that the Gascons would be moved to act in the knowledge that the French had possession of his son and heir.

Charles IV was enabled to raise taxes from his subjects as a result of the renewed outbreak of war. In October 1326 he told the barons and others in Mâcon, Lyon and the duchy of Burgundy that an assembly held at Meaux had promised him 'certaine aide' to resist Edward II on land and sea. As was normal, *réformateurs* were to be sent to levy the tax and to redress any grievances held by the inhabitants against royal officers.[108] War in the south-west evoked requests from Charles IV's subjects to fortify their dwellings and to be exempted from war taxes. In June 1326, the inhabitants of the *bastide* at Luc-de-Bigorre were granted the right to fortify their town, for it lay on the frontiers of the *comtés* of Astarac, Armagnac and Comminges, close to Béarn and the duchy of Aquitaine. An enclosure of stakes, ditches and a moat was to be constructed for the settlement was in a very exposed position.[109] On the other side, Ingham's administration concentrated upon the defence of selected strongholds, such as Penne d'Agenais, Dax and the castles and towns which lay along the southern boundaries of the duchy. At Penne a large garrison was retained, including an English maker of banners and standards called Master William of Winchelsea, who worked them with heraldic devices between 11 June 1326 and 8 March 1327.[110] At Dax, the *prévôt*, Raymond de Vaux, served in the town garrison with six men-at-arms and thirty foot-serjeants during the same period, and received 600 *l.t.* to effect an exchange of prisoners with the French in June 1327.[111] Individuals on both sides evidently made private profit from the situation: Raymond de Vaux, for example, had captured Menaud de Testa (alias the Borc de Montpezat), a valuable prisoner, for whose exchange he received compensation from Ingham.[112] One price of loyalty was the pursuit of profit, as well as honour,

---

[106]C 61/38, m. 6ᵛ (23 September 1326).

[107]C 61/38, m. 4ᵛ (27 June 1326). The letters were sent to Bordeaux, Bayonne, Sorde, Libourne, St Sever, Bonnegarde, Dax, Hastingues, Labourt, Pimbo, St Emilion, St Macaire, Penne, Bourg and St Gien.

[108]AN, J 634, no. 18 (20 October 1326); and JJ 64, fos 18ᵛ–19ᵛ for an agreement with the consuls of towns in Rivière-Basse to raise subsidies for the war of St Sardos (18 January 1325).

[109]AN, JJ 64, fo. 104ᵛ (June 1326).

[110]E 101/165/8, A, unnumbered; E, unnumbered; G, unnumbered; 166/1, fo. 83ʳ.

[111]E 101/165/6, D, no. 6 (15 May 1327).

[112]E 101/165/6, D, no. 51 (6 June 1327).

and the survival of the Plantagenet regime partly depended upon it. The payment of debts to Gascon nobles for their services and losses in war continued to exercise Ingham and John de Weston, constable of Bordeaux, who had apparently received an ultimatum from a large group of 'barons and nobles' on 24 April 1327, pointing out the danger of disinheritance to the king-duke if such payments were not made. Ingham referred to the 'unbridled perseverance' of these nobles and ordered immediate satisfaction, at least in part, of their demands.[113]

A previous peace-making attempt, through the mediation of Henri de Sully, had failed to produce a settlement between England and France in July 1325, although Edward had agreed to Sully's appointment as interim seneschal of Aquitaine as a concession to Charles IV.[114] Ingham replaced him in October and it was not until February 1327 that a truce, followed by a peace proposal in March, was established. The lands and goods confiscated from alien priories during the war were to be restored (4 February 1327), but preparations for further warfare in Aquitaine were still being considered.[115] Edward III wrote to the seneschal of Aquitaine and constable of Bordeaux on 27 February, urging them to continue negotiations for military aid from certain Aragonese nobles, because there was as yet no certainty that peace would be made between him and Charles IV.[116] Edward was anxious that these overtures should not be broken off. He was also concerned that old resentments in Aquitaine should be forgiven, pardons issued and lands restored to his loyal subjects there. But caution and dissimulation were essential. The possibility of further French aggression in the duchy was in fact very real, and a budget for a proposed invasion of Aquitaine in 1327 has survived among the papers of Charles IV's Burgundian counsellor, Miles de Noyers.[117] It advises Charles IV about a war in the south-west, 'supposing that war is made', estimating that a total of 843,900 *l.t.* was required to wage war for fourteen months, excluding the cost of supplies and provisions obtained in the Toulousain, Agenais and Albigeois 'from rich prelates and abbeys', so that the common people might be spared. The estimated total annual revenues of the French crown at this time were 275,609 *l.t.*, so that the proposed war expenditure was over three times the annual receipts of the monarchy.[118] Without heavy taxation – of the kind which developed during

---

[113]E 101/165/5/ G, no. 4; 165/10, N, no. 2. The notarial instrument in which the requests of the barons and nobles were made, dated 24 April 1327, does not appear to survive.

[114]C 61/38, m. 7 (13 July 1325); see above, p. 229.

[115]*Foedera*, II, ii, pp. 684–5, 693–4.

[116]C 61/39, m. 6 (27 February 1327); SC 1/38, no. 33 for an Aragonese noble's petition on this subject.

[117]M. Jusselin, 'Comment la France se préparait à la guerre de Cent Ans', *BEC*, lxxiii (1912), pp. 211, 213, 220–1.

[118]See H. Moranvillé, 'Rapports à Philippe VI sur l'état de ses finances', *BEC*, xlviii (1887), pp. 382–3.

the Hundred Years War – a prolonged campaign in Aquitaine was scarcely feasible.

However, negotiations in the spring and summer of 1327 barely affected the state of war, punctuated by armed truces, in the duchy. The marshal of France, Robert-Bertrand de Briquebec, was besieging the castle of Madaillan in May 1327, moving on to La Réole in August and September, where he eventually negotiated terms with the commissioners appointed to hand over castles and other places occupied by Anglo-Gascon forces.[119] On 16 September Sir John Hausted, seneschal of Aquitaine, sent messengers to proclaim the 'peace' between England and France at certain places in the duchy.[120] The settlement was not particularly favourable to Edward III. Its financial clauses were particularly onerous, requiring payment of the 60,000 *l.t.* relief demanded for Edward's seisin of the duchy in 1325 plus an indemnity of 50,000 marks for French losses during the war.[121] Charles IV was to hold the Agenais and much of the Bazadais. Sentences of banishment from the realm of France, pronounced against Edward's subjects in Aquitaine, were now subject to an amnesty, although its terms were disputed. Banishment had obliged Edward to remove Ingham from the seneschalship, and he was not to be reappointed until June 1331.[122] The other banished Gascons were those who had been conspicuously loyal to the Plantagenet regime during the St Sardos war and its sequel: Arnaud-Guillaume de Béarn, lord of Lescun, Bertrand Caillau, Anessans and Guillaume de Caumont, Rainfroi de Durfort, Amanieu de Fossat, Guillaume de Galard, Gerard de Tastes, Raymond-Bernard de Ste-Foy and other nobles.[123] Although banished from the kingdom of France, some of these men, including Arnaud-Guillaume de Béarn and Amanieu de Fossat, were paid wages and compensation by the constable of Bordeaux. Anessans de Caumont promised to absent himself but claimed wages for men-at-arms and foot-serjeants to defend his lordships during his absence.[124] These were duly paid, and his loyalty thereby assured.

The course of diplomatic proceedings during this period has been described in detail by Déprez, Cuttino and other scholars and I do not intend to retrace their steps here.[125] The young Edward III was not fully master in

[119]AN, JJ 66, fo. 386ʳ (24 May 1327); APA, E 27, no. 8 (7 August 1327), where he received an oath of fealty from Bernard-Ezi d'Albret.

[120]E 101/309/36, m. 3. Hausted was communicating with Briquebec in August and September (mm. 1–2).

[121]Déprez, *Les Préliminaires*, pp. 59–60; *Foedera*, II, ii, pp. 693–4.

[122]C 61/39, m. 3 (1 June 1327) for the pardon issued by Edward to Ingham for all actions committed by him in Aquitaine or elsewhere under Edward II. He was again appointed seneschal on 29 June 1331 (C 61/43, m. 10).

[123]Déprez, *Les Préliminaires*, p. 56, n. 3; C 61/39, m. 3.

[124]C 61/40, m. 1 (10 December 1328); C 47/24/4, no. 2 (17 September 1327); E 36/78, pp. 22, 25, 27; SC 8/282, nos 14061–2; E 101/165/5, E, no. 8.

[125]Déprez, *Les Préliminaires*, pp. 38–82; Cuttino, *English Diplomatic Administration*, pp. 100–11.

his own house until the fall of Isabella and Mortimer in October and November 1330. His external relations often bore the stamp of others' machinations and we can never be certain that the king-duke's own wishes were expressed and executed until after that date. The accession of Philip VI of Valois to the French throne in May 1328 was probably the most significant event in this confused and confusing phase of Anglo-French relations. The new reign witnessed increasing pressure on the Plantagenet regime, expressed by the assertion of sovereignty over Aquitaine in various guises. Threats to confiscate the duchy if Edward III's activities elsewhere – in the Low Countries, the Franco-imperial borderland or Scotland – harmed Valois interests were frequently applied. A far greater degree of interference than hitherto in Edward III's affairs as duke of Aquitaine was reflected in the letters issued by the French Chancery after 1328.[126] Edward's actions in Aquitaine were thus increasingly subject to unwelcome intervention by the French monarchy. There was an increasing element of threat and duress behind Anglo-French diplomatic dealings after 1328, prompted partly by the strength of the Valois monarchy but also by its relative weakness.

In one sense, the French were clearly in a position of supremacy. They held the Agenais and subjected Edward III's officers in Aquitaine to such humiliations as the loss of powers to appoint officials (such as the *prévôt* of Bazas) which had previously been within their competence.[127] Safeguards and protections to those supporters of the French crown who were menaced and harrassed by their neighbours flowed forth in profusion. At Langon the French imposed a *maltôte* of 10 *s.t.* on every tun of wine and forbade the wine merchants to sell their wares to anyone who would export it to England.[128] Loyalists such as the Servat family of Port-Ste-Marie in the Agenais were liberally rewarded for their sufferings 'for the good of the French crown'. Gaillard and Bernard Servat were also pardoned by Philip VI on 20 January 1336 for excesses committed during a nocturnal *charivari* outside the house of a newly married inhabitant of the town, in which they had illicitly borne arms. The French seneschal of the Agenais confirmed that no deaths or woundings had taken place and all penalties against them were thus remitted.[129] Men who had formerly been subject to the jurisdiction of the king-duke of Aquitaine now escaped it entirely. Financially, Edward III was in a difficult position. Non-performance of his homage to the newly elected Philip VI might entail seizure of the duchy's revenues as well as confiscation of Aquitaine. An assembly of peers and barons of France, reported by the *Grandes Chroniques* in 1328, declared that Philip should not confiscate the duchy for default of homage, but could sequestrate Edward's revenues there

---

[126]See *La Gascogne dans les Régistres du Trésor des Chartes*, ed. C. Samaran (Paris, 1966), nos 403, 416, 442, 513, 514, 520, 523, 529.

[127]APA, E 27, no. 1 (8 April 1328).

[128]SC 8/283, no. 14105.

[129]AN, JJ 66, fo. 17ʳ (March 1329); JJ 69, fo. 111ᵛ (20 January 1336).

until the ceremony had taken place.[130] Given the value of the territory, this was no small matter. When the unpaid relief and indemnity for war losses was added to this, Edward stood to lose a very substantial sum. He was therefore constrained to pay homage, sooner rather than later, to Philip of Valois.

In the second place, it could be argued that the assertion of sovereignty over Aquitaine was partly a product of Philip VI's relative weakness. The new Valois monarch was in effect an elected king, his title was open to contest, and a show of strength might therefore be thought imperative. By demanding homage for Aquitaine, Philip could demonstrate his authority to the other magnates who had chosen him as Charles IV's successor. Like the young Edward III, Philip was not 'absolute master of decisions' made in his name during his early years. He represented the Valois interest at the court of France, inherited his father's policies and promoted the hegemony of Burgundy in the early 1330s.[131] Contemporary observers remarked upon the limitations imposed on Philip's authority by powerful interests. In c.1329, an English diplomatic memorandum, probably drawn up by Master Henry of Canterbury, observed that:

> the king of France's power is so restricted that he is unable to restore lands and franchises recently seized into the hands of his predecessor [Charles IV] by force of arms to our . . . lord [Edward III] . . . without the assent of the inhabitants of the said lands and of the peers of France.[132]

Philip, it was claimed, was not powerful enough to prevent his own officers, the peers of France and the presidents of the Paris Parlement from intervening in Aquitaine. These attitudes handicapped Anglo-French relations. A later memorandum dating from May 1333 alleged that the personnel of his Chambre des Comptes were preventing the king from administering justice to English merchants.[133] If Philip IV found his counsellors and courtiers difficult to control in 1294, Philip VI's fundamental insecurity lay in his obligations to those who had chosen him and in the growth of powerful interests within his own bureaucracy. His lawyers were easily bribed: in 1334–5, Master Jean Amici was paid by the constable of Bordeaux for obtaining letters and *arrêts* from the Parlement and for 'dinners and gifts to the advocates, *huissiers* and other officials of the French court . . . to expedite [Edward III's] business more profitably there'.[134] In the duchy itself, officials of the seneschal of Périgord were once again found to be

---

[130]Déprez, *Les Préliminaires*, p. 40.

[131]R. Cazelles, *La Société politique et la crise de la royauté sous Philippe de Valois* (Paris, 1958), pp. 71, 435.

[132]C 47/28/5, no. 18.

[133]Cazelles, *La Société politique*, pp. 72–3.

[134]E 101/166/5, m. 7.

persuadable by material inducements: Ingham paid bribes to a French serjeant-at-arms to refrain from implementing a fine on the king-duke, to the treasurer of Agenais's lieutenant and to two French notaries charged with recording the restitution of lands seized in the last Gascon war because 'they acted courteously [*curialiter*] and obligingly [*benigne*]'.[135] When the most skilled advocates of the Parlement (such as Eudes de Sens or Guillame de Breuil, author of the *Stilus curie Parliamenti*) pleaded cases for the king-duke of Aquitaine, and sometimes won them, the exercise of Valois sovereignty could be undermined in the king's own court.[136] A display of extrajudicial authority was therefore desirable.

An alternative means of demonstrating Valois authority, and emphasizing the new dynasty's affinity with the Capetians, was the vigorous espousal of crusading schemes. To some extent, pressure upon the Plantagenet presence in Aquitaine between 1329 and 1336 was relieved by Philip's preoccupation with the Crusade.[137] If there was to be no Valois-led Crusade, a war with England might serve as an alternative method of promoting Philip's superiority. But the first objective was to gain a firm acknowledgement of Edward III's vassalic status as duke of Aquitaine. As is well known, Edward paid simple homage to Philip at Amiens on 6 June 1329, largely, it seems, as a means of preventing a French invasion of the duchy.[138] Plans had certainly been made in February–March for a Gascon campaign, in which 5000 men-at-arms and 16,000 infantry from France and Languedoc were to serve, at a total cost to Philip VI of about 455,000 *l.t.*[139] At the same time Edward III was preparing to resist an expected invasion of Aquitaine, and an expeditionary force was assembled in England. Oliver Ingham and Simon de Bereford were commissioned to lead the army, but the expedition was called off and the fines taken for non-performance of military service were pardoned.[140] On 25 March 1329 Philip VI told the seneschal of Beaucaire to levy an aid for war against the English, as Edward III was 'disobedient and rebellious', refusing to pay homage for Aquitaine.[141] Edward meanwhile gathered together all documents concerning Anglo-French relations, including interviews between kings and the homage of the counts of Armagnac.[142]

[135]E 101/166/5, mm. 16, 17.

[136]See above, p. 241; AN, JJ 66, fo. 38ᵛ (2 July 1329) for Breuil's annual pension of 100 *l.t.* from Jean I of Armagnac. See also R. Delachenal, *Histoire des avocats au Parlement de Paris, 1300–1600* (Paris, 1885), pp. 340–1; and *Stilus curie Parliamenti*, ed. F. Aubert (Paris, 1909), pp. i–iv, 99, 179: 'ita fuit obtentum per magistrum Guillelmum de Breolio pro duce Acquitanie'.

[137]See C. J. Tyerman, 'Philip VI and the recovery of the Holy Land', *EHR*, c (1985), pp. 25–52, esp. p. 49: 'while the prospect lasted, the crusade restrained overt hostilities between England and France'.

[138]AN, J 634, no. 21 (6 June 1329); Déprez, *Les Préliminaires*, pp. 44–6.

[139]Jusselin, 'Comment la France se préparait', pp. 222–8.

[140]See SC 8/285, no. 14228.

[141]AN, J 918, no. 20 (25 March 1329).

[142]*Foedera*, II, ii, p. 761 (22 April 1329).

In the event the meeting in Amiens cathedral on 6 June put an end to the preparations and deprived Philip of a war tax.

The homage ceremony did not put an end to the problem of restitutions in Aquitaine. It was proving impossible to restore the pre-1324 position because dispossessions carried out during the St Sardos war could not be satisfactorily resolved. An agreement was eventually reached at Bois-de-Vincennes on 8 May 1330, but it remained unfulfilled until September, when Philip VI issued a virtual ultimatum to Edward III.[143] Edward was to perform liege homage or lose his inheritance, while Philip reserved to himself the Agenais and other French-occupied territories. Disorder in England and the imminent fall of Mortimer ruled out resistance on Edward's part. On 20 September 1330 he wrote to his Gascon officials telling them to offer no resistance to French officers sent to execute the terms of the Vincennes agreement. Edward was beginning to display evidence of diplomatic skill and the effective use of dissimulation. He told Hausted and other officers in the duchy to

> soeffrez, si debonnerement, par bel parler, les execucions, sans y mettre grant debat on resistence, nient necessaire, pur paisser la malice de temps, *issint que nous puissoms autrefoitz empescher mesmes les execucions, quant nous averoms plus grant covenablete de temps* et que par tiele dissimulation, nous et nos subgetz puissaent escheure les sodeins damages qu'ils purront resceivre.[144]

Edward was playing for time, and there was little doubt that he considered the terms agreed upon in May 1330 as little more than formal but temporary assurances which might in due course be relinquished. The subsequent agreement on 30 March 1331, in which he acknowledged that his homage should be considered liege, although he never attended a homage ceremony, was also nothing more than a diplomatic device to secure his lordship over Aquitaine. Edward stated that 'although [at Amiens in 1329] we performed homage in general terms it was, is and should be understood as liege, and that we should give him [Philip VI] faith and loyalty'.[145] The French were especially concerned to confirm the authenticity of this statement, and the document in which it was expressed, at later stages of the Hundred Years War.[146] Three days before his letter was written at Eltham on 30 March, Edward wrote to the constable of Bordeaux, ordering him to send him information about the state of Aquitaine, so that the duchy might be better set in order and reduced to good government. He was especially concerned by its financial state and in July replaced Pierre de Galician with John

---

[143] AN, J 635, no. 1; Déprez, *Les Préliminaires*, pp. 59–61, 63, 64.

[144] *Foedera*, II, iii, pp. 50–1 (20 September 1330) (Italics mine).

[145] AN, J 635, no. 2 (30 March 1331); *Foedera*, II, ii, p. 61.

[146] AN, J 635, no. 6 (inspeximus of 9 March 1340).

Travers as constable of Bordeaux.[147] Travers was ordered not to honour any bills or recognizances of debts issued to creditors by his predecessor, for the king-duke needed the money for 'certain difficult matters'. In any case, the constable's debts were as much as the duchy's revenues would yield for long into the future. On 29 June 1331 Sir Oliver Ingham began the last phase of his somewhat chequered career when he was appointed seneschal of Aquitaine for a second term of office.[148] Ingham had supported Mortimer's regime and his presence in England was perhaps not pleasing to the king, who had recently arrested Ingham. He was to serve his way back into favour in an area where his military and administrative expertise had already been put to the test. On 15 July Edward ordered Ingham and Travers to conduct an inquiry into office-holding in the duchy and to remove all unsuitable and incompetent officers.[149] A degree of personal control by the king-duke was now being exercised and he had chosen agents of ability and experience to implement his desires. While acknowledging the duchy's tenure by a form of homage which was never actually paid to Philip VI, Edward had not only retained his continental inheritance but left the way open for a more confident assertion of his own claims when the time was ripe.

A strengthening of bonds with the nobility of the duchy was also imperative. From March 1328 onwards, Edward attempted to consolidate existing alliances, recruit new allies and pardon former rebels among the Gascon nobility. He was determined to recover his rights and inheritances in the duchy but was prepared to bide his time. This might be done *quand temps sera*.[150] By September 1328, he had promised to indemnify members of the Albret, Armagnac and Foix-Béarn families so that they might aid him to recover his 'rights and inheritances in the kingdom of France and duchy of Aquitaine'.[151] Lands lost or damaged by war with France were to be restored or an equivalent sum given to them, and they were to be included in all truces made with Edward's enemies. In September 1330 nobles of the Agenais were wooed with pardons for their previous behaviour which, Edward declared, had been the result of a *fait accompli* and the application of duress by the French.[152] During the St Sardos war the leading members of the senior branches of Albret, Armagnac and Foix-Béarn had served the French. Edward III could not rely upon any of them to support him in the

---

[147]C 61/43, m. 15 (27 March 1331); m. 12 (5 July 1331); m. 4 (30 November 1331). Pierre de Galician petitioned Edward III for his losses in Edward II's service, including his capture by the French and the destruction of his 'manors and vines'. He claimed to have lost ecclesiastical benefices worth 1000 *l.t.* per year (SC 8/287, no. 14305).

[148]C 61/43, m. 10 (29 June and 15 July 1331).

[149]C 61/43, m. 12 (15 July 1331). Ingham had been arrested, with Mortimer and Simon de Bereford, during the Nottingham Parliament of October 1330 (Déprez, *Les Préliminaires*, p. 71, n. 9). For Ingham's earlier pardon see above, n. 122.

[150]*Foedera*, II, ii, pp. 736, 737 (28 March 1328).

[151]C 61/40, mm. 2, 3 (16 September 1328).

[152]C 61/42, m. 4 (17 September 1330).

south-west. It was fortunate that all these houses had important political concerns outside the duchy during the 1330s: Albret and Foix in the Crusading schemes of Philip VI and the war against the Moors in Granada; Armagnac in the wars of the Italian peninsula where he fought for John of Luxembourg, king of Bohemia.[153] In the course of the wars Jean I of Armagnac was captured by the Este of Ferrara and ransomed for the enormous sum of 42,760 *réaux d'or* (17,000 *l.t.*). In July 1334 Jean appointed representatives to negotiate a loan for the repayment of his ransom from Bernard-Ezi d'Albret and, on 20 December, he recognized that he owed Albret not merely the 20,000 *réaux d'or* loaned him for his ransoming but a further 21,760 *réaux* as the residue of his sister's dowry.[154] Mathe d'Armagnac had married Albret but was still owed her dowry. Armagnac was deeply in debt to many creditors, who had begun to seize and detain his possessions in Armagnac and Fézensac. Philip VI intervened and placed the two *comtés* in royal custody, so that aids could be taken from the count's men there to pay off his debts to Albret.[155] It was not surprising that Armagnac's political behaviour was to a large extent determined by his relationship to Albret. Armagnac's indebtedness helped to precipitate a crisis in Anglo-French relations which was to lead to war.

In September 1334 a 'process' held at Langon, between representatives of Edward III and Philip VI, broke up in disarray.[156] One of the issues that prompted its collapse was the refusal of the Plantagenets' proctors to surrender the lordships of Blanquefort and Veyrines to the French crown.[157] These were lordships in the Bordelais previously held by Bertrand de Goth, and inherited by Jean I of Armagnac from his wife Régine. On 26 March 1335, an agreement was reached between Jean I and Philip VI's counsellors Guillaume Flote, lord of Ravel, and Guy Cherier that Philip and his heirs should hold all Armagnac's rights in the *vicomtés* of Lomagne and Auvillars, with the lordships and castles of Blanquefort, Veyrines 'without the *maison-forte*', Villandraut, Montségur and other strongholds in the dioceses of Bordeaux and Bazas.[158] The de Goth inheritance was to be annexed to the French crown and distributed to Philip's allies and supporters in Aquitaine. Armagnac was to be compensated with the *comté* of Gaure in the *sénéchaussée* of Toulouse, held from the French crown in liege homage, from which an annual revenue of at least 2000 *l.t.* would be forthcoming. All fines imposed

---

[153]Tyerman, 'Philip VI and the recovery of the Holy Land', pp. 26–7; *Chroniques romanes des comtes de Foix composées au xve siècle par Arnaud Esquerrier et Miègeville*, ed. F. Pasquier and H. Courteault (Foix, Paris, Toulouse and Pons, 1895), pp. 49–51. See above, pp. 130–1.

[154]APA, E 28, nos 18 (at Ferrara, July 1334), 20 (at Paris, 20 December 1334); E 240, no. 3.

[155]APA, E 240, no. 8 (9 December 1334).

[156]Cuttino, 'The process of Agen', p. 170; C 47/30/3/8.

[157]See AN, JJ 70, nos 78, 170.

[158]AN, J 298, no. 5 (at Avignon, 26 March 1335). The agreement was confirmed by Philip VI at Paris on 13 November 1336. It was annulled in August 1343 (no. 6). See above, pp. 94–6.

upon Armagnac for alleged disobedience and damage to the king's officers in
the Toulousain, Bigorre and Rivière-Basse were remitted. Philip VI proceeded to distribute that portion of the de Goth inheritance which lay at the
heart of Plantagenet Aquitaine in October 1336. Blanquefort was awarded to
Aymeric de Durfort, lord of Duras in the Agenais, a middling baron of
considerable authority in the south-west.[159] As Blanquefort lay very near to
Bordeaux and, claimed Philip, was held from the crown of France 'without
intermediate lord', it was deemed 'necessary and profitable' to defend it in
this way against aggressors. The royal grant stated:

> that should it happen in future that war or threat of war should arise between us
> or our heirs . . . and the duke of Aquitaine and his heirs, by reason of which it
> should be necessary to garrison and defend our castles in that land, which God
> forbid, we and our heirs . . . shall be held to furnish to the said Aymeric . . . five
> men-at-arms and 15 foot-serjeants . . . for as long as the war shall last . . . and to
> pay their wages.[160]

By a second grant, similarly dated at Bois-de-Vincennes in October 1336,
Philip gave Durfort Villandraut and Veyrines, but retained all lands and
goods which had escheated to him through rebellion at Villandraut and
Blanquefort.[161] Some of these were already in his possession, but others were
to be recovered as a result of agreements made with the duke of Aquitaine.
Durfort was to hold all these lordships in liege homage from the crown of
France. In effect, such measures brought the direct lordship and sovereign
authority of the French crown into the very heart of Edward III's duchy. His
proctors at Langon in 1334 had understandably refused to surrender these
lordships, and there were also local interests opposed to such high-handed
actions on Philip's part. Amanieu de Vayres, lord of Montferrand, was not
slow to raise his protest at Armagnac's 'usurpation' of his rights to Veyrines
and their subsequent assumption by the French crown.[162] Not until the
Durfort showed themselves loyal vassals of Edward III were the former
lordships of Bertrand de Goth to be securely held by them.

Philip VI's intentions in Aquitaine were further exemplified in an agreement made between him and Gaston II, count of Foix, on 23 October
1336.[163] For a sum of 3000 *l.t.* Gaston was to provide 100 men-at-arms and

[159] See *Documents sur la maison de Durfort (xi*ᵉ*–xv*ᵉ *siècles)*, ed. N. de Peña, pp. xxv–xxvi, and nos 730, 788, 810; see above, pp. 101–2, 105.
[160] AN, JJ 70, fo. 38ʳ (at Bois-de-Vincennes, October 1336).
[161] AN, JJ 70, fos 37ᵛ–38ʳ (October 1336). For the castles at Blanquefort, Villandraut and Veyrines see above, pp. 106–7.
[162] SC 8/282, no. 1469. Blanquefort passed to the cadet branch of the Durfort, who were in Edward III's allegiance. See *Documents sur la maison de Durfort*, pp. xxxi–xxxii; C 61/49, m. 12 (27 August 1337) for Arnaud de Durfort as captain of Penne for Edward.
[163] AN, J 332, no. 17ᵇⁱˢ (23 October 1336, witnessed by Gaston II on 26 October).

500 infantry for two months' service commencing on 24 November 1336. The agreement was to come into force 'if we shall have need of them in Gascony, and if we do not have war there within the said two months, the said 3000 *l.t.* shall remain in the hands of the count or of those to whom he shall have given them'. Gaston was also to serve Philip with all his vassals from Béarn, 'at our pleasure during the wars which we shall wage, if any shall take place, within two years from the date of these present letters, in the parts of Gascony'.[164]

The fact that two of Gaston's Béarnais vassals – Fortaner, lord of Lescun, and Raymond, lord of Miossens – were said to be outside the agreement left little doubt as to whom the wars were to be directed against. Lescun and Miossens were vassals of Edward III as duke of Aquitaine for lands they held in the duchy. Gaston promised Philip VI, however, that he would try to win them over to the best of his ability.[165] It seems clear that by attempting to establish an immediate presence within Aquitaine, excluding the king-duke from lordship over castles and strongpoints in the Bordelais and Bazadais, and by recruiting substantial military aid against Edward III from one of the great Pyrenean houses, the aims of the Valois monarchy in the autumn of 1336 were in no way peaceable. Much has been made in the past of Edward III's war preparations at this time, but the other side was also laying its plans and marshalling its resources in Aquitaine.

There is evidence for an intensification of military activity in the duchy during the years 1335–6. Between 17 April and 29 September 1335 Niccolo Usumare, the Genoese constable of Bordeaux, inspected ducal castles and other fortresses with 'a great company of horse and foot', and supervised their victualling and defensive equipment.[166] At the castle of Montendre in the Charente, the keeper of victuals and artillery was paid the costs of retaining 140 foot-serjeants during the same period and meeting the dangers ensuing from any aggressive actions. Repairs to the castle were under way in 1335, including the rebuilding of a ruined wall, the construction of a new tower and repairs to the hall.[167] Works were also undertaken at Penne, Puymirol and St Macaire, while between September 1335 and September 1336, a new crenellated wall-walk was constructed at the barbican of Montendre castle and a well was dug next to that outwork.[168] Montendre stood in an exposed position, guarding one of the northern approaches to the

---

[164] AN, J 332, no. 17[bis]; Monlezun, *Histoire de Gascogne*, vi, pp. 188–9 for Foix's musters for Philip VI. By October 1338 he was owed 28, 842 *l.t.* for his military service by the king (AN, J 332, no. 17[1]).

[165] See C 61/50, m. 4 (January 1338); C 61/49, m. 5 (12 September 1337) for Miossens's defence of the castle of Mauléon-de-Soule against the French. Gaston II of Foix was granted Mauléon by Philip VI in November 1339, but only if he could conquer it at his own expense from Edward III: APA, E 355, no. 9 (at Vincennes, November 1339).

[166] E 101/166/5, m. 11. He was paid 65 *l.b.* for twenty-six days' service between those dates.

[167] E 101/166/5, mm. 12, 18–19.

[168] E 101/166/8, no. 2.

duchy, and the expenditure incurred there was not to be in vain. Crossbows, supplies and other defensive weapons were bought for Blaye, Bourg, Bordeaux, Penne, Puymirol, St Macaire and the former castle of Jourdain de L'Isle at Casaubon at the same time.[169] Edward III was sufficiently concerned for the duchy's security in August 1336 that he ordered Ingham to forbid all men-at-arms to leave it without his licence, for it would be gravely endangered if troops were lacking.[170]

An intensification of French jurisdictional activity could also be observed at this time. In July 1334 the abbot and convent of La Sauve-Majeure in the Entre-deux-Mers recognized that the monastery and its daughter-houses were held immediately from Philip VI, although Edward III's proctor in the Paris Parlement objected that the king-duke possessed rights over the abbey.[171] Philip VI took the house and its *membra* into his special protection on 13 August 1335, reasserting the claim that they were directly subject to his lordship.[172] A roll of charges against French officers in the *sénéchaussées* of Périgord, Quercy and Limousin, which was delivered to Master Raymond Durand, Edward III's Gascon lawyer, and probably dates from 1336, also survives.[173] Durand had himself lost a lordship in the Toulousain through confiscation in 1327 and certified that the incursions listed in the roll were true. At St Astier, Beauregard, Limeuil and Roffignac, the king-duke's rights had been violated, and the French seneschal of Périgord had cited his subjects before him and condemned them for non-appearance. Bergerac castle had been seized early in 1336[174] and a castellan appointed, while one of the king-duke's subjects had been condemned to death for sorcery, a crime which, it was claimed, fell within the king-duke's jurisdiction. Four others had been condemned to death and their lands seized, and the French seneschal of Périgord had erected gallows at St Astier, Beauregard and Molières, while complex jurisdictional issues were unresolved in the *bailliage* of Villefranche. Edward II had been assigned 3000 *l.t.* in rents there but these had never been handed over, and appeals had been obstructed by Philip VI's proctors. It was clear that pressure of a new and intolerable kind was being exerted upon the Plantagenet administration in Aquitaine and upon its representatives at Paris.

This was borne out by events at the court of France in the spring and summer of 1336. After Pope Benedict XII's refusal to support his enterprise in March, Philip VI's Crusading fleet was transferred from Marseilles to the

---

[169]E 101/166/8, no. 2. A total sum of 275 *l.* 12 *s.* 6 *d.b.* were spent on munitions.

[170]*Foedera* II, ii, p. 944 (20 August 1336).

[171]AN, X^{1a}7, fo. 47^v (4 July 1334).

[172]AN, JJ fo. 3^r (13 August 1335).

[173]E 30/137, mm. 1–2. In March 1334 and April 1335, Master William Brun, Edward III's proctor, was at Libourne replying to summonses by French officials in the *sénéchaussées* of Périgord and Quercy (E 101/166/5, m. 6).

[174]APA, E 622, no. 33; E 30/1374, mm. 1, 2.

Norman ports,[175] Edward III's reactions to this event, mobilizing his resources in the Channel Islands and putting the English coast into a state of
readiness for war, are well known.[176] Richard de Bury, Edward's former
tutor and close adviser, began a diplomatic mission to Paris on 12 July 1336
to treat with Philip VI over Anglo-Scots truces.[177] On 11 August he paid a
messenger for taking letters to England informing the king and his counsellors of the manner of proceeding in the council of France and warning them
of the 'extraordinary requests' (*peticionibus mirabilibus*) made by the councils of
France and Scotland. The English feared that the letter might be intercepted
by the French, and duplicates were made which were to be taken under the
guarantee of the Italian banking house of Bardi. On 12 August Bury sent a
spy to the Norman ports to discover the state of French ships and galleys
there, while on 8 August a king's esquire was dispatched to Burgundy (from
which Edward was anxious to recruit allies) to discover the state of the war
there between the duke and Jean de Châlon. The 'final reply' of Philip VI
and his council to Edward's envoys was sent to England on 20 August, and
the messenger was empowered to tell the king and council *vive voce* those
things which Bury dared not write about the defence of the realm.

War was by now virtually unavoidable. Edward's representatives at the
Paris Parlement were subject to threats and assaults, and Masters John Piers
and Andrew Ufford refused to take charge of cases there surrendered by the
aged Elias Johnston.[178] The French had begun so many actions against
Edward's subjects that the seneschal of Aquitaine was unable to defend their
liberties and privileges without fear of banishment from the realm of France.
Gascon nobles were about to be coerced into obedience to Philip VI, on pain
of disinheritance and banishment. Elias Johnston had prepared a statement,
to be made 'at his peril' before the court of France, in which he alleged that
French officers were behaving in such a way that 'the sovereignty which your
[Edward III's] ancestors were wont to have in ... Gascony' was breached.[179]
Unless a speedy solution was found, Gascon castles and towns which refused
entry to French officials faced imminent annexation to the French crown.
Johnston feared that Edward would have to buy his way back into Philip VI's
favour by payment of 100,000 marks in unpaid fines and indemnities. A dam-
aging peace with the Scots was also necessary, and greater subjection to the
French crown in Aquitaine was unavoidable unless 'competent clerks' could
be found who were willing to defend Edward's interests. But it was unlikely

---

[175]Tyerman, 'Philip VI and the recovery of the Holy Land', pp. 44–47, 48; Déprez, *Les
Préliminaires*, pp. 127–35.

[176]*Foedera*, II, ii, pp. 150, 153–4.

[177]E 101/311/22 for his account (12 July–13 September 1336) and for the following sentences.

[178]C 47/30/5, no. 14; printed by G. C. Cuttino, 'Historical revision: the causes of the Hundred
Years War', *Speculum*, xxxi (1956), pp. 476–7.

[179]Cuttino, 'Historical revision', p. 476: 'en blemissement de la sovereinte que voz auncestres
soloient aver en ... Gascoigne'.

that such would come forward, and Johnston declined to remain in office as Keeper of the Processes.

Anglo-French diplomacy had collapsed in 1336. The two kingdoms were precipitated into war by many issues, not least of which was the appeal and rebellion of Garcie-Arnaud, lord of Sault-de-Navailles. The appeal of Navailles against Edward III stemmed from a fine of 31,000 *l.t.* apparently imposed by Philip the Fair on Edward I for damages sustained by Navailles's father in Edward I's French war.[180] The English claimed in 1336 that the fine had been pardoned and remitted but could not find reference to it in any 'peace or pact' with France. If the parlement's *arrêt* on the matter were opposed, then a general proclamation of arms would be made by the French in the duchy of Aquitaine, as they had done in the case of the castle of Montpezat in 1324.[181] Edward III's proctors at Paris were most anxious to avoid an inquiry into the war of 1294–8, because they felt that this would prejudice the king-duke's position and lead to additional French demands for payment of the remainder of the 600,000 *l.t.* required for damages sustained by Philip the Fair's subjects before the outbreak of war in 1294. To probe into pre-war damages was to 'enter upon a great sea', for Boniface VIII's arbitration of Anglo-France disputes as a private person in 1298 had required Edward I to compensate Philip the Fair for all damages done on land and sea to his subjects, including Navailles, before the war of 1294.[182] Navailles was declared a rebel by Edward III, and his possessions in the duchy were confiscated, but he died shortly afterwards.[183] He was among the very last Gascon appellants to the French crown before the severing of all feudal relationships between England and France in 1340. But his appeal well illustrated the impasse into which Anglo-French relations had been led by the unrestrained exercise of appellate jurisdiction by the new Valois monarchy. In the event, the *arrêt* of the Parlement was resisted in Aquitaine and a declaration of war followed in Gascony and the Agenais.

From the very outset of the events which were to lead to the Valois confiscation of Aquitaine on 24 May 1337, Edward III's status as duke was crucial. Philip's famous letter of 26 December 1336, demanding the surrender of the exiled Robert of Artois (whom Edward was harbouring), was an explicit expression of the feudal relationship. That summons, addressed to the seneschal of Aquitaine, emphasized the inferior status of a vassal and called upon Edward III as a liegeman to hand over a 'mortal enemy' of his lord.[184] There was nothing dynastic or nationalistic about the manner in

---

[180]M. W. Labarge, *Gascony: England's First Colony* (London, 1980) p. 120; C 47/28/4, nos 8, 9.

[181]C 47/28/4, no. 10ʳ; see above, pp. 235–6.

[182]C 47/28/4, nos. 8: 'qar parler des damages donnetz en guerres ceo serait entrer en la graunt meer'; 10ʳˉᵛ, 11.

[183]APA, E 194, no. 11 (inspeximus, dated 22 February 1344, of Ingham's letters on Navailles's rebellion, 17 September 1340).

[184]Printed by Déprez, *Les Prèliminaires*, pp. 414–15. For the affair of Robert of Artois, see H. S.

which the Hundred Years War began. Edward certainly possessed a strong claim to the French throne through his mother, and was a nephew of Charles IV. He was also the son and grandson of a king, unlike his rival Philip of Valois who was merely the son of a count. Although Edward had expressed his claim to the throne in May 1328, he was content to suspend its prosecution until a later date.[185] He was biding his time and first used the title in October 1337 in letters appointing Jean, duke of Brabant, his lieutenant and vicar-general in the kingdom of France.[186] But, significantly, Edward refrained from using the French royal style again until 1340. It could be argued that the balance of forces in the Low Countries, and Robert of Artois's persuasive advocacy, combined to impel Edward to assume the title on 8 February 1340 and declare Philip VI a usurper.[187] But until that date, he was not prepared to take the decisive step which converted a feudal dispute between lord and vassal into a war between two sovereigns of equal and independent authority.

Philip VI confiscated Aquitaine on 24 May 1337. His commissioners arrived in the duchy in June, and met Ingham at Libourne. He refused to surrender the duchy, and requested at least eight days' delay in which to take advice and notify the Gascons. On 17 June Ingham told Philip's commissioners that he could not execute the order and cited Philip's earlier letters requiring him to surrender Robert of Artois.[188] Ingham professed ignorance of Robert's whereabouts and failed to see why the matter should concern him. He threatened an appeal to the court of France, but this was declared invalid by the commissioners.[189] They departed for Penne-d'Agenais and Puymirol to proclaim the confiscation of the duchy. On 17 July Puymirol castle was seized into Philip VI's hands after resistance from the garrison. Operations began, largely confined to the Agenais, where local support was most likely

Lucas, *The Low Countries and the Hundred Years War, 1326–47* (Ann Arbor, 1929), pp. 176–81; B. J. Whiting, 'The "Vows of the Heron"', *Speculum* xx (1945), pp. 261–78; G. T. Diller, 'Robert d'Artois et l'historicité des *Chroniques* de Froissart', *MA*, lxxxvi (1980), pp. 217–31. I hope to devote a separate study to a re-examination of the affair.

[185] See *Foedera*, II, ii, pp. 736, 737, 743. On 29 January 1327, Edward had incorporated two fleurs-de-lis 'of the arms of France' into the lower part of his great seal: *Foedera*, II, ii, p. 683. His claim was vigorously supported by some of the Flemings, including William de Deken, burgomaster of Bruges, who was executed at Paris in 1328.

[186] *Foedera*, II, ii, p. 1001 where Edward used the style: 'dei gratia, rex Anglie et Francie, dominus Hibernie et dux Aquitanie' (7 October 1337). The retention of the title 'duke of Aquitaine' in conjunction with that of king of France is noteworthy. His first regnal year as king of France was formally dated 25 January 1340 to 24 January 1341.

[187] See Lucas, *The Low Countries and the Hundred Years War*, pp. 358–67; *Foedera*, II, ii, pp. 1108–10, 1111, 1115; P. Chaplais, *English Medieval Diplomatic Practice* (London, 1980), I, ii, no. 236 (26 and 27 July 1340).

[188] A. Lancelot, 'Mémoires pour servir à l'histoire de Robert d'Artois', *Mémoires de littérature tirez des registres de l'Académie Royale des Inscriptions et Belles Lettres*, x (1736), pp. 642–4; Déprez, *Les Préliminaires de la guerre de Cent Ans*, p. 154, n. 1.

[189] Lancelot, 'Memoires', pp. 643–4; AN, JJ 68, no. 147; Diller, 'Robert d'Artois et l'historicité des *Chroniques* de Froissart', pp. 217–19.

to be forthcoming. Meanwhile Raoul, count of Eu, commenced sieges at St Macaire and Marmande.[190] The warfare undertaken in Aquitaine at this juncture had a desultory and inconclusive character, determined by siege and counter-siege. Edward III had anticipated military action in the duchy for some time and his officers there were not unprepared. Between 9 April 1337 and 29 September 1339 saltpetre and sulphur for cannon were bought in increasingly large quantities for the castles at St Macaire, Penne, Caumont and Montgaillard.[191] The raw materials for making gunpowder cost the constable of Bordeaux 143 *l.b.* during that period, and 70 pounds were bought in the accounting year 1338–9. Total expenditure on saltpetre and sulphur for cannon represented 2.45 per cent of all military expenses – not a large sum, but one that was significant at such an early stage in the history of firearms.[192]

The garrisons of Aquitaine were well provided with modern weapons against the French, and Oliver Ingham's defence of the duchy, mobilizing local forces, was creditable. Munitions and supplies were almost entirely of local origin, although foreign experts were also employed. Between November 1336 and September 1339, for example, certain 'master iron-workers' came from Genoa and made bolts for crossbows (and perhaps for early guns) at Bordeaux castle for the defence of the duchy's castles and towns.[193] The Usumare family, who held the constableship of Bordeaux, were no doubt responsible for the recruitment of their compatriots who were skilled in the manufacture of weapons. In July 1338 Jean Dassi, 'master of the cannon', was retained with one foot-serjeant at the castle of Penne.[194] That these measures resulted in some successes was evident from Ingham's custody of prisoners taken at his sieges of Suirac and Montlaur, and from the town of Bonnegarde's protracted resistance to the French.[195] During the

---

[190]Déprez, *Les Préliminaires*, p. 154, n. 1; AN, JJ 68, no. 147; JJ 72, no. 2.

[191]E 101/166/11, mm. 41–4.

[192]The earliest recorded European references to guns occur in north Italian sources in 1326, and an illustration of an early cannon, firing a bolt, is found in Walter de Milemetes's *De nobilitatibus sapientiis et prudenciis regum* of *c*.1326 (Oxford, Christ Church, MS 92, fo. 70ᵛ). See J.-F. Finò, *Forteresses de la France médiévale* (Paris, 1967), pp. 273–5. The accounts of the constables of Bordeaux in 1337–9 contain some of the earliest surviving documentary records of the use of firearms in France. Cf. T. F. Tout, 'Firearms in England in the fourteenth century', *EHR*, xxvi (1911), pp. 669–70, 688.

[193]E 101/166/11, m. 44, where 312 *l.* 10 *s.* 11 *d.b.* was paid to them. For missions to Genoa in Edward III's name, undertaken by the Usumare family, see mm. 12, 36, 37; negotiations for Genoese galleys were also in progress (E 101/311/25; *Foedera*, II, iii, p. 151). Antonio di Pessagno of Genoa re-emerged in Edward III's service in 1332 and was paid for his labours at Paris in May 1337 (C 61/44, mm. 4, 7; E 403/294, m. 15). He had entered Philip VI's service by December 1338 when he was pardoned for his previous behaviour (AN, JJ 71, fo. 137ᵛ).

[194]E 101/166/11, m. 17. He was paid 38 *l.* 16 *s.* 8 *d.b.* for his services (20 July–13 November 1338).

[195]E 101/166/11, mm. 12, 32, 37; *Foedera*, II, ii, p. 1128 for Edward's payment for the restoration of the walls, bridge and *maison-forte* at Bonnegarde, in stone, because it lay 'on the frontier of our enemies' (21 June 1340).

financial year 1338–9, moreover, the constable of Bordeaux paid for the production of fifteen standards, nine of them worked with the arms of St George, the remainder with Edward III's arms, which had been set up 'in recently acquired places and castles'.[196]

Despite setbacks such as the treasonable surrender of Penne in December 1338 and the fall of Bourg to the French in 1339, Ingham held the line in Aquitaine while Edward campaigned in the north.[197] Edward was in constant communication with his seneschal in Aquitaine whilst he stayed at Antwerp, Ghent and elsewhere in the Low Countries during 1338 and 1339–40.[198] The defence of Aquitaine was costly, however, and many expedients were resorted to in order to raise money, including the compulsory purchase of wool and cloth, and the levy of subsidies and loans in the duchy.[199] Dire straits even justified the imposition of a tax on wine grown by the bourgeois and inhabitants of Bordeaux which was apparently paid without opposition. Once again, members of the Gascon nobility provided the great majority of troops to serve the Plantagenet cause. Gascon defence was very largely self-defence, and few English men-at-arms and archers were found in the duchy at this time. John de Norwich, knight, served with a small company between July 1337 and February 1338; John of York, archer, was garrisoned at Libourne with fifty-nine other archers and twelve foot-serjeants on 17 May 1338, with Jordan the Tailor, another Englishman, and twenty archers.[200] No English expeditionary force of any size was to be dispatched to Aquitaine before the campaign by Henry, earl of Derby, in 1345. The duchy's defence rested in the hands of Gascon nobles such as Jean de Grailly, captal de Buch. He was owed 29,790 *l.b.* in wages for himself, seventy-seven men-at-arms and 685 foot-serjeants from 16 June 1337 to 13 November 1338 at Castelnau-de-Médoc, Buch, la Teste and other castles.[201] Such men were to be the props of the English war effort, and the captal's services were rewarded by founder-membership of the order of the Garter. Bérard d'Albret, lord of Rions and Vayres had eight knights, thirty-nine mounted and thirty-seven unmounted men-at-arms and 340 foot-serjeants at Blaye,

---

[196]E 101/166/11, m. 44; cf. E 101/166/1, fo. 83ʳ (1326–7).

[197]For Fortaner de Gerrenaque's imprisonment for his treason at Penne, see E 101/166/11, mm. 3, 12, 14. He was arrested and made to surrender money received from an agreement between him and Gaston II, count of Foix, to deliver the castle there on 13 November 1338: Déprez, *Les Préliminaires*, p. 154. Bourg was taken by the French on 23 April 1339 (E 101/166/11, m. 10).

[198]E 36/202, fos 92ʳ, 98ʳ⁻ᵛ, 99ʳ, 101ʳ⁻ᵛ, 104ᵛ (July 1338–January 1340).

[199]See E 101/166/11, mm. 7, 13, 29. Ingham raised over 4700 *l.b.* from subsidies and compulsory purchase of cloth, and received 9120 *l.* 2 *s.b.* from the sale of 196 sacks of wool sent from England (m. 7).

[200]A proposed English expeditionary force to Aquitaine in 1337 was called off (E 101/166/10). For English troops in the duchy see E 101/166/11, m. 19 and 11 (relief of Montendre by John de Norwich, Ingham and their companies).

[201]E 101/166/11, m. 16.

Vayres, Puynormand, Rions and elsewhere 'as the greatest necessity required' between August and December 1338.[202] His elder brother and head of the senior branch of the Albret, Bernard-Ezi, was playing a double game between Edward III and Philip VI but acted as a broker for Jean I, count of Armagnac, whose alliance with Edward he negotiated in June 1340.[203] By November, Albret had clearly been won over by Edward. The fact that the Foix–Armagnac feud flared up again at this time was not irrelevant to Albret's decision.[204] Like Armagnac, Albret was in conflict with Gaston II, count of Foix, and allied with Jean I against him in March 1341.[205] The traditional patterns of regional politics thus greatly influenced the alignments adopted by the Gascon nobility during the greater conflict between England and France.

By assuming the title to the French throne in June 1340 Edward III broke with the past. His previous homages to Philip VI were renounced. They had been performed when he was a minor, or under threat of confiscation of his continental possessions by 'sire Philippe de Valois'.[206] He would act as guardian of the 'customs of St Louis' in the kingdom of France, resist monetary debasement and refrain from exercising arbitrary powers.[207] His assumption of the French title would in no way violate the rights and privileges of those upon whose support he depended. On 21 June 1340, Edward declared that his faithful subjects in Aquitaine would enjoy all their ancient liberties and privileges, including rights of appeal in the *dernier ressort*.[208] Similar letters were dispatched to his new subjects in the *comtés* of Flanders and Artois.[209] Yet recourse to a source of appeal outside their immediate lord's jurisdiction was now denied them. Edward's assumption of the French crown meant that any Gascon (or Fleming) who appealed to the court of Philip of Valois was acknowledging the authority of a usurper. The exemptions from ducal jurisdiction which appellants had previously enjoyed were eliminated at a stroke. Finally, a long-standing source of Anglo-French

---

[202]E 101/166/11, m. 18 (1 August–11 December 1338); APA, E 202, nos 6 (29 May 1339), 19 (15 May 1340) for Albret's tenure of Puynormand.

[203]APA, E 27, no. 6; AN, JJ 71, fo. 34ᵛ; APA, E 30, nos 4, 17; E 240, no. 11ᵇⁱˢ for Armagnac's alliance with Edward III (1 June 1340).

[204]The dispute broke out over rights to the lordship of Miramont-en-Tursan in August 1339: APA, E 278, nos 9 (22 August 1339); 6 (27 October and 24 December 1340). For the sequel to these events see APA, E 405; 477, nos 31, 41, 44, 45 (1341–2).

[205]APA, E 31, no. 4 (at Bordeaux, 20 March 1341).

[206]Déprez, *Les Préliminaires*, pp. 155–6.

[207]*Foedera*, II, ii, pp. 1108–9. A memorandum drawn up in c. 1336 reminded Edward of the events of 1314–15 in France, when certain magnates and nobles conspired to restore 'St Louis' laws and liberties': C 47/28/5, no. 44. In August 1340 Benedict XII told Philip VI that there were some in France who desired war as they 'felt themselves burdened by taxes': *Calendar of Papal Registers. Papal Letters*, ii, p. 581.

[208]*Foedera*, II, iii, pp. 1127–8.

[209]ADN, B 265, no. 7374.

tension was also removed. The financial implications of a settlement with France, under the terms of agreements negotiated in a spirit of dissimulation and insincerity, were at last resolved.[210] Rather than pay his way back into the grace of his liege lord as duke of Aquitaine and count of Ponthieu, Edward III went to war.

Material considerations, as well as a concern for honour and status, thus led to the final Anglo-French rupture of 1340. The conflict was a product of the Angevin legacy: it stemmed from Edward's tenure of the Plantagenet dominions and from the wars that his predecessors had fought in their defence. The armed clashes which began in 1294 need not have developed into a 'Hundred Years War'. But intransigence of the kind displayed by the Valois crown of France after 1328 was in part a product of dynastic insecurity. When the rival claimant to the throne was both king of England and duke of Aquitaine, Philip of Valois had much to fear. This conjuction of circumstances was to deprive the Valois of much of the ground gained by the Capetians from the reign of Philip Augustus onwards.

The events of 1337–40, however, marked the end of a phase in Plantagenet tactics against France. Edward III initially reactivated the old coalitions of encirclement which had been created in 1212–16 and 1294–8 in order to pressurize Philip VI.[211] While the defence of Aquitaine was entrusted largely to its own inhabitants, alliances were made with the German Empire and the nobilities of Brabant, Limburg, Bar, Alsace, Lorraine, the Rhineland, the Franche-Comté and Savoy to ensure the isolation of the French. The Plantagenets had exploited existing relationships with the ruling houses of these regions to encircle the French and establish bridgeheads for attack upon them. The loss of Normandy to Philip Augustus in 1204 had hampered Plantagenet attempts to campaign in northern France ever since. The recruitment of imperial vassals and other allies was therefore imperative. Although there are parallels between the Anglo-imperial alliances of 1294 and 1338, there are clear differences between them. Edward I had no imperial title, for instance, while Edward III was created vicar-general of the Empire by Lewis of Bavaria in September 1338. He was to act '*per Alemanniam et Galliam et universas earum provincias sive partes*' ('throughout Alemannia and Gallia and throughout all their provinces and regions').[212] Edward's powers as vicar over imperial lands to the west of the Rhine were to be used to resist French encroachments upon fiefs and rights claimed by the

[210]C 47/30/5, no. 14; 28/4, nos 10^v–11.

[211]F. M. Powicke, *The Thirteenth Century* (Oxford, 1954), pp. 246–47; B. D. Lyon, *From Fief to Indenture: The Transition from Feudal to Non-feudal Contract in Western Europe* (Cambridge, Mass., 1957), pp. 207–8; J. W. Baldwin, *The Government of Philip Augustus. Foundations of French Royal Power in the Middle Ages* (Berkeley, Los Angeles and London, 1986), pp. 207–16.

[212]H. S. Offler, 'England and Germany at the beginning of the Hundred Years War', *EHR*, liv (1939), pp. 611–12; F. Trautz, *Die Könige von England und das Reich, 1272–1377, mit einem Rückblick auf ihr Verhältnis zu den Staufern Reich* (Heidelberg, 1961), pp. 274–5.

emperor, just as Edward's assumption of the title to the throne of France in 1340 was intended to prevent further Valois intervention, through the hearing of appeals and granting of *sauvegardes* and *paréages*, in his own duchy of Aquitaine.

But both Edward I's and Edward III's imperial alliances and contracts with the *nobiles Alemanni* failed to bring about the ends they were designed to achieve. As a result of these negotiations both kings faced immense financial problems: Edward I spent at least 142,026 *l.st.* on allies and mercenaries between June 1294 and April 1298, while Edward III spent about 130,112 *l.st.* on them between November 1337 and January 1341.[213] Despite this huge outlay, neither was able to discharge his obligations to the Empire, nor to the imperial vassals he had recruited. The nobility of the Franco-imperial borderlands had set so high a monetary value upon their services to the English crown that they had effectively priced themselves out of the market. Edward III may well have tried to learn from his grandfather's mistakes. He attempted, for example, to enforce service from his allies by exploiting his newly assumed titles of king of France and imperial vicar-general. His imperial vicariate of 1338 was a 'potential means of making his avowed allies stand by their obligations'.[214] He failed, and the collapse of the Anglo-imperial pact between 1338 and 1341 was both a symptom and a cause of a shift in English war aims on the continent. Despite the vicariate, the elaborate system of alliances and military contracts with Netherlandish and Rhenish nobles fell apart. It was the last act in a drama begun under Richard I and John, and played with a larger cast under Edward I. Plantagenet intervention now turned from the Franco-imperial frontier towards Brittany, the March of Calais, Spain and Aquitaine.

Nevertheless, although many campaigns were to be launched and fought in northern France, the defence of Aquitaine remained a constant preoccupation of the Plantagenets and their successors. The king-duke's most ancient inheritance and firmest continental power-base lay in south-west France. The durability of the Plantagenet regime in Aquitaine bore witness to the degree of support which it commanded. As every French schoolchild knows, the 'English' were expelled from 'France' as a result of the battle at Castillon-sur-Dordogne, in the duchy of Aquitaine, fought by Anglo-Gascon against French forces in July 1453. The last remnant of the Angevin legacy then fell into the hands of the Valois monarchy. English continental possessions (with the exception of the town and March of Calais) were lost for ever.

---

[213]See E. B. Fryde, 'Financial resources of Edward I in the Netherlands, 1294–8: main problems and some comparisons with Edward III in 1337–40', in *Studies in Medieval Trade and Finance* (London, 1983), pt II, pp. 1174–5.

[214]Offler, 'England and Germany', p. 618; Fryde, 'Financial resources of Edward III in the Netherlands, 1337–40', in *Studies in Medieval Trade and Finance*, pt VII, pp. 1142–3, 1175–81.

8

Epilogue

The war between England and France which broke out in 1337 differed from previous Anglo-French conflicts in two respects: by its length, and by the introduction of a Plantagenet claim to the throne of France into the quarrel which divided the two kingdoms. Despite these differences, continuities were apparent in the war aims and methods of warfare adopted by both protagonists. If the 'origins' of the war lay in the implications and non-fulfilment of the Peace of Paris in 1259, a good case can be made for its beginning in 1294. If Anglo-French rivalry over sovereignty in Aquitaine was a major cause of sustained conflict, then there is a clear line of continuity from Edward I's French war through Edward III's successes to Henry VI's defeat. French civil war in the fifteenth century allowed Henry V and John, duke of Bedford, to aim for nothing less than the French crown, but the enormously expensive Lancastrian occupation of northern France ultimately crippled the English war effort. Edward IV and Henry VIII fell back upon earlier tactics of raid or *chevauchée* but failed to re-establish a foothold outside Calais, in either northern or southern France. This book has therefore tried to see the so-called Hundred Years War as one phase in a longer, intermittent conflict between England and France, in which the exercise of authority over the duchy of Aquitaine was a fundamental issue. Not only did the Plantagenets' homage for the duchy and the feudal relationship which stemmed from that homage produce friction, but other problems, deriving from its political, economic and social condition, served to make Aquitaine a constant source of Anglo-French tension.

The quarrel which was to spill over into sustained warfare after 1337 was to some extent a struggle in which the power of myth was pitted against political reality. Both Capetians and Valois shared the myth of an inherited Carolingian sovereignty over a greater *Francia*, extending to the Pyrenees.[1] During the crises of 1294–8, 1324–5 and 1337–40 attempts were made to translate that myth into reality by force. During the intervening periods varying forms and degrees of pressure were brought to bear on the Plan-

---

[1] See P. S. Lewis, 'France and England: the growth of the nation state', *Essays in Later Medieval French History*, p. 236.

tagenets, depending upon the balance of forces or influences upon the French crown at a given moment. In the end, this pressure became intolerable and Edward III categorically denied Valois sovereignty over Aquitaine by assuming the title to the French throne. But a claim to *ducal* sovereignty which did not necessarily depend upon the royal title also continued to exist, as it had since Edward I's lawyers argued in the late 1290s for the allodial and autonomous status of Aquitaine. Edward III was therefore prepared to renounce his title to the French crown in 1360 in return for full sovereignty over a greatly expanded Aquitaine.[2] This was not to be, but claims to ducal sovereignty were to gain a new lease of life among French princes, such as the dukes of Burgundy or Brittany, in the unstable political conditions of the later fourteenth and early fifteenth centuries. Edward III's assumption of the French royal style after 1340 was to some extent a tactical device. Full sovereignty over Aquitaine and the consequent elimination of Gascon appeals to the Valois crown of France could not at that juncture be achieved by any other means. But that did not mean that Edward's claim was undertaken frivolously nor that he had a weak case in law. It was to prove a valuable, but ultimately unrealizable instrument of English war aims.

On the other side, the French myth (expressed both in propaganda and jurisdictional activity) that Capetian–Valois sovereignty could be effectively exercised over Aquitaine before 1340 was challenged and often denied by political realities. Both Philip the Fair and Charles IV failed to occupy the whole duchy by force, and their Valois successors were to fare no better until the mid-fifteenth century. The Plantagenets' Gascon subjects were quite prepared to appeal to the crown of France as a means of delaying or preventing ducal justice but would not brook its direct and immediate lordship. Political and economic reality ran counter to the more extravagant claims of Capetian and Valois propaganda. Loyalties that had developed during the Anglo-French war and French occupation of Aquitaine between 1294 and 1303 were to be built upon at later stages of the conflict. Regional and local privileges and immunities were perceived to be threatened by the unwelcome prospect of Valois sovereignty with its apparatus of taxation, confiscation and dispossession. The Anglo-Gascon union was strong enough to defy all efforts to break it until the débâcles of the 1440s and 1450s. A similar denial of the French monarchy's claims led the rulers and inhabitants of Flanders and Artois to sustain an even longer and more successful resistance to French expansionism.[3] The Valois possessed no monopoly of dynastic loyalties at the extremities of their kingdom. Edward III's war effort was to be partly sustained by internal dissension and disaffection from the

---

[2] J. Le Patourel, 'The treaty of Brétigny, 1360', in *Feudal Empires. Norman and Plantagenet*, ed. M. Jones (London, 1984), pt XIII, pp. 20–2, 29–32, 39.

[3] See W. Blockmans, 'La position de la Flandre dans le royaume à la fin du xve siècle', in *La France de la fin du xv siècle. Renouveau et apogée*, ed. B. Chevalier and P. Contamine (Paris, 1985), pp. 71–89.

Valois monarchy within the French kingdom. Some elements of continuity with the past nevertheless remained. The Gascon nobility, who had served consistently under all three Edwards, helped to further Edward III's and the Black Prince's aims in the remaining Plantagenet possessions.[4] At one point in the 1360s the re-creation of a large part of the Angevin Empire appeared to be a realistic ambition. The old arena of Plantagenet–Capetian rivalry – Poitou, Limousin, Angoumois – once more became a major theatre of Anglo-French war.

The century before 1340, which had begun with the Plantagenet loss of Poitou, witnessed changes in Anglo-French relations which worsened the political and diplomatic climate in which divisive issues were resolved. To stress the inevitability of conflict, however, ignores the unexpected and unpredictable aspects of human nature. If Philip VI and his advisers had been less adamant in their demands for liege homage from the young Edward III; if the two kings had not harboured each others' 'mortal enemies' Robert of Artois and David of Scotland; or if papal mediation had been as effective under Benedict XII as it was under Clement V, Anglo-French war might have been averted. But the imbroglio into which both kingdoms had been drawn by 1337, which also brought Flemish, Scottish and imperial issues into their quarrel, meant that the impasse over Aquitaine was in the end broken by force. Benedict XII might warn both sides about the dire consequences of conflict with reference to the past, but his words fell on deaf ears.[5] There was no other viable source of mediation, and the dearth of secular intermediaries between England and France made reconciliation impossible. The 'cross-Channel' connections of the English nobility and knightly class had become steadily weaker, especially after the Anglo-French wars of 1294–8 and 1324–6. Edward III's marriage into the house of Hainault in 1326 and the accession of the Valois to the French throne in 1328 accentuated this tendency. The English court began to look towards the Low Countries rather than France; a development reinforced and perpetuated in the fifteenth century through closer contacts between England and the Burgundian Netherlands. It was arrested for a time by Henry V's and Bedford's occupation of northern France. But Anglo-French civilization was not destined to survive the strains of Anglo-French conflict.

Cultural divergence was slow to develop, however. Only in 1524 did John Bourchier, Lord Berners translate Froissart's *Chroniques* 'out of Frenche into our maternal englysshe tonge' at Henry VIII's command, for a readership

---

[4] See P. Capra, 'Les bases sociales du pouvoir anglo-gascon au milieu du xive siècle', *MA*, lxxxi (1975), pp. 273–99, 447–73; N. de Peña, 'Vassaux gascons au service du roi d'Angleterre dans la première moitié du xive siècle: fidelité ou esprit de profit?' *AM*, lxxxviii (1976), pp. 5–21; K. Fowler, *The King's Lieutenant, Henry of Grosmont, first duke of Lancaster, 1310–61* (London, 1969), pp. 54–74; Barber, *Edward, Prince of Wales and Aquitaine* (London, 1978), pp. 112–14, 117–19.

[5] *Calendar of Papal Registers. Papal Letters*, ii, pp. 581–3 (26 August 1340).

which had formerly read them in French.[6] Awareness of Anglo-French differences was probably sharpened by the Lancastrian occupation of northern France between 1420 and 1449 and keener hostility grew. But in the period covered by this book there was little spontaneous expression of mutual hatred. The fact that Edward III's attempts to recruit armies of a cosmopolitan kind, drawn from the nobilities of the Low Countries and the Franco-imperial frontier, failed between 1337 and 1341 may have done more to make the Hundred Years War a war between nations than the forces of incipient nationalism detected by some historians. His victories were to be won largely by English and Gascon forces raised among his own subjects. These men, including the rank-and-file, had a stake in the king's war with France; by and large they profited from it. The creation of a 'national' chivalry, sustained by a form of joint-stock enterprise between king, magnates and knightly class, was to overcome their resistance to foreign service in the crown's wars. The age of Beauchamp, Chandos, Fastolf and Talbot was about to begin.

[6] *The Chronicles of Froissart, Translated by John Bourchier, Lord Berners*, ed. G. C. Macaulay (London, 1908), p. xxvii.

Appendix I Family Trees

Table 1. The houses of Plantagenet, Capet and Valois

Table 2. The houses of Plantagenet and Lusignan and their affiliation

Table 3a. The house of Albret

Table 3b. The house of Armagnac

Table 3c. The houses of Bigorre, Béarn and Foix

Table 3d. The Soler and Colom of Bordeaux

Table 3e. The family of Bordeaux (captaux de Buch)

Table 3f. The family of Caillau

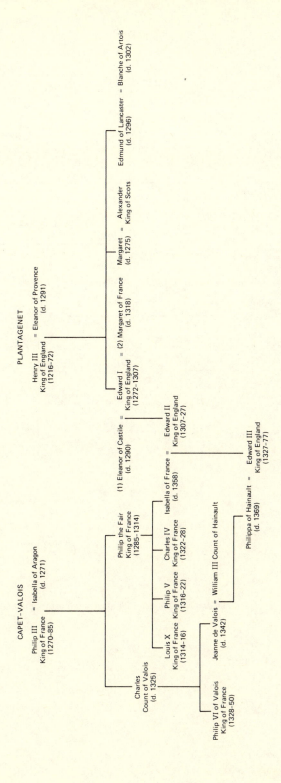

Table 1. The houses of Plantagenet, Capet and Valois

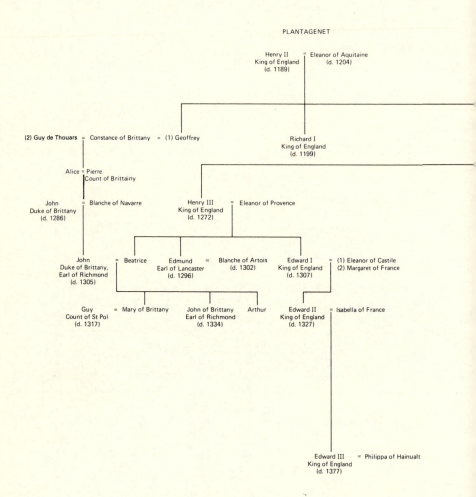

Table 2. The houses of Plantagenet and Lusignan and their affiliation

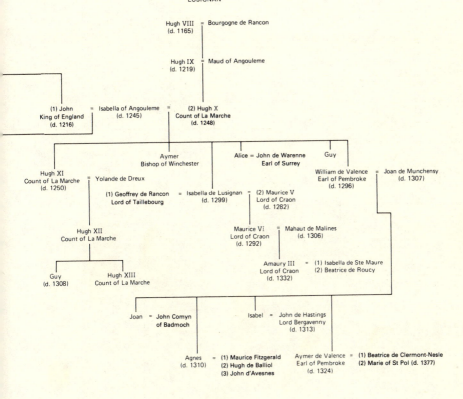

LUSIGNAN

Hugh VIII = Bourgogne de Rancon
(d. 1165)

Hugh IX = Maud of Angouleme
(d. 1219)

(1) John = Isabella of Angouleme = (2) Hugh X
King of England (d. 1245) Count of La Marche
(d. 1216) (d. 1248)

Aymer   Alice = John de Warenne   Guy
Bishop of Winchester   Earl of Surrey

Hugh XI   William de Valence = Joan de Munchensy
Count of La Marche = Yolande de Dreux   Earl of Pembroke   (d. 1307)
(d. 1250)   (d. 1296)

(1) Geoffrey de Rancon = Isabella de Lusignan = (2) Maurice V
Lord of Taillebourg   (d. 1299)   Lord of Craon
(d. 1282)

Hugh XII   Maurice VI = Mahaut de Malines
Count of La Marche   Lord of Craon   (d. 1306)
(d. 1292)

Guy   Hugh XIII   Amaury III = (1) Isabella de Ste Maure
(d. 1308) Count of La Marche   Lord of Craon   (2) Beatrice de Roucy
(d. 1332)

Joan = John Comyn   Isabel = John de Hastings
of Badmoch   Lord Bergavenny
(d. 1313)

Agnes = (1) Maurice Fitzgerald   Aymer de Valence = (1) Beatrice de Clermont-Nesle
(d. 1310)   (2) Hugh de Balliol   Earl of Pembroke   (2) Marie of St Pol (d. 1377)
(3) John d'Avesnes   (d. 1324)

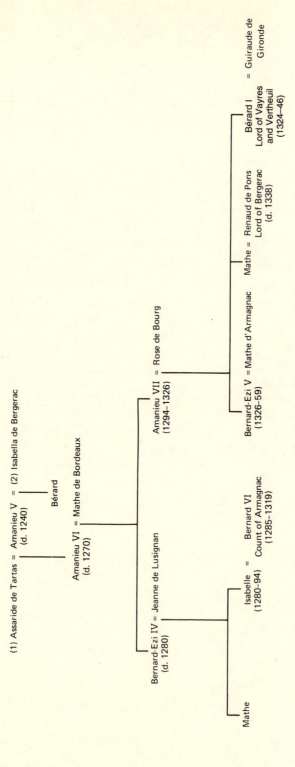

Table 3a. The house of Albret

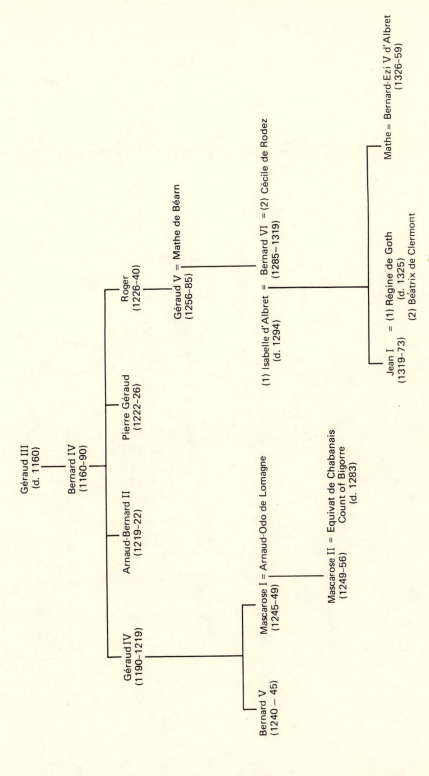

Table 3b. The house of Armagnac

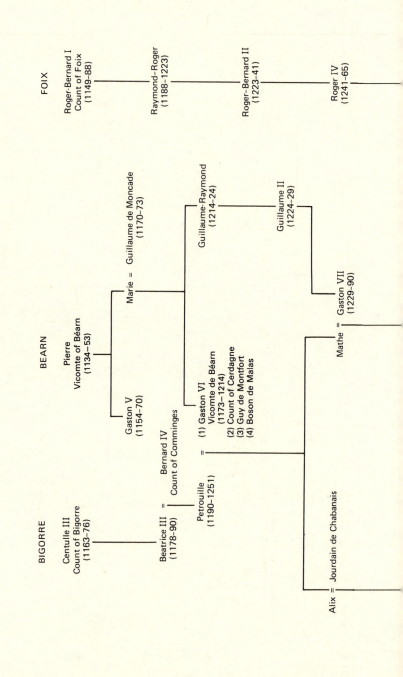

BIGORRE

Centulle III
Count of Bigorre
(1163–76)

Beatrice III
(1178–90)
=
Bernard IV
Count of Comminges

Petrouille
(1190–1251)

Alix = Jourdain de Chabanais

BEARN

Pierre
Vicomte de Béarn
(1134–53)

Gaston V
(1154–70)

Marie = Guillaume de Moncade
(1170–73)

(1) Gaston VI
Vicomte de Béarn
(1173–1214)
(2) Count of Cerdagne
(3) Guy de Montfort
(4) Boson de Malas

=

Guillaume-Raymond
(1214–24)

Guillaume II
(1224–29)

Mathe = Gaston VII
(1229–90)

FOIX

Roger-Bernard I
Count of Foix
(1149–88)

Raymond-Roger
(1188–1223)

Roger-Bernard II
(1223–41)

Roger IV
(1241–65)

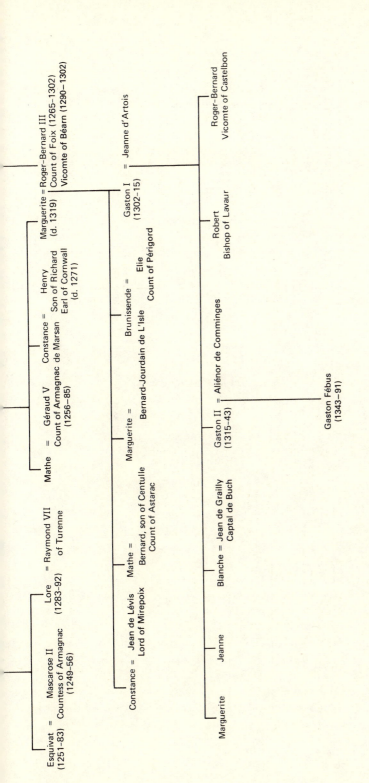

Table 3c. The houses of Bigorre, Béarn and Foix

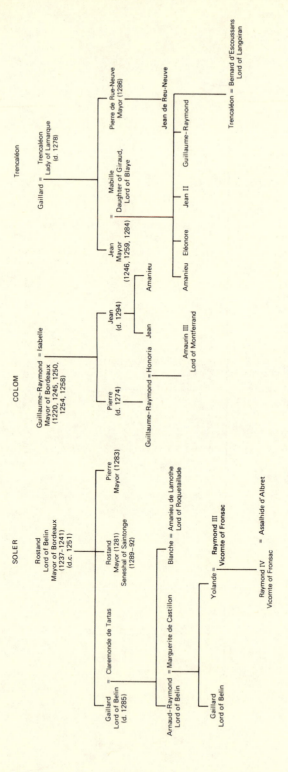

Table 3d. The Soler and Colom of Bordeaux

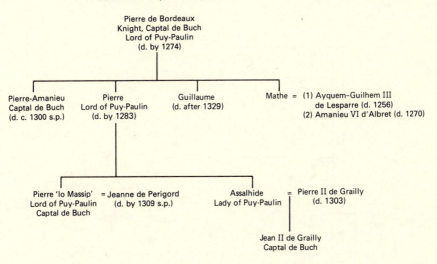

BORDEAUX (Captaux de Buch)

Pierre de Bordeaux
Knight, Captal de Buch
Lord of Puy-Paulin
(d. by 1274)

Pierre-Amanieu
Captal de Buch
(d. c. 1300 s.p.)

Pierre
Lord of Puy-Paulin
(d. by 1283)

Guillaume
(d. after 1329)

Mathe = (1) Ayquem–Guilhem III
de Lesparre (d. 1256)
(2) Amanieu VI d'Albret (d. 1270)

Pierre 'lo Massip'   = Jeanne de Perigord
Lord of Puy-Paulin   (d. by 1309 s.p.)
Captal de Buch

Assalhide   = Pierre II de Grailly
Lady of Puy-Paulin   (d. 1303)

Jean II de Grailly
Captal de Buch

Table 3e.   The family of Bordeaux (captaux de Buch)

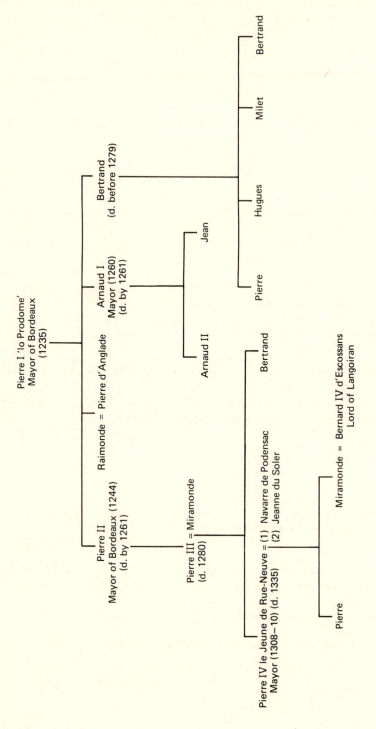

Table 3f. The family of Caillau

Appendix II   The Costs of the Gascon War, 1294–1299[1]

English expenditure on the war

Total expenditure 1294–9	Average annual expenditure	Total estimated annual income
1,440,000 l.t. (£360,000 st.)	238,000 l.t. (£59,500 st.) (i.e. 83.8% of total estimated annual income)	120,000 l.t. + 164,400 l.t. = 284,400 l.t[2] (£30,000 st. + £41,000 st = £71,100 st.)

French expenditure on the war

Total expenditure 1294–9 (estimate)	Average annual expenditure	Total estimated annual income
1,730,000 l.t.[3] (£432,500 st.)	346,000 l.t. (£86,500 st.) (i.e. 61.5% of total estimated annual income)	562,500 l.t. (£140,625 st.)

English expenditure on troops' wages and compensation for lost horses, 1294–9

	£st.	% of total expenditure
Wages of Gascon men-at-arms (cavalry) during war (1294–8)	£137,595	38.22
Wages of Gascon men-at-arms during truce (1298–9)	£ 30,690	8.53
Wages of English men-at-arms (cavalry) during war (1294–8)	£ 37,050	10.29
Total cavalry wages	£205,335	57.04

Wages of Gascon infantry	£ 17,928	4.98
Restaur of horses killed or lost during war (1294–8) (mainly to Gascons)	£ 25,816	7.17
Total expenditure on wages and *restaur*	£249,079	69.19

[1] These figures do not include expenditure on campaigns in Flanders or on Netherlandish, imperial or other alliances.

[2] Total estimated income from ordinary revenues and the customs.

[3] 76.5% contributed by urban, commercial and mercantile sources.

Abbreviations: l.t., *livres tournois*; l. st., pounds sterling.

Sources: English Exchequer accounts (PRO, E.101 and E.372/160); French Chambre des Comptes and other accounts (printed in *Revue Historique*, xxxix (1889), 326–48 and in *Comptes Royaux, 1285–1314*, ed. R. Fawtier and F. Maillard, iii (Paris, 1956).

Note: An exchange rate of £1 *st.* = £4 *t.* has been adopted. This represents a very approximate equivalent, as the rate oscillated between £4 *t.* and £6 *t.* to the pound sterling throughout the period from 1294 to 1299.

Appendix III   Maps

Map 1.   The duchy of Aquitaine, c. 1307 (based on *Rôles Gascons* ed. C. Bémont, iii (Paris, 1906)).

Map 2.   The *comté* of Ponthieu, 1279–1337 (based on S. Storey-Challenger, *L' Administration anglaise du Ponthieu* (Abbeville, 1975).

Map 3.   Principal lordships of south-west France, 1290–1340 (based on P. Tucoo-Chala, *Gaston Fébus et la Vicomté de Béarn, 1343–1391* (Bordeaux, 1960), Carte I).

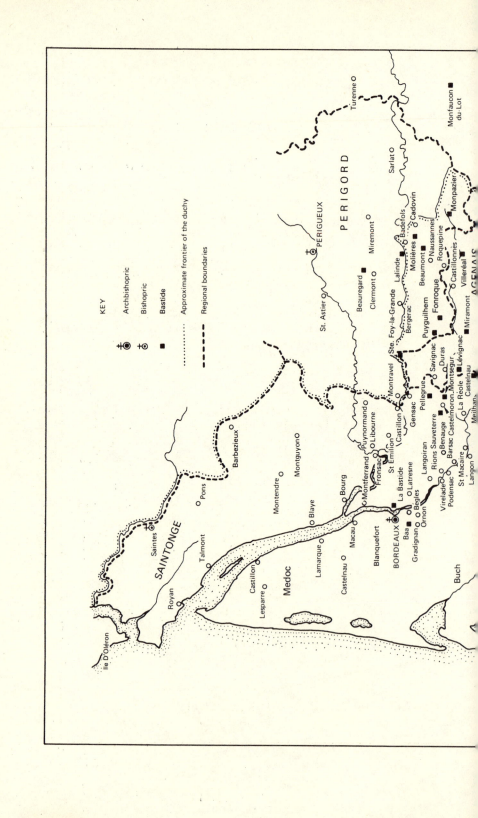

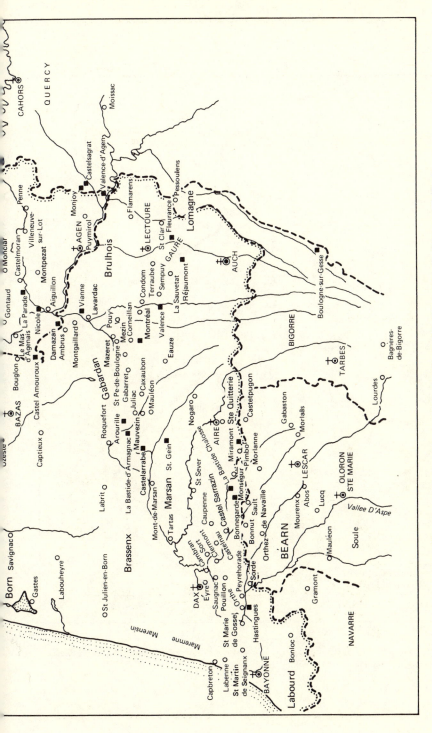

Map 1. The duchy of Aquitaine, c. 1307 (based on *Rôles Gascons* ed. C. Bémont, iii (Paris, 1906)).

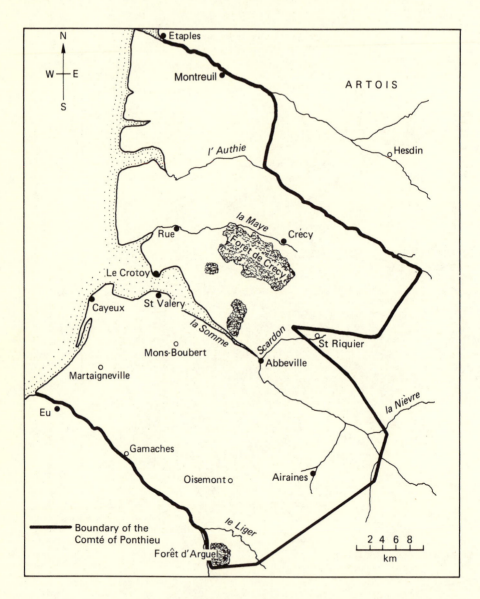

Map 2. The *comté* of Ponthieu, 1279–1337 (based on S. Storey-Challenger, *L' Administration anglaise du Ponthieu* (Abbeville, 1975).

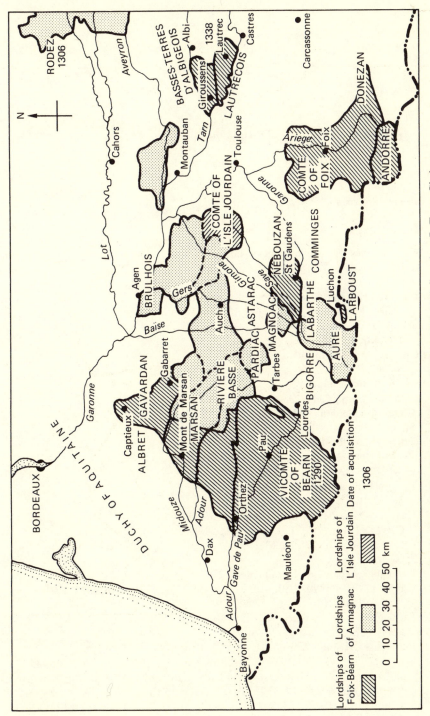

Map 3. Principal lordships of south-west France, 1290–1340 (based on P. Tucoo-Chala, *Gaston Fébus et la Vicomté de Béarn, 1343–1391* (Bordeaux, 1960), Carte I).

Bibliography

Primary Sources

Manuscript Sources

Agen, Archives Départementales de Lot-et-Garonne
  2 J 1
  6 J 43
Arras, Archives Départementales de Pas-de-Calais
  A 2, 38–42, 49, 135–7, 140, 144–5, 181, 1015
Auch, Archives Départementales du Gers
  E 476, 482, I 2248
Bordeaux, Archives Municipales
  MSS 207, 209, 211, 361
London, British Library
  Additional MSS 7965, 7966A, 7967, 17363, 26891
  Cotton MS Caligula D III
  Stowe MS 553
London, Public Record Office
  Ancient Correspondence (SC 1)
    SC 1/2–4, 12–21, 23–4, 37, 39, 31–4, 27–9, 45, 47–50, 55, 58
  Ancient Petitions (SC 8)
    SC 8/281–93, nos 14000–635
  Chancery Miscellanea; Diplomatic Documents, Chancery (C 47)
    C 47/25/1, 17, 27; 26/6–7; 27/3–5, 8; 28/4–5; 29/3–5; 30/6–7; 31/5, 7
  Chancery, Gascon Rolls (C 61)
    C 61/32–51
  Exchequer, Diplomatic Documents (E 30)
    E 30/44 (A, B), 1207, 1217–18, 1343, 1348, 1369, 1374, 1418, 1473, 1521, 1530, 1553–7, 1588, 1610, 1654
  Exchequer, Treasury of the Receipt, Miscellaneous Books (E 36)
    E 36/78, 81, 201, 203
  Exchequer, Accounts Various (E 101)
    E 101/3/27; 5/2, 20–1, 25; 7/26–30; 8/2–3; 9/5; 10/16, 23; 13/30; 14/4, I0; 15/24; 16/35–40; 17/1–6, 38–9; 18/18; 35/8; 68/25, 43; 152/3; 153/1–15; 154/1–15, 24–6; 155/1–13, 15, 24–8; 157/5; 159/4–5, 7, 10–14, 20; 160/1–2, 4, 6, 15; 161/15–17, 23–5; 162/2; 163/3; 164/1–2, 5–8, 10, 15–18; 165/1–3,

5–11; 166/1, 3–11; 182/4; 309/9, 36; 310/23, 25, 37; 619/11–12; 684/22; 688/1

Exchequer, King's Remembrancer, Memoranda Rolls (E 159)
E 159/93

Exchequer, Lord Treasurer's Remembrancer, Pipe Rolls (E 372)
E 372/160, 183, 185

Exchequer, Exchequer of the Receipt, Issue Rolls (E 403)
E 403/294

Montauban, Archives Départementales de Tarn-et-Garonne
A 23–8, 73, 297

Paris, Archives Nationales
Layettes du Trésor des Chartes (J)
J 292–4, 299, 332, 392, 397, 620, 631–6, 654, 918
Registres du Trésor des Chartes (JJ)
JJ 38, 40–50, 52–6, 58–9, 61–6, 69–73
Monuments historiques (K)
K 36–7, 41

Pau, Archives Départementales des Pyrénées-Atlantiques
Fonds d' Albret
E 17–31, 124–9, 131–3, 138, 142, 150–1, 153, 161, 165–6, 170–1, 188, 190, 194, 198–200, 202, 206–9, 216, 221–2, 225, 227
Fonds d' Armagnac
E 237, 240, 269, 278, 281
Fonds de Foix-Béarn
E 288–292, 295–6, 298, 350–2, 355, 369–71, 374, 382, 389, 399, 401–3, 405, 419, 470, 477, 486, 507, 510–11, 613, 618, 622, 842

1 Printed Sources

Actes du Parlement de Paris, ed. E. Boutaric, 2 vols (Paris, 1863–7).

Annales Gandenses, ed. H. Johnstone (2nd edn, Oxford, 1985).

Annales Monastici, H. R. Luard, 5 vols (RS, London, 1864–9).

Archives Municipales d'Agen. Chartes (1189–1328), ed. A. Magen and G. Tholin (Villeneuve-sur-Lot, 1876).

Archives Municipales de Bayonne. Livre des Etablissements, ed. E. Dulaurens (Bayonne, 1892).

Archives Municipales de Bordeaux. Livre des Coutumes, ed. H. Barckhausen (Bordeaux, 1890).

Beaumanoir, Philippe de Rémi, sire de, *Ouevres poétiques*, ed. H. Suchier, 2 vols (Paris, 1884).

——, *Coutumes de Beauvaisis*, ed. A. Salmon, 2 vols (Paris, 1900, repr. 1970).

Breuil, Guillaume de, *Stilus curie Parlamenti*, ed. F. Aubert (Paris, 1909).

Bury, Richard de, *Philobiblon*, ed. M. Maclagan (Oxford, 1960).

——, *The Liber Epistolaris*, ed. N. Denholm Young (Roxburghe Club, Oxford, 1950).

Calendar of Close Rolls.

Calendar of Patent Rolls.

Calendar of Entries in the Papal Registers Relating to Great Britain and Ireland. Papal Letters, ii *(1305–42)*, ed. W. H. Bliss (London, 1895).

Canterbury, Gervase of, *Historical Works*, ed. W. Stubbs, 2 vols (RS, London, 1879–80).

Chaplais, P. (ed.), *English Medieval Diplomatic Practice*, 2 vols (London, 1980).

Chronica Monasterii de Melsa, ed. E. A. Bond, 2 vols (RS, London, 1867).

The Chronicle of Walter of Guisborough, ed. H. Rothwell, Camden Society, 3rd ser., lxcxix (London, 1957).

Chronicles of the Reigns of Edward I and Edward II, ed. W. Stubbs, 2 vols (RS, London, 1882–3).

Chronicles of the Reigns of Stephen, Henry II and Richard I, ed. R. Howlett (RS, London, 1885).

Chronicon de Lanercost, ed. J. Stevenson (Edinburgh, 1839).

Chronique Artésienne (1295–1304), ed. F. Funck-Brentano (Paris, 1899).

Chroniques romanes des comtes de Foix composées au xve siècle par Arnaud Esquerrier et Miègeville, ed. F. Pasquier and H. Courteault (Foix, Paris, Toulouse and Pons. 1895).

Complete Peerage, ed. G. E. Cokayne et al., 12 vols (London, 1910–59).

Comptes Royaux (1285–1314), ed. R. Fawtier and F. Maillard, 3 vols (Paris, 1953–6).

Confessions et jugements de criminels au Parlement de Paris, ed. M. Langlois and Y. Lanhers (Paris, 1971).

Diplomatic Documents, 1101–1272, ed. P. Chaplais, i (London, 1964).

Documents illustrating the Crisis of 1297–8 in England, ed. M. Prestwich, Camden Society. 4th ser., xxiv (London, 1980).

Documents of the Baronial Movement of Reform and Rebellion, 1258–67, ed. R. F. Treharne and I. J. Sanders (Oxford, 1973).

'Documents pontificaux sur la Gascogne', ed. L. Guerard, in *Archives Historiques de la Gascogne*, 2me sér., ii (1896), vi (1903).

Documents sur la maison de Durfort (xie–xve siècles), ed. N. de Peña (Bordeaux, 1977).

Le Dossier de l'affaire des Templiers, ed. G. Lizerand (repr. Paris, 1964).

Dubois, P., *Summaria brevis et compendiosa doctrina felicis expedicionis et abbreacionis guerrarum ac litium regni Francorum*, ed. H. Kämpf (Berlin and Leipzig, 1936).

Dupuy, P., *Histoire du différend d'entre le pape Boniface VIII et Philippe le Bel Roy de France. Preuves* (Paris, 1655).

Flores Historiarum, ed. H. R. Luard, 3 vols (RS, London, 1890).

Foedera, conventiones, litterae et cuiuscunque generis acta publica, ed. T. Rymer. 4 vols (London, 1816–30).

La Gascogne dans les Registres du Trésor des Chartes, ed. C. Samaran (Paris, 1966).

The Gascon Calendar of 1322, ed. G. P. Cuttino, Camden Society, 3rd ser., lxx (London, 1949).

Gascon Register A (Series of 1318–19), ed. G. P. Cuttino and J.-P. Trabut-Cussac. 3 vols (Oxford, 1975).

Grandes Chroniques de France, ed. J. Viard, viii, ix (Paris, 1934, 1939).

Guiart, G. *Branche des royaux lignages*, ed. J. A. Buchon (Paris, 1828).

Emden, A. B., *A Biographical Register of the University of Oxford to 1500*, 2 vols (Oxford 1957, 1958).

Enquêtes administratives d'Alfonse de Poitiers (1249–71), ed. P. Fournier and P. Guerin (Paris, 1959).

Joinville, Jean de, *Histoire de St Louis*, ed. J. Natalis de Wailly (Paris, 1868).

Le Livre d'Agenais, ed. G. P. Cuttino (Toulouse, 1956).

Mémoire relatif au paréage de 1307 conclu entre l'evêque Guillaume Durand II et le roi Philippe le Bel, ed. A. Maisonobe (Mende, 1896).

Monlezun, J. J., *Histoire de la Gascogne depuis les temps les plus reculés jusqu'à nos jours, vi, Preuves* (Auch, 1850).

Les Olim ou registres des arrêts rendus par le Cour du roi, ed. A. Beugnot, 4 vols (Paris, 1839–48).

Ordonnances des rois de France de la troisième race, ed. E. J. de Laurière et al., 22 vols (Paris, 1723–1849).

Paris, Matthew, *Chronica Majora*, ed. H. R. Luard, v (RS, London, 1880).

Recogniciones feodorum in Aquitania, ed. C. Bémont (Paris, 1914).

Records of the Trial of Walter Langton . . . 1307–12, ed. A. Beardwood, Camden Society, 4th ser., vi (London, 1969).

Regestum Clementis papae V, ed. Monachorum OSB, 8 vols (Rome, 1885–92).

Registres du Trésor des Chartes, ed. R. Fawtier, J. Glénisson and J. Guerout, 3 vols (Paris, 1958–79).

'Rôles . . . de l'armée assemblée à Morlaas par Gaston Phoebus, comte de Foix en 1376', ed. P. Raymond, *AHG*, xii (1870), pp. 167–73.

Rôles Gascons, ed. F. Michel, C. Bémont and Y. Renouard, 4 vols (Paris and London, 1885–1964).

The Rolls of Arms of the Princes, Barons and Knights who Attended King Edward I to the Siege of Caerlaverock, ed. T. Wright (London, 1864).

Rotuli Parliamentaorum, ii (London, 1783).

'Rouleaux d'arrêts de la cour du roi au xiiie siècle', *BEC*, xlviii (1887), pp. 535–65; 1 (1889), pp. 41–52.

Treaty Rolls, i, 1234–1325, ed. P. Chaplais (London, 1955).

Le Trésor des Chartes d'Albret. I. Les Archives de Vayres, ed. J.-B. Marquette (Paris, 1973).

Vic, C. de and Vaissete, J., *Histoire générale de Languedoc, avec des notes et les pièces justificatives*, re-ed. A. Molinier, 16 vols (Toulouse, 1872–1904).

Vitae paparum Avenionensium, ed. S. Baluze, re-ed. G. Mollat, 3 vols (Paris, 1914).

The War of St Sardos (1323–25). Gascon Correspondence and Diplomatic Documents, ed. P. Chaplais, Camden Society, 3rd ser., lxxxvii (London, 1954).

Wyon, A. B. and A. W., *Great Seals of England* (London, 1887).

2 Secondary Sources

Age of Chivalry. Art in Plantagenet England, 1200–1400, ed. J. Alexander and P. Binski (London, 1987).

Albe, E., *Autour de Jean XXII. Les familles du Quercy* (Rome, 1903–6).

——, 'Les suites du traité de Paris de 1259 pour le Quercy', *AM*, xxviii (1911), pp. 492–91.

Alexander, J. J. G., 'Painting and manuscript illumination for royal patrons in the later Middle Ages', in *English Court Culture in the Later Middle Ages*, ed. V. J. Scattergood and J. W. Sherborne (London, 1983).

——, 'The Making of the "Age of Chivalry"', *HT*, xxxvii (1987), pp. 3–11.

Allmand, C., *The Hundred Years War. England and France at War, c. 1300–c.1450* (Cambridge, 1988).

Art and the Courts. France and England from 1259 to 1328, ed. P. Verdier, P. Brieger and M. F. Montpetit, 2 vols (Ottawa, 1972).

Aubenas, R., 'Documents notariés provençaux du xiiiᵉ siècle', *Annales de la Faculté de droit d'Aix*, xxv (1935), pp. 82–90.

Aubert, F., *Histoire du Parlement de Paris*, i (Paris, 1894).

Avril, F., *Manuscript Painting at the Court of France. The Fourteenth Century* (London, 1978).

Ayton, A., *Knights and Warhorses. Military Service and the English Aristocracy under Edward III* (Woodbridge, 1994).

Balasque, J. and Dulaurens, E., *Etudes historiques sur la ville de Bayonne* (Bayonne, 1862).

Baldwin, J. W., *The Government of Philip Augustus. Foundations of French Royal Power in the Middle Ages* (Berkeley, Los Angeles and London, 1986).

Barber, R., *Edward, Prince of Wales and Aquitaine* (London, 1978).

Baron, F., 'Enlumineurs, peintres et sculpteurs parisiens des xiiiᵉ et xivᵉ siècles, d'après les rôles de la taille', *BACTH*, n.s., iv (1969), pp. 37–121.

——, 'Le décor sculpté et peint de l'Hôpital St-Jacques-aux-Pélerins', *Bulletin Monumental*, cxxxiii (1975), pp. 29–72.

Bascher, J. de, 'La chronologie des visites pastorales de Simon de Beaulieu, archevêque de Bourges', *Revue d'Histoire de l'Eglise de France*, lvii (1972), pp. 73–89.

Bautier, R.-H. 'Diplomatique et histoire politique: ce que la critique diplomatique nous apprend sur la personnalité de Philippe le Bel', *RH*, dcxxv (1978), pp. 3–27.

Beardwood, A., 'The trial of Walter Langton, bishop of Coventry and Lichfield', *Transactions of the American Philosophical Society*, n.s., liv (1964), pp. 1–45.

Bémont, C., 'La Campagne de Poitou (1242–1243), Taillebourg et Saintes', *AM*, v (1893), pp. 289–314.

——, 'Les factions et les troubles à Bordeaux de 1300 à 1330 environ. Documents inédits', *BPH* (1916), pp. 121–80.

——, 'Les institutions municipales de Bordeaux au Moyen Age: la mairie et la jurade', *RH*, cxxiii (1916), pp. 274–90.

——, 'La mairie et la jurade dans les villes de la Guyenne anglaise: Le Réole', *AM*, xxi (1919), pp. 23–33.

——, *La Guyenne pendant la domination anglaise, 1152–1453* (London and New York, 1920).

Beresford, M., *New Towns of the Middle Ages. Town Plantation in England, Wales and Gascony* (London, 1967).

Bernard, J., 'Les types de navires ibériques et leur influence sur la construction navale dans les ports du sud-ouest de la France (xvᵉ–xviᵉ siècles)', in *Les aspects internationaux de la découverte océanique aux xvᵉ et xviᵉ siècles*, ed. M. Mollat and P. Adam (Paris, 1968), pp. 195–220.

——, *Navires et gens de mer à Bordeaux (vers 1400–vers 1550)*, 3 vols (Paris, 1968).

——, 'Le nepotisme de Clément V et ses complaisances pour la Gascogne', *AM*, lxi (1968–9), pp. 369–413.

——, 'Trade and finance in the Middle Ages', in *Fontana Economic History of Europe*, ed. C. M. Cipolla (London, 1972), pp. 274–338.

Binski, P., *The Painted Chamber at Westminster*, Society of Antiquaries Occasional Paper, n.s., ix (London, 1986).

—— *Westminster Abbey and the Plantagenets. Kingship and the Representation of Power, 1200–1400* (New Haven and London, 1995).

Black, J. G., 'Edward I and Gascony in 1300', *EHR*, xvii (1902), pp. 518–27.

Black-Michaud, J., *Feuding Societies* (Oxford, 1975).

Bloch, M., *The Historian's Craft*, tr. P. Putnam (Manchester, 1954).

——, *Les Rois Thaumaturges* (Paris, 1961).

Blockmans, W., 'La position de la Flandre dans le royaume à la fin du xvᵉ siècle', in *La France de la fin du xvᵉ siècle. Renouveau et apogée*, ed. B. Chevalier and P. Contamine (Paris, 1985), pp. 71–89.

Boase, T. S. R., *Boniface VIII* (London, 1933).

——, 'Fontevrault and the Plantagenets', *Journal of the British Archaelogical Association*, 3rd ser., xxxiv (1971), pp. 1–10.

Bossuat, A., 'La formule "Le roi est empereur en son royaume"', *RHDFE*, xxxix (1961), pp. 371–81.

Boutruche, R., *La crise d'une société: seigneurs et paysans du Bordelais pendant la guerre de Cent Ans*, 2nd edn (Paris, 1963).

Branner, R., 'The Montjoies of St Louis', in *Essays in the History of Architecture Presented to Rudolf Wittkower*, ed. D. Fraser, H. Hibbard and M. Lewine (London, 1967), pp. 13–16.

Broussillon, B. de, *La Maison de Craon, 1050–1480*, 2 vols (Paris, 1893).

Brown, E. A. R., 'Gascon subsidies and the finances of the English dominions, 1315–24', *Studies in Medieval and Renaissance History*, viii (1971), pp. 33–146.

——, 'The tyranny of a construct: feudalism and historians of medieval Europe', *AHR*, lxxix (1974), pp. 1063–88.

—— 'The political repercussions of family ties in the early fourteenth century: the marriage of Edward II of England and Isabelle of France', *Speculum*, lxiii (1988), pp. 573–95.

—— 'Diplomacy, adultery and domestic politics at the court of Philip the Fair: Queen Isabelle's mission to France in 1314' in *Documenting the Past. Essays in Medieval History Presented to George Peddy Cuttino*, ed. J. S. Hamilton and P. J. Bradley (Woodbridge, 1989).

—— and Regalado, N. F., '*La grant feste*: Philip the Fair's celebration of the knighting of his sons in Paris at Pentecost of 1313', in *City and Spectacle in Medieval Europe*, ed. B. A. Hanawalt and K. L. Reyerson (Minneapolis and London, 1994), pp. 56–86.

Brutails, J., 'Les fiefs du roi et les alleux en Guienne', *AM*, xxix (1917), pp. 55–86.

Buck, M., *Politics, Finance and the Church in the Reign of Edward II* (Cambridge, 1983).

Burias, J., 'Géographie historique du comté d'Angoulême, 1308–1531', *Bulletin et Mémoires de la société archéologique et historique de la Charente* (Angoulême, 1957).

Burrows, M., *The Family of Brocas of Beaurepaire and Roche Court* (London, 1886).

Cadis, L., *Le Château de Villandraut* (Paris, 1942).

The Cambridge History of Medieval Political Thought, ed. J. H. Burns (Cambridge, 1988).

Campbell, J., 'England, Scotland and the Hundred Years War in the fourteenth century', in *Europe in the Late Middle Ages*, ed. J. R. Hale, J. R. L. Highfield and B. Smalley (London, 1965), pp. 184–216.

Capra, P., 'Les bases sociales du pouvoir anglo-gascon au milieu du xivᵉ siècle', *MA*, lxxxi (1975), pp. 273–99, 447–73.

Carus-Wilson, E. M. and Coleman, O., *England's Export Trade, 1275–1547* (Oxford, 1963).

Cazelles, R., *La société politique et la crise de la royauté sous Philippe de Valois* (Paris, 1958).

——, 'La règlementation royale de la guerre privée de St Louis à Charles V et la precarité des ordonnances', *RHDFE*, xxxviii (1960), pp. 530–48.

——, *Paris de la fin du règne de Philippe Auguste à la mort de Charles V 1223–1380* (Paris, 1972).

Chaplais, P., 'English arguments concerning the feudal status of Aquitaine in the 14th Century', *BIHR*, xxi (1946–8), pp. 203–13.

——, *Essays in Medieval Diplomacy and Administration* (London, 1981).

—— *Piers Gaveston. Edward II's Adoptive Brother* (Oxford, 1994).

Clanchy, M. T., *From Memory to Written Record. England, 1066–1307* (London, 1979).

——, *England and its Rulers, 1066–1272* (London, 1983).

Contamine, P., *La Guerre au Moyen Age* (Paris, 1980).

Coulson, C., 'Rendability and castellation in medieval France', *Chateau Gaillard. Etudes de castellogie médiévale*, vi (1972), pp. 59–67.

Coulson, C., 'Structural symbolism in medieval castle architecture', *Journal of the British Archaelogical Association*, cxxxii (1979), pp. 73–90.

Courteault, H., 'Un archiviste des comtes de Foix au xve siècle. Le chroniqueur Michel du Bernis', vi (1894), pp. 281–300.

Curry, A., *The Hundred Years War* (Basingstoke, 1993).

Cursente, B., *Les castelnaux de la Gascogne médiévale* (Bordeaux, 1980).

——, 'Les habitats fortifiés en Gascogne: une mise à jour', in *Habitats fortifiés et organisation de l'espace en Mediterranée médiévale*, ed. A. Bazzana, P. Guichard and J. M. Poisson (Lyon, 1983), pp. 57–61.

Cuttino, G. C., 'Henry of Canterbury', *EHR*, lvii (1942), pp. 298–311.

——, 'The process of Agen', *Speculum*, xix (1944), pp. 161–78.

——, 'Historical revision: the causes of the Hundred Years War', *Speculum*, xxxi (1956), pp. 463–77.

——, *English Diplomatic Administration, 1259–1339* (2nd edn, Oxford, 1971).

——, 'A chancellor of the Lord Edward', *BIHR*, (1977–8), pp. 229–32.

——, *English Medieval Diplomacy* (Bloomington, Ind., 1985).

Davies, R. R., *Lordship and Society in the March of Wales, 1282–1400* (Oxford, 1978).

Day, J., *The Medieval Market Economy* (Oxford, 1988).

Delachenal, R., *Histoire des avocats au Parlement de Paris, 1300–1600* (Paris, 1885).

Delisle, L., 'Mémoire sur une lettre inédite addressée à la Reine Blanche par un habitant de La Rochelle', *BEC*, xvii (1856), pp. 513–33.

Denholm-Young, N., 'Richard de Bury (1287–1345)', *TRHS*, xx (1937), pp. 135–68.

——, *Richard of Cornwall* (Oxford, 1947).

Denton, J. H., 'Pope Clement V's early career as a royal clerk', *EHR*, lxxxiii (1968), pp. 303–14.

Déprez, E., *Les Préliminaires de la guerre de Cent Ans (1328–42)*, (Paris, 1902).

Diller, G. T., 'Robert d'Artois et l'historicité des *Chroniques* de Froissart', *MA*, lxxxvi (1980), pp. 217–31.

Drouyn, L., *La Guienne militaire*, 2 vols (Bordeaux and Paris, 1865).

Dubled, H., 'Noblesse et féodalité en Alsace du xie au xiiie siècle', *Tijdscrift voor Rechtgeschiednis*, xxvii (1960), pp. 129–80.

Dunbabin, J., 'From clerk to knight: changing orders', in *The Ideals and Practice of Medieval Knighthood II*, ed., C. Harper-Bill and R. Harvey (Woodbridge, 1988), pp. 26–39.

Duplès-Agier, H., 'Ordonnance somptuaire de Philippe le Hardi (1279)', *BEC*, xv (1854), pp. 176–82.

Durrieu, P., 'Documents relatifs à la chute de la maison Armagnac-Fézensaguet et la mort du comte de Pardiac', *Archives Historique de la Gascogne* (1883), pp. 71–87.

Edwards, J. G., 'The treason of Thomas Turberville, 1295', in *Studies in Medieval History Presented to F. M. Powicke*, ed. R. W. Hunt, W. A. Pantin and R. W. Southern (Oxford, 1948), pp. 296–309.

England and her Neighbours, 1066–1453. Essays in Honour of Pierre Chaplais, ed. M. Jones and M. Vale (London, 1989).

England and the Low Countries in the Late Middle Ages, ed. C. Barron and N. Saul (Stroud and New York, 1995).

England in Europe, 1066–1453, ed. N. Saul (London, 1994).

Evans-Pritchard, E. E., *Essays in Social Anthropology* (London, 1969).

Les Fastes du Gothique. Le siècle de Charles V (Paris, 1981).

Favier, J., 'Les légistes et le gouvernement de Philippe le Bel', *Journal des Savants* (1969), pp. 92–108.

Fawtier, R., 'Un incident diplomatique franco-allemand au temps de Philippe le Bel', *Annuaire-Bulletin de la Société de l'Histoire de France* (1946–7), pp. 27–38.

——, 'Comment le roi de France, au début du xive siècle, pouvait-il se representer son royaume?', *Mélanges . . . P.-E. Martin* (Geneva, 1961), pp. 65–77.

Finò, J.-F., *Forteresses de la France médiévale* (Paris, 1967).

Fourgous, M., *L'Arbitrage dans le droit français aux xiiie et xive siècles* (Paris, 1906).

Fournier, P., 'Note complémentaire pour l'histoire des canonistes au xive siècle. III. Gaillard de Durfort, canoniste et seigneur féodal', *Nouvelle revue du droit français et étranger* (1920), pp. 516–24.

Freeman, A. Z., 'A moat defensive: the coast defence scheme of 1295', *Speculum*, xlii (1967), pp. 442–62.

Fryde, E. B., *Studies in Medieval Trade and Finance* (London, 1983).

Fryde, N., 'Antonio Pessagno of Genoa, king's merchant of Edward II of England', *Studi in memoria de Federigo Melis*, ii (Naples, 1978), pp. 159–78.

——, *The Tyranny and Fall of Edward II, 1321–1326* (Cambridge, 1979).

Funck-Brentano, F., 'Les luttes sociales aux xive siècle: Jean Colomb de Bordeaux', *MA*, x (1897), pp. 289–320.

——, *Les Origines de la Guerre de Cent Ans. Philippe le Bel en Flandre* (Paris, 1897).

Galbraith, V. H., 'The Tower as an exchequer record office in the reign of Edward I', in *Essays in Medieval History presented to T. F. Tout* (Manchester, 1925), pp. 232–40.

Gardeau, L. and Trabut-Cussac, J.-P., 'Les premiers Grailly et la tombe de Pierre I de Grailly à Uzeste', *BPH* (1960), pp. 713–22.

Gardelles, J., *Les Châteaux du Moyen Age dans la France du Sud-Ouest (1216–1327)* (Geneva, 1972).

Gavrilovitch, M., *Etude sur le traité de Paris de 1259* (Paris, 1899).

Genicot, L., 'Les grandes villes d'Occident en 1300', in *Economies et Sociétés au Moyen Age. Mélanges offerts à Edouard Perroy* (Paris, 1973), pp. 199–219.

Geremek, B., 'Paris, la plus grande ville de l'Occident médiéval', *Acta Poloniae Historica*, xviii (1968), pp. 18–37.

Gillingham, J., *Richard the Lionheart* (London, 1978).

——, *The Angevin Empire* (London, 1984).

Giry, A., *Les Etablissements de Rouen*, 2 vols (Paris, 1885).

Glénisson, J., 'Notes d'histoire militaire. Quelques lettres de défi du xivᵉ siècle', *BEC*, cvii (1947–8), pp. 235–54.

Gluckman, M., 'The peace in the feud', in *Custom and Conflict in Africa* (Oxford, 1965), pp. 1–26.

Gouron, A., 'Les archives notariales des anciens pays de droit écrit au Moyen Age', *Recueil de Mémoires et travaux par la société d'histoire du droit et des institutions des ancien pays de droit écrit*, v (1966), pp. 47–60.

Guenée, B., *States and Rulers in Later Medieval Europe*, trans. J. Vale (Oxford, 1985).

Guerout, J., 'Le Palais de la Cité à Paris des origines à 1417: essai topographique et archéologique', *Mémoires de la Fédération des Sociétés Historiques et Archéologiques de Paris et de l'Ile-de-France*, ii (1950), pp. 23–44.

Guillemain, B., 'Les recettes et les dépenses de la Chambre Apostolique pour la quatrième année du pontificat de Clement V (1308–9)', *Collections de l'Ecole française de Rome*, xxxix (Rome, 1978).

Hamilton, J. S., *Piers Gaveston, Earl of Cornwall, 1307–1312. Politics and Patronage in the Reign of Edward II* (Detroit, 1988).

Harriss, G. L., *King, Parliament and Public Finance in Medieval England to 1369* (Oxford, 1975).

Harvey, R., *Moriz von Craûn and the Chivalric World* (Oxford, 1961).

Heers, J., *Le Clan familial au Moyen Age* (Paris, 1974).

Henderson, G., 'Studies in English manuscript illumination', *JWCI*, xxx (1967), pp. 91–120.

Higounet, C., *Le comté de Comminges de ses origines à l'annexation à la couronne* (Toulouse and Paris, 1949).

——, 'Cistercians et bastides', *MA*, lvi (1950), pp. 69–84.

——, 'Le groupe aristocratique en Aquitaine et en Gascogne', in *Les structures sociales de l'Aquitaine, du Languedoc et de l'Espagne au premier age féodal* (Toulouse and Paris, 1969), pp. 221–37.

——, *Paysages et villages neufs du Moyen Age* (Bordeaux, 1975).

——, 'La société nobiliaire en Bordelais à la fin du xiiiᵉ siècle', in *Société et groupes sociaux en Aquitaine et Angleterre* (Bordeaux, 1976).

Hillgarth, J. N., *The Spanish Kingdoms, 1250–1516*, 2 vols (Oxford, 1976).

Histoire de Bordeaux, III. Bordeaux sous les rois d'Angleterre, 1152–1453, ed. Y. Renouard (Bordeaux, 1965).

The History of the King's Works, ed. H. M. Colvin, i (London, 1963).

Hollister, C. W., 'Normandy, France and the Anglo-Norman *Regnum*', *Speculum*, li (1976), pp. 202–42.

Holt, J. C., 'The end of the Anglo-Norman realm', *PBA*, lxi (1975), pp. 223–65.

——, 'The loss of Normandy and royal finances', in *War and Government in the Middle Ages. Essays in Honour of J. O. Prestwich*, ed. J. Gillingham and J. C. Holt (Woodbridge, 1984), pp. 92–105.

James, M. K., 'Fluctuations of the Anglo-Gascon wine trade in the fourteenth century', *EcHR*, 2nd ser., iv (1951), pp. 170–96.

——, 'Les activités commerciales des negociants en vins gascons en Angleterre à la fin du Moyen Age', *AM*, lxv (1953), pp. 35–49.

Jenkinson, H., 'Mary de Sancto Paulo, foundress of Pembroke College, Cambridge', *Archaeologia*, lxvi (1915), pp. 401–46.

Johnstone, H., 'The county of Ponthieu, 1279–1307', *EHR*, xxvi (1914), pp. 435–52.

——, *Edward of Caernarvon* (Manchester, 1946).

Jusselin, M., 'Comment la France se preparait à la guerre de Cent Ans', *BEC*, lxxxiii (1912), pp. 209–36.

Keen, M. H., *The Laws of War in the Late Middle Ages* (London, 1965).

Kershaw, I., 'The great famine and agrarian crisis in England, 1315–1322', *PP*, lix (1973), pp. 3–50.

Kicklighter, J. A., 'Les monastères de Gascogne et le conflit franco-anglais (1270–1327)', *AM*, xci (1979), pp. 121–33.

——, 'French jurisdictional supremacy in Gascony: one aspect of the ducal government's response', *JMH*, v (1979), pp. 127–34.

——, 'English Bordeaux in conflict: the execution of Pierre Vigier de la Rousselle and its aftermath, 1312–24', *JMH*, ix (1983), pp. 1–14.

——, 'The nobility of English Gascony: the case of Jourdain de L'Isle', *JMH*, xiii (1987), pp. 327–42.

Kingsford, C. L., 'Sir Otho de Grandison', *TRHS*, 3rd ser., iii (1909), pp. 125–95.

Labarge, M. W., *Gascony: England's First Colony* (London, 1980).

Lalou, E., 'Les négociations diplomatiques avec l'Angleterre sous le règne de Philippe le Bel', in *La 'France anglaise' au Moyen Age*, ed. R.-H. Bautier (Paris, 1988), pp. 325–55.

—— 'Les questions militaires sous le règne de Philippe le Bel', in *Guerre et société en France, en Angleterre et en Bourgogne, xive–xve siècle*, ed. P. Contamine, C. Giry-Deloison, and M. H. Keen (Lille, 1991), pp. 37–62.

Lancelot, A., 'Mémoires pour servir à l'histoire de Robert d'Artois', *Mémoires de littérature tirez des registres de l'Academie Royale des Inscriptions et Belles Lettres*, x (1736), pp. 571–663.

Larenaudie, M.-J., 'Les famines en Languedoc aux xive et xve siècles', *AM*, lxiv (1952), pp. 21–40.

Le Goff, J., 'The town as an agent of civilisation', in *The Fontana Economic History of Europe. The Middle Ages*, ed., C. M. Cipolla (London, 1972), pp. 71–106.

Le Marignier, J. F., *Recherches sur l'hommage en marche et les frontières féodales* (Lille, 1945).

Le Patourel, J., 'The Norman Conquest, 1066, 1106, 1154', in *Proceedings of the Battle Conference on Anglo-Norman Studies*, i, 1978 (Woodbridge, 1979).

——, *Feudal Empires. Norman and Plantagenet*, ed. M. Jones (London, 1984).

Lewis, F. R., 'Beatrice of Falkenburg, 3rd wife of Richard of Cornwall', *EHR*, lii (1937), pp. 274–82.

Lewis, P. S., *Essays in Later Medieval French history* (London, 1985).

Lizerand, G., *Clément V et Philippe IV le Bel* (Paris, 1910).

Loirette, G., 'La charte de coutumes de la bastide de Créon (1315)', *AM*, lxiv (1952), pp. 283–95.

Lubimenko, I., *Jean de Bretagne, comte de Richmond (1266–1334)* (Lille, 1908).

Lucas, H. S., *The Low Countries and the Hundred Years War, 1326–47* (Ann Arbor, 1929, repr. Philadelphia, 1976).

——, 'The great European famine of 1315, 1316 and 1317', *Speculum*, v (1930), pp. 343–77.

Lyon, B. D., *From Fief to Indenture: The Transition from Feudal to Non-feudal Contract in Western Europe* (Cambridge, Mass., 1957).

Mackay, A., *Spain in the Middle Ages. From Frontier to Empire, 1000–1500* (London, 1977).

McFarlane, K. B., *The Nobility of Later Medieval England* (Oxford, 1973).

McIsack, M., *The Fourteenth Century* (Oxford, 1959).

Maddicott, J. R., *Thomas of Lancaster, 1307–22* (Oxford, 1970).

——, 'The origins of the Hundred Years War', *HT*, xxxvi (1986), pp. 31–37.

Marquette, J.-B., 'Les Albret. I. Les origines (xiᵉ siècle – 1240)', *Cahiers du Bazadais*, xxx, xxxi (1975), pp. 5–107.

Marsh, F. B., *English Rule in Gascony, 1199–1259* (Ann Arbor, 1912).

Medieval Statecraft and the Perspectives of History. Essays by Joseph R. Strayer, ed. J. F. Benton and T. N. Bisson (Princeton, 1971).

Meuret, R., *Les Peintures murales du sud-ouest de la France du xiᵉ au xviᵉ siècles* (Paris, 1967).

Mezières, Philippe de, *Le Songe du vieil pélerin*, ed. G. W. Coopland, 2 vols (Cambridge, 1969).

Millar, E. G., *The Parisian Miniaturist Honoré* (London, 1959).

Mollat, G., *Les Papes d'Avignon, 1305–1376* (Paris, 1949).

Morand, K., *Jean Pucelle* (Oxford, 1962).

Morel, H., 'Jean de Labarthe et la maison d'Armagnac, un épisode de la concentration féodale au xivᵉ siècle', *AM*, lxi (1949), pp. 257–311.

Nicholas, D., *Medieval Flanders* (London and New York, 1992).

La Noblesse au Moyen Age, ed. P. Contamine (Paris, 1976).

Offler, H. S., 'England and Germany at the beginning of the Hundred Years War', *EHR*, liv (1939), pp. 608–31.

Ormrod, W. M., 'Edward III and his family', *Journal of British Studies*, xxvi (1987), pp. 398–422.

—— *The Reign of Edward III. Crown and Political Society in England, 1327–1377* (New Haven and London, 1990).

Offler, H. S., 'England and Germany at the beginning of the Hundred Years War', *EHR*, liv (1939), pp. 608–31.

Ormrod, W. M., 'Edward III and his family', *Journal of British Studies*, xxvi (1987), pp. 398–422.

Parisse, M., *La Noblesse lorraine, xiᵉ–xiiiᵉ siècles* (Lille and Paris, 1976).

Parkes, M. B., 'The literacy of the laity', in *The Medieval World*, ed. D. Daiches and A. Thorlby (London, 1973), pp. 555–62.

Pegues, F. J., *The Lawyers of the Last Capetians* (Princeton, 1962).

Peña, N. de, 'Vassaux gascons au service du roi d'Angleterre dans la première moitié du xivᵉ siècle: fidelité ou esprit de profit?', *AM*, lxxxviii (1976), pp. 5–21.

Perroy, E., *The Hundred Years War*, trans. W. B. Wells (London, 1945).

——, 'Social mobility among the French *noblesse* in the later Middle Ages', *PP*, xxi (1962), pp. 25–38.

Petit, J., 'Un capitaine du règne de Philippe le Bel', *MA*, 2nd ser., i (1897), pp. 224–39.

——, *Charles de Valois, 1270–1325* (Paris, 1900).

Phillips, J. R. S., *Aymer de Valence, Earl of Pembroke, 1308–24. Baronial Politics in the Reign of Edward II* (Oxford, 1972).

Pocquet du Haut-Jussée, B. A., 'Une idée politique de Louis XI: la sujétion éclipse la vassalité', *RH*, ccxxvi (1961), pp. 383–98.

Pole-Stuart, E., 'The interview between Philip V and Edward II at Amiens in 1320', *EHR*, xli (1926), pp. 413–15.

Poumarède, J., *Les Successions dans le sud-ouest de la France au Moyen Age* (Toulouse, 1972).

Powicke, F. M., *Henry III and the Lord Edward*, 2 vols (Oxford, 1947).

——, *The Thirteenth Century* (Oxford, 1954).

——, *The Loss of Normandy, 1189–1204. Studies in the History of the Angevin Empire* (2nd edn, Manchester, 1961).

Prestwich, J., 'The military household of the Norman kings', *EHR*, xcvi (1981), pp. 1–35.

Prestwich, M., *War, Politics and Finance under Edward I* (London, 1972).

——, *The Three Edwards. War and State in England, 1272–1377* (London, 1980).

——, *Edward I* (London, 1988).

Renouard, Y., *Etudes d'histoire médiévale*, 2 vols (Paris, 1968).

Représentation, pouvoir et royauté à la fin du Moyen Age, ed. J. Blanchard (Paris, 1995).

Reynolds, S., *Kingdoms and Communities in Western Europe, 900–1300* (Oxford, 1984).

Rhodes, W. E., 'Edmund, earl of Lancaster', *EHR*, x (1895), pp. 19–40, 209–37.

Richard, A., *Histoire des comtes de Poitou, 778–1204*, 2 vols (Paris, 1903).

Rickard, P., *Britain in Medieval French Literature* (Cambridge, 1956).

Ridgeway, H., 'William de Valence and his "familiares" ', *Historical Research*, lxv (1992), pp. 239–57.

Robson, J., 'The Catalan fleet and Moorish sea-power (1337–1344)', *EHR*, lxxiv (1959), pp. 386–408.

Rocadier, J., *St Bertrand-de-Comminges* (Toulouse, 1987).

Rogers, C. J., 'The military revolutions of the Hundred Years War', *Journal of Military History*, lvii (1993), pp. 249–57.

—— 'Edward III and the dialectics of strategy', *TRHS*, 6th ser., iv (1994), pp. 83–102.

Rogozinski, J., *Power, Caste and Law. Social Conflict in Fourteenth-century Montpellier* (Cambridge, Mass., 1982).

Roncière, C. de la, 'Le blocus continental de l'Angleterre sous Philippe le Bel', *RQH*, lx (1896), pp. 401–41.

Rothwell, H., 'Edward I's case against Philip the Fair over Gascony in 1298', *EHR*, xiii (1927), pp. 572–82.

St-Blanquat, O. de, 'Comment se sont créées les bastides du sud-ouest de la France?', *Annales*, iv (1949), pp. 278–89.

Samaran, C., 'Un texte historique à rétrouver: les chroniques de la maison d'Armagnac (xive siècle)', in *Recueil . . . Clovis Brunel*, ii (Paris, 1955), pp. 501–6.

Sandler, L. F., *The Peterborough Psalter in Brussels and other Fenland Manuscripts* (London, 1974).

——, *Gothic Manuscripts, 1285–1385. A Survey of Manuscripts Illuminated in the British Isles*, v (London, 1986).

Sapori, A., *La compagnia dei Frescobaldi in Inghliterra* (Florence, 1947).

Sivery, G., 'La description du royaume de France par les conseillers de Philippe Auguste et par leurs successeurs', *MA*, xc (1984), pp. 65–85.

Smalley, B., *English Friars and Antiquity in the Early Fourteenth Century* (Oxford, 1960).

Southern, R. W., 'England's first entry into Europe', in *Medieval Humanism and Other Essays* (Oxford, 1970), pp. 135–57.

Stacey, R.C., *Politics, Policy and Finance under Henry III, 1216–45* (Oxford, 1987).

Steinberg, S. H., 'A portrait of Beatrix of Falkenburg', *Antiquaries Journal*, xviii (1938), pp. 142–5.

Stone, L., *Sculpture in Britain: The Middle Ages* (Harmondsworth, 1955).

Strayer, J. R., *The Administration of Normandy under St Louis* (Cambridge, Mass., 1932).

——, 'The costs and profits of war: the Anglo-French conflict of 1294–1303', in *The Medieval City*, ed. H. A. Miskimin, D. Herlihy and A. L. Udovitch (Yale, 1977), pp. 269–91.

——, *The Reign of Philip the Fair* (Princeton, 1980).

Studd, J. R., 'The Lord Edward and Henry III', *BIHR*, 1 (1977–8), pp. 4–19.

——, 'The "privilegiati" and the treaty of Paris, 1259', in *La 'France Anglaise' au Moyen Age*, ed. R.-H. Bautier (Paris, 1988), pp. 175–89.

Sturler, J. de, *Les Relations politiques et les échanges commerciaux entre le duché de Brabant et l'Angleterre au Moyen Age* (Paris, 1936).

Suggett, H., 'The use of French in England in the later Middle Ages', *TRHS*, 4th ser., xxvi (1946), pp. 60–83.

Sumption, J., *The Hundred Years War. Trial by Battle* (London, 1990).

Taylor, A. J., *Studies in Castles and Castle-building* (London, 1985).

Tout, T. F., 'Firearms in England in the fourteenth century', *EHR*, xxvi (1911), pp. 666–702.

——, *France and England: Their Relations in the Middle Ages and Now* (Manchester, 1922).

——, *Chapters in the Administrative History of Medieval England*, 6 vols (Manchester, 1928–37).

Trabut-Cussac, J.-P., 'Les coutumes ou droits de douane perçus à Bordeaux', *AM*, lxii (1950), pp. 135–50.

——, 'Itinéraire d'Edouard Ier en France, 1286–1289', *BIHR*, xxv (1952), pp. 170–200.

——, 'La fondation de Sauveterre-de-Guyenne (1281–3)', *RHB*, n.s., ii (1953), pp. 181–217.

——, 'Bastides ou forteresses?' *MA*, (1954), pp. 81–135.

——, 'Créon, bastide administrative', *AM*, lxvi (1954), pp. 343–50.

——, 'Date, fondation et identification de la bastide de Baa', *RHB*, n.s., x (1961), pp. 133–44.

——, *'L'Administration anglaise en Gascogne sous Henry III et Edouard I de 1254 à 1307* (Geneva, 1972).

Trautz, F., *Die Könige von England und das Reich, 1292–1377, mit einem Rückblick auf ihr verhältnis zu den Staufern* (Heidelberg, 1961).

Tuck, A., *Crown and Nobility, 1272–1461* (London, 1985).

Tucoo-Chala, P., 'Les relations économiques entre le Béarn et les pays de la couronne d'Aragon', *BPH*, 1957 (1958), pp. 115–36.

——, *Gaston Fébus et la vicomté de Béarn (1343–1391)* (Bordeaux, 1960).

Tummers, H. A., *Early Secular Effigies in England. The Thirteenth Century* (Leiden, 1980).

Tyerman, C. J., 'Philip VI and the recovery of the Holy Land', *EHR*, c (1985), pp. 25–52.

Vale, J., *Edward III and Chivalry. Chivalric Society and its Context, 1270–1350* (Woodbridge, 1982).

Vale, M., *English Gascony, 1399–1453* (Oxford, 1970).

——, 'Warfare and the life of the French and Burgundian nobility in the late Middle Ages', in *Adelige Sachkultur des Spätmittelalters. Internationaler Kongress, Krems an der Donau, 22 bis. 25 September 1980* (Vienna, 1982), pp. 169–94.

——, 'The Gascon nobility and the Anglo-French war, 1294–98', in *War and Government in the Middle Ages*, ed. J. Gillingham and J. C. Holt (Woodbridge and Totowa, 1984), pp. 134–46.

——, 'Nobility, bureaucracy and the "state" in English Gascony, 1250–1340: a prosopographical approach', in *Genèse de l'Etat moderne: prosopographie et histoire*, ed. F. Autrand (Paris, 1985).

——, 'Seigneurial fortification and private war in later medieval Gascony', in *Gentry and Lesser Nobility in Late Medieval Europe*, ed. M. Jones (Gloucester, 1986), pp. 133–58.

——, 'The Gascon nobility and crises of loyalty, 1294–1337', in *La 'France Anglaise' au Moyen Age*, (Paris, 1988), pp. 207–16.

Vale, M. G. A., 'The Anglo-French wars, 1294–1340: allies and alliances' in *Guerre et société en France, en Angleterre et en Bourgogne, xive–xve siècle*, ed. P. Contamine, C. Giry-Deloison, and M. H. Keen (Lille, 1991), pp. 15–35.

Vidal, J.-M., *Histoire des Evêques de Pamiers. I. Bernard Saisset (1232–1311)* (Toulouse and Paris, 1926).

Wathey, A., 'The marriage of Edward III and the transmission of French motets to England', *Journal of the American Musicological Society*, xlv, I (1992), pp. 1–29.

Watson, G. W., 'The families of Lacy, Geneva, Joinville and La Marche', *The Genealogist*, xxi (1904), pp. 1–16, xxii (1905), pp. 163–72, 234–43.

Waugh, S. L., *England in the Reign of Edward III* (Cambridge, 1991).

Whiting, B. J., 'The "Vows of the Heron"', *Speculum*, xx (1945), pp. 261–78.

Williams, G. A., *Medieval London: From Commune to Capital* (London, 1963).

Wolff, P., 'The Armagnacs in southern France (14th–15th centuries)', *BIHR*, xx (1945), pp. 186–91.

——, 'Un problème d'origines: la Guerre de Cent Ans', in *Eventail de l'histoire vivante: Hommage à Lucien Fèbvre*, ii (Paris, 1953), pp. 141–8.

Wood, C. T., '*Regnum Francie*: a problem in Capetian administrative usage', *Traditio*, xxii (1967), pp. 117–47.

——, 'The Mise of Amiens and St Louis' theory of Kingship', *French Historical Studies*, vi (1970), pp. 300–10.

Wright, J. R., *The Church and the English Crown, 1305–34* (Toronto, 1980).

Index

Aachen 13
Abbeville 71, 73
Aberdeen 209
Acre 81, 188
Adenet le Roi 39
Adhérens 129, 130
Adour 115, 149, 157, 204
Agen 1, 8, 58, 101, 105–6, 125, 128,
    141–2, 144, 147, 150–1, 180–1,
    185–6, 205, 211, 216–17, 218–19,
    220–1, 228, 233–4, 237–8
  Guillaume de Cambrai, *bailli* of
  216
  process of 218
Agenais 11, 12, 22, 53, 57–8, 68–70,
    77–8, 83, 87–8, 94–5, 98, 100–2,
    105, 109–10, 115–16, 122, 131–5,
    138, 151–3, 156, 158, 179, 180–1,
    183, 186, 199, 208, 216–17, 219,
    225, 232–5, 237–8, 243, 247–9,
    252–3, 255, 259, 260
  Achard de Montguidon, seneschal of
  the 233
  Jean de Maignelay, seneschal of the
  208
Ailhan d', family of 145
Aire, bishop of 88, 91, 129, 230, 232
Alagone, Artoldo of 178, 199
Albi 147, 150
Albigensian crusades 81, 98
Albigeois 148, 150, 204, 247
Albret, family of 8, 75, 83, 95–7,
    100–1, 108, 116, 118, 131, 168,
    170–1, 174, 240, 241, 253–4, 263
  Amanieu VI, lord of 85, 134

Amanieu VII, lord of 95–8, 121, 132,
    134, 137, 164, 166–7, 173, 205,
    219, 240
  Bérard d', lord of Rions and Vayres
  95, 262
  Bernard-Ezi V, lord of 96, 101, 113,
    240, 254, 263
  Guichard d' 97
  Isabelle d' 96
Alençon 197
Alfonso IV, king of Aragon 178, 197
Alliances 85, 130
Alliés 123, 129
Alphonso Psalter 38
Alphonso X, king of Castile 57
Alsace 110, 264
Ambrus 181
Amesbury 26
Amici, Master Jean 250
Amiennois 12
Amiens 14, 16, 51, 71, 77, 178–9, 233,
    251–2
  Mise of 178
Ancona, marquisate of 94
Andorra 125
Angers 11
Angevin Empire 9, 11, 12, 13, 15, 19,
    46, 56, 59
Anglo-Norman 5
Angoulême 27, 29, 208, 211
  comté of 29
Angoumois 30, 208, 268
Anjou 10–12, 32–3, 53, 56, 67, 177–8,
    197
  Fulk Nerra, count of 12

Annales of London 196
Annales of Dunstable 196
Antequam essent clerici 191, 193
Antwerp 262
Appeals 68, 78, 79
Appellants 182, 188, 263
Aquitaine 2, 4, 6–7, 9–10, 12–20, 22,
    26–7, 30–4, 39, 42–3, 48, 50,
    52–4, 56–67, 69–71, 73–5, 77–8,
    80–2, 85, 88, 91, 95, 99–100, 103,
    108, 110–15, 118, 121–2, 131,
    134–5, 138–40, 142, 144, 147–8,
    150, 152–3, 157–8, 160, 164–5,
    168, 170, 173, 176–7, 179–81,
    183–5, 188–9, 191, 193, 196,
    199–208, 211–21, 215–20, 224–5,
    228, 232, 236–7, 241–5, 247–52,
    255, 260, 262, 264–5, 267
  duchy of 15, 100
  dukes of 4, 17, 43
Aragon, kingdom of 32, 42, 52, 57, 176,
    177–8, 194, 197–8, 237
Archier, Jean, knight 158
Armagnac, house of 8, 75, 86–7, 91–2,
    95–6, 100–1, 106, 108, 116, 118,
    121, 124–5, 127–32, 196, 241, 253–
    5, 263
  Bernard VI, count of 87, 93–4, 96,
      113, 124, 126, 130
  comté of 246
  counts of 84, 92, 123, 199, 215, 242, 251
  Géraud V, count of 92
  Jean I, count of 91, 94–5, 125, 263
  Mathe, countess of 96, 128, 254
  Régine de Goth, countess of 94–6
  Roger of, bishop of Lavaur 132
Armagnac and Fézensac, *comtés* of 93
Arras 212
Arthus, abbot of 157
Articuli super Cartas 164
Artois 12, 33, 67, 200–1, 208, 263, 267
  Blanche of 25, 179
  Jeanne of 90, 91, 95, 229–31
  Robert of 71–2, 259–60
  Robert II, count of 98, 183, 196,
      198–9, 200–1, 205, 207–12,
      214–15, 217, 219, 225

Arundel Psalter 1, 39
Ashanti 118
Assisi 176
Astarac, comté of 93, 115, 118, 246
Atlantic 147, 149
Auch 15, 93, 94, 101, 106, 128, 220
Auch, Arnaud de Goth, cardinal of 107
Auch, archbishop of 92
Audenge, Bernard de Blanquefort, lord
    of 103
Audoin, Guillaume, lord of 230
Audoins 87
Auge, Richard Leneveu, archdeacon of
    224
Auribat 101
Auros 103
Auros, Baudoin d' 217
Auvergne 11, 184, 208
Auvillars 93, 105, 254
Avignon 35, 38, 40, 91, 94, 165, 167,
    227
  papacy 408, 131
Ayquem, Gaillard 210

Baa 154
Bachen 123
Bagnières, Jean de, siege engineer 239
Bakewell, John 72
Balanger, Raymond 216
Baldock, Robert, bishop of London 139
Baleine, Gerard 216, 224, 225
Balet, Guillaume de, canon of Agen 143
Balliol, Edward 197
Bannockburn, battle of 143
Bapaume 12
Bar, comté of 60, 176, 264
Barbarès, Arnaud de, *prévôt* of Dax
Bardi 258
Barentin, Dreu de 64
Basque country 100
Basset, Ralph, of Drayton 69, 234, 235,
    236
Bastides 68–9, 75, 103, 105, 118, 125,
    142, 153–8, 160, 180, 183, 208,
    230–1, 233–4, 239, 246
Bavaria, Emperor Lewis of 264
Bayonnais 193

Bayonne 8, 11, 13, 18–19, 26, 62, 117, 126, 142–4, 149–50, 157, 163, 172, 183, 196–8, 202–4, 206, 209–12, 215, 218, 223, 226, 235, 239
  cathedral of Ste-Marie at 142
Bazadais 82–3, 95–7, 101–3, 105–7, 110, 136, 156, 163, 240, 243–4, 248, 256
Bazas 66, 105, 112, 126, 144, 211, 216, 232, 249, 254
Béarn 61, 82, 86, 88, 94, 99, 115–16, 118, 124–7, 156, 171, 197, 230, 239, 246, 251
  Arnaud-Guillaume de, lord of Lescun 239, 248
  Bernard de, lord of Arrudy 239
  Gaston VII, *vicomte* of 15, 17, 63, 84–9, 92, 124, 125, 126
  Mathe de, daughter of Gaston VII 92
  Raymond-Arnaud, bastard of 124
  vicomté of 98
  vicomtes of 83, 84, 87, 88, 89, 115
Béarn and Marsan, Margaret, *vicomtesse* of 81, 90–2
Beatrice, daughter of Raoul de Clermont-Nesle, constable of France 27
Beatrix, daughter of Henry III 12, 26
Béatrix de Clermont 95
Beaucaire 251
Beaumanoir, Philippe de Rémy, sire de 17, 44, 45, 112
Beaumarchais, Eustache de, seneschal of Toulouse 89, 154, 194
Beaumaris 106
Beaumont-de-Périgord 153
Beauregard 257
Beauvaisis 112
Bedford, John, duke of 266, 268
Bègles 239
Béguey, family of 145, 161, 221
  Pierre 169
Belhus, Thomas de, knight 72
Bellac 29
Belleperche, Pierre de 100, 190, 223
Belleperche, abbot of 189
Bénauges 32, 116

Benedict XII, Pope 41, 257, 268
Benon 184
Bereford, Simon de 251
Bergerac 158, 211, 257
Berners, John Bourchier, Lord 268
Berwick-upon-Tweed 109, 143, 149
Bible Moralisé 38
Bigod 164
Bigorre 77, 88–90, 92–3, 124–5, 184, 196, 205, 255
  Bernard, count of 89
  comté of 82, 84
  Esquivat, count of 86
  Mathe de 86, 124
  Petronilla, countess of 86
Biscay, bay of 19, 149
Black Death 144
Blankharden, Van den 160
Blanquefort 94, 95, 106, 182, 254, 255
Blasimont, abbot of 155
Blaye 95, 108, 149, 184–6, 203–4, 206, 208–10, 218, 223, 230, 238, 239, 257, 262
Blyth 98
Boccanegra, Simon 221
Bois-de-Vincennes 252, 255
Bologna 191
Boniface VIII, Pope 35, 121, 141, 150, 184, 189, 193, 214, 217, 219–20, 227, 259
Bonnegarde 186, 206, 209, 215, 225, 261
Bordeaux 6, 7, 11, 13–15, 18–19, 31, 57, 62, 64–5, 72–4, 78, 85, 93–107, 123–4, 127, 131–2, 135–6, 141–50, 153, 160–4, 166–9, 173, 178, 182–3, 185–6, 196, 203, 207, 209–11, 216, 220–1, 223, 231, 235–6, 238–9, 242, 245, 248, 250, 252–4, 256–7, 261–2
  Assalhide de, lady of Puy-Paulin 146
  cathedral of St André at 142
  constables of 63; Elsfield, Richard de 163; Limber, Adam 232, 238; Mège, Aubert 169; Mirailh, Raymond de 155; Morant, Jourdain 169; Travers, John 237, 253; Weston, John de 247

Bordeaux (*continued*)
  Faubourg St-Eloi at 146, 160
  La Rousselle at 160, 163
  Palais Gallien at 136
  Porte de Caillau at 238
  Robert de Shirland, mayor of 232
  Rue-Neuve at 160
Bordeaux, Pierre de 103, 219
Boulogne 16, 30, 51
Bourg 95, 108, 149, 183, 203–4, 206,
    208–12, 218, 223, 239, 257, 262
Bourges 96
Bouvines 12
Brabant 27, 176, 264
Brabant, Jean, duke of 34, 268
Brabourne 30
Branches des royaux lignages 177, 193
Brane, Vidau 103
Brassenx 103
Breuil, Master Guillaume de 241, 251
Briquebec, Robert-Bertrand de 248
Bristol 149, 150, 238
Brittany: duchy of 11, 27, 67, 68, 265, 267
    Arthur of 26
    Blanche, duchess of 26
    Eleanor of 26
Bruges, bishop of 22
Brulhois, *vicomté* of 93
Brutails, Guillaume de 97
Bruxelles, Gautier de 212
Buch, *captaux de* 103, 146, 262
    Jean de Grailly, *captal de* 262
    Pierre 'lo Massip', lord of Puy-Paulin
      and *captal de* 146
    Pierre-Amanieu, *captal de* 81, 210
Buch 262
Budos 106
Burgundian 31
Burgundian Netherlands 268
Burgundy 67, 68, 113, 176, 201, 246,
    250, 258, 267
    duke of 31, 53
Burnell, Robert, bishop of Bath and
    Wells 92, 154, 179
Bury, Richard de, bishop of Durham
    41–2, 46, 258
Buzet 181

Caerphilly 106
Cahors 53, 67, 91, 150–1, 183, 187,
    214, 233
    Bernard Tixier of 151
    Pont Valentré at 152
Caillau 20, 96, 145, 146, 160, 163
Caillau, Arnaud III de 161, 163–4,
    168–9, 173, 221
Caillau, Bernard 248
Caillau, Pierre IV de 163–4, 167
Calais 72, 199, 200, 201, 245, 266
Calais, the March of 265
Cambes, Alexandre de 161
Cambrai 30
Cambridge 43
Cambridge, Thomas of 110, 170, 206
Campagne, Raymond de, knight 186,
    219
Canfranc 194
Canteloupe 101
Canterbury 97
Canterbury, Gervase of 55
Canterbury, Master Henry of 43, 180,
    232, 250
Capbreton 101
Capet 14
Capetian 54, 60, 66, 70, 71, 77
Capetians 1, 2, 4–6, 10, 12–13, 15–16,
    22, 25, 30, 34, 39, 47–8, 61, 69, 80,
    83–4, 90, 92, 112–13, 124, 127,
    140–1, 148, 152, 158, 172–3, 176–7,
    179–80, 182–5, 187, 198, 201, 205,
    207, 212, 228–9, 236, 251, 256
Captieux 215, 230
Carcassonne 202, 221, 205, 208
Carolles, Master Hugues de 167
Casaubon, 138, 257
Casaux, Arnaud-Guillaume de, lord of
    St Martin 123
Casenave 85
Casenave, Odo de 217
Castandet, Sanche-Loup, lord of 155
Casteljaloux 131, 167, 240
Castelnau, Arnaud de, esquire 224
Castelnau, Arnaud de, *prévôt* of St
    Sever 169
Castelnau, Pierre de 131

Castelnau-de-Médoc 262

Castelnau-de-Rivière 90, 186

Castelnau-en-Tursan, Pierre, lord of 123, 155

Castelnaux 105, 108, 154, 156

Castelsarrasin 225

Castetpugon, Gaillard de 131

Castile, kingdom of 21, 35, 52, 57, 121, 124, 176, 237

Castillon 32, 116

Castillon, Pons de, 103, 131, 210, 219, 239

Castillon-de-Médoc 204

Castillon-sur-Dordogne 265

Castillonès 69, 225

Catalans 178, 199, 203

Catalonia 84

Cathars 81

Caudaresse, Bernard de, 'baron' 225

Caudaresse, Raymond-Arnaud de, bishop of Cahors 225

Caumont, family of 131, 261
   Alexandre de 132, 134, 136
   Anessans de, knight 116, 248
   Guillaume de, lord of 245, 248
   Guillaume-Raymond de 239
   Marguerite de 101

Caupenne, lordship of 110
   Arnaud de, knight 97, 219
   Elie de 131
   Garcie-Arnaud de 224

Celestine V, Pope 227

Central Massif 11

Cépoy, Thibaut de 208, 216

Cernés 102

Châlon, Hugues de 121

Châlon, Jean de 258

Chalosse 202, 206

Champagnac 29

Champagne 26, 32, 33, 176, 179
   comté of 25

Channel Islands 59, 258

Charente 256

Charivari 249

Charles IV, king of France 22, 34, 87, 98, 113–14, 120, 137–9, 200, 228–32, 234, 236, 240–1, 245–8, 250, 260, 267

Charles V, king of France 30

Charles of Anjou, king of Sicily 21, 49, 54, 126, 178

Chartres 197

Châtelet 138

Châtillon, Gautier de 138

Chauvency 34

Chester, Edward, earl of 241

Chevauchée 211, 266

Cinque Ports 19, 149

Ciron 102

Cistercians 100–1, 154

Clement V, Pope 31, 35, 87, 94–7, 105–8, 111, 121, 127, 137, 143, 165, 170–1, 223, 227, 268

Clermont-Nesle, Raoul de, constable of France 23, 189, 198, 227

Clifford, Robert lord 34

Clinton, John of Maxstoke 72

Cliquat, Bernard 223

co-seigneurie 83

Cobham, Thomas 42

Coignet, Renaud 211

Cok, Van den 160

Cologne 36

Colom, family of 20, 145–6, 160, 162–3, 221, 238
   Amanieu 161
   Jean 161, 164, 167–9, 173, 223
   Mabille 133

Comminges 75, 83, 86, 93, 118, 131
   Bernard IV, count of 128
   comté of 84, 246
   counts of 137, 215, 236

Compiègne 34

Compostella 100, 151

Comtat Venaissin 94

Condom 126, 141, 151, 239

Condominium 102

Cornwall 30

Cornwall, Richard, earl of 12–13, 21, 54

Courtrai 184, 219, 221, 227

Craon, lordship of 31, 32
   Amaury III de, seneschal of Aquitaine 27, 33–4, 59, 74, 112, 123, 125–6, 156, 169, 172
   Maurice de 74

Creil 200
Créon 156, 158, 159
Crespin, Guillaume 212
Croyland, Geoffrey of, abbot of
    Peterborough 43
Crusades 14, 82, 178, 191, 251, 254,
    257
Cuerden Psalter 39
Curia, Roman 47
Curton, Amanieu de 131

D'Ailhan, family of 161
Dartmouth 209
Dassi, Jean 261
Dauphiné 184
David II, king of Scotland 268
Dax 66, 126, 172, 203, 205, 221, 225,
    235, 239, 242
De Tallagio non concedendo 164
Dene, Master Peter de 35
Derby, earldom of 164, 170
    Henry of Grosmont, earl of 262
Despenser, family of 98, 232, 241–2
    Hugh le 34, 240
Devon, William of, Bible of 39
Doazit, Odo, lord of 235
Doncaster, Roger de, king's clerk
    39
Donezan 125
Donzac 94, 95
Dordogne, river 19, 147, 185–6, 194
Dorset 143
Douai, Salomon Boinebroke, merchant
    of 208
Douce Apocalypse 39
Dover 4
Dreux, count of 31
Droit de guerre 112, 119, 126
Droit de vengeance 119
Dubois, Pierre 203
Duèse, family of 91, 92, 134, 139
    Cardinal Gaucelme 43, 136
Dunes 94, 95
Dunwich, Peter of 58
Durand, Master Raymond 257
Duras, lordship of 94
    Aymeric de Durfort, lord of 255

Durfort, family of 98, 100, 106–7
    Arnaud de 105, 240–1
    Gaillard I de 101
    Rainfroi de 248
    Raymond de, bishop of Périgueux
    105

East Anglia 150
East Sutton 30
Edward I, king of England 1, 3, 4, 9,
    12, 15, 17, 19–23, 26–7, 31–2, 34–8,
    41, 50–2, 54–5, 62–4, 66, 68–75,
    77, 83–4, 87, 89, 92, 93, 97–100,
    103, 105–6, 108, 115–17, 121–2,
    125–7, 131, 151, 153–6, 158, 162,
    164–6, 169, 174, 176–8, 180–3,
    185–8, 190–1, 193, 196–7,
    199–200, 201–2, 204–6, 209, 211,
    215–18, 223–4, 226–7, 229, 233,
    237, 240, 259, 265–7
Edward II, king of England 20–2, 27,
    31, 33–5, 42–3, 50–1, 58, 60, 69–
    74, 91, 95, 98–9, 102–3, 108–10,
    112–13, 114, 118, 121–2, 125–6,
    134, 136, 138, 143, 148–52, 155,
    157–8, 162–7, 169, 172, 173–4,
    223, 225, 227–33, 235–8, 240–2,
    245–6, 257
Edward III, king of England 3, 5–6,
    9, 20–1, 27, 31, 36, 41, 46, 50, 68,
    71, 83, 95, 98–9, 116, 150, 157,
    160, 225, 241–4, 247–52, 253–9,
    261–9
Edward, prince of Wales, the Black
    Prince 20, 50, 268
Edward the Confessor, king of England
    25, 36
Egerton 30
Eleanor of Aquitaine 9, 63
Eleanor of Castile, queen of England
    37, 54, 71
    commemorative crosses of 1, 37
Eltham 252
Ely, Master Nicholas de 56
Empire, German 12, 35, 227, 264–5
Entre-deux-Mers 95, 239, 257
Escaude 65

Escoussan, family of 146
  Guillaume de Seguin d', canon of St
    Seurin at Bordeaux 218
  Mabille d' 96
Esquerrier, Arnaud 124
Estivaux, Arnaud-Loup, lord of 103,
  154
Etablissements de Rouen 18, 19
Etienne de Rouen 16
Eu, Raoul, count of 261
Evreux, Louis of 31, 136
Eymet 208

Faide 119
Fargues 106
Fargues, Gaillard de, esquire 245
Fauquemont 12
fealty 48–53, 68
Fehde 119
Felton, John 138
Ferrara, Este, lords of 254
Ferre, Guy 133, 169, 170, 172
Ferrers of Chartley, John, seneschal of
  Gascony 116, 164
Fézensac 92, 115, 254
Fézensaguet, Géraud, *vicomte* of 130
Fiennes 31
Fiennes, Jean, sire de 72
Fiennes, Michel de 72
Fiennes and Tingry, Guillaume de
  72
Flanders 12, 18, 34, 40, 52, 58–9, 67,
  136, 176, 180, 196, 201, 215, 227,
  236, 263, 267
  comté of 141
  counts of 53, 62, 67
Fleurance 125, 126
Florence 237
Flores Historiarum 164
Flote, Pierre 89, 183–4, 187, 191, 196,
  198, 201, 220, 227
Foix-Béarn, house of 8, 75, 84–7, 90–2,
  95, 125, 129–30, 253
Foix, Agnes, daughter of Roger IV,
  count of 86
  Brunissende de, countess of Périgord
    132

comté of 86–7, 91, 108, 118, 121,
  124–9, 131–2, 254
  counts of 83–4, 90, 92–4, 120, 194,
    215, 236
  Gaston I, count of 90–1, 95, 125, 127
  Gaston II, count of 87, 90–1, 99,
    130, 229–30, 232, 255, 263
  Margaret, countess of 81–2, 127–9,
    158, 171
  Margaret, daughter of Roger-Bernard
    III of 87
  Roger-Bernard III, count of and
    vicomte of Béarn 84–6, 98, 124,
    126, 130, 198, 204
Fontevrault 9
Forez 110, 113
Forz, Isabel de, lady of Aumale 88
Fossat, Amanieu de, lord of Madaillan
  102, 109, 116, 128, 135, 163, 225,
  241, 248
Fowey 209
France, Archives Départmentales 7
Francesco Accursius of Bologna 63
Franche-Comté 264
Francia 266
Francs, Robert de 172
Frederick Barbarossa, Emperor 16
Frescobaldi 166
Froissart, Jean, *Chroniques* of 268
Frondeboeuf 230
Fronsac 183, 186, 208
  Raymond, *vicomte* of 146
  vicomtes of 186
Fulcher, Pierre 136

Gabardan 90, 101, 125, 128, 129
Gabaston 87
  Arnaud, lord of 166
Gages de bataille 113, 132, 135
Galard, Guillaume de 248
Galician, Master Pierre de, canon of
  Agen 121–2, 252
Garges 65
Garland, Guillaume de, baron 239
Garonne, river 15, 19, 61, 103, 147,
  150, 151, 168, 217, 239
Garonne basin 141

Garter, order of the 262
Gascon Calendar 181
Gascony 6, 11, 15, 20, 42, 50, 54–5,
    57–9, 61–6, 68, 73, 75, 78, 81, 84–5,
    92, 94, 99, 107, 114–15, 122, 128,
    132, 134, 137, 143–4, 153, 156,
    162, 164–5, 169, 186, 191, 197,
    206–8, 221, 244, 256, 259
  allodial status of 60
  appeals from 69, 100, 259, 267
  nobility of 8, 16, 31, 66, 80–1, 97–8,
    101–3, 109–10, 217, 242, 243, 253
Gaure, comté of 254
Gavarret 127, 128
  Pierre de 103, 217
Gave de Pau, river 115, 157
Gaveston, Piers, earl of Cornwall 27,
    30, 98, 116, 165–7, 170, 240
Gavre, bailli of 207
Gayrosse 87
Geaune 231
Geneva 31
Geneville 31
Genoa 201, 221, 261
Gensac 116
  Alexandre de la Pebrée, lord of 158
  Guillaume-Raymond de 97
Gerderest 87
Germany 12, 13
Gers 94, 108, 158, 171, 186
Gervais, Bernard 229
Ghent 144, 218, 262
Gironde, river 57, 209, 223, 240
Gisors 201
Gîte right of 66
Gloucester 165
  Statute of (1280) 64
Gloucester, Richard de Clare, earl of 55
Godorie, Bertrand de 132
Goth, family of, de 96, 101, 105–6, 146,
    254–5
  Arnaud-Garcie de vicomte of
    Lomagne and Auvillars 97, 105
  Bertrand de, vicomte of Lomagne and
    Auvillars, marquis of Ancona
    94–5, 105, 107–8, 122, 132–3, 135,
    137, 254–5

Gaillard de 105
  Régine de, countess of Armagnac 94–6
Gramont 118
  Arnaud-Guillaume de 85
Granada 254
Grandes Chroniques de France 200, 249
Grandisson, John de, bishop of Exeter
    31–2
Grandselve 100
  abbot of 189
Grandson, family of 30, 106
  Odo de 31–2, 75, 92, 219, 224
Gratian's Decretum 40
Graves 102
Gregorian reforms 100
Grilly (later Grailly), family of 31, 106–7
  Catherine de 132, 139
  Jean de 32, 57, 62, 74, 86, 88, 92–3,
    99, 106, 153, 158
  Jean de, captal de Buch 262
  Pierre de 32, 34, 57
  Pierre II de 146
  Pierre III de 116
Guelf–Ghibelline conflict 124
Guiart, Guillaume 178, 193
Guisborough, Walter of 210

Hagetmau 225
Hailes abbey 242
Hainault, comté of 21, 241, 268
Harlech 106
Hastings, John of, seneschal of Gascony
    75, 122, 128, 157, 169, 221, 223
Hastingues 75, 118, 157
Hausted, John, seneschal of Aquitaine
    248, 252
Haut pays 19, 147, 148, 242
Havering, John of, seneschal of
    Gascony 67, 93, 127, 131, 169, 181,
    186, 223
Hemingburgh, Walter of 196
Henry II, king of England 9, 11, 13,
    16, 20, 56, 61, 63
Henry III, king of England 1, 9–14,
    20–1, 23, 25, 27, 31, 35–7, 39–40,
    48–56, 59–60, 61–4, 68–9, 73,
    88–9, 146, 162

Henry V, king of England 3, 266, 268
Henry VI, king of England 266
Henry VIII, king of England 3, 266, 268
Henry le Waleys 19
Henry, son of Richard of Cornwall 88
Henry the Lion, duke of Saxony 16
Hereford, Humphrey de Bohun, earl of 72, 164
Herefordshire 32
Hérisson, Master Thierry d' 212, 214
Hesdin 200, 227
Hildesley, John de 42
Hohenstaufen 12
Homage 16, 48, 50–4, 56, 59, 60, 62, 68
Hontonx 230
Hotham, John, bishop of Ely 114, 138, 230, 232
Huire 225
Hull 238
Hundred Rolls 63, 64, 65
Hundred Years War 1–5, 20, 22, 34, 41, 46, 59, 63, 65, 71, 88, 115–16, 140–1, 201, 204, 210–11, 215, 218, 226, 244, 248, 252, 260, 264, 266, 269
Huntingdon 97

Iberian peninsula 11, 19, 81, 265
Ightham 97
Ile-de-la-Cité 35, 51
Ile-de-France 45, 60
India 75
Inge, William 170
Ingham, Oliver, seneschal of Aquitaine 240–8, 251, 253, 257, 260–2
Innocent IV, Pope 54
Ippegrave, Thomas de 74
Ireland 56, 65, 73, 77, 134, 204
Isabella of Angoulême, queen of England 9, 13
Isabella of Aragon, queen of France 197
Isabella of France, queen of England 21–2, 172, 241, 245, 249
Isabella Psalter 38

Isle of Oléron 59, 216
Italy 12, 13, 96, 160, 227

Jean de Dammartin et Blonde d'Oxford 44
Jean, canon of St Victor-de-Paris 143
Jeanne of Navarre, queen of France 21, 22, 25–6, 179
Jerusalem 35
Jews 207, 225, 226
John, king of England 12, 18, 54, 265
John XXI, Pope 121
John XXII, Pope 43, 82, 90–2, 95, 108, 112, 121–3, 128–9, 131–2, 134, 136–8, 141, 229, 232
John of Luxembourg, king of Bohemia 130, 254
John of Reading 36
Johnston, Elias 258
Joinville, family of 31–2, 44, 49, 54
    Gauthier de 33
    Geoffroi de 23, 27, 32, 46
    Jean de 32–3
    Pierre de 32
    Simon de 33
Jourdain, Master Austence 229, 232

Kent 30
    Edmund, earl of 237, 238, 242
    William Trussel, sheriff of 209
King's Lynn 149
Kingson, William 209
Kirkby, John de, chancellor 39

L'Isle-Caumont quarrel 137
L'Isle-Jourdain, family of 8, 86–7, 92–3, 130, 133, 138
    Bernard-Jourdain de 87, 133, 136–7, 236
    Jourdain de 8, 86, 93, 130, 132–9, 172, 230, 257
La Marche, *comté* of 29
    Hugh X de Lusignan, count of 13
La Mote de Villeneuve 103
La Mothe, family of 107
    Bertrand, lord of 122
La Pebrée, Isabella de 116

La Réole 19, 65, 131, 135, 144, 147, 172, 209, 211, 230, 238–9, 248
La Rochelle 11, 13, 18–19, 59, 147, 183–4, 194, 232
La Romieu 107
La Rousselle 146
La Sauve-Majeure 156, 257
La Teste 262
La Trave 106
Labarthe, Seignoran de 235
Labatut 225
Labourt 95, 110
Labrit 95
Lacy, family of 27, 30
    Maud de 32
Lados, Odo de 158, 163, 167, 169
Lados, Raymond Fort de 103, 217
Lambert, family of 106, 145–6, 161
Lancaster, earldom of 30
    Edmund, earl of 1, 20, 25–6, 77, 164, 177, 187–91, 200, 206, 210, 212, 218
    John of Gaunt, duke of 50
    Thomas, earl of 136, 186
Landes 70, 77, 101–2, 110, 115, 123, 144, 156, 186, 206, 218, 231, 240
Landévennec, Master Yves de 167, 224
Lanercost-Chronicle 197, 198
Langoiran 96, 108
Langon 82, 103, 128, 147, 168, 208, 239, 249, 254–5
Langton, Walter, bishop of Coventry and Lichfield 88, 164–5, 167
Languedoc 18, 94, 98, 147, 198, 201, 204–5, 210, 220, 236, 240, 251
Larboust 125
Laserrade 128
Laurent, Brother, confessor to Philip III 38
Le Crotoy 71
Le Mas 131
Le Mas d'Agenais, Bernard Pelet, prior of 224
Le Mas Ste-Quitterie 242
Le Puy, bishop and chapter of 89–90
Lectoure 93, 95, 106, 118, 158, 186
Lens 33

Lescun, family of 87
    Arnaud-Guillaume, lord of 230, 241
    Fortaner de 133, 225, 256
Lesparre, lordship of 65, 116
    Guillaume-Ayquem, lord of 116, 167–8, 171
    Senebron, lord of 65
Lestrange, Fulk, lord of Whitchurch, seneschal of Aquitaine 91, 112, 123–4, 133, 138, 229–32
Lettres de défi 119
Lévis-Mirepoix, Robert de 205
Ley, Thomas de la 39
Leyburne, Roger de 75
Libourne 19, 75, 144, 153, 170, 185–7, 239, 260, 262
Limburg 12, 264
Limeuil 11, 16, 29, 38, 53, 67, 183, 212, 233, 257
Limoges, Pierre de 54
Limoges, Raymond de 168–9
Limousin 11, 30, 53, 70, 77, 158, 194, 208, 219, 257, 268
Lincoln, Henry Lacy, earl of 20, 77, 122, 202, 205–6, 209–10, 219, 224–5, 227
Lisieux 224
Lobinger 225
Loire, river 11
Lomagne 93, 105, 254
Lombards 226
London 21, 44, 144–5, 150, 218
    Public Record Office 7
    Tower Royal at 145
    Vintry ward of 19, 145
Looe 209
Lorraine 110, 264
Lot, river 147, 150
Louis VII, king of France 10, 16, 61
Louis VIII, king of France 15
Louis IX, king of France 10, 13–15, 21, 32, 35–7, 39, 48–9, 51–62, 64, 68–9, 113, 177, 179, 263
Louis X, king of France 34, 58, 72, 90, 108
Louis XI, king of France 49
Loup, Blaise de 217

Louvain 160
Louvre 35
Low Countries 7, 12, 34, 119, 143, 160, 176, 201, 249, 260, 262, 268–9
Luc, Arnaud-Sanche de 163
Luc-de-Bigorre 246
Lusignan, family of 16, 27, 29–30, 32–3
Lyon 60, 106, 246

Macau 204
Mâcon 246
Mâconnais 98, 121
Madaillan 116, 248
Magnoac 125
Maine 11, 33, 53, 197
Marciac 120, 157
Marensin, *vicomte* of 123
Margaret, duchess of Brabant 34
Margaret, queen of England 21, 41
Margaret, queen of France 55, 188
Marie of Brabant, queen of France 22, 39
Marie de St Pol 27, 30, 46
Marigny, Enguerrand de 170
Marmande 135, 144, 209, 212, 221, 230, 237, 261
Marmande, Raymond-Bernard de, esquire 243
Marsan 88, 90, 101, 115, 123, 125, 171, 231–2, 239
    Arnaud de, lord of Cauna 122
    Arnaud-Guillaume de 109, 116, 166
    Arnaud-Raymond de 122
    Constance de Béarn, *vicomtesse* de 82, 88–90, 92, 127, 205
    Garcie-Arnaud, *vicomte* of 171
    vicomté of 84, 88, 91, 129, 230
Marseilles 257
Martel, Master Philip 68
Martheleye, William de, clerk 238
Master Honoré, illuminator 38
Maubuisson 90
Mauléon, lordship of 117, 186, 230
    Auger de, esquire 202, 225
Mauvezin 89
Meaux 246
Meaux, Chronicler of 55

Mediterranean 147
Médoc 65
Meilhan 96, 97
Mercoeur, Béraud de 121
Merle, Jean 239
Merton, Walter de, chancellor of England 54
Meurin 231
Mézières, Philippe de 124
Mézin 108
Midi 19
Midouze, river 115
Miossens, lordship of 87
    Raymond, lord of 109, 256
Miramont 118, 225, 230, 231
Mirande 157
Mise 14
Missenden, Roger de 39
Moissac 100, 212
Molières 257
Monadey 145, 221
Monflanquin 93
Monlaur, Pons de, knight 216
Mons 34
Mons-Boubert, Gerard d'Abbeville, lord of 73
Mont-de-Marsan 205, 208, 211, 239
Montauban 151, 212
Montaut, Isnard de 121
Montaut, Odo de, knight 205, 207, 208, 217
Montclar 156
Montclar-d'Agenais 102
Montendre 256
Montendre, Alain de 208
Montesquieu, Gentille de 120
Monteux, lordship of 94–5
Montferrand, lordship of 107, 146
    Amanieu de Vayres, lord of 255
Montflanquin 156
Montfort 230
Montfort, Eleanor de, countess of Leicester 55
Montfort, Simon de 44, 55, 77, 81, 153, 162
Montgaillard 138, 231, 261
Montignac 29
Montlaur 261

Montpellier 191, 202
Montpezat, castle and lordship of 116,
    233, 235–6, 238, 259
  Menaud de Testa (alias the Borc de)
    246
  Raymond-Bernard de 116, 233–5
Montréjeau 147
Montreuil 58, 71–3
  process of 218, 228
Montségur 94, 95, 153, 155–6, 208,
    216, 254
Morizès 65
Morlaas 129
Mortimer, Roger, lord of Wigmore 249,
    252–3
Mothe, Auger de 96
Muslims 81, 254

Nantes 11
Nanteuil, Guy de 185
Narbonne 201–2, 220
  Gilles Aicelin, archbishop of 184, 223
Nassau, Adolf of 183, 200
Navailles, Garcie-Arnaud, lord of 117,
    202, 259
Navarre, kingdom of 35, 52, 84, 118,
    176, 197
Nébouzan, *vicomté* of 84, 125
Nérac 132, 166
Nesle, Jean de 34
Newcastle upon Tyne 109
Nîmes 214
Niort 194
Nogaret, Guillaume de 49, 60, 184
Normandy 11–12, 53–6, 60–1, 67–8,
    183, 193, 264
North Africa 19
Norwich, John of 262
Norwich, William of 40
Noyers, Miles de 247
Nuer 118
Nuremberg 38

Oléron, island of 18, 56, 232, 245
Oloron-Ste-Marie 178, 194
Ombrière, castle of the 163, 168, 216
  prévôt of the 149

Orthe, Arnaud-Raymond, *vicomte* of 171
Outremer 81
Oxford 42, 43
  Franciscan convent at 13
  Provisions of 15
Ozourt 154

Palazols, Guillaume de 102
Palazols, Raymond-Guillaume de 102
Palmier, Master, physician 211
Pamiers 141, 147
  Bernard Saisset, bishop of 85, 198,
    207, 220
Pardiac 93, 115
  comté of 157
  Géraud, count of 113
Paréage 83, 154–7, 166, 233, 265
Paris 11–13, 16–17, 33, 35, 37, 39–41,
    43, 46–7, 56, 61, 67–9, 93, 100,
    113–14, 134, 138, 152, 165, 173, 179,
    184, 187–8, 190–1, 202–3, 212,
    223–4, 228–9, 235, 241, 257, 259
  Archives Nationales 7
  Chambre des Comptes at 250
  chapel of St James of Compostella at
    40
  Guillaume de Hangest, *prévôt* of 198
  Notre-Dame of 96
  Parlement of 7, 17, 22, 33, 43, 49, 58,
    63–4, 67–70, 72, 78, 89, 113, 134,
    139, 150, 156, 158, 162, 164–5,
    169, 179, 180–1, 193, 229, 233–5,
    241, 250–1, 257–9
  Treaty of 21, 40, 54, 58, 63, 68, 179,
    266
  University of 40, 42, 179, 191
Paris, Matthew 55
Pas-de-Calais 30
Pays d'Albret 101
Péage 96, 100, 157
Pecche, Gilbert, knight 134
Pedro III, king of Aragon 126
Pellegrue 153
Pembroke, earldom of 27, 30, 46
  Aymer de Valence, earl of 1, 23, 27,
    29–30, 32–3, 46, 136, 170, 172, 229
  William Marshal, earl of 55

Penguy, Philippe de Vienne, lord of 201
Penne d'Agenais 147, 150–1, 230, 239, 246, 256–7, 260–2
Périgord 11, 53, 77–8, 95, 115, 122, 131–2, 134, 152, 160, 163, 168, 179, 182–3, 186–7, 205, 208, 219, 234–6, 250, 257
Périgord, Jean d'Arrablaye, seneschal of 185, 186–7, 194
Périgord, Jeanne de, lady of Lavardac 132, 146
Périgueux 53, 58, 67, 101, 144, 152, 183, 228, 233
  bishop of 105
  process of 216, 218
Péronne 92, 103
Peruzzi 237
Pessagno, Antonio di 69, 99, 134–6, 155
Peterborough Psalter 1
Pevensey, Richard of 72
Peyrehorade 202, 225
Philip II Augustus, king of France 10, 12–13, 15–16, 53, 56, 61, 201, 264
Philip III, king of France 15, 17, 26, 34, 52, 55, 57, 71, 78, 92–4, 111, 121, 177, 194, 197
Philip IV the Fair, king of France 17, 21–3, 25–6, 29, 31, 33, 35–6, 49, 51–2, 56, 58, 60, 62, 68, 70, 72, 82, 85–7, 89, 90, 93, 103, 105, 113, 116, 126–8, 133, 135, 150, 152, 158, 162, 166–73, 176–91, 193, 196–8, 200, 201, 203–5, 207–8, 210, 212, 216–17, 219, 221, 223–6, 250, 259, 267
Philip V, king of France 51, 121, 129, 136, 137, 228, 233
Philip VI of Valois, king of France 33, 43, 50, 51, 113, 249–58, 260, 263–4, 268
Philip III of Evreux, king of Navarre 130
Philippa of Hainault, queen of England 44, 258
Philobiblon 42
Picardy 98, 218

Piers, Master John 258
Pimbo 225, 231
Pins, Doat de 217
Pins, Sansaner de 106, 121, 132, 137
Plantagenets 1, 2, 4, 6, 7, 9–22, 25, 29, 30, 32–4, 37, 42–3, 48–9, 52, 54, 60, 62–4, 66–9, 71, 77, 80, 83–5, 87–8, 90–1, 98, 100, 108, 110, 115–16, 122, 128, 140–1, 143, 145, 147–8, 150, 153–4, 158, 163–4, 173–4, 176–7, 182–4, 187, 193–4, 199, 201, 206–7, 212, 216, 223–4, 228, 231, 237–40, 244–5, 247, 249, 265–6
Podensac, lordship and castle of 96, 104, 117, 146, 204
  Adam d'Abbeville, captain of 216
  Bertrand d'Escossans, lord of 96, 104, 117
Poissy 33, 173, 228
Poitiers 11, 15–16, 18, 194
Poitiers, Alphonse de 14, 64, 68, 153, 154
Poitou 11, 13, 16, 30, 53, 54, 131, 147, 153, 184, 194, 205, 268
  comté of 61
  Pierre de Molet, receiver of 212
Pommiers 65–6
  Guillaume-Sanche de 65
  Pierre de 65
  Pierre-Amanieu de 65
Pons, Elie-Rudel, lord of 33
Pons, Renaud de, lord of 95
Pont-à-Vendin 33
Ponthieu, comté of 9, 26, 42, 57–9, 71–3, 75, 179, 232, 241, 264
  counts of 4, 43
Pontonx-sur-l'Adour 45, 90, 202, 218
Port d'armes 112, 208
Port-Ste-Marie 237, 249
  Huard de Dune, bailli of 216
Portsmouth 202, 218
Portugal, kingdom of 124, 237
Poudenx, Auger de 122
Poudenx, Sansaner de, esquire 225
Poudenx, Vidal de 123
Pouillon 225

Poujols, Gérard de 150–1
Preyssac 106
Prie, Jean de 34
Prouille, nuns of Notre-Dame at 207
Provence 21, 35, 95, 176, 201
Pucelle, Jean 40
Puch, Jourdain de, esquire 155
Puch-de-Gontaud 138
Puy-Calvary 102
Puy-Paulin 103, 146
Puyguilhem, lordship of 94, 186
  Eble de 187, 210
Puymirol 256, 257, 260
Puynormand 263
Pyrenees 60, 61, 84, 85, 115, 266

Queen Mary Psalter 38
Quercy 11, 53, 70, 77, 115, 153, 158,
  205, 208, 219, 257
Quia Emptores (1290) 73
Quo warranto proceedings 63, 64

Rançon 29
Ravel, lordship of 184
  Guillaume Flote, lord of 254
Ravignan, Bernard de, co-seigneur of
  the castle of Buzet 180–2
Recogniciones feodorum 63–4, 66, 73, 78,
  83, 99, 108
Redort 66
Reims 35
Rhineland 264
Rhône 94·
Richard I, king of England 9, 12, 16,
  61, 62, 63, 265
Richard II, king of England 50
Richmond, Jean of Brittany, earl of 26,
  27, 30, 204
Rions 198, 203, 240, 263
Rivière-Basse 125, 255
Rocamadour 214
Rodez, Cécile, daughter of Henri, count
  of 94
Roffignac 257
Rôles d'Oléron 149
Roman law 17, 19, 191
Romans, kings of the 12, 13, 35, 193

Rome 38, 220
Roncevaux 100
Roquefort-de-Marsan, lordship of 116,
  230
  Arnaud-Guillaume de Marsan, lord
  of 231
Roquetaillade 102, 106
Rose de Bourg 95
Rostain 145, 161, 221
Rouen 11, 19, 61, 202
Rouergue 94, 208
  Gui de Cabrières, seneschal of 208
Roussel, Guillaume, serjeant 168
Rousselle, Pierre Béguey (Vigier) de la 168
Roussillon 84

Sablé 34
Saint-Astier 257
Saint-Bertrand-de-Comminges 86, 101,
  105
Saint-Denis 35, 37, 96, 232
  abbot of 182
St Edmund, Hugh de 235
St Edward 230
Saint-Emilion 19, 147, 186–7, 208, 224,
  239
Saint-Fort, Guillaume de, seneschal of
  the Landes 231
Saint-Gein-en-Marsan 155, 158, 231
St George 138, 262
  Master James of 144
Saint-Gilles 214
St John, Sir John, of Halnaker,
  lieutenant and seneschal of
  Aquitaine 75, 185–6, 189–90, 199,
  204, 206, 209
Saint-Luc-de-Bigorre 118
Saint-Macaire 144, 147, 189–90, 203,
  206, 210–11, 230, 239, 256–7, 261
Saint-Maurin, abbot of 88
Saint-Médard-en-Jalle, Gombaud de
  Tiran, lord of 180, 182
Saint-Omer 72, 199, 208
Saint-Sardos 91, 158, 232, 234–7, 245
  war of 44, 87, 98, 110, 120, 139, 158,
  160, 173, 219, 227–9, 241, 243–4,
  252–3

Saint-Sever 64, 66, 78, 116, 122, 124, 156, 181, 198, 202–3, 231, 239
  prévôté of 101
Saint-Sixte-del-Douple 133, 138
Sainte-Bazeille 116, 133–5
Sainte-Foy, Bernard de 248
Ste-Foy-la-Grande 208, 211, 214
Sainte-Gemme 129
Sainte-Quitterie 225
Saintes 11, 101, 230, 232
Saintonge 11, 68, 77, 87, 122, 131, 179, 184, 196, 205, 208, 232, 237–8
  Pierre de Bailleul, seneschal of 184, 208
Salas, Arnaud de las 239
Salerno, Charles of 178
Salisbury 38
Salmon, John, bishop of Norwich 148
Sandale, John de 110, 206
Sandwich 209
Sandwich, Thomas of, knight 72
Sarlat 233, 234
  abbot of 233
Saubrusse 215
Sauveterre-de-Béarn 85, 231
Sauveterre-de-Guyenne 155, 158, 230
  Guillaume de Charenton, castellan of 216
Sauviac, lordship of 106
  Bertrand de 97
Savage, Roger 58
Savoy 107, 176, 264
  Amadeus V, count of 39, 41, 227
Savoyards 31–2
Scotland, kingdom of 26, 33, 44, 58, 97, 109–10, 165, 176–7, 197, 249, 258
  war in 23, 137, 220, 231, 237, 238
Scotti, family of 212
Séailles, Garcie-Arnaud, lord of 120
Seguin, Etienne 239
Seine, river 11–12
Sempuy 230
Sens, Eudes de 251
Servat, family of 249
  Bernard 249
  Gaillard 249
Sescas, Amanieu de 97

Sescas, Barrau de, knight and admiral of Bayonne 96–7, 204
Sescas, Guillaume de, esquire 97
Shoreham 209
Shropshire 32
Sicilian Vespers, war of the 178
Sicily and Naples, kingdom of 13, 54, 178
Societas navium baionensium 150
Soirin, Austorge de 132
Soler, family of 145–6, 160, 162–3, 221
  Rostand del 162
Somerset 143
Somme le Roi, Le 38
Somme, river 71
Song of Caerlaverock 23, 97
Songe du vieil pélerin 124
Sorde-l'Abbaye 157, 231
  abbot of 215
Souillac 147
Soule, *vicomté* of 95, 110
Southampton 209
sovereignty 4, 6, 16–17, 48–50, 54, 56, 58–9, 62, 68, 70, 114, 138, 250, 258, 266
Spoleto 220
Stapleton, Walter, bishop of Exeter 139, 237
Stilus curie Parliamenti 251
Stirling 23
Stud, Robert 238
Suirac 261
Sully, Henri de, *grand bouteiller* of France 129, 136, 228, 247
Summaria Brevis 203
Sutton Valence 30

Taillebourg expedition 13
Tailor, Jordan the 262
Talence 239
Tarbes 88, 130
Tarn, river 147
Tartas, 146, 208–9, 211
Tartas, *vicomté* of 146, 242
  Arnaud-Raymond, vicomte of 81
Tastes, Gérard de 248
Temple, order of the 170–1, 207, 226–7

Terraube 118
Thames, river 145, 218
Thérouanne, Michel, bishop of 72
Thomas, Master, seige engineer 238
Thornham, Robert of, seneschal of
    Poitou and Gascony 20
Tickhill Psalter 1
Tonneins 237
Toulousain 126, 131, 148, 150, 204,
    210, 220, 247, 255, 257
Toulouse 53, 120, 128, 139, 144, 152,
    169, 183, 190, 202, 205, 207–8,
    210, 212, 221, 235–6, 254
  comté of 64, 85–6, 154
  counts of 84
  Jean d'Archevêque, viguier of 208
  Parlement of 184
  sénéchaussée of 89
  seneschal of 93
Touraine 11, 33, 53
Tournoi de Chauvency, Le 45
Tournon 230
  Guillaume de Gisors, castellan of 216
Tours 11
Tours-en-Vimeu 30
Tremblet 65
Trim 32
Tunis 37
Turberville, Thomas 198
Turenne 61
Turenne, Assaride de, lady of Aguérac
    and Gensac 116
Tursan 101, 231–2
Tweed, river 19

Ufford, Master Andrew 258
Urdinale, Elie de 229
Urgel, count of 199
Usumare, family of 261
  Niccolo 256
Uzeste 101, 107

Valedors et adhérens 122, 129–30
Valence, family of 27, 29–31, 44
  William de 27, 153
Valence d'Agen 121, 153
Valenciennes 60

Valentin Pascau 202
Valkenburg (Fauquemont), Dirk II,
    lord of 12
Valois, Charles, count of 183, 196–8,
    200, 202–3, 223, 227, 229–30, 235,
    237–8, 240, 242
Valois, house of 1, 5, 46, 112, 249, 256,
    259, 264–8
Vaquarissa, Peregrin de 235
Vaur 208, 210
  bailli of 207
  Raymond Martin de 207
  Sicard de 190
Vauvert 214
Vaux, Jean de 67
Vaux, Pierre de, esquire 125
Vaux, Raymond de 246
Vayres 95, 240, 263
Velay 89
Verlinghem, Robert de 208
Vertheuil 95
Veyrines 94, 187, 254–5
Vic, Master Pierre-Arnaud de 172
Vic-de-Bigorre 89
Vielle, Bernard de 150
Vienne, Cluniac priory of 133
Vienne, Council of 170
Vienne, Dauphin Humbert of 184
Vignoles, Bernard de 117
Villandraut 101, 105–6, 108, 254–5,
    257
Villenueve-sur-Lot 118, 150
Villeréal 183
Virelade 204
Vita Edwardi Secundi 170
Vye-St-Bavon 215

Wales 19, 26, 57–8, 75, 109, 115
Waltham, abbey of 237
Wardrobe, office of the 7, 176
Ware (Herts) 218
Warenne 30
Warwick 170
Wavrin, Robert de, lord of Saint-
    Venant 203, 216
Welyfedd, William, king's merchant
    143

Westminster 13, 25, 35–8, 40, 56, 58,
    63, 171, 205, 217, 237
  abbey of 1, 35–8
  Exchequer at 58, 176
  Painted Chamber at 23, 25, 38,
    177
  St Stephen's Chapel at 36
Westminster, Matthew of 164
Weymouth 209
Wibert, Adam 209

Wickham 30
Winchelsea 209
  Master William of 246
Wissant 30
Wolsey, Cardinal 3
Wymondeswold, Thomas de 40

York 58, 101, 217
  John of 262
  Minster 35